W9-AWU-669

A New Reader
of the
OLD SOUTH

Also edited by Ben Forkner and Patrick Samway, S.J.

A MODERN SOUTHERN READER:
*Major Stories, Drama, Poetry, Essays, Interviews
and Reminiscences from the Twentieth Century South*
(Peachtree)

STORIES OF THE MODERN SOUTH

STORIES OF THE OLD SOUTH

Also edited by Ben Forkner

MODERN IRISH SHORT STORIES

A NEW BOOK OF DUBLINERS

LOUISIANA STORIES

Also by Patrick Samway, S.J.

FAULKNER'S "INTRUDER IN THE DUST":
A Critical Study of the Typescripts

FAULKNER AND IDEALISM:
Perspectives from Paris
(Co-editor with Michel Gresset)

WALKER PERCY:
Signposts in a Strange Land
(Editor)

A New Reader
of the
OLD SOUTH

Major Stories, Tales, Slave Narratives,
Diaries, Essays, Travelogues,
Poetry and Songs: 1820-1920

Edited by Ben Forkner
and Patrick Samway, S.J.

PEACHTREE PUBLISHERS, LTD.
Atlanta

Published by
PEACHTREE PUBLISHERS, LTD.
494 Armour Circle, NE
Atlanta, Georgia 30324

Text © 1991 by Ben Forkner and Patrick Samway, S.J.

All rights reserved. No part of this book may be reproduced in any form or by any means without the prior written permission of the Publisher, excepting brief quotes used in connection with reviews, written specifically for inclusion in a magazine or newspaper.

Manufactured in the United States of America

First printing (1991)

Text composition by Kathryn D. Mothershed
Cover design by Candace J. Magee and Laurie Warlick

Library of Congress Cataloging-in-Publication Data

A New Reader of the Old South : major stories, tales, poetry, essays, slave narratives, diaries, and travelogues, 1820-1920 / Ben Forkner and Patrick Samway, S.J. [editors]
     p. cm.
    ISBN 1-56145-019-7 (hardcover) : $34.95. -- ISBN 1-56145-020-0 (trade paper) : $24.95
    1. Southern States--Literary collections. 2. American literature--Southern States. 3. American literature--19th century. 4. American literature--20th century.   I. Forkner, Ben.   II. Samway, Patrick H.
PS551.N46 1991
810'.8'0975--dc20   90-26836
                                               CIP

CONTENTS

A New Reader
of the
OLD SOUTH

Introduction

Even in the midst of assembling the selections for *A Modern Southern Reader* (1986), we were attracted by the idea of a companion volume of related Southern writing from the nineteenth century. At the time, there seemed to be at least one good reason for contemplating such a collection: Many of the writers included in *A Modern Southern Reader* had discovered their major themes only after a long, deliberate, dramatic grappling with the native written and unwritten versions of Southern identity handed down to them by the "Old South." In order to study better the more acclaimed Southern literature of our own century, we could readily argue that it would be useful to put together a fairly comprehensive choice of earlier Southern stories, essays, poems, speeches, songs, travelogues, and assorted literary efforts.

From the beginning, however, we wanted a collection that was not merely representative of the period; this was important, but equally important was the esthetic desire to remain alert to what was most original and most lasting in the mass of Southern writing the century produced. The literary skill and insight of the writer were at least as important as the subject and purpose of his or her work. We were primarily interested in what Ford Maddox Ford once called the "humaner letters," and not in a thick compendium of any and every historical document that might reflect the "spirit of the times."

We were especially watchful for any expression of individual human life in a period that often sacrificed the individual for the sake of high-sounding political rhetoric and were prepared to accept that the best writing of the period would no doubt be found well outside the realms of popular fiction. This was often the case, and some of the most revealing pieces we include, notably from the slave narratives and diaries, were written by men and women whose ordinary vocation or condition placed them at a considerable distance from the literary professionals. But at the same time, we soon realized that there was far more good fiction than we had counted on, particularly in the short stories of the time; they do not rival the power, completeness, and probing realism of the great modern works, but they were often innovative, independent, and far-reaching, and many of them could be read and praised on their own merits. And here we were given a second good reason for putting together the collection.

But to return to our first reason. It is worth taking a closer look at the odd half-antagonistic way the imagination of modern Southern writers finally took possession of itself by working its way backward toward the full meaning of the Old South. Actually, the various selections of *A New Reader of the Old South* are best appreciated with this modern critical attitude always in mind. And this is the case even when their unexpected qualities openly fly in the face of received opinion. For young intellectual

Southerners at the beginning of the twentieth century had one certain conviction: Even though they might be racked by all sorts of doubts and competing emotions—kinship, loyalty, love, emulation, disbelief, guilt, alienation—there was little question, as far as such intellectuals were concerned, that the professional, or semi-professional, Old South writers, above all the novelists, had never completely succeeded. These writers had been unable or unwilling to penetrate the deeper life of Southern character, white and black, male and female, and their novels had thus betrayed not only the demands of literary art, but the Southern community as well.

Of course, when modern Southerners thought of the earlier writing, what they usually had in mind were the countless numbing romantic portraits of plantation life that followed each other in novel after novel from about the 1830's on, and that continued with a vengeance after the antebellum South and the short-lived Confederacy had fallen and given way to the far more resistant Lost Cause: entire books, shelves, and libraries filled with "dreams, dramas, and dust," a literature that Ellen Glasgow damningly described as "sentimental decay." It took little effort for Southern writers at the beginning of the twentieth century to perceive the stark contrasts between the fictional legends and the "real" South. The contrasts were only faintly less stark when the recent Southern past was taken into consideration. Here, too, genuine personal knowledge was offended and perplexed by the evasions and simple reductions of the genteel old fiction.

The personal knowledge of a tragic collective fate of young modern Southerners cannot be overemphasized; it became in time the distinguishing mark and measure of everything they would eventually write. As early as their own first memories, they knew they had inherited a household of living history, a family of compelling stories each with its own rich mixture of exploits, accommodations, inner rebellions, and unhealed scars. And behind all these separate voices were always the dominant and hammering echoes of actual war and actual defeat, a chorus of public and private claims that did not always make sense, but that demanded attention and that remained a permanent fascination. The first paragraph of William Faulkner's third novel, *Sartoris* (1929), reveals just such an attitude: "As usual, old man Falls had brought John Sartoris into the room with him, had walked the three miles in from the county Poor Farm, fetching, like an odor, like the clean dusty smell of his faded overalls, the spirit of the dead man into that room where the dead man's son sat and where the two of them, pauper and banker, would sit for a half an hour in the company of him who had passed beyond death and then returned." And again for the intent, searching young Southern writers, the fascination was edged with the vexing, but perhaps also inspiring, recognition that the South had yet to create a literature worthy of what it had experienced, and worthy especially of the multitude of individual lives caught up by a tragic history and never completely released.

What the young writers found above all else when they read the historical romances of William Alexander Caruthers, William Gilmore Simms, John Esten Cooke, and Thomas Nelson Page, among others, was an overwhelmingly consistent parade of uncomplicated Southern types: the high-toned planter and gracious but spirited plantation mistress, the gallant soldier-son, the domestic slave or faithful retainer (once the Civil War was over), and the large marginal population of half-wild, hand-to-mouth hunters and poor-white stick-farmers who inhabited a vast Southern backcountry of mountains, pine barrens, and swamps. There were other types, too, who occasionally made an appearance, but they remained types and seldom diverged from the predictable pattern.

The limitations of such a list were obvious to the young writers looking back, and even had they agreed to the game of making categories, they would have had little trouble naming the many Southern groups the early novels excluded. The immense majority of slaves, of course, worked in the fields and had little commerce with the plantation household. Only a chosen few enjoyed the status and privileges of body servants or domestic help, and by far the most numerous class of whites were the working families on their small or middle-size farms, representatives of what Thomas Jefferson referred to as "solid independent yeomanry," and what the twentieth-century social historians Frank Owsley and W. J. Cash respectively called the "plain folk" of the South and the "man in the center."

It was not the limited cast of the standard nineteenth-century novel that disturbed modern writers the most, nor even the fact that the novels served themselves so shamelessly of conventional types. These writers would have been the first to acknowledge that society is often best revealed in the extremes it creates, and that in the Old South the extremes generated by the plantation regime offered the most direct means of portraying Southern life. Even recent studies of the Old South, professionally attuned to all sorts of subtle qualifications of caste, class, creed, and race, have not been able to avoid the powerful magnetic field of plantation hierarchies. And no one would deny, or need to deny, that such hierarchies, even when isolated and exaggerated, were based on certain physical, cultural, and historical conditions that actually existed. At any rate, almost from the beginning of a Southern sense of separate identity, the oppositions between the gentleman planter and the non-gentleman or the non-planter have entered into every published definition of Southern character, and not merely, nor even most emphatically, into the nineteenth-century novel.

What did disturb modern writers, such as Allen Tate and William Faulkner, was the fact that given the wide-spread recognition of fixed Southern types and oppositions, the nineteenth-century novelist refused to do anything with them other than to put them on display. The dramatic possibilities of playing them against each other as a way of exposing their limits and revealing signs of hidden individual life were successfully attempted in the best short stories of the period, as readers of *A New Reader of the Old South* can judge for themselves, but they were rarely convincing in the long narrative. There was, of course, the vigorous tradition of native Southern humor and satire; it, too, is at its best in the short sketch or story in which stock characters, pretenders, rogues, and hypocrites abound. But the virtues of satire are also its liabilities, and it can seldom do anything more with a character after it has gone behind his back or turned him on his head.

Even in *The Adventures of Huckleberry Finn* (1884), one of the very few Southern novels of the nineteenth century that fully conveys the dramatic image of a living human presence—through the independent voice and troubled, uncertain conscience of Huck—Mark Twain is not always able to escape the stubborn inertia of the long-standing Southern sterotypes, especially when he deals with the extremes of Southern society and turns his attention toward the Southern adult. Twain obviously took great pains with the other characters in the novel, particularly with Jim whose very survival depends on slipping in and out of the roles imposed by black slavery. And one of Twain's revolutionary achievements derives from his conscious desire to include a wide but specific variety of Southern speech. Throughout the novel, in fact, there are many signs that Twain deliberately attempted to counter, as far as possible, the romantic ellipses of popular Southern fiction by presenting a complete vision of Southern life, up and down the social scale. Unlike the other Southern novels of the period, *The Adventures of Huckleberry Finn* makes room for ordinary townsfolk and farm families notable for their natural courtesy, good humor, and common sense, even though they stand firmly, and for the most part, uncritically, in the midst of the antebellum Southern community. Twain's description of the Phelps' farm at the end of the novel, "a little one-horse cotton plantation," could have applied with little alteration well into the twentieth century all throughout the South.

At the bottom and at the top of white Southern society, however, there are occasions when Twain found it difficult to budge the stage Southerner from his habitual roles and set scenes. As far as the lowest level "poor white trash" were concerned, Twain's attitude is not that much different from the antebellum Southern humorist, nor the various social commentators in the journals and newspapers. Twain is generally more caustic and far less inclined to see even the slightest quality of shrewdness and comic mother wit, but in other respects his portraits conform to the conventional type. Most readers of this novel will remember Twain's stage picture of the shiftless, tobacco-chewing men in a small town in Arkansas whose idea of recreation consists in watching the pigs wallow in the mud and in tormenting stray dogs by putting turpentine on them and setting them on fire. This is straightforward satirical scorn: effective, instructive, convincing as far as it goes, but finally damning its way to a dramatic dead end. Of course, Twain never lets the reader forget that Huck himself comes from this despised, degraded class, one of the wonderful ironies of the novel, and one of the reasons it appealed so strongly to modern Southern writers.

At the opposite end of the social scale, Twain gives his version of the patrician Southerner in two major episodes: the murderous feud between the Grangerfords and Shepherdsons, and the isolated story of Colonel Sherburn facing down a cowardly mob after he has calmly killed a defenseless drunkard. Twain's portraits are full of moral ironies and contradictions, but at the same time they are heavily dependent on popular conventions. Attitudes toward the Southern planter had become polarized during the decades before the Civil War, and were deeply divided between the image of the respectable, high-minded, independent country gentleman of the Southern nationalist and the brutal, slave-driving patriarch of the anti-slavery crusaders. An even greater influence on Twain was the sentimental literary revival of the plantation romance after the collapse of the South, a revival that tended to idealize the planter beyond all credibility. Twain's melodramatically plotted love affair between the children of the Grangerfords and Shepherdsons, his overcharged, cliché-packed descriptions of the Grangerfords' rituals, books, furniture, even their physical appearance, are clearly meant to be an ironic pastiche of the postbellum romance. And yet Twain leaves absolutely no doubt in the reader's mind that the Grangerfords' demonstrations of kindness and hospitality are genuine and that Huck's admiration for these qualities is well-deserved.

The evil underside of Twain's humorous mockery of the fashionable fictional planter is the deadly feud in which even a boy is gunned down like a rat in the river. At this point the contradictions begin to overwhelm. We are confronted with the spectacle of apparently courageous and civilized men capable of committing cold-blooded murder behind the blind mask of a debased code of honor. The origins of the feud have been long forgotten. And later on, in the Sherburn episode, we are faced with the confounding sight of a killer who is also a proud man standing unflinchingly on his own and openly haranguing the mob that has come to lynch him. And if that were not enough, Sherburn's very speech is a model of strong-minded satirical oratory, in the style and spirit of an honored Southern tradition, and echoes to a syllable Twain's own thoughts. The best one can say about these violently clashing conventions, and it is saying a lot compared to the usual novel of the period, is that Twain reveals his own distrust of simple caricature, and that he does provide at least an ironic suggestion of the Old South's overdramatically divided mind. For all his skill, however, Twain's portraits of the Southern planter never fully convince, and were evidently not meant to convince. In kind, if not in attitude, they belong to the same category of often shrewd, often merely emphatic generalizations put forward by such social critics and pundits in the South as Hinton Rowan Helper in *The Impending Crisis of the South* (1857) and Daniel Hundley in *Social Relations in Our Southern States* (1860), or in the North by John W. De Forest in his essay "Chivalrous and Semi-Chivalrous Southrons" (1869).

To return to modern Southern writers and their search through the novels of the Old South for some dramatic insight into their own condition, we must remember that they sought above all else two closely linked qualities: an honest vision of the full range of Southern experience, faithful to their own personal knowledge, and proof of particular human beings alive in a concrete world. *The Adventures of Huckleberry Finn* provided much of what they were looking for, most forcefully in the wholly compelling creation of Huck Finn himself, but modern Southerners realized, too, that the Southern planter and the plantation world were central to Southern history and to the tragic succession of events they had to grasp finally in order to assess their own troubled Southern identities. In this respect, they would have to look elsewhere than in Twain's novel.

Still, it should go almost without saying that we have insisted on *The Adventures of Huckleberry Finn* because it stands out entirely by itself as one of the great novels of the Old South. Had space allowed us to include it in *A New Reader of the Old South*, we would have done so without the slightest qualm or hesitation. Actually, as we already noted in *A Modern Southern Reader, Huckleberry Finn* is not only the major novel of the Old South, but also a direct influence on much of the best writing of the twentieth-century South. Allen Tate called it the "first modern novel by a Southerner," and every important Southern writer since has singled it out as the first fully accomplished work in a legitimate Southern literary tradition. Looking back from the vantage point of the end of the twentieth century, we should not be too surprised at the problems that faced Twain when he turned his own thoughts toward the Southern upper class. Even the poor white and the black slave, as vulnerable as they were to caricature and prejudice, did not have the additional burden of a full-scale myth to overcome.

Readers of Southern fiction are familiar enough with the rough chronology of the plantation myth. As the South moved toward the final separation from the Union in mid-century, a growing movement of pro-Southern apologists began to praise the planter and project his life back into an old-world civilization, improved and humanized by its new setting and its uncorrupted agrarian virtues. Opposing the plantation to the crowded, industrialized, materialistic Northern city with its unhappy mass of wage-slaves, these novelists and journalists and public spokesmen created an image of plantation existence as slow-paced, high-spirited, good-natured, and respectful of God-given natural hierarchies, a world in which time-honored traditions were cherished and in which white masters and black slaves lived in Christian communal harmony, each content with his appointed tasks and responsibilities.

The Civil War, with its monumental shocks, privations, and loss of life, crushed the South, but instead of crushing the antebellum image, magnified it into one of the permanent romantic myths of American history. Of course, the postbellum version of the myth was intensified almost beyond endurance by the collective Southern sense of a tragic fall, an arrested destiny of greatness, and a dead future doomed to guilt, grief, and remembrance. As Lewis Simpson has demonstrated in a number of remarkable studies, the culture of the Lost Cause replaced the culture of Southern nationalism and created an uncertain spiritual Southern identity trapped between a redemptive acceptance of suffering and a bewildered desire to believe that the past was not yet past. The idea of the Old South itself is defined by the two chronological halves of the plantation myth, before and after the Civil War, and only at the beginning of a greater and more universal reminder of tragic human fate, World War I, does the myth cease to play an active and dominant role in a collective Southern identity.

As with any "national" myth, the plantation myth was a mixture of historical fact, natural human will for a larger purpose, and defensive self-promotion. There is little point here in retracing every step of its development, or in pointing out again and again its all-too-obvious divergences from the concrete particulars of plantation reality, which itself was far more various than constant. One of the reasons *A New Reader of the Old South* includes a cross-selection from diaries and other non-fictional documents is the desire to reveal and highlight these very divergences. On the other hand, we should not be too quick to dismiss the way myth itself enters deeply into the full reality of the human mind. In the Old South, whether before, after, or during the Civil War, no Southerner could stand untouched by the persuasive cultural ideal of a separate destiny, and more often than such a Southerner perhaps might easily admit, this striving after a public demonstration of Southern difference strained a sense of private identity to the breaking point.

Inner tension between public and private realms was not the kind of problem openly addressed in the fictional versions of the plantation myth, as modern Southern writers were the first to notice and to lament. But actually the very existence of the myth-making impulse points to an undercurrent of doubt, especially when we consider that even from the beginning of the nineteenth century the Southern plantation had become a legend imbued with a haunting sense of loss and falling away.

Almost everywhere we look in the writing and memoirs of the Old South, a longing for an older, more self-assured South of the eighteenth century can be found. It should not be forgotten that the first Southern romances were historical, and that the Southern imagination long before the Lost Cause, and a full century before the first generation of Southern modernists, was under the spell of the "backward look." The colonial and revolutionary novels of John Pendleton Kennedy, Caruthers, and Simms spring readily to mind. The model was usually the eighteenth-century planter, with a strong strain of Cavalier blood, and this is especially true when we read the leading writers and intellectuals of the twin centers of plantation society: Virginia and South Carolina. Even in a work that brings us up into the nineteenth century, Kennedy's *Swallow Barn* (1832), the original and the best "plantation romance," the eighteenth century remains the ideal standard of judgment. Kennedy, despite his light-hearted mockery concerning the more fantastic feudal rituals of the Virginians, primarily the over-romanticized, Walter Scott-enchanted younger generation, expresses a keen regret that a superior society has been irreversibly reduced.

Outside the novels, elegiac comments on a disappearing world appear over and over again with the insistence of a refrain that cannot be forgotten. As early as 1814, John Randolph, wittily described by Lewis Simpson as the "first last gentleman," for whom even Thomas Jefferson was a symbol of patrician decline, complains in a letter: "I made a late visit to my birthplace. At the end of a journey through a wilderness, I found desolation & stillness as if of death—the fires of hospitality long since quenched—the hearth cold—& the parish church tumbling to pieces, not more from natural decay than sacrilegious violence. This is a faithful picture of this state from the falls of the great river to the sea-board." Further south, in South Carolina, not long after the publications of *Swallow Barn,* the well-known statesman and man of letters, Hugh Swinton Legaré, painted a comparably gloomy picture in a letter of 1833: "We are (I am quite sure) the *last* of the *race* of South Carolina; I see nothing before us but decay and downfall,—but, on that very account, I cherish its precious relics the more."

Even the wide-spread aspiration to own a plantation as a sign of having reached the ultimate level of Southern success was undermined by the knowledge that the new estate could never rival the old. William J. Grayson, proslavery author of "The Hireling and the Slave," wrote in his memoir of James Louis Petigru, published in 1866, the following account of antebellum ambition: "No matter how one might begin, as lawyer, physician, clergyman, mechanic, or merchant, he ended, if prosperous, as proprietor of a rice or cotton plantation. It was the condition that came nearest to the shadow of the colonial aristocracy which yet remained." Without much hunting around, many similar remarks could be added to the list. It is interesting to note that there is little sense of self-delusion in these expressions of regret, but instead a very human desire to commit oneself to a culture and a community that seemed worth defending. The point to be made is that the simple, almost sacred propositions of the plantation myth had a definite appeal and exerted a tremendous pressure on individual members of the upper and middle classes, chiefly the sons and grandsons of those who still had memories of an earlier South. On one hand, there was the growing sectional urge to assert a social and cultural superiority to the North, and on the other, a constant reminder that the Southern planter of the nineteenth century was the last of a dying breed, whose gentlemanly codes and ceremonies were forced to call attention to themselves in an exaggerated manner in order not to betray the tradition.

James Henry Hammond, the brilliant but flawed South Carolina governor and U.S. congressman and senator, and the man who popularized the phase "cotton is king" on the floor of the Senate in 1858, browbeat his sons mercilessly with their failure to meet his almost impossible standards. One of his severest complaints was that they could never prove themselves to be "well-bred independent South Carolina Country Gentlemen," but remained, even when fully grown and entrusted with their own plantations, "mere dilettanti—theatrical planters." Such theatrical planters were encountered more than once in the Old South, years before the postbellum "professional Southerner" was taken to task by Mark Twain, Walter Hines Page, O. Henry, and others. Early in his political career in the House of Representatives, Hammond rejected as unconstitutional any petitions concerning slavery. He maintained that if slavery were an evil, which he denied it was, then it was an evil for the South alone and no outsider should interfere with the South's internal problems. He countered his opponents, as did many of his compatriots, by saying that slavery, in fact, brought with it many blessings. A tough-minded supremacist at heart who believed that the white aristocracy, looking back to early Egyptian civilization or the feudal society of the Middle Ages, could be preserved best on a foundation or "mudsill" of black slavery, Hammond never expressed any guilt in his diaries about being a slave owner; in fact, it is suprising how little he mentions slavery in these pages. For him, the Civil War—the modern Armageddon—destroyed all that he held dear. In his eyes, then, to deviate from his rigid code was not merely a family disgrace, or a source of ridicule, but a failing that could approach the gravity of a public sin. It is perhaps not surprising that the call to arms was answered so eagerly by large numbers of planters' sons. Here at last was the ultimate proof of living up to the code, by fighting and dying for it.

There were far less demanding fathers than James Henry Hammond, and many more sons than not who fought and died without playing, George Pickett-style, the glory-seeking Cavalier heir to the hilt. But throughout the Old South, the proper public rites and roles held sovereign sway over all other considerations. The plantation myth set forward by the Old South novel both reflected and helped create this overall impression that public life was all that really counted in human existence. As modern Southerners were quick to notice, almost all signs of private struggle, inner reality, or even individual difference, had been suppressed in the overwhelming majority of novels they read.

Edmund Wilson, in his monumental study *Patriotic Gore* (1962), expressed a similar opinion, but went on to say that there was, however, outside the novels, a remarkable literary culture made up of "speeches and pamphlets, private letters and diaries, personal memoirs and journalistic reports." He was speaking more narrowly of the Civil War period, but his own copious illustrations are by no means confined to the literature of the Civil War itself, and his observations would apply equally well to the full sweep of nineteenth-century Southern writing. They are also an excellent argument for presenting the Old South in the form of an anthology. Since there is no single work of fiction that does justice to the full reality of the period, or represents its best literary insights, with the possible exception of *The Adventures of Huckleberry Finn,* there is good reason to claim, as Wilson does, that the momentous story of the Old South is best told from a variety of different perspectives and modes—not all of which need come from the literary artist—dramatized through a deliberate juxtaposition of individual pieces.

Wilson also goes to some lengths to single out several neglected Southern short stories, praised by him for their realism and independence when compared to the better-known novels, and this brings us to another general esthetic principle behind the putting together of the *A New Reader of the Old South.* Without taking too many critical risks, we can mildly suggest that each literary genre has its own special virtues, limitations, and relationships to the culture it springs from and seeks to represent. The novel is spacious enough to speak for an entire society, but the impulse to do so, as the Old South novel so often proved, can be a disadvantage in a society dominated by a powerful public ideology.

The short story, on the other hand, is limited in its presentation of society, and is usually tempted to pierce through rather than to spread out. Every prose narrative involves some sort of dramatic tension between private and public lives, but the short story is certainly at its most characteristic, and most convincing, when it concentrates on the private drama of the single individual. And even when an extremely socially conscious writer such as Thomas Nelson Page aims at giving the impression that his individual characters are representative figures, the very fact of an isolated narrative voice in his best dialect stories thrusts the question of private identity forward in surprising and revealing, if not always intentional, ways.

It may be going too far to insist that the form of the short story itself saved several major Southern writers from repeating the flaws and complacencies of their novels, but there can be no question that the most original fiction of the Old South is found in the succession of short stories going back to the early humorists and reaching up to some of the remarkable, and too-little known, stories of the local colorists. Here is the valid literary tradition that modern Southerner writers found lacking in the Southern novel and the official rhetoric. And here is perhaps the most compelling argument for *A New Reader of the Old South* that gives the lion's share of its space, not to extracts from novels, but to an opening section that collects a large number of some of the best stories we could find.

The Southern short story first found a distinctive voice in a series of comic tales and sketches published during the three decades before the Civil War. Beginning with Augustus Baldwin Longstreet's *Georgia Scenes* in 1835, praised and promoted by Edgar Allan Poe as a comic masterpiece, and as a sure sign of "better days for the literature of the South," Southern or "Southwestern" humor became eagerly sought after and quickly printed by major Northern magazines and publishing houses. Soon after *Georgia Scenes* had launched the fashion, other Southern writers followed with their own popular collections: *Major Jones's Courtship* (1843) by William Tappan Thompson, *Some Adventures of Simon Suggs* (1845) by Johnson Jones Hooper, *Odd*

Leaves from the Life of a Louisiana "Swamp Doctor" (1850) by Henry Clay Lewis, *The Flush Times of Alabama and Mississippi* (1853) by Joseph G. Baldwin, and *Sut Lovingood's Yarns* (1867) by George Washington Harris. Many of their stories were first published in the widely circulated New York sporting journal *Spirit of the Times* whose editor, William T. Porter, was an enthusiastic champion of the wild exploits and raw independence of the untamed Southern backwoods. Porter himself put together two anthologies of humorous stories, including the influential *The Big Bear of Arkansas and Other Sketches* (1845) whose title story by Thomas Bangs Thorpe, a Northern expatriot who spent twenty years in Louisiana, began a long line of Southern hunting tales that reach from William Elliott's "The Fire Hunter," Henry Clay Lewis's "The Indefatigable Bear Hunter," and William Gilmore Simms's "How Sharp Snaffles Got his Capital and Wife" on up to the Aleck Maury stories of Caroline Gordon and William Faulkner's modern masterpiece "The Bear."

In reading the Southern humorists today, it is easy enough to understand their wide-spread appeal as sheer comic entertainment. This was their primary aim, and to a surprising degree the outrageous gestures, low cunning, and inventive verbal wit are still almost impossible to resist. Poe described his own immediate reaction to *Georgia Scenes* as one of outright "immoderate laughter." But Poe was also quick to point out two other qualities in Longstreet's sketches that bring them closer in spirit and form to the modern short story: a skill in expressing character through a single dramatic action, and a faithful, if somewhat exaggerated, description of the sights and sounds that were actually observed, no matter how preposterous, violent, unseemly, or vulgar they appeared to the observer.

It may seem odd that Southern self-mockery and local realism appeared and began to ripen in the very period when Southern nationalism raised and fixed its banners, and that in almost every case the major Southern humorists were devoted defenders of the Southern cause. But the two movements were perhaps not as contradictory as they seem. In his pioneering study, *Augustus Baldwin Longstreet: A Study of the Development of Culture in the South* (1924), John Donald Wade suggests that Longstreet's willingness to cast a half-satirical and often highly critical eye on his own native Georgia reflects an independence of spirit that itself was a natural consequence of strongly affirmed sectional rights.

One common explanation for Southern humor emerging when it did has been that the humorists themselves stood apart from the uneducated, unsophisticated world they described. Their professional and social status as lawyer, doctor, or newspaper owner gave them a moral superiority and freedom to look down and beyond that in no way jeopardized their position as acknowledged community leaders. In fact their comic literary powers probably strengthened that position and certainly conferred on them a special authority as Southern spokesmen both within and without the boundaries of the South. But a careful reading of the four stories we have chosen to represent the humorist movement, Longstreet's "The Fight," Hooper's "The Widow Rugby's Husband," Simms's "Ephraim Bartlett, the Edisto Raftsman," and Harris's "Mrs. Yardley's Quilting," should leave no doubt that the superior attitude of the author-observer was never wholly untouched by genuine amusement, and even certain feelings of admiration and pride.

In Longstreet's "The Fight," for example, the thrust of the satire is aimed at Ransy Sniffles, a wonderful vision of the lowest grade poor-white who has, in his earlier days, "fed copiously on red clay and blackberries," and who strikes a universal chord of recognition in his pathetic need to foment violence as long as he himself can remain safely out of the way when the dust begins to fly. Along with Ransy, however, are Longstreet's other characters, the local noncommittal sage, Uncle Tommy Loggins, and especially the two fighters, Billy Stallings and Bob Durham. These are all rough, unpolished, country-town natives, but they are easily distinguishable from each other and they have their commendable qualities. Even ill-favored Ransy is capable of near-eloquence when inspired. Longstreet gives us a bloody, no-holds-barred battle, but both fighters emerge as powerful physical specimens who prove they have earned their reputations. They are hard-skinned and fierce, but at the same time show courage and, when the fight is done, an honest, good-natured lack of spite. There is no question where Longstreet's own sympathies lie, even though he rather feebly tries to have it both ways in the final moralizing paragraph.

For all his cowardly cunning in stirring up trouble, Longstreet's Ransy Sniffles would have been no match for the resourceful rogues created by two of the most gifted Southern humorists, Johnson Jones Hooper and George Washington Harris. Hooper introduced his character Simon Suggs in a series of newspaper sketches in the 1840's and gained a national reputation in 1845 with his first collection, *Some Adventures of Captain Simon Suggs, Late of the Tallapoosa Volunteers; Together with "Taking the Census," and Other Alabama Sketches.* Captain Suggs is a consummate hypocrite and opportunist with a flair for seeing through the less shrewd hypocrisies of others. His motto, "It's good to be shifty in a new country," became one of the catch phrases of the antebellum South. "The Widow Rugby's Husband" is a later Suggs story and a rather unusual example of political satire finding its way into the earlier fiction. Hooper, himself an ardent secessionist, begins the narrative with an ironic presentation of "The Union Hotel" and its owners during the divisive days of the nullification crisis. The heart of the story, however, as is always the case when Captain Suggs is on the scene, lies in his genius for plotting, cheating, and outfoxing his way out of debt and out of trouble.

Hooper shared with Longstreet a receptive ear for native speech and emphatic Southernisms, but as narrators they always maintained a respectable verbal restraint. There is no verbal restraint, or restraint of any other kind, in the Sut Lovingood stories of George Washington Harris, who lived most of his life in and around Knoxville, Tennessee, and forged a richly imagined dialect based on the mountain speech of East Tennessee that gives his hero, or anti-hero, Sut Lovingood, a literary originality that had to wait for the age of John Millington Synge and Sean O'Casey before being fully appreciated. Sut has no illusions about the world or about his own animal pleasure and spends his time drinking, telling stories, chasing women, fleeing women, playing practical jokes, and exposing anyone and everyone who does not agree with his coarse but straightforward philosophy of life: "Man wer made a-purpus jis' to eat, drink, and fur staying awake in the yearly part ove the nites, an' wimen were made to cook the vittils, mix the spirits, an help the men du the staying awake." We can add to this list Sut's own self-delight in the creative power of outrageous metaphor and ripe invective all too sadly lacking in the bloodless, sexless, sentimental prose that would soon engulf the South along with much of the rest of the Victorian English-speaking world.

Obviously, Sut was not meant to represent the typical Southerner, nor even the typical Southern mountaineer, but in reading his stories and the wildlife adventures of Simon Suggs and others, it is difficult not to think that the comic horseplay and frank earthiness of the Southern humorists, no matter how careful they might be in establishing a moral distance from their characters, were a not-too-subtle means of exaggerating a sensual, loud-laughing, all-too-human South in opposition to the standard dour image of the holier-than-thou Yankee Puritan.

William Gilmore Simms's sketch, "Ephraim Bartlett, the Edisto Raftsman," was published in 1852 as the fourth installment of a magazine series titled "Home Sketches, or Life along the Highways and Byways of the South." As the most prominent professional novelist and man of letters in the antebellum South, Simms worked ceaselessly in almost every literary form, and his novels, essays, poems, and stories touched on almost every level of Southern life, up and down the social scale, from the South Carolina low country to the remote, barely settled backwoods border regions. Though he was best known in his lifetime for his numerous historical romances, his interests in native humor and dialect are displayed to better effect in his stories than in his novels. Two of his dialect stories, "How Sharp Snaffles Got His Capital and Wife" and "Bald-Head Bill Bauldy," are masterpieces of Southern humor. Both these stories were too long for *A New Reader of the Old South,* but "Ephraim Bartlett," despite its "occasional" nature and somewhat unsteady narrative focus, clearly demonstrates Simms's skill in the genre. As a partially "recorded" tall tale, it definitely belongs in the company of the early Southern humorists, but what makes "Ephraim Bartlett" rather exceptional for its time is Simms's sympathetic treatment of the bonds between the white raftsman and his black helper, bonds that look forward to the ones more consciously explored a generation later by several of the Southern local colorists.

Actually, local color is a term that probably should be avoided when considering the largest group of stories in *A New Reader of the Old South,* those written by Southern writers who made their reputations after the Civil War, and who did more than all the other writers in *A New Reader of the Old South* combined to define the character of the Old South. Certainly such writers as Joel Chandler Harris in Georgia and George Washington Cable and Grace King in Louisiana were often associated with other American writers who helped create a new national interest in regional identities during the last decades of the nineteenth century: Sarah Orne Jewett in Maine, Bret Harte in California, and Hamlin Garland in the Middle West, to name three of the most popular. Along with Harris, Cable, and King, the South had more than its share of popular regionalists who concentrated on well-defined pockets of Southern life: Charles Egbert Craddock (Mary Noailles Murfree) in Tennessee and James Lane Allen in Kentucky, for example. But to suggest that there was a unified literary school of local colorists masks enormous differences in style, aim, and originality among the individual writers, and these differences are striking and important when we turn to the following six stories: "Posson Jone'" by Cable,

"Mingo: A Sketch of Life in Middle Georgia" by Harris, "Unc' Edinburg's Drowndin': A Plantation Echo" by Thomas Nelson Page, "Bayou l'Ombre" by Grace King, "A Night in Acadie" by Kate Chopin, and "Sis' Becky's Pickaninny" by Charles Waddell Chesnutt.

Still, there are several strands that bind these writers together, and that deserve to be mentioned. To begin with, they were all highly conscious of themselves as Southern writers, writing out of a land more united by suffering and defeat than it had been in the years before the Civil War when public proclamations of Southern unity could often sound artificial and abstract. As children, these writers had lived through the murderous war years, and one of them, George Washington Cable, barely out of childhood, had fought in the Confederate calvary. Another, Charles Waddell Chesnutt, had followed the news of the war from his home in Cleveland, Ohio, where his parents, free blacks from North Carolina, had moved several years before the South seceded. At the age of eight, in 1866, Chesnutt was back in North Carolina where his father had returned to open a grocery store.

As mature men and women, all personally attached to the South in one way or another, these same writers addressed themselves to a society that would remain confused, deeply afflicted, and haunted by racial divisions for much of their lifetimes. As we have already suggested, the short story form perhaps encouraged them to aim their insights at sharp, glancing angles in a world that everyone knew, or thought they knew, but that was difficult for the writer to confront head-on, and with any conviction of doing it full justice. In any event, they all established their reputations with well-received first collections of short stories, beginning with Cable's *Old Creole Days* in 1879, and followed by Harris's *Uncle Remus: His Songs and Sayings* (1880), Page's *In Ole Virginia* (1887), King's *Tales of a Time and Place* (1892), Chopin's *Bayou Folk* (1894), and Chesnutt's *The Conjure Woman* (1899). With all due allowances for four remarkable novels, Cable's *The Grandissimes* (1880), Chopin's *The Awakening* (1899), Chesnutt's *The Marrow of Tradition* (1901), and King's *The Pleasant Ways of St. Médard* (1916), the stories of these six writers have remained their most lasting work.

A final argument for looking at them as a group, and for considering their attraction to the short story, stems from the fact that they each began their career by giving a literary voice to isolated individuals from two distinct Southern communities who had been largely ignored in Southern fiction up to then, and whose culture and character opened up new, far-reaching literary avenues into the meaning of the South as a whole: the Southern black and the Louisiana French.

Of the three writers in this group—Harris, Page, and Chesnutt—who introduced black culture into Southern fiction, Page presents by far the most difficult case to appraise today. He is still remembered as the nineteenth-century writer most fully engaged in reviving the plantation romance after the Civil War and in glorifying what he felt were the supreme qualities of the Old South regime before they were destroyed by the collapse of the Confederacy. There is no question that he used his stories and novels to portray plantation life as a noble dream of honor, loyalty, courage, triumphant benevolence, and heroic self-sacrifice, and that his ability to weave these fading virtues into melodramatic plots filled with romantic old-time portraits helps explain the enormous appeal his work had in both the South and the North.

Page can be called a stubborn idealist, but despite his genuine regret of a lost past, and despite his tireless efforts in defending the Southern cause, he was no blind apologist, and he had a sound knowledge of Southern realities. One of the intriguing features of his fiction, however, is that his prose is most convincing when he has taken on the voice of the black narrators in his dialect stories. In "Unc' Edinburg's Drowndin'," for example, we need only note Unc' Edinburg's energetic account of the Christmas dance, with the black fiddler "rockin' like boat rockin' on the water," his frank appraisal of sexual politics, both black and white, his worldly irony at the expense of his masters ("white folks' 'ligion ain' like niggers', you know; dee got so much larnin dee kin dance an' fool de devil too"); these are the natural gifts of a supple, emphatic, unrestrained language that Page was not free to use when speaking in his own voice. There are many unintended ironies in the story, but one of the strangest is that a white dream of the plantation becomes, at the same time, a white dream of the fuller existence of the black slave, almost as if Page obscurely sensed his only access to the real world was through the back door. At any rate, his dialect stories are the best things he wrote, and it is understandable that Joel Chandler Harris wrote to Page praising "Marse Chan" and "Unc' Edinburg's Drowdin'" as stories he would have liked to have written himself.

Joel Chandler Harris is often paired with Page as a nostalgic defender of antebellum plantation life, yet Harris himself was much more of an outsider in this world than Page. He was the illegitimate son of a mother who had been deserted by his father, and who had to struggle to survive in the small town of Eatonton, Georgia. Harris did have a taste of plantation life as a boy when he worked during the Civil War on the Turnwold plantation owned by Joseph Addison Turner, who by all accounts was a model of the benevolent slave owner. He was also the editor of a weekly paper, *The Countryman,* and his literary encouragement and well-stocked library convinced Harris that his own future lay in the world of letters. After his stay at Turnwold, where he became close friends with many of the slaves, Harris entered into a lifetime of newspaper work and an eventual career as one of the most beloved and admired Southern writers of his time. His best-known writings were the long series of black folk tales beginning with the collection, *Uncle Remus: His Songs and Sayings,* in 1880.

The Uncle Remus tales were based on animal stories, songs, and superstitions he had listened to as a boy, and he always insisted that his own role as a writer was merely to record them as accurately as possible. Praised by Mark Twain and Rudyard Kipling as a main influence in their own careers, Harris is recognized today as the first writer to fully appreciate and express the vigorous oral tradition of the Southern black. He considered himself a "Georgia humorist" in the fertile tradition of Longstreet, William Tappan Thompson (whom he worked for on *The Savannah News*), Charles Henry Smith, and Richard Malcolm Johnston, but he surpassed all of them in his sympathetic understanding of both the Georgia black and the struggling Georgia white farmer. Along with "Free Joe and the Rest of the World," "Mingo" is one of his most surprising and independent studies of Southern ironies, and a showcase for his celebrated ear for local dialects. With Mingo and Mrs. Feratia Bivins, Harris paints the portrait of an unlikely, but convincing partnership. Mrs. Bivins is a strong-willed Georgia "cracker": "She had evidently seen sorrow and defied it. There was no suggestion of compromise in manner or expression. Even her hospitality was uncompromising." And Mingo, the former carriage driver for Judge Junius Wornum and his wife Emily, in his decision to remain in the South after the Civil War, shows more strength of character and family loyalty than his masters.

Charles Waddell Chesnutt obviously owed more than a spark of inspiration to Harris and the Uncle Remus tales when he began in the late 1880's to write his own series of dialect stories based on the language and culture of the Southern black. Chesnutt had spent much of his boyhood and young adulthood in North Carolina during the Reconstruction period, but when he began writing he returned to Cleveland, Ohio, and to a lifetime career as a lawyer and successful businessman. Unlike Harris's Uncle Remus, who only rarely suggests the suffering of the plantation slave, Chesnutt's black spokesman and tale teller, Uncle Julius, freely exposes the injustices and inhumanity that threatened the slave every day of his life, which Chesnutt as a youth must have felt deeply as part of his own racial inheritance. Chesnutt's first story, "The Goophered Grapevine," was published in *The Atlantic Monthly* in August 1887. Twelve years later Chestnutt joined it with six other related tales in the collection *The Conjure Woman,* which derive their narrative power from the vivid dramatic voice and sly moral undertones of Uncle Julius, who demonstrates, in such stories as "Mars Jeems's Nightmare" and "Sis' Becky's Pickaninny," that Chesnutt was far more conscious of the hidden dimensions of black folk beliefs and magical lore than the white writers of his day.

When George Washington Cable began his literary career in the 1870's, Louisiana was already recognized as a fertile field overgrown with the exotic local color Northern magazines and publishers were actively seeking. Cable actually got his start when he read a few of his unpublished stories to Edward King, a young journalist visiting New Orleans who had come down from New York to write a series of articles on the South under Reconstruction for *Scribner's Magazine.* In one of these articles, later collected in his book *The Great South* (1875), King suggests the central drama that Cable himself was the first to explore fully: "Louisiana today is Paradise Lost. In twenty years it may be Paradise Regained. It has unlimited, magnificent possibilities. Upon its bayou-penetrated soil, on its rich uplands and its vast prairies, a gigantic struggle is in progress; it is the battle of race with race, of the *picturesque* and unjust civilisation of the past with the prosaic and leveling civilisation of the present." It is clear that Cable realized early in his writing that the lingering presence of the Old Creole plantation society, now out of power and in steady decline, with a stubborn pride in its past that decades of bad fortune had done little to diminish, gave him a special historical perspective on the current tragedy of the entire South. The Creoles had generally been ardent defenders of Confederate interests, not only because they rightly considered themselves legitimate Southerners who happened to speak French, but also because the Civil War reminded them of an earlier "invasion" when the traditional Creole world was shaken to its roots by the Louisiana Purchase in 1803.

To Cable's credit, he was never satisfied with merely displaying the colorful contrast and rich cultural and racial mixtures of Louisiana life, though he did so with a sympathy, a flair, and an accuracy that can still be enjoyed and admired. Almost always in his fiction the initial impression of a half-amused, half-sentimental, theatrical intelligence slowly setting the scene of a left-behind age gradually gives way to a dramatic sense of moral struggle forcing the individual to reveal, defend, revise, or abandon his old inherited rituals and beliefs. In any event, he is made to confront them, face to face. In Cable's mind, and in the minds of his readers, the comparisons between old Louisiana and the recent Confederacy were not perhaps always overwhelming, but they were obvious and disturbing. They became so disturbing to Cable himself that his own literary career increasingly moved toward the courageous personal stand, especially in the South of the 1880's, of writing polemical essays and speaking out in public against segregation and racial injustice. Because of this, even though as a devoted Southerner he continued to hope that the "silent South" was on his side, he was so roundly condemned by the New Orleans press that he finally decided to take his family and move North. Though Grace King and Kate Chopin never became the public figure Cable was, and though they concerned themselves more with the role of the Southern woman than with the debate on racial segregation, they shared with Cable a tough-minded moral independence and a willingness to challenge that set them apart from the majority of other writers in the Old South.

Neither Cable, King, nor Chopin belonged by birth to the Creole community, but all three spoke French and were deeply sensitive to the cultural differences between the Louisiana French and the other Louisiana natives. There can be little question that their attraction to Creole culture awakened them to puzzling perceptions of their own hidden identities and led them toward a literature in which public certitudes are often called into question, and in which personal allegiances are often forced to measure themselves against the racial, religious, social, and sexual assumptions of the rest of the world. In any case, all three writers have in common a Louisiana-inspired combination of self-irony and cultural awareness that deepened their visions of the Old South and helped them take an impressive stride toward the major Southern themes of the modern era. In reading through their stories, we were faced with a much wider choice than with the other Southern writers of the century. Chopin herself, in a writing career that lasted barely fifteen years, wrote over a hundred stories. And both Cable and King could have been well represented with a number of stories other than the ones we finally selected.

Cable was capable of writing stories in more somber strains, as in his tragic study of a former slave-trader, "Jean-ah Poquelin," or in his too-little-known Civil War narrative, "Carancro," but in "Posson Jone'," the comical confrontation between the self-indulgent, carefree Creole Jules St.-Ange and the physically powerful, forthright backwoods preacher Parson Jones gives a good idea of Cable's dramatic skills and his mastery of Southern dialects. What is noteworthy in this story is Cable's ability to make the humorous clash of very recognizable types reveal a common ground of individual tolerance and friendship that public conventions would have been reluctant to imagine and accept.

Grace King continues to be best known for her two short stories, "Monsieur Motte," her first published work, later expanded into a short novel, and "The Little

Convent Girl." Both, it is true, are good examples of her polished skill at undercutting melodramatic plots with sharp thrusts of psychological realism. "Monsieur Motte," a story of a black Creole servant who secretly provides for a white schoolgirl orphaned by the war, was acclaimed immediately when it first appeared anonymously in *The New Princeton Review* in January 1886. "The Little Convent Girl," a highly symbolic study of Southern innocence overcome by Southern experience, was singled out by Edmund Wilson in *Patriotic Gore,* a book that did a great deal to revive interest in King's other work. "The Little Convent Girl" has also been recently praised by Anne Goodwyn Jones in her fine analysis of Southern women writers, *Tomorrow is Another Day* (1981). But surprisingly little attention has been given to "Bayou l'Ombre," a long, dense narrative of three romantic Creole-educated sisters during the Civil War. The slow-moving, wearisome pace of an isolated, waterbound plantation kept going by the women and a handful of unpredictable domestic slaves is wonderfully captured in this story, but what lifts it above much of the literature of the Old South is King's ironic perception of a romanticism and a blind faith that is all the more convincing for being rooted in the psychological fact of what she wisely called New Orleans realism.

Kate Chopin was born in St. Louis, Missouri, but everything she wrote was centered in the Louisiana she moved to when she married a cotton trader and plantation owner a few years after the Civil War. Her family was sympathetic to the Confederate cause, and one of her brothers died of typhoid fever after having been imprisoned by the Union army. Though her own attachments to the South were strong, they were not political, and she could challenge such sacred Southern claims as unmixed blood, in her story "Désirée's Baby," for example, with a directness that approaches derision. In a different vein, no reader of *The Awakening* will forget that Edna Pontellier is a Southern belle from a Presbyterian Kentucky family with a passion for race horses. Edna herself proves to be a fine judge of horse flesh in one of the crucial scenes of the book. Her father, a colonel in the Confederacy, is described as one of the theatrical Southerners Mark Twain and Walter Hines Page were fond of attacking. When Edna receives him on a visit to New Orleans, he is now padded in the shoulders and an expert at making strong "toddies." It is interesting to remember, too, that among Edna's final thoughts are the sound of her father's voice and the image of the young Southern cavalry officer she had been enamored of in her youth.

Though *The Awakening* has been Chopin's most frequently praised work, several of her stories are equally, if not more, accomplished. "A Night in Acadie" is one of her best and an excellent example of her manner of entering directly, and with complete authority, into the local sensual reality of the close-knit Louisiana French community. In this instance, the story takes place, not among the plantation or New Orleans Creoles, but among the more remote Acadian (or "Cajun") farms and small hamlets toward the end of the century. One of Chopin's minor subjects in this story is Telèsphore's modern impulse away from the old ways of his uncle, but the heart of the narrative action turns on a demanding arousal of sexual will that, as *The Awakening* confirms, must be considered one of Chopin's most compulsive and serious themes.

In 1900, the year after *The Awakening* was published, a thirty-six-year-old Virginia woman, Ellen Glasgow, brought out her third novel, *The Voice of the People.* This would be the first of her long series of strong-minded, realistic Virginia novels on the last days of the Old South, including *The Battle-Ground* (1902), her Civil War novel, *Virginia* (1913), her first great study of a Southern woman's inherited roles, and *Barren Ground* (1925), her first masterpiece. In each case, the Southern ideal of woman's place in society is thoroughly sounded out; and in each case, the ideal is found to be painfully deficient in dealing with real life. It continues to serve, however, even if it is no longer unconsciously obeyed, and this is one of the self-conscious Southern woman's ambiguous strengths after the trials of the Civil War that Glasgow was the first writer to realize fully. She continued her chronicle of Virginia life and manners with a trilogy of sophisticated Richmond comedies, *The Romantic Comedians* (1926), *They Stooped to Folly* (1929), and her second masterpiece, *The Sheltered Life* (1932). Her last works included two further novels, *Vein of Iron* (1935) and *In This Our Life* (1941), and a posthumous autobiography, *The Woman Within* (1954).

As editors, we would be the first to admit that Glasgow could have been included, without the slightest scruple, in *A Modern Southern Reader.* Especially after *Barren Ground,* she is clearly one of the major writers of the modern South. But it is arguable, too, that she owes as much to the Old South as she does to the new; she was often held, as she herself admitted, by the same traditions her novels so revealingly questioned. At any rate, we had considered using her story "Jordan's End" in the modern collection, but decided then, and continue to believe, that it is a story more in the spirit of her earlier fiction whose rightful place as a representative piece of the major transitional figure in Southern letters has been respected. Glasgow was far more at ease in the novel than in the short story, but "Jordan's End" is a well-crafted, haunting tale of Southern isolation, inbreeding, and madness, written with a care for the exactly observed sight and sound that never falters; it provides a brief, searing glimpse of a very typical self-sacrificial Glasgow heroine. Chronologically, "Jordan's End" is the last story of our short story section. Appropriately, for more reasons than mere esthetic justice, especially when we consider that the authentic literary voice of the Southern woman was rarely heard or valued during much of the nineteenth century, "Jordan's End" completes a powerful trinity of stories whose authors, King, Chopin, and Glasgow, by themselves alone, fully justify a long new look at the Old South.

Most of these postbellum writers were keenly aware that before the Civil War, many Southern whites had been gripped by a terrible fear and anxiety that their way of life, based to a large extent on slavery, would be radically changed; as a result, they became defensive as they sought more and more isolation from the forces of abolitionism. In extreme cases, as noted historian John Hope Franklin points out in his essay "Slavery and the Martial South," a climate of intense conflict could be felt within the plantation system itself: "If the relationship between master and slave was that of a superior and a subordinate, a despot or tyrant and a powerless subject, or an armed victor and a vanquished foe, it can almost be described as a state of war. At least it is possible to recognize the martial spirit that pervaded the entire plantation atmosphere....Slaves enjoyed no well-defined body of rights; for their infractions there was summary punishment; and there was, of course, no appeal." It should be recalled that the attempted revolt of Nat Turner in 1831 was stopped by both local and federal forces, so adamant was the desire of the white ruling class to prevent any disruption of their society. When the whites thought of the bloody nature of such possible insurrections, they became traumatized.

If anyone in the United States could have set a truly moral course toward the abolition of slavery, it would have been Thomas Jefferson, who died on July 4, 1826. Yet Jefferson never fully resolved the dilemma of slavery, and perhaps because he left an ambiguous legacy in this regard, many of his successors, even down to recent times it could be argued, never felt absolutely sure of what moral, legal, and political positions to take. Jefferson put the dilemma most succinctly in his letter to John Holmes, dated April 22, 1820: "Justice is in one scale, and self-preservation in the other." This author of *The Declaration of Independence,* founder of the University of Virginia, and translator of the Bible, owned himself numerous slaves, only two of whom he freed, even though he publicly denounced slavery. Still, who would doubt that Jefferson had a profound sense of freedom, as evidenced in the "Bill for Establishing Religious Freedom," based on a philosophy of the natural rights of mankind, which he introduced into the Virginia Assembly on June 13, 1779. When this bill met considerable opposition, Jefferson prudently lobbied for its passage until it was finally adopted in 1786. In his study titled *Mind and the American Civil War: A Meditation on Lost Causes* (1989), Lewis Simpson likewise stresses the importance of Jefferson's *Notes on the State of Virginia* (privately printed, 1785; publicly printed, 1787), which represents the ideals of the Enlightenment in juxtapostion with the interests of a provincial slave society that had "without any real intention of abolishing its own slave system, paradoxically committed itself to the rejection of slavery to a king in the name of the sovereignty of self." With more than a modicum of doubt, and with a good dose of pathos as well, Jefferson's implicit thesis is that the mind cannot by itself serve as history's guiding instrument of reason. In emphasizing the freedom that Virginians knew as a result of their break with England, Jefferson praised the General Assembly for banning the future importation of slaves from beyond national boundaries. He wrote: "This will in some measure stop the increase of this great political and moral evil, while the minds of our citizens may be ripening for a complete emancipation of human nature." After reading this enigmatic sentence, one can only wonder whether Jefferson actually believed that the corporate social human intellect would ever accept blacks and whites as total equals.

In underscoring the possibility that human nature might not always accept the moral imperatives of the rational will, Jefferson, in the noted Query XVIII of *Notes on the State of Virginia,* in which he affirms, at least in this one instance, that the slave is intellectually and morally equal with a white person, suggests an ironic reversal: Those who own slaves may not be able to sever the bonds they have with their slaves. And though in this document Jefferson actually called for the emancipation of slaves, he undercut this view by postulating that the mind could probably not extricate itself, except with the aid of divine intervention, from the forces of history that had brought it into existence up to this point in time: "The spirit of the master is abating, that of the slave rising from the dust, his condition mollifying the way I hope preparing, under the auspices of heaven, for a total emancipation, and that this is disposed, in the order of events, to be with the consent of the masters, rather than by their extirpation." In his letter to Edward Coles, dated August 25, 1814, Jefferson stated that "the hour of emancipation is advancing, in the march of time." Believing that good intentions and good deeds would prevail in the end, Jefferson thought it best that the younger generations solve the problem. In subsequent years, many who followed Jefferson, however, did not deal as seriously with the philosophical subtleties of the mind, land, and slavery equation as he did, however inconclusive his argument; rather, they sought to justify the institution of slavery more as a theological given, though their impassioned rhetoric rarely served as convincing argument.

Differing views of society could not help, in spite of political lobbying and intellectual analyses, but come to a critical point, as happened in October 1859 when John Brown attacked a government weapons factory in Harpers Ferry, situated fifty miles northwest of Washington, D.C., at the confluence of the Shenandoah and the Potomac Rivers. This antislavery hardliner and his motley crew of eighteen men soon became a symbol of Northern hostility. Fueled, in part, by the growing abolitionist movement within the Republican Party and by popular fiction, such as Harriet Beecher Stowe's *Uncle Tom's Cabin* (1851) and Edmund Ruffin's curiously prophetic *Anticipations of the Future: To Serve as Lesson for the Present Time* (1860), unresolved abstruse arguments over slavery continued to find outlets in violence; both Northerners and Southerners intuited in such incidents as Brown's raid what could easily happen if a solution to the question of slavery were not found. One politician, John C. Calhoun, a native South Carolinian, who served in the House of Representatives and the Senate, and as Secretary of War, Secretary of State, and Vice President for two terms, had suggested an approach that he thought addressed the more legitimate concerns of American citizens. A defender of slavery, supporter of states' rights, and believer in nullification, a legal opinion that held the South could veto any federal legislation that would hinder Southern prosperity or the continuance of slavery, Calhoun's essays "The Discourse on the Constitution" and "The Disquisition on Government" and the posthumously published *A Disquisition on Government* (1851) clearly develop his thesis that the North had received a larger portion of the common territory than the South, that the North had benefited from the system of taxation at the expense of the South, and that the original character of the United States government had radically changed and, therefore, was in need of revision.

Denying the natural rights philosophy of Thomas Jefferson and the other signers of *The Declaration of Independence,* Calhoun proposed a legal formula based on his perception of democracy in ancient Greece, namely that a "concurrent majority," in which each individual state retains the right to veto a decision made by the numerical majority of other states, decide what is best for the United States, thereby protecting society from those who think illogically and have debased passions. As Calhoun explains in his *Disquisition on Government,* the concurrent majority is better suited to enlarge and secure the bounds of liberty because it is capable of protecting the community and preventing it from passing beyond its proper limits: "It is only through an organism which vests each with a negative, in some one form or another, that those who have like interests in preventing the government from passing beyond its proper sphere, and encroaching on the rights and liberty of individuals, can co-operate peaceably and effectually in resisting the encroachments of power, and thereby preserve their rights and liberty." Calhoun's arguments, however, unlike the more generous and moderate views of his peer, Alexander H. Stephens, a member of the House of Representatives and Vice President of the Confederacy, were hardly persuasive to Northern legislators.

From an academic viewpoint, George Fitzhugh of Virginia had surveyed and presented prior to John Brown's fiasco a good deal of sociopolitical literature in *Sociology for the South; or, the Failure of a Free Society* (1854) and *Cannibals All!, or Slaves Without Masters* (1857). As a slave owner himself, Fitzhugh saw slavery as good and natural for both whites and blacks; whites could protect slaves from their inherent weaknesses, and the South as a whole might eventually lead to an improved traditional humanism, something the capitalistic cannibals of the industrial North were incapable of achieving. In his books and essays, Fitzhugh felt that he had honestly studied society and had a firm grasp on the implications of Southern nationality; those in power have an obligation to protect the weak and, as he contends in "Southern Thought Again," be benevolent to the poor. His imperious decree of those in need of protection—"wives, apprentices, inmates of poor houses, idiots, lunatics, children, sailors, soldiers, and domestic slaves"—is a mild example of his often intoxicated, always demagogical rhetoric. In similar fashion, Edmund Ruffin's proslavery work, *The Political Economy of Slavery* (1858), builds on some of the ideas of Fitzhugh, though Ruffin carried his views to a logical extreme by committing suicide rather than accepting Northern victory.

As white writers of fiction and nonfiction held center stage before and directly after the Civil War, black writers, too, gradually felt the need to express themselves, primarily in autobiographical essays and narratives. Slave narratives and autobiographies written by nineteenth-century blacks should be seen as literary documents that proclaim the black community's dignity and desire for freedom. Since slave narratives, in particular, were meant both to inform influential black leaders and convert white readers, they had a calculated rhetorical cast to them, yet they provide moments for revelation and reflection.

The tradition of the African-American autobiographical narrative began in the second half of the eighteenth century and in the early part of the nineteenth century in England and America, most notably with the accounts by James Gronniosaw (1770), John Marrant (1785), and George White (1810). Yet the quest for freedom was not bound by gender. As the slave population in the South grew and as the country expanded westward into territories and states, such as Kansas and Nebraska, that had to decide whether they wanted to admit slaves, women, too, spoke out and added their voices to a growing chorus seeking a change in American attitudes. In *The Life and Religious Experience of Janena Lee, A Coloured Lady* (1836), the author, a widowed freewoman and mother of two children, explains how she followed her religious calling, even at the expense of separating herself from her children. As an itinerant Methodist preacher, Mrs. Lee appeared indefatigable in sharing her abolitionist views. Similarly, Zilpha Elaw in her *Memoirs* (1846) reveals a missionary zeal that one expected at that time of an ordained male presbyterate but not of women who saw no chance of being admitted to an ecclesial hierarchy and establishing church polity.

As Mrs. Elaw went from one slave state to another risking arrest and bondage in the days before the Civil War, she shared the fruits of her spiritual visions. Her zeal even took her to England where, before the final days of her life became lost in obscurity, she preached over a thousand sermons. Thus it should not be a surprise to learn that one of the first significant slave narratives, *Incidents in the Life of a Slave Girl, Written by Herself* (1861), was written by a woman, Harriet Jacobs, whose work stands as startling vindication of her life as a black slave mother and a valiant woman.

Born a slave in Edenton, North Carolina, about 1813, young Harriet had a troubled childhood and became in her teens the mother of two children. She eventually ran away and stayed for seven years in her grandmother's house where she sought inner consolation by reading the Bible. In 1842, she moved to New York City and began working for a white couple. Still fearing that she would be captured by her owner, she fled to Rochester, New York, and there joined a circle of abolitionists. Jacobs's letters to Amy Post, a Quaker reformer, not only give an insight into Jacobs's political and religious views, but provide parallel texts that can be used to measure the authenticity and authority of her narrative, which, when read today, however diachronologically, has an impact achieved by few modern feminists.

In order to understand the nature of autobiographies and narratives written by nineteenth-centry blacks and ex-slaves, one has only to contrast them with similar works written by whites during the same period, foremost of which is *Walden, or Life in the Woods* (1854), by Henry David Thoreau, which records the two years (July 4, 1845 to September 6, 1847) he spent in a small building on the shore of Walden Pond. Actually, in the book, these two years were imaginatively reduced to one, meant to symbolize the entire span of a person's life. Thoreau took great pains to structure his work, rewriting sections of it over and over; the final result is a wide-ranging treatise on a multitude of topics. Walden Pond became for Thoreau not only a source of water (in the form of ice) that would sustain people throughout the world, but also a source of eternal and common-sensical ideas. Whatever was in the firmament above was reflected in the blue waters of this pond, which became a world in microcosm. Using the skill of a phrenologist, Thoreau measured the breadth and width and depth of Walden Pond in order to understand its inner psyche, and the validity of his observations and insights could be compared, either explicitly or implicitly, with those of Greek, German, and English poets and philosophers. Unlike the authors of slave narratives, Thoreau felt no need to travel to other places to find his ecological niche on earth.

For the nineteenth-century African-American autobiographer, such as Henry Bibb, William Wells Brown, Josiah Henson, and Solomon Northup, the aim lay not so much in discovering the hidden permanent truth in the natural world, but in revealing to a white reader the degrading life of a slave and appealing for a universal change of attitudes in white society. As black writers entered the literate white world, their major task was to show that their insights, based on years of trial and defeat, could compete with what was being written by their intelligent white counterparts. Thus, these black writers needed to create a style and shape the content of their works so that white readers—and blacks for that matter—would believe what they had written; their challenge was to persuade through artful means, often indirect and disguised, a conversion of hearts and minds in such a way that their white readers would not think that former slaves, too often considered as lustful and depraved children in adult bodies, were about to subdue and control their world. Why should whites, the argument went, believe blacks whom they knew to be inveterate liars? Given this distrustful environment, black writers were obliged to select those experiences that would reveal that they were simple, honest people who had suffered and wanted only what was due all human beings everywhere.

But the process of persuasion was not simple since initially few traditional maps existed to lead the way. Each black writer had to learn to organize disparate experiences, some collective in nature that reached back to earlier times in Africa, and put them through many linguistic filters until the final image became clear. As Henry Louis Gates, Jr., says in his introduction to *"Race," Writing, and Difference* (1987), blacks, when accused of lacking a formal and collective history, "published individual histories which, taken together, were intended to narrate in segments the larger yet fragmented history of blacks in Africa, now dispersed through a cold New World. The narrated, descriptive 'eye' was put into service as a literary form to posit both the individual 'I' of the black author as well as the collective 'I' of the race. Text created author; and black authors, it was hoped would create, or re-create, the image of the race in European discourse. The very *face* of the race was contingent upon the recording of the black *voice*." The genre of the slave narrative developed gradually, not in any uniform or programmatic way as James Olney reminds us, though many of the narratives have remarkable stereotypical points of contact, and at times one text seems to backloop on another and pull the other forward. Although Olney notes in his essay "'I Was Born': Slave Narratives, Their Status as Autobiography and as Literature" (1985) that the slave narrative is "most often a non-memorial description fitted to a pre-formed mold, a mold with regular depressions here and equally regular prominences there—virtually obligatory fixtures, scenes, turns of phrases, observances, and authentications—that carry over from narrative to narrative and give to them as a group the species character that we designate by the phrase 'slave narrative',," individual authors, such as Booker T. Washington and Frederick Douglass, strove to achieve an ongoing greater perspective on their lives: Washington in *The Story of My Life and Work* (1900), then in *Up From Slavery* (1901), *Working with the Hands* (1904), and finally in *My Larger Education* (1911); Douglass in his *Narrative of Frederick Douglass, an American Slave, Written by Himself* (1845), then in *My Bondage and My Freedom* (1855), and finally in *The Life and Times of Frederick Douglass* (1881).

As the black writer of this period battled toward an authentic voice, often not without a polemicism that could sustain subtle, but highly charged, arguments, a discerning reader had to notice what was said, how it was said, and what was omitted. The lacunae in slave narratives often indicated dark holes that were too difficult for the writer to illuminate and plumb. The first-person voice of the ex-slave would prove to be most powerful because it allowed the reader (and listener) to judge whether the nature of the scenes and episodes being portrayed actually fit into a pattern of both a possible and probable slave environment. The first-person narrative, unlike that of the third-person, which can assume a factual, dispassionate, systematic, and rationale xxxiv • A NEW READER OF THE OLD SOUTH •

mode of discourse, seeks to reach within the individual and pull up fears, aspirations, and paradigmatic events and images that convey great personal psychological depth. When reaching into the past, an author can find images that he or she had not suspected, but which, in turn, can be accepted, discarded, or modified; or to put it another way, one in-vents (in the Latin sense of *invenire*) inner myths, and in finding them, the author can hold them up to the light of day to test their acceptability.

By reaching down and back, an ex-slave writer can come into proximity with the universal core of humanity, as Frederick Douglass certainly did in his *Narrative,* and show that he or she has known and can freely admit rage, sin, despair, hopelessness, and a kind of prolonged indifference that could lead to suicide. In living with Edward Covey, the slave-breaker, Douglass acknowledged that he reached the bottom: "I was broken in body, soul, and spirit. My natural elasticity was crushed, my intellect languished, the disposition to read departed, the cheerful spark that lingered about my eye died; the dark nights of slavery closed in upon me; and behold a man transformed into a brute!" From this common ground, the ex-slave could then rise above it and could measure his or her growth by how far he or she had traveled physically and spiritually from a life of degradation. Such writers piece together scraps of their past lives to give the impression that their works, however naive, incomplete or unbalanced, are made out of whole cloth. By withdrawing into the self, a land of chiaroscuro, the ex-slave transforms the obvious black-and-white world and replaces it with outlines and shadows. As William L. Andrews has expressed it in his excellent *To Tell a Free Story: The First Century of Afro-American Autobiography, 1760-1865* (1986), when "the unconscious finds vehicles of expression and engages the conscious mind in creative interaction, black autobiography begins to redefine freedom as the power to integrate the unknown and the known within the self, not just the black into the white in the broader social context." Like Virgil, the ex-slave can lead his Dante through an inferno and point out the suffering that has taken place and the punishment that will undoubtedly occur if changes are not made.

To this end, many narratives tended to employ the journey motif, which served as a sub-text, particularly those journeys rooted in biblical stories; slaves considered themselves the chosen people leaving Egypt and entering the land of milk and honey. Although *A Narrative of Some Remarkable Incidents in the Life of Solomon Bayley, Formerly a Slave* (1825), *The Confessions of Nat Turner* (1831), and *The Life, Experience and Gospel Labors of the Rt. Reverend Richard Allen* (1833) are quite explicit in their use of Christian topology, others are more implicit. Solomon Northup, for example, recounts how he often read the Bible to Sam, a fellow slave belonging to his master William Ford. In relying on the Bible, the ex-slaves were only indirectly attacking their white masters (who certainly were familiar with Colossians 4:1); their intention was to explain how all men and women on this earth participate in the biblical journey, a spiritual pilgrimage whose goal one could reach by following a real or imaginary North Star. Frederick Douglass in his *Narrative* notes how he felt, even as a child, a spiritual presence in his life: "From my earliest recollection, I date the entertainment of a deep conviction that slavery would not always be able to hold me within its foul embrace; and in the darkest hours of my career in slavery, this living word of faith and spirit of hope departed not from me, but remained like ministering angels to cheer me through the gloom." In addition, arguments based on the Bible, as evidenced clearly in Angelina Emily Grimké's essay "Appeal to the Christian Women of the South," supplied a revered, age-old context whose imagery, vocabulary, personages, locales, and conflicts could evoke mutual sympathetic reactions between blacks and whites.

Yet the ex-slave writer, true to the narrator's craft, still had to tell his or her particular story, however sacred or secular it might be, and in the telling of it explain honestly and, to gain sympathy, humbly that he or she was inadequate to the task; the object was to draw the white reader into the verbal world the ex-slave had created and show that the story being told was nevertheless quite true. In a country united by a single religion, however, an ex-slave had an advantage over a white master; since the ex-slave knew intuitively that *praxis* formed a significant component of Christianity and that the moral dilemma inherent in slavery could not be contemplated or discussed forever, but needed to be resolved by personal and corporate action, he or she realized that eventually the leaders within the white society must react in some morally responsible way. Both blacks and whites likewise knew that many Gospel pericopes and parables, for example, invite the reader to imitate divine goodness and accept the invitation to improve one's lot and build a society in conformity with biblical imperatives.   Former slaves, however, had to rely mostly on the implicit sweep and flow of their religious arguments and not pose as scholars by explicating specific passages lest they be quickly refuted by the more scripturally agile.

Nineteenth-century letters and diaries, unlike slave narratives, tend to be more spontaneous and personal, since letters are directed, for the most part, to specific individuals and, as such, evoke a calculated response from the recipient, who, in turn, can choose to answer the various points made in the letter and even initiate new ones. In short, letters are written private conversations. Diaries tend to be even more intimate, though one always suspects that, deep down, a person who expends time and effort in keeping a diary, as did Frances Anne Kemble in her *Journal of a Residence on a Georgian Plantation in 1838-1839* (published in 1863), would like to see it circulated eventually in some way so his or her life would be appreciated and validated. Rather than build up a consistent picture, however artful and persuasive, a letter writer is in a position to see his or her missive as communicating something partial and often cryptic. When all is said and done, there really are no rules for writing either letters or diaries, and that is often the source of their imaginative strengths.

Some collections of letters are rather innovative: In editing the two volumes of letters of Walter Hines Page, for example, the editor, Burton J. Hendrick, daringly quotes from Page's autobiographical novel, *The Southerner: A Novel, Being the Autobiography of Nicholas Worth* (1909), in order to reveal the drama he thought lacking in the letters. The correspondence between Samuel L. Clemens (in his own marvelous proper *persona*) and William Dean Howells, dated from 1872 to 1910, are fairly typical of the spontaneity and warmth of letter writers who express themselves in relatively short, informative, honest, bounding sentences that come from the heart. In writing from Elmira, New York, to Howells on July 20, 1883, Clemens shares his unusual writing schedule: "I wrote 4000 words to-day & I touch 3000 & upwards pretty often, & don't fall below 2600 on any working day. And when I get fagged out,

I lie abed a couple of days & read & smoke, & then go it again for 6 or 7 days." In a similar vein, but more emotive, are Paul Hamilton Hayne's letters to Sidney Lanier, his friend Margaret J. Preston, and his wife affectionally called "My Beloved Minna" or "Carissima." Hayne's letters are gossipy, exclamative, at times apodictic, but always allow his genuine personality to show through. They also allow us to feel the pang and tether of the particular moment, something that no amount of forced recollection can really establish. At the other end of the scale, where a letter merges into a formal treatise, is Hammond's letter to an English abolitionist, dated January 28, 1845, in which he explains in logical order the religious, political, and social arguments that attempt to refute antislavery views by taking the high road; though Hammond believes that slaves from Africa have moved from darkness to light, from death to life, he blithely passes over the growing body of black literature that would easily demolish many of his deeply felt views.

The problem with much of the correspondence of the period, at least for the anthologist, is the injustice of wrenching a few letters from an exchange that sometimes lasts several decades, and that involves all sorts of interlocking family allusions essential to a full appreciation. On principle we decided against extracts from novels, and on the same principle we decided against extracts from such remarkable collections as *The Hammonds of Redcliffe* (1981), edited by Carol Bleser, *The Granite Farm Letters* (1988), edited by John Rozier, and the immense collection of letters written from 1860 to 1868 by members of the family of the Reverend Charles Colcock Jones (1804-1863), selected and edited by Robert Manson Myers in his *Children of Pride* (1972), and recently published (1984) in a new, abridged edition. These informative and lively letters give a detailed account of what happened before, during, and after the Civil War mostly in Liberty County, thirty miles south of Savannah, Georgia; collectively, they serve as an epistolary film depicting in vivid detail both the landscape and the mindscape of an extended nineteenth-century Southern family. In particular, the multiple perspectives, like so many movie cameras about one scene, add a type of depth and perspective sometimes missing in the back-and-forth correspondence between two individuals. When Frederick Law Olmsted journeyed on horseback through this marshy area, rank with myrtle, cypress, and palmetto, he wrote of the harmony and benevolence of whites toward the blacks in his two-volume *The Cotton Kingdom* (1861) ("...the planters of that [Liberty] county are as a body remarkably intelligent, liberal, and thoughtful of the moral welfare of the childlike wards Providence has placed under their care and tutorship."), an indirect tribute to Reverend Jones, a wealthy, educated man known for his apostolic work among the slave communities. Whether in Montevideo, a 941-acre cotton plantation south of the North Newport River near Riceboro, or in Maybank, their summer retreat (itself a 700-acre plantation), Reverend and Mrs. Jones and their three children, Charles, Joseph, and Mary Sharpe, were held in affectionate esteem by their friends and relatives. Among the most moving letters are those written by Charles to his parents, and vice versa, during the Civil War; most importantly, from a critical perspective, they show a reasoned, controlled, and sensitive use of language in a time of great anxiety, an accomplishment rarely seen in even the best poets of the age.

In parallel fashion, Mary Boykin Chesnut's diaries offer a rich source for investigating how one writer reinterpreted her life to give it the coherence her artistic sensibilities demanded. Her original posthumously published diary, incomplete and poorly edited, was titled *A Diary from Dixie* (1905, 1949); the authoritative edition, edited by C. Vann Woodward, entitled *Mary Chesnut's Civil War,* appreared in 1981. This work is based on diary entries she wrote between 1861 and 1865, as she lived in various cities such as Camden, New Jersey, Columbia and Charleston, South Carolina, and Montgomery, Alabama. An articulate woman, widely read, influential in social circles, both candid and caustic at times, her diary entries, sometimes incorporating letters, newspaper accounts, and public documents, became a large mirror she could privately converse with. Since she wrote during the entire sweep of the Civil War, her poignant texts intersect with what we read in the standard histories of this period, rendering them more accessible and human. Ten years after finishing her diaries, Mrs. Chesnut returned to them in order to extend, polish, fill in the gaps, and give them a fluidity and continuity she felt had been lacking; her efforts, at least in her mind, were not totally successful.

Driven by a desire to find a form to capture the totality of her experience, Mrs. Chesnut attempted for a while fiction and even poetry. As Woodward notes, the genre that she looked for would be the one that "would enable her to speak in her own colloquial and ironic style, to be analytical and opinionated, and to express her responses to events in ways that fiction did not permit, but yet it must also allow the events themselves, rather than her emotional peaks and valleys, to predominate." And thus, in 1881, she returned, not surprisingly, to the diary form. The published 1905 book is not a transcript of her original work, but a reconception and represents a new level of reflection. Unfortunately, it omits some significant antislavery observations, such as those she made on March 18, 1861: "I wonder if it be a sin to think slavery a curse to any land. [Charles] Sumner said not one word of this hated institution which is not true. Men & women are punished when their masters & mistresses are brutes & and not when they do wrong—& then we live surrounded by prostitutes. An abandoned woman is sent out of any decent house elsewhere. Who thinks any worse of a Negro or Mulatto woman for being a thing we can't name. God forgive *us,* but ours is a *monstrous* system & wrong & iniquity." Nurtured in a patriarchal society, but keenly aware of its limitations and potential destructiveness, Chesnut and her complex voice with its incredible range should be given, we believe, a more prominent place in American letters.

Like a latter-day Boethius, Alexander H. Stephens in his diary that he kept while imprisoned in Fort Warren in Boston Harbor in 1865 maintained a studied calmness far different from anything Mrs. Chesnut wrote; this quiet tone removes the immediacy from the events surrounding the Civil War. Whether commenting on Prescott's books about Ferdinand and Isabella or about the conquest of Mexico, Stephens always has a thoughtful point of view to share. He knew that while he had suffered enormously—and experienced some extremely dark and bitter moments in life—he was not about to proclaim in prison total and abject defeat. "I still have," he wrote, "unshaken confidence in the people under God. They do not always do right. The late horrible war on both sides may be attributed to a considerable extent to popular passions spurred to excess; but reaction will come sooner or later. I have strong hopes that, after this generation will have passed away, if not before, a new order will arise, from which still further progress in civilization will be made and still higher and grander career entered upon by the people of this continent." In one section, a dreamlike playlet that has a free-floating quality rarely seen in diaries, Stephens responds to disturbing questions about the Civil War. When read in tandem with contemporary battle diaries, such as the informative one written by John Mosby about his involvement with the campaigns of General J.E.B. Stuart, one can more readily appreciate the depth of the emotional toll this war exacted on its soldiers of whatever rank.

In "The New South," a speech delivered at the New England Club of New York on December 21, 1886, Henry W. Grady, who became managing editor of *The Atlanta Constitution* in the early 1880's, draws a large picture of what it must have been like for a Southern soldier to return home after the Civil War and find his house in ruin, his slaves vanished, his farm devastated, and his whole way of life lost. Yet Grady portrays this soldier as valiantly picking up the pieces of his life and putting them together. Likewise, in Grady's mind, the freed black has reason to hope for success as he learns to deal in new and inventive ways with white society: "Our future, our very existence," Grady stressed, "depend on our working out his problem in full and exact justice." The New South, he believed, offers a clear-cut opportunity for a perfect democracy, and though this new society will be less splendid on the surface than was the old, it will be compact and stronger at the core; there will be a hundred farms for every plantation and a diversified industry to meet the needs of the next century. Part cheerleader, part preacher, part economic forecaster, Grady challenged New Englanders, in particular, not to permit the prejudices of war to remain in their hearts, but to accept the South's wounded, but honorably outstretched hand in friendship and trust. Needless to say, that when Grady died on December 23, 1889, he did not see his wished-for prosperous South.

Quick to respond, Thomas Nelson Page delivered the following year at The College of Washington and Lee a speech titled "The Old South" (with interesting variations in subsequent printings) in which he traced the history of the Old South. Throughout its long and glorious history, the South "held by its old tenets when they were no longer tenable, by its ancient customs when, perhaps, they were no longer defensible." Slavery had forced the South into a position either to fight or surrender her rights. While citing statistics of the number of slaves in both the North and the South, Page noted that the problem in both parts of the country was "stupendous." In 1790, for example, the Northern states had fewer than 42,000 slaves, while Virginia alone, in the same year, had 293,427 slaves. For Page, it all boiled down to the difference between a literal reading of the U.S. Constitution by Southerners or a more liberal reading by Northerners. Not surprisingly, Page leaps over a discussion of the Civil War and consoles and strokes his audience: "That the Old South was honest, no sensible man who reads the history of that time can doubt, and no honest man will deny. Its whole course throughout its existence, whatever other criticism it may be subjected to, was one of honesty and honor. Even under the perils of public life, which try men's souls, the personal integrity which was the fruit of the civilization in which it flourished was never doubted." Though Cable had covered the same ground in his stirring address before the American Social Sciences Association at Saratoga, New York, on September 11, 1884, Page, who later became interested in industrial problems, never felt compelled to ask forthrightly the basic human questions about freedom and citizenship. He seemed content to allow his tired voice to drift off asymptotically, afraid to enter into dialogue with others who might challenge his views.

As did Cable, Walter Hines Page distanced himself from Thomas Nelson Page (it is thought by some that they were distantly related) by not recalling a nostalgic, romanticized past, but by sketching a blueprint of twentieth-century industry, agriculture, and education. As editor of both *The Forum* and *The Atlantic Monthly,* as founder of Doubleday, Page and Company, and as Ambassador to the Court of St. James (1913-1918), Walter Hines Page came to symbolize the progressive Southern thinker in touch with a multitude of changing realities; one can almost imagine him ripping up the pages of Civil War history so that his influential peer group in both the North and South would not have to rehearse and refight old battles. Page committed himself wholeheartedly to educational reform in the South. He once said, "I have no sentimental stuff in me about the Negro, but I have a lot of economic stuff in me about the necessity of training him." At the end of the century, he joined such distinguished educators as Edwin A. Alderman, the President of the University of North Carolina at Chapel Hill, and Charles D. McIver, the President of the Southern Educational Association, in their meetings at Capon Springs, West Virginia, to set up policies and programs that would benefit both races.

After leaving the South in 1885, Walter Hines Page was able to gain an exile's perspective on what was happening in the South in the 1890's and into the twentieth century. In a November 1893 issue of *The Forum,* titled "The Last Hold of the Southern Bully," he lashes out at the legal and moral aspects of a problem that in one form or another never seems to extricate itself from the Southern psyche: the inequity of severely condemning or even lynching a black man who sexually attacks a white woman, when, in similar circumstances, a white man who attacks a black woman would receive a lighter sentence. Page's plea, directed mostly at politicians, preachers, and the press, is for the abolition of inequitable laws. For a more personal view of how Page took on the burden of the South, and how he imaginatively pictured himself spearheading progressive leadership, not, of course, without defeats and reversals, we recommend his novel about Nicholas Worth, who returns after graduating from Harvard College to his native state of North Carolina to promote justice and education. Though Page's *The Southerner* is a lesser *The Education of Henry Adams* (1907), to which it has been compared, it does portray his alter ego confronting the problems of Reconstruction and grappling with the enormous difficulties individuals in the South had to face as they entered a new era that their traditional heritage had not adequately prepared them for.

From studies done in the past twenty years, it is clear that interest in nineteenth-century Southern short stories, essays, slave narratives, and diaries has dramatically increased. This has not been the case with the poetry of this period. Many contemporary readers might find themselves recalling, though struggling to forget, the unfortunate couplet of J. Gordon Coogler, the self-promoting versifier from Columbia, South Carolina, who despite his secure position at the bottom of any list of Southern poets, happened to write two of the most unforgettable lines of the century: "Alas for the South! Her books have grown fewer, / She was never much given to literature." Thankfully, Coogler is in a category by himself, and there are genuine poets, such as Poe or Timrod or Lanier, an anthologist can turn to in order to do justice to the period. The problem, however, is that even much of the best poetry rarely escapes some dependence on popular poetic conventions, or on borrowed themes from the great English Romantics. There are very few strong, independent, wholly original poems to choose from. Southern songs are another matter, and once we admitted the principle of including the best songs of the Old South, we had some trouble stopping where we did.

The published poetry of the nineteenth-century South seldom rises above the level of spirited amateur competence for the good reason that it was largely written by part-time poets when they could spare the time from their non-literary professional commitments. In fact, the amateur status of much of the poetry was often insisted on by the writer himself, especially during the antebellum times. As a lawyer, statesman, or even a professional soldier, he might legitimately cultivate a taste for verse and for the great poets of the English language, but he would never presume to place his own efforts in their company. For such a poet, the occasional poem was the genteel accomplishment of leisure and of a certain sense of social class, something every well-rounded and well-read individual could try his or her hand at.

William Grayson, the author of "The Hireling and the Slave," the 1851 proslavery poem he began only after retiring from active political life past the age of sixty, suggests the gentlemanly "poet" in just these terms when, in his *Autobiography,* he contrasts Davy Crockett and Richard Henry Wilde, both of whom happened to be Representatives in the same 1833 U.S. Congress: "Among those most remarkable in 1833, David Crockett was not the least famous. He was a dull, heavy, almost stupid man, in appearance. I never heard him utter a word that savoured of wit or sense. To judge from his features one would have supposed such an event impossible. Yet by some freak of fortune he became the reputed author of innumerable queer sayings and stories, a man of infinite joke, an incarnation of frontier oddity....He was a good natured, kindhearted man and a general favourite in the house. He was a brave soldier too and had seen service in the Texan war with Mexico, but he was the last man in the house that a stranger would have pitched upon as a wit and humorist. At a desk not far from Crockett, Wilde of Georgia, presented a thorough contrast to the Western member. One was stout and clumsy in person with a blotchy fair complexion and light eye, ungainly in address and manners; the other dark, of good figure, with black eyes, easy, sprightly, engaging in conversation, a good speaker and, still more, a poet."

Wilde was the author of "My Life is Like a Summer Rose" (also known as "The Lament of the Captive") and "To the Mocking-Bird," both graceful, popular lyrics more or less indistinguishable in subject and style from those written by a large company of comparable talents: Samuel Henry Dickson, Mirabeau B. Lamar, Edward Coote Pinkney, Philip Pendleton Cooke, Theodore O'Hara, and James Mathewes Legaré. We represent this group with Pinkney's well-known "Song" and Alexander Beaufort Meek's "The Mocking-Bird," both of which convey the limited, but non-negligible lyrical skills of the occasional, gentleman poet.

One antebellum Southern poet who in certain respects should be considered is Edgar Allan Poe. Raised in Richmond, Virginia, with a reputation in his youth as an exceptional and daring athlete, educated in upper-class English schools, forced to leave Thomas Jefferson's University of Virginia for gambling debts, praised as a soldier in the U.S. Army before he decided to have himself expelled from the U.S. Military Academy at West Point, Poe had all the trappings of a Virginia gentleman, or aspiring gentleman, since his origins as an orphaned son of impoverished traveling actors placed him on the margins of society from the beginning.

The difference, of course, between Poe and the other romantic gentleman poets of the antebellum South was that Poe was a genius and intensely committed to the art of poetry as a sacred calling. His own lyrics are deeply influenced by the English Romantics, but they have a hypnotic verbal music and a compelling symbolic logic that are all his own. As the most original, inventive, and far-reaching antebellum Southern writer, Poe is somewhat of an embarrassment to Southern scholars and to anthologists because little of what he wrote is conspicuously Southern. The best one can do is offer a couple of his most celebrated poems, and rather quickly assert that they are at least characteristic of the Southern poet's love of poetic technique, musical mood-setting, and a tendency to escape immediate Southern reality by cultivating an ideal world of abstract art. We did consider, of course, that Poe's reputation today is based far more on several of his brilliant short stories than on his poetry. And he did write at least one powerful story with a Southern locale, "The Gold Bug." But it would be difficult to argue that this story is a central work in the history of the South's literary development, no matter how intriguing its presentation of well-defined Southern types engaged in an obsessive hunt for a life of riches and ease hidden in a long-buried treasure contaminated from the beginning by human evil. Other well-known stories by Poe have been examined as obscure demonic parables of the Southern condition, including, rather convincingly, "The Fall of the House of Usher," and future speculation may very well argue that his stories are more "Southern" than they seem on the surface. We came close, in fact, to including "The Man Who Was Used Up" as the single contribution by Poe. Finally, however, we took the reasonable, perhaps too reasonable, decision to represent Poe with his poetry, a decision that does have the advantage of thrusting into view other Southern poets who do not have Poe's world-wide reputation, but who did address certain themes of Southern life and culture more openly and more directly.

Of these latter, the most important were the four writers and friends who gathered at Russell's Bookstore in Charleston, South Carolina, in the years just before the Civil War: William Grayson, William Gilmore Simms, Henry Timrod, and Paul Hamilton Hayne. They all contributed to *Russell's Magazine,* a short-lived journal (1857-1860) edited by Hayne and founded to promote Southern letters at a time when the South was becoming more and more isolated from the rest of the United States. Once we make the usual qualifications, that is, that their idea of poetry was defined by a extreme devotion to a conservative, overly "poetic" diction, and to the standard classical forms, that they were derivative and tradition-bound, rather than willing to work through the traditions toward more original poetic voices and themes, we must admit, too, that each of these men wrote effective poems of enduring quality and, in the case of Timrod, a handful of Civil War poems that are close to perfection.

William Grayson and William Gilmore Simms were the senior members and guiding lights of the Charleston group. Simms was the best-known Southern writer of the day, but a more confident writer of prose than of poetry. Still, despite the strained, overblown diction, Simms's "The Edge of the Swamp" is a rather powerful evocation of the poetic sensibility trying to inhabit a hostile Southern landscape. Grayson's proslavery "The Hireling and the Slave" was too long to include here, and more fired by polemics than by poetry, but in places his ringing heroic couplets are able to overcome the ideological cast of his inspiration and create some sharply etched social portraits, especially when he turned his mind to England's miserable "hireling" poor.

Henry Timrod had already published a collection of poems before the Civil War began, but his major poetry was written around the rise and fall of the Confederacy. His remarkable "Ethnogenesis" is a resounding nationalistic Pindaric Ode celebrating Southern independence, and sustained throughout by the solemn conviction that Southern humanism in a benighted world will eventually spread its benefactions to all parts of the globe. His best poems, however, were written after these grand hopes were utterly shattered once the war began to take its toll. As the Confederacy foundered, and as Timrod witnessed first-hand, for a time as a war correspondent, the loss of life and the immense suffering that accompanied Southern collapse, his poetry became graver, more direct, and more inspired. The brooding priestly sadness and restraint that underlie his elegiac "Unknown Dead" and his commemorative "Ode," the last stanza of which is the first hymn to the new Lost Cause, must place them both among the moving war poems of the century.

The youngest member of the Charleston group, Paul Hamilton Hayne, may well have possessed the most dedicated poetical faith of all. He continued to write long after he had lost almost everything in the war, and retired with his wife, son, and mother to a remote Georgia farm he called "Copse Hill." He will probably be remembered less for his verse, however, than as a spirited chronicler of the Charleston literary scene and as an energetic and voluminous correspondent.

One of Hayne's correspondents was Sidney Lanier, who had also suffered greatly in the war, having contracted tuberculosis in a Union prison, and who resembled Hayne in never realizing his full promise as a major Southern poet. Unlike Hayne, however, Lanier did write several major poems, including the Whitmanesque "The Marshes of Glynn." Lanier was a professional musician deeply interested in the musical properties and powers of verse. One of the last things he wrote was a study of English prosody, *The Science of English Verse* (1880). Though he was not always successful in his various experiments with "musical" language and rhythms in his own poetry, his fascination with the way words actually sounded when spoken or sung made him more alert than most of his contemporaries to the poetic possibilities of Southern dialect. Along with his Robert Burns-inspired, rural white dialect poem "Thar's More in the Man Than Thar is in the Land," Lanier wrote several poems in black dialect and carried his interest in black culture to such a point that in his handbook guide to Florida, written primarily to bring some money into his impoverished household, he took the pains to present what was probably the first musical notation of improvised black whistling.

Lanier recognized, even earlier than most of the Southern local colorists, that the spoken language of the uneducated Southerner was capable of poetry and of the full range of human emotions. It need not be limited to the comic exaggerations of the Southern humorists before the Civil War, or, as far as the Southern black was concerned, to the simple clownish reductions of the black-face minstrel shows that had begun in the 1820's and 1830's, and by the late 1840's had become a well-established theatrical tradition. Most of the black dialect in the antebellum novels seldom goes beyond the conventional, simple-minded speech of the minstrelized slave.

For all their limitations and distortions, however, the minstrel songs and dances at least had the merit of making the general public aware of the vast hidden resources of Southern black culture. Clearly some of the lyrics and melodies were based on actual slave songs. Many others were no more than clever urban imitations of the way the song writers imagined they should sound. Making the situation even more complex is the fact that some of the most popular minstrel and parlor songs of the antebellum period freely flowed back into the Southern folk culture that had distantly inspired them. Stephen Foster is the best and most brilliant example. Born in Pennsylvania in 1826, and with little immediate contact with the rural Southern black, Foster so effectively captured the American imagination with his nostalgic lyrical versions of the plantation myth that his songs were often mistaken for genuine folk songs and were sung as such throughout the South. Along with Daniel Emmett's "Dixie," many of Foster's Southern-inspired songs must be considered part of the South's permanent lyrical tradition, a tradition we only barely suggest in our restricted choice of a few of the best minstrel songs packed in, side by side, with more authentic Southern ballads and songs such as "John Henry," "Omie Wise," and James Innes Randolph's "I'm A Good Old Rebel."

We have been even more restrictive in our choice of Southern religious songs, though we do try to do justice to the astonishing black spirituals, proof of the capacity of rural black and white traditions, even in antebellum times, to converge in the creation of a wholly original Southern art. The exact history of the black spirituals is just as confused as the development of the secular song. We do know that both blacks and whites in large numbers attended the revivalist camp meetings during the first half of the nineteenth century. The singing of Protestant hymns, of the kind found in such popular collections as the shape-note hymnals, *The Southern Harmony* (1835) and *The Sacred Harp* (1844), went on day and night and was characterized by highly emotional, often improvised variations on the standard texts and well-known biblical passages. And we know, too, that the contributions by the black congregations at these meetings and in regular church services were recognized by everyone as original and clearly distinguishable from the hymns sung by the Southern whites.

These spirituals, what Mary Boykin Chesnut called in an 1861 diary entry "soul-stirring Negro camp-meeting hymns," were well known before the Civil War and often mentioned in letters, diaries, and slave narratives. But they did not reach a wide public until the pioneer collection *Slave Songs of the United States* was published in

1867 by William Francis Allen, Charles Pickard Ware, and Lucy McKim Garrison (all Northern enthusiasts), and until the successful Reconstruction tours of the Fisk Jubilee Singers from Fisk University in Nashville, Tennessee.

Sidney Lanier was not the only poet of the Old South to turn his attention to the poetic possibilities of native dialects. On the whole, however, Southern poets were late in recognizing a distinctive Southern folk culture, and especially late in tapping into the creative currents of the Southern black. Before the Civil War, the Georgia poet Thomas Holley Chivers, better known for his highly romantic lyrics and his claim that Poe had stolen "The Raven" from him, made several successful attempts to recreate black dialect. His rather slight, but convincing "Corn Shucking Song" of 1855 suggests that he might well have rescued his own verse from its unfortunate idealistic excess had he concentrated more on the familiar sights and sounds of his daily Georgia existence:

> Jinny broke de hoecake, Sally make de cawphy,
> Nancy bile de bakyon wid de bracky-ey pea;
> Cuffy blow de Ram's Hawn, Juba beat de banjo —
> Dinah ring de Tin Pan to cawl us awl to Tea.

Chivers had accused such popular Northern writers as Harriet Beecher Stowe and Stephen Foster of ignoring Southern black culture; it may have been a combination of national public interest and a private desire to demonstrate their greater familiarity and knowledge that led several Southerners to make a serious effort to introduce black music and language in their own poetry. In most cases, these poems are only halfway between popular entertainment and literature, but they do at least point in the direction of the more varied, complex, and fuller expression of the Southern black in twentieth-century poetry. Our selections include three of the better known writers to make substantial use of black dialect in verse form: Irwin Russell, whose "Christmas Night in the Quarters" was published in 1878 and had a strong influence not only on the subsequent dialect poetry, but also on some of the major short story writers; Paul Laurence Dunbar, not Southern-born, but son of a former slave, and haunted by his Southern origins, and Joel Chandler Harris, whose versification of "Brer Rabbit and the Tar-Baby" should be compared to his earlier, and more effective, prose version.

Some mention should be made of James Weldon Johnson, who, like Ellen Glasgow, is another major transitional figure between the Old South and the twentieth century, and whose two sermon-poems, "The Creation" and "The Crucifixion," help mark the chronological limits of this anthology. Johnson experimented with black dialect in some of his early popular songs and poems, but he eventually came to the conclusion that too much emphasis on pronunciation alone obscured the deeper verbal life of the Southern black. He appreciated accurate representation of the way the spoken words sounded, but for Johnson, writing when he did, the very presence of phonetic transcription made the black stereotypes of the minstrel shows leap too automatically to mind. For this reason alone, he preferred composing his sermons celebrating the "old time Negro preacher" not in dialect, but in poems whose images, rhythms, and narrative power are more than enough to evoke the preacher's voice.

One of the important truths underlying Johnson's later poetry, and his various reflections on black identity and what can be found emerging out of the best Southern writing after the Civil War, is the gradual realization that the living folk traditions of both black and white Southerners will be, along with the permanent impact of slavery and the war, the great sustaining force of Southern difference. If Southern history was all too often destructive, bewildering, and heavy a burden to carry into the modern world, the creative counter-current of the South's varied folk culture was a constant and reassuring source of affirmation. There can surely be no doubt that one of the remarkable qualities of the history of Southern literature, and especially as we move closer to the great figures of the twentieth century, has been that the whole positive thrust of its imaginative life springs from the powerful marriage, between equals, of a thriving confident communal culture and the independent self-questioning artist and intellectual.

Ben Forkner
Patrick Samway, S.J.

STORIES,
SHORT
NARRATIVES
and
TALES

GEORGE WASHINGTON CABLE

Posson Jone'

To Jules St.-Ange—elegant little heathen—there yet remained at manhood a remembrance of having been to school, and of having been taught by a stony-headed Capuchin that the world is round—for example, like a cheese. This round world is a cheese to be eaten through, and Jules had nibbled quite into his cheese-world already at twenty-two.

He realized this as he idled about one Sunday morning where the intersection of Royal and Conti Streets some seventy years ago formed a central corner of New Orleans. Yes, yes, the trouble was he had been wasteful and honest. He discussed the matter with that faithful friend and confidant, Baptiste, his yellow body-servant. They concluded that, papa's patience and *tante's* pin-money having been gnawed away quite to the rind, there were left open only these few easily-enumerated resorts: to go to work—they shuddered; to join Major Innerarity's filibustering expedition; or else—why not?—to try some games of confidence. At twenty-two one must begin to be something. Nothing else tempted; could that avail? One could but try. It is noble to try; and, besides, they were hungry. If one could "make the friendship" of some person from the country, for instance, with money, not expert at cards or dice, but, as one would say, willing to learn, one might find cause to say some "Hail Marys."

The sun broke through a clearing sky, and Baptiste pronounced it good for luck. There had been a hurricane in the night. The weed-grown tile-roofs were still dripping, and from lofty brick and low adobe walls a rising steam responded to the summer sunlight. Up-street, and across the Rue du Canal, one could get glimpses of the gardens in Faubourg Ste.-Marie standing in silent wretchedness, so many tearful Lucretias, tattered victims of the storm. Short remnants of the wind now and then came down the narrow street in erratic puffs heavily laden with odors of broken boughs and torn flowers, skimmed the little pools of rain-water in the deep ruts of the unpaved street, and suddenly went away to nothing, like a juggler's butterflies or a young man's money.

It was very picturesque, the Rue Royale. The rich and poor met together. The locksmith's swinging key creaked next door to the bank; across the way, crouching, mendicant-like, in the shadow of a great importing-house, was the mud laboratory of the mender of broken combs. Light balconies overhung the rows of showy shops and stores open for trade this Sunday morning, and pretty Latin faces of the higher class glanced over their savagely pronged railings upon the passers below. At some windows hung lace curtains, flannel duds at some, and at others only the scraping and sighing one-hinged shutter groaning toward Paris after its neglectful master.

M. St.-Ange stood looking up and down the street for nearly an hour. But few ladies, only the inveterate mass-goers, were out. About the entrance of the frequent *cafés* the masculine gentility stood leaning on canes, with which now one and now another beckoned to Jules, some even adding pantomimic hints of the social cup.

M. St.-Ange remarked to his servant without turning his head that somehow he felt sure he should soon return those *bons* that the mulatto had lent him.

"What will you do with them?"

"Me!" said Baptiste, quickly; "I will go and see the bull-fight in the Place Congo."

"There is to be a bull-fight? But where is M. Cayetano?"

"Ah, got all his affairs wet in the tornado. Instead of his circus, they are to have a bull-fight—not an ordinary bull-fight with sick horses, but a buffalo-and-tiger fight. I would not miss it"—

Two or three persons ran to the opposite corner, and commenced striking at something with their canes. Others followed. Can M. St.-Ange and servant, who hasten forward—can the Creoles, Cubans, Spaniards, St. Domingo refugees, and other loungers—can they hope it is a fight? They hurry forward. Is a man in a fit? The crowd pours in from the side-streets. Have they killed a so-long snake? Bareheaded shopmen leave their wives, who stand upon chairs. The crowd huddles and packs. Those on the outside make little leaps into the air, trying to be tall.

"What is the matter?"

"Have they caught a real live rat?"

"Who is hurt?" asks some one in English.

"*Personne,*" replies a shopkeeper; "a man's hat blow' in the gutter; but he has it now. Jules pick it. See, that is the man, head and shoulders on top the res'."

"He in the homespun?" asks a second shopkeeper. "Humph! an *Américain*—a West-Floridian; bah!"

"But wait; 'st! he is speaking; listen!"

"To who is he speak—?"

"Sh-sh-sh! to Jules."

"Jules who?"

"Silence, you! To Jules St.-Ange, what howe me a bill since long time. Sh-sh-sh!"

Then the voice was heard.

Its owner was a man of giant stature, with a slight stoop in his shoulders, as if he was making a constant, good-natured attempt to accommodate himself to ordinary doors and ceilings. His bones were those of an ox. His face was marked more by weather than age, and his narrow brow was bald and smooth. He had instantaneously formed an opinion of Jules St.-Ange, and the multitude of words, most of them lingual curiosities, with which he was rasping the wide-open ears of his listeners, signified, in short, that, as sure as his name was Parson Jones, the little Creole was a "plum gentleman."

M. St.-Ange bowed and smiled, and was about to call attention, by both gesture and speech, to a singular object on top of the still uncovered head, when the nervous motion of the *Américain* anticipated him, as, throwing up an immense hand, he drew down a large roll of bank-notes. The crowd laughed, the West-Floridian joining, and began to disperse.

"Why, that money belongs to Smyrny Church," said the giant.

"You are very dengerous to make your money expose like that, Misty Posson Jone'," said St.-Ange, counting it with his eyes.

The countryman gave a start and smile of surprise.

"How d'dyou know my name was Jones?" he asked; but, without pausing for the Creole's answer, furnished in his reckless way some further specimens of West-Floridian English; and the conciseness with which he presented full intelligence of his home, family, calling, lodging-house, and present and future plans, might have passed for consummate art, had it not been the most run-wild nature. "And I've done been to Mobile, you know, on busi*ness* for Bethesdy Church. It's the on'yest time I ever been from home; now you wouldn't of believed that, would you? But I admire to have saw you, that's so. You've got to come and eat with me. Me and my boy ain't been fed yit. What might one call yo' name? Jools? Come on, Jools. Come on, Colossus. That's my niggah—his name's Colossus of Rhodes. Is that yo' yallah boy, Jools? Fetch him along, Colossus. It seems like a special provi*dence.*—Jools, do you believe in a special provi*dence?*"

Jules said he did.

The new-made friends moved briskly off, followed by Baptiste and a short, square, old negro, very black and grotesque, who had introduced himself to the mulatto, with many glittering and cavernous smiles, as "d'body-sarvant of d'Rev'n' Mr. Jones."

Both pairs enlivened their walk with conversation. Parson Jones descanted upon the doctrine he had mentioned, as illustrated in the perplexities of cotton-growing, and concluded that there would always be "a special provi*dence* again' cotton untell folks quits a-pressin' of it and haulin' of it on Sundays!"

"*Je dis,*" said St.-Ange, in response, "I thing you is juz right. I believe, me, strong-strong in the improvidence, yes. You know my papa he hown a sugah-plantation, you know. 'Jules, me son,' he say one time to me, 'I goin' to make one baril sugah to fedge the moze high price in New Orleanz.' Well, he take his bez baril sugah—I neveh see a so careful man like me papa always to make a so beautiful sugah *et sirop.* 'Jules, go at Father Pierre an' ged this lill pitcher fill with holy-water, an' tell him sen' his tin bucket, and I will make it fill with *quitte.*' I ged the holy-water; my papa sprinkle it over the baril, an' make one cross on the 'ead of the baril."

"Why, Jools," said Parson Jones, "that didn't do no good."

"Din do no good! Id broughd the so great value! You can strike me dead if thad baril sugah din fedge the more high cost than any other in the city. *Parce-que,* the man what buy that baril sugah he make a mistake of one hundred pound"—falling back—"*Mais certainlee!*"

"And you think that was growin' out of the holy-water?" asked the parson.

"*Mais,* what could make it else? Id could not be the *quitte,* because my papa keep the bucket, an' forget to sen' the *quitte* to Father Pierre."

Parson Jones was disappointed.

"Well, now, Jools, you know, I don't think that was right. I reckon you must be a plum Catholic."

M. St.-Ange shrugged. He would not deny his faith.

"I am a *Catholique, mais*"—brightening as he hoped to recommend himself anew—"not a good one."

"Well, you know," said Jones—"where's Colossus? Oh! all right. Colossus strayed off a minute in Mobile, and I plum lost him for two days. Here's the place; come in. Colossus and this boy can go to the kitchen.—Now, Colossus, what *air* you a-beckonin' at me faw?"

He let his servant draw him aside and address him in a whisper.

"Oh, go 'way!" said the parson with a jerk. "Who's goin' to throw me? What? Speak louder. Why, Colossus, you shayn't talk so, saw. 'Pon my soul, you're the mightiest fool I ever taken up with. Jest you go down that alley-way with this yalla boy, and don't show yo' face untell yo' called!"

The Negro begged; the master wrathily insisted.

"Colossus, will you do ez I tell you, or shell I hev' to strike you, saw?"

"Oh Mahs Jimmy, I—I's gwine; but"—he ventured nearer—"don't on no account drink nothin', Mahs Jimmy."

Such was the negro's earnestness that he put one foot in the gutter, and fell heavily against his master. The parson threw him off angrily.

"Thar, now! Why, Colossus, you most of been dosted with sumthin'; yo' plum crazy.—Humph, come on, Jools, let's eat! Humph! to tell me that when I never taken a drop, exceptin' for chills, in my life—which he knows so as well as me!"

The two masters began to ascend a stair.

"Mais, he is a sassy; I would sell him, me," said the young Creole.

"No, I wouldn't do that," replied the parson; "though there is people in Bethesdy who says he is a rascal. He's a powerful smart fool. Why, that boy's got money, Jools; more money that religion, I reckon. I'm shore he fallen into mighty bad company"— they passed beyond earshot.

Baptiste and Colossus, instead of going to the tavern kitchen, passed to the next door and entered the dark rear corner of a low grocery, where, the law notwithstanding, liquor was covertly sold to slaves. There, in the quiet company of Baptiste and the grocer, the colloquial powers of Colossus, which were simply prodigious, began very soon to show themselves.

"For whilst," said he, "Mahs Jimmy has eddication, you know—whilst he has eddication, I has 'scretion. He has eddication and I has 'scretion, an' so we gits along."

He drew a black bottle down the counter, and, laying half his length upon the damp board, continued:

"As a p'rinciple I discredits de imbimin' of awjus liquors. De imbimin' of awjus liquors, de wiolution of de Sabbaf, de playin' of de fiddle, and de usin' of by-words, dey is de fo' sins of de conscience; an' if any man sin de fo' sins of de conscience, de debble done sharp his fork fo' dat man.—Ain't that so, boss?"

The grocer was sure it was so.

"Neberdeless, mind you"—here the orator brimmed his glass from the bottle and swallowed the contents with a dry eye—"mind you, a roytious man, sech as ministers of de gospel and dere body-sarvants, can take a *leetle* for de weak stomach."

But the fascinations of Colossus's eloquence must not mislead us; this is the story of a true Christian; to wit, Parson Jones.

The parson and his new friend ate. But the coffee M. St.-Ange declared he could not touch; it was too wretchedly bad. At the French Market, near by, there was some noble coffee. This, however, would have to be bought, and Parson Jones had scruples.

"You see, Jools, every man has his conscience to guide him, which it does so in—"

"Oh, yes!" cried St.-Ange, "conscien'; thad is the bez, Posson Jone'. Certainlee! I am a *Catholique*, you is a *schismatique*; you thing it is wrong to dring some coffee—well, then, it *is* wrong; you thing it is wrong to make the sugah to ged the so large price—well, then, it *is* wrong; I thing it is right—well, then, it *is* right; it is all 'abit; *c'est tout.* What a man thing is right, *is right*; 'tis all 'abit. A man muz nod go again' his conscien'. My faith! do you thing I would go again' my conscien'? *Mais allons,* led us go and ged some coffee."

"Jools."

"W'at?"

"Jools, it ain't the drinkin' of coffee, but the buyin' of it on a Sabbath. You must really excuse me, Jools, it's again' conscience, you know."

"Ah!" said St.-Ange, "*c'est* very true. For you it would be a sin, *mais* for me it is only 'abit. Rilligion is a very strange; I know a man one time, he thing it was wrong to go to cock-fight Sunday evening. I thing it is all 'abit. *Mais,* come, Posson Jone'; I have got one friend, Miguel; led us go at his house and ged some coffee. Come; Miguel have no familie; only him and Joe—always like to see friend; *allons,* led us come yonder."

"Why, Jools, my dear friend, you know," said the shamefaced parson, "I never visit on Sundays."

"Never w'at?" asked the astounded Creole.

"No," said Jones, smiling awkwardly.

"Never visite?"

"Exceptin' sometimes amongst church-members," said Parson Jones.

"*Mais,*" said the seductive St.-Ange, "Miguel and Joe is church-member'—certainlee! They love to talk about rilligion. Come at Miguel and talk about some rilligion. I am nearly expire for me coffee."

Parson Jones took his hat from beneath his chair and rose up.

"Jools," said the weak giant, "I ought to be in church right now."

"*Mais,* the church is right yonder at Miguel, yes. Ah!" continued St.-Ange, as they descended the stairs, "I thing every man muz have the rilligion he like the bez—me, I like the *Catholique* rilligion the bez—for me it *is* the bez. Every man will sure go to heaven if he likes his rilligion the bez."

"Jools," said the West-Floridian, laying his great hand tenderly upon the Creole's shoulder, as they stepped out upon the *banquette*, "do you think you have any shore hopes of heaven?"

"Yass!" replied St.-Ange; "I am sure-sure. I thing everybody will go to heaven. I thing you will go, *et* I thing Miguel will go, *et* Joe—everybody, I thing—*mais,* hof course, not if they not have been christen'. Even I thing some niggers will go."

"Jools," said the parson, stopping in his walk—"Jools, I *don't* want to lose my niggah."

"You will not loose him. With Baptiste he *cannot* ged loose."

But Colossus's master was not re-assured.

"Now," said he, still tarrying, "this is jest the way; had I of gone to church"—

"Posson Jone'," said Jules.

"What?"

"I tell you. We goin' to church!"

"Will you?" asked Jones, joyously.

"*Allons*, come along," said Jules, taking his elbow.

They walked down the Rue Chartres, passed several corners, and by and by turned into a cross street. The parson stopped an instant as they were turning, and looked back up the street.

"W'at you lookin'?" asked his companion.

"I thought I saw Colossus," answered the parson, with an anxious face; "I reckon 'twa' n't him, though." And they went on.

The street they now entered was a very quiet one. The eye of any chance passer would have been at once drawn to a broad, heavy, white brick edifice on the lower side of the way, with a flagpole standing out like a bowspit from one of its great windows, and a pair of lamps hanging before a large closed entrance. It was a theatre, honey-combed with gambling-dens. At this morning hour all was still, and the only sign of life was a knot of little barefoot girls gathered within its narrow shade, and each carrying an infant relative. Into this place the parson and M. St.-Ange entered, the little nurses jumping up from the sills to let them pass in.

A half-hour may have passed. At the end of that time the whole juvenile company were laying alternate eyes and ears to the chinks, to gather what they could of an interesting quarrel going on within.

"I did not, saw! I given you no cause of offence saw! It's not so, saw! Mister Jools simply mistaken the house, thinkin' it was a Sabbath-school! No such thing, saw; I *ain't* bound to bet! Yes, I kin git out! Yes, without bettin'! I hev a right to my opinion; I reckin I'm a *white man*, saw! No saw! I on'y said I didn't think you could get the game on them cards. 'Sno such thing, saw! I do *not* know how to play! I wouldn't hev a rascal's money ef I should win it! Shoot, ef you dare! You can kill me, but you can't scare me! No, I shayn't bet! I'll die first! Yes, saw; Mr. Jools can bet for me if he admires to; I ain't his mostah."

Here the speaker seemed to direct his words to St.-Ange.

"Saw, I don't understand you, saw. I never said I'd loan you money to bet on me. I didn't suspicion this from you, saw. No, I won't take any more lemonade; it's the most notorious stuff I ever drank, saw!"

M. St.-Ange's replies were in *falsetto* and not without effect; for presently the parson's indignation and anger began to melt. "Don't ask me, Jools, I can't help you. It's no use; it's a matter of conscience with me, Jools."

"*Mais oui!* 'tis a matt' of conscien' wid me, the same."

"But, Jools, the money's none o' mine, nohow; it belongs to Smyrny, you know."

"If I could make just *one* bet," said the persuasive St.-Ange, "I would leave this place, fas'-fas', yes. If I had thing—*mais* I did not soupspicion this from you, Posson Jone'"—

"Don't, Jools, don't!"

"No! Posson Jone'."

"You're bound to win?" said the parson, wavering.

"*Mais certainement!* But it is not to win that I want; 'tis me conscien'—me honor!"

"Well, Jools, I hope I'm not a-doin' no wrong. I'll loan you some of this money if you say you'll come right out 'thout takin your winnin's."

All was still. The peeping children could see the parson as he lifted his hand to his breastpocket. There it paused a moment in bewilderment, then plunged to the bottom. It came back empty, and fell lifelessly at his side. His head dropped upon his breast, his eyes were for a moment closed, his broad palms were iifted and pressed against his forehead, a tremour seized him, and he fell all in a lump to the floor. The children ran off with their infant-loads, leaving Jules St.-Ange swearing by all his deceased relatives, first to Miguel and Joe, and then to the lifted parson, that he did not know what had become of the money "except if" the black man had got it.

In the rear of ancient New Orleans, beyond the sites of the old rampart, a trio of Spanish forts, where the town has since sprung up and grown old, green with all the luxuriance of the wild Creole summer, lay the Congo Plains. Here stretched the canvas of the historic Cayetano, who Sunday after Sunday sowed the sawdust for his circus-ring.

But to-day the great showman had fallen short of his printed promise. The hurricane had come by night, and with one fell swash had made an irretrievable sop of everything. The circus trailed away its bedraggled magnificence, and the ring was cleared for the bull.

Then the sun seemed to come out and work for the people. "See," said the Spaniards, looking up at the glorious sky with its great, white fleets drawn off upon the horizon—"see—heaven smiles upon the bull-fight!"

In the high upper seats of the rude amphitheatre sat the gayly-decked wives and daughters of the Gascons, from the *métairies* along the Ridge, and the chattering Spanish women of the Market, their shining hair unbonneted to the sun. Next below were their husbands and lovers in Sunday blouses, milkmen, butchers, bakers, black-bearded fishermen, Sicilian fruiterers, swarthy Portugese sailors, in little woolen caps, and strangers of the graver sort; mariners of England, Germany, and Holland. The lowest seats were full of trappers, smugglers, Canadian *voyageurs*, drinking and singing; *Américains*, too—more's the shame—from the upper rivers—who will not keep their seats—who ply the bottle, and who will get home by and by and tell how wicked Sodom is; broad-brimmed, silver-braided Mexicans, too, with their copper cheeks and bat's eyes, and their tinkling spurred heels. Yonder, in that quieter section, are the quadroon women in their black lace shawls—and there is Baptiste; and below them are the turbaned black women, and there is—but he vanishes—Colossus.

The afternoon is advancing, yet the sport, though loudly demanded, does not begin. The *Américains* grow derisive and find pastime in gibes and raillery. They mock the various Latins with their national inflections, and answer their scowls with laughter. Some of the more aggressive shout pretty French greetings to the women of Gascony, and one bargeman, amid peals of applause, stands on a seat and hurls a kiss to the quadroons. The mariners of England, Germany, and Holland, as spectators, like the fun, while the Spaniards look back and cast defiant imprecations upon their persecutors. Some Gascons, with timely caution, pick their women out and depart, running a terrible fire of gallantries.

In hope of truce, a new call is raised for the bull: "The bull, the bull—hush!"

In a tier near the ground a man is standing and calling—standing head and shoulders above the rest—calling in the *Américaine* tongue. Another man, big and red, named Joe, and a handsome little Creole, in elegant dress and full of laughter, wish to stop him, but the flat-boatmen, ha-ha-ing and cheering, will not suffer it. Ah, through some shameful knavery of the men, into whose hands he has fallen, he is drunk! Even the women can see that; and now he throws his arms wildly and raises his voice until the whole great circle hears it. He is preaching!

Ah! kind Lord, for a special providence now! The men of his own nation—men from the land of the open English Bible and temperance cup and song are cheering him on to mad disgrace. And now another call for the appointed sport is drowned by the flat-boatmen singing the ancient tune of Mear. You can hear the words—

"Old Grimes is dead, that good old soul"

—from ribald lips and throats turned brazen with laughter, from singers who toss their hats aloft and roll in their seats; the chorus swells to the accompaniment of a thousand brogans—

"He used to wear an old gray coat
All buttoned down before."

A ribboned man in the arena is trying to be heard, and the Latins raise one mighty cry for silence. The big red man gets a hand over the parson's mouth, and the ribboned man seizes his moment.

"They have been endeavoring for hours," he says, "to draw the terrible animals from their dens, but such is their strength and fierceness, that"—

His voice is drowned. Enough has been heard to warrant the inference that the beasts cannot be whipped out of the storm-drenched cages to which menagerie-life and long starvation have attached them, and from the roar of indignation the man of ribbons flies. The noise increases. Men are standing up by hundreds, and women are imploring to be let out of the turmoil. All at once, like the bursting of a dam, the whole mass pours down into the ring. They sweep across the arena and over the showman's barriers. Miguel gets a frightful trampling. Who cares for gates or doors? They tear the beasts' houses bar from bar, and, laying hold of the gaunt buffalo, drag him forth by feet, ears, and tail; and in the midst of the *mêlée*, still head and shoulders above all, wilder, with the cup of the wicked, than any beast, is the man of God from the Florida parishes!

In his arms he bore—and all the people shouted at once when they saw it—the tiger. He had lifted it high up with its back to his breast, his arms clasped under its shoulders; the wretched brute had curled up caterpillar-wise, with its long tail against its belly, and through its filed teeth grinned a fixed and impotent wrath. And Parson Jones was shouting:

"The tiger and the buffler *shell* lay down together! You dah to say they shayn't and I'll comb you with this varmint from head to foot! The tiger and the buffler *shell* lay down together. They *shell!* Now, you, Joe! Behold! I am here to see it done. The lion and the buffler *shell* lay down together!"

Mouthing these words again and again, the parson forced his way through the surge in the wake of the buffalo. This creature the Latins had secured by a lariat over his head, and were dragging across the old rampart and into a street of the city.

The northern races were trying to prevent, and there was pommelling and knocking down, cursing and knife-drawing, until Jules St.-Ange was quite carried away with the fun, laughed, clapped his hands, and swore with delight, and ever kept close to the gallant parson.

Joe, contrariwise, counted all this child's-play an interruption. He had come to find Colossus and the money. In an unlucky moment he made bold to lay hold of the parson, but a piece of the broken barriers in the hands of the flat-boatman felled him to the sod, the terrible crowd swept over him, the lariat was cut, and the giant parson hurled the tiger upon the buffalo's back. In another instant both brutes were dead at the hands of the mob; Jones was lifted from his feet, and prating of Scripture and the millennium, of Paul at Ephesus and Daniel in the "buffler's" den, was borne aloft upon the shoulders of the huzzaing *Américains.* Half an hour later he was sleeping heavily on the floor of a cell in the *calaboza.*

When Parson Jones awoke, a bell was somewhere tolling for midnight. Somebody was at the door of his cell with a key. The lock grated, the door swung, the turnkey looked in and stepped back, and a ray of moonlight fell upon M. Jules St.-Ange. The prisoner sat upon the empty shackles and ring-bolt in the centre of the floor.

"Misty Posson Jone'," said the visitor, softly.

"O Jools!"

"*Mais,* w'at de matter, Posson Jone'?"

"My sins, Jools, my sins!"

"Ah! Posson Jone', is that something to cry, because a man get sometime a litt' bit intoxicate? *Mais,* if a man keep *all the time* intoxicate, I think that is again' the conscien'."

"Jools, Jools, your eyes is darkened—oh! Jools, where's my pore old niggah?"

"Posson Jone', never min'; he is wid Baptiste."

"Where?"

"I don' know w'ere—*mais* he is wid Baptiste. Baptiste is a beautiful to take care of somebody."

"Is he as good as you, Jools?" asked Parson Jones, sincerely.

Jules was slightly staggered.

"You know, Posson Jone', you know, a nigger cannot be good as a w'ite man— *mais* Baptiste is a good nigger."

The parson moaned and dropped his chin into his hands.

"I was to of left for home to-morrow, sun-up, on the Isabella schooner. Pore Smyrny!" He deeply sighed.

"Posson Jone'," said Jules, leaning against the wall and smiling, "I swear you is the moz funny man I ever see. If I was you I would say, me, 'Ah! 'ow I am lucky! the money I los', it was not mine, anyhow!' My faith! shall a man make hisse'f to be the more sorry because the money he los' is not his? Me, I would say, 'it is a specious providence.'

"Ah! Misty Posson Jone'," he continued, "you make a so droll sermon ad the bull-ring. Ha! ha! I swear I thing you can make money to preach thad sermon many time ad the theatre St. Philippe. Hah! you is the moz brave dat I never see, *mais* ad the same time the moz rilligious man. Where I'm goin' to fin' one priest to make like dat? *Mais*, why you can't cheer up an' be 'appy? Me, if I should be miserabl' like that I would kill meself."

The countryman only shook his head.

"*Bien*, Posson Jone', I have the so good news for you."

The prisoner looked up with eager inquiry.

"Las' evening when they lock' you, I come right off at M. De Blanc's house to get you let out of de calaboose; M. De Blanc he is the judge. So soon I was entering—'Ah! Jules, me boy, juz the man to make complete the game!' Posson Jone', it was a specious providence! I win in t'ree hours more dan six hundred dollah! Look." He produced a mass of bank-notes, *bons*, and due-bills.

"And you got the pass?" asked the parson, regarding the money with a sadness incomprehensible to Jules.

"It is here; it take the effect so soon the daylight."

"Jools, my friend, your kindness is in vain."

The Creole's face became a perfect blank.

"Because," said the parson, "for two reasons: firstly, I have broken the laws, and ought to stand the penalty; and secondly—you must really excuse me, Jools, you know, but the pass has been got onfairly, I'm afeerd. You told the judge I was innocent; and in neither case it don't become a Christian (which I hope I can still stay I am one) to 'do evil that good may come.' I muss stay."

M. St.-Ange stood up aghast, and for a moment speechless, at this exhibition of moral heroism; but an artifice was presently hit upon. "*Mais*, Posson Jone'!"—in his old *falsetto*—"de order—you cannot read it, it is in French—compel you to go hout, sir!"

"Is that so?" cried the parson, bounding up with radiant face—"is that so, Jools?"

The young man nodded, smiling; but, though he smiled, the fountain of his tenderness was opened. He made the sign of the cross as the parson knelt in prayer, and even whispered "Hail Mary," etc., quite through, twice over.

Morning broke in summer glory upon a cluster of villas behind the city, nestled under live-oaks and magnolias on the banks of a deep bayou, and known as Suburb St. Jean.

With the first beam came the West-Floridian and the Creole out upon the bank below the village. Upon the parson's arm hung a pair of antique saddle-bags. Baptiste limped wearily behind; both his eyes were encircled with broad, blue rings, and one cheek-bone bore the official impress of every knuckle of Colossus's left hand. The "beautiful to take care of somebody" had lost his charge. At mention of the negro he became wild, and half in English, half in the "gumbo" dialect, said murderous things. Intimidated by Jules to calmness, he became able to speak confidently on one point; he could, would, and did swear that Colossus had gone home to the Florida parishes; he was almost certain; in fact, he thought so.

There was a clicking of pulleys as the three appeared upon the bayou's margin, and Baptiste pointed out, in the deep shadow of a great oak, the Isabella, moored among the bulrushes, and just spreading her sails for departure. Moving down to where she lay, the parson and his friend paused on the bank, loath to say farewell.

"O Jools!" said the parson, "supposin' Colossus ain't gone home! O Jools, if you'll look him out for me, I'll never forget you—I'll never forget you nohow, Jools. No, Jools, I never will believe he taken that money. Yes, I know all niggahs will steal"— he set foot upon the gangplank—"but Colossus wouldn't steal from me. Good-by."

"Misty Posson Jone'," said St.-Ange, putting his hand on the parson's arm with genuine affection, "hol' on. You see dis money—w'at I win las' night? Well, I win' it by a specious providence, ain't it?"

"There's no tellin'," said the humbled Jones. "Providence
      'Moves in a mysterious way
      His wonders to perform'."

"Ah!" cried the Creole, "*c'est* very true. I ged this money in the mysterieuze way. *Mais*, if I keep dis money, you know where it goin' be to-night?"

"I really can't say," replied the parson.

"Goin' to the dev'," said the sweetly-smiling young man.

The schooner-captain, leaning against the shrouds, and even Baptiste, laughed outright.

"O Jools, you mustn't!"

"Well, den, w'at I shall do wid *it?*"

"Any thing!" answered the parson; "better donate it away to some poor man"—

"Ah! Misty Posson Jone', dat is w'at I want. You los' five hondred dollar'—'twas me fault."

"No, it wa'n't, Jools."

"*Mais*, it was!"

"No!"

"It *was* me fault! I *swear* it was me fault! *Mais*, here is five hondred dollar'; I wish you shall take it. Here! I don't got no use for money.—Oh, my faith! Posson Jone', you must not begin to cry some more."

Parson Jones was choked with tears. When he found voice he said:

"O Jools, Jools, Jools! my pore, noble, dear, misguidened friend! ef you hed of hed a Christian raisin'! May the Lord show you your errors better'n I kin, and bless you for your good intentions—oh, no! I cayn't touch that money with a ten-foot pole; it wa'n't rightly got; you must really excuse me, my dear friend, but I cayn't touch it."

St.-Ange was petrified.

"Good-by, dear Jools," continued the parson. "I'm in the Lord's haynds, and he's very merciful, which I hope and trust you'll find it out. Good-by!"—the schooner swung slowly off before the breeze—"good-by!"

St.-Ange roused himself.

"Posson Jone'! make me hany'ow *dis* promise: you never, never, *never* will come back to New Orleans."

"Ah Jools, the Lord willin', I'll never leave home again!"

"All right!" cried the Creole; "I thing he's willin'. Adieu, Posson Jone'. My faith'! you are the so fighting an' moz rilligious man as I never saw! Adieu! Adieu!"

Baptiste uttered a cry and presently ran by his master toward the schooner, his hands full of clods.

St.-Ange looked just in time to see the sable form of Colossus of Rhodes emerge from the vessel's hold, and the pastor of Smyrna and Bethesda seize him in his embrace.

"O Colossus! you outlandish old nigger! Thank the Lord! Thank the Lord!"

The little Creole almost wept. He ran down the tow-path, laughing and swearing, and making confused allusion to the entire *personnel* and furniture of the lower regions.

By odd fortune, at the moment that St.-Ange further demonstrated his delight by tripping his mulatto into a bog, the schooner came brushing along the reedy bank with a graceful curve, the sails flapped, and the crew fell to poling her slowly along.

Parson Jones was on the deck, kneeling once more in prayer. His hat had fallen before him; behind him knelt his slave. In thundering tones he was confessing himself "a plum fool," from whom "the conceit had been jolted out," and who had been made to see that even his "nigger had the longest head of the two."

Colossus clasped his hands and groaned.

The parson prayed for a contrite heart.

"Oh, yes!" cried Colossus.

The master acknowledged countless mercies.

"Dat's so!" cried the slave.

The master prayed that they might still be "piled on."

"Glory!" cried the black man, clapping his hands; "pile on!"

"An' now," continued the parson, "bring this pore backslidin' jackace of a parson and this pore ole fool nigger back to thar home in peace!"

"Pray fo' de money!" called Colossus.

But the parson prayed for Jules.

"Pray fo' de *money!*" repreated the negro.

"And oh, give thy servant back that there lost money!"

Colossus rose stealthily, and tiptoed by his still shouting master. St.-Ange, the captain, the crew, gazed in silent wonder at the strategist. Pausing but an instant over the master's hat to grin an acknowledgment of his beholders' speechless interest, he softly placed in it the faithfully-mourned and honestly-prayed-for Smyrna fund; then, saluted by the gesticulative, silent applause of St.-Ange and the schooner-men, he resumed his first attitude behind his roaring master.

"Amen!" cried Colossus, meaning to bring him to a close.

"Onworthy though I be"—cried Jones.

"*Amen!*" reiterated the negro.

"A-a-amen!" said Parson Jones.

He rose to his feet, and, stooping to take up his hat, beheld the well-known roll.

As one stunned he gazed for a moment upon his slave, who still knelt with clasped hands and rolling eyeballs; but when he became aware of the laughter and cheers that greeted him from both deck and shore, he lifted eyes and hands to heaven, and cried like the veriest babe. And when he looked at the roll again, and hugged and kissed it, St.-Ange tried to raise a second shout, but choked, and the crew fell to their poles.

And now up runs Baptiste, covered with slime, and prepares to cast his projectiles. The first one fell wide of the mark; the schooner swung round into a long reach of water, where the breeze was in her favor; another shout of laughter drowned the maledictions of the muddy man; the sails filled; Colossus of Rhodes, smiling and bowing as hero of the moment, ducked as the main boom swept round, and the schooner, leaning slightly to the pleasant influence, rustled a moment over the bulrushes, and then sped far away down the rippling bayou.

Mr. Jules St.-Ange stood long, gazing at the receding vessel as it now disappeared, now re-appeared beyond the tops of the high undergrowth; but, when an arm of the forest hid it finally from sight, he turned townward, followed by that fagged-out spaniel, his servant, saying, as he turned, "Baptiste."

"*Miché?*"

"You know w'at I goin' do wid dis money?"

"*Non, m'sieur.*"

"Well, you can strike me dead if I don't goin' to pay hall my debts! *Allons!*"

He began a merry little song to the effect that his sweetheart was a wine-bottle, and master and man, leaving care behind, returned to the picturesque Rue Royale. The ways of Providence are indeed strange. In all Parson Jones's after-life, amid the many painful reminiscences of his visit to the City of the Plain, the sweet knowledge was withheld from him that by the light of the Christian virtue that shone from him even in his great fall, Jules St.-Ange arose, and went to his father an honest man.

(1876)

CHARLES W. CHESNUTT

Sis' Becky's Pickaninny

We had not lived in North Carolina very long before I was able to note a marked improvement in my wife's health. The ozone-laden air of the surrounding piney woods, the mild and equable climate, the peaceful leisure of country life, had brought about in hopeful measure the cure we had anticipated. Toward the end of our second year, however, her ailment took an unexpected turn for the worse. She became the victim of a settled melancholy, attended with vague forebodings of impending misfortune.

"You must keep up her spirits," said our physician, the best in the neighboring town. "This melancholy lowers her tone too much, tends to lessen her strength, and, if it continues too long, may be fraught with grave consequences."

I tried various expedients to cheer her up. I read novels to her. I had the hands on the place come up in the evening and serenade her with plantation songs. Friends came in sometimes and talked, and frequent letters from the North kept her in touch with her former home. But nothing seemed to rouse her from the depression into which she had fallen.

One pleasant afternoon in spring, I placed an armchair in a shaded portion of the front piazza, and filling it with pillows led my wife out of the house and seated her where she would have the pleasantest view of a somewhat monotonous scenery. She was scarcely placed when old Julius came through the yard, and, taking off his tattered straw hat, inquired, somewhat anxiously:—

"How is you feelin' dis afternoon, ma'm?"

"She is not very cheerful, Julius," I said. My wife was apparently without energy enough to speak for herself.

The old man did not seem inclined to go away, so I asked him to sit down. I had noticed, as he came up, that he held some small object in his hand. When he had taken his seat on the top step, he kept fingering this object,—what it was I could not quite make out.

"What is that you have there, Julius?" I asked, with mild curiosity.

"Dis is my rabbit foot, suh."

This was at a time before this curious superstition had attained its present jocular popularity among white people, and while I had heard of it before, it had not yet outgrown the charm of novelty.

"What do you do with it?"

"I kyars it wid me fer luck, suh."

"Julius," I observed, half to him and half to my wife, "your people will never rise in the world until they throw off these childish superstitions and learn to live by the light of reason and common sense. How absurd to imagine that the fore-foot of a poor dead rabbit, with which he timorously felt his way along through a life surrounded by snares and pitfalls, beset by enemies on every hand, can promote happiness or success, or ward off failure or misfortune!"

"It is ridiculous," assented my wife, with faint interest.

"Dat's w'at I tells dese niggers roun' heah," said Julius. "De fo'-foot ain' got no power. It has ter be de hin'-foot, suh,—de lef' hin'-foot er a grabeya'd rabbit, killt by a cross-eyed nigger on a da'k night in de full er de moon."

"They must be very rare and valuable," I said.

"Dey is kinder ska'ce, suh, en dey ain' no 'mount er money could buy mine, suh. I mought len' it ter anybody I sot sto' by, but I would n' sell it, no indeed, suh, I would n'."

"How do you know it brings good luck?" I asked.

"'Ca'se I ain' had no bad luck sence I had it, suh, en I's had dis rabbit foot fer fo'ty yeahs. I had a good marster befo' de wah, en I wa'n't sol' erway, en I wuz sot free; en dat 'uz all good luck."

"But that doesn't prove anything," I rejoined. "Many other people have gone through a similar experience, and probably more than one of them had no rabbit's foot."

"Law, suh! you doan hafter prove 'bout de rabbit foot! Eve'ybody knows dat; leas'ways eve'ybody roun' heah knows it. But ef it has ter be prove' ter folks w'at wa'n't bawn en raise' in dis naberhood, dey is a' easy way ter prove it. Is I eber tol' you de tale er Sis' Becky en her pickaninny?"

"No," I said, "let us hear it." I thought perhaps the story might interest my wife as much or more than the novel I had meant to read from.

"Dis yer Becky," Julius began, "useter b'long ter ole Kunnel Pen'leton, who owned a plantation down on de Wim'l'ton Road, 'bout ten miles fum heah, des befo' you gits ter Black Swamp. Dis yer Becky wuz a fiel'-han', en a monst'us good 'un. She had a husban' oncet, a nigger w'at b'longed on de nex' plantation, but de man w'at owned her husban' died, en his lan' en his niggers had ter be sol' fer ter pay his debts. Kunnel Pen'leton 'lowed he'd 'a' bought dis nigger, but he had be'n bettin' on hoss races, en did n' hab no money, en so Becky's husban' wuz sol' erway ter Fughinny.

"Co'se Becky went on some 'bout losin' her man, but she coul n' he'p herse'f; en 'sides dat, she had her pickaninny fer ter comfo't her. Dis yer little Moze wuz de cutes', blackes', shiny-eyedes' little nigger you eber laid eyes on, en he wuz ez fon' er his mammy ez his mammy wuz er him. Co'se Becky had ter wuk en did n' hab much time ter was'e wid her baby. Ole Aun' Nancy, de plantation nuss down at de qua'ters, useter take keer er little Mose in de daytime, en atter de niggers come in fum de cotton-fiel' Becky 'ud git her chile en kiss 'im en nuss 'im, en keep 'im 'tel mawnin'; en on Sundays she'd hab 'im in her cabin wid her all day long.

"Sis' Becky had got sorter useter gittin' 'long widout her husban', w'en one day Kunnel Pen'leton went ter de races. Co'se w'en he went ter de races, he tuk his hosses, en co'se he bet on 'is own hosses, en co'se he los' his money; fer Kunnel Pen'leton did n' nebber hab no luck wid his hosses, ef he did keep hisse'f po' projeckin' wid 'em. But dis time dey wuz a hoss name' Lightnin' Bug, w'at b'longed ter ernudder man, un dis hoss won de sweep-stakes; en Kunnel Pen'leton tuck a lackin' ter dat hoss, en ax' his owner w'at he wuz willin' ter take fer 'im.

"'I'll take a thousan' dollahs fer dat hoss,' sez dis yer man, who had a big plantation down to'ds Wim'l'ton, whar he raise' hosses fer ter race en ter sell.

"Well, Kunnel Pen'leton scratch' 'is head, en wonder whar he wuz gwine ter raise a thousan' dollahs; en he did n' see des how he could do it, fer he owed ez much ez he could borry a'ready on de skyo'ity he could gib. But he wuz des boun' ter hab dat hoss, so sezee:—

"'I'll gib you my note fer 'leven hund'ed dollahs fer dat hoss.'

"De yuther man shuck 'is head, en sezee:—

"'Yo' note, suh, is better'n gol', I doan doubt; but I is made it a rule in my bizness not ter take no notes fum nobody. Howsomeber, suh, ef you is kinder sho't er fun's, mos' lackly we kin make some kin' er bahg'in. En w'iles we is talkin', I mought 's well say dat I needs ernudder good nigger down on my place. Ef you is got a good one ter spar', I mought trade wid you.'

"Now, Kunnel Pen'leton did n' r'ally hab no niggers fer ter spar', but he 'lowed ter hisse'f he wuz des bleedzd ter hab dat hoss, en so he sez, sezee:—

"'Well, I doan lack ter, but I reckon I'll haf ter. You come out ter my plantation ter-morrer en look ober my niggers, en pick out de one you wants.'

"So sho' 'nuff nex' day dis yer man come out ter Kunnel Pen'leton's place en rid roun' de plantation en glanshed at de niggers, en who sh'd he pick out fum 'em all but Sis' Becky.

"'I needs a noo nigger 'oman down ter my place,' sezee, 'fer ter cook en wash, en so on; en dat young 'oman 'll des fill de bill. You gimme her, en you kin hab Lightnin' Bug.'

"Now, Kunnel Pen'leton did n' lack ter trade Sis' Becky, 'ca'se she wuz nigh 'bout de bes' fiel'-han' he had; en 'sides, Mars Dugal' did n' keer ter take de mammies 'way fum dey chillun w'iles de chillun wuz little. But dis man say he want Becky, er e'se Kunnel Pen'leton could n' hab de race hoss.

"'Well,' sez de kunnel, 'you kin hab de 'oman. But I doan lack ter sen' her 'way fum her baby. W'at 'll you gimme fer dat nigger baby?'

"'I doan want de baby,' sez de yuther man. 'I ain' got no use fer de baby.'

"'I tell yer w'at I'll do,' 'lows Kunnel Pen'leton, 'I'll th'ow dat pickaninny in fer good measure.'

"But de yuther man shuck his head. 'No,' sezee, 'I's much erbleedzd, but I doan raise niggers; I raises hosses, en I doan wanter be both'rin' wid no nigger babies. Nemmine de baby. I'll keep dat 'oman so busy she'll fergit de baby; fer niggers is made ter wuk, en dey ain' got no time fer no sich foolis'ness ez babies.'

"Kunnel Pen'leton did n' wanter hu't Becky's feelin's,—fer Kunnel Pen'leton wuz a kin'-hea'ted man, en nebber lack' ter make no trouble fer nobody,—en so he tol' Becky he wuz gwine sen' her down ter Robeson County fer a day er so, ter he'p out his son-in-law in his wuk; en bein' ez dis yuther man wuz gwine dat way, he had ax' 'im ter take her 'long in his buggy.

"'Kin I kyar little Mose wid me, marster?' ax' Sis' Becky.

"'N-o,' sez de kunnel, ez ef he wuz studyin' whuther ter let her tak 'im er no; 'I reckon you better let Aun' Nancy look atter yo' baby fer de day er two you'll be gone, en she'll see dat he gits ernuff ter eat 'tel you gits back.'

"So Sis' Becky hug' en kiss' little Mose, en tol' 'im ter be a good little pickaninny, en take keer er hisse'f, en not fergit his mammy w'iles she wuz gone. En little Mose put his arms roun' his mammy en lafft en crowed des lack it wuz monst'us fine fun fer his mammy ter go 'way en leabe 'im.

"Well, dis yer hoss trader sta'ted out wid Becky, en bimeby, atter dey'd gone down de Lumbe'ton Road fer a few miles er so, dis man tu'nt roun' in a diffe'nt d'rection, en kep' goin' dat erway, 'tel bimeby Sis' Becky up 'n ax' 'im ef he wuz gwine ter Robeson County by a noo road.

"'No, nigger,' sezee, 'I ain' gwine ter Robeson County at all. I's gwine ter Bladen County, whar my plantation is, en whar I raises all my hosses.'

"'But how is I gwine ter git ter Mis' Laura's plantation down in Robeson County?' sez Becky, wid her hea't in her mouf, fer she 'mence' ter git skeered all er a sudden.

"'You ain' gwine ter git dere at all,' sez de man. 'You b'longs ter me now, fer I done traded my bes' race hoss fer you, wid you' ole marster. Ef you is a good gal, I'll treat you right, en ef you doan behabe yo'se'f,—w'y, w'at e'se happens 'll be yo' own fault.'

"Co'se Sis' Becky cried en went on 'bout her pickaninny, but co'se it did n' do no good, en bimeby dey got down ter dis yer man's place, en he put Sis' Becky ter wuk, en fergot all 'bout her habin' a pickaninny.

"Meanwi'les, w'en ebenin' come, de day Sis' Becky wuz tuk 'way, little Mose 'mence' ter git res'less, en bimeby, w'en his mammy did n' come, he sta'ted ter cry fer 'er. Aun' Nancy fed 'im en rocked 'im en rocked 'im, en fin'lly he des cried en cried 'tel he cried hisse'f ter sleep.

"De nex' day he did n' 'pear ter be as peart ez yushal, en w'en night come he fretted en went on wuss'n he did de night befo'. De nex' day his little eyes 'mence' ter lose dey shine, en he would n' eat nuffin, en he 'mence' ter look so peaked dat Aun' Nancy tuk'n kyared 'im up ter de big house, en showed 'im ter her ole missis, en her ole missis gun her some med'cine fer 'im, en 'lowed ef he did n' git no better she sh'd fetch 'im up ter de big house ag'in, en dey'd hab a doctor, en nuss little Mose up dere. Fer Aun' Nancy's ole missis 'lowed he wuz a lackly little nigger en wu'th raisin'.

"But Aun' Nancy had l'arn' ter lack little Mose, en she did n' wanter hab 'im tuck up ter de big house. En so w'en he did n' git no better, she gethered a mess er green peas, and tuk de peas en de baby, en went ter see ole Aun' Peggy, de cunjuh 'oman down by de Wim'l'ton Road. She gun Aun' Peggy de mess er peas, en tol' her all 'bout Sis' Becky en little Mose.

"'Dat is a monst'us small mess er peas you is fotch' me,' sez Aun' Peggy, sez she.

"'Yas, I knows,'' lowed Aun' Nancy, 'but dis yere is a monst'us small pickaninny.'

"'You'll hafter fetch me sump'n mo',' sez Aun' Peggy, 'fer you can't 'spec' me ter was'e my time diggin' roots en wukkin' cunj'ation fer nuffin.'

"'All right,' sez Aun' Nancy, 'I'll fetch you sump'n mo' nex' time.'

"'You bettah,' sez Aun' Peggy, 'er e'se dey'll be trouble. W'at dis yer little pickaninny needs is ter see his mammy. You leabe 'im heah 'tel ebenin' en I'll show 'im his mammy.'

"So w'en Aun' Nancy had gone 'way, Aun' Peggy tuk'n wukked her roots, en tu'nt little Mose ter a hummin'-bird, en sont 'im off fer ter fin' his mammy.

"So little Mose flewed, en flewed, en flewed away, 'tel bimeby he got ter de place whar Sis' Becky b'longed. He seed his mammy wukkin' roun' de ya'd, en he could tel fum lookin' at her dat she wuz trouble' in her min' 'bout sump'n, en feelin' kin' er po'ly. Sis' Becky heared sump'n hummin' roun' en roun' her, sweet en low. Fus' she 'lowed it wuz a hummin'-bird; den she thought it sounded lack her little Mose croonin' on her breas' way back yander on de ole plantation. En she des 'magine' it wuz her little Mose, en it made her feel bettah, en she went on 'bout her wuk pearter 'n she'd done sence she'd be'n down dere. Little Mose stayed roun' 'tel late in de ebenin', en den flewed back ez hard ez he could ter Aun' Peggy. Ez fer Sis' Becky, she dremp all dat night dat she wuz holdin' her pickaninny in her arms, en kissin' him, en nussin' him, des lack she useter do back on de ole plantation whar he wuz bawn. En fer th'ee er fo' days Sis' Becky went 'bout her wuk wid mo' sperrit dan she'd showed sence she'd be'n down dere ter dis man's plantation.

"De nex' day atter he come back, little Mose wuz mo' pearter en better 'n he had be'n fer a long time. But to'ds de een' er de week he 'mence' ter git res'less ag'in, en stop' eatin', en Aun' Nancy kyared 'im down ter Aun' Peggy once mo', en she tu'nt 'im ter a mawkin'-bird dis time, en sont 'im off ter see his mammy ag'in.

"It did n' take him long fer ter git dere, en w'en he did, he seed his mammy standin' in de kitchen, lookin' back in de d'rection little Mose wuz comin' fum. En dey wuz tears in her eyes, en she look' mo' po'ly en peaked 'n she had w'en he wuz down dere befo'. So little Mose sot on a tree in de ya'd en sung, en sung, en sung, des fittin' ter split his th'oat. Fus' Sis' Becky did n' notice 'im much, but dis mawkin'-bird kep' stayin' roun' de house all day, en bimeby Sis' Becky des 'magine' dat mawkin'-bird wuz her little Mose crowin' en crowin', des lack he useter do w'en his mammy would come home at night fum de cotton-fiel'. De mawkin'-bird stayed roun' dere 'mos' all day, en w'en Sis' Becky went out in de ya'd one time, dis yer mawkin'-bird lit on her shoulder en peck' at de piece er bread she wuz eatin', en fluttered his wings so dey rub' up agin de side er her head. En w'en he flewed away 'long late in de ebenin', des 'fo' sundown, Sis' Becky felt mo' better'n she had sence she had heared dat hummin'-bird a week er so pas'. En dat night she dremp 'bout ole times ag'in, des lack she did befo'.

"But dis yer totin' little Mose down ter ole Aun' Peggy, en dis yer gittin' things fer ter pay de cunjuh 'oman, use' up a lot er Aun' Nancy's time, en she begin ter git kinder ti'ed. 'Sides dat, w'en Sis' Becky had be'n on de plantation, she had useter he'p Aun' Nancy wid de young uns ebenin's en Sundays; en Aun' Nancy 'mence' ter miss 'er monst'us, 'speshly sence she got a tech er de rheumatiz herse'f, en so she 'lows ter ole Aun' Peggy one day:—

"'Aun' Peggy, ain' dey no way you kin fetch Sis' Becky back home?'

"'Huh!' sez Aun' Peggy, 'I dunno 'bout dat. I'll hafter wuk my roots en fin' out whuther I kin er no. But it'll take a monst'us heap er wuk, en I can't was'e my time fer nuffin. Ef you'll fetch me sump'n ter pay me fer my trouble, I reckon we kin fix it.'

"So nex' day Aun' Nancy went down ter see Aun' Peggy ag'in.

"'Aun' Peggy,' sez she, 'I is fotch' you my bes' Sunday head-hankercher. Will dat do?'

"Aun' Peggy look' at de head-hankercher, en run her han' ober it, en sez she:—

"'Yas, dat'll do fus'-rate. I's be'n wukkin' my roots sence you be'n gone, en I 'lows mos' lackly I kin git Sis' Becky back, but it's gwine take fig'rin' en studyin' ez well ez cunj'in'. De fus' thing ter do'll be ter stop fetchin' dat pickaninny down heah, en not sen' 'im ter see his mammy no mo'. Ef he gits too po'ly, you lemme know, en I'll gib you some kin' er mixtry fer ter make 'im fergit Sis' Becky fer a week er so. So 'less'n you comes fer dat, you neenter come back ter see me no mo' 'tel I sen's fer you.'

"So Aun' Peggy sont Aun' Nancy erway, en de fus' thing she done wuz ter call a hawnet fum a nes' unner her eaves.

"'You go up ter Kunnel Pen'leton's stable, hawnet,' sez she, 'en sting de knees er de race hoss name' Lightnin' Bug. Be sho' en git de right one.'

"So de hawnet flewed up ter Kunnel Pen'leton's stable en stung Lightnin' Bug roun' de laigs, en de nex' mawnin' Lightnin' Bug's knees wuz all swoll' up, twice't ez big ez dey oughter be. W'en Kunnel Pen'leton went out ter de stable en see de hoss's laigs, hit would 'a' des made you trimble lack a leaf fer ter heah him cuss dat hoss trader. Howesomeber, he cool' off bimeby en tol' de stable boy fer ter rub Lightnin' Bug's laigs wid some linimum. De boy done ez his marster tol' 'im, en by de nex' day de swellin' had gone down consid'able. Aun' Peggy had sont a sparrer, w'at had a nes' in one er de trees close ter her cabin, fer ter watch w'at wuz gwine on 'roun' de big house, en w'en dis yer sparrer tol' 'er de hoss wuz gittin' ober de swellin', she sont de hawnet back fer ter sting 'is knees some mo', en de nex' mawnin' Lightnin' Bug's laigs wuz swoll' up wuss 'n befo'.

"Well, dis time Kunnel Pen'leton wuz mad th'oo en th'oo, en all de way 'roun', en he cusst dat hoss trader up en down, fum *A* ter *Izzard*. He cusst so ha'd dat de stable boy got mos' skeered ter def, en went off en hid hisse'f in de hay.

"Ez fer Kunnel Pen'leton, he went right up ter de house en got out his pen en ink, en tuk off his coat en roll' up his sleeves, en writ a letter ter dis yer hoss trader, en sezee:—

"'You is sol' me a hoss w'at is got a ringbone er a spavin er sump'n, en w'at I paid you fer wuz a soun' hoss. I wants you ter sen' my nigger 'oman back en take yo' ole hoss, er e'se I'll sue you, sho's you bawn.'

"But dis yer man wa'n't skeered a bit, en he writ back ter Kunnel Pen'leton dat a bahg'in wuz a bahg'in; dat Lightnin' Bug wuz soun' w'en he sol' 'im, en ef Kunnel Pen'leton did n' knowed ernuff 'bout hosses ter take keer er a fine racer, dat wuz his own fune'al. En he say Kunnel Pen'leton kin sue en be cusst fer all he keer, but he ain' gwine ter gib up de nigger he bought en paid fer.

"W'en Kunnel Pen'leton got dis letter he wuz madder'n he wuz befo', 'speshly 'ca'se dis man 'lowed he did n' know how ter take keer er fine hosses. But he could n' do nuffin but fetch a lawsuit, en he knowed, by his own 'spe'ience, dat lawsuits wuz slow ez de seben-yeah eetch and cos' mo'd'n dey come ter, en he 'lowed he better go slow en wait awhile.

"Aun' Peggy knowed w'at wuz gwine on all dis time, en she fix' up a little bag wid some roots en one thing en ernudder in it, en gun it ter dis sparrer er her'n, en tol' 'im ter take it 'way down yander whar Sis' Becky wuz, en drap it right befo' de do' er her cabin, so she'd be sho' en fin' it de fus' time she come out'n de do'.

"One night Sis' Becky dremp' her pickaninny wuz dead, en de nex' day she wuz mo'nin' en groanin' all day. She dremp' de same dream th'ee nights runnin', en den, de nex' mawnin' atter de las' night, she foun' dis yer little bag de sparrer had drap' in front her do'; en she 'lowed she'd be'n cunju'd, en wuz gwine ter die, en ez long ez her pickaninny wuz dead dey wa'n't no use tryin' ter do nuffin nohow. En so she tuk 'n went ter bed, en tol' her marster she'd be'n cunju'd en wuz gwine ter die.

"Her marster lafft at her, en argyed wid her, en tried ter 'suade her out'n dis yer fool notion, ez he called it,—fer he wuz one er dese yer w'ite folks w'at purten' dey doan b'liebe in cunj'in',—but hit wa'n't no use. Sis' Becky kep' gittin' wusser en wusser, 'tel fin'lly dis yer man 'lowed Sis' Becky wuz gwine ter die, sho' 'nuff. En ez he knowed dey had n' be'n nuffin de matter wid Lightnin' Bug w'en he traded 'im, he 'lowed mebbe he could kyo' 'im en fetch 'im roun' all right, leas'ways good 'nuff ter sell ag'in. En anyhow, a lame hoss wuz better 'n a dead nigger. So he sot down en writ Kunnel Pen'leton a letter.

"'My conscience,' sezee, 'has be'n troublin' me 'bout dat ringbone' hoss I sol' you. Some folks 'lows a hoss trader ain' got no conscience, but dey doan know me, fer dat is my weak spot, en de reason I ain' made no mo' money hoss tradin'. Fac' is,' sezee, 'I is got so I can't sleep nights fum studyin' 'bout dat spavin' hoss; en I is made up my min' dat, w'iles a bahg'in is a bahg'in, en you seed Lightnin' Bug befo' you traded fer 'im, principle is wuth mo'd'n money er hosses er niggers. So ef you'll sen' Lightnin' Bug down heah, I'll sen' yo' nigger 'oman back, en we'll call de trade off, en be ez good frien's ez we eber wuz, en no ha'd feelin's.'

"So sho' 'nuff, Kunnel Pen'leton sont de hoss back. En w'en de man w'at come ter bring Lightnin' Bug tol' Sis' Becky her pickaninny wa'n't dead, Sis' Becky wuz so glad dat she 'lowed she wuz gwine ter try ter lib 'tel she got back whar she could see little Mose once mo'. En w'en she retch' de ole plantation en seed her baby kickin' en crowin' en holdin' out his little arms to'ds her, she wush' she wuz n' cunju'd en did n' hafter die. En w'en Aun' Nancy tol' 'er all 'bout Aun' Peggy, Sis' Becky went down ter see de cunjuh 'oman, en Aun' Peggy tol' her she had conju'd her. En den Aun' Peggy tuk de goopher off'n her, en she got well, en stayed on de plantation, en raise' her pickaninny. En w'en little Mose growed up, he could sing en whistle des lack a mawkin'-bird, so dat de w'ite folks useter hab 'im come up ter de big house at night, en whistle en sing fer 'em, en dey useter gib 'im money en vittles en one thing er ernudder, w'ich he alluz tuk home ter his mammy; fer he knowed all 'bout w'at she had gone th'oo. He tu'nt out ter be a sma't man, en l'arnt de blacksmif trade; en Kunnel

Pen'leton let 'im hire his time. En bimeby he bought his mammy en sot her free, en den he bought hisse'f, en tuk keer er Sis' Becky ez long ez dey bofe libbed."

My wife had listened to this story with greater interest than she had manifested in any subject for several days. I had watched her furtively from time to time during the recital, and had observed the play of her countenance. It had expressed in turn sympathy, indignation, pity, and at the end lively satisfaction.

"That is a very ingenious fairy tale, Julius," I said, "and we are much obliged to you."

"Why, John!" said my wife severely, "the story bears the stamp of truth, if ever a story did."

"Yes," I replied, "especially the humming-bird episode, and the mocking-bird digression, to say nothing of the doings of the hornet and the sparrow."

"Oh, well, I don't care," she rejoined, with delightful animation; "those are mere ornamental details and not at all essential. The story is true to nature, and might have happened half a hundred times, and no doubt did happen, in those horrid days before the war."

"By the way, Julius," I remarked, "your story doesn't establish what you started out to prove,—that a rabbit's foot brings good luck."

"Hit's plain 'nuff ter me, suh," replied Julius. "I bet young misses dere kin 'splain it herse'f."

"I rather suspect," replied my wife promptly, "that Sis' Becky had no rabbit's foot."

"You is hit de bull's-eye de fus' fire, ma'm," assented Julius. "Ef Sis' Becky had had a rabbit foot, she nebber would 'a' went th'oo all dis trouble."

I went into the house for some purpose, and left Julius talking to my wife. When I came back a moment later, he was gone.

My wife's condition took a turn for the better from this very day, and she was soon on the way to ultimate recovery. Several weeks later, after she had resumed her afternoon drives, which had been interrupted by her illness, Julius brought the rockaway round to the front door one day, and I assisted my wife into the carriage.

"John," she said, before I had taken my seat, "I wish you would look in my room, and bring me my handkerchief. You will find it in the pocket of my blue dress."

I went to execute the commission. When I pulled the handkerchief out of her pocket, something else came with it and fell on the floor. I picked up the object and looked at it. It was Julius's rabbit's foot.

(1899)

KATE CHOPIN

A Night in Acadie

There was nothing to do on the plantation so Telèsphore, having a few dollars in his pocket, thought he would go down and spend Sunday in the vicinity of Marksville.

There was really nothing more to do in the vicinity of Marksville than in the neighborhood of his own small farm; but Elvina would not be down there, nor Amaranthe, nor any of Ma'me Valtour's daughters to harass him with doubt, to torture him with indecision, to turn his very soul into a weather-cock for love's fair winds to play with.

Telèsphore at twenty-eight had long felt the need of a wife. His home without one was like an empty temple in which there is no altar, no offering. So keenly did he realize the necessity that a dozen times at least during the past year he had been on the point of proposing marriage to almost as many different young women of the neighborhood. Therein lay the difficulty, the trouble which Telèsphore experienced in making up his mind. Elvina's eyes were beautiful and had often tempted him to the verge of declaration. But her skin was overly swarthy for a wife; and her movements were slow and heavy; he doubted she had Indian blood, and we all know what Indian blood is for treachery. Amaranthe presented in her person none of these obstacles to matrimony. If her eyes were not so handsome as Elvina's, her skin was fine, and being slender to a fault, she moved swiftly about her household affairs, or when she walked the country lanes in going to church or to the store. Telèsphore had once reached the point of believing that Amaranthe would make him an excellent wife. He had even started out one day with the intention of declaring himself, when, as the god of chance would have it, Ma'me Valtour espied him passing in the road and enticed him to enter and partake of coffee and "baignés." He would have been a man of stone to have resisted, or to have remained insensible to the charms and accomplishments of the Valtour girls. Finally there was Ganache's widow, seductive rather than handsome, with a good bit of property in her own right. While Telèsphore was considering his chances of happiness or even success with Ganache's widow, she married a younger man.

From these embarrassing conditions, Telèsphore sometimes felt himself forced to escape, to change his environment for a day or two and thereby gain a few new insights by shifting his point of view.

It was Saturday morning that he decided to spend Sunday in the vicinity of Marksville, and the same afternoon found him waiting at the country station for the south-bound train.

He was a robust young fellow with good, strong features and a somewhat determined expression—despite his vacillations in the choice of a wife. He was dressed rather carefully in navy-blue "store clothes" that fitted well because anything would have fitted Telèsphore. He had been freshly shaved and trimmed and carried an umbrella. He wore—a little tilted over one eye—a straw hat in preference to the conventional gray felt; for no other reason than that his uncle Telèsphore would have worn a felt, and a battered one at that. His whole conduct of life had been planned on lines in direct contradistinction to those of his uncle Telèsphore, whom he was thought in early youth to greatly resemble. The elder Telèsphore could not read nor write, therefore the younger had made it the object of his existence to acquire these accomplishments. The uncle pursued the avocations of hunting, fishing and moss-picking; employments which the nephew held in detestation. And as for carrying an umbrella, "Nonc" Telèsphore would have walked the length of the parish in a deluge before he would have so much as thought of one. In short, Telèsphore, by advisedly shaping his course in direct opposition to that of his uncle, managed to lead a rather orderly, industrious, and respectable existence.

It was a little warm for April but the car was not uncomfortably crowded and Telèsphore was fortunate enough to secure the last available window-seat on the shady side. He was not too familiar with railway travel, his expeditions being usually made on horse-back or in a buggy, and the short trip promised to interest him.

There was no one present whom he knew well enough to speak to: the district attorney, whom he knew by sight, a French priest from Natchitoches and a few faces that were familiar only because they were native.

But he did not greatly care to speak to anyone. There was a fair stand of cotton and corn in the fields and Telèsphore gathered satisfaction in silent contemplation of the crops, comparing them with his own.

It was toward the close of his journey that a young girl boarded the train. There had been girls getting on and off at intervals and it was perhaps because of the bustle attending her arrival that this one attracted Telèsphore's attention.

She called good-bye to her father from the platform and waved good-bye to him through the dusty, sunlit window pane after entering, for she was compelled to seat herself on the sunny side. She seemed inwardly excited and preoccupied save for the attention which she lavished upon a large parcel that she carried religiously and laid reverentially down upon the seat before her.

She was neither tall nor short, nor stout nor slender; nor was she beautiful, nor was she plain. She wore a figured lawn, cut a little low in the back, that exposed a round, soft nuque with a few little clinging circles of soft, brown hair. Her hat was of white straw, cocked up on the side with a bunch of pansies, and she wore gray lisle-thread gloves. The girl seemed very warm and kept mopping her face. She vainly sought her fan, then she fanned herself with her handkerchief, and finally made an attempt to open the window. She might as well have tried to move the banks of Red River.

Telèsphore had been unconsciously watching her the whole time and perceiving her strait he arose and went to her assistance. But the window could not be opened. When he had grown red in the face and wasted an amount of energy that would have driven the plow for a day, he offered her his seat on the shady side. She demurred— there would be no room for the bundle. He suggested that the bundle be left where it was and agreed to assist her in keeping an eye upon it. She accepted Telèsphore's place at the shady window and he seated himself beside her.

He wondered if she would speak to him. He feared she might have mistaken him for a Western drummer, in which event he knew that she would not; for the women of the country caution their daughters against speaking to strangers on the trains. But the girl was not one to mistake an Acadian farmer for a Western traveling man. She was not born in Avoyelles parish for nothing.

"I wouldn' want anything to happen to it," she said.

"It's all right w'ere it is," he assured her, following the direction of her glance, that was fastened upon the bundle.

"The las' time I came over to Foché's ball I got caught in the rain on my way up to my cousin's house, an' my dress! J' vous réponds! it was a sight. Li'le mo', I would miss the ball. As it was, the dress looked like I'd wo' it weeks without doin'-up."

"No fear of rain to-day," he reassured her, glancing out at the sky, "but you can have my umbrella if it does rain; you jus' as well take it as not."

"Oh, no! I wrap' the dress roun' in toile-cirée this time. You goin' to Foché's ball? Didn' I meet you once yonda on Bayou Derbanne? Looks like I know yo' face. You mus' come f'om Natchitoches pa'ish."

"My cousins, the Fédeau family, live yonda. Me, I live on my own place in Rapides since '92."

He wondered if she would follow up her inquiry relative to Foché's ball. If she did, he was ready with an answer, for he had decided to go to the ball. But her thoughts evidently wandered from the subject and were occupied with matters that did not concern him, for she turned away and gazed silently out of the window.

It was not a village; it was not even a hamlet at which they descended. The station was set down upon the edge of a cotton field. Near at hand was the post office and store; there was a section house; there were a few cabins at wide intervals, and one in the distance the girl informed him was the home of her cousin, Jules Trodon. There lay a good bit of road before them and she did not hesitate to accept Telèsphore's offer to bear her bundle on the way.

She carried herself boldly and stepped out freely and easily, like a negress. There was an absence of reserve in her manner; yet there was no lack of womanliness. She had the air of a young person accustomed to decide for herself and for those about her.

"You said yo' name was Fédeau?" she asked, looking squarely at Telèsphore. Her eyes were penetrating, but earnest and dark, and a little searching. He noticed that they were handsome eyes; not so large as Elvina's but finer in their expression. They started to walk down the track before turning into the lane leading to Trodon's house. The sun was sinking and the air was fresh and invigorating by contrast with the stifling atmosphere of the train.

"You said yo' name was Fédeau?" she asked.

"No," he returned. "My name is Telèsphore Baquette."

"An' my name; it's Zaïda Trodon. It looks like you ought to know me; I don' know w'y."

"It looks that way to me, somehow," he replied. They were satisfied to recognize this feeling—almost conviction—of pre-acquaintance, without trying to penetrate its cause.

By the time they reached Trodon's house he knew that she lived over on Bayou de Glaize with her parents and a number of younger brothers and sisters. It was rather dull where they lived and she often came to lend a hand when her cousin's wife got tangled in domestic complications; or, as she was doing now, when Foché's Saturday ball promised to be unusually important and brilliant. There would be people there even from Marksville, she thought; there were often gentleman from Alexandria. Telèsphore was as unreserved as she, and they appeared like old acquaintances when they reached Trodon's gate.

Trodon's wife was standing on the gallery with a baby in her arms, watching for Zaïda; and four little bare-footed children were sitting in a row on the step, also waiting, but terrified and struck motionless and dumb at sight of a stranger. He opened the gate for the girl but stayed outside himself. Zaïda presented him formally to her cousin's wife, who insisted upon his entering.

"Ah, b'en, pour ça! you got to come in. It's any sense you goin' to walk yonda to Foché's! Ti Jules, run call yo' pa." As if Ti Jules could have run or walked even, or moved a muscle!

But Telèsphore was firm. He drew forth his silver watch and looked at it in a business-like fashion. He always carried a watch; his uncle Telèsphore always told the time by the sun, or by instinct, like an animal. He was quite determined to walk on to Foché's a couple of miles away, where he expected to secure supper and a lodging, as well as the pleasing distraction of the ball.

"Well, I reckon I see you all tonight," he uttered in cheerful anticipation as he moved away.

"You'll see Zaïda; yes, an' Jules," called out Trodon's wife good-humoredly. "Me, I got no time to fool with balls, J'vous réponds! with all them chil'ren."

"He's good-lookin'; yes," she exclaimed, when Telèsphore was out of ear-shot. "An' dressed! it's like a prince. I didn' know you knew any Baquettes, you, Zaïda."

"It's strange you don' know 'em yo' se'f, cousine." Well, there had been no question from Ma'me Trodon, so why should there be an answer from Zaïda?

Telèsphore wondered as he walked why he had not accepted the invitation to enter. He was not regretting it; he was simply wondering what could have induced him to decline. For it surely would have been agreeable to sit there on the gallery waiting while Zaïda prepared herself for the dance; to have partaken of supper with the family and afterward accompanied them to Foché's. The whole situation was so novel, and had presented itself so unexpectedly that Telèsphore wished in reality to become acquainted with it, accustomed to it. He wanted to view it from this side and that in comparison with other, familiar situations. The girl had impressed him—affected him in some way; but in some new, unusual way, not as the others always had. He could not recall details of her personality as he could recall such details of Amaranthe or the Valtours, or any of them. When Telèsphore tried to think of her he could not think at all. He seemed to have absorbed her in some way and his brain was not so occupied with her as his senses were. At that moment he was looking forward to the ball; there was no doubt about that. Afterwards, he did not know what he would look forward to; he did not care; afterward made no difference. If he had expected the crash of doom to come after the dance at Foché's, he would only have smiled in his thankfulness that it was not to come before.

There was the same scene every Saturday at Foché's! A scene to have aroused the guardians of the peace in a locality where such commodities abound. And all on account of the mammoth pot of gumbo that bubbled, bubbled, bubbled out in the open air. Foché in shirt-sleeves, fat, red and enraged, swore and reviled, and stormed at old black Douté for her extravagance. He called her every kind of a name of every kind of animal that suggested itself to his lurid imagination. And every fresh invective that he fired at her she hurled it back at him while into the pot went the chickens and the pans-full of minced ham, and the fists-full of onion and sage and piment rouge and piment vert. If he wanted her to cook for pigs he had only to say so. She knew how to cook for pigs and she knew how to cook for people of les Avoyelles.

The gumbo smelled good, and Telèsphore would have liked a taste of it. Douté was dragging from the fire a stick of wood that Foché had officiously thrust beneath the simmering pot, and she muttered as she hurled it smouldering to one side:

"Vaux mieux y s'méle ces affaires, lui; si non!" But she was all courtesy as she dipped a steaming plate for Telèsphore, though she assured him it would not be fit for a Christian or a gentleman to taste till midnight.

Telèsphore having brushed, "spruced" and refreshed himself, strolled about, taking a view of the surroundings. The house, big, bulky and weather-beaten, consisted chiefly of galleries in every state of decrepitude and dilapidation. There were a few chinaberry trees and a spreading live oak in the yard. Along the edge of the fence, a good distance away was a line of gnarled and distorted mulberry trees; and it was there, out in the road, that the people who came to the ball tied their ponies, their wagons and carts.

Dusk was beginning to fall and Telèsphore, looking out across the prairie, could see them coming from all directions. The little Creole ponies galloping in a line looked like hobby horses in the faint distance; the mule-carts were like toy wagons. Zaïda might be among those people approaching, flying, crawling ahead of the darkness that was creeping out of the far wood. He hoped so, but he did not believe so; she would hardly have had time to dress.

Foché was noisily lighting lamps, with the assistance of an inoffensive mulatto boy whom he intended in the morning to butcher, to cut into sections, to pack and salt down in a barrel, like the Colfax woman did to her old husband—a fitting destiny for so stupid a pig as the mulatto boy. The negro musicians had arrived: two fiddlers and an accordion player, and they were drinking whiskey from a black quart bottle which was passed socially from one to the other. The musicians were really never at their best till the quart bottle had been consumed.

The girls who came in wagons and on ponies from a distance wore, for the most part, calico dresses and sun-bonnets. Their finery they brought along in pillow-slips or pinned up in sheets and towels. With these they at once retired to an upper room; later to appear be-ribboned and be-furbelowed; their faces masked with starch powder, but never a touch of rouge.

Most of the guests had assembled when Zaïda arrived—"dashed up" would better express her coming—in an open, two-seated buckboard, with her cousin Jules driving. He reined the pony suddenly and viciously before the time-eaten front steps, in order to produce an impression upon those who were gathered around. Most of the men had halted their vehicles outside and permitted their women folk to walk up from the mulberry trees.

But the real, the stunning effect was produced when Zaïda stepped upon the gallery and threw aside her light shawl in the full glare of half a dozen kerosene lamps. She was white from head to foot—literally, for her slippers even were white. No one would have believed, let alone suspected that they were a pair of old black ones which she had covered with pieces of her first communion sash. There is no describing her dress; it was fluffy, like a fresh powder-puff, and stood out. No wonder she had handled it so reverentially! Her white fan was covered with spangles that she herself had sewed all over it; and in her belt and in her brown hair were thrust small sprays of orange blossom.

Two men leaning against the railing uttered long whistles expressive equally of wonder and admiration.

"Tiens! t'es-pareille comme ain mariée, Zaïda;" cried out a lady with a baby in her arms. Some young women tittered and Zaïda fanned herself. The women's voices were almost without exception shrill and piercing, the men's, soft and low-pitched.

The girl turned to Telèsphore, as to an old and valued friend:

"Tiens! c'est vous?" He had hesitated at first to approach, but at this friendly sign of recognition he drew eagerly forward and held out his hand. The men looked at him suspiciously, inwardly resenting his stylish appearance, which they considered intrusive, offensive and demoralizing.

How Zaïda's eyes sparkled now! What very pretty teeth Zaïda had when she laughed, and what a mouth! Her lips were a revelation, a promise; something to carry away and remember in the night and grow hungry thinking of next day. Strictly speaking, they may not have been quite all that; but in any event, that is the way Telèsphore thought about them. He began to take account of her appearance: her nose, her eyes, her hair. And when she left him to go in and dance her first dance with cousin Jules, he leaned up against a post and thought of them: nose, eyes, hair, ears, lips and round, soft throat.

Later it was like Bedlam.

The musicians had warmed up and were scraping away indoors and calling the figures. Feet were pounding through the dance; dust was flying. The women's voices were piped high and mingled discordantly, like the confused, shrill chatter of waking birds, while the men laughed boisterously. But if some one had only thought of gagging Foché, there would have been less noise. His good humor permeated everywhere, like an atmosphere. He was louder than all the noise; he was more visible than the dust. He called the young mulatto (destined for the knife) "my boy" and sent him flying hither and thither. He beamed upon Douté as he tasted the gumbo and congratulated her: "C'est-toi qui s'y connais, ma fille! 'cré tonnerre!"

Telèsphore danced with Zaïda and then he leaned out against the post; then he danced with Zaïda, and then he leaned against the post. The mothers of the other girls decided that he had the manners of a pig.

It was time to dance again with Zaïda and he went in search of her. He was carrying her shawl, which she had given him to hold.

"W'at time it is?" she asked him when he had found and secured her. They were under one of the kerosene lamps on the front gallery and he drew forth his silver watch. She seemed to be still laboring under some suppressed excitement that he had noticed before.

"It's fo'teen minutes pas' twelve," he told her exactly.

"I wish you'd fine out w'ere Jules is. Go look yonda in the card-room if he's there, an' come tell me." Jules had danced with all the prettiest girls. She knew it was his custom after accomplishing this agreeable feat, to retire to the card-room.

"You'll wait yere till I come back?" he asked.

"I'll wait yere; you go on." She waited but drew back a little into the shadow. Telèsphore lost no time.

"Yes, he's yonda playin' cards with Foché an' some others I don' know," he reported when he had discovered her in the shadow. There had been a spasm of alarm when he did not at once see her where he had left her under the lamp.

"Does he look—look like he's fixed yonda fo' good?"

"He's got his coat off. Looks like he's fixed pretty comf'table fo' the nex' hour or two."

"Gi' me my shawl."

"You cole?" offering to put it around her.

"No, I ain't cole." She drew the shawl about her shoulders and turned as if to leave him. But a sudden generous impulse seemed to move her, and she added:

"Come along yonda with me."

They descended the few rickety steps that led down to the yard. He followed rather than accompanied her across the beaten and trampled sward. Those who saw them thought they had gone out to take the air. The beams of light that slanted out from the house were fitful and uncertain, deepening the shadows. The embers under the empty gumbo-pot glared red in the darkness. There was a sound of quiet voices coming from under the trees.

Zaïda, closely accompanied by Telèsphore, went out where the vehicles and horses were fastened to the fence. She stepped carefully and held up her skirts as if dreading the least speck of dew or of dust.

"Unhitch Jules' ho'se an' buggy there an' turn 'em 'roun' this way, please." He did as instructed, first backing the pony, then leading it out to where she stood in the half-made road.

"You goin' home?" he asked her, "betta let me water the pony."

"Neva mine." She mounted and seating herself grasped the reins. "No, I ain't goin' home," she added. He, too, was holding the rein gathered in one hand across the pony's back.

"W'ere you goin?" he demanded.

"Neva you mine w'ere I'm goin'."

"You ain't goin' anyw'ere this time o' night by yo'se'f?"

"W'at you reckon I'm 'fraid of?" she laughed. "Turn loose that ho'se," at the same time urging the animal forward. The little brute started away with a bound and Telèsphore, also with a bound, sprang into the buckboard and seated himself beside Zaïda.

"You ain't goin' anyw'ere this time o' night by yo'se'f." It was not a question now, but an assertion, and there was no denying it. There was even no disputing it, and Zaïda recognizing the fact drove on in silence.

There is no animal that moves so swiftly across a 'Cadian prairie as the little Creole pony. This one did not run nor trot; he seemed to reach out in galloping bounds. The buckboard creaked, bounced, jolted and swayed. Zaïda clutched her shawl while Telèsphore drew his straw hat further down over his right eye and offered to drive. But he did not know the road and she would not let him. They had soon reached the woods.

If there is any animal that can creep more slowly through a wooded road than the little Creole pony, that animal has not yet been discovered in Acadie. This particular animal seemed to be appalled by the darkness of the forest and filled with dejection. His head drooped and he lifted his feet as if each hoof were weighted with a thousand pounds of lead. Any one unacquainted with the peculiarities of the breed would sometimes have fancied that he was standing still. But Zaïda and Telèsphore knew better. Zaïda uttered a deep sigh as she slackened her hold on the reins and Telèsphore, lifting his hat, let it swing from the back of his head.

"How you don' ask me w'ere I'm goin'?" she said finally. These were the first words she had spoken since refusing his offer to drive.

"Oh, it don' make any diff'ence w'ere you goin'."

"Then if it don' make any diff'ence w'ere I'm goin', I jus' as well tell you." She hesitated, however. He seemed to have no curiosity and did not urge her.

"I'm goin' to get married," she said.

He uttered some kind of an exclamation; it was nothing articulate—more like the tone of an animal that gets a sudden knife thrust. And now he felt how dark the forest was. An instant before it had seemed a sweet, black paradise; better than any heaven he had ever heard of.

"W'y can't you get married at home?" This was not the first thing that occurred to him to say, but this was the first thing he said.

"Ah, b'en oui! with perfec' mules fo' a father an' mother! it's good enough to talk."

"W'y couldn' he come an' get you? W'at kine of a scound'el is that to let you go through the woods at night by yo'se'f?"

"You betta wait till you know who you talkin' about. He didn' come an' get me because he knows I ain't 'fraid; an' because he's got too much pride to ride in Jules Trodon's buckboard afta he done been put out o' Jules Trodon's house."

"W'at's his name an' w'ere you goin' to fine 'im?"

"Yonda on the other side the woods up at ole Wat Gibson's—a kine of justice of the peace or something. Anyhow he's goin' to marry us. An' afta we done married those têtes-de-mulets yonda on Bayou de Glaize can say w'at they want."

"W'at's his name?"

"André Pascal."

The name meant nothing to Telèsphore. For all he knew, André Pascal might be one of the shining lights of Avoyelles; but he doubted it.

"You betta turn 'roun'," he said. It was an unselfish impulse that prompted the suggestion. It was the thought of this girl married to a man whom even Jules Trodon would not suffer to enter his house.

"I done give my word," she answered.

"W'at's the matta with 'im? W'y don't yo' father and mother want you to marry 'im?"

"W'y? Because it's always the same tune! W'en a man's down eve'ybody's got stones to throw at 'im. They say he's lazy. A man that will walk from St. Landry plumb to Rapides lookin' fo' work; an' they call that lazy. Then, somebody's been spreadin' yonda on the Bayou that he drinks. I don' b'lieve it. I neva saw 'im drinkin', me. Anyway, he won't drink afta he's married to me; he's too fon' of me fo' that. He say he'll blow out his brains if I don' marry 'im."

"I reckon you betta turn roun'."

"No, I done give my word." And they went creeping on through the woods in silence.

"W'at time is it?" she asked after an interval. He lit a match and looked at his watch.

"It's quarta to one. W'at time he say?"

"I tole 'im I'd come about one o'clock. I knew that was a good time to get away f'om the ball."

She would have hurried a little but the pony could not be induced to do so. He dragged himself, seemingly ready at any moment to give up the breath of life. But once out of the woods he made up for lost time. They were on the open prairie again, and he fairly ripped the air; some flying demon must have changed skins with him.

It was a few minutes of one o'clock when they drew up before Wat Gibson's house. It was not much more than a rude shelter, and in the dim starlight it seemed isolated, as if standing alone in the middle of the black, far-reaching prairie. As they halted at the gate a dog within set up a furious barking, and an old negro who had been smoking his pipe at that ghostly hour, advanced toward them from the shelter of the gallery. Telèsphore descended and helped his companion to alight.

"We want to see Mr. Gibson," spoke up Zaïda. The old fellow had already opened the gate. There was no light in the house.

"Marse Gibson, he yonda to ole Mr. Bodel's playin' kairds. But he neva' stay atter one o'clock. Come in, ma'am; come in, suh; walk right 'long in." He had drawn his own conclusions to explain their appearance. They stood upon the narrow porch waiting while he went inside to light the lamp.

Although the house was small, as it comprised but one room, that room was comparatively a large one. It looked to Telèsphore and Zaïda very large and gloomy when they entered it. The lamp was on a table that stood against the wall, and that held further a rusty looking ink bottle, a pen and an old blank book. A narrow bed was off in the corner. The brick chimney extended into the room and formed a ledge that served as mantel shelf. From the big, low-hanging rafters swung an assortment of fishing tackle, a gun, some discarded articles of clothing and a string of red peppers. The boards of the floor were broad, rough and loosely joined together.

Telèsphore and Zaïda seated themselves on opposite sides of the table and the Negro went out to the wood pile to gather chips and pieces of bois-gras with which to kindle a small fire.

It was a little chilly; he supposed the two would want coffee and he knew that Wat Gibson would ask for a cup the first thing on his arrival.

"I wonder w'at's keepin' 'im," muttered Zaïda impatiently. Telèsphore looked at his watch. He had been looking at it at intervals of one minute straight along.

"It's ten minutes pas' one," he said. He offered no further comment.

At twelve minutes past one Zaïda's restlessness again broke into speech.

"I can't imagine, me, w'at's become of André! He said he'd be yere sho' at one." The old negro was kneeling before the fire that he had kindled, contemplating the cheerful blaze. He rolled his eyes toward Zaïda.

"You talkin' 'bout Mr. André Pascal? No need to look fo' him. Mr. André he b'en down to de P'int all day raisin' Cain."

"That's a lie," said Zaïda. Telèsphore said nothing.

"Tain't no lie, ma'am; he be'n sho' raisin' de ole Nick." She looked at him, too contemptuous to reply.

The negro told no lie so far as his bald statement was concerned. He was simply mistaken in his estimate of André Pascal's ability to "raise Cain" during an entire afternoon and evening and still keep a rendezvous with a lady at one o'clock in the morning. For André was even then at hand, as the loud and menacing howl of the dog testified. The negro hastened out to admit him.

André did not enter at once; he stayed a while outside abusing the dog and communicating to the negro his intention of coming out to shoot the animal after he had attended to more pressing business that was awaiting him within.

Zaïda arose, a little flurried and excited when he entered. Telèsphore remained seated.

Pascal was partially sober. There had evidently been an attempt at dressing for the occasion at some early part of the previous day but such evidences had almost wholly vanished. His linen was soiled and his whole appearance was that of a man who, by an effort, had aroused himself from a debauch. He was a little taller than Telèsphore, and more loosely put together. Most women would have called him a handsomer man. It was easy to imagine that when sober, he might betray by some subtle grace of speech or manner, evidences of gentle blood.

"W'y did you keep me waitin', André? w'en you knew—" she got no further, but backed up against the table and stared at him with earnest, startled eyes.

"Keep you waiting, Zaïda? my dear li'le Zaïda, how can you say such a thing! I started up yere an hour ago an' that—w'ere's that damned ole Gibson?" He had approached Zaïda with the evident intention of embracing her, but she seized his wrist and held him at arm's length away. In casting her eyes about for old Gibson his glance alighted upon Telèsphore.

The sight of the 'Cadian seemed to fill him with astonishment. He stood back and began to contemplate the young fellow and lose himself in speculation and conjecture

before him, as if before some unlabeled wax figure. He turned for information to
Zaïda.

"Say, Zaïda, w'at you call this? W'at kine of damn fool you got sitting yere? Who
let him in? W'at you reckon he's lookin' fo'? trouble?"

Telèsphore said nothing; he was awaiting his cue from Zaïda.

"André Pascal," she said, "you jus' as well take the do' an' go. You might stan' yere
till the day o' judgment on yo' knees befo' me; an' blow out yo' brains if you a mine
to. I ain't neva goin' to marry you."

"The hell you ain't!"

He had hardly more than uttered the words when he lay prone on his back.
Telèsphore had knocked him down. The blow seemed to complete the process of
sobering that had begun in him. He gathered himself together and rose to his feet; in
doing so he reached back for his pistol. His hold was not yet steady, however, and the
weapon slipped from his grasp and fell to the floor. Zaïda picked it up and laid it on
the table behind her. She was going to see fair play.

The brute instinct that drives men at each other's throat was awake and stirring in
these two. Each saw in the other a thing to be wiped out of his way—out of existence
if need be. Passion and blind rage directed the blows which they dealt, and steeled the
tension of muscles and clutch of fingers. They were not skillful blows, however.

The fire blazed cheerily; the kettle which the negro had placed upon the coals was
steaming and singing. The man had gone in search of his master. Zaïda had placed the
lamp out of harm's way on a high mantel ledge and she leaned with her hands
behind her upon the table.

She did not raise her voice or lift her finger to stay the combat that was acting before
her. She was motionless, and white to the lips; only her eyes seemed to be alive and
burning and blazing. At one moment she felt that André must have strangled
Telèsphore; but she said nothing. The next instant she could hardly doubt that the blow
from Telèsphore's doubled fist could be less than a killing one; but she did nothing.

How the loose boards swayed and creaked beneath the weight of the struggling
men! The very old rafters seemed to groan; and she felt that the house shook.

The combat, if fierce, was short, and it ended out on the gallery whither they had
staggered through the open door—or one had dragged the other—she could not tell.
But she knew when it was over, for there was a long moment of utter stillness. Then
she heard one of the men descend the steps and go away, for the gate slammed after
him. The other went out to the cistern; the sound of the tin bucket splashing in the
water reached her where she stood. He must have been endeavoring to remove traces
of the encounter.

Presently Telèsphore entered the room. The elegance of his apparel had been
somewhat marred; the men over at the 'Cadian ball would hardly have taken
exception now to his appearance.

"W'ere is André?" the girl asked.

"He's gone," said Telèsphore.

She had never changed her position and now when she drew herself up her wrists
ached and she rubbed them a little. She was no longer pale; the blood had come back
into her cheeks and lips, staining them crimson. She held out her hand to him. He took

it gratefully enough, but he did not know what to do with it; that is, he did not know what he might dare do with it, so he let it drop gently away and went to the fire.

"I reckon we betta be goin', too," she said. He stooped and poured some of the bubbling water from the kettle upon the coffee which the negro had set upon the hearth.

"I'll make a li'le coffee firs'," he proposed, "an' anyhow we betta wait till ole man w'at's-his-name comes back. It wouldn't look well to leave his house that way without some kine of excuse or explanation."

She made no reply, but seated herself submissively beside the table.

Her will, which had been overmastering and aggressive, seemed to have grown numb under the disturbing spell of the last few hours. An illusion had gone from her, and had carried her love with it. The absence of regret revealed this to her. She realized, but could not comprehend it, not knowing that the love had been part of the illusion. She was tired in body and spirit, and it was with a sense of restfulness that she sat all drooping and relaxed and watched Telèsphore make the coffee.

He made enough for them both and a cup for old Wat Gibson when he should come in and also one for the negro. He supposed the cups, the sugar and spoons were in the safe over there in the corner, and that is where he found them.

When he finally said to Zaïda, "Come, I'm going to take you home now," and drew her shawl around her, pinning it under the chin, she was like a little child and followed whither he led in all confidence.

It was Telèsphore who drove on the way back, and he let the pony cut no capers, but held him to a steady and tempered gait. The girl was still quiet and silent; she was thinking tenderly—a little tearfully of those two old têtes-de-mulets yonder on Bayou de Glaize.

How they crept through the woods! And how dark it was and how still!

"W'at time it is?" whispered Zaïda. Alas! he could not tell her; his watch was broken. But almost for the first time in his life, Telèsphore did not care what time it was.

(1897)

ELLEN GLASGOW

Jordan's End

At the fork of the road there was the dead tree where buzzards were roosting, and through its boughs I saw the last flare of the sunset. On either side the November woods were flung in broken masses against the sky. When I stopped they appeared to move closer and surround me with vague, glimmering shapes. It seemed to me that I had been driving for hours; yet the ancient negro who brought the message had told me to follow the Old Stage Road till I came to Buzzard's Tree at the fork. "F'om dar on hit's moughty nigh ter Marse Jur'dn's place," the old man had assured me, adding tremulously, "en young Miss she sez you mus' come jes' ez quick ez you kin." I was young then (that was more than thirty years ago), and I was just beginning the practice of medicine in one of the more remote counties of Virginia.

My mare stopped, and leaning out, I gazed down each winding road, where it branched off, under half bared boughs, into the autumnal haze of the distance. In a little while the red would fade from the sky, and the chill night would find me still hesitating between those dubious ways which seemed to stretch into an immense solitude. While I waited uncertainly there was a stir in the boughs overhead, and a buzzard's feather floated down and settled slowly on the robe over my knees. In the effort to drive off depression, I laughed aloud and addressed my mare in a jocular tone:

"We'll choose the most God-forsaken of the two, and see where it leads us."

To my surprise the words brought an answer from the trees at my back. "If you're goin' to Isham's store, keep on the Old Stage Road," piped a voice from the underbrush.

Turning quickly, I saw the dwarfed figure of a very old man, with a hunched back, who was dragging a load of pine knots out of the woods. Though he was so stooped that his head reached scarcely higher than my wheel, he appeared to possess unusual vigour for one of his age and infirmities. He was dressed in a rough overcoat of some wood brown shade, beneath which I could see his overalls of blue jeans. Under a thatch of grizzled hair his shrewd little eyes twinkled cunningly, and his bristly chin jutted so far forward that it barely escaped the descending curve of his nose. I remember thinking that he could not be far from a hundred; his skin was so wrinkled and weather-beaten that, at a distance, I had mistaken him for a negro.

I bowed politely. "Thank you, but I am going to Jordan's End," I replied.

He cackled softly. "Then you take the bad road. Thar's Jur'dn's turnout." He pointed to the sunken trail, deep in mud, on the right. "An' if you ain't objectin' to a little comp'ny, I'd be obleeged if you'd give me a lift. I'm bound thar on my own o' count, an' it's a long ways to tote these here lightwood knots."

While I drew back my robe and made room for him, I watched him heave the load of resinous pine into the buggy, and then scramble with agility to his place at my side.

"My name is Peterkin," he remarked by way of introduction. "They call me Father Peterkin along o' the gran'child'en." He was a garrulous soul, I suspected, and would not be averse to imparting the information I wanted.

"There's not much travel this way," I began, as we turned out of the cleared space into the deep tunnel of the trees. Immediately the twilight enveloped us, through now and then the dusky glow in the sky was still visible. The air was sharp with the tang of autumn; with the effluvium of rotting leaves, the drift of wood smoke, the ripe flavour of crushed apples.

"Thar's nary a stranger, thoughten he was a doctor, been to Jur'dn's End as fur back as I kin recollect. Ain't you the new doctor?"

"Yes, I am the doctor." I glanced down at the gnomelike shape in the wood brown overcoat. "Is it much farther?"

"Naw, suh, we're all but thar jest as soon as we come out of Whitten woods."

"If the road is so little travelled, how do you happen to be going there?"

Without turning his head, the old man wagged his crescent shaped profile. "Oh, I live on the place. My son Tony works a slice of the farm on shares, and I manage to lend a hand at the harvest or corn shuckin', and, now-and-agen, with the cider. The old gentleman used to run the place that away afore he went deranged, an' now that the young one is laid up, thar ain't nobody to look arter the farm but Miss Judith. Them old ladies don't count. Thar's three of 'em, but they're all addle-brained an' look as if the buzzards had picked 'em. I reckon that comes from bein' shut up with crazy folks in that thar old tumbledown house. The roof ain't been patched fur so long that the shingles have most rotted away, an' thar's times, Tony says, when you kin skearcely hear yo' years fur the rumpus the wrens an' rats are makin' overhead."

"What is the trouble with them—the Jordans, I mean?"

"Jest run to seed, suh, I reckon."

"Is there no man of the family left?"

For a minute Father Peterkin made no reply. Then he shifted the bundle of pine knots, and responded warily. "Young Alan, he's still livin' on the old place, but I hear he's been took now, an' is goin' the way of all the rest of 'em. 'Tis a hard trial for Miss Judith, po' young thing, an' with a boy nine year old that's the very spit an' image of his pa. Wall, wall, I kin recollect away back yonder when old Mr. Timothy Jur'dn was the proudest man anywhar aroun' in these parts; but arter the War things sorter begun to go down hill with him, and he was obleeged to draw in his horns."

"Is he still living?"

The old man shook his head. "Mebbe he is, an' mebbe he ain't. Nobody knows but the Jur'dn's, an' they ain't tellin' fur the axin'."

"I suppose it was this Miss Judith who sent for me?"

"'Twould most likely be she, suh. She was one of the Yardlys that lived over yonder at Yardly's Field; an' when young Mr. Alan begun to take notice of her, 'twas the first time sence way back that one of the Jur'dn's had gone courtin' outside the family. That's the reason the blood went bad like it did, I reckon. Thar's a sayin' down aroun' here that Jur'dn an' Jur'dn won't mix." The name was invariably called Jurdin by all classes; but I had already discovered that names are rarely pronounced as they are spelled in Virginia.

"Have they been married long?"

"Ten year or so, suh. I remember as well as if 'twas yestiddy the day young Alan brought her home as a bride, an' thar warn't a soul besides the three daft old ladies to welcome her. They drove over in my son Tony's old buggy, though 'twas spick an' span then. I was goin' to the house on an arrant, an' I was standin' right down thar at the ice pond when they come by. She hadn't been much in these parts, an' none of us had ever seed her afore. When she looked up at young Alan her face was pink all over and her eyes war shinin' bright as the moon. Then the front do' opened an' them old ladies, as black as crows, flocked out on the po'ch. Thar never was anybody as peart-lookin' as Miss Judith was when she come here; but soon arterwards she begun to peak an' pine, though she never lost her sperits an' went mopin' roun' like all the other women folks at Jur'dn's End. They married sudden, an' folks do say she didn't know nothin' about the family, an' young Alan didn't know much mo' than she did. The old ladies had kep' the secret away from him, sorter believin' that what you don't know cyarn' hurt you. Anyways they never let it leak out tell arter his chile was born. Thar ain't never been but that one, an' old Aunt Jerusly declars he was born with a caul over his face, so mebbe things will be all right fur him in the long run."

"But who are the old ladies? Are their husbands living?"

When Father Peterkin answered the question he had dropped his voice to a hoarse murmur. "Deranged. All gone deranged," he replied.

I shivered, for a chill depression seemed to emanate from the November woods. As we drove on, I remembered grim tales of enchanted forests filled with evil faces and whispering voices. The scents of wood earth and rotting leaves invaded my brain like a magic spell. On either side the forest was as still as death. Not a leaf quivered, not a bird moved, not a small wild creature stirred in the underbrush. Only the glossy leaves and the scarlet berries of the holly appeared alive amid the bare interlacing branches of the trees. I began to long for an autumn clearing and the red light of the afterglow.

"Are they living or dead?" I asked presently.

"I've hearn strange tattle," answered the old man nervously, "but nobody kin tell. Folks do say as young Alan's pa is shut up in a padded place, and that his gran'pa died thar arter thirty years. His uncles went crazy too, an' the daftness is beginnin' to crop out in the women. Up tell now it has been mostly the men. One time I remember old Mr. Peter Jur'dn tryin' to burn down the place in the dead of the night. Thar's the end of the wood, suh. If you'll jest let me down here, I'll be gittin' along home across the old-field, an' thanky too."

At last the woods ended abruptly on the edge of an abandoned field which was thickly sown with scrub pine and broomsedge. The glow in the sky had faded now to a thin yellow-green, and a melancholy twilight pervaded the landscape. In this twilight I looked over the few sheep huddled together on the ragged lawn, and saw the old brick house crumbling beneath its rank growth of ivy. As I drew nearer I had the feeling that the surrounding desolation brooded there like some sinister influence.

Forlorn as it appeared at this first approach, I surmised that Jordan's End must have possessed once charm as well as distinction. The proportions of the Georgian front were impressive, and there was beauty of design in the quaint doorway, and in the steps of rounded stone which were brocaded now with a pattern of emerald moss. But the whole place was badly in need of repair. Looking up, as I stopped, I saw that the eaves were falling away, that crumbled shutters were sagging from loosened hinges, that odd scraps of hemp sacking or oil cloth were stuffed into windows where panes were missing. When I stepped on the floor of the porch, I felt the rotting boards give way under my feet.

After thundering vainly on the door, I descended the steps, and followed the beaten path that led round the west wing of the house. When I had passed an old boxwood tree at the corner, I saw a woman and a boy of nine years or so come out of a shed, which I took to be the smokehouse, and begin to gather chips from the woodpile. The woman carried a basket made of splits on her arm, and while she stooped to fill this, she talked to the child in a soft musical voice. Then, at a sound that I made, she put the basket aside, and rising to her feet, faced me in the pallid light from the sky. Her head was thrown back, and over her dress of some dark calico, a tattered gray shawl clung to her figure. That was thirty years ago; I am not young any longer; I have been in many countries since then, and looked on many women; but her face, with that wan light on it, is the last one I shall forget in my life. Beauty! Why, that woman will be beautiful when she is a skeleton, was the thought that flashed into my mind.

She was very tall, and so thin that her flesh seemed faintly luminous, as if an inward light pierced the transparent substance. It was the beauty, not of earth, but of triumphant spirit. Perfection, I suppose, is the rarest thing we achieve in this world of incessant compromise with inferior forms; yet the woman who stood there in that ruined place appeared to me to have stepped straight out of legend or allegory. The contour of her face was Italian in its pure oval; her hair swept in wings of dusk above her clear forehead; and, from the faintly shadowed hollows beneath her brows, the eyes that looked at me were purple-black, like dark pansies.

"I had given you up," she began in a low voice, as if she were afraid of being overheard. "You are the doctor?"

"Yes, I am the doctor. I took the wrong road and lost my way. Are you Mrs. Jordan?"

She bowed her head. "Mrs. Alan Jordan. There are three Mrs. Jordans besides myself. My husband's grandmother and the wives of his two uncles."

"And it is your husband who is ill?"

"My husband, yes. I wrote a few days ago to Doctor Carstairs." (Thirty years ago Carstairs, of Baltimore, was the leading alienist in the country.) "He is coming to-morrow morning; but last night my husband was so restless that I sent for you to-day." Her rich voice, vibrating with suppressed feeling, made me think of stained glass windows and low organ music.

"Before we go in," I asked, "will you tell me as much as you can?"

Instead of replying to my request, she turned and laid her hand on the boy's shoulder. "Take the chips to Aunt Agatha, Benjamin," she said, "and tell her that the doctor has come."

While the child picked up the basket and ran up the sunken steps to the door, she watched him with breathless anxiety. Not until he had disappeared into the hall did she lift her eyes to my face again. Then, without answering my question, she murmured, with a sigh which was like the voice of that autumn evening, "We were once happy here." She was trying, I realized, to steel her heart against the despair that threatened it.

My gaze swept the obscure horizon, and returned to the mouldering woodpile where we were standing. The yellow-green had faded from the sky, and the only light came from the house where a few scattered lamps were burning. Through the open door I could see the hall, as bare as if the house were empty, and the spiral staircase which crawled to the upper story. A fine old place once, but repulsive now in its abject decay, like some young blood of former days who has grown senile.

"Have you managed to wring a living out of the land?" I asked, because I could think of no words that were less compassionate.

"At first a poor one," she answered slowly. "We worked hard, harder than any negro in the fields, to keep things together, but we were happy. Then three years ago this illness came, and after that everything went against us. In the beginning it was simply brooding, a kind of melancholy, and we tried to ward it off by pretending that it was not real, that we imagined it. Only of late, when it became so much worse, have we admitted the truth, have we faced the reality—"

This passionate murmur, which had almost the effect of a chant rising out of the loneliness, was addressed, not to me, but to some abstract and implacable power. While she uttered it her composure was like the tranquillity of the dead. She did not lift her hand to hold her shawl, which was slipping unnoticed from her shoulders, and her eyes, so like dark flowers in their softness, did not leave my face.

"If you will tell me all, perhaps I may be able to help you," I said.

"But you know our story," she responded. "You must have heard it."

"Then it is true? Heredity, intermarriage, insanity?"

She did not wince at the bluntness of my speech. "My husband's grandfather is in an asylum, still living after almost thirty years. His father—my husband's, I mean—died there a few years ago. Two of his uncles are there. When it began I don't know, or how far back it reaches. We have never talked of it. We have tried always to forget it—Even now I cannot put the thing into words—My husband's mother died of a broken heart, but the grandmother and the two others are still living. You will see them when you go into the house. They are old women now, and they feel nothing."

"And there have been other cases?"

"I do not know. Are not four enough?"

"Do you know if it has assumed always the same form?" I was trying to be as brief as I could.

She flinched, and I saw that her unnatural calm was shaken at last. "The same, I believe. In the beginning there is melancholy, moping, Grandmother calls it, and then—" She flung out her arms with a despairing gesture, and I was reminded again of some tragic figure of legend.

"I know, I know," I was young, and in spite of my pride, my voice trembled. "Has there been in any case partial recovery, recurring at intervals?"

"In his grandfather's case, yes. In the others none. With them it has been hopeless from the beginning."

"And Carstairs is coming?"

"In the morning. I should have waited, but last night—" Her voice broke, and she drew the tattered shawl about her with a shiver. "Last night something happened. Something happened," she repeated, and could not go on. Then, collecting her strength with an effort which made her tremble like a blade of grass in the wind, she continued more quietly, "To-day he has been better. For the first time he has slept, and I have been able to leave him. Two of the hands from the fields are in the room." Her tone changed suddenly, and a note of energy passed into it. Some obscure resolution brought a tinge of colour to her pale cheek. "I must know," she added, "if this is as hopeless as all the others."

I took a step toward the house. "Carstairs's opinion is worth as much as that of any man living," I answered.

"But will he tell me the truth?"

I shook my head. "He will tell you what he thinks. No man's judgment is infallible."

Turning away from me, she moved with an energetic step to the house. As I followed her into the hall the threshold creaked under my tread, and I was visited by an apprehension, or, if you prefer, by a superstitious dread of the floor above. Oh, I got over that kind of thing before I was many years older; though in the end I gave up medicine, you know, and turned to literature as a safer outlet for a suppressed imagination.

But the dread was there at that moment, and it was not lessened by the glimpse I caught, at the foot of the spiral staircase, of a scantily furnished room, where three lean black-robed figures, as impassive as the Fates, were grouped in front of a wood fire. They were doing something with their hands. Knitting, crocheting, or plaiting straw?

At the head of the stairs the woman stopped and looked back at me. The light from the kerosene lamp on the wall fell over her, and I was struck afresh not only by the alien splendour of her beauty, but even more by the look of consecration, of impassioned fidelity that illumined her face.

"He is very strong," she said in a whisper. "Until this trouble came on him he had never had a day's illness in his life. We hoped that hard work, not having time to brood, might save us; but it has only brought the thing we feared sooner."

There was a question in her eyes, and I responded in the same subdued tone. "His health, you say, is good?" What else was there for me to ask when I understood everything?

A shudder ran through her frame. "We used to think that a blessing, but now—" She broke off and then added in a lifeless voice, "We keep two field hands in the room day and night, lest one should forget to watch the fire, or fall asleep."

A sound came from a room at the end of the hall, and, without finishing her sentence, she moved swiftly toward the closed door. The apprehension, the dread, or whatever you choose to call it, was so strong upon me, that I was seized by an impulse to turn and retreat down the spiral staircase. Yes, I know why some men turn cowards in battle.

"I have come back, Alan," she said in a voice that wrung my heartstrings.

The room was dimly lighted; and for a minute after I entered, I could see nothing clearly except the ruddy glow of the wood fire in front of which two negroes were seated on low wooden stools. They had kindly faces, these men; there was a primitive humanity in their features, which might have been modelled out of the dark earth of the fields.

Looking round the next minute, I saw that a young man was sitting away from the fire, huddled over in a cretonne-covered chair with a high back and deep wings. At our entrance the negroes glanced up with surprise; but the man in the winged chair neither lifted his head nor turned his eyes in our direction. He sat there, lost within the impenetrable wilderness of the insane, as remote from us and from the sound of our voices as if he were the inhabitant of an invisible world. His head was sunk forward; his eyes were staring fixedly at some image we could not see; his fingers, moving restlessly, were plaiting and unplaiting the fringe of a plaid shawl. Distraught as he was, he still possessed the dignity of mere physical perfection. At his full height he must have measured not under six feet three; his hair was the colour of ripe wheat, and his eyes, in spite of their fixed gaze, were as blue as the sky after rain. And this was only the beginning, I realized. With that constitution, that physical frame, he might live to be ninety.

"Alan!" breathed his wife again in her pleading murmur.

If he heard her voice, he gave no sign of it. Only when she crossed the room and bent over his chair, he put out his hand, with a gesture of irritation, and pushed her away, as if she were a veil of smoke which came between him and the object at which he was looking. Then his hand fell back to its old place, and he resumed his mechanical plaiting of the fringe.

The woman lifted her eyes to mine. "His father did that for twenty years," she said in a whisper that was scarcely more than a sigh of anguish.

When I had made my brief examination, we left the room as we had come, and descended the stairs together. The three old women were still sitting in front of the wood fire. I do not think they had moved since we went upstairs; but, as we reached the hall below, one of them, the youngest, I imagine, rose from her chair, and came out to join us. She was crocheting something soft and small, an infant's sacque, I perceived as she approached, of pink wool. The ball had rolled from her lap as she stood up, and it trailed after her now, like a woolen rose, on the bare floor. When the skein pulled at her, she turned back and stooped to pick up the ball, which she rewound with caressing fingers. Good God, an infant's sacque in that house!

"Is it the same thing?" she asked.

"Hush!" responded the younger woman kindly. Turning to me she added, "We cannot talk here," and opening the door, passed out on the porch. Not until we had reached the lawn, and walked in silence to where my buggy stood beneath an old locust tree, did she speak again.

Then she said only, "You know now?"

"Yes, I know," I replied, averting my eyes from her face while I gave my directions as briefly as I could. "I will leave an opiate," I said. "To-morrow, if Carstairs should not come, send for me again. If he does come," I added, "I will talk to him and see you afterward."

"Thank you," she answered gently; and taking the bottle from my hand, she turned away and walked quickly back to the house.

I watched her as long as I could; and then getting into my buggy, I turned my mare's head toward the woods, and drove by moonlight, past Buzzard's Tree and over the Old Stage Road, to my home. "I will see Carstairs to-morrow," was my last thought that night before I slept.

But, after all, I saw Carstairs only for a minute as he was taking the train. Life at its beginning and its end had filled my morning; and when at last I reached the little station, Carstairs had paid his visit, and was waiting on the platform for the approaching express. At first he showed a disposition to question me about the shooting, but as soon as I was able to make my errand clear, his jovial face clouded.

"So you've been there?" he said. "They didn't tell me. An interesting case, if it were not for that poor woman. Incurable, I'm afraid, when you consider the predisposing causes. The race is pretty well deteriorated, I suppose. God! what isolation! I've advised her to send him away. There are three others, they tell me, at Staunton."

The train came; he jumped on it, and was whisked away while I gazed after him. After all, I was none the wiser because of the great reputation of Carstairs.

All that day I heard nothing more from Jordan's End; and then, early next morning, the same decrepit negro brought me a message.

"Young Miss, she tole me ter ax you ter come along wid me jes' ez soon ez you kin git ready."

"I'll start at once, Uncle, and I'll take you with me."

My mare and buggy stood at the door. All I needed to do was to put on my overcoat, pick up my hat, and leave word, for a possible patient, that I should return before noon. I knew the road now, and I told myself, as I set out, that I would make as quick a trip as I could. For two nights I had been haunted by the memory of that man in the armchair, plaiting and unplaiting the fringe of the plaid shawl. And his father had done that, the woman had told me, for twenty years!

It was a brown autumn morning, raw, windless, with an overcast sky and a peculiar illusion of nearness about the distance. A high wind had blown all night, but at dawn it had dropped suddenly, and now there was not so much as a ripple in the broomsedge. Over the fields, when we came out of the woods, the thin trails of blue smoke were as motionless as cobwebs. The lawn surrounding the house looked smaller than it had appeared to me in the twilight, as if the barren fields had drawn closer since my last visit. Under the trees, where the few sheep were browsing, the piles of leaves lay in windrifts along the sunken walk and against the wings of the house.

When I knocked the door was opened immediately by one of the old women, who held a streamer of black cloth or rusty crape in her hands.

"You may go straight upstairs," she croaked; and, without waiting for an explanation, I entered the hall quickly, and ran up the stairs.

The door of the room was closed, and I opened it noiselessly, and stepped over the threshold. My first sensation, as I entered, was one of cold. Then I saw that the windows were wide open, and that the room seemed to be full of people, though, as I made out presently, there was no one there except Alan Jordan's wife, her little son, the two old aunts, and an aged crone of a negress. On the bed there was something under a yellowed sheet of fine linen (what the negroes call "a burial sheet," I suppose), which had been handed down from some more affluent generation.

When I went over, after a minute, and turned down one corner of the covering, I saw that my patient of the other evening was dead. Not a line of pain marred his features, not a thread of gray dimmed the wheaten gold of his hair. So he must have looked, I thought, when she first loved him. He had gone from life, not old, enfeebled and repulsive, but enveloped still in the romantic illusion of their passion.

As I entered, the two old women, who had been fussing about the bed, drew back to make way for me, but the witch of a negress did not pause in the weird chant, an incantation of some sort, which she was mumbling. From the rag carpet in front of the empty fireplace, the boy, with his father's hair and his mother's eyes, gazed at me silently, broodingly, as if I were trespassing; and by the open window, with her eyes on the ashen November day, the young wife stood as motionless as a statue. While I looked at her a redbird flew out of the boughs of a cedar, and she followed it with her eyes.

"You sent for me?" I said to her.

She did not turn. She was beyond the reach of my voice, of any voice, I imagine; but one of the palsied old women answered my question.

"He was like this when we found him this morning," she said. "He had a bad night, and Judith and the two hands were up with him until daybreak. Then he seemed to fall asleep, and Judith sent the hands, turn about, to get their breakfast."

While she spoke my eyes were on the bottle I had left there. Two nights ago it had been full, and now it stood empty, without a cork, on the mantelpiece. They had not even thrown it away. It was typical of the pervading inertia of the place that the bottle should still be standing there awaiting my visit.

For an instant the shock held me speechless; when at last I found my voice it was to ask mechanically.

"When did it happen?"

The old woman who had spoken took up the story. "Nobody knows. We have not touched him. No one but Judith has gone near him." Her words trailed off into unintelligible muttering. If she had ever had her wits about her, I dare-say fifty years at Jordan's End had unsettled them completely.

I turned to the woman at the window. Against the gray sky and the black intersecting branches of the cedar, her head, with its austere perfection, was surrounded by that visionary air of legend. So Antigone might have looked on the day of her sacrifice, I reflected. I had never seen a creature who appeared so withdrawn, so detached, from all human associations. It was as if some spiritual isolation divided her from her kind.

"I can do nothing," I said.

For the first time she looked at me, and her eyes were unfathomable. "No, you can do nothing," she answered. "He is safely dead."

The negress was still crooning on; the other old women were fussing helplessly. It was impossible in their presence, I felt, to put in words the thing I had to say.

"Will you come downstairs with me?" I asked. "Outside of this house?"

Turning quietly, she spoke to the boy. "Run out and play, dear. He would have wished it."

Then, without a glance toward the bed, or the old women gathered about it, she followed me over the threshold, down the stairs, and out on the deserted lawn. The ashen day could not touch her, I saw then. She was either so remote from it, or so completely a part of it, that she was impervious to its sadness. Her white face did not become more pallid as the light struck it; her tragic eyes did not grow deeper; her frail figure under the thin shawl did not shiver in the raw air. She felt nothing, I realized suddenly.

Wrapped in that silence as in a cloak, she walked across the windrifts of leaves to where my mare was waiting. Her step was so slow, so unhurried, that I remember thinking she moved like one who had all eternity before her. Oh, one has strange impressions, you know, at such moments!

In the middle of the lawn, where the trees had been stripped bare in the night, and the leaves were piled in long mounds like double graves, she stopped and looked in my face. The air was so still that the whole place might have been in a trance or asleep. Not a branch moved, not a leaf rustled on the ground, not a sparrow twittered in the ivy; and even the few sheep stood motionless, as if they were under a spell. Farther away, beyond the sea of broomsedge, where no wind stirred, I saw the flat desolation of the landscape. Nothing moved on the earth, but high above, under the leaden clouds, a buzzard was sailing.

I moistened my lips before I spoke. "God knows I want to help you!" At the back of my brain a hideous question was drumming. How had it happened? Could she have killed him? Had that delicate creature nerved her will to the unspeakable act? It was incredible. It was inconceivable. And yet. . . .

"The worst is over," she answered quietly, with that tearless agony which is so much more terrible than any outburst of grief. "Whatever happens, I can never go through the worst again. Once in the beginning he wanted to die. His great fear was that he might live too long, until it was too late to save himself. I made him wait then. I held him back by a promise."

So she had killed him, I thought. Then she went on steadily, after a minute, and I doubted again.

"Thank God, it was easier for him than he feared it would be," she murmured.

No, it was not conceivable. He must have bribed one of the negroes. But who had stood by and watched without intercepting? Who had been in the room? Well, either way! "I will do all I can to help you," I said.

Her gaze did not waver. "There is so little that any one can do now," she responded, as if she had not understood what I meant. Suddenly, without the warning of a sob, a cry of despair went out of her, as if it were torn from her breast. "He was my life," she cried, "and I must go on."

So full of agony was the sound that it seemed to pass like a gust of wind over the broomsedge. I waited until the emptiness had opened and closed over it. Then I asked as quietly as I could:

"What will you do now?"

She collected herself with a shudder of pain. "As long as the old people live, I am tied here. I must bear it out to the end. When they die, I shall go away and find work. I am sending my boy to school. Doctor Carstairs will look after him, and he will help me when the time comes. While my boy needs me, there is no release."

While I listened to her, I knew that the question on my lips would never be uttered. I should always remain ignorant of the truth. The thing I feared most, standing there alone with her, was that some accident might solve the mystery before I could escape. My eyes left her face and wandered over the dead leaves at our feet. No, I had nothing to ask her.

"Shall I come again?" That was all.

She shook her head. "Not unless I send for you. If I need you, I will send for you," she answered; but in my heart I knew that she would never send for me.

I held out my hand, but she did not take it; and I felt that she meant me to understand, by her refusal, that she was beyond all consolation and all companionship. She was nearer to the bleak sky and the deserted fields than she was to her kind.

As she turned away, the shawl slipped from her shoulders to the dead leaves over which she was walking; but she did not stoop to recover it, nor did I make a movement to follow her. Long after she had entered the house I stood there, gazing down on the garment that she had dropped. Then climbing into my buggy, I drove slowly across the field and into the woods.

(1923)

GEORGE WASHINGTON HARRIS

Mrs. Yardley's Quilting

"Thar's one durn'd nasty muddy job, an' I is jis' glad enuf tu take a ho'n ur two, on the straingth ove hit."

"What have you been doing, Sut?"

"Helpin tu salt ole Missis Yardley down."

"What do you mean by that?"

"Fixin her fur rotten cumfurtably, kiverin her up wif sile, tu keep the buzzards frum cheatin the wurms."

"Oh, you have been helping to bury a woman."

"That's hit, by golly! Now why the devil can't I 'splain mysef like yu? I ladles out my words at random, like a calf kickin at yaller-jackids; yu jis' rolls em out tu the pint, like a feller a-layin bricks—every one fits. How is it that bricks fits so clost enyhow? Rocks won't ni du hit."

"Becaze they'se all ove a size," ventured a man with a wen over his eye.

"The devil yu say, hon'ey-head! haint reapin-mersheens ove a size? I'd like tu see two ove em fit clost. Yu wait ontil yu sprouts tuther ho'n, afore yu venters tu 'splain mix'd questions. George, did yu know ole Missis Yardley?"

"No."

"Well, she wer a curious 'oman in her way, an' she wore shiney specks. Now jis' listen: Whenever yu see a ole 'oman ahine a par ove *shiney* specks, yu keep yer eye skinn'd; they am dang'rus in the extreme. Thar is jis' no knowin what they ken du. I hed one a-stradil ove me onst, fur kissin her gal. She went fur my har, an' she went fur my skin, ontil I tho't she ment tu kill me, an' wud a-dun hit, ef my hollerin hadent fotch ole Dave Jordan, a *bacheler*, tu my aid. He, like a durn'd fool, cotch her by the laig, an' drug her back'ards ofen me. She jis' kivered him, an' I run, by golly! The nex time I seed him he wer bald headed, an' his face looked like he'd been a-fitin wild-cats.

"Ole Missis Yardley were a great noticer ove littil things, that nobody else ever seed. She'd say right in the middil ove sumbody's serious talk: 'Law sakes! thar goes that yaller slut ove a hen, a-flingin straws over her shoulder; she's arter settin now, an' haint laid but seven aigs. I'll disapint *her*, see ef I don't; I'll put a punkin in her ne's, an' a feather in her nose. An' bless my soul! jis' look at that cow wif the wilted ho'n, a-flingin up dirt an' a-smellin the place whar hit cum frum, wif the rale ginuine still-wurim twis' in her tail, too; what upon the face ove the yeath kin she be arter now, the ole fool? watch her, Sally. An' sakes alive! jis' look at that ole sow; she's a-gwine in a fas' trot, wif her empty bag a-floppin agin her sides. Thar, she hes stop't, an's a-listenin! massy on us! what a long yearnis grunt she gin; hit cum frum way back ove her kidneys. Thar she goes agin; she's arter no good, sich kerryin on means no good.'

"An' so she wud gabble, no odds who wer a-listenin. She looked like she mout been made at fust 'bout four foot long, an' the common thickness ove wimen when they's at tharsefs, an' then had her har tied tu a stump, a par ove steers hitched to her heels, an' then straiched out a-mos' two foot more—mos' ove the straichin cumin outen her laigs an' naik. Her stockins, a-hangin on the clothes-line tu dry, looked like a par ove sabre scabbards, an' her naik looked like a dry beef shank smoked, an' mout been ni ontu es tough. I never felt hit mysef, I didn't, I jis' jedges by looks. Her darter Sal wer bilt at fust 'bout the laingth ove her mam, but wer never straiched eny by a par ove steers an' she wer fat enuf to kill; she wer taller lyin down than she wer a-standin up. Hit wer her who gin me the 'hump shoulder.' Jis' look at me; haint I'se got a tech ove the dromedary back thar bad? haint I humpy? Well, a-stoopin tu kiss that squatty lard-stan ove a gal is what dun hit tu me. She wer the fairest-lookin gal I ever seed. She allers wore thick woolin stockins 'bout six inches too long fur her laig; they rolled down over her garters, lookin like a par ove life-presarvers up thar. I tell yu she wer a tarin gal enyhow. Luved kissin, wrastlin, an' biled cabbige, an' hated tite clothes, hot weather, an' suckit-riders. B'leved strong in married folk's ways, cradles, an' the remishun ove sins, an' didn't b'leve in corsets, fleas, peaners, nur the fashun plates."

"What caused the death of Mrs. Yardley, Sut?"

"Nuffin, only her heart stop't beatin 'bout losin a nine dimunt quilt. True, she got a skeer'd hoss tu run over her, but she'd a-got over that ef a quilt hadn't been mix'd up in the catastrophy. Yu see quilts wer wun ove her speshul gifts; she run strong on the bed-kiver question. Irish chain, star ove Texas, sun-flower, nine dimunt, saw teeth, checker board, an' shell quilts; blue, an' white, an' yaller an' black coverlids, an' callickercumfurts reigned triumphan' 'bout her hous'. They wer packed in drawers, layin in shelfs full, wer hung four dubbil on lines in the lof, packed in chists, piled on cheers, an' wer everywhar, even ontu the beds, an' wer changed every bed-makin. She told everybody she cud git tu listen tu hit that she ment tu give every durn'd one ove them tu Sal when she got married. Oh, lordy! what es fat a gal es Sal Yardley cud ever du wif half ove em, an' sleepin wif a husbun at that, is more nor I ever cud see through. Jis' think ove her onder twenty layer ove quilts in July, an' yu in thar too. Gewhillikins! George, look how I is sweatin' now, an' this is December. I'd 'bout es lief be shet up in a steam biler wif a three hundred pound bag ove lard, es tu make a bisiness ove sleepin wif that gal—'twould kill a glass-blower.

"Well, tu cum tu the serious part ove this conversashun, that is how the old quilt-mersheen an' coverlid-loom cum tu stop operashuns on this yeath. She hed narrated hit thru the neighborhood that nex Saterday she'd gin a quiltin—three quilts an' one cumfurt tu tie. 'Goblers, fiddils, gals, an' whisky,' wer the words she sent tu the men-folk, an' more tetchin ur wakenin words never drap't ofen an 'oman's tongue. She sed tu the gals, 'Sweet toddy, huggin, dancin, an' huggers in 'bundunce.' Them words struck the gals rite in the pit ove the stumick, an' spread a ticklin sensashun bof ways, ontil they scratched thar heads wif one han, an' thar heels wif tuther.

"Everybody, he an' she, what wer baptized b'levers in the righteousnes ove quiltins wer thar, an' hit jis' so happen'd that everybody in them parts, frum fifteen summers tu fifty winters, wer unannamus b'levers. Strange, warn't hit? Hit wer the bigges' 'quiltin ever Missis Yardley hilt, an' she hed hilt hundreds; everybody wer thar, 'scept the constibil an' suckit-rider, two dam easily-spared pussons; the numbers ni ontu even too; jis' a few more boys nur gals; that made hit more exhitin, fur hit gin the gals a chance tu kick an' squeal a littil, wifout runnin eny risk ove not gittin kissed at all, an' hit gin reasonabil grouns fur a few scrimmages amung the he's. Now es kissin an' fitin am the pepper an' salt ove all soshul getherins, so hit wer more espishully wif this ove ours. Es I swung my eyes over the crowd, George, I thought quiltins, managed in a morril an' sensibil way, truly am good things—good fur free drinkin, good fur free eatin, good fur free huggin, good fur free dancin, good fur free fitin, an' goodest ove all fur poperlatin a country fas'.

"Thar am a fur-seein wisdum in quiltins, ef they hes proper trimmins: 'vittils, fiddils, an' sperrits in 'bundunce.' One holesum quiltin am wuf three old pray'r-meetins on the poperlashun pint, purtickerly ef hits hilt in the dark ove the moon, an' runs intu the night a few hours, an' April ur May am the time chosen. The moon don't suit quiltins whar everybody is well acquainted an' already fur along in courtin. She dus help pow'ful tu begin a courtin match onder, but when hit draws ni ontu a head, nobody wants a moon but the ole mammys.

"The mornin cum, still, saft, sunshiney; cocks crowin, hens singin, birds chirpin, tuckeys gobblin—jis' the day tu sun quilts, kick, kiss, squeal, an' make love.

"All the plow-lines an' clothes-lines wer straiched tu every post an' tree. Quilts purvailed. Durn my gizzard ef two acres roun that ar house warn't jis' one solid quilt, all out a-sunnin, an' tu be seed. They dazzled the eyes, skeered the hosses, gin wimen the heart-burn, an' perdominated.

"To'ards sundown the he's begun tu drap in. Year-nis' needil-drivin cummenced tu lose ground; threads broke ofen, thimbils got los', an' quilts needed anuther roll. Gigglin, winkin, whisperin, smoofin ove har, an' gals a-ticklin one anuther, wer a-gainin every inch ove ground what the needils los'. Did yu ever notis, George, at all soshul getherins, when the he's begin tu gather, that the young she's begin tu tickil one anuther an' the ole maids swell thar tails, roach up thar backs, an' sharpen thar nails ontu the bedposts an' door jams, an' spit an' groan sorter like cats a-courtin? Dus hit mean *rale* rath, ur is hit a dare tu the he's, sorter kivered up wif the outside signs ove danger? I honestly b'leve that the young she's ticklin means, 'Cum an' take this job ofen our hans.' But that swellin I jis' don't onderstan; dus yu? Hit looks skeery, an' I never tetch one ove em when they am in the swellin way. I may be mistaken'd 'bout the ticklin bisiness too; hit may be dun like a feller chaws poplar bark when he haint got eny terbacker, a-sorter better nur nun make-shif. I dus know one thing tu a certainty: that is, when the he's take hold the ticklin quits, an' ef yu gits one ove the ole maids out tu hersef, then she subsides an' is the smoofes, sleekes, saft thing yu ever seed, an' dam ef yu can't hear her purr, jis' es plain!

"But then, George, gals an' ole maids haint the things tu fool time away on. Hits widders, by golly, what am the rale sensibil, steady-goin, never-skeerin, never-kickin, willin, sperrited, smoof pacers. They cum clost up tu the hoss-block, standin still wif thar purty silky years playin, an' the naik-veins a-throbbin, an' waits fur the word, which ove course yu gives, arter yu finds yer feet well in the stirrup, an' away they moves like a cradil on cushioned rockers, ur a spring buggy runnin in damp san'. A tetch ove the bridil, an' they knows yu wants em tu turn, an' they dus hit es willin es ef the idear wer thar own. I be dod rabbited ef a man can't 'propriate happiness by the skinful ef he is in contack wif sumbody's widder, an' is smart. Gin me a willin widder, the yeath over: what they don't know, haint worth larnin. They hes all been tu Jamakey an' larnt how sugar's made, an' knows how tu sweeten wif hit; an' by golly, they is always ready tu use hit. All yu hes tu du is tu find the spoon, an' then drink cumfort till yer blind. Nex tu good sperrits an' my laigs, I likes a twenty-five year ole widder, wif roun ankils, an' bright eyes, honestly an' squarly lookin intu yurn, an' sayin es plainly es a partrige sez 'Bob White,' 'Don't be afraid ove me; I hes been thar; yu know hit ef yu hes eny sense, an' thar's no use in eny humbug, ole feller—cum ahead!'

"Ef yu onderstans widder nater, they ken save yu a power ove troubil, onsartinty, an' time, an' ef yu is interprisin yu gits mons'rous well paid fur hit. The very soun ove thar littil shoeheels speak full trainin, an' hes a knowin click as they tap the floor; an' the rustil ove thar dress sez, 'I dar yu tu ax me.'

"When yu hes made up yer mind tu court one, jis' go at hit like hit wer a job ove rail-maulin. Ware yer workin close, use yer common, every-day moshuns an' words, an' abuv all, fling away yer cinamint ile vial an' burn all yer love songs. No use in tryin tu fool em, fur they sees plum thru yu, a durn'd sight plainer than they dus thru thar veils. No use in a pasted shut; she's been thar. No use in borrowin a cavortin fat hoss; she's been thar. No use in har-dye; she's been thar. No use in cloves, tu kill whisky breff; she's been thar. No use in buyin clost curtains fur yer bed, fur she has been thar. Widders am a speshul means, George, fur ripenin green men, killin off weak ones, an makin 'ternally happy the soun ones.

"Well, es I sed afore, I flew the track an' got ontu the widders. The fellers begun tu ride up an' walk up, sorter slow, like they warn't in a hurry, the durn'd 'saitful raskils, hitchin thar critters tu evything they cud find. One red-comb'd, long-spurr'd, dominecker feller, frum town, in a red an' white grid-iron jackid an' patent leather gaiters, hitched his hoss, a wild, skeery, wall-eyed devil, inside the yard palins, tu a cherry tree lim'. Thinks I, that hoss hes a skeer intu him big enuf tu run intu town, an' perhaps beyant hit, ef I kin only tetch hit off; so I sot intu thinkin.

"One aind ove a long clothes-line, wif nine dimunt quilts ontu hit, wer tied tu the same cherry tree that the hoss wer. I tuck my knife and socked hit thru every quilt, 'bout the middil, an' jis' below the rope, an' tied them thar wif bark, so they cudent slip. Then I went tu the back aind, an' ontied hit frum the pos', knottin in a hoe-handil, by the middil, tu keep the quilts frum slippin off ef my bark strings failed, an' laid hit on the groun. Then I went tu the tuther aind: thar wer 'bout ten foot tu spar, a-lyin on the groun arter tyin tu the tree. I tuck hit atwix Wall-eye's hine laigs, an' tied hit fas' tu bof stirrups, an' then cut the cherry tree lim' betwix his bridil an' the tree, almos' off. Now, mine yu thar wer two ur three uther ropes full ove quilts atween me an' the hous', so I wer purty well hid frum thar. I jis' tore off a palin frum the fence, an' tuck hit in bof hans, an' arter raisin hit 'way up yander, I fotch hit down, es hard es I cud, flatsided to'ards the groun, an' hit acksidentally happen'd tu hit Wall-eye, 'bout nine inches ahead ove the root ove his tail. Hit landed so hard that hit made my hans tingle, an' then busted intu splinters. The first thing I did, wer tu feel ove mysef, on the same spot whar hit hed hit the hoss. I cudent help duin hit tu save my life, an' I swar I felt sum ove Wall-eye's sensashun, jis' es plain. The fust thing he did, wer tu tare down the lim' wif a twenty foot jump, his head to'ards the hous'. Thinks I, now yu hev dun hit, yu durn'd wall-eyed fool! tarin down that lim' wer the beginin ove all the troubil, an' the hoss did hit hissef; my conshuns felt clar es a mountin spring, an' I wer in a frame ove mine tu obsarve things es they happen'd, an' they soon begun tu happen purty clost arter one anuther rite then, an' thar, an' tharabouts, clean ontu town, thru hit, an' still wer a-happenin, in the woods beyant thar ni ontu eleven mile frum ole man Yardley's gate, an' four beyant town.

"The fust line ove quilts he tried tu jump, but broke hit down; the nex one he ran onder; the rope cotch ontu the ho'n ove the saddil, broke at bof ainds, an' went along wif the hoss, the cherry tree lim' an' the fust line ove quilts, what I hed proverdensally tied fas' tu the rope. That's what I calls foresight, George. Right furnint the frunt door he cum in contack wif ole Missis Yardley hersef, an' anuther ole 'oman; they were a-holdin a nine dimunt quilt spread out, a-'zaminin hit, an' a-praisin hits purfeckshuns. The durn'd onmanerly, wall-eyed fool run plum over Missis Yardley, frum ahine, stompt one hine foot through the quilt, takin hit along, a-kickin ontil he made hits corners snap like a whip. The gals screamed, the men hollered wo! an' the ole 'oman wer toted intu the hous' limber es a wet string, an' every word she sed wer, 'Oh, my preshus nine dimunt quilt!'

"Wall-eye busted thru the palins, an' Dominicker sed 'im, made a mortal rush fur his bitts, wer too late fur them, but in good time fur the strings ove flyin quilts, got tangled amung em, an' the gridiron jackid patren wer los' tu my sight amung star an' Irish chain quilts; he went frum that quiltin at the rate ove thuty miles tu the hour. Nuffin lef on the lot ove the hole consarn, but a nine biler hat, a par ove gloves, an' the jack ove hearts.

"What a onmanerly, suddin way ove leavin places sum folks hev got, enyhow.

"Thinks I, well, that fool hoss, tarin down that cherry tree lim', hes dun sum good, enyhow; hit hes put the ole 'oman outen the way fur the balance ove the quiltin, an' tuck Dominicker outen the way an' outen danger, fur that gridiron jackid wud a-bred a scab on his nose afore midnite; hit wer morrily boun tu du hit.

"Two months arterwards, I tracked the route that hoss tuck in his kalamatus skeer, by quilt rags, tufts ove cotton, bunches ove har, (human an' hoss,) an' scraps ove a gridiron jackid stickin ontu the bushes, an' plum at the aind ove hit, whar all signs gin out, I foun a piece ove watch chain an' a hosses head. The places what know'd Dominicker, know'd 'im no more.

"Well, arter they'd tuck the ole 'oman up stairs an' camfired her tu sleep, things begun to work agin. The widders broke the ice, an' arter a littil gigglin, goblin, an' gabblin, the kissin begun. *Smack!*—'Thar, now,' a widder sed that. *Pop!*—'Oh, don't!' *Pfip!*—'Oh, yu quit!' *Plosh!*—'Go *way* yu awkerd critter, yu kissed me in the eye!' anuther widder sed that. *Bop!* 'Now yu ar satisfied, I recon, big mouf!' *Vip!*— 'That haint fair!' *Spat!*—'Oh, lordy! May, cum pull Bill away; he's a-tanglin my har.' *Thut!*—'I jis' d-a-r-e yu tu du that agin!' a widder sed that, too. Hit sounded all 'roun that room like poppin co'n in a hot skillet, an' wer pow'ful sujestif.

"Hit kep on ontil I be durn'd ef *my* bristils didn't begin tu rise, an' sumthin like a cold buckshot wud run down the marrow in my back-bone 'bout every ten secons, an' then run up agin, tolerabil hot. I kep a swallerin wif nuthin tu swaller, an' my face felt swell'd; an' yet I wer fear'd tu make a bulge. Thinks I, I'll ketch one out tu hersef torreckly, an' then I guess we'll rastil. Purty soon Sal Yardley started fur the smoke-'ous, so I jis' gin my head I few short shakes, let down one ove my wings a-trailin, an' sirkiled roun her wif a side twis' in my naik, steppin sidewise, an' a-fetchin up my hinmos' foot wif a sorter jerkin slide at every step. Sez I, 'Too coo-took a-too.' She onderstood hit, an stopt, sorter spreadin her shoulders. An' jis' es I hed pouch'd out my mouf, an' wer a-reachin forrid wif hit, fur the article hitsef, sunthin interfared wif me, hit did. George, wer yu ever ontu yer hans an' knees, an' let a hell-tarin big, mad ram, wif a ten-yard run, but yu yearnis'ly, jis' onst, right squar ontu the pint ove yer back-bone?"

"No, you fool; why do you ask?"

"Kaze I wanted tu know ef yu cud hev a realizin' noshun ove my shock. Hits scarcely worth while tu try to make yu onderstan the case by words only, onless yu hev been tetched in that way. Gr-eat golly! the fust thing I felt, I tuck hit to be a back-ackshun yeathquake; an' the fust thing I seed wer my chaw'r terbacker a-flyin over Sal's head like a skeer'd bat. My mouf wer pouch'd out, ready fur the article hitsef, yu know, an' hit went outen the roun hole like the wad outen a pop-gun—thug! an' the fust thing I know'd, I wer a flyin over Sal's head too, an' a-gainin on the chaw'r terbacker fast. I wer straitened out strait, toes hinemos', middil finger-nails foremos', an' the fust thing I hearn wer, 'Yu dam Shanghi!' Great Jerus-a-lam! I lit ontu my all fours jis' in time tu but the yard gate ofen hits hinges, an' skeer loose sum more hosses—kep on in a four-footed gallop, clean acrost the lane afore I cud straiten up, an' yere I cotch up wif my chaw'r terbacker, stickin flat agin a fence-rail. I hed got so good a start that I thot hit a pity tu spile hit, so I jis' jump'd the fence an' tuck thru the orchurd. I tell yu I dusted these yere close, fur I tho't hit wer arter me.

"Arter runnin a spell, I ventured tu feel roun back thar, fur sum signs ove what hed happened tu me. George, arter two pow'ful hardtugs, I pull'd out the vamp an' sole ove one ove ole man Yardley's big brogans, what he hed los' amung my coat-tails. Dre'-ful! dre'ful! Arter I got hit away frum thar, my flesh went fas' asleep, frum abuv my kidneys tu my knees; about now, fur the fust time, the idear struck me, what hit wer that hed interfar'd wif me, an' los' me the kiss. Hit wer ole Yardley hed kicked me. I walked fur a month like I wer straddlin a thorn hedge. Sich a shock, at sich a time, an' on sich a place—jis' think ove hit! hit am tremenjus, haint hit? The place feels num, right now."

"Well, Sut, how did the quilting come out?"

"How the hell du yu 'speck me tu know? I warn't thar eny more."

(1867)

JOEL CHANDLER HARRIS

The Wonderful Tar-Baby Story

"Didn't the fox *never* catch the rabbit, Uncle Remus?" asked the little boy the next evening.

"He come mighty nigh it, honey, sho's you bawn—Brer Fox did. One day atter Brer Rabbit fool 'im wid dat calamus root, Brer Fox went ter wuk en got 'im some tar, en mix it wid some turkentime, en fix up a contrapshun wat he call a Tar-Baby, en he tuck dish yer Tar-Baby en he sot 'er in de big road, en den he lay off in de bushes fer ter see wat de news wuz gwineter be. En he didn't hatter wait long, nudder, kaze bimeby here come Brer Rabbit pacin' down de road—lippity-clippity, clippity-lippity—dez ez sassy ez a jay-bird. Brer Fox, he lay low. Brer Rabbit come prancin' 'long twel he spy de Tar-Baby, en den he fotch up on his behime legs like he wuz 'stonished. De Tar-Baby, she sot dar, she did, en brer Fox, he lay low.

"'Mawnin'!' sez Brer Rabbit, sezee—'nice wedder dis mawnin',' sezee.

"Tar-Baby ain't sayin' nuthin', en Brer Fox, he lay low.

"'How duz yo' smy'tums seem ter segashuate?' sez Brer Rabbit, sezee.

"Brer Fox, he wink his eye slow, en lay low, en de Tar-Baby, she ain't sayin' nuthin'.

"'How you come on, den? Is you deaf?' sez Brer Rabbit, sezee. 'Kaze if you is, I kin holler louder,' sezee.

"Tar-Baby stay still, en Brer Fox, he lay low.

"'Youer stuck up, dat's w'at you is,' sez Brer Rabbit, sezee, 'en I'm gwineter kyore you, dat's w'at I'm a gwineter do,' sezee.

"Brer Fox, he sorter chuckle in his stummuck, he did, but Tar-Baby ain't sayin' nuthin'.

"'I'm gwineter larn you howter talk ter 'specttubble fokes ef hit's de las' ack,' sez Brer Rabbit, sezee. 'Ef you don't take off dat hat en tell me howdy, I'm gwineter bus' you wide open,' sezee.

"Tar-Baby stay still, en Brer Fox, he lay low.

"Brer Rabbit keep on axin' 'im, en de Tar-Baby, she keep on sayin' nuthin', twel present'y Brer Rabbit draw back wid his fis', he did, en blip he tuck 'er side er de head.

Right dar's whar he broke his merlasses jug. His fis' stuck, en he can't pull loose. De tar hilt 'im. But Tar-Baby, she stay still, en Brer Fox, he lay low.

"'Ef you don't lemme loose, I'll knock you agin,' sez Brer Rabbit, sezee, en wid dat he fotch 'er a wipe wid de udder han', en dat stuck. Tar-Baby, she ain't sayin' nuthin', en Brer Fox he lay low.

"'Tu'n me loose, fo' I kick de natal stuffin' outen you,' sez Brer Rabbit, sezee, but de Tar-Baby, she ain't sayin' nuthin'. She des hilt on, en den Brer Rabbit lose de use er his feet in de same way. Brer Fox, he lay low. Den Brer Rabbit squall out dat ef de Tar-Baby don't tu'n 'im loose he butt 'er cranksided. En den he butted, en his head got stuck. Den Brer Fox, he sa'ntered fort', lookin' des ez innercent ez wunner yo' mammy's mockin' birds.

"'Howdy, Brer Rabbit,' sez Brer Fox, sezee. 'You look sorter stuck up dis mawnin',' sezee, en den he rolled on de groun', en laft en laft twel he couldn't laff no mo'. 'I speck you'll take dinner wid me dis time, Brer Rabbit. I done laid in some calamus root, en I ain't gwineter take no skuse,' sez Brer Fox, sezee."

Here Uncle Remus paused, and drew a two-pound yam out of the ashes.

"Did the fox eat the rabbit?" asked the little boy to whom the story had been told.

"Dat's all de fur de tale goes," replied the old man. "He mout, en den agin he moutent. Some say Jedge B'ar come 'long en loosed 'im—some say he didn't. I hear Miss Sally callin'. You better run 'long."

How Mr. Rabbit Was Too Sharp for Mr. Fox

"Uncle Remus," said the little boy one evening, when he had found the old man with little or nothing to do, "did the fox kill and eat the rabbit when he caught him with the Tar-Baby?"

"Law, honey, ain't I tell you 'bout dat?" replied the old darkey, chuckling slyly. "I 'clar ter grashus I ought er tole you dat, but ole man Nod wuz ridin' on my eyeleds 'twel a leetle mo'n I'd a dis'member'd my own name, en den on to dat here come yo' mammy a hollerin' atter you.

"W'at I tell you w'en I fus' begin? I tole you Brer Rabbit wuz a monstus soon creetur; leas'ways dat's w'at I laid out fer ter tell you. Well, den, honey, don't you go en make no udder calkalashuns, kaze in dem days Brer Rabbit en his family wuz at de head er de gang w'en enny racket wuz on han', en dar dey stayed. 'Fo' you begins fer ter wipe yo' eyes 'bout Brer Rabbit, you wait en see whar'bouts Brer Rabbit gwineter fetch up at. But dat's needer yer ner dar.

"W'en Brer Fox fine Brer Rabbit mixt up wid de Tar-Baby, he feel mighty good, en he roll on de groun' en laff. Bimeby he up'n say, sezee:

"'Well, I speck I got you dis time, Brer Rabbit,' sezee; 'maybe I ain't, but I speck I is. You been runnin' roun' here sassin' after me a mighty long time, but I speck you done come ter de een' er de row. You bin cuttin' up yo' capers en bouncin' 'roun' in dis neighberhood ontwel you come ter b'leeve yo'sef de boss er de whole gang. En den youer allers som'ers whar you got no bizness,' sez Brer Fox, sezee. 'Who ax you fer ter come en strike up a 'quaintance wid dish yer Tar-Baby? En who stuck you up dar whar you iz? Nobody in de roun' worril. You des tuck en jam yo'se'f on dat Tar-Baby widout waitin' fer enny invite,' sez Brer Fox, sezee, 'en dar you is, en dar you'll stay twel I fixes up a bresh-pile and fires her up, kaze I'm gwineter bobbycue you dis day, sho,' sez Brer Fox, sezee.

"Den Brer Rabbit talk mighty 'umble.

"'I don't keer w'at you do wid me, Brer Fox,' sezee, 'so you don't fling me in dat brier-patch. Roas' me, Brer Fox,' sezee, 'but don't fling me in dat brier-patch,' sezee.

"'Hit's so much trouble fer ter kindle a fier,' sez Brer Fox, sezee, ''dat I speck I'll hatter hang you,' sezee.

"'Hang me des ez high as you please, Brer Fox,' sez Brer Rabbit, sezee, 'but do fer de Lord's sake don't fling me in dat brier-patch,' sezee.

"'I ain't got no string,' sez Brer Fox, sezee, 'en now I speck I'll hatter drown you,' sezee.

"'Drown me des ez deep ez you please, Brer Fox,' sez Brer Rabbit, sezee, 'but do don't fling me in dat brier-patch,' sezee.

"'Dey ain't no water nigh,' sez Brer Fox, sezee, 'en now I speck I'll hatter skin you,' sezee.

"'Skin me, Brer Fox,' sez Brer Rabbit, sezee, 'snatch out my eyeballs, t'ar out my years by de roots, en cut off my legs,' sezee, 'but do please, Brer Fox, don't fling me in dat brier-patch,' sezee.

"Co'se Brer Fox wanter hurt Brer Rabbit bad ez he kin, so he cotch 'im by de behime legs en slung 'im right in de middle er de brier-patch. Dar wuz a considerbul flutter whar Brer Rabbit struck de bushes, en Brer Fox sorter hang 'roun' fer ter see w'at wuz gwineter happen. Bimeby he hear somebody call 'im, en way up de hill he see Brer Rabbit settin' cross-legged on a chinkapin log koamin' de pitch outen his har wid a chip. Den Brer Fox know dat he bin swop off mighty bad. Brer Rabbit wuz bleedzed fer ter fling back some er his sass, en he holler out:

"'Bred en bawn in a brier-patch, Brer Fox—bred en bawn in a brier-patch!' en wid dat he skip out des ez lively ez a cricket in de embers."

(1880)

Mingo: A *Sketch* of Life in Middle Georgia

I

In 1876, circumstances, partly accidental and partly sentimental, led me to revisit Crooked Creek Church, near the little village of Rockville, in Middle Georgia. I was amazed at the changes which a few brief years had wrought. The ancient oaks ranged roundabout remained the same, but upon everything else time had laid its hand right heavily. Even the building seemed to have shrunk; the pulpit was less massive and imposing, the darkness beyond the rafters less mysterious. The preacher had grown gray, and feebleness had taken the place of that physical vigor which was formerly the distinguishing feature of his interpretations of the larger problems of theology. People I had never seen sat in the places of those I had known so well. There were only traces here and there of the old congregation, whose austere simplicity had made so deep an impression upon my youthful mind. The blooming girls of 1860 had grown into careworn matrons, and the young men had developed in their features the strenuous uncertainty and misery of the period of desolation and disaster through which they had passed. Anxiety had so ground itself into their lives that a stranger to the manner might well have been pardoned for giving a sinister interpretation to these pitiable manifestations of hopelessness and unsuccess.

I had known the venerable preacher intimately in the past; but his eyes, wandering vaguely over the congregation, and resting curiously upon me, betrayed no recognition. Age, which had whitened his hair and enfeebled his voice, seemed also to have given him the privilege of ignoring everything but the grave and the mysteries beyond.

These swift processes of change and decay were calculated to make a profound impression, but my attention was called away from all such reflections. Upon a bench near the pulpit, in the section reserved for the colored members, sat an old negro man whose face was perfectly familiar. I had known him in my boyhood as Mingo, the carriage-driver and body-servant of Judge Junius Wornum. He had changed but little. His head was whiter than when I saw him last; but his attitude was as firm and as erect, and the evidences of his wonderful physical strength as apparent, as ever. He sat with his right hand to his chin, his strong serious face turned contemplatively toward the rafters. When his eye chanced to meet mine, a smile of recognition lit up his features, his head and body drooped forward, and his hand fell away from his face, completing a salutation at once graceful, picturesque, and imposing.

I have said that few evidences of change manifested themselves in Mingo; and so it seemed at first, but a closer inspection showed one remarkable change. I had known him when his chief purpose in life seemed to be to enjoy himself. He was a slave, to be sure, but his condition was no restraint upon his spirits. He was known far and wide as "Laughing Mingo," and upon hundreds of occasions he was the boon companion of the young men about Rockville in their wild escapades. Many who read this will remember the "possum suppers" which it was Mingo's delight to prepare for these young men, and he counted among his friends and patrons many who afterward became distinguished both in war and in the civil professions. At these gatherings Mingo, bustling around and serving his guests, would keep the table in a roar with his quaint sayings and local satires in the shape of impromptu doggerel; and he would also repeat snatches of orations which he had heard in Washington when Judge Wornum was a member of Congress. But his chief accomplishments lay in the wonderful ease and fluency with which he imitated the eloquent appeals of certain ambitious members of the Rockville bar, and in his travesties of the bombastic flights of the stump-speakers of that day.

It appeared, however, as he sat in the church, gazing thoughtfully and earnestly at the preacher, that the old-time spirit of fun and humor had been utterly washed out of his face. There was no sign of grief, no mark of distress, but he had the air of settled anxiety belonging to those who are tortured by an overpowering responsibility. Apparently here was an interesting study. If the responsibilities of life are problems to those who have been trained to solve them, how much more formidable must they be to this poor negro but lately lifted to his feet! Thus my reflections took note of the pathetic associations and suggestions clustering around this dignified representative of an unfortunate race.

Upon this particular occasion church services were to extend into the afternoon, and there was an interval of rest after the morning sermon, covering the hour of noon. This interval was devoted by both old and young to the discussion of matters seriously practical. The members of the congregation had brought their dinner baskets, and the contents thereof were spread around under the trees in true pastoral style. Those who came unprovided were, in pursuance of an immemorial custom of the section and the occasion, taken in charge by the simple and hearty hospitality of the members.

Somehow I was interested in watching Mingo. As he passed from the church with the congregation, and moved slowly along under the trees, he presented quite a contrast to the other negroes who were present. These, with the results of their rural surroundings superadded to the natural shyness of their race, hung upon the outskirts of the assembly, as though their presence was merely casual, while Mingo passed along from group to group of his white friends and acquaintances with that familiar and confident air of meritorious humility and unpretentious dignity which is associated with good-breeding and gentility the world over. When he lifted his hat in salutation, there was no servility in the gesture; when he bent his head, and dropped his eyes upon the ground, his dignity was strengthened and fortified rather than compromised. Both his manners and his dress retained the flavor of a social system the exceptional features of which were too often, by both friend and foe, made to stand for the system itself. His tall beaver, with its curled brim, and his blue broadcloth dress-coat, faded and frayed, with its brass buttons, bore unmistakable evidence of their age and origin; but they seemed to be a reasonable and necessary contribution to his individuality.

Passing slowly through the crowd, Mingo made his way to a double-seated buggy shielded from all contingencies of sun and rain by an immense umbrella. From beneath the seat he drew forth a large hamper, and proceeded to arrange its contents upon a wide bench which stood near.

While this was going on, I observed a tall, angular woman, accompanied by a bright-looking little girl, making her way toward Mingo's buggy. The woman was plainly, even shabbily, dressed, so that the gay ribbons and flowers worn by the child were gaudy by contrast. The woman pressed forward with decision, her movements betraying a total absence of that undulatory grace characteristic of the gentler sex, while the little girl dancing about her showed not only the grace and beauty of youth, but a certain refinement of pose and gesture calculated to attract attention.

Mingo made way for these with ready deference, and after a little I saw him coming toward me. He came forward, shook hands, and remarked that he had brought me an invitation to dine with Mrs. Feratia Bivins.

"Miss F'raishy 'members you, boss," he said, bowing and smiling, "en she up 'n' say she be mighty glad er yo' comp'ny ef you kin put up wid cole vittles an' po' far'; en ef you come," he added on his own account, "we like it mighty well."

II

Accepting the invitation, I presently found myself dining with Mrs. Bivins, and listening to her remarkable flow of small talk, while Mingo hovered around, the embodiment of active hospitality.

"Mingo 'lowed he'd ast you up," said Mrs. Bivins, "an' I says, says I, 'Don't you be a-pesterin' the gentulmun, when you know thar's plenty er the new-issue quality ready an' a-waitin' to pull an' haul at 'im,' says I. Not that I begrudges the vittles,— not by no means; I hope I hain't got to that yit. But somehow er 'nother folks what hain't got no great shakes to brag 'bout gener'ly feels sorter skittish when strange folks draps in on 'em. Goodness knows, I hain't come to that pass wher' I begrudges the vittles that folks eats, bekaze anybody betweenst this an' Clinton, Jones County, Georgy, 'll tell you the Sanderses wa'n't the set to stint the'r stomachs. I was a Sanders 'fore I married, an' when I come 'way frum pa's house hit was thes like turnin' my back on a barbecue. Not by no means was I begrudgin' of the vittles. Says I, 'Mingo,' says I, 'ef the gentulmun is a teetotal stranger, an' nobody else hain't got the common perliteness to ast 'im, shorely you mus' ast 'im,' says I; 'but don't go an' make no great to-do,' says I, 'bekaze the little we got mightent be satisfactual to the gentulmun,' says I. What we got may be little enough, an' it may be too much, but hit's welcome."

It would be impossible to convey an idea of the emphasis which Mrs. Bivins imposed upon her conversation. She talked rapidly, and yet with a certain deliberation of manner which gave a quaint interest to everything she said. She had thin gray hair, a prominent nose, firm thin lips, and eyes that gave a keen and sparkling individuality to sharp and homely features. She had evidently seen sorrow and defied it. There was no suggestion of compromise in manner or expression. Even her hospitality was uncompromising. I endeavored to murmur my thanks to Mrs. Bivins for Mingo's thoughtfulness, but her persistent conversation drowned out such poor phrases as I could hastily frame.

"Come 'ere, Pud Hon," continued Mrs. Bivins, calling the child, and trimming the demonstrative terms of "Pudding" and "Honey" to suit all exigencies of affection,— "come 'ere, Pud Hon, an' tell the gentulmun howdy. Gracious me! don't be so *countrified.* He ain't a-gwine to *bite* you. No, sir, you won't fine no begrudgers mixed up with the *Sanderses.* Hit useter be a *common* sayin' in Jones, an' cle'r 'cross into Jasper, that pa would 'a' bin a rich man an' a' owned *niggers* if it had n't but 'a' bin bekase he sot his head ag'in stintin' of his stomach. That's what they useter say,—use n't they, Mingo?"

"Dat w'at I year tell, Miss F'raishy—sho'," Mingo assented, with great heartiness. But Mrs. Bivins's volubility would hardly wait for this perfunctory indorsement. She talked as she arranged the dishes, and occasionally she would hold a piece of crockery suspended in the air as she emphasized her words. She dropped into a mortuary strain:—

"Poor pa! I don't never have nothin' extry an' I don't never see a dish er fried chicken but what pa pops in my mind. A better man hain't never draw'd the breath of life,—that they hain't. An' he was thes as gayly as a kitten. When we gals 'd have comp'ny to dinner, pore pa he'd cut his eye at me, an' up an' say, says he, 'Gals, this 'ere turkey's mighty nice, yit I'm reely afeared you put too much inguns in the dressin'. Maybe the young men don't like 'em as good as you all does;' an' then pore pa'd drap his knife an' fork, an' laugh tell the tears come in his eyes. Sister Prue she uster run off an' have a cry, but I let you know I was one er the kind what wa'n't so easy sot back.

"I'd 'a' bin mighty glad if Pud yer had er took airter pa's famerly, but frum the tip end er her toe nails to the toppermust ha'r of her head she's a Wornum. Hit ain't on'y thes a streak yer an' a stripe thar,—hit's the whole bolt. I reckon maybe you know'd ole Jedge June Wornum; well, Jedge June he was Pud's gran'pa, an' Deely Wornum was her ma. Maybe you might 'a' seed Deely when she was a school-gal."

Cordelia Wornum! No doubt my astonishment made itself apparent, for Mrs. Bivins bridled up promptly, and there was a clearly perceptible note of defiance in her tone as she proceeded.

"Yes, sir-ree! *An' make no mistake!* Deely Wornum married my son, an' Henry Clay Bivins made 'er a good husbun', if I do have to give it out myse'f. Yes, 'ndeed! An' yit if you'd 'a' heern the rippit them Wornums kicked up, you'd 'a' thought the pore chile'd done took 'n' run off 'long of a whole passel er high pirates frum somewheres er 'nother. In about that time the ole Jedge he got sorter fibbled up, some say in his feet, an' some say in his head; but his wife, that Em'ly Wornum, she taken on awful. I never seen her a-gwine on myse'f; not that they was any hidin' out 'mongst the Bivinses er the Sanderses,—bless you, no! bekaze here's what wa'n't afeared er all the Wornums in the continental State er Georgy, not if they'd 'a' mustered out under the lead er ole Nick hisse'f, which I have my doubts if he wa'n't somewheres aroun'. I never seen 'er, but I heern tell er how she was a-cuttin' up. You may n't think it, but that 'oman taken it on herse'f to call up all the niggers on the place an' give 'em her forbiddance to go an' see the'r young mistiss."

"Yit I lay dey tuck 'n' sneak 'roun' en come anyhow, ain't dey, Miss F'raishy?" inquired Mingo, rubbing his hands together and smiling blandly.

"*That* they did,—*that* they did!" was Mrs. Bivin's emphatic response. "Niggers is niggers, but them Wornum niggers was a cut er two 'bove the common run. I'll say that, an' I'll say it on the witness stan'. Freedom might 'a' turned the'r heads when it come to t' other folks, but hit did n't never turn the'r heads 'bout the'r young mistiss. An' if Mingo here hain't done his juty 'cordin' to his lights, then I dunner what juty is. I'll say that open an' above-board, high an' low."

The curious air of condescension which Mrs. Bivins assumed as she said this, the tone of apology which she employed in paying this tribute to Mingo and the Wornum negroes, formed a remarkable study. Evidently she desired me distinctly to understand that in applauding these worthy colored people she was in no wise compromising her own dignity.

Thus Mrs. Bivins rattled way, pausing only long enough now and then to deplore my lack of appetite. Meanwhile Mingo officiated around the improvised board with gentle affability; and the little girl, bearing strong traces of her lineage in her features,—a resemblance which was confirmed by a pretty little petulance of temper,—made it convenient now and again to convey a number of tea cakes into Mingo's hat, which happened to be sitting near, the conveyance taking place in spite of laughable pantomimic protests on the part of the old man ranging from appealing nods and grimaces to indignant gestures and frowns.

"When Deely died," Mrs. Bivins went on, waving a towel over a tempting jar of preserves, "they wa' n't nobody but what was afeared to break it to Emily Wornum, an' the pore chile'd done been buried too long to talk about before her ma heern tell of it, an' then she drapped like a clap er thunder had hit 'er. Airter so long a time, Mingo thar he taken it 'pun hisse'f to tell 'er, an' she flopped right down in 'er tracks, an' Mingo he hepped 'er into the house, an', bless your life, when he come to he'p 'er out'n it, she was a changed 'oman. 'T wa' n't long 'fore she taken a notion to come to my house, an' one mornin' when I was a-washin' up dishes, I heern some un holler at the gate, an' thar sot Mingo peerched up on the Wornum carry-all, an' of all livin' flesh, who should be in thar but ole Emily Wornum!

"Hit's a sin to say it,' continued Mrs. Bivins, smiling a dubious little smile that was not without its serious suggestions, "but I tightened up my apern strings, an' flung my glance aroun' tell hit drapped on the battlin'-stick, 'bekaze I flared up the minnit I seen 'er, an' I says to myse'f, says I, 'If hit's a fracas you er huntin', my lady, I lay you won't hafter put on your specs to fine it.' An' then I says to Pud, says I,—

"'Pud Hon, go in the shed-room thar, chile, an' if you hear anybody a-hollerin' an' a-squallin' ther', shet your eyeleds an' grit your teeth, bekaze hit'll be your pore ole granny a-tryin' to git even with some er your kin.'

"An' then I taken a cheer an' sot down by the winder. D'reckly in come Emily Wornum, an' I wish I may die if I'd 'a' know'd 'er if I'd saw 'er anywheres else on the face er the yeth. She had this 'ere kinder dazzled look what wimmen has airter they bin baptized in the water. I helt my head high, but I kep' my eye on the battlin'-stick, an' if she'd 'a' made fight, I'd be boun' they'd 'a' bin some ole sco'es settled then an' thar if ole sco'es ken be settled by a frailin'. But, bless your heart, they wa' n't never no cammer 'oman than what Emily Wornum was; an' if you'd 'a' know'd 'er, an' Mingo wa' n't here to b'ar me out, I wish I may die if I would n't be afeared to tell you how ca'm an' supjued that 'oman was, which in her young days she was a tarrifier. She up an' says, says she,—

"'Is Mizzers Bivins in?'

"'Yessum,' says I, 'she is that-away. An' more 'n that, nobody don't hafter come on this hill an' holler more 'n twicet 'thout gittin' some kinder answer back. *Yessum!* An' what's more, Mizzers Bivins is come to that time er life when she's mighty proud to git calls from the big-bugs. If I had as much perliteness, ma'am, as I is cheers, I'd ast you to set down,' says I.

"She stood thar, she did, thes as cool as a cowcumber; but d'reckly she ups an' says, says she,—

"'Might I see my little gran'chile?' says she.

"'Oho, ma'am!' says I; 'things is come to a mighty purty pass when quality folks has to go frum house to house a-huntin' up pore white trash, an' a-astin' airter the'r kin. Tooby shore! tooby shore! Yessum, a mighty purty pass,' says I."

I cannot hope to give even a faint intimation of the remarkable dramatic fervor and earnestness of this recital, nor shall I attempt to describe the rude eloquence of attitude and expression; but they seemed to represent the real or fancied wrongs of a class, and to spring from the pent-up rage of a century.

"I wa' n't lookin' fer no compermise, nuther," Mrs. Bivins continued. "I fully spected 'er to flar' up an' fly at me; but 'stedder that, she kep' a-stan'in' thar lookin' thes like folks does when they er runnin' over sump'n in the'r min'. Then her eye lit on some er the pictur's what Deely had hung up on the side er the house, an' in pertic'lar one what some er the Wornum niggers had fetched 'er, whar a great big dog was a-watchin' by a little bit er baby. When she seen that, bless your soul, she thes sunk right down on the floor, an' clincht 'er han's, an' brung a gasp what looked like it might er bin the last, an' d'reckly she ast, in a whisper, says she,—

"'Was this my dear daughter's room?'

"Maybe you think," said Mrs. Bivins, regarding me coldly and critically, and pressing her thin lips more firmly together, if that could be,—"maybe you think I oughter wrung my han's, an' pitied that 'oman kneelin' thar in that room whar all my trouble was born an' bred. Some folks would 'a' flopped down by 'er, an' I won't deny but what hit come over me; but the nex' minnit hit flashed acrost me as quick an hot as powder how she'd 'a' bin a'houndin' airter me an' my son, an' a-treatin' us like as we'd 'a' bin the offscourin's er creation, an' how she cast off her own daughter, which Deely was a good a gal as ever draw'd the breath er life,—when all this come over me, hit seem like to me that I could n't keep my paws off'n 'er. I hope the Lord 'll forgive me,—that I do,—but if hit hadn't but 'a' bin for my raisin', I'd 'a' jumped at Emily Wornum an' 'a' spit in 'er face an' 'a' clawed 'er eyes out'n 'er. An' yit, with ole Nick a-tuggin' at me, I was a Christun 'nuff to thank the Lord that they was a tender place in that pore mizerbul creetur's soul-case.

"When I seen her a-kneelin' thar, with 'er year-rings a-danglin' an' 'er fine feathers atossin' an' a-trimblin', leetle more an' my thoughts would 'a' sot me afire. I riz an' I stood over her, an' I says, says I,—

"'Emily Wornum, whar you er huntin' the dead you oughter hunted the livin'. What's betwix' you an' your Maker *I* can't tell,' says I, 'but if you git down on your face an' lick the dirt what Deely Bivins walked on, still you won't be humble enough for to go whar *she's* gone, nor good enough nuther. She died right yer while you was a-traipsin' an' a-trollopin' roun' frum pos' to pillar a-upholdin' your quality idees. These arms helt 'er,' says I, 'an' ef hit had n't but 'a' bin for *her*, Emily Wornum,' says I, 'I'd 'a' strangled the life out 'n you time your shadder darkened my door. An' what's more,' says I, 'ef you er come to bother airter Pud, *thes make the trial of it. Thes so much as lay the weight er your little finger on 'er,'* says I, *'an I'll grab you by the goozle an' t'ar your haslet out,'* says I."

Oh, mystery of humanity! It was merely Mrs. Feratia Bivins who had been speaking, but the voice was the voice of Tragedy. Its eyes shone; its fangs glistened and gleamed; its hands clutched the air; its tone was husky with suppressed fury; its rage would have stormed the barriers of the grave. In another moment Mrs. Bivins was brushing the crumbs from her lap, and exchanging salutations with her neighbors and acquaintances; and a little later, leading her grandchild by the hand, she was making her way back to the church, where the congregation had begun to gather.

III

For my own part, I preferred to remain under the trees, and I soon found that this was the preference of Mingo. The old man had finished his dinner, and sat at the foot of a gigantic oak, gazing dreamily at the fleecy clouds that sailed across the sky. His hands were clasped above his head, and his attitude was one of reflection. The hymn with which the afternoon services were opened came through the woods with a distinctness that was not without a remote and curious suggestion of pathos. As it died away, Mingo raised himself slightly, and said, in a tone that was intended to be explanatory, if not apologetic,—

"Miss F'raishy, ef she ain't one sight, den I ain't never seed none. I s'pec' it seem sorter funny ter you, boss, but dat w'ite 'oman done had lots er trouble; she done had bunnunce er trouble—she sholy is! Look mighty cu'us dat some folks can't git useter yuther folks w'at got Ferginny ways, but dat's Miss F'raishy up en down. Dat's her, sho'! Ole Miss en ole Marster dey had Ferginny ways, en Miss F'raishy she would n't 'a' stayed in a ten-acre fiel' wid um,—dat she would n't. Folks w'at got Ferginny ways, Miss F'raishy she call um big-bugs, en she git hos*tile* w'en she year der name call. Hit's de same way wid niggers. Miss F'raishy she hate de common run er niggers like dey wuz pizen. Yit I ain't makin' no complaints, kaze she mighty good ter me. I goes en I suns myse'f in Miss F'raishy back peazzer all day Sundays, w'en dey ain't no meetin's gwine on, en all endurin' er de week I hangs 'roun' en ploughs a little yer, en hoes a little dar, en scratches a little yander, en looks arter ole Miss' gran'chile. But des let 'n'er nigger so much ez stick der chin cross de yard palin's, en, bless yo' soul, you'll year Miss F'raishy blaze out like de woods done cotch afire."

Mingo paused here to chuckle over the discomfiture and alarm of the imaginary negro who had had the temerity to stick his supposititious chin over the fence. Then he went on:—

"I dunner whar Miss F'raishy git de notion 'bout dat child a-faverin' er de Wornums, kaze she de ve'y spit en image er ole Miss, en ole Miss wuz a full-blood Bushrod. De Bushrods is de fambly what I cum fum myse'f, kaze w'en ole Miss marry

Marster, my mammy fell ter her, en w'en I got big 'nuff, dey tuck me in de house fer ter wait on de table en do er'n's, en dar I bin twel freedom come out. She 'uz mighty high-strung, ole Miss wuz, yit I sees folks dese days put on mo a'rs dan w'at ole Miss ever is. I ain't 'sputin' but w'at she hilt 'er head high, en I year my mammy say dat all the Bushrods in Ferginny done zactly dat a way.

"High-strung yer, headstrong yander," continued Mingo, closing one eye, and gazing at the sun with a confidential air. "Ef it had n't er bin fer de high-strungity-head-strongityness er de Bushrod blood, Miss Deely would n't 'a' never runn'd off wid Clay Bivins in de roun' worril, dough he 'uz des one er de nicest w'ite mens w'at you 'mos' ever laid yo' eyes on. Soon ez she done dat, wud went 'roun' fum de big house dat de nigger w'at call Miss Deely name on dat plantation would be clap on de cote-house block, en ole Miss she shot 'erse'f up, she did, en arter dat mighty few folks got a glimpse un 'er, 'ceppin' hit 'uz some er de kin, en bless yo' soul, *dey* hatter look mighty prim w'en dey come whar she wuz. Ole Marster he ain't say nothin', but he tuck a fresh grip on de jimmy-john, en it got so dat, go whar you would, dey wa' n't no mo' lonesomer place on de face er de yeth dan dat Wornum plantation, en hit look like ruination done sot in. En den, on top er dat, yer come de war, en Clay Bivins he went off en got kilt, en den freedom come out, en des 'bout dat time Miss Deely she tuck 'n' die.

"I 'clar' ter gracious," exclaimed Mingo, closing his eyes and frowning heavily, "we'n I looks back over my shoulder at dem times, hit seem like it mighty funny dat any un us pull thoo. Some did en some did n't, en dem w'at did, dey look like deyer mighty fergitful. W'en de smash come, ole Marster he call us niggers up, he did, en 'low dat we 'uz all free. Some er de boys 'low dat dey wuz a-gwineter see ef dey wuz free sho 'nuff, en wid dat dey put out fer town, en some say ef dey wuz free dey wuz free ter stay. Some talk one way en some talk 'n'er. I let you know I kep' my mouf shot, yit my min' 'uz brim-ful er trouble.

"Bimeby soon one mornin' I make a break. I wrop up my little han'ful er duds in a hankcher, en I tie de hankcher on my walkin'-cane, en I put out arter de army. I walk en I walk, en 'bout nine dat night I come ter Ingram Ferry. De flat wuz on t'er side er de river, en de man w'at run it look like he gone off some'r's. I holler en I whoop, en I whoop en I holler, but ef dey wuz any man 'roun', he wuz hidin' out fum me. Arter so long I got tired er whoopin' en hollerin', en I went ter de nighest house en borrer'd a chunk, en built me a fier by de side er de road, en I set dar en nod twel I git sleepy, en den I pull my blanket 'cross my head en quile up—en when I do dat, it's good-by, Mingo!

"Boss," said Mingo, after a little pause, "you don't b'leeve in no ghos'es en ha'nts en sperrits, does you?"

An apparently irrelevant inquiry, suddenly put, is sometimes confusing, and I fear I did not succeed in convincing Mingo of my unbelief.

"Some does en some don't," he continued, "but ez fer me, you kin des put me sorter 'twix' en 'tween. Dey mout be ghos'es en den ag'in dey moutent. Ole nigger like me ain't got no bizness takin' sides, en dat w'at make I say w'at I does. I ain't mo'n kivver my head wid dat blanket en shot my eyes, 'fo' I year somebody a-callin' un me. Fus' hit soun' way off yander.

"'*Mingo!—O Mingo!*' en den hit got nigher—'*Mingo!—O Mingo!*'

"I ain't 'spon' ter dat, but I lay dar, I did, en I say ter myse'f,—

"'Bless gracious! de man on t'er side done come; but how in de name er goodness is he know Mingo?'

"I lay dar, en I study en I lissen, en I lissen en I study; en den I doze off like, en fus' news I know yer come de call,—

"'*Mingo!—O Mingo!*'

"Hit soun' nigher, yit hit seem like it come fum a mighty fur ways, en den wiles I wundin' en studyin', yer she come mo' plainer dan befo',—

"'O MINGO!'

"I snatch de blanket off 'n my head, en sot up en lissen, I did, en den I make answer,—

"'Who dat callin' Mingo 'way out yer?'

"I lissen en I lissen, but nobody ain't callin'. I year de water sneakin' 'long under de bank, en I year de win' squeezin' en shufflin' 'long thoo de trees, en I year de squinch-owl shiver'n' like he cole , but I ain' year no callin'. Dis make me feel sorter jubous like, but I lay down en wrop up my head.

"I ain't bin dar long 'fo' bimeby yer come de call, en it soun' right at me. Hit rise en it fall, en de wud wuz,—

"'*Mingo!—O Mingo! Whar my little baby? My little baby, Mingo! Whar my little baby?*'

"En den, boss, hit seem like I year sump'n like a 'oman cryin' in de dark like 'er heart gwineter break. You kin laff ef you mineter, but I ain't dast ter take dat blanket off 'n my head, kaze I know my young mistiss done come back, en mo'n dat, I know she uz stannin' dar right over me.

"Tooby sho', I wuz skeer'd; but I wa' n't so skeer'd dat I dunner w'at she mean, en I des broke inter de bigges' kinder boo-hoo, en I say, sez I,—

"'Make yo' peace, Miss Deely! make yo' peace, honey! kaze I gwine right back ter dat baby ef de Lord spar' me. I gwine back, Miss Deely! I gwine back!'

"Bless yo' soul, boss, right den en dar I know'd w'at bin a-pester'n' un me, kaze des time I make up my min' fer ter come back ter dat baby, hit look like I see my way mo' cle'r dan w'at it bin belo'. Arter dat I lay dar, I did, en I lissen en I lissen, but I ain't year no mo' callin' en no mo' cryin'; en bimeby I tuck de blanket fum off 'n my head, en lo en beholes, de stars done fade out, en day done come, en dey wa' n't no fuss nowhars. De squinch-owl done hush, en de win' done gone, en it look like de water done stop sneakin' en crawlin' und' de bank.

"I riz up, I did, en shuck de stiffness out 'n my bones, en I look 'way 'cross de river ter de top er de hill whar de road lead. I look en I say, sez I,—

"'Maybe you leads ter freedom, but, bless God! I gwine back.'

"Des 'bout dat time I see de fe'ymun come down ter de flat en onloose de chain, en make ez he wuz comin' 'cross arter me. Wid dat I raise up my hat en tip 'im a bow, en dat's de las' I seed un 'im.

"I come back, I did," continued Mingo, reflectively, "en yer I is, en yer I bin; en I ain't come none too soon, en I ain't stay none too close, n'er, kaze I dunner w'at mout er happin. Miss F'raishy been mighty good, too, sho'. She ain't useter niggers like some w'ite folks, en she can't git 'long wid um, but she puts up wid me mighty well. I tuck holt er de little piece er groun' w'at she had, en by de he'p er de Lord we bin gittin' on better dan lots er folks. It bin nip en tuck, but ole tuck come out ahead, en it done got so now dat Miss F'raishy kin put by some er de cotton money fer ter give de little gal a chance w'en she git bigger. 'T won't b'ar tellin' how smart dat chile is. She got Miss Deely peanner, en, little ez she is, she kin pick mos' all de chunes w'at 'er mammy useter pick. She sets at de peanner by de hour, en whar she larnt it I be bless ef *I* kin tell you,—dat I can't!"

The little girl had grown tired of the services in the church, and ran out just as the old man had put my horse to the buggy. Mingo knew a shorter road to Rockville than that by which I had come, and, taking the child by the hand, he walked on ahead to show me the way. In a little while we came to the brow of a hill, and here I bade the old man and his charge good-by, and the two stood watching me as I drove away. Presently a cloud of dust rose between us, and I saw them no more; but I brought away a very pretty picture in my mind,—Mingo with his hat raised in farewell, the sunshine falling gently upon his gray hairs, and the little girl clinging to his hand and daintily throwing kisses after me.

(1884)

JOHNSON JONES HOOPER

The Widow Rugby's Husband: A *Story of 'Suggs'*

Some ten or twelve years agone, one Sumeral Dennis kept the "Union Hotel," at the seat of justice of the county of Tallapoosa. The house took its name from the complexion of the politics of its proprietor; he being a true-hearted Union man, and opposed—as I trust all my readers are—at all points, to the damnable heresy of *nullification.* In consequence of the candid exposition of his political sentiments upon his signboard, mine host of the Union was liberally patronized by those who coincided with him in his views. In those days, party spirit was, in that particular locality, exceedingly bitter and proscriptive; and had Sumeral's chickens been less tender, his eggs less impeachable, his coffee more sloppy, the "Union Hotel" would still have lost no guest—its keeper no dimes. But, as Dennis was wont to remark, "*the party* relied on his honour; and as an honest man—but more especially as an honest *Union* man—he was bound to give them the value of their money." Glorious fellow, was Sumeral! Capital landlady, was his good wife, in all the plenitude of her *embonpoint!* Well-behaved children, too, were Sumeral's—from the shaggy and red-headed representative of paternal peculiarities, down to little Solomon of the sable locks, whose "favour" puzzled the neighbours, and set at defiance all known physiological principles. Good people, all, were the Dennises! May a hungry man never fall among worse!

Among the political friends who had for some years bestowed their patronage, semi-annually, during Court week, upon the proprietor of the "Union," was Captain Simon Suggs, whose deeds of valour and of strategy are not unknown to the public. The captain had "put up" with our friend Sumeral, time and again—had puffed the "Union," both "before the face and behind the back" of its owner, until it seemed a miniature of the microcosm that bears the name of Astor—and, in short, was so generally useful, accommodating, and polite, that nothing short of long-continued and oft-repeated failures to *settle his bills*, could have induced Sumeral to consider Suggs in other light than as the best friend the "Union" or any other house ever had. But alas! Captain Suggs had, from one occasion to another, upon excuses the most plausible, and with protestations of regret the most profound, invariably left the fat larder and warm beds of the Union without leaving behind the slightest pecuniary remuneration with Sumeral. For a long time the patient innkeeper bore the imposition with a patience that indicated some hope of eventual payment. But year in and year out, and the money did not come. Mrs. Dennis at length spoke out, and argued the necessity of a tavern-keeper's collecting his dues, if he was disposed to do justice to himself and family.

"Suggs is a nice man in his talk," she said. "Nobody can fault him, as far as that's concerned; but smooth talk never paid for flour and bacon;" and so she recommended to her leaner half that the *"next time"* summary measures should be adopted to secure the amount in which the Captain was indebted to the "Union Hotel."

Sumeral determined that his wife's advice should be strictly followed; for he had seen, time and again, that *her* suggestions had been the salvation of the establishment.

"Hadn't she kept him from pitchin' John Seagrooves, neck and heels, out of the window, for sayin' that nullification *warn't* treason, and John C. Calhoun *warn't* as bad as Benedict Arnold! And hadn't John been a good payin' customer ever since? That was what he wanted to know!"

The next session of the Circuit Court, after this prudent conclusion had been arrived at in Dennis's mind—the Circuit Court, with all its attractions of criminal trials, poker-playing lawyers, political caucuses and possible monkey-shows—found Captain Suggs snugly housed at the "Union." Time passed on swiftly for a week. The judge was a hearty, liquor-loving fellow, and lent the Captain ten dollars, "on sight." The Wetumpka and Montgomery lawyers bled freely. In short everything went bravely on for the Captain, until a man with small-pox pits and a faro-box came along. The Captain yielded to the temptation—yielded, with a presentiment on his mind that he should be "slain." The "tiger" *was* triumphant, and Suggs was left without a dollar!

As if to give intensity to his distress, on the morning after his losses at the faro bank, the friendly Clerk of the Court hinted to Suggs, that the Grand Jury had found an indictment against him for gaming. Here was a dilemma! Not only out of funds, but obliged to decamp, before the adjournment of Court!—obliged to lose all opportunity of redeeming his "fallen fortunes," by further plucking the greenhorns in attendance.

"This here," said Simon, "is h—l! h—l! a mile and a quarter square, and fenced in all round! What's a *reasonable* man to do? Ain't I done my duty? Cuss that mahogany box? I wish the man that started it had had his head sawed off with a cross-cut, *just* afore he thought on't! Now thar's sense in *short cards.* All's fair, and cheat and cheat alike is the order; and the longest pole knocks down the persimmon! But whar's the reason in one of your d—d boxes, full of springs and the like, and the better *no* advantages, except now and then when he kin kick up a squabble, *and the dealer's afeard of him!*

"I'm for doin' things on the squar. What's a man without his honour? Ef natur give me a gift to beat a feller at 'old sledge' and the like, it's all right! But whar's the justice in a thing like farrer, that ain't got but one side! It's strange what a honin' I have for the cussed thing! No matter how I make an honest rise, I'm sure to 'buck it off' at farrer. As my wife says, *farrer's my besettin' sin.* It's a weakness—a soft spot—it's—a—a—let me see!—it's a way I've got of a runnin' agin Providence! But hello! here's

Dennis."

When the inn-keeper walked up, Captain Suggs remarked to him, that there was a "little paper out, signed by Tom Garrett, in his *official capacity,* that was calculated to hurt feelins," if he remained in town; and so he desired that his horse might be saddled and brought out.

Sumeral replied to this by presenting to the Captain a slip of paper containing entries of many charges against Suggs, and in favour of the Union Hotel.

"All right," said Suggs; "I'll be over in a couple of weeks, and settle."

"Can't wait; want money to buy provisions; account been standing two years; thirty-one dollars and fifty cents is money, these days," said Dennis, with unusual firmness.

"Blast your ugly face," vociferated Suggs, "*I'll give you my note!* that's enough amongst gentlemen, I suppose."

"Hardly," returned the inn-keeper, "hardly: we want the cash; your note ain't worth the trouble of writin' it."

"D—n you!" roared Suggs; "d—n you for a biscuit-headed *nullifier!* I'll give you a mortgage on the best half section of land in the county: south half of 13, 21, 29!"

"Captain Suggs," said Dennis, drawing off his coat, "you've called me a nullifier, and *that's* what I *won't* stand from *no* man! Strip, and I'll whip as much *dog* out of you as 'll make a full pack of hounds! You swindlin' robber!"

This hostile demonstration alarmed the Captain, and he set in to soothe his angry landlord.

"Sum, old fel!" he said, in his most honeyed tones: "Sum, old fel! be easy. I'm not a fightin' man"—and here Suggs drew himself up with dignity; "I'm not a fightin' man, *except* in the cause of my country! *Thar* I'm *allers* found! Come old fellow— do you reckon ef you'd been a nullifier, *I'd* ever been ketched at your house! No, no! You *ain't* no part of a nullifier, but you *are* reether hard down on your Union friends that allers puts up with you. Say, won't you take that mortgage—the land's richly worth $1,000—and let me have old Bill?"

The heart of Dennis was melted at the appeal thus made. It was to his good fellowship and his party feelings. So, putting on his coat, he remarked, that he "rather thought he would take the mortgage. However," he added, seeing Mrs. Dennis standing at the door of the tavern watching his proceedings, "he would see his wife about it."

The Captain and Dennis approached the landlady of the Union, and made known the state of the case.

"You see, cousin Betsy"—Suggs always *cousined* any lady whom he wished to cozen—"you see, cousin Betsy, the fact is, I'm down, just now, in the way of money, and you and Sumeral bein' afraid I'll run away and never come back——"

"Taint *that* I'm afraid of," said Mrs. Dennis.

"What then?" asked Suggs.

"Of your comin' back, eatin' us out o' house and home, and *never payin' nothin'.*"

"Well," said the Captain, slightly confused at the lady's directness; "well, seein' that's the way the mule kicks, as I was sayin', I proposed to Sum here, as long as him and you distrusts an old *Union* friend that's stuck by your house like a tick, even when the red-mouthed nullifiers swore you was feedin' us *soap-tails* on *bull-beef and blue collards*—I say, as long as that's the case, I propose to give you a mortgage on the south half of 21, 13, 29. It's the best half section in the county, and it's worth forty times the amount of your bill."

"It looks like that ought to do," said Sumeral, who was grateful to the Captain for defending his house against the slanders of the nullifiers; "and seein' that Suggs has always patronized the Union and *voted the whole ticket*——"

"Never *split* in my life," dropped in Suggs, with emphasis.

"I," continued Dennis, "am for takin the mortgage and lettin' him take old Bill and go; for I know it would be a satisfaction to the nullifiers to have him put in jail."

"Yes," quoth the Captain, sighing, "I'm about to be tuk up and made a martyr of, on account of the Union, but I'll die true to my prin*sipp*les, d—d if I don't."

"They *shan't* take you," said Dennis, his long lank form stiffening with energy as he spoke; "as long as they put it on *that* hook, d—d ef they shall! Give us the mortgage and slope!"

"Thar's a true-hearted Union man," exclaimed Suggs, "that's not got a drop of pizen of treason in his veins!"

"You ain't got no rights to that land…I jist know it—or you wouldn't want to mortgage it for a tavern bill," shouted Mrs. Dennis; "and I tell you and Sumeral *both*, that old Bill don't go out of that stable till the money's paid—mind I say *money*—into *my* hand;" and here the good lady turned off and called Bob, the stable boy, to bring her the stable key.

The Captain and Sumeral looked at each other like two chidden school-boys. It was clear that no terms short of payment in money would satisfy Mrs. Dennis. Suggs saw that Dennis had become interested in his behalf; so, acting upon the idea, he suggested:

"Dennis, *suppose you loan me the money?*"

"Egad, Suggs, I've been thinking of that; but as I have only a fifty dollar bill, and my wife's key bein' turned on that, there's no chance. D—n it, I'm sorry for you."

"Well the Lord'll purvide," said Suggs.

As Captain Suggs could not get away *that* day, evidently, he arranged, through his friend Sumeral, with the Clerk not to issue a capias until the next afternoon. Having done this, he cast around for some way of raising the wind; but the fates were against him; and at eleven o'clock that night, he went to bed in a fit of the blues that three pints of whiskey had failed to dissipate.

An hour or two after the Captain had got between his sheets, and after every one else was asleep, he heard some one walk unsteadily, but still softly, up stairs. An occasional hiccup told that it was some fellow drunk; and this was confirmed by a heavy fall which the unfortunate took as soon as, leaving the railing, he attempted to travel *suis pedibus.*

"Oh, good Lord!" groaned the fallen man; "who'd a-thought it! Me, John P. Pullum, drunk and fallin' down! I never was so before. The world's a-turnin' over—*and*—over! Oh, Lord!—Charley Stone got me into it! What will Sally say ef she hears it—oh, Lord!"

"That thar feller," said the Captain to himself, "is the victim of vice! I wonder ef he's got any money?" and the Captain continued his soliloquy *inaudibly.*

Poor Mr. Pullum, after much tumbling about and sundry repetitions of his fall, at length contrived to get into bed, in a room adjoining that occupied by the Captain, and only separated from it by a thin partition. The sickening effects of his debauch increased, and the dreadful nausea was likely to cause him to make both a "clean breast" and a clean stomach.

"I'm very—very—oh, Lord!—drunk! Oh, me, is this John P. Pullum that—good Heavens! I'll faint—married Sally Rugby!—oh! oh!"

Here the poor fellow got out of bed, and, poking his head through a vacant square, in the window-sash, began his ejaculations of supper and of grief.

"Ah! I'm so weak!—wouldn't have Sally—aw—owh—wha—oh, Lord!—to hear of it for a hundred dollars. She said—it's comin' agin—awh—ohg—who—o—o—gracious Lord, how sick!—she said when she agreed for me to sell the cotton, I'd be certain—oh, Lord, I believe I'll die!"

The inebriate fell back on his bed, almost fainting, and Captain Suggs thought he'd try an experiment.

Disguising his voice, with his mouth close to the partition, he said:

"You're a liar! you didn't marry Widow Rugby; you're some d—d thief tryin' to pass off for something!"

"Who am I then, if I ain't John P. Pullum that married the widow, Sally Rugby, Tom Rugby's widow, old Bill Stearn's only daughter? Oh, Lord, if it ain't me, who is it! Where's Charley Stone—can't he tell if it's John P. Pullum?"

"No, it ain't you, you lyin' swindler—you ain't got a dollar in the world—and never married no rich widow," said Suggs, still disguising his voice.

"I did—I'll be d—d ef I didn't —I know it now: Sally Rugby with the red head— all of the boys said I married her for her money, but it's a—oh, Lord, I'm sick again— augh!"

Mr. Pullum continued his maudlin talk, half asleep, half awake, for some time; and all the while Captain Suggs was analyzing the man—conjecturing his precise circumstances—his family relations—the probable state of his purse, and the like.

"It's a plain case," he mused, "that this feller married a red-headed widow for her money—no man ever married sich for anything else. It's plain again, she's got the property settled upon her, or fixed some way, for he talked about her 'agreein' for him to sell the cotton. I'll bet that he's the new feller that's dropped in down thar by Tallassee, that Charley Stone used to know. And I'll bet he's been down to Wetumpky to sell the cotton—got on a bust thar—and now's on another here.—He's afraid of his wife, too; leastways, his voice trimbled like it, when he called her red-headed, Pullum! Pullum! Pull-um!" Here Suggs studied—"That's surely a Talbot county name—I'll ventur' on it, any how."

Having reached a conclusion, the Captain turned over in bed, and composed himself to sleep.

At nine o'clock the next morning, the bar-room of the Union contained only Dennis and our friend the Captain. Breakfast was over, and the most of the temporary occupants of the tavern were on the public square. Captain Suggs was watching for Mr. Pullum, who had not yet come down to breakfast.

At length an uncertain step was heard on the stairway, and a young man, whose face showed indisputable evidence of a frolic on the previous night, descended. His eyes were bloodshot, and his expression was a mingled one of shame and fear.

Captain Suggs walked up to him, as he entered the bar-room, gazed at his face earnestly, and, slowly placing his hand on his shoulder, as slowly, and with a stern expression, said:

"Your—name—is—Pullum!"

"I know it is," said the young man.

"Come this way, then," said Suggs, pulling his victim out into the street, and still gazing at him with the look of a stern but affectionate parent. Turning to Dennis, as they went out, he said: "Have a cup of coffee ready for this young man in fifteen minutes, and his horse by the time he's done drinking it!"

Mr. Pullum looked confounded, but said nothing, and he and the Captain walked over to a vacant blacksmith shop, across the street, where they could be free from observation.

"You're from Wetumpky last," remarked Suggs, with severity, and as if his words charged a crime.

"What if I am?" replied Pullum with an effort to appear bold.

"What's cotton worth?" asked the Captain, with an almost imperceptible wink.

Pullum turned white, and stammered out:

"Seven or eight cents."

"Which will you tell your wife you sold yours—*hers*—for?"

John P. turned blue in the face.

"What do *you* know about my wife?" he asked.

"Never mind about *that*—was you in the habit of gettin' drunk before you left Talbot county, Georgy?"

"I never lived in Talbot; I was born and raised in Harris," said Pullum, with something like triumph.

"Close to the line though," rejoined Suggs, confidently, relying on the fact that there was a large family of Pullums in Talbot; "most of your connexions lived in Talbot."

"Well, what of all that?" asked Pullum, with impatience: "what is it to you whar I come from, or whar my connexion lived?"

"Never mind—I'll show you—no man that married Billy Stearns's daughter can carry on the way *you've been doin'*, without *my* interferin' for the int'rust of the family!"

Suggs said this with an earnestness, a sternness, that completely vanquished Pullum. He tremulously asked:

"How did you know that I married Stearns's daughter?"

"That's a fact 'most anybody could a known that was intimate with the family in old times. You'd better ask how I knowed that you tuk *your wife's* cotton to Wetumpky—sold it—*got on a spree*—after Sally give you a caution too—and then come by here—*got on another spree*. What do you reckon Sally will say to you when you git home?"

"She won't know it," replied Pullum, "unless somebody tells her."

"Somebody *will* tell her," said Suggs; "*I'm* going home with you as soon as you've had breakfast. My poor Sally Rugby shall not be trampled on in this way. I've only got to borrow fifty dollars from some of the boys to make out a couple of thousand I need to make the last payment on my land. So go over and eat your breakfast, quick."

"For God's sake, sir, don't tell Sally about it; you don't know how unreasonable she is."

Pullum was the incarnation of misery.

"The devil I don't! She bit this piece out of my face"—here Suggs pointed to a scar on his cheek—"when I had her on my lap, a little girl only five years old. She was always game."

Pullum grew more nervous at this reference to his wife's mettle.

"My dear sir, I don't even know your name—"

"Suggs, sir, Capt. Simon Suggs."

"Well, my dear Captain, ef you'll jist let me off this time, I'll lend you the fifty dollars."

"*You'll—lend—me—the—fifty—dollars! Who* asked *you* for your money—or rather *Sally's* money?"

"I only thought," replied the humble husband of Sally, "that it might be an accommodation. I meant no harm; I know Sally wouldn't mind my lending it to an old friend of the family."

"Well," said Suggs, and here he mused, shutting his eyes, biting his lips, and talking very slowly, "ef I knowed you would do better."

"I swear I will," said Pullum.

"No swearin', sir!" roared Suggs, with a dreadful frown; "no swearin' in *my* presence!"

"No, sir, I won't any more."

"Ef," continued the Captain, "I *knowed* you'd do better—*go right home*"—(the Captain didn't wish Pullum to stay where his stock of information might be increased)—and treat Sally like a wife all the rest of your days, I might, *may be*, borrow the fifty, (seein' it's Sally's, any way,) and let you off this time."

"Ef you will, Captain Suggs, I'll never forget you—I'll think of you all the days of my life."

"I ginnally makes my mark, so that I'm hard to forget," said the Captain, *truthfully.* "Well, turn me over a fifty for a couple of months, and go home."

Mr. Pullum handed the money to Suggs, who seemed to receive it reluctantly. He twisted the bill in his fingers, and remarked:

"I reckon I'd better not take this money—you won't go home, and do as you said."

"Yes, I will," said Pullum; "yonder's my horse at the door—I'll start this minute."

The Captain and Pullum returned to the tavern, where the latter swallowed his coffee and paid his bill.

As the young man mounted his horse, Suggs took him affectionately by the hand—

"John," said he, "go home, give my love to cousin Sally, and kiss her for me. Try and do better, John, for the futur'; and if you have any children, John, bring 'em up in the way of the Lord. Good by!"

Captain Suggs now paid *his* bill, and had a balance on hand. He immediately bestrode his faithful "Bill," musing thus as he moved homeward:

"Every day I git more insight into scriptur'. It used to be I couldn't understand the manna in the wilderness, and the ravens feedin' Elishy; now, it's clear to my eyes. Trust in Providence—that's the lick! Here was I in the wilderness, sorely oppressed, and mighty nigh despar. Pullum come to me, like a 'raven,' in my distress—and a *fat* one, at that! Well, as I've *allers* said, Honesty and Providence will never fail to fetch a man out! Jist give me that for a *hand*, and I'll 'stand' agin all creation!"

(1849)

GRACE KING

Bayou l'Ombre:
An Incident of the War

Of course they knew all about war—soldiers, flags, music, generals on horseback
brandishing swords, knights in armor escalading walls, cannons booming through
clouds of smoke. They were familiarized with it pictorially and by narrative long
before the alphabet made its appearance in the nursery with rudimentary accounts of
the world they were born into, the simple juvenile world of primary sensations and
colors. Their great men, and great women, too, were all fighters; the great events of
their histories, battles; the great places of their geography, where they were fought
(and generally the more bloody the battle, the more glorious the place); while their
little chronology—the pink-covered one—stepped briskly over the centuries solely
on the names of kings and sanguinary saliencies. Sunday added the sabbatical
supplement to week-day lessons, symbolizing religion, concreting sin, incorporating
evil, for their better comprehension, putting Jehovah himself in armor, to please their
childish faculties—the omnipotent Intervener of the Old Testament, for whom they
waved banners, sang hymns, and by the brevet title, "little *soldiers* of the cross," felt
committed as by baptism to an attitude of expectant hostility. Mademoiselle Couper,
their governess, eased the cross-stitching in their samplers during the evenings, after
supper, with traditions of "le grand Napoléon," in whose army her grandfather was
a terrible and distinguished officer, le Capitaine Césaire Paul Picquet de Montignac;
and although Mademoiselle Couper was most unlovable and exacting at times, and
very homely, such were their powers of sympathetic enthusiasm even then that they
often went to bed envious of the possessor of so glorious an ancestor, and dreamed
fairy tales of him whose gray hair, enshrined in a brooch, reposed comfortably under
the folds of mademoiselle's fat chin—the hair that Napoleon had looked upon!

When a war broke out in their own country they could hardly credit their good-
fortune; that is, Christine and Régina, for Lolotte was still a baby. A wonderful
panorama was suddenly unfolded before them. It was their first intimation of the
identity of the world they lived in with the world they learned about, their first
perception of the existence of an entirely novel sentiment in their hearts—patriotism,
the *amour sacré de la patrie,* over which they had seen mademoiselle shed tears as

copiously as her grandfather had blood. It made them and all their little companions feel very proud, this war; but it gave them a heavy sense of responsibility, turning their youthful precocity incontinently away from the books, slates, and pianos towards the martial considerations that befitted the hour. State rights, Federal limits, monitors and fortresses, proclamations, Presidents, recognitions, and declarations, they acquired them all with facility, taxing, as in other lessons, their tongue to repeat the unintelligible on trust for future intelligence. As their father fired his huge after-dinner bombs, so they shot their diminutive ammunition; as he lighted brands in the great conflagration, they lighted tapers; and the two contending Presidents themselves did not get on their knees with more fervor before their colossal sphinxes than these little girls did before their doll-baby presentment of "Country." It was very hard to realize at times that histories and story-books and poetry would indeed be written about them; that little flags would mark battles all over the map of their country—the country Mademoiselle Couper despised as so hopelessly, warlessly insignificant; that men would do great things and women say them, teachers and copy-books reiterate them, and children learn them, just as they did of the Greeks and Romans, the English and French. The great advantage was having God on their side, as the children of Israel had; the next best thing was having the finest country, the most noble men, and the bravest soldiers. The only fear was that the enemy would be beaten too easily, and the war cease too soon to be glorious; for, characteristic of their sex, they demanded nothing less than that their war should be the longest, bloodiest, and most glorious of all wars ever heard of, in comparison with which even "le grand Napoleon" and his Capitaine Picquet would be effaced from memory. For this were exercised their first attempts at extempore prayer. God, the dispenser of inexhaustible supplies of munitions of war, became quite a different power, a nearer and dearer personality, than "Our Father," the giver of simple daily bread, and He did not lack reminding of the existence of the young Confederacy, nor of the hearsay exigencies they gathered from the dinner-table talk.

Titine was about thirteen, Gina was twelve, and Lolotte barely eight years old, when this, to them, happy break in their lives occurred. It was easily comprehensible to them that their city should be captured, and that to escape that grim ultimatum of Mademoiselle Couper, *"passées au fil de l'épée,"* they should be bundled up very hurriedly one night, carried out of their home, and journey in troublesome roundabout ways to the plantation on Bayou l'Ombre.

That was all four years ago. School and play and city life, dolls and fêtes and Santa Claus, had become the property of memory. Peace for them hovered in that obscurity which had once enveloped war, while "'61," "'62," "'63," "'64," filled immeasurable spaces in their short past. Four times had Christine and Régina changed the date in their diaries—the last token of remembrance from Mademoiselle Couper—altering the numerals with naïve solemnity, as if under the direction of the Almighty himself, closing with conventional ceremony the record of the lived-out twelve months, opening with appropriate aspirations the year to come. The laboriously careful chronicle that followed was not, however, of the growth of their bodies advancing by inches, nor the expansion of their minds, nor of the vague forms that began to people the shadow-land of their sixteen and seventeen year old hearts. Their own budding and leafing and growing was as unnoted as that of the trees and weeds about them. The progress of the war, the growth of their hatred of the enemy, the expansion of the *amour sacré* germ—these were the confidences that filled the neatly-stitched foolscap volumes. If on comparison one sister was found to have been happier in the rendition of the common sentiment, the coveted fervor and eloquence were plagiarized or imitated the next day by the other, a generous emulation thus keeping the original flame not only alight, but burning, while from assimilating each other's sentiments the two girls grew with identity of purpose into identity of mind, and effaced the slight difference of age between them.

Little Lolotte responded as well as she could to the enthusiastic exactions of her sisters. She gave her rag dolls patriotic names, obediently hated and loved as they required, and learned to recite all the war songs procurable, even to the teeming quantities of the stirring "Men of the South, our foes are up!" But as long as the squirrels gambolled on the fences, the blackbirds flocked in the fields, and the ditches filled with fish; as long as the seasons imported such constant variety of attractions— persimmons, dewberries, blackberries, acorns, wild plums, grapes, and muscadines; as long as the cows had calves, the dogs puppies, the hogs pigs, and the quarters new babies to be named; as long as the exasperating negro children needed daily subjugation, regulation, and discipline—the day's measure was too well filled and the night's slumber too short to admit of her carrying on a very vigorous warfare for a country so far away from Bayou l'Ombre—a country whose grievances she could not understand.

But—there were no soldiers, flags, music, parades, battles, or sieges. This war was altogether distinct from the wars contained in books or in Mademoiselle Couper's memory. There was an absence of the simplest requirements of war. They kept awaiting the familiar events for which they had been prepared; but after four years the only shots fired on Bayou l'Ombre were at game in the forest, the only blood shed was from the tottering herds of Texas beeves driven across the swamps to them, barely escaping by timely butchery the starvation they came to relieve, and the only heroism they had been called upon to display was still going to bed in the dark. Indeed, were it not that they knew there was a war they might have supposed that some malignant fairy had transported them from a state of wealth and luxury to the condition of those miserable Hathorns, the pariahs of their childhood, who lived just around the corner from them in the city, with whom they had never been allowed to associate. If they had not so industriously fostered the proper feelings in their hearts, they might almost have forgotten it, or, like Lolotte, been diverted from it by the generous overtures of nature all around them. But they kept on reminding each other that it was not the degrading want of money, as in the Hathorns' case, that forced them to live on salt meat, corn-bread, and sassafras tea, to dress like the negro women in the quarters, that deprived them of education and society, and imprisoned them in a swamp-encircled plantation, the prey of chills and fever; but it was for love of country, and being little women now, they loved their country more, the more they suffered for her. Disillusion might have supervened to disappointment and bitterness have quenched hope, experience might at last have sharpened their vision, but for the imagination, that ethereal parasite which fattens on the stagnant forces of youth and garnishes with tropical luxuriance the abnormal source of its nourishment. Soaring aloft, above the prosaic actualities of the present, beyond the rebutting evidence of earth, was a fanciful stage where the drama of war such as they craved was unfolded; where neither homespun, starvation, overflows, nor illness were allowed to enter; where the heroes and heroines they loved acted roles in all the conventional glitter of costume and conduct, amid the dazzling pomps and circumstances immortalized in history and romance. Their hearts would bound and leap after these phantasms, like babes in nurses' arms after the moon, and would almost burst with longing, their ripe little hearts, Pandora-boxes packed with passions and pleasures for a lifetime, ready to spring open at a touch! On moonlit nights in summer, or under the low gray clouds of winter days, in the monotony of nothingness about them, the yearning in their breasts was like that of hunting dogs howling for the unseen game. Sometimes a rumor of a battle "out in the Confederacy" would find its way across the swamps to them, and months afterwards a newspaper would be thrown to them from a passing skiff, some old, useless, tattered, disreputable, journalistic tramp, garrulous with mendacities; but it was all true to them, if to no one else in the world—the factitious triumphs, the lurid glories, the pyrotechnical promises, prophecies, calculations, and Victory with the laurel wreath always in the future, never out of sight for an instant. They would con the fraudulent evangel, entranced; their eyes would sparkle, the blood color their cheeks, their voices vibrate, and a strange strength excite and nerve their bodies. Then would follow wakeful nights and restless days; Black Margarets, Jeanne d'Arcs, Maids of Saragossa, Katherine Douglases, Charlotte Cordays, would haunt them like the goblins of a delirium; then their prayers would become imperious demands upon Heaven, their diaries would almost break into spontaneous combustion from the incendiary material enmagazined in their pages, and the South would have conquered the world then and there could their hands but have pointed the guns and their hearts have recruited the armies. They would with mingled pride and envy read all the names, barely decipherable in the travel-stained record, from the President and Generals in big print to the diminishing insignificance of smallest-type privates; and they would shed tears, when the reaction would come a few days later, at the thought that in the whole area of typography, from the officers gaining immortality to the privates losing lives, there was not one name belonging to them; and they would ask why, of all the families in the South, precisely their father and mother should have no relations, why, of all the women in the South, they should be brotherless.

There was Beau, a too notorious guerilla captain; but what glory was to be won by raiding towns, wrecking trains, plundering transports, capturing couriers, disobeying orders, defying regulations? He was almost as obnoxious to his own as to the enemy's flag.

Besides, Beau at most was only a kind of a cousin, the son of a deceased step-sister of their father's; the most they could expect from him was to keep his undisciplined crew of "'Cadians," Indians, and swampers away from Bayou l'Ombre.

"Ah, if we were only men!" But no! They who could grip daggers and shed blood, they who teemed with all the possibilities of romance or poetry, they were selected for a passive, paltry contest against their own necessities; the endurance that would have laughed a siege to scorn ebbing away in a never-ceasing wrangle with fever and ague—willow-bark tea at odds with a malarious swamp!

It was now early summer; the foliage of spring was lusty and strong, fast outgrowing tenderness and delicacy of shade, with hints of maturity already swelling the shape. The day was cloudless and warm, the dinner-hour was long past, and supper still far off. There were no appetizing varieties of menu to make meals objects of pleasant anticipation; on the contrary, they had become mournful effigies of a convivial institution of which they served at most only to recall the hours, monotonously measuring off the recurring days which passed like unlettered mileposts in a desert, with no information to give except that of transition. To-day the meal-times were so far apart as to make one believe that the sun had given up all forward motion, and intended prolonging the present into eternity. The plantation was quiet and still; not the dewy hush of early dawn trembling before the rising sun, nor the mysterious muteness of midnight, nor yet the lethargic dullness of summer when the vertical sun-rays pin sense and motion to the earth. It was the motionless, voiceless state of unnatural quietude, the oppressive consciousness of abstracted activity, which characterized those days when the whole force of Bayou l'Ombre went off into the swamps to cut timber. Days that began shortly after one midnight and lasted to the other; rare days, when neither horn nor bell was heard for summons; when not a skiff, flat-boat, nor pirogue was left at the "gunnels;" when old Uncle John alone remained to represent both master and men in the cares and responsibilities devolving upon his sex. The bayou lived and moved as usual, carrying its deceptive depths of brackish water unceasingly onward through the shadow and sunshine, rippling over the opposite low, soft banks, which seemed slowly sinking out of sight under the weight of the huge cypress-trees growing upon it. The long stretch of untilled fields back of the house, feebly kept in symmetrical proportion by crumbling fences, bared their rigid, seedless furrows in despairing barrenness to the sun, except in corner spots where a rank growth of weeds had inaugurated a reclamation in favor of barbarism. The sugar-house, superannuated and decrepit from unwholesome idleness, tottered against its own massive, smokeless chimney; the surrounding sheds, stables, and smithy looked forsaken and neglected; the old blind mule peacefully slept in the shade of his once flagellated course under the corn-mill. Afar off against the woods the huge wheel of the draining-machine rose from the underbrush in the big ditch. The patient buzzards, roosting on the branches of the gaunt, blasted gum-tree by the bayou, would raise their heads from time to time to question the loitering sun, or, slowly flapping their heavy wings, circle up into the blue sky, to fall again in lazy spirals to their watch-tower, or they would take short flights by twos and threes over the moribund plantation to see if dissolution had not yet set in, and then all would settle themselves again to brood and sleep and dream, and wait in tranquil certainty the striking of their banqueting hour.

The three girls were in the open hall-way of the plantation house, Christine reading, Régina knitting, both listlessly occupied. Like everything else, they were passively quiet, and, like everything else, their appearance advertised an unwholesome lack of vitality, an insidious anamorphosis from an unexplained dearth or constraint. Their meagre maturity and scant development clashed abnormally with the surrounding prodigality of insensible nature. Though tall, they were thin; they were fair, but sallow; their gentle deep eyes were reproachful and deprived-looking. If their secluded hearts ventured even in thought towards the plumings natural to their age, their coarse, homely, ill-fitting garments anathematized any coquettish effort or naïve expression of a desire to find favor. Like the fields, they seemed hesitating on the backward path from cultivation. Lolotte stood before the cherry-wood armoire that held the hunting and fishing tackle, the wholesome receptacle of useful odds and ends. Not old enough to have come into the war with preconceptions, Lolotte had no reconciliations or compromises to effect between the ideal and the real, no compensations to solicit from an obliging imagination, which so far never rose beyond the possibilities of perch, blackbirds, and turtle eggs. The first of these occupied her thoughts at the present moment. She had made a tryst with the negro children at the draining-machine this afternoon. If she could, unperceived, abstract enough tackle from the armoire for the crowd, and if they could slip away from the quarters, and she evade the surveillance of Uncle John, there would be a diminished number of "brim" and "goggle-eye" in the ditch out yonder, and such a notable addition to the plantation supper to-night as would crown the exploit a success, and establish for herself a reputation above all annoying recollections of recent mishaps and failures. As she tied the hooks on to the lines she saw herself surrounded by the acclaiming infantile populace, pulling the struggling perch up one after the other; she saw them strung on palmetto thongs, long strings of them; she walked home at the head of her procession; heard Peggy's exclamations of surprise, smelt them frying, and finally was sitting at the table, a plate of bones before her, the radiant hostess of an imperial feast.

"Listen!" Like wood-ducks from under the water, the three heads rose simultaneously above their abstractions. "Rowlock! Rowlock!" The eyes might become dull, the tongue inert, and the heart languid on Bayou l'Ombre, but the ears were ever assiduous, ever on duty. Quivering and nervous, they listened even through sleep for that one blessed echo of travel, the signal from another and a distant world. Faint, shadowy, delusive, the whispering forerunner of on-coming news, it overrode the rippling of the current, the hooting of the owls, the barking of dogs, the splash of the gar-fish, the grunting of the alligator, the croaking of frogs, penetrating all turmoil, silencing all other sounds. "Rowlock! Rowlock!" Slow, deliberate, hard, and strenuous, coming up-stream; easy, soft, and musical, gliding down. "Rowlock! Rowlock!" Every stroke a very universe of hope, every oar frothing a sea of expectation! Was it the bayou or the secret stream of their longing that suggested the sound today?" "Rowlock! Rowlock!" The smouldering glances brightened in their eyes, they hollowed their hands behind their ears and held their breath for greater surety. "Rowlock! Rowlock!" In clear, distinct reiteration. It resolved the moment of doubt.

"Can it be papa coming back?"

"No; it's against stream."

"It must be swampers."

"Or hunters, perhaps."

"Or Indians from the mound."

"Indians in a skiff?"

"Well, they sometimes come in a skiff."

The contingencies were soon exhausted, a cut-off leading travellers far around

Bayou l'Ombre, whose snaggy, rafted, convoluted course was by universal avoidance relegated to an isolation almost insulting. The girls, listening, not to lose a single vibration, quit their places and advanced to the edge of the gallery, then out under the trees, then to the levee, then to the "gunnels," where they stretched their long, thin, white necks out of their blue and brown check gowns, and shaded their eyes and gazed down-stream for the first glimpse of the skiff—their patience which had lasted months fretting now over the delay of a few moments.

"At last we shall get some news again."

"If they only leave a newspaper!"

"Or a letter," said Lolotte.

"A letter! From whom?"

"Ah, that's it!"

"What a pity papa isn't here!"

"Lolotte, don't shake the gunnels so; you are wetting our feet."

"How long is it since the last one passed?"

"I can tell you," said Lolotte—"I can tell you exactly: it was the day Lou Ann fell in the bayou and nearly got drowned."

"You mean when you both fell in."

"I didn't fall in at all; I held on to the pirogue."

The weeping-willow on the point below veiled the view; stretching straight out from the bank, it dropped its shock of long, green, pliant branches into the water, titillating and dimpling the surface. The rising bayou bore a freight of logs and drift from the swamps above; rudely pushing their way through the willow boughs, they tore and bruised the fragile tendrils that clung to the rough bark, scattering the tiny leaves which followed hopelessly after in their wake or danced up and down in the hollow eddies behind them. Each time the willow screen moved, the gunnels swayed under the forward motion of the eager bodies of the girls.

"At last!"

They turned their eyes to the shaft of sunlight that fell through the plantation clearing, bridging the stream. The skiff touched, entered, and passed through it with a marvellous revelation of form and color, the oars, silvering and dripping diamonds, arrows and lances of light scintillating from polished steel, golden stars rising like dust from tassels, cordons, button, and epaulets, while the blue clouds themselves seemed to have fallen from their empyrean heights to uniform the rowers with their own celestial hue—blue, not gray!

"Rowlock! Rowlock!" What loud, frightful, threatening reverberations of the oars! And the bayou flowed on the same, and the cypress-trees gazed stolidly and steadfastly up to the heavens, and the heavens were serenely blue and white! But the earth was sympathetic, the ground shook and swayed under their feet; or was it the rush of thoughts that made their heads so giddy? They tried to arrest one and hold it for guidance, but on they sped, leaving only wild confusion of conjecture behind.

"Rowlock! Rowlock!" The rudder headed the bow for the gunnels.

"Titine! Gina! Will they kill us all?" whispered Lolotte, with anxious horror.

The agile Lou Ann, Lolotte's most efficient co-adjutor and Uncle John's most successful tormentor, dropped her bundle of fishing-poles (which he had carefully spread on his roof to "cure"), and while they rolled and rattled over the dry shingles she scrambled with inconceivable haste to her corner of descent. Holding to the eaves while her excited black feet searched and found the top of the window that served as a step, she dropped into the ash-hopper below. Without pausing, as usual, to efface betraying evidences of her enterprise from her person, or to cover her tracks in the wet ashes, she jumped to the ground, and ignoring all secreting offers of bush, fence, or ditch, contrary to her custom, she ran with all the speed of her thin legs down the shortest road to the quarters. They were, as she knew, deserted. The doors of the cabins were all shut, with logs of wood or chairs propped against them. The chickens and dogs were making free of the galleries, and the hogs wallowed in peaceful immunity underneath. A waking baby from a lonely imprisoned cradle sent cries for relief through an open window. Lou Ann, looking neither to the right nor the left, slackened not her steps, but passed straight on through the little avenue to the great white-oak which stood just outside the levee on the bank of the bayou.

Under the wide-spreading, moss-hung branches, upon the broad flat slope, a grand general washing of the clothes of the small community was in busy progress by the women, a proper feminine consecration of this purely feminine day. The daily irksome routine was broken, the men were all away, the sun was bright and warm, the air soft and sweet. The vague recesses of the opposite forest were dim and silent, the bayou played under the gunnels in caressing modulations. All furthered the hearkening and the yielding to a debonair mood, with disregard of concealment, license of pose, freedom of limb, hilarity, conviviality, audacities of heart and tongue, joyous indulgence in freak and impulse, banishment of thought, a return, indeed, for one brief moment to the wild, sweet ways of nature, to the festal days of ancestral golden age (a short retrogression for them), when the body still had claims, and the mind concessions, and the heart owed no allegiance, and when god and satyr eyes still might be caught peeping and glistening from leafy covert on feminine midsummer gambols. Their skirts were girt high around their broad full hips, their dark arms and necks came naked out of their low, sleeveless, white chemise bodies, and glistened with perspiration in the sun as if frosted with silver. Little clouds of steam rose from the kettles standing around them over heaps of burning chips. The splay-legged battling-boards sank firmer and firmer into the earth under the blows of the bats, pounding and thumping the wet clothes, squirting the warm suds in all directions, up into the laughing faces, down into the panting bosoms, against the shortened, clinging skirts, over the bare legs, out in frothy runnels over the soft red clay corrugated with innumerable toe-prints. Out upon the gunnels the water swished and foamed under the vigorous movements of the rinsers, endlessly bending and raising their flexible, muscular bodies, burying their arms to the shoulders in the cool, green depths, piling higher and higher the heaps of tightly-wrung clothes at their sides. The water-carriers, passing up and down the narrow, slippery plank-way, held the evenly filled pails with the ease of coronets upon their heads. The children, under compulsion of continuous threats and occasional chastisement, fed the fire with chips from distant wood-piles, squabbling for the possession of the one cane-knife to split kindlers, imitating the noise and echoing with absurd fidelity the full-throated laughter that interrupted from time to time the work around the wash-kettles.

High above the slop and tumult sat old Aunt Mary, the official sick-nurse of the plantation, commonly credited with conjuring powers. She held a corn-cob pipe between her yellow protruding teeth, and her little restless eyes travelled inquisitively from person to person as if in quest of professional information, twinkling with amusement at notable efforts of wit, and with malice at the general discomfiture expressed under their gaze. Heelen sat near, nursing her baby. She had taken off her kerchief, and leaned her uncovered head back against the trunk of the tree; the long wisps of wool, tightly wrapped in white knitting-cotton, rose from irregular sections all over her elongated narrow skull, and encircled her wrinkled, nervous, toothless face like some ghastly serpentine chevulure.

"De Yankees! de Yankees! I seed 'em—at de big house! Little mistus she come for Uncle John. He fotched his gun—for to shoot 'em."

Lou Ann struggled to make her exhausted breath carry all her tidings. After each item she closed her mouth and swallowed violently, working her muscles until her little horns of hair rose and moved with the contortions of her face.

"An' dey locked a passel o' men up in de smoke-house—Cornfedrits."

The bats paused in the air, the women on the gunnels lifted their arms out of the water, those on the gang-plank stopped where they were; only the kettles simmered on audibly.

Lou Ann recommenced, this time finishing in one breath, with the added emphasis of raising her arm and pointing in the direction from whence she came, her voice getting shriller and shriller to the end:

"I seed 'em. Dey was Yankees. Little mistus she come for Uncle John; he fotched his gun for to shoot 'em; and they locked a passel o' men up in the smoke-house—Cornfedrits."

The Yankees! What did it mean to them? How much from the world outside had penetrated into the unlettered fastnesses of their ignorance? What did the war mean to them? Had Bayou l'Ombre indeed isolated both mind and body? Had the subtle time-spirit itself been diverted from them by the cut-off? Could their rude minds draw no inferences from the gradual loosening of authority and relaxing of discipline? Did they neither guess nor divine their share in the shock of battle out there? Could their ghost-seeing eyes not discern the martyr-spirits rising from two opposing armies, pointing at, beckoning to them? If, indeed, the water-shed of their destiny was forming without their knowledge as without their assistance, could not maternal instinct spell it out of the heart-throbs pulsing into life under their bosoms, or read from the dumb faces of the children at their breast the triumphant secret of their superiority over others born and nourished before them?

Had they, indeed, no gratifications beyond the physical, no yearnings, no secret burden of a secret prayer to God, these bonded wives and mothers? Was this careless, happy, indolent existence genuine, or only a fool's motley to disguise a tragedy of suffering? What to them was the difference between themselves and their mistresses? their condition? or their skin, that opaque black skin which hid so well the secrets of life, which could feel but not own the blush of shame, the pallor of weakness.

If their husbands had brought only rum from their stealthy midnight excursions to distant towns, how could the child repeat it so glibly—"Yankees—Cornfedrits?" The women stood still and silent, but their eyes began to creep around furtively, as if seeking degrees of complicity in a common guilt, each waiting for the other to confess comprehension, to assume the responsibility of knowledge.

The clear-headed children, profiting by the distraction of attention from them, stole away for their fishing engagement, leaving cane-knife and chips scattered on the ground behind them. The murmuring of the bayou seemed to rise louder and louder; the cries of the forsaken baby, clamorous and hoarse, fell distinctly on the air.

"My Gord A'mighty!"

The exclamation was uncompromising; it relieved the tension and encouraged rejoinder.

"My Lord!—humph!"

One bat slowly and deliberately began to beat again—Black Maria's. Her tall, straight back was to them, but, as if they saw it, they knew that her face was settling into that cold, stern rigidity of hers, the keen eyes beginning to glisten, the long, thin nostrils nervously to twitch, the lips to open over her fine white teeth—the expression they hated and feared.

"O-h! o-h! o-h!"

A long, thin, tremulous vibration, a weird, haunting note: what inspiration suggested it?

"Glo-o-ry!"

Old Aunt Mary nodded her knowing head affirmatively, as if at the fulfillment of a silent prophecy—she quietly shook the ashes out of her pipe, hunted her pocket, put it in, and, rising stiffly from the root, hobbled away on her stick in the direction of her cabin.

"Glo-o-ry!"

Dead-arm Harriet stood before them, with her back to the bayou, her right arm hanging heavy at her side, her left extended, the finger pointing to the sky. A shapely arm and tapering finger; a comely, sleek, half-nude body; the moist lips, with burning red linings, barely parting to emit the sound they must have culled in uncanny practices. The heavy lids drooped over the large sleepy eyes, looking with languid passion from behind the thick black lashes.

"Glo-o-ry!" It stripped their very nerves and bared secret places of sensation! The "happy" cry of revival meetings—as if midnight were coming on, salvation and the mourners' bench before them, Judgment-day and fiery flames behind them, and "Sister Harriet" raising her voice to call them on, on, through hand-clapping, foot-stamping, shouting, groaning, screaming, out of their sins, out of their senses, to rave in religious inebriation, and fall in religious catalepsy across the floor at the preacher's feet. With a wild rush, the hesitating emotions of the women sought the opportune outlet, their hungry blood bounding and leaping for the mid-day orgy. Obediently their bodies began the imperceptible motion right and left, and the veins in their throats to swell and stand out under their skins, while the short, fierce, intense responsive exclamations fell from their lips to relieve their own and increase the exaltation of the others.

"Sweet Christ! sweet Christ!"

"Take me, Saviour!"

"Oh, de Lamb! de Lamb!"

"I'm a-coming! I'm a-coming!"

"Hold back, Satan! we's a-catching on!"

"De blood's a-dripping! de blood's a-dripping!"

"Let me kiss dat cross! let me kiss it!"

"Sweet Master!"

"Glo-o-ry! Fre-e-dom!" It was a whisper, but it came like a crash, and transfixed them; their mouths stood open with the last words, their bodies remained bent to one side or the other, the febrile light in their eyes burning as if from their blood on fire. They could all remember the day when Dead-arm Harriet, the worst worker and most violent tongue of the gang, stood in the clearing, and raising that dead right arm over her head, cursed the overseer riding away in the distance. The wind had been blowing all day; there was a sudden loud crack above them, and a limb from a deadened tree broke, sailed, poised, and fell crashing to her shoulder, and deadening her arm forever. They looked instinctively now with a start to the oak above them, to the sky—only moss and leaves and blue and white clouds. And still Harriet's voice rose, the words faster, louder, bolder, more determined, whipping them out of their awe, driving them on again down the incline of their own passions.

"Glory! Freedom! Freedom! Glory!"

"I'm bound to see 'em! Come along!"

Heelen's wild scream rang shrill and hysterical. She jerked her breast from the sucking lips, and dropped her baby with a thud on the ground. They all followed her up the levee, pressing one after the other, slipping in the wet clay, struggling each one not to be left behind. Emmeline, the wife of little Ben, the only yellow woman on the place, was the last. Her skirt was held in a grip of iron; blinded, obtuse, she pulled forward, reaching her arms out after the others.

"You stay here!"

She turned and met the determined black face of her mother-in-law.

"You let me go!" she cried, half sobbing, half angry.

"You stay here, I tell you!" The words were muttered through clinched teeth.

"You let me go, I tell you!"

"Glory! Freedom!"

The others had already left the quarters, and were on the road. They two were alone on the bank now, except Heelen's baby, whimpering under the tree; their blazing eyes glared at each other. The singing voices grew fainter and fainter. Suddenly the yellow face grew dark with the surge of blood underneath, the brows wrinkled, and the lips protruded in a grimace of animal rage. Grasping her wet bat tightly with both hands, she turned with a furious bound, and raised it with all the force of her short muscular arms. The black woman darted to the ground; the cane-knife flashed in the air and came down pitilessly towards the soft fleshy shoulder. A wild, terrified scream burst from Emmeline's lips; the bat dropped; seizing her skirt with both hands, she pulled forward, straining her back out of reach of the knife; the homespun tore, and she fled up the bank, her yellow limbs gleaming through the rent left by the fragment in the hand of the black woman.

The prisoners were so young, so handsome, so heroic; the very incarnation of the holy spirit of patriotism in their pathetic uniform of brimless caps, ragged jackets, toeless shoes, and shrunken trousers—a veteran equipment of wretchedness out of keeping with their fresh young faces. How proud and unsubdued they walked through the hall between the file of bayonets! With what haughty, defiant eyes they returned the gaze of their insultingly resplendent conquerors! Oh, if girls' souls had been merchantable at that moment! Their hands tied behind their backs like runaway slaves! Locked up in the smoke-house! that dark, rancid, gloomy, mouldy depot of empty hogs-heads, barrels, boxes, and fetid exhalations.

They were the first soldiers in gray the girls had ever seen; their own chivalrous knights, the champions of their radiant country. What was the story of their calamity? Treacherously entrapped? Overpowered by numbers? Where were their companions—staring with mute, cold, upturned faces from pools of blood? And were these to be led helplessly tethered into captivity, imprisoned; with ball and chain to gangrene and disgrace their strong young limbs, or was solitary confinement to starve their hearts and craze their minds, holding death in a thousand loathsome, creeping shapes ever threateningly over them?

The smoke-house looked sinister and inimical after its sudden promotion from keeper of food to keeper of men. The great square whitewashed logs seemed to settle more ponderously on the ground around them, the pointed roof to press down as if the air of heaven were an emissary to be dreaded; the hinges and locks were so ostentatiously massive and incorruptible. What artful, what vindictive security of carpenter and lock-smith to exclude thieves or immure patriots!

The two eldest girls stood against the open armoire with their chill fingers interlaced. Beyond the wrinkled back of Uncle John's copperas-dyed coat before them lay the region of brass buttons and blue cloth and hostility; but they would not look at it; they turned their heads away; the lids of their eyes refused to lift and reveal the repugnant vision to them. If their ears had only been equally sensitive!

"And so you are the uncle of the young ladies? Brother of the father or mother?" What clear, incisive nasal tones! Thank Heaven for the difference between them of the voice at least!

The captain's left arm was in a sling, but his hand could steadily hold the note-book in which he carefully pencilled Uncle John's answers to his minute cross-examination—a dainty, fragrant, Russia-leather note-book, with monogram and letters and numbers emblazoned on the outside in national colors. It had photographs inside, also, which he would pause and admire from time to time, reading the tender dedications aloud to his companions.

"And the lady in the kitchen called mammy? She is the mother, I guess?"

"P-p-p-peggys' a nigger, and my mistresses is white," stuttered Uncle John.

"Ah, indeed! Gentlemen in my uniform find it difficult to remember these trifling distinctions of color."

What tawdry pleasantry! What hypocritical courtesy! What exquisite ceremony and dainty manual for murderous dandies!

"Ef-ef-ef-ef I hadn't done gone and forgot dem caps!"

Uncle John stood before his young mistresses erect and determined, his old double-barrel shotgun firmly clasped in his tremulous hands, his bleary, bloodshot eyes fearlessly measuring the foe. If it were to be five hundred lashes on his bare back under the trees out there (terms on which he would gladly have compromised), or, his secret fear, a running noose over one of the branches, or the murderous extravagance of powder and shot for him, he had made up his mind, despite every penalty, to fulfil his duty and stand by his word to Marse John. Ever since the time the little crawling white boy used to follow the great awkward black boy around like a shadow, John made a cult of Marse John. He had taught him as a child to fish, hunt, trap birds, to dress skins, knit gloves, and play cards on the sly, to fight cocks on Sunday, to stutter, to cut the "pigeon wing" equal to any negro in the State—and other personal accomplishments besides. He had stood by him through all his scrapes as a youth, was valet to all his frolics as a young man, and now in his old age he gardened for him, and looked after the young ladies for him, stretching or contracting his elastic moral code as occasion required; but he had never deceived him nor falsified his word to him. He knew all about the war: Marse John had told him. He knew what Marse John meant when he left the children to him, and Marse John knew what to expect from John. He would treat them civilly as long as they were civil, but his gun was loaded, both barrels with bullets, and—

"Ef-ef-ef-ef I hadn't done gone and forgot dem caps!"

There was his powder-horn under one arm, there was his shot-flask filled with the last batch of slugs under the other; but the caps were not in his right-hand coat-pocket, they were in his cupboard, hidden for safety under a pile of garden "truck."

The busy martins twittered in and out of their little lodge under the eaves of the smoke-house. Régina and Christine were powerless to prevent furtive glances in that direction. Could the *prisoners* hear it inside? Could *they* see the sun travelling westward, crack by crack, chink by chink, in the roof? Could they feel it sinking, and with it sinking all their hopes of deliverance? Or did they hope still?

Maidens had mounted donjon towers at midnight, had eluded Argus-eyed sentinels, had drugged savage blood-hounds, had crossed lightning-flashed seas, had traversed robber-infested forests; whatever maidens had done they would do, for could ever men more piteously implore release from castle keep than these gray-clad youths from the smoke-house? And did ever maiden hearts beat more valiantly than theirs? (and did ever maiden limbs tremble more cowardly?) Many a tedious day had been lightened by their rehearsal of just such a drama as this; they had prepared roles for every imaginable sanguinary circumstance, but prevision, as usual, had overlooked the unexpected. The erstwhile feasible conduct, the erstwhile feasible weapons, of a Jeanne d'Arc or Charlotte Corday, the defiant speeches, the ringing retorts— how inappropriate, inadequate, here and now! If God would only help them! but, like the bayou, the cypresses, and the blue sky, He seemed to-day eternally above such insignificant human necessities as theirs.

Without the aid of introspection or the fear of capital punishment, Lolotte found it very difficult to maintain the prolonged state of rigidity into which her sisters had frozen themselves. All the alleviations devised during a wearisome experience of compulsory attendance on plantation funerals were exhausted in the course of this protracted, hymnless, prayerless solemnity. She stood wedged in between them and the armoire which displayed all its shelves of allurements to her. There were her bird-traps just within reach; there was the fascinating bag of nux-vomica root—crow poison; there was the little old work-box filled with ammunition, which she was forbidden to touch, and all the big gar-fish lines and harpoons and decoy-ducks. There were her own perch lines, the levy she had raised in favor of her companions; they were neatly rolled, ready to tie on the rods, only needing sinkers; and there was the old Indian basket filled with odds and ends, an unfailing treasure of resource and surprise. She was just about searching in it for sinkers when this interruption occurred.

The sky was so bright over the fields! Just the evening to go fishing whether they caught anything or not. If the enemy would only hurry and go, there might still be time; they would leave, they said, as soon as mammy cooked them something to eat. She had seen mammy chasing a chicken through the yard. She wondered how the nice, fat little round "doodles" were getting on in their tin can under the house; she never had such a fine box of bait; she wondered if the negro children would go all the same without her; she wondered if she could see them creeping down the road. How easy she could have got away from Uncle John! Anything almost would do for sinkers—bits of iron, nails; they had to do since her father and Uncle John made their last moulding of bullets. She thought they might have left her just one real sinker simply as a matter of distinction between herself and the little darkies. Her eyes kept returning to the Indian basket, and if she stopped twisting her fingers one over the other but a moment they would take their way to rummaging among the rusty contents.

"Glory! Freedom!"

In came the negresses, Bacchantes drunk with the fumes of their own hot blood, Dead-arm Harriet, like a triumphant sorceress, leading them, waving and gesticulating with her one "live" arm, all repeating over and over again the potent magical words, oblivious of the curious looks of men, their own exposure, the presence of their mistresses, of everything but their own ecstasy.

"Freedom! Master! Freedom!"

Christine and Régina raised their heads and looked perplexed at the furious women in the yard, and the men gazing down to them.

What was the matter with them? What did they mean? What was it all about?

"Freedom! Freedom!"

Then light broke upon them; their fingers tightened in each other's clasp, and their cheeks flushed crimson.

"How dared they? What insolence! What—"

The opposite door stood open; they rushed across the hall and closed it between them and the humiliating scene. This, this they had not thought of, this they had never read about, this their imagination in wildest flights had not ventured upon. This was not a superficial conflict to sweep the earth with cannons and mow it with sabres; this was an earthquake which had rent it asunder, exposing the quivering organs of hidden life. What a chasm was yawning before them! There was no need to listen one to the other; the circumstances could wring from the hearts of millions but one sentiment, the tongue was left no choice of words.

"Let them go! let them be driven out! never, never to see them again!"

The anger of outraged affection, betrayed confidence, abandoned trust, traitorous denial, raged within them.

These were their servants, their possessions! From generation to generation their lives had been woven together by the shuttle of destiny. How flimsy and transparent the fabric! How grotesque and absurd the tapestry, with its vaunted traditions of mutual loyalty and devotion! What a farce, what a lying, disgusting farce it had all been! Well, it was over now; that was a comfort—all over, all ended. If the hearts had intergrown, they were torn apart now. After this there was no return, no reconciliation possible! Through the storm of their emotions a thought drifted, then another; little detached scenes flitted into memory; familiar gestures, speeches, words, one reminiscence drawing another. Thicker and thicker came little episodes of their pastoral existence together; the counter interchanges of tokens, homely presents, kind offices, loving remembrances; the mutual assistance and consolation in all the accidents of life traversed together, the sicknesses, the births, the deaths; and so many thousand trivial incidents of long, long ago—memory had not lost one—down to the fresh eggs and the pop-corn of that very morning; they were all there, falling upon their bruised hearts.

In the hearts of the women out there were only shackles and scourges. What of the long Sundays of Bible-reading and catechism, the long evenings of woodland tales; the confidences; the half-hours around the open fireplaces when supper was cooking, the potatoes under their hillocks of ashes, the thin-legged ovens of cornbread with their lids of glowing coals, the savory skillets of fried meat, the— Was it indeed all of the past, never again to be present or future? And those humble, truthful, loving eyes, which had looked up to them from the first moment of their lives: did they look with greater trust up to God Himself? It was all over, yes, all over! The color faded from their faces, the scornful resolution left their lips; they laid their faces in their hands and sobbed.

"Do you hear, Titine?" Lolotte burst into the room. "They are all going to leave, every one of them; a transport is coming to-night to take them off. They are going to bundle up their things and wait at the steamboat-landing; and they are not going to take a child, and not a single husband. The captain says the government at Washington will give them the nicest white husbands in the land; that they ought to be glad to marry them. They carried on as if they were drunk. Do you believe it, Titine? Oh, I do wish Jeff Davis would hurry up and win!"

The door opened again; it was Black Maria, still holding the cane-knife in her hand. She crossed the room with her noiseless barefooted tread, and placed herself behind them. They did not expect her to say anything; Black Maria never talked much; but they understood her, as they always did.

Her skirts were still tied up, her head-kerchief awry; they saw for the first time that the wool under it was snow-white.

Black Maria! They might have known it! They looked at her. No! She was not! She was not negro, like the others. Who was she? What was she? Where did she come from, with her white features and white nature under her ebon skin? What was the mystery that enveloped her? Why did the brain always torture itself in surmises about her? Why did she not talk as the others did, and just for a moment uncover that coffin heart of hers? Why was she, alone of all the negroes, still an alien, a foreigner, and exile among them? Was she brooding on disgrace, outrage, revenge? Was she looking at some mirage behind her—a distant equatorial country, a princely rank, barbaric state, some inherited memory transmitted by that other Black Maria, her mother? Who was the secret black father whom no one had discovered? Was it, as the negroes said, the Prince of Darkness? Who was her own secret consort, the father of Ben? What religion had she to warrant her scornful repudiation of Christianity? What code that enabled her to walk as if she were free through slavery, to assume slavery now when others hailed freedom, to be loyal in the midst of treason?

"Look!" Lolotte came into the room, and held up a rusty, irregular piece of iron. "I found this in the old Indian basket where I was looking for sinkers. Don't you see what it is? It is the old key of the smoke-house, and I am going to let those Confederates out." She spoke quietly and decidedly. There was something else in the other hand, concealed in the folds of her dress. She produced it reluctantly. It was the gun-wrench that filled so prominent a part in her active life—always coveting it, getting possession of it, being deprived of it, and accused unfailingly for its every absence and misplacement. "You see, it is so convenient; it screws so nicely on to everything," she continued, apologetically, as she demonstrated the useful qualification by screwing it on to the key. "There! it is as good as a handle. All they've got to do is to slip away in the skiff while the others are eating. And I would like to know how they can ever be caught, without another boat on the place! But oh, girls"—her black eyes twinkled maliciously—"what fools the Yankees are!"

If the Federals, as they announced, were only going to remain long enough for the lady in the kitchen to prepare them something to eat, the length of their stay clearly rested in Peggy the cook's hands, as she understood it. She walked around her kitchen with a briskness rarely permitted by her corpulent proportions, and with an intuitive faith in the common nature of man regardless of political opinion, she exerted her culinary skill to the utmost. She knew nothing of the wholesale quarrelling and fighting of a great war, but during her numerous marital experiments, not counting intermittent conjugalities for twenty-five years with Uncle John, she had seen mercy and propitiation flow more than once after a good meal from the most irate; and a healthy digestion aiding, she never despaired of even the most revengeful. The enemy, in her opinion, were simply to be treated like furious husbands, and were to be offered the best menu possible under the trying circumstances. She worked, inspired by all the wife-lore of past ages, the infiltrated wisdom that descends to women in the course of a world of empirical connubiality, that traditionary compendium to their lives by which they still hope to make companionship with men harmonious and the earth a pleasant abiding-place. With minute particularity Peggy set the table and placed the dishes. The sun was now sinking, and sending almost horizontal rays over the roof of the smoke-house, whose ugly square frame completely blocked the view of the dining-room window. Peggy carefully drew the red calico curtain across it, and after a moment's rehearsal to bring her features to the conventional womanly expression of cheerful obtuseness to existing displeasure, she opened the dining-room door.

Gina and Lolotte stood close under the window against the dwelling, looking at the locked door of the smoke-house before them, listening to the sounds falling from the dining-room above. Once in the skiff, the prisoners were safe; but the little red curtain of the window fluttering flimsily in the breeze coquetted with their hopes and the lives of three men. If the corners would but stay down a second! Titine and Black Maria were in front, busy about the skiff. Peggy's culinary success appeared, from the comments of the diners, to be complimentary to her judgment. But food alone, however, does not suffice in the critical moments of life; men are half managed when only fed. There was another menu, the ingredients of which were not limited or stinted by blockade of war. Peggy had prepared that also; and in addition to the sounds of plates, knives, forks, and glasses, came the tones of her rich voice dropping from a quick tongue the *entremets* of her piquant imagination. The attention in the room seemed tense, and at last the curtain hung straight and motionless.

"Now! now!" whispered Gina. "We must risk something."

Woman-like, they paused midway and looked back; a hand stretched from the table was carelessly drawing the curtain aside, and the window stared unhindered at the jail.

Why had they waited? Why had they not rushed forward immediately? By this time their soldiers might have been free! The could hear Peggy moving around the table; they could see her bulky form push again and again across the window.

"Mammy! Mammy!"

Could she hear them? They clasped their hands and held their faces up in imploring appeal. The sun was setting fast, almost running down the west to the woods. The dinner, if good, was not long. It all depended upon Peggy now.

"Mammy! Mammy!" They raised their little voices, then lowered them in agony of apprehension. "Mammy, do something! Help us!"

But still she passed on and about, around the table, and across the window, blind to the smokehouse, deaf to them, while her easy, familiar voice recited the comical gyrations of "old Frizzly," the half-witted hen, who had set her heart against being killed and stewed, and ran and hid, and screamed and cackled, and ducked and flew, and then, after her silly head was twisted off, "just danced, as if she were at a 'Cadian' ball, all over the yard."

It would soon be too late! It was, perhaps, too late now!

Black Maria had got the skiff away from the gunnels, but they might just as well give it up; they would not have time enough now.

"Mammy!" The desperate girls made a supreme effort of voice and look. The unctuous black face, the red bead ear-rings, the bandanna head-kerchief, appeared at the window with "old Frizzly's" last dying cackle. There was one flashing wink of the left eye.

Her nurslings recognized then her *pièce de résistance oratoire*—a side-splitting prank once played upon her by another nursling, her pet, her idol, the plague of her life—Beau.

Who could have heard grating lock or squeaking hinges through the boisterous mirth that followed? Who could have seen the desperate bound of the three imprisoned soldiers for liberty through that screen of sumptuous flesh—the magnificent back of Mammy that filled to overlapping the insignificant little window?

They did not wait to hear the captain's rapturous toast to Peggy in sassafras tea, nor his voluble protestations of love to her, nor could they see him in his excitement forgetting his wounded arm, bring both clinched fists with a loud bravo to the table, and then faint dead away.

"I knew it!"

"Just like him!"

"Take him in the air—quick!"

"No, sir! You take him in there, and put him on the best bed in the house." Peggy did not move from the window, but her prompt command turned the soldiers from the door in the hall, and her finger directed them to the closed bed-chamber.

Without noticing Christine standing by the open window, they dropped their doughty burden—boots, spurs, sword, epaulets, and all—on the fresh, white little bed, the feather mattress fluffing up all around as if to submerge him.

"Oh, don't bother about that; cut the sleeve off!"

"Who has a knife?"

"There."

"That's all right now."

"He's coming round."

"There's one nice coat spoiled."

"Uncle Sam has plenty more."

"Don't let it drip on the bed."

"Save it to send to Washington—trophy—wet with rebel blood."

The captain was evidently recovering.

"You stay here while I keep 'em eating," whispered Peggy, authoritatively, to Christine.

Titine trembled as if she had an ague.

"How could they help seeing the tall form of Black Maria standing in the prow of the boat out in the very middle of the bayou? Suppose she, Titine, had not been there to close the window quick as thought? Suppose instead of passing through her room she had run through the basement, as she intended, after pushing off the skiff?"

Rollicking, careless, noisy, the soldiers went back to their interrupted meal, while the boat went cautiously down the bayou to the meeting place beyond the clearing.

"How far was Black Maria now?" Titine opened the window a tiny crack. "Heavens! how slowly she paddled! lifting the oar deliberately from side to side, looking straight ahead. How clear and distinct she was in the soft evening light! Why did she not hurry? Why did she not row? She could have muffled the oars. But no, no one thought of that; that was always the way—always something overlooked and forgotten. The soldiers could finish a dozen dinners before the skiff got out of sight at this rate. Without the skiff the prisoners might just as well be locked still in the smoke-house. Did he on the bed suspect something, seeing her look out this way?" She closed the window tight.

"How dark the room was! She could hardly see the wounded man. How quiet he was! Was he sleeping, or had he fainted again? In her bed! her enemy lying in her bed! his head on her pillow, her own little pillow, the feverish confidant of so many sleepless nights! How far were they now on the bayou? She must peep out again. Why, Maria had not moved! not moved an inch! Oh, if she could only scream to her! If she were only in the skiff!

"How ghastly pale he looked on the bed! his face as white as the coverlet, his hair and beard so black; how changed without his bravado and impertinence! And he was not old, either; not older than the boys in gray. She had fancied that age and ugliness alone could go with violence and wrong. How much gold! how much glitter! Why, the sun did not rise with more splendor of equipment. Costumed as if for the conquest of worlds. If the Yankees dressed their captains this way, what was the livery of their generals? How curious the sleeveless arm looked! What a horrible mark the gash made right across the soft white skin! What a scar it would leave! What a disfigurement! And this, this is what men call love of country!"

On Saturday nights sometimes, in the quarters, when rum had been smuggled in, the negroes would get to fighting and beating their wives, and her father would be sent for in a hurry to come with his gun and separate them. Hatchets, axes, cane-knives—anything they would seize, to cut and slash one another, husbands, wives, mothers, sons, sisters, brothers; but they were negroes, ignorant, uneducated, barbarous, excited; they could not help it; they could not be expected to resist all at once the momentum of centuries of ancestral ferocity. But for white men, gentlemen, thus furiously to mar and disfigure their own mother-given bodies! All the latent maternal instinct in her was roused, all the woman in her revolted against the sacrilegious violence of mutilation. "Love of country to make her childless, or only the mother of invalids! This was only one. What of the other thousands and hundreds of thousands? Are men indeed so inexhaustible? Are the pangs of maternity so cheap? Are women's hearts of no account whatever in the settlement of disputes? O God! cannot the world get along without war? But even if men want it, even if God permits it, how can the women allow it? If the man on the bed were a negro, she could do something for his arm. Many a time, early Sunday mornings, Saturday night culprits had come to her secretly, and she had washed off the thick, gummy blood, and bandaged up their cuts and bruises; they did not show so on black skin. . . . This man had a mother somewhere among the people she called 'enemies': a mother sitting counting day by day the continued possession of a live son, growing gray and old before that terrible next minute ever threatening to take her boy and give her a corpse. Or perhaps, like her own, his mother might be dead. They might be friends in that kingdom which the points of the compass neither unite nor divide; together they might be looking down on this quarrelling, fighting world; mothers, even though angels, looking, looking through smoke and powder and blood and hatred after their children. Their eyes might be fixed on this lonely little spot, on this room. . . ." She walked to the bed.

The blood was oozing up through the strips of plaster. She stanched and bathed and soothed the wound as she well knew how with her tender, agile fingers, and returned to the window. Maria had disappeared now; she could open the window with impunity. The trackless water was flowing innocently along, the cooling air was rising in mist, the cypress-trees checked the brilliant sky with the filigree and network of their bristly foliage. The birds twittered, the chickens loitered and dallied on their way to roost. The expectant dogs were lying on the levee waiting for the swampers, who, they ought to know, could not possibly return before midnight. And Molly was actually on time this evening, lowing for mammy to come and milk her;

what was the war to her? How happy and peaceful it all was! What a jarring contrast to swords and bayonets! Thank God that Nature was impartial, and could not be drilled into partisanship! If humanity were like Nature! If—if there had been no war! She paused, shocked at her first doubt; of the great Circumstance of her life it was like saying, "If there had been no God!"

As she stood at the window and thought, all the brilliant coloring of her romantic fantasies, the stories of childhood, the perversions of education, the self-delusions, they all seemed to fade with the waning light, and with the beautiful day sink slowly and quietly into the irrevocable past. "Thank God, above all, that it is a human device to uniform people into friends and enemies! The heart (her own felt so soft and loving)—the heart repudiates such attempts of blue and gray; it still clings to Nature, and belongs to God." She thought the wound must need tending again, and returned to the bed. The patient, meanwhile, went in and out of the mazes of unconsciousness caused by weakness.

"Was that really he on this foamy bed? What a blotch his camp-battered body made down the centre of it! It was good to be on a bed once more, to look up into a mosquito-bar instead of the boughs of trees, to feel his head on a pillow. But why did they put him there? Why did they not lay him somewhere on the floor, outside on the ground, instead of soiling and crumpling this lily-white surface?"

He could observe his nurse through his half-closed lids, which fell as she approached the bed, and closed tight as she bent above him. When she stood at the window he could look full at her. "How innocent and unsuspecting she looked!" The strained rigidity had passed away from her face. Her transparent, child-like eyes were looking with all their life of expression in the direction of the bed, and then at something passing in her own mind. "Thank Heaven, the fright had all gone out of them! How horrible for a gentleman to read fear in the eyes of a woman! Her mind must be as pure and white, yes, and as impressionable, too, as her bed. Did his presence lie like a blot upon it also? How she must hate him! how she must loathe him! Would it have been different if he had come in the other uniform—if he had worn gray? Would she then have cared for him, have administered to him? How slight and frail she was! What a wan, wistful little face between him and the gloomy old bayou! He could see her more plainly now since she had opened the window and let in the cool, fragrant air. There was no joyous development of the body in her to proclaim womanhood, none of the seductive, confident beauty that follows coronation of youth; to her had only come the care and anxiety of maturity. This—this," he exclaimed to himself, "is the way women fight a war." Was she coming this way? Yes. To the bed? Hardly. Now she was pressing against it, now bending over him, now dropping a cooling dew from heaven on his burning arm, and now—oh, why so soon?—she was going away to stand and look out of the window again. ʹ

The homely little room was filled with feminine subterfuges for ornament, feminine substitutes for comfort. How simple women are! how little they require, after all! Only peace and love and quiet, only the impossible in a masculine world. What was she thinking of? If he could only have seen the expression of her eyes as she bent over him! Suppose he should open his and look straight up at her? but no, he had not the courage to frighten her again. He transplanted her in his mind to other surroundings, her proper surroundings by birthright, gave her in abundance all of which this war had deprived her, presented to her assiduous courtiers, not reckless soldiers like himself, but men whom peace had guided in the lofty sphere of intellectual pursuits. He held before her the sweet invitations of youth, the consummations of life. He made her smile, laugh.

"Ah!"—he turned his face against the pillow—"had that sad face ever laughed? Could any woman laugh during a war? Could any triumph, however glorious, atone for battles that gave men death, but left the women to live? This was only one; how many, wan and silent as she, were looking at this sunset—the sunset not of a day, but a life? When it was all over, who was to make restitution to them, the women? Was any cost too great to repurchase for them simply the privilege of hoping again? What an endless chain of accusing thoughts! What a miserable conviction tearing his heart! If he could get on his knees to her, if he could kiss her feet, if he could beg pardon in the dust—he, a man for all men, of her, a woman for all women. If he could make her his country, not to fight, but to work for, it. . . ."

She came to his side again, she bent over him, she touched him.

Impulsive, thoughtless, hot-headed, he opened his eyes full, he forgot again the wounded arm. With both hands he stayed her frightened start; he saw the expression of her eyes bending over him.

"Can you forgive me? It is a heartless, cowardly trick! I am not a Yankee; I am Beau, your cousin, the guerilla."

The door of the smoke-house opened, the escaped soldiers ran like deer between the furrows of Uncle John's vegetable garden, where the waving corn leaves could screen them; then out to the bank of the bayou—not on the levee, but close against the fence—snagging their clothes and scratching their faces and hands on the cuckleburs; Lolotte in front, with a stick in her hand, beating the bushes through habit to frighten the snakes, calling, directing, animating, in excited whispers; Régina in the rear, urging, pressing, sustaining the young soldier lagging behind, but painfully striving with stiffened limbs to keep up with the pace of his older, more vigorous companions. Ahead of them Black Maria was steadily keeping the skiff out in the current. The bayou narrowed and grew dark as it entered between the banks of serried cypress-trees, where night had already begun.

Régina looked hurriedly over her shoulder. "Had they found out yet at the house? How slowly she ran! How long it took to get to the woods! Oh, they would have time over and over again to finish their dinner and catch them. Perhaps at this very moment, as she was thinking of it, some forgotten article in the skiff was betraying them! Perhaps a gun might even now be pointing down their path! Or, now! the bullet could start and the report come too late to warn them."

She looked back again and again.

From the little cottage under the trees the curtains fluttered, but no bayonet nor smooth-bore was visible.

She met her companion's face, looking back also, but not for guns—for her. "If it had been different! If he had been a visitor, come to stay; days and evenings to be passed together!" The thought lifting the sulphurous war-clouds from her heart, primitive idyls burst into instantaneous fragrant bloom in it like spring violets. He was not only the first soldier in gray she had ever seen, but the first young man; or it seemed so to her.

Again she looked back.

"How near they were still to the house! how plainly they could yet be seen! He could be shot straight through the back, the gray jacket getting one stain, one bullet-hole, more, the country one soldier less. Would they shoot through a woman at him? Would they be able to separate them if she ran close behind him, moving this way and that way, exactly as he did? If she saw them in time she could warn him; he could lie flat down in the grass; then it would be impossible to hit him."

Increasing and narrowing the space between them at the hest of each succeeding contradictory thought, turning her head again and again to the house behind her, she lost speed. Lolotte and the two men had already entered the forest before she reached it. Coming from the fields, the swamps seemed midnight dark. Catching her companion's hand, they groped their way along, tripped by the slimy cypress knees that rose like evil gnomes to beset and entangle their feet, slipping over rolling logs, sinking in stagnant mire, noosed by the coils of heavy vines that dropped from unseen branches overhead. Invisible wings of startled birds flapped above them, the croaking of frogs ebbed and flowed around them, owls shrieked and screamed from side to side of the bayou. Lolotte had ceased her beating; swamp serpents are too sluggish to be frightened away. In the obscurity, Black Maria could be dimly seen turning the skiff to a half-submerged log, from which a turtle dropped as if ballasted with lead. A giant cypress-tree arrested them; the smooth, fluted trunk, ringed with whitish watermarks, recording floods far over their heads; where they were scrambling once swam fish and serpents. The young soldier turned and faced her, the deliverer, whose manœvers in the open field had not escaped him.

She had saved him from imprisonment, insult, perhaps death—the only heir of a heroic father, the only son of a widowed mother; she had restored him to a precious heritage of love and honor, replaced him in the interrupted ambitious career of patriotic duty; she had exposed her life for him—she was beautiful. She stood before him, panting, tremulous, ardent, with dumb, open red lips, and voluble, passionate eyes, and with a long scratch in her white cheek from which the blood trickled. She had much to say to him, her gray uniformed hero; but how in one moment express four years—four long years—and the last long minutes. The words were all there, had been rushing to her lips all day; her lips were parted; but the eager, overcrowded throng were jammed on the threshold; and her heart beat so in her ears! He could not talk; he could not explain. His companions were already in the boat, his enemies still in gunshot. He bent his face to hers in the dim light to learn by heart the features he must never forget—closer, closer, learning, knowing more and more, with the eager precocity of youth.

Bellona must have flown disgusted away with the wings of an owl, Columbia might have nodded her head as knowingly as old Aunt Mary could, when the callow hearts, learning and knowing, brought the faces closer and closer together, until the lips touched.

"I shall come again; I shall come again. Wait for me. Surely I shall come again."

"Yes! Yes!"

Black Maria pushed the skiff off. "Rowlock! Rowlock!" They were safe and away.

A vociferous group stood around the empty gunnels. Uncle John, with the daring of desperation, advanced, disarmed as he was, towards them.

"I-I-I-I don't keer ef you is de-de-de President o' de United States hisself, I ain't gwine to 'low no such cussin' an' swearin' in de hearin' o' de-de-de young ladies. Marse John he-he-he don't 'low it, and when Marse John ain't here I-I-I- don't 'low it."

His remonstrance and heroic attitude had very little effect, for the loud talk went on, and chiefly by ejaculation, imprecation, and self-accusation published the whole statement of the case; understanding which, Uncle John added his voice also:

"Good Gord A'mighty! Wh-wh-what's dat you say? Dey-dey-dey Yankees, an' you Cornfedrits? Well, sir, an' are you Marse Beau—you wid your arm hurted? Go 'long! You can't fool me; Marse Beau done had more sense en dat. My Gord! an' dey wuz Yankees? You better cuss—cussin's about all you kin do now. Course de boat's gone. You'll never ketch up wid 'em in Gord's world now. Don't come along arter me about it? 'Tain't my fault. How wuz I to know? You wuz Yankees enough for me. I declar', Marse Beau, you ought to be ashamed o' yourself! You wanted to l'arn dem a lesson! I reckon dey l'arnt you one! You didn't mean 'em no harm! Humph! dey've cut dey eye-teeth, dey have! Lord! Marse Beau, I thought you done knowed us better. Did you really think we wuz a-gwine to let a passel o' Yankees take us away off our own plantation? You must done forgot us. We jes cleaned out de house for 'em, we did—clo'es, food, tobacco, rum. De young ladies 'ain't lef' a mossel for Marse John. An'—an'—an' 'fore de good Gord, my gun! Done tuck my gun away wid "em! Wh-wh-wh-what you mean by such doin's? L-l-look here, Marse Beau, I don't like dat, nohow! Wh-wh-what! you tuck my gun and gin it to de Yankees? Dat's my gun! I done had dat gun twenty-five year an' more! Dog-gone! Yes, sir, I'll cuss—I'll cuss ef I wants to! I 'ain't got no use for gorillas, nohow! Lem me 'lone, I tell you! lem me 'lone! Marse John he'll get de law o' dat! Who's 'sponsible? Dat's all I want to know—who's 'sponsible? Ef-ef-ef-ef— No, sir; dar ain't nary boat on de place, nor hereabouts. Yes, sir; you kin cross de swamp ef you kin find de way. No, sir—no, sir; dar ain't no one to show you. I ain't gwine to leave de young ladies twell Marse John he comes back. Yes, I reckon you kin git to de cut-off by to-morrow mornin', ef you ain't shot on de way for Yankees, an' ef your company is fool enough to wait for you. No, sir, I don't know nothin' 'bout nothin'; you better wait an' arsk Marse John…My Gord! I'm obleeged to laugh; I can't help it. Dem fool nigger wimen a-sittin' on de brink o' de byer, dey clo'es tied up in de bedquilts, an' de shotes an' de pullits all kilt, a-waitin' for freedom! I lay de'll git freedom enough to-night when de boys come home. Dey git white gentlemen to marry 'em! Dey'll git five hundred apiece. Marse Beau, Gord 'll punish you for dis—He surely will. I done tole Marse John long time ago he oughter sell dat brazen nigger Dead-arm Harriet, an' git shet o' her. Lord! Lord! Lord! Now you done gone to cussin' an' swearin' agin. Don't go tearin' off your jackets an' flingin' em at me. We don't want 'em; we buys our clo'es—what we don't make. Yes, Marse John 'll be comin' along pretty soon now. What's your hurry, Marse Beau? Well, so long, ef you won't stay. He ain't got much use for gorillas neither, Marse John hain't."

The young officer wrote a few hasty words on a leaf torn from the pretty Russia-leather note-book, and handed it to the old darky. "For your Marse John."

"For Marse John—yes, sir; I'll gin hit to him soon 's he comes in."

They had dejectedly commenced their weary tramp up the bayou; he called him back, and lowered his voice confidentially: "Marse Beau, when you captured dat transport and stole all dem fixin's an' finery, you didn't see no good chawin' tobacco layin' round loose, did you? Thanky! thanky, child! Now I looks good at you, you ain't so much changed sence de times Marse John used to wallop you for your tricks. Well, good-bye, Marse Beau."

On the leaf were scrawled the words:

"All's up! Lee has surrendered.—BEAU."

(1892)

AUGUSTUS BALDWIN LONGSTREET

The Fight

In the younger days of the Republic there lived in the county of——two men, who were admitted on all hands to be the very *best men* in the county; which, in the Georgia vocabulary, means they could flog any other two men in the county. Each, through many a hard-fought battle, had acquired the mastery of his own battalion; but they lived on opposite sides of the Courthouse, and in different battalions: consequently, they were but seldom thrown together. When they met, however, they were always very friendly; indeed, at their first interview, they seemed to conceive a wonderful attachment to each other, which rather increased than diminished as they became better acquainted; so that, but for the circumstance which I am about to mention, the question, which had been a thousand times asked, "Which is the best man, Billy Stallions (Stallings) or Bob Durham?" would probably never have been answered.

Billy ruled the upper battalion, and Bob the lower. The former measured six feet and an inch in his stockings, and, without a single pound of cumbrous flesh about him, weighed a hundred and eighty. The latter was an inch shorter than his rival, and ten pounds lighter; but he was much the most active of the two. In running and jumping he had but few equals in the county; and in wrestling, not one. In other respects they were nearly equal. Both were admirable specimens of human nature in its finest form. Billy's victories had generally been achieved by the tremendous power of his blows, one of which had often proved decisive of his battles; Bob's, by his adroitness in bringing his adversary to the ground. This advantage he had never failed to gain at the onset, and, when gained, he never failed to improve it to the defeat of his adversary. These points of difference have involved the reader in a doubt as to the probable issue of a contest between them. It was not so, however, with the two battalions. Neither had the least difficulty in determining the point by the most natural and irresistible deductions *a priori;* and though, by the same course of reasoning, they arrived at directly opposite conclusions, neither felt its confidence in the least shaken by this circumstance. The upper battalion swore "that Billy only wanted one lick at him to knock his heart, liver, and lights out of him; and if he got two at him, he'd knock him into a cocked hat." The lower battalion retorted, "that he wouldn't have time to double his fist before Bob would put his head where his feet ought to be; and that, by the time he hit the ground, the meat would fly off his face so quick, that people would think it was shook off by the fall." These disputes often led to the *argumentum ad hominem*, but with such equality of success on both sides as to leave the main question just where they found it. They usually ended, however, in the common way, with a bet; and many a quart of old Jamaica (whiskey had not then supplanted rum) were staked upon the issue. Still, greatly to the annoyance of the curious, Billy and Bob continued to be good friends.

Now there happened to reside in the county just alluded to a little fellow by the name of Ransy Sniffle: a sprout of Richmond, who, in his earlier days, had fed copiously upon red clay and blackberries. This diet had given to Ransy a complexion that a corpse would have disdained to own, and an abdominal rotundity that was quite unprepossessing. Long spells of the fever and ague, too, in Ransy's youth, had conspired with clay and blackberries to throw him quite out of the order of nature. His shoulders were fleshless and elevated; his head large and flat; his neck slim and translucent; and his arms, hands, fingers, and feet were lengthened out of all proportion to the rest of his frame. His joints were large and his limbs small; and as for flesh, he could not, with propriety, be said to have any. Those parts which nature usually supplies with the most of this article—the calves of the legs, for example—presented in him the appearance of so many well-drawn blisters. His height was just five feet nothing; and his average weight in blackberry season, ninety-five. I have been thus particular in describing him, for the purpose of showing what a great matter a little fire sometimes kindleth. There was nothing on this earth which delighted Ransy so much as a fight. He never seemed fairly alive except when he was witnessing, fomenting, or talking about a fight. Then, indeed, his deep-sunken gray eyes assumed something of a living fire, and his tongue acquired a volubility that bordered upon eloquence. Ransy had been kept for more than a year in the most torturing suspense as to the comparative manhood of Billy Stallings and Bob Durham. He had resorted to all his usual expedients to bring them in collision, and had entirely failed. He had faithfully reported to Bob all that had been said by the people in the upper battalion "agin him," and "he was sure Billy Stallings started it. He heard Billy say himself to Jim Brown, that he could whip him, *or any other man in his battalion;*" and this he told to Bob; adding, "Dod darn his soul, if he was a little bigger, if he'd let any man *put upon* his battalion in such a way." Bob replied, "If he (Stallings) thought so, he'd better come and try it." This Ransy carried to Billy, and delivered it with a spirit becoming his own dignity and the character of his battalion, and with a colouring well calculated to give it effect. These, and many other schemes which Ransy laid for the gratification of his curiosity, entirely failed of their object. Billy and Bob continued friends, and Ransy had begun to lapse into the most tantalizing and hopeless despair, when a circumstance occurred which led to a settlement of the long-disputed question.

It is said that a hundred gamecocks will live in perfect harmony together if you do not put a hen with them; and so it would have been with Billy and Bob, had there been no women in the world. But there were women in the world, and from them each of our heroes had taken to himself a wife. The good ladies were no strangers to the prowess of their husbands, and, strange as it may seem, they presumed a little upon it.

The two battalions had met at the Courthouse upon a regimental parade. The two champions were there, and their wives had accompanied them. Neither knew the other's lady, nor were the ladies known to each other. The exercises of the day were just over, when Mrs. Stallings and Mrs. Durham stepped simultaneously into the store of Zephaniah Atwater, from "down east."

"Have you any Turkey-red?" said Mrs. S.

"Have you any curtain calico?" said Mrs. D. at the same moment.

"Yes, ladies," said Mr. Atwater, "I have both."

"Then help me first," said Mrs. D., "for I'm in a hurry."

"I'm in as great a hurry as she is," said Mrs. S., "and I'll thank you to help me first."

"And, pray, who are you, madam?" continued the other.

"Your betters, madam," was the reply.

At this moment Billy Stallings stepped in. "Come," said he, "Nancy, let's be going; it's getting late."

"I'd a been gone half an hour ago," she replied, "if it hadn't a' been for that impudent huzzy."

"Who do you call an impudent huzzy, you nasty, good-for-nothing, snaggle-toothed gaub of fat, you?" returned Mrs. D.

"Look here, woman," said Billy, "have you got a husband here? If you have, I'll *lick* him till he learns to teach you better manners, you *sassy* heifer you." At this moment something was seen to rush out of the store as if ten thousand hornets were stinging it; crying, "Take care—let me go—don't hold me—where's Bob Durham?" It was Ransy Sniffle, who had been listening in breathless delight to all that had passed.

"Yonder's Bob, setting on the Courthouse steps," cried one. "What's the matter?"

"Don't talk to me!" said Ransy. "Bob Durham, you'd better go long yonder, and take care of your wife. They're playing h—l with her there, in Zeph Atwater's store. Dod etarnally darn my soul, if any man was to talk to my wife as Bill Stallions is talking to yours, if I wouldn't drive blue blazes through him in less than no time."

Bob sprang to the store in a minute, followed by a hundred friends; for the bully of a county never wants friends.

"Bill Stallions," said Bob, as he entered, "what have you been saying to my wife?"

"Is that your wife?" inquired Billy, obviously much surprised and a little disconcerted.

"Yes, she is, and no man shall abuse her, I don't care who he is."

"Well," rejoined Billy, "it an't worth while to go over it; I've said enough for a fight: and, if you'll step out, we'll settle it!"

"Billy," said Bob, "are you for a fair fight?"

"I am," said Billy. "I've heard much of your manhood, and I believe I'm a better man than you are. If you will go into a ring with me, we can soon settle the dispute."

"Choose your friends," said Bob; "make your ring, and I'll be in with mine as soon as you will."

They both stepped out, and began to strip very deliberately, each battalion gathering round its champion, except Ransy, who kept himself busy in a most honest endeavour to hear and see all that transpired in both groups at the same time. He ran from one to the other in quick succession; peeped here and listened there; talked to this one, then to that one, and then to himself; squatted under one's legs and another's arms; and, in the short interval between stripping and stepping into the ring, managed to get himself trod on by half of both battalions. But Ransy was not the only one interested upon this occasion; the most intense interest prevailed everywhere. Many were the conjectures, doubts, oaths, and imprecations uttered while the parties were preparing for the combat. All the knowing ones were consulted as to the issue, and they all agreed, to a man, in one of two opinions: either that Bob would flog Billy, or Billy would flog Bob. We must be permitted, however, to dwell for a moment upon the opinion of Squire Thomas Loggins; a man who, it was said, had never failed to predict the issue of a fight in all his life. Indeed, so unerring had he always proved in this regard, that it would have been counted the most obstinate infidelity to doubt for a moment after he had delivered himself. Squire Loggins was a man who said but little, but that little was always delivered with the most imposing solemnity of look and cadence. He always wore the aspect of profound thought, and you could not look at him without coming to the conclusion that he was elaborating truth from its most intricate combinations.

"Uncle Tommy," said Sam Reynolds, "you can tell us all about it if you will; how will the fight go?"

The question immediately drew an anxious group around the squire. He raised his teeth slowly from the head of his walking cane, on which they had been resting; pressed his lips closely and thoughtfully together; threw down his eyebrows, dropped his chin, raised his eyes to an angle of twenty-three degrees, paused about half a minute, and replied, "Sammy, watch Robert Durham close in the beginning of the fight; take care of William Stallions in the middle of it; and see who has the wind at the end." As he uttered the last member of the sentence, he looked slyly at Bob's friends, and winked very significantly; whereupon they rushed, with one accord, to tell Bob what Uncle Tommy had said. As they retired, the squire turned to Billy's friends, and said, with a smile, "Them boys think I mean that Bob will whip."

Here the other party kindled into joy, and hastened to inform Billy how Bob's friends had deceived themselves as to Uncle Tommy's opinion. In the mean time, the principals and seconds were busily employed in preparing themselves for the combat. The plan of attack and defence, the manner of improving the various turns of the conflict, "the best mode of saving wind," &c., &c., were all discussed and settled. At length Billy announced himself ready, and his crowd were seen moving to the centre of the Courthouse Square; he and his five seconds in the rear. At the same time, Bob's party moved to the same point, and in the same order. The ring was now formed, and for a moment the silence of death reigned through both battalions. It was soon interrupted, however, by the cry of "Clear the way!" from Billy's seconds; when the ring opened in the centre of the upper battallion (for the order of march had arranged the centre of the two battalions on opposite sides of the circle), and Billy stepped into the ring from the east, followed by his friends. He was stripped to the trousers, and exhibited an arm, breast, and shoulders of the most tremendous portent. His step was firm, daring, and martial; and as he bore his fine form a little in advance of his friends, an involuntary burst of triumph broke from his side of the ring; and, at the same moment, an uncontrollable thrill of awe ran along the whole curve of the lower battalion.

"Look at him!" was heard from his friends; "just look at him."

"Ben, how much you ask to stand before that man two seconds?"

"Pshaw, don't talk about it! Just thinkin' about it's broke three o' my ribs a'ready!"

"What's Bob Durham going to do when Billy let's that arm loose upon him?"

"God bless your soul, he'll think thunder and lightning a mint julep to it."

"Oh, look here, men, go take Bill Stallions out o' that ring, and bring in Phil Johnson's stud horse, so that Durham may have some chance! I don't want to see the man killed right away."

These and many other like expressions, interspersed thickly with oaths of the most modern coinage, were coming from all points of the upper battalion, while Bob was adjusting the girth of his pantaloons, which walking had discovered not to be exactly right. It was just fixed to his mind, his foes becoming a little noisy, and his friends a little uneasy at his delay, when Billy called out, with a smile of some meaning, "Where's the bully of the lower battalion? I'm getting tired of waiting."

"Here he is," said Bob, lighting, as it seemed, from the clouds into the ring, for he had actually bounded clear of the head of Ransy Sniffle into the circle. His descent was quite as imposing as Billy's entry, and excited the same feelings, but in opposite bosoms.

Voices of exultation now rose on his side.

"Where did he come from?"

"Why," said one of his seconds (all having just entered), "we were girting him up, about a hundred yards out yonder, when he heard Billy ask for the bully; and he fetched a leap over the Courthouse, and went out of sight; but I told them to come on, they'd find him here."

Here the lower battalion burst into a peal of laughter, mingled with a look of admiration, which seemed to denote their entire belief of what they had heard.

"Boys, widen the ring, so as to give him room to jump."

"Oh, my little flying wild-cat, hold him if you can! and, when you get him fast, hold lightning next."

"Ned, what do you think he's made of?"

"Steel springs and chicken-hawk, God bless you!"

"Gentlemen," said one of Bob's seconds, "I understand it is to be a fair fight; catch as catch can, rough and tumble: no man touch till one or the other halloos."

"That's the rule," was the reply from the other side.

"Are you ready?"

"We are ready."

"Then blaze away, my game cocks!"

At the word, Bob dashed at his antagonist at full speed; and Bill squared himself to receive him with one of his most fatal blows. Making his calculation, from Bob's velocity, of the time when he would come within striking distance, he let drive with tremendous force. But Bob's onset was obviously planned to avoid this blow; for, contrary to all expectations, he stopped short just out of arm's reach, and, before Billy could recover his balance, Bob had him "all under-hold." The next second, sure enough, "found Billy's head where his feet ought to be." How it was done no one could tell; but, as if by supernatural power, both Billy's feet were thrown full half his own height in the air, and he came down with a force that seemed to shake the earth. As he struck the ground, commingled shouts, screams, and yells burst from the lower battalion, loud enough to be heard for miles. "Hurra, my little hornet!" "Save him!" "Feed him!" "Give him the Durham physic till his stomach turns!" Billy was no sooner down than Bob was on him, and lending him awful blows about the face and breast. Billy made two efforts to rise by main strength, but failed. "Lord bless you, man, don't try to get up! *Lay* still and take it! you *bleege* to have it!"

Billy now turned his face suddenly to the ground, and rose upon his hands and knees. Bob jerked up both his hands and threw him on his face. He again recovered his late position, of which Bob endeavoured to deprive him as before; but, missing one arm, he failed, and Billy rose. But he had scarcely resumed his feet before they flew up as before, and he came again to the ground. "No fight, gentlemen!" cried Bob's friends; "the man can't stand up! Bouncing feet are bad things to fight in." His fall, however, was this time comparatively light; for, having thrown his right arm round Bob's neck, he carried his head down with him. This grasp, which was obstinately maintained, prevented Bob from getting on him, and they lay head to head, seeming, for a time, to do nothing. Presently they rose, as if by mutual consent; and, as they rose, a shout burst from both battalions. "Oh, my lark!" cried the east, "has he foxed you? Do you begin to feel him! He's only beginning to fight; he ain't got warm yet."

"Look yonder!" cried the west; "didn't I tell you so! He hit the ground so hard it jarred his nose off. Now ain't he a pretty man as he stands? He shall have my sister Sal just for his pretty looks. I want to get in the breed of them sort o' men, to drive ugly out of my kinfolks."

I looked, and saw that Bob had entirely lost his left ear, and large piece from his left cheek. His right eye was a little discoloured, and the blood flowed profusely from his wounds.

Bill presented a hideous spectacle. About a third of his nose, at the lower extremity, was bit off, and his face so swelled and bruised that it was difficult to discover in it anything of the human visage, much more the fine features which he carried into the ring.

They were up only long enough for me to make the foregoing discoveries, when down they went again, precisely as before. They no sooner touched the ground than Bill relinquished his hold upon Bob's neck. In this he seemed to all to have forfeited the only advantage which put him upon an equality with his adversary. But the movement was soon explained. Bill wanted this arm for other purposes than defence; and he had made arrangements whereby he knew that he could make it answer these purposes; for, when they rose again, he had the middle finger of Bob's left hand in his mouth. He was now secure from Bob's annoying trips; and he began to lend his adversary tremendous blows, every one of which was hailed by a shout from his friends. "Bullets!" "*Hoss*-kicking!" "Thunder!" "That'll do for his face; now feel his short ribs, Billy!"

I now considered the contest settled. I deemed it impossible for any human being to withstand for five seconds the loss of blood which issued from Bob's ear, cheek, nose, and finger, accompanied with such blows as he was receiving. Still he maintained the conflict, and gave blow for blow with considerable effect. But the blows of each became slower and weaker after the first three or four; and it became obvious that Bill wanted the room which Bob's finger occupied for breathing. He would therefore, probably, in a short time, have let it go, had not Bob anticipated his politeness by jerking away his hand, and making him a present of the finger. He now seized Bill again, and brought him to his knees, but he recovered. He again brought him to his knees, and he again recovered. A third effort, however, brought him down, and Bob on top of him. These efforts seemed to exhaust the little remaining strength of both; and they lay, Bill undermost and Bob across his breast, motionless, and panting for breath. After a short pause, Bob gathered his hand full of dirt and sand, and was in the act of grinding it in his adversary's eyes, when Bill cried "ENOUGH!" Language cannot describe the scene that followed; the shouts, oaths, frantic gestures, taunts, replies, and little fights, and therefore I shall not attempt it. The champions were borne off by their seconds and washed; when many a bleeding wound and ugly bruise was discovered on each which no eye had seen before.

Many had gathered round Bob, and were in various ways congratulating and applauding him, when a voice from the centre of the circle cried out, "Boys, hush and listen to me!" It proceeded from Squire Loggins, who had made his way to Bob's side, and had gathered his face up into one of its most flattering and intelligible expressions. All were obedient to the squire's command. "Gentlemen," continued he, with a most knowing smile, "is—Sammy—Reynolds—in—this—company—of—gentlemen?"

"Yes," said Sam, "here I am."

"Sammy," said the squire, winking to the company, and drawing the head of his cane to his mouth with an arch smile as he closed, "I—wish—you—to tell—cousin—Bobby—and—these—gentlemen here present—what—your—Uncle—Tommy—said—before—the—fight—began?"

"Oh! get away, Uncle Tom," said Sam, smiling (the squire winked), "you don't know nothing about *fighting*." (The squire winked again.) "All you know about it is how it'll begin, how it'll go on, how it'll end; that's all. Cousin Bob, when you going to fight again, just go to the old man, and let him tell you all about it. If he can't, don't ask nobody else nothing about it, I tell you."

The squire's foresight was complimented in many ways by the by-standers; and he retired, advising "the boys to be at peace, as fighting was a bad business."

Durham and Stallings kept their beds for several weeks, and did not meet again for two months. When they met, Billy stepped up to Bob and offered his hand, saying, "Bobby, you've *licked* me a fair fight; but you wouldn't have done it if I hadn't been in the wrong. I oughtn't to have treated your wife as I did; and I felt so through the whole fight; and it sort o' cowed me."

"Well, Billy," said Bob, "let's be friends. Once in the fight, when you had my finger in your mouth, and was pealing me in the face and breast, I was going to halloo; but I thought of Betsy, and knew the house would be too hot for me if I got whipped when fighting for her, after always whipping when I fought for myself."

"Now that's what I always love to see," said a by-stander. "It's true I brought about the fight, but I wouldn't have done it if it hadn't o' been on account of *Miss* (Mrs.) Durham. But dod etarnally darn my soul, if I ever could stand by and see any woman put upon, much less *Miss* Durham. If Bobby hadn't been there, I'd o' took it up myself, be darned if I wouldn't, even if I'd o' got whipped for it. But we're all friends now." The reader need hardly be told that this was Ransy Sniffle.

Thanks to the Christian religion, to schools, colleges, and benevolent associations, such scenes of barbarism and cruelty as that which I have been just describing are now of rare occurrence, though they may still be occasionally met with in some of the new counties. Wherever they prevail, they are a disgrace to that community. The peace-officers who countenance them deserve a place in the Penitentiary.

(1835)

THOMAS NELSON PAGE

Unc' Edinburg's Drowndin': A Plantation Echo

"Well, suh, dat's a fac—dat's what Marse George al'ays said. 'Tis hard to spile Christmas anyways."

The speaker was "Unc' Edinburg," the driver from Werrowcoke, where I was going to spend Christmas; the time was Christmas Eve, and the place the muddiest road in eastern Virginia—a measure which, I feel sure, will to those who have any experience establish its claim to distinction.

A half-hour before, he had met me at the station, the queerest-looking, raggedest old darky conceivable, brandishing a cedar-staffed whip of enormous proportions in one hand, and clutching a calico letter-bag with a twisted string in the other; and with the exception of a brief interval of temporary suspicion on his part, due to the unfortunate fact that my luggage consisted of only a hand-satchel instead of a trunk, we had been steadily progressing in mutual esteem.

"Dee's a boy standin' by my mules; I got de ker'idge heah for you," had been his first remark on my making myself known to him. "Mistis say as how you might bring a trunk."

I at once saw my danger, and muttered something about "a short visit," but this only made matters worse.

"Dee don' nobody nuver pay short visits dyah," he said, decisively, and I fell to other tactics.

"You couldn' spile Christmas den noways," he said, decisively, and I fell to other tactics.

"You couldn' spile Christmas den noways," he repeated, reflectingly, while his little mules trudged knee-deep through the mud. "Twuz Christmas den, sho' 'nough," he added, the fires of memory smouldering, and then, as they blazed into sudden flame, he asserted, positively: "Dese heah free-issue niggers don' know what Christmas is. Hog meat an' pop crackers don' meck Christmas. Hit tecks ole times to meck a sho-'nough, tyahin'-down Christmas. Gord! I's seen 'em! But de wuss Christmas I ever seen tunned out de best in de een," he added, with sudden warmth, "an' dat wuz de Christmas me an' Marse George an' Reveller all got drowned down at Braxton's Creek. You's hearn 'bout dat?"

As he was sitting beside me in solid flesh and blood, and looked as little ethereal in his old hat and patched clothes as an old oak stump would have done, and as Colonel Staunton had made a world-wide reputation when he led his regiment through the Chickahominy thickets against McClellan's intrenchments, I was forced to confess that I had never been so favored, but would like to hear about it now; and with a hitch of the lap blanket under his outside knee, and a supererogatory jerk of the reins, he began:

"Well, you know, Marse George was jes eighteen when he went to college. I went wid him, 'cause me an' him wuz de same age; I was born like on a Sat'day in de Christmas, an' he wuz born in de new year on a Chuesday, an' my mammy nussed us bofe at one breast. Dat's de reason maybe huccome we took so to one nurr. He sutney set a heap o' sto' by me; an' I 'ain' nuver see nobody yit wuz good to me as Marse George."

The old fellow, after a short reverie, went on:

"Well, we growed up togerr, jes as to say two stalks in one hill. We cotch ole hyahs togerr, an' we hunted 'possums togerr, an' 'coons. Lord! he wuz a climber! I 'member a fight he had one night up in de ve'y top o' a big poplar-tree wid a 'coon, whar he done gone up after, an' he flung he hat over he head; an' do' de varmint leetle mo' tyah him all to pieces, he fotch him down dat tree 'live; an' me an' him had him at Christmas. 'Coon meat mighty good when dee fat, you know?"

As this was a direct request for my judgment, I did not have the moral courage to raise an issue, although my views on the subject of 'coon meat are well known to my family, so I grunted something which I doubt not he took for assent, and he proceeded:

"Dee warn' nuttin he didn' lead de row in; he wuz de bes' swimmer I ever see, an' he handled a skiff same as a fish handle heself. An' I wuz wid him constant; wherever you see Marse George, dyah Edinburg sho, jes' like he shadow. So twuz, when he went to de university; 'twarn' nuttin would do but I got to go too. Marster he didn' teck much to de notion, but Marse George wouln' have it no urr way, an' co'se mistis she teck he side. So I went 'long as he body-servant to teck keer on him an' help meck him a gent'man. An' he wuz, too. From time he got dyah tell he come 'way he wuz de head man.

"Dee warn' but one man dyah didn' compliment him, an' dat wuz Mr. Darker. But he warn' nuttin! not dat he didn' come o' right good fambly—'cep' dee politics; but he wuz sutney pitted, jes like sometimes you see a weevly runty pig in a right good litter. Well, Mr. Darker he al'ays 'ginst Marse George; he hate me an' him bofe, an' he sutney act mischeevous todes us; 'cause he know he warn' as we all. De Stauntons dee wuz de populariest folks in Virginia; an' dee wuz high-larnt besides. So when Marse George run for de medal, an' wuz to meck he gret speech, Mr. Darker he speak 'ginst him. Dat's what Marse George whip him 'bout. 'Ain' nobody nuver told you 'bout dat?"

I again avowed my misfortune; and although it manifestly aroused new doubts, he worked it off on the mules, and once more took up his story:

"Well, you know, dee had been speakin' 'ginst one nurr ev'y Sat'dy night; an' ev'ybody knowed Marse George wuz de bes' speaker, but dee give him one mo' sho', an' dee was bofe gwine spread deeselves, an' dee wuz two urr gent'mens also gwine speak. An' dat night when Mr. Darker got up he meck sich a fine speech ev'ybody wuz s'prised; an' some on 'em say Mr. Darker done beat Marse George. But shuh! I know better'n dat; an' Marse George face look so curious; but, suh, when he riz I knowed der wuz somen gwine happen—I wuz leanin' in de winder. He jes step out in front an' throwed up he head like a horse wid a rank kyurb on him, an' den he begin; an' twuz jes like de river when hit gits out he bank. He swep' ev'ything. When he fust open he mouf I knowed twuz comin'; he face wuz pale, an' he wuds tremble like a fiddle-string, but he eyes wuz blazin', an' in a minute he wuz jes reshin'. He voice soun' like a bell; an' he jes wallered dat turr man, an' wared him out; an' when he set down dee all yelled an' hollered so you couldn' heah you' ears. Gent'mans, twuz royal!

"Den dee tuck de vote, an' Marse George got it munanimous, an' dee all hollered agin, all 'cep' a few o' Mr. Darker friends. An' Mr. Darker he wuz de second. An' den dee broke up. An' jes den Marse George walked thoo de crowd straight up to him, an' lookin' him right in de eyes, says to him, 'You stole dat speech you made to-night.' Well, suh, you ought to 'a hearn 'em; hit soun' like a mill-dam. You couldn' heah nuttin 'cep' roarin', an' you couldn' see nuttin 'cep' shovin'; but, big as he wuz, Marse George beat him; an' when dee pull him off, do' he face wuz mighty pale, he stan' out befo' 'em all, dem whar wuz 'ginst him, an' all, an' as straight as an arrow, an' say: 'Dat speech wuz written an' printed years ago by somebody or nurr in Congress, an' this man stole it; had he beat me only, I should not have said one word; but as he has beaten others, I shall show him up!' Gord, suh, he voice wuz clear as a game rooster. I sutney wuz proud on him.

"He did show him up, too, but Mr. Darker ain' wait to see it; he lef' dat night. An' Marse George he wuz de popularest gent'man at dat university. He could handle dem students dyah same as a man handle a hoe.

"Well, twuz de next Christmas we meet Miss Charlotte an' Nancy. Mr. Braxton invite we all to go down to spen' Christmas wid him at he home. An' sich a time as we had!

"We got dyah Christmas Eve night—dis very night—jes befo' supper, an' jes natchelly froze to death," he pursued, dealing in his wonted hyperbole, "an' we jes had time to git a apple toddy or two when supper was ready, an' wud come dat dee wuz waitin' in de hall. I had done fix Marse George up gorgeousome, I tell you; an' when he walked down dem stairs in dat swaller-tail coat, an' dem paten'-leather pumps on, dee warn nay one dyah could tetch him; he looked like he own 'em all. I jes rest my mind. I seen him when he shake hands wid 'em all roun', an' I say, 'Um-m-m! he got 'em.'

"But he ain' teck noticement o' none much tell Miss Charlotte come. She didn' live dyah, had jes come over de river dat evenin' from her home, 'bout ten miles off, to spen' Christmas like we all, an' she come down de stairs jes as Marse George finish shakin' hands. I seen he eye light on her as she come down de steps smilin', wid her dim blue dress trainin' behind her, an' her little blue foots peepin' out so pretty, an' holdin' a little hankcher, lookin' like a spider-web, in one hand, an' a gret blue fan in turr, spread out like a peacock tail, an' jes her roun' arms an' th'oat white, an' her gret dark eyes lightin' up her face. I say, 'Dayh 'tis!' an' when de ole Cun'l stan' aside an' interduce 'em, an' Marse George step for'ard an' meck he grand bow, an' she sort o' swing back an' gin her curtchy, wid her dress sort o' dammed up 'ginst her, an' her arms so white, an' her face sort o' sunsetty, I say, 'Yes, Lord! Edinburg, dyah you mistis.' Marse George look like he think she done come down right from de top o' de blue sky an' bring piece on it wid her. He ain' nuver took he eyes from her dat night. Dee glued to her, mun! an' she—well, do' she mighty rosy, an' look mighty unconsarned, she sutney ain' hender him. Hit look like kyarn nobody else tote dat fan an' pick up dat hankcher skuzin o' him; an' after supper, when dee all playin' blindman's-buff in de hall—I don' know how twuz—but do' she jes as nimble as a filly, an' her ankle jes as clean, an' she kin git up her dress an' dodge out de way o' ev'ybody else, somehow or nurr she kyarn help him ketchin' her to save her life; he always got her corndered; an' when dee'd git fur apart, dat ain' nuttin, dee jes as sure to come togerr agin as water is whar you done run you hand thoo. An' do' he kiss ev'ybody else under de mestletow, 'cause dee be sort o' cousins, he ain' nuver kiss her, nor nobody else nurr, 'cep' de ole Cun'l. I wuz standin' down at de een de hall wid de black folks, an' I notice it 'tic'lar, 'cause I done meck de 'quaintance o' Nancy; she wuz Miss Charlotte's maid; a mighty likely young gal she wuz den, an' jes as impident as a fly. She see it too, do' she ain' 'low it.

"Fust thing I know I seen a mighty likely light-skinned gal standin' dyah by me, wid her hyah mos' straight as white folks, an' a mighty good frock on, an' a clean apron, an' her hand mos' like a lady, only it brown, an' she keep on 'vidin her eyes twix me an' Miss Charlotte; when I watchin' Miss Charlotte she watchin' me, an' when I steal my eye roun' on her she noticin' Miss Charlotte; an' presney I sort o' sidle 'longside her, an' I say, 'Lady, you mighty sprightly tonight.' An' she say she 'bleeged to be sprightly, her mistis look so good; an' I ax her which one twuz, an' she tell me, 'Dat queen one over dyah,' an' I tell her dee's a king dyah too, she got her eye set for; an' when I say her mistis tryin' to set her cap for Marse George, she fly up, an' say she an' her mistis don' have to set dee cap for nobody; *dee* got to set dee cap an' all dee clo'es for dem, an' den dee ain' gwine cotch 'em, 'cause dee ain' studyin' 'bout no up-country folks whar dee ain' nobody know nuttin 'bout.

"Well, dat oudaciousness so aggrivate me, I lite into dat nigger right dyah. I tell her she ain' been no whar 'tall ef she don' know we all; dat we wuz de bes' o' quality, de ve'y top de pot; an' den I tell her 'bout how gret we wuz; how de ker'idges wuz al'ays hitched up night an' day, an' niggers jes thick as weeds; an' how Unc' Torm he wared he swaller-tail ev'y day when he wait on de table; an' Marse George he won' wyah a coat mo'n once or twice anyways, to save you life. Oh! I sutney 'stonish dat nigger, 'cause I wuz teckin up for de fambly, an' I meck out like dee use gold up home like urr folks use wood, an' sow silver like urr folks sow wheat; an' when I got thoo dee wuz all on 'em listenin', an' she 'lowed dat Marse George he were ve'y good, sho 'nough, ef twarn for he nigger; but I ain' tarrifyin' myself none 'bout dat, 'cause I know she jes projickin, an' she couldn' help bein' impident ef you wuz to whup de frock off her back.

"Jes den dee struck up de dance. Dee had wheel de pianer out in de hall, an' somebody say Jack Forester had come 'cross de river, an' all on 'em say dee mus' git Jack; an' presney he come in wid he fiddle, grinnin' an' scrapin', 'cause he wuz a notable fiddler, do' I don' think he wuz equal to we all's Tubal, an' I know he couldn' tetch Marse George, 'cause Marse George wuz a natchel fiddler, jes like 'coons is natchel pacers, an' mules an womens is natchel kickers. Howsomever, he sutney jucked a jig sweet, an' when he shake dat bow you couldn' help you foot switchin' a leetle—not ef you wuz a member of de chutch. He wuz a mighty sinful man, Jack wuz, an' dat fiddle had done drawed many souls to torment.

"Well, in a minute dee wuz all flyin', an' Jack he wuz rockin' like boat rockin' on de water, an' he face right shiny, an' he teef look like ear o' corn he got in he mouf, an' he big foot set 'way out keepin' time, an' Marse George he wuz in de lead row dyah too; ev'y chance he git he tunned Miss Charlotte—'petchel motion, right hand across, an' cauliflower, an' croquette—dee croquette plenty o' urrs, but I notice dee ain' nuver fail to tun one nurr, an' ev'y tun he gin she wrappin' de chain roun' him; once when dee wuz 'prominadin-all' down we all's een o' de hall, as he tunned her somebody step on her dress an' to' it. I heah de screech o' de silk, an' Nancy say, 'O Lord!' den she say, 'Nem mine! now I'll git it!' an' dee stop for a minute for Marse George to pin it up, while turrers went on, an' Marse George wuz down on he knee, an' she look down on him mighty sweet out her eyes, an' say, 'Hit don' meck no difference,' an' he glance up an' cotch her eye, an', jes dout a wud, he tyah a gret piece right out de silk an' slipt it in he bosom, an' when he got up, he say, right low, lookin' in her eyes right deep, 'I gwine wyah dis at my weddin';' an' she jes look sweet as candy; an' ef Nancy ever wyah dat frock I ain' see it.

"Den presney dee wuz talkin' 'bout stoppin'. De ole Cun'l say hit time to have prars, an' dee wuz beggin' him to wait a leetle while; an' Jack Forester lay he fiddle down nigh Marse George, an' he picked 't up an' drawed de bow 'cross it jes to try it, an' den jes projeckin' he struck dat chune 'bout 'You'll ermember me.' He hadn' mo'n tetch de string when you could heah a pin drop. Marse George he warn noticin', an' he jes lay he face on de fiddle, wid he eyes sort o' half shet, an' drawed her out like he'd do some nights at home in de moonlight on de gret porch, tell on a sudden he looked up an' cotch Miss Charlotte eye leanin' for'ards so earnest, an' all on 'em list'nin', an' he stopt, an' dee all clapt dee hands, an' he sudney drapt into a jig. Jack Forester ain' had to play no mo' dat night; even de ole Cun'l ketched de fever, an' he stept out in de flo', in he long-tail coat an' high collar, an' knocked 'em off de 'Snow-bud on de Ash-bank,' an' 'Chicken in de Bread-tray,' right natchel. Oh, he could jes plank 'em down!

"Oh, dat wuz a Christmas like you been read 'bout! An' twuz hard to tell which gittin cotch most, Marse George or me, 'cause dat nigger she jes as confusin' as Miss Charlotte. An' she sutney wuz sp'ilt dem days; ev'y nigger on dat place got he eye on her, an' she jes as oudacious an' aggrivatin as jes womens kin be.

"Dees monsus 'ceivin' critters, womens is, jes as onreliable as de hind-leg of a mule; a man got to watch 'em all de time; you kyarn break 'em like you kin horses.

"Now dat off mule dyah" (indicating, by a lazy but not light lash of his whip the one selected for his illustration), "dee ain' no countin' on her at all; she go 'long all day, or maybe a week, jes dat easy an' sociable, an' fust thing you know you ain' know nuttin, she done knock you brains out; dee ain' no 'pendence to be placed in 'em 'tall, suh; she jes as sweet as a kiss one minute, an' next time she come out de house she got her head up in de air, an' her ears backed, an' goin' 'long switchin' herself like I ain' good 'nough for her to walk on.

"'Fox-huntin's?' oh, yes, suh, ev'y day mos'; an' when Marse George didn' git de tail, twuz 'cause twuz a bob-tail fox—you heah me! He play de fiddle for he pastime, but he fotched up in de saddle—dat he cradle!

"De fust day dee went out I heah Nancy quoilin 'bout de tail layin' on Miss Charlotte dressin'-table gittin' hyahs over ey'ything.

"One day de ladies went out too, Miss Charlotte 'mongst 'em, on Miss Lucy gray myah Switchity, an' Marse George he rid Mr. Braxton's chestnut Willful.

"Well, suh, he stick so close to dat gray myah, he leetle mo' los' dat fox; but, Lord! he know what he 'bout—he monsus 'ceivin' 'bout dat!—he know de way de fox gwine jes as well as he know heself; an' all de time he leadin' Miss Charlotte whar she kin heah de music, but he watchin' him too, jes as narrow as a ole hound. So, when de fox tun de head o' de creek, Marse George had Miss Charlotte on de aidge o' de flat, an' he de fust man see de fox tun down on turr side wid de hounds right rank after him. Dat sort o' set him back, 'cause by rights de fox ought to 'a double an' come back dis side; he kyarn git out dat way, an' two or three gent'mens dee had see it too, an' wuz jes layin' de horses to de groun' to git roun' fust, 'cause de creek wuz heap too wide to jump, an' wuz 'way over you head, an' hit cold as Christmas, sho 'nough; well, suh, when dee tunned, Mr. Clarke he wuz in de lead (he wuz ridin' for Miss Charlotte too), an' hit fyah set Marse George on fire; he ain' said but one wud, 'Wait,' an' jes set de chestnut's head straight for de creek, whar de fox comin' wid he tail up on he back, an' de dogs ravlin mos' on him.

"De ladies screamed, an' some de gent'mens hollered for him to come back, but he ain' mind; he went 'cross dat flat like a wild-duck; an' when he retch de water he horse try to flinch, but dat hand on de bridle, an' dem rowels in he side, an' he 'bleeged to teck it.

"Lord! suh, sich a screech as dee set up! But he wuz swimmin' for life, an' he wuz up de bank an' in de middle o' de dogs time dee tetched ole Gray Jacket; an' when Mr. Clarke got dyah Marse George wuz stan'in' holdin' up de tail for Miss Charlotte to see, turrer side de creek, an' de hounds wuz wallerin' all over de body, an' I don' think Mr. Clarke done got up wid 'em yit.

"He cotch de fox, an' he cotch some'n' else besides, in my 'pinion, 'cause when de ladies went upstairs dat night Miss Charlotte had to wait on de steps for a glass o' water, an' couldn' nobody git it but Marse George; an' den when she tell him goodnight over de banisters, he couldn' say it good enough; he got to kiss her hand; an' she ain' do nuttin but jes peep upstairs ef anybody dyah lookin'; an' when I come thoo de do' she juck her hand 'way an' ran upstairs jes as farst as she could. Marse George look at me sort o' laughin', an' say: 'Confound you! Nancy couldn' been very good to you.' An' I say, 'She le' me squench my thirst kissin' her hand'; an' he sort o' laugh an' tell me to keep my mouf shet.

"But dat ain' de on'y time I come on 'em. Dee al'ays gittin' corndered; an' de evenin' befo' we come 'way I wuz gwine in thoo de conservity, an' dyah dee wuz sort o' hide 'way. Miss Charlotte she wuz settin' down, an' Marse George he wuz leanin' over her, got her hand to he face, talkin' right low an' lookin' right sweet, an' she ain' say nuttin; an' presney he drapt on one knee by her, an' slip he arm round her, an' try to look in her eyes, an' she so 'shamed to look at him she got to hide her face on he shoulder, an' I slipt out.

"We come 'way next mornin'. When marster heah 'bout it he didn' teck to de notion at all, 'cause her pa—dat is, he warn' her own pa, 'cause he had married her ma when she wuz a widder after Miss Charlotte pa died, an' he politics warn' same as ourn. 'Why, you kin never stand him, suh,' he said to Marse George. 'We won't mix any mo'n fire and water; you ought to have found that out at college; dat fellow Darker is his son.'

"Marse George he say he know dat; but he on'y de step-brurr of de young lady, an' ain' got a drap o' her blood in he veins, an' he didn' know it when he meet her, an' anyhow hit wouldn' meck any diffence; an' when de mistis see how sot Marse George is on it she teck he side, an' dat fix it; 'cause when ole mistis warn marster to do a thing, hit jes good as done. I don' keer how much he rar roun' an' say he ain' gwine do it, you jes well go 'long an' put on you hat; you gwine see him presney doin' it jes peaceable as a lamb. She tun him jes like she got bline-bridle on him, an' he ain' nuver know it.

"So she got him jes straight as a string. An' when de time come for Marse George to go, marster he mo' consarned 'bout it 'n Marse George; he ain' say nuttin 'bout it befo', but now he walkin' roun' an' roun' axin mistis mo' questions 'bout he cloes an' he horse an' all; an' dat mornin' he gi' him he two Sunday razors, an' gi' me a pyah o' boots an' a beaver hat, 'cause I wuz gwine wid him to kyar he portmanteau, an' git he shavin' water, sence marster say ef he wuz gwine marry a Locofoco, he at least must go like a gent'man; an' me an' Marse George had done settle it 'twixt us, 'cause we al'ays set bofe we traps on de same hyah parf.

"Well, we got 'em, an' when I ax dat gal out on de wood-pile dat night, she say bein' as her mistis gwine own me, an' we bofe got to be in de same estate, she reckon she ain' nuver gwine to be able to git shet o' me; an' den I clamp her. Oh, she wuz a beauty!"

A gesture and guffaw completed the recital of his conquest.

"Yes, suh, we got 'em sho!" he said, presently. "Dee couldn' persist us; we crowd 'em into de fence an' run 'em off dee foots.

"Den come de 'gagement; an' ev'ything wuz smooth as silk. Marse George an' me wuz ridin' over dyah constant, on'y we nuver did git over bein' skeered when we wuz ridin' up dat turpentine road facin' all dem winders. Hit 'pear like ev'ybody in de wull 'mos' wuz lookin' at us.

"One evenin' Marse George say, 'Edinburg, d'you ever see as many winders p'intin' one way in you' life? When I git a house' he say, 'I gwine have all de winders lookin' turr way.'

"But dat evenin', when I see Miss Charlotte come walkin' out de gret parlor wid her hyah sort o' rumpled over her face, an' some yaller roses on her bres, an' her gret eyes so soft an' sweet, an' Marse George walkin' 'long hinst her, so peaceable, like she got chain roun' him, I say, 'Winders ain' nuttin.'

"Oh, twuz jes like holiday all de time! An' den Miss Charlotte come over to see mistis, an' of co'se she bring her maid wid her, 'cause she 'bleeged to have her maid, you know, an' dat wuz de bes' of all.

"Dat evenin', 'bout sunset, dee come drivin' up in de big ker'idge, wid dee gret hyah trunk stropped on de seat behind, an' Nancy she settin' by Billy, an' Marse George settin' inside by he rose-bud, 'cause he had done gone down to bring her up; an' marster he done been drest in he blue coat an' yallow westket ever sence dinner, an' walkin' roun', watchin' up de road all de time, an' tellin' de mistis he reckon dee ain' comin', an' ole mistis she try to pacify him, an' she come out presney drest, an' rustlin' in her stiff black silk an' all, an' when de ker'idge come in sight, ev'ybody wuz runnin'; an' when dee draw up to de do', Marse George he help her out an' in'duce her to marster an' ole mistis; an' marster he start to meck her a gret bow, an' she jes put up her mouf like a little gal to be kissed, an' dat got him. An' mistis teck her right in her arms an' kiss her twice, an' de servants dee wuz all peepin' an' grinnin'.

"Ev'ywhar you tun you see a nigger teef, 'cause dee all warn see de young mistis whar good 'nough for Marse George.

"Dee ain' gwine be married tell de next fall, 'count o' Miss Charlotte bein' so young; but she jes good as b'longst to we all now; an' ole marster an' mistis dee jes as much in love wid her as Marse George. Hi! dee warn pull de house down an' buil' it over for her! An' ev'y han' on de place he peepin' to try to git a look at he young mistis whar he gwine b'longst to. One evenin' dee all on 'em come roun' de porch an' send for Marse George, an' when he come out, Charley Brown (he al'ays de speaker, 'cause he got so much mouf, kin talk pretty as white folks), he say dee warn interduce to de young mistis, an' pay dee bespects to her; an' presney Marse George lead her out on de porch laughin' at her, wid her face jes rosy as a wine-sap apple, an' she meck 'em a beautiful bow, an' speak to 'em ev'y one, Marse George namin' de names; an' Charley Brown he meck her a pretty speech, an' tell her we mighty proud to own her; an' one o' dem impident gals ax her to gin her dat white frock when she git married; an' when she say, 'Well, what am I goin' weah?' Sally say, 'Lord, honey, Marse George gwine dress you in pure gol'!' an' she look up at him wid sparks flashin' out her eyes, while he look like dat ain' good 'nough for her. An' so twuz, when she went 'way, Sally Marshall got dat frock, an' proud on it I tell you.

"Oh yes; he sutney mindin' her tender. Hi! when she go to ride in evenin' wid him, de ain' no horse-block good 'nough for her! Marse George got to have her step in he hand; an' when dee out walkin' he got de umbreller holdin' 't over her all de time, he so feared de sun 'll kiss her; an' dee walk so slow down dem walks in de shade you got to sight 'em by a tree to tell ef dee movin' 'tall. She use' to look like she used to it too, I tell you, 'cause she wuz quality, one de white-skinned ones; an' she'd set in dem big cheers, wid her little foots on de cricket whar Marse George al'ays set for her, he so feared dee'd tetch de groun', jes like she on her throne; an' ole marster he'd watch her 'mos' edmirin as Marse George; an' when she went 'way hit sutney was lonesome. Hit look like daylight gone wid her. I don' know which I miss mos', Miss Charlotte or Nancy.

"Den Marse George was 'lected to de Legislature, an' ole Jedge Darker run for de Senator, an' Marse George vote gin him an' beat him. An' dat commence de fuss; an' den dat man gi' me de whuppin, an' dat breck 'tup an' breck he heart.

"You see, after Marse George wuz 'lected ('lections wuz 'lections dem days; dee warn' no bait-gode 'lections, wid ev'y sort o' worms squirmin' up 'ginst one nurr, wid piece o' paper d' ain' know what on, drappin' in a chink; didn' nuttin but gent'mens vote den, an' dee took dee dram, an' vote out loud, like gent'mens)—well, arter Marse George wuz 'lected, de parties wuz jes as even balanced as stilyuds, an' wen dee ax Marse Geroge who wuz to be de Senator, he vote for de Whig, 'ginst de ole jedge, an' dat beat him, of co'se. An' dee ain' got sense to know he 'bleeged to vote wid he politics. Dat he sprinciple; he kyarn vote for Locofoco, I don' keer ef he is Miss Charlotte pa, much less her step-pa. Of co'se de ole jedge ain' speak to him arter dat, nur is Marse George ax him to. But who dat gwine s'pose woman-folks got to put dee mouf in too? Miss Charlotte she write Marse George a letter dat pester him mightily; he set up all night answerin' dat letter, an' he mighty solemn, I tell you. An' I wuz gittin' right grewjousome myself, 'cause I studyin' 'bout dat gal down dyah whar I done gi' my wud to, an' when dee ain' no letters come torectly hit hard to tell which one de anxiouser, me or Marse George. Den presney I so 'straughted 'long o' it I ax Aunt Haly 'bouten it; she know all sich things, 'cause she 'mos' a hundred years ole, an' seed evil sperits, an' got skoripins up her chimney, an' knowed cunjure; an' she ax me what wuz de signication, an' I tell her I ain' able nuther to eat nor to sleep, an' dat gal come foolin' 'long me when I sleep jes as natchel as ef I see her sho 'nough. An' she way I done conjured; dat de gal done tricked me.

"Oh, Gord! dat skeered me!

"You white folks, marster, don' b'lieve nuttin like dat; y'all got too much sense, 'cause y' all kin read; but niggers dee ain' know no better, an' I sutney wuz skeered, 'cause Aunt Haly say my coffin done seasoned, de planks up de chimney.

"Well, I got so bad Marse George ax me 'bout it, an' he sort o' laugh an' sort o' cuss, an' he tell Aunty Haly ef she don' stop dat foolishness skeerin' me he'll sell her an' teah her ole skoripin house down. Well, co'se he jes talkin' an he ax me next day how'd I like to go' an' see my sweetheart. Gord! suh, I got well torectly. So I set off next evenin', feelin' jes big as ole marster, wid my pass in my pocket, which I warn' to show nobody 'douten I 'bleeged to, 'cause Marse George didn' warn nobody to know he le' me go. An' den, dat rascallion teck de shut off my back. But ef Marse George didn' pay him de wuth o' it!

"I done git 'long so good, too.

"When Nancy see me she sutney was 'stonished. She come roun' de cornder in de back yard whar I settin' in Nat's do' (he wuz de gardener) wid her hyah all done ontwist, an' breshed out might fine, an' a clean ap'on wid fringe on it, meckin' out she so s'prised to see me (whar wuz all a lie, 'cause some on 'em done notify her I dyah), an' she say, 'Hi! what dis black nigger doin' heah?'

"An' I say, 'Who you callin' nigger, you impident kercumber-faced thing you?' Den we shake hands, an' I tell her Marse George done set me free—dat I done buy myself; dat's de lie I done lay off to tell her.

"An' when I tole her dat, she bust out laughin', an' say, well, I better go 'long 'way, den, dat she don' warn no free nigger to be comp'ny for her. Dat sort o' set me back, an' I tell her she kickin' fo' she spurred, dat I ain' got her in my mine; I got a nurr gal at home whar grievin' 'bout me dat ve'y minute. An' after I tell her all sich lies as dat, presney she ax me ain' I hongry; an' ef dat nigger didn't git her mammy to gi' me de bes' supter! Umm-m! I kin 'mos' tas'e it now. Wheat bread off de table, and 'zerves, an' fat bacon, tell I couldn' 'a put a nurr moufful nowhar sep'n' I'd teck my hat. Dat night I tote Nancy water for her, an' I tell her all 'bout ev'ything, an' she jes sweet as honey. Next mornin', do', she done sort o' tunned some, an' ain' so sweet. You know how milk gits sort o' bonny-clabberish? An' when she see me she 'gin to 'buse me— say I jes tryin' to fool her, an' all de time got nurr wife at home, or gittin' ready to git one, for all she know, an' she ain' know wherr Marse George an' jes 'ceivin' as I is; an' nem mine, she got plenty warn marry her; an' as to Miss Charlotte, she got de whole wull; Mr. Darker he ain' got nobody in he way now, dat he deah all de time, an ain' gwine West no mo'. Well, dat aggrivate me so I tell her ef she say dat 'bout Marse George I gwine knock her; an' wid dat she got so oudacious I meck out I gwine 'way, an' lef' her, an' went up todes de barn; an' up dyah, fust thing I know, I come across dat ar man Mr. Darker. Soon as he see me he begin to cuss me, an' he ax me what I doin' on dat land, an' I tell him, 'Nuttin'.' An' he say, well, he gwine to gi' me some'n; he gwine teach me to come prowlin' round gent'men's houses. An' he meck me go in de barn an' teck off my shut, an' he beat me wid he whup tell de blood run out my back. He sutney did beat me scandalous 'cause he done hate me an' Marse George ever since we wuz at college togurr. An' den he say: 'Now you git right off dis land. Ef either you or your marster ever put you foot on it, you'll git de same thing agin.' An' I tell you, Edinburg he come 'way, 'cause he sutney had worry me. I ain' stop to see Nancy or nobody; I jes come 'long, shakin' de dust, I tell you. An' as I come 'long de road I pass Miss Charlotte walkin' on de lawn by herself, an' she call me: 'Why, hi! ain' dat Edinburg?'

"She look so sweet, an' her voice soun' so cool, I say, 'Yes'm; how you do, missis?' An' she say, she ve'y well, an' how I been, an' whar I gwine? I tell her I ain' feelin' so well, dat I gwine home. 'Hi!' she say, 'is anybody treat you bad?' An' I tell her, 'Yes'm.' An' she say, 'Oh! Nancy don' mean nuttin by dat; dat you mus'n mine what womens say an'do, 'cause dee feel sorry for it next minute; an' sometimes dee kyarn help it, or maybe hit you fault; an', anyhow, you ought to be willin' to overlook it; an' I better go back an' wait till to-morrow—ef—ef I ain' 'bleeged to git home to-day.'

"She got mighty mixed up in de een part o' dat, an' she looked mighty anxious 'bout me an' Nancy; an' I tell her, 'Nor'm, I 'bleeged to git home.'

"Well, when I got home Marse George he warn know all dat gwine on; but I mighty sick—dat man done beat me so; an' he ax me what de marter, an' I upped an' tell him.

"Gord! I nuver see a man in sich a rage. He call me in de office an' meck me teck off my shut, an' he fyah bust out cryin'. He walked up an' down dat office like a caged lion. Ef he had got he hand on Mr. Darker den, he'd a kilt him, sho'!

"He wuz most 'stracted. I don' know what he'd been ef I'd tell him what Nancy tell me. He call for Peter to git he horse torectly, an' he tell me to go an' git som'n from mammy to put on my back, an' to go to bed torectly, an' not to say nuttin to nobody, but to tell he pa he'd be away for two days, maybe; an' den he got on Reveller an' galloped 'way hard as he could wid he jaw set farst, an' he heaviest whip clamped in he hand. Gord! I wuz most hopin' he wouldn' meet dat man, 'cause I feared ef he did he'd kill him; an' he would, sho, ef he had meet him right den; dee say he leetle mo' did when he fine him next day, an' he had done been ridin' den all night; he cotch him at a sto' on de road, an' dee say he leetle mo' cut him all to pieces; he drawed a weepin on him, but Marse George wrench it out he hand an' flung it over de fence; an' when dee got him 'way he had weared he whup out on him; an' he got dem whelps on him now, ef he ain' dead. Yes, suh, he ain' let nobody else do dat he ain' do heself, sho!

"Dat done de business!

"He sont Marse George a challenge, but Marse George sont him wud he'll cowhide him agin ef he ever heah any mo' from him, an' he ain't. Dat perrify him, so he shet he mouf. Den come he ring an' all he pictures an' things back—a gret box on 'em, and not a wud wid 'em. Marse George, I think he know'd dee wuz comin', but dat ain' keep it from huttin' him, 'cause he done been a'gaged to Miss Charlotte, and' got he mine riveted to her; an' do' befo' dat dee had stop writin', an' a riff done git 'twixt 'em, he ain' satisfied in he mine dat she ain't gwine 'pologizee—I know by Nancy; but now he got de confirmation dat he done for good, an' dat de gret gulf fixed 'twix him an' Abraham bosom. An', Gord, suh, twuz torment, sho' 'nough! He ain' say nuttin 'bout it, but I see de light done pass from him, an' de darkness done wrap him up in it. In a leetle while you wouldn' 'a knowed him.

"Den ole mistis died.

"B'lieve me, ole marster he 'most much hut by Miss Charlotte as Marse George. He meck a 'tempt to buy Nancy for me, so I find out arterward, an' write Jedge Darker he'll pay him anything he'll ax for her, but he letter wuz sont back 'dout any answer. He sutney was mad 'bout it—he say he'd horsewhip him as Marse George did dat urr young puppy, but ole mistis wouldn' let him do nuttin, and den he grieve heself to death. You see he mighty ole, anyways. He nuver got over ole mistis death. She had been failin' a long time, an' he ain' tarry long 'hinst her; hit sort o' like breckin up a holler—de ole 'coon goes 'way soon arter dat; an' marster nuver could pin he own collar or buckle he own stock—mistis she al'ays do dat; an' do' Marse George do de bes' he kin, an' mighty willin', he kyarn handle pin like a woman; he hand tremble like a p'inter dog; an' anyways he ain' ole mistis. So ole marster foller her dat next fall, when dee wuz gittin in de corn, an' Marse George he ain' got nobody in de wull left; he all alone in dat gret house, an' I wonder sometimes he ain' die too, he sutney was fond o' ole marster.

"When ole mistis wuz dyin', she tell him to be good to ole marster, an' patient wid him, 'cause he sutney wuz fond o' ole marster. When ole mistis wuz dyin' she tell him to be good to ole marster an' patient wid him 'cause he ain' got nobody but him now (ole marster he had jes step out de room to cry); an' Marse George he lean over her an' kiss her an' promise her faithful he would. An' he sutney wuz tender wid him as a woman; an' when ole marster die he set by him an' hol' his hand an' kiss him sorf, like he was ole mistis.

"But, Gord! twuz lonesome arter dat, an' Marse George eyes look wistful, like he al'ays lookin' far 'way; an' Aunt Haly say he see harnts whar walk 'bout in de gret house. She say dee walk dyah constant of nights sence ole marster done alterate de rooms from what dee wuz when he gran'pa buil' 'em, an' dat dee huntin' for dee ole chambers an' kyarn git no rest 'cause dee kyarn fine 'em. I don't know how dat wuz. I know Marse George *he* used to walk about heself mightily of nights. All night long, all night long, I'd heah him tell de chickens crowin' dee second crow, an' some mornin's I'd go dyah an' he ain' even rumple de bed. I thought sho he wuz gwine die, but I suppose he done 'arn he days to be long in de land, an' dat save him. But hit sutney wuz lonesome, an' he nuver went off the plantation, an' he got older an' older, tell we all thought he wuz gwine die.

"An' one day come jes befo' Christmas, 'bout nigh two year after marster die, Mr. Braxton ride up to de do'. He had done come to teck Marse George home to spen' Christmas wid him. Marse George warn git out it, but Mr. Braxton won' teck no disapp'intment; he say he gwine baptize he boy, an' he done name him after Marse George (he had marry Marse George cousin, Miss Peggy Carter, an' he 'vite Marse George to de weddin', but he wouldn' go, do' I sutney did want him to go, 'cause I heah Miss Charlotte was nominated to marry Mr. Darker, an' I warn know what done 'come o' dat bright–skinned nigger gal whar I used to know down dyah); an' he say Marse George got to come an' stan' for him, an' gi' him a silver cup an' a gol' rattle. So Marse George he finally promise to come an' spend Christmas Day, an' Mr. Braxton went 'way next mornin', an' den hit tun in an' rain so I feared we couldn' go, but hit cler off de day befo' Christmas Eve an' tun cold. Well, suh, we ain' been nowhar for so long I wuz skittish as a young filly; an' den you know twuz de same ole place.

"We didn't git dyah till supper-time, an' twuz a good one, too, 'cause seventy miles dat cold a weather hit whet a man's honger jes like a whetstone.

"Dee sutney wuz glad to see we all. We rid roun' by de back yard to gi' Billy de horses, an' we see dee wuz havin' gret fixin's; an' den we went to de house, jest as some o' de folks run in an' tell 'em we wuz come. When Marse George stept in de hall dee all clustered roun' him like dee gwine hug him, dee faces fyah dimplin' wid pleasure, an' Miss Peggy she jes retched up an' teck him in her arms an' hug him.

"Dee tell me in de kitchen dat dee wuz been 'spectin' of Miss Charlotte over to spend Christmas too, but de river wuz so high dee s'pose dee couldn' git 'cross. Chile, dat sutney disapp'int me!

"Well, after supper de niggers had a dance. Hit wuz down in de laundry, an' de table wuz set in de carpenter shop jes 'by. Oh, hit sutney wuz beautiful! Miss Lucy an' Miss Ailsy dee had superintend ev'ything wid dee own hands. So dee wuz down dyah wid dee ap'ons up to dee chins, an' dee had de big silver strandeliers out de house, two on each table, an' some o' ole mistiss's best damas' tablecloths, an' ole marster's gret bowl full o' eggnog; hit look big as a mill-pond settin' dyah in de cornder; an' dee had flowers out de greenhouse on de table, an' some o' de chany out de gret house, an' de dinin'-room cheers set roun' de room. Oh! oh! nuttin warn too good for niggers dem times; an' de little niggers wuz runnin' roun' right 'stracted, squealin' an' peepin' an' gittin in de way onder you foots; an' de mens dee wuz totin' in de wood— gret hickory logs, look like stock whar you gwine saw—an' de fire so big hit look like you gwine kill horgs, 'cause hit sutney wuz cold dat night. Dis nigger ain' nuver gwine forgit it! Jack Forester he had come 'cross de river to lead de fiddlers, an' he say he had to put he fiddle onder he coat an' poke he bow in he breeches leg to keep de strings from poppin', an' dat de river would freeze over sho ef twarn so high; but twuz jes snortin', an' he had hard wuck to git over in the skiff, an' Unc' Jeems say he ain' gwine come out he boathouse no mo' dat night—he done tempt Providence often 'nough dat day.

"Den ev'ything wuz ready, an' de fiddlers got dee dram an' chuned up, an' twuz lively, I tell you! Twuz jes as thick in dyah as blackberries on de blackberry bush, 'cause ev'y gal on de plantation wuz dyah, shakin' her foot for some young buck, an' back-steppin' for to go 'long. Dem ole sleepers wuz jes a-rockin', an' Jack Forester he wuz callin' de figgers for to wake 'em up. I warn' dancin', 'cause I done got 'ligion an' longst to de chutch since de trouble done tetch us up so rank; but I tell you my foots wuz pintedly eechchin for a leetle sop on it, an' I had to come out to keep from crossin' 'em onst, anyways. Den, too, I had a tetch o' misery in my back, an' I lay off to git a tas'e o' dat eggnog out dat big bowl wid snow-drift on it from Miss Lucy—she al'ays mighty fond o' Marse George; so I slip into de carpenter shop, an' ax her kyarn I do nuttin for her, an' she laugh an' say, yes, I kin drink her health, an' gi' me a gret gobletful, an' jes den de white folks come in to 'spec' de tables, Marse George in de lead, an' dee all fill up dee glasses an' pledge dee health, an' all de servants', an' a merry Christmas, an' den dee went in de wash-house to see de dancin', an' maybe to teck a hand deeself, 'cause white folks' 'ligion ain' like niggers', you know; dee got so much larnin dee kin dance an' fool de devil, too. An' I stay roun' a little while, an' den went in de kitchen to see how supper gittin on, 'cause I wuz so hongry when I got dyah I ain' able to eat 'nough at one time to 'commodate it, an' de smell o' de tuckeys an' de gret saddlers o' mutton in de two kitchens wuz mos' 'nough by deeself to feed a right hongry man; an' dyah wuz a whole parcel o' niggers cookin' an' tunnin' 'bout for life, an' dee faces jes as shiny as ef dee done bas'e 'em wid gravy; an' dyah, settin' back in a cheer out de way, wid her clean frock up off de flo', wuz dat gal. I sutney did feel curious.

"I say, 'Hi! name o' Gord! whar'd you come from?' She say, 'Oh, Marster! ef heah ain' dat free nigger!' An' ev'ybody laughed.

"Well, presney we come out, 'cause Nancy warn me see de dancin', an' we stop a leetle while 'hind de cornder out de wind while she tell me 'bout ev'ything. An' she say dat's all a lie she tell me dat day 'bout Mr. Darker an' Miss Charlotte; an' he done gone 'way now for good, 'cause he so low-down an' wuthless dee kyarn nobody stand him; an' all he warn marry Miss Charlotte for is to git her niggers. But Nancy say Miss Charlotte nuver could abide him, he so'sateful, spressly sence she fine out what a lie he told 'bout Marse George. You know, Mr. Darker he done meck'em think Marse George sont me dyah to fine out ef he done come home, an' den dat he fall on him wid he weepin when he ain' noticin' him, an' sort o' out de way too, an' git two urr mens to hold him while he beat him, all 'cause he in love wid Miss Charlotte. D'you ever, ever heah sich a lie? An' Nancy say, do' Miss Charlotte ain' b'lieve it all togerr, hit look so reasonable she done le' de ole jedge an' her ma, who wuz 'pending on what she heah, 'duce her to send back he things; an' dee ain' know no better not tell after de ole jedge die; den dee fine out 'bout de whuppin me, an' all; an' den Miss Charlotte know huccome I ain' gwine stay dat day; an' she say dee wuz sutney outdone 'bout it, but it too late den, an' Miss Charlotte kyarn do nuttin but cry 'bout it, an' dat she did, pintedly, 'cause she done lost Marse George, an' done 'stroy his life; an' she nuver keer 'bout nobody else sep Marse George, Nancy say. Mr. Clarke he hangin' on, but

Miss Charlotte she done tell him pintedly she ain' nuver gwine marry nobody. An' dee jes done come, she say, 'cause dee had to go 'way round by de rope-ferry 'long o' de river bein' so high, an' dee ain' know tell dee done git out de ker'idge an' in de house dat we all wuz heah; an' Nancy say she glad dee ain', 'cause she 'feared ef dee had, Miss Charlotte wouldn' 'a come.

"Den I tell her all 'bout Marse George, 'cause I know she 'bleeged to tell Miss Charlotte. Twuz powerful cold out dyah, but I ain' mine dat, chile. Nancy she done had to wrop her arms up in her ap'on, an' she kyarn meck no zistance 'tall, an' jes dis nigger ain' keerin nuttin 'bout cold den.

"An' jes den two ladies come out de carpenter shop an' went 'long to de wash-house, an' Nancy say, 'Dyah Miss Charlotte now'; an' twuz Miss Lucy an' Miss Charlotte; an' we heah Miss Lucy coaxin' Miss Charlotte to go, tellin' her she kin come right out; an' jes den dee wuz a great shout, an' we went in hinst 'em. Twuz Marse George had done teck de fiddle, an' ef he warn' natchelly layin' hit down! he wuz up at de urr een o' de room, 'way from we all, 'cause we wuz at de do', nigh Miss Charlotte whar she wuz standin' 'hind some on 'em, wid her eyes on him mighty timid, like she hidin' from him, an' ev'y nigger in de room wuz on dat flo'. Gord! suh, dee wuz grinnin' so dee warn' a toof in dat room you couldn' git you tweezers on; an' you couldn' heah a wud, dee so proud o' Marse George playin' for 'em.

"Well, dee danced tell you couldn' tell which wuz de clappers an' which de back-steppers; de whole house look like it wuz rockin'; an' presney somebody say supper, an' dat stop 'em, an' dee wuz a spell for a minute, an' Marse George standin' dyah wid de fiddle in he hand. He face wuz tunned away, an' he wuz studyin'—studyin' 'bout dat urr Christmas so long ago—'an' sudney he face drapt down on de fiddle, an' he drawed he bow 'cross de strings, an' dat chune 'bout 'You'll ermember me' begin to whisper right sorf. Hit begin so low ev'ybody had to stop talkin' an' hold dee mouf to heah it; an' Marse George he ain' know nuttin 'bout it, he done gone back, an' standin' dyah in de gret hall playin' it for Miss Charlotte whar done come down de steps wid her little blue foots an' gret fan, an' standin' dyah in her dim blue dress an' her fyah arms, an' her gret eyes lookin' in he face so earnest, what he ain' gwine nuver speak to no mo'. I see it by de way he look—an' de fiddle wuz jes pleadin'. He drawed it out jes as fine as a stran' o' Miss Charlotte's hyah.

"Hit so sweet, Miss Charlotte, mun, she couldn' stan' it; she made to de do'; an' jes while she watchin' Marse George to keep him from seein' her he look dat way, an' he eyes fall right into hern.

"Well, suh, de fiddle drapt down on de flo'—perlang!, an' he face wuz white as a sycamore limb.

"Dee say twuz a swimmin' in de head he had: an' Jack say de whole fiddle warn' wuff de five dollars.

"Me an' Nancy followed 'em tell dee went in de house, an' den we come back to de shop whar de supper wuz gwine on, an' got we all supper an' a leetle sop o' dat yaller gravy out dat big bowl, an' den we all rejourned to de wash-house agin, an' got onder de big bush o' misseltow whar hangin' from de jice, an' ef you ever see scufflin', dat's de time.

"Well, me an' she had jes done lay off de whole Christmas, when wud come dat

Marse George want he horses.

"I went, but it sutney breck me up; an' I wonder whar de name o' Gord Marse George gwine sen' me dat cold night, an' jes as I got to de do' Marse George an' Mr. Braxton come out, an' I know torectly Marse George wuz gwine 'way. I seen he face by de light o' de lantern, an' twuz set jes rigid as a rock.

"Mr. Braxton he wuz beggin' him to stay; he tell him he ruinin' he life, dat he sho dee's some mistake, an' 'twill be all right. An' all de answer Marse George meck wuz to swing heself up in de saddle, an' Reveller he look like he gwine fyah 'stracted. He al'ays mighty fool anyway when he git cold, dat horse wuz.

"Well, we come 'long 'way, an' Mr. Braxton an' two mens come down to de river wid lanterns to see us cross, 'cause twuz dark as pitch, sho 'nough.

"An' jes 'fo' I started I got one o' de mens to hol' my horses, an' I went in de kitchen to git warm, an' dyah Nancy wuz. An' she say Miss Charlotte upsteairs cryin' right now, 'cause she think Marse George gwine cross de river 'count o' her, an' she whimper a little herself when I tell her good-by. But twuz too late den.

"Well, de river wuz jes natchelly b'ilin', an' hit soun' like a mill-dam roarin' by; an' when we got dyah Marse George tunned to me an' tell me he reckon I better go back. I ax him whar he gwine, an' he say, 'Home.' 'Den I gwine wid you,' I says. I wuz mighty skeered, but me an' Marse George wuz boys togerr; an' he plunged right in, an' I arter him.

"Gord! Twuz cold as ice; an' we hadn' got in befo' bofe horses wuz swimmin' for life. He holler to me to byah de myah head up de stream; an' I did try, but what's a nigger to dat water! Hit jes pick me up an' dash me down like I ain' no mo'n a chip, an' de fust thing I know I gwine down de stream like a piece of bark, an' water washin' all over me. I knowed den I gone, an' I hollered for Marse George for help. I heah him answer me not to get skeered, but to hold on; but de myah wuz lungin' an' de water wuz all over me like ice, an' den I washed off de myah back, an' got drownded.

"I 'member comin' up an' hollerin' agin for help, but I know den, 'tain' no use, dee ain' no help den, an' I got to pray to Gord, an' den some'n hit me an' I went down agin, an' de next thing I know, I wuz in de bed, an' I heah 'em talkin 'bout wherr I dead or not, an' I ain' know myself tell I taste de whiskey dee po'rin' down my jugular.

"An' den dee tell me 'bout how when I hollered Marse George tun back an' struck out for me for life, an' how jes as I went down de last time he cotch me an' helt on to me tell we wash down to whar de bank curve, an' dyah de current was so rapid hit yuck him off Reveller back, but he helt on to de reins tell de horse lunge so he hit him wid he fo'foot an' breck he collar-bone, an' den he had to let him go, an' jes helt on to me; an' jes den we wash up agin de bank an' cotch in a tree, an' de mens got dyah quick as dee could, and when dee retched us Marse George wuz holdin' on to me, an' had he arm wropped roun' a limb, an' we wuz lodged in de crotch, an' bofe jes as dead as a nail; an' de myah she got out, but Reveller he wuz drownded, wid his foot cotch in de rein an' de saddle tunned onder he side; an' dee ain' know wherr Marse George ain' dead too, 'cause he not only drownded, but he lef' arm broke up nigh de shoulder.

"An' dee say Miss Charlotte she 'mos' 'stracted; dat de fust thing anybody know 'bout it wuz when some de servants bust in de hall an' holler, and say Marse George an' me done bofe washed 'way an' drownded, an' dat she drapt down dead on de flo', an' when dee bring her to she 'low to Miss Lucy dat she de 'casion on he death; an' dee say dat when de mens wuz totin' him in de house, an' wuz shufflin' de feets not to meck no noige, an' a little piece o' blue silk drapt out he breast whar somebody picked up an' gin Miss Lucy, Miss Charlotte breck right down agin; an' some on 'em say she sutney did keer for him; an' now when he layin' upsteairs dyah dead, hit too late for him ever to know it.

"Well, suh, I couldn' teck it in dat Marse George and Reveller wuz dead, an' jes den somebody say Marse George done comin' to, an' dee gi' me so much whiskey I went to sleep.

"An' next mornin' I got up an' went to Marse George room, an' see him layin' dyah in de bed, wid he face so white an' he eyes so tired-lookin', an' he ain' know me no mo' 'n ef he nuver see me, an' I couldn' stan' it; I jes drap down on de flo' an' bust out cryin'. Gord! suh, I couldn' help it, 'cause Reveller wuz drownded, an' Marse George he wuz mos' gone.

"An' he came nigher goin' yit, 'cause he had sich a strain, an' been so long in de water, he heart done got numbed, an' he got 'lirium, an' all de time he thought he was tryin' to git 'cross de river to see Miss Charlotte, an' hit so high, he kyarn git dyah.

"Hit sutney wuz pitiful to see him layin' dyah tossin' an' pitchin', not knowin' whar he wuz, tell it took all Mr. Braxton an' me could do to keep him in de bed, an' de doctors say he kyarn hol' out much longer.

"An' all dis time Miss Charlotte she wuz gwine 'bout de house wid her face right white, an' Nancy say she don' do nuttin all day long in her room but cry an' say her pra'rs, prayin' for Marse George, whar dyin' upsteairs by 'count o' not knowin' she love him, an' I tell Nancy how he honin' all de time to see her, an' how he constant callin' her name.

"Well, so twuz, tell he mos' done weah heself out; an' jes lay dyah wid his face white as de pillow, an' he gret pitiful eyes rollin' 'bout so restless, like he still lookin' for her whar he all de time callin' her name, an' kyarn git 'cross dat river to see; an' one evenin' 'bout sunset he 'peared to be gwine; he weaker'n he been at all, he ain' able to scuffle no mo', an' jes layin' dyah so quiet, an' presney he say, lookin' mighty wistful,

"'Edinburg, I'm goin' to-night; ef I don' git 'cross dis time, I'll gin't up.'

"Mr. Braxton wuz standin' nigh de head o' de bed, an' he say, 'Well, by Gord! he *shell* see her!'—jes so. An' he went out de room, an' to Miss Charlotte do', an' call her, an' tell her she got to come, ef she don't he'll die dat night; an' fust thing I know, Miss Lucy bring Miss Charlotte in, wid her face right white, but jes as tender as an angel's, an' she come an' stan' by de side de bed, an' lean down over him, an' call he name, 'George!'—' jes so.

"An' Marse George he ain' answer; he jes look at her studdy for a minute, an' den he forehead got smooth, an' he tun he eyes to me, an' say, 'Edinburg, I'm 'cross.'"

(1886)

WILLIAM GILMORE SIMMS

Ephraim Bartlett:
The Edisto Raftsman

I resume my narrative. In my last, we had just hurried across the common road, once greatly travelled, leading along the Ashley, to the ancient village of Dorchester. Something was said of the fine old plantations along this river. It was the aristocratic region during the Revolution; and when the Virginians and Marylanders, at the close of the war, who had come to the succor of Carolina against the British, drew nigh to Charleston, their hearts were won and their eyes ravished, by the hospitalities and sweets of this neighborhood. Many brave fellows found their wives along this river, which was bordered by flourishing farms and plantations, and crowned by equal luxury and refinement. Here, too, dwelt many of those high-spirited and noble dames whose courage and patriotism contributed so largely to furnish that glorious chapter in Revolutionary history, which has been given to the women of that period. The scene is sadly changed at this season. The plantations along the Ashley are no longer flourishing as then. The land has fallen in value, not exhausted, but no longer fertile and populous. The health of the country is alleged to be no longer what it was. This I regard as all absurdity. The truth is that the cultivation was always inferior; and the first fertile freshness of the soil being exhausted, the opening of new lands in other regions naturally diverted a restless people from their old abodes. The river is still a broad and beautiful one, navigable for steamers and schooners up to Dorchester, which, by land, is twenty-one miles from Charleston. There is abundant means for restoring its fertility. Vast beds of marl, of the best quality, skirt the river all along the route, and there is still a forest growth sufficiently dense to afford the vegetable material necessary to the preparation of compost. As for the health of the neighborhood, I have no sort of question, that, with a dense population, addressed to farming, and adequate to a proper drainage, it would prove quite as salubrious as any portion of the country. Staple culture has been always the curse of Carolina. It has prevented thorough tillage, without which no country can ever ascertain its own resources, or be sure of its health at any time.

Cooper river, on the right, is at a greater distance from us. This, too, was a prosperous and well cultivated region in the Revolution. In a considerable degree it still remains so, and is distinguished by flourishing country seats which their owners only occupy during spring and winter. The cultivation is chiefly rice, and the rice plantation is notoriously and fatally sickly, except among the negroes. They flourish in a climate which is death to the European. But of this river hereafter. I may persuade you, in future pages, to a special journey in this quarter, when our details and descriptions may be more specific. Between the two rivers the country is full of interest and full of game, to those who can delay to hunt for it. He who runs over the railroad only, sees nothing and can form no conception of it. A few miles further, on the right, there is a stately relic of the old British parochial establishment, a church edifice dedicated to St. James, which modern veneration has lately restored with becoming art, and re-awakened with proper rituals. Built of brick, with a richly painted interior and tesselated aisles, surrounded by patriarchal oaks, and a numerous tenantry of dead in solemn tomb and ivy-mantled monument, you almost fancy yourself in the midst of an antiquity which mocks the finger of the historian. In this neighborhood flourished a goodly population. Large estates and great wealth were associated with equally large refinement and a liberal hospitality, and the land was marked by peculiar fertility. The fertility is not wanting now, but the population is gone—influenced by similar consideration with those which stripped the sister river of its thousands.

Until late years, the game was abundant in this region. The swamps which girdled the rivers afforded a sure refuge, and the deer stole forth to the ridges between, to browse at midnight, seeking refuge in the swamps by day. We have just darted through an extensive tract named Izard's camp, which used to be famous hunting-ground for the city sportsmen. Twenty years ago I have cracked away at a group of deer, myself, in these forest pastures, and even now you may rouse the hunt profitably in the ancient ranges. There are a few sportsmen who still know where to seek with certainty for the buck at the proper season. The woods, though mostly pine, have large tracts of oak and hickory. The scrubby oak denotes a light sandy soil, of small tenacity, and, most usually, old fields which have been abandoned. Along the smaller water-courses, the creeks and branches, long strips of fertile territory may be had; and the higher swamp lands only need drainage to afford tracts of inexhaustible fertility, equal to any Mississippi bottom. The introduction of farming culture will find these and reclaim them, and restore the poorer regions.

A thousand stories of the Revolution, peculiar to this country, would reward the seeker. Nor is it wanting in other sources of interest. Traditions are abundant which belong more to the spiritual nature of the people than their national history. The poorer classes in the low country of the South were full of superstition. Poverty, for that matter, usually is so, but more particularly when it dwells in a region which is distinguished by any natural peculiarities. Thus the highlands of Scotland cherish a faith in spectral forms that rise in the mist and vapor of the mountain; and the Brownie is but the grim accompaniment of a life, that, lacking somewhat in human association, must seek its companions among the spiritual; and these must derive their aspects from the gloomy fortunes of the seeker. The Banshee of Ireland is but the finally speaking monitor of a fate that has always more or less threatened the fortunes of the declining family; and the Norwegian hunting demons are such as are equally evoked by the sports which he pursues and the necessities by which he is pursued himself. In the wild, deep, dark, and tangled masses of a Carolina swamp region, where, even by daylight, mystic shadows harbor and walk capriciously with every change of the always doubtful sunlight, the mind sees and seeks a spiritual presence, which, though it may sometimes oppress, always affords company. Here, solitude, which is the source of the spiritual and contemplative, is always to be found; and forces herself— certainly at one season of the year—upon the scattered forester and farmer. The man who lives by pursuit of the game, the deer or turkey, will be apt to conjure up, in the silent, dim avenues through which he wanders, some companion for his thought, which will, in time, become a presence to his eye; and, in the secluded toils of the farmer, on the borders of swamp and forest, he will occasionally find himself disturbed by a visitor or spectator which his own loneliness of life has extorted from his imagination, which has shaped it to a becoming aspect with the scene and climate under which he dwells. Many of these wild walkers of the wood are supposed to have been gods and spirits of the Indian tribes, who have also left startling memories behind them; and though reluctant to confess his superstitions—for the white hunter and forester dread ridicule more than anything beside—yet a proper investigation might find treasures of superstition and grim tradition among our people of this region, such as would not discredit any of the inventions of imagination.

One of these traditions occurs to me at this moment, the scene of which is at hand but a short distance from us, but not visible from the railroad. Here is not only a haunted house, but a haunted tract of forest. The tale was told me many years ago, as derived from the narrative of a raftsman of the Edisto. The Edisto, of which we may speak hereafter, is the great *lumber* river of South Carolina. Its extent is considerable, penetrating several district divisions of the State, and upon its two great arms or arteries, and its tributary creeks or branches, it owns perhaps no less than one hundred and fifty mills for sawing lumber. It supples Charleston, by a sinuous route, almost wholly; and large shipments of its timber are made to the island of Cuba, to Virginia, and recently to New York, and other places. Its navigation is difficult, and, as it approaches the sea, somewhat perilous. Many of its rafts have been driven out to sea and lost, with all on board. It requires, accordingly, an experienced pilot to thread its intricacies, and such an one was Ephraim Bartlett, a worthy fellow, who has passed pretty much out of the memories of the present generation.

Ephraim was a good pilot of the Edisto, one of the best; but he had an unfortunate faith in whiskey, which greatly impaired his standing in society. It did not injure his reputation, however, as a pilot; since it was well known that Ephraim never drank on the voyage, but only on the return; and as this was invariably by land, no evil could accrue from his bad habit to anybody but himself. He rewarded himself for his abstinence on the river, by free indulgence when on shore. His intervals of leisure were given up wholly to his potations; and between the sale of one fleet of rafts, and the preparation for the market of another, Ephraim, I am sorry to say, was a case which would have staggered the temperance societies. But the signal once given by his employers, he would shake himself free from the evil spirit, by a plunge into the river. Purification followed—his head was soon as clear for business as ever; and, wound about with a bandanna handkerchief of flaming spot in place of a hat, it would be seen conspicuous on the raft, making for the city. With cheerful song and cry he made his way down, pole in hand, to ward off the overhanging branches of the trees, or to force aside the obstructions. Accompanied by a single negro, still remembered by many as old 'Bram Geiger, his course was usually prosperous. His lumber usually found the best market, and Ephraim and Bram, laying in their little supplies in Charleston, with a sack over their shoulders, and staff or gun in hand, would set out from the city on their return to Lexington, the district of country from which they descended. On these occasions, Ephraim never forgot his jug. This was taken with him empty on the raft, but returned filled, upon his or Bram's shoulders. They took turns in carrying it, concealing it from too officious observers by securing it in one end of the sack. In the other might be found a few clothes, and a fair supply of tobacco.

On the particular occasion when Ephraim discovered for himself that the ancient house and tract were haunted, it happened that he left the city about mid-day. It was Saturday, at twelve or one o'clock, according to his account, when they set out, laden as usual. They reached the house, which was probably twelve or thirteen miles from town, long before sundown; and might have stretched away a few miles farther, but for a cramp in the stomach, which seized upon Old 'Bram. Ephraim at once had resort to his jug, and a strong noggin was prepared for the relief of the suffering negro. At the same time, as Bram swore that he must die, that nothing could possibly save him under such suffering as he experienced, Ephraim concluded to take lodgings temporarily in the old house, which happened to be within a few hundred yards of the spot, and to lie by for the rest of the day. The building was of brick, two stories in height, but utterly out of repair—doors and windows gone, floors destroyed, and the entire fabric within quite dismantled. It was a long time before Bram was relieved from his suffering and fright. Repeated doses of the potent beverage were necessary to a cure; and, by the time this was effected, the old fellow was asleep. In the meantime, Ephraim had built a rousing fire in the old chimney: had gathered *lightwood* (resinous pine) sufficient to keep up the fire all night; had covered the old negro with his own blanket, which he bore strapped beneath the sack upon his shoulders; and had opened his wallet of dried meat and city bread for his supper. Meanwhile, the fumes of the whiskey had ascended gratefully to his own nostrils; and it seemed only reasonable that he should indulge himself with a dram, having bestowed no less than three upon his companion. He drank accordingly, and as he had no coffee to his supper, he employed the whiskey, which he thought by no means a bad substitute. He may have swallowed three several doses in emulation of Bram, and in anticipation of a similar attack, before he had quite finished supper. He admits that he certainly drank again when his meal was ended, by way of washing down the fragments. Bram, meanwhile, with the blazing fire at his feet, continued to sleep on very comfortably. When Ephraim got to sleep is not so certain. He admits that he was kept awake till a late hour by the fumes of the whiskey, and by strange noises that reached him from the forest. He recalled to memory the bad character of the dwelling and neighborhood as haunted; and is not so sure, but thinks it possible that this recollection prompted him to take another drought, a stirrup cup, as it were, before yielding himself to sleep. But he denies that he was in any way affected by the whiskey. To use his own language, he had none of the "how-come-you-so" sensation upon him, but insists that he said his prayers, rationally, like any other Christian, put several fresh brands upon the fire, and sank into the most sober of all mortal slumbers.

I am the more particular in stating these details, since a question has been made in regard to them. Bram had his story also. He admits that he was sick, and physicked as described—that Ephraim had gathered the fuel, made the fire, and covered him with his blanket, while he slept—but he alleges that he awoke at midnight, when Ephraim himself was asleep, and being still a little distressed in the abdominal region, he proceeded to help himself out of the jug, without disturbing the repose of his comrade; and he affirms, on his honesty, that he then found the jug fully half emptied, which had been quite full when he left the city; and he insisted that, in giving him his several doses, Ephraim had always been very careful not to make them over strong. Bram admits that, when he had occasion to help himself, as the attack was still threatening, he preferred to take an over dose rather than peril his safety by mincing the matter. It is very certain, from the united testimonies of the two, the whiskey had, one half of it, most unaccountably disappeared before the night was half over. I must suffer Ephraim to tell the rest of the story for himself, and assert his own argument.

"Well, now, you see, my friends," telling his story to a group, "as I said afore, it was mighty late that night afore I shut my eyes. I reckon twarn't far from day-peep when I slipped off into a hearty sleep, and then I slept like a cat after a supper. Don't you be thinking now 'twas owing to the whiskey that I was wakeful, or that I slept so sound at last. 'Bram's troubles in the stomach made me oneasy, and them strange noises in the woods helped the matter."

"But what were the noises like, Ephraim?"

"Oh! like a'most anything and everything. Horns a-blowing, horses a-snorting, cats a-crying, and then sich a rushing and a trampling of four-footed beasts, that I could 'a-swore it was a fox hunt for all the world. But it warn't that! No! 'Twas a hunt agin natur'. The hounds, and horses, and horns that made that racket, warn't belonging to this world. I felt suspicions about it then, and I reckon I knows it now, if such a matter ever is to be made known. Well, as I was a-saying, I got to sleep at last near upon day-light. How long I did sleep there's no telling. 'Twas mighty late when I waked, and then the noise was in my ears again. I raised myself on end, and sat up in my blanket. The fire was gone out clean, and I was a little coldish. 'Bram, the nigger, had scruged himself into the very ashes, and had quite kivered up his head in the blanket. How he drawed his breath there's no telling, since the tip of his nose warn't to be seen nowhere. Says I, ''Bram, do you hear them noises?' But never a word did he answer. Says I, to myself, 'the nigger's smothered.' So I onwraped him mighty quick, and heard him grunt. Then I know'd there was no harm done. The nigger was only drunk."

"Nebber been drunk dat time," was the usual interruption of 'Bram, whenever he was present at the narration.

"'Bram, you was most certainly drunk, sense I tried my best to waken you, and couldn't get you up."

"Ha! da's 'cause I bin want for sleep, so I nebber consent for ye'r (hear). I bin ye'r berry well all de time; but a man wha's bin trouble wid 'fliction in the stomach all night, mus' hab he sleep out in de morning. I bin ye'r well enough, I tell you."

"You old rascal, if I had thought so, I'd ha' chunk'd you with a lightwood knot!—but the nigger *was* asleep, my friends, in a regular drunk sleep, if ever he was; for when I hearn the noises coming nigh—the hounds and the horses—I drawed him away from the ashes by the legs, and laid him close up agin' the wall t'other side of the fire-place, and pretty much out of sight. I kivered him snug with the blanket, and let him take his sleep out, though I was beginning to be more and more jub'ous about them noises. You see, 'twas the regular noises of a deer-hunt. I could hear the drivers beating about in the thick; then the shout; then the dogs, yelping out whenever they struck upon the trail; I know'd when they nosed the cold trail, and when the scent got warm; and then I heerd the regular rush, when the deer was started, all the dogs in full blast, and making the merriest music. Then I heerd the crack of the gun—first one gun, then another, then another, and another, a matter of four shots—and I felt sure they must ha' got the meat. The horns sounded; the dogs were stopped, and, for a little while, nothing but silence. Oh! I felt awful all over, and monstrous jub'ous of something strange!"

"But why should you feel awful, and what should there be so strange about a deer-hunt near Izard's Camp—a place where you may start deer even at this day?"

"Why, 'twas Sunday, you see, and nobody now, in our times, hunts deer, or anything, a-Sundays; and it 'twan't till after midnight on Saturday that I heer'd the noises. That was enough to make me jub'ous. But when I remember'd how they used to tell me of the rich English gentleman, named Lumley, that once lived in the neighborhood, long afore the old Revolution; what a wicked man he was, and how he used to hunt a-Sundays; and how a judgment come upon him; and how he was lost, in one of his huntings, for a matter of six months or more; and when he was found, 'twas only his skileton. Well I reckon, to think of all that, was enough to give me a bad scare—and it did. People reckoned he must have been snake-bit, for there were the bones of a snake beside him, with the rattles on, eleven and the button; he must have killed the snake after he was struck. But it didn't help him. He never got away from the spot till they found his skileton, and they know'd him by the ring upon his finger, and his knife, and horn, and gun; but all the iron was ruined, eaten up by the rust. Well, when I heer'd the horns a-Sunday, I recollected all about Squire Lumley, and his wickedness; and, before I seed anything, I was all over in a shiver. Well, presently I heerd the horns blowing merrily again, and the sounds come fresher than ever to my ears. I was oneasy enough, and I made another trial to wake up 'Bram, but 'twas of no use. He was sounder than ever."

"I 'speck I bin sleep den, for true," was the modest interruption of 'Bram, at this stage of the narrative. With a grave shake of the head, Ephraim continued—

"I went out then in front of the house, and the horns were coming nigher from behind it. I was a-thinking to run and hide in the bushes, but I was so beflustered that I was afeer'd I should run right into the jaws of the danger. Though, when I thought of the matter agin', I got a little bolder, and I said to myself, 'what's the danger, I wonder. I'm in a free country. I'm troubling no man's property. I've let down no man's fence. I've left no man's gate open to let in the cattle. This old house nobody lives in, and I wouldn't ha' troubled it, ef so be Bram hadn't been taken sick in his bowels. What's the danger?' When I thought, in this way, to myself, I went in and took a sup of whiskey—a small sup—only a taste—by way of keeping my courage up. I tried to waken Bram again, for I said, 'two's always better than one, though one's a nigger,' but 'twas no use; Bram's sleep was sounder than ever. It was pretty cl'ar that he had soak'd the whiskey mighty deep that night!"

"Ki! Mass Ephraim! How you talk! Ef you nebber been drink more than me, dat night, you nebber been scare wid de hunters dat blessed Sunday morning."

"The nigger will talk!" said Ephraim, contemptuously, as he continued his narrative.

"Well, I felt stronger after I had taken that little sup, and went out again. Just then there came a blast of the horns almost in my very ears, and in the next minute I hear'd the trampling of horses. Soon a matter of twenty dogs burst out of the woods, and pushed directly for the house as if they knowed it; and then came the riders—five in all—four white men and one nigger. Ef I was scared at the sounds afore, the sight of these people didn't make me feel any easier. They were well enough to look at in the face, but Lord bless you they were dressed in sich an outlandish fashion! Why, even the nigger had on short breeches, reaching only to his knees, and then stockings blue and red streaked, fitting close to his legs;—and sich a leg, all the calf turned in front, and the long part of his foot pretty much where the heel ought to be. Then he had buckles at his knees, and buckles on his shoes, jest for all the world like his master. And he wore a cap like his master, though not quite so handsome, and a great coat of bright indigo blue, with the cuffs and collar trimmed with yellow. His breeches were of a coarse buff, the same color with the gentlemen, only theirs were made with a finer article—the raal buff, I reckon. They had on red coats that were mighty pretty, and all their horns were silver mounted. Our Governor and his officers, nowadays, never had on prettier regimentals. Well, up they rode, never taking any more notice of me than ef I was a dog; and I saw the nigger throw down a fine buck from his saddle. There was only one, but he had a most powerful head of horns. While they were all getting off their horses, and the nigger was taking 'em, I turned quietly into the house ag'in to try if a kick or two could get Bram out of his blankets. But, lord have mercy, when I look in, what should I see but another nigger there spreading a table with a cloth as white as the driven snow, and a-setting plates, and knives, and forks, and spoons, and bottles, and salt, and pepper, and mustard, and horse-radish, all as ef he had a cupboard somewhere at his hand. I was amazed, and worse than amazed, when I seed my own jug among the other things. But I hadn't the heart to touch it. For that matter, the nigger that was setting out the things kept as sharp an eye upon me as ef I was a thief. But soon the dishes began to show upon the table. There were the pots upon the fire, the gridiron, the Dutch oven, and everything, and the most rousing fire, and Bram still asleep in the corner, and knowing nothing about it. I was all over in a sweat. Soon, the gentlemen began to come in, but they took no sort of notice of me; and I slipped out and looked at their horses; but as the nigger was standing by 'em, and looking so strange, I didn't go too nigh. But the deer was still a-lying where he first threw it, and I thought I'd turn the head over and see the critter fairly, when, as I'm a living man, the antlers slipped through my fingers jest as fast as I tried to take 'em,—like so much water or smoke. There was a feel to me as ef I had touched something, but I couldn't take hold no how, and while I was a-trying, the nigger holla'd, in a gruff voice, from the horses—'Don't you touch Maussa's meat!' I was getting desp'rate mighty fast, and I thought I'd push back, and try what good another sup of whiskey would do. Well, when I went into the house, the gentlemen were all a-setting round the table, and busy with knife and fork, jest as ef they were the commonest people. There was a mighty smart chance for feeding at the table. Ham and turkey, a pair of as fine wild ducks, English, as you ever seed; a beef tongue, potetters (potatoes), cabbage, eggs, and other matters, and all for jest five men and their servants. Jest then, one of the gentlemen set his eyes on me, and p'inted to one of the bottles—says he, jest as if I had been his own servant—

"'Hand the bottle.'

"And somehow, I felt as ef I couldn't help myself, but must hand it, sure enough. When he had poured out the liquor, which was a mighty deep red, yet clear as the sunshine, he gin me back the bottle, and I thought I'd take a taste of the stuff, jest to see what it was. I got a chance, and poured out a tolerable dram—supposing it was a sort of red bald face (whiskey)—into a cup and tossed it off in a twinkle. But it warn't bald face, nor brandy, nor wine, nor any liquor that I ever know'd before. It hadn't a strong taste, but was something like a cordial, with a flavor like fruit and essence. 'Twarn't strong, I say; so I tried it ag'in an' ag'in, whenever I could git a chance; for I rather liked the flavor; and I warn't mealy-mouthed at helping myself, as they had enough of the critter, and, by this time, they had begun upon my own old bald-face. They seemed to like it well enough. They tried it several times, as if 'twas something new to them, and they didn't find it hard to make the acquaintance. I didn't quarrel with them, you may be sure, for I never was begrudgeful of my liquor; and, besides, wasn't I trying their'n? Well, I can't tell you how long this lasted. 'Twas a good while; and they kept me busy; one after the other on 'em calling out to me to hand 'em this, and hand 'em that, and even the nigger motioning me to help him with this thing and the other. He didn't say much, and always spoke in a whisper. But, it so happened, that, when I was stretching out for one of the bottles, to try another taste of the cordial, one of the cursed dogs would come always in my way. At last, I gin the beast a kick; and, would you believe it, my foot went clean through him—through skin, and ribs, and body, jest the same as if I had kicked the wind or the water. I did not feel him with my foot. I was all over in a trimble; and the dog yelped, jest as if I had hurt him. Sure enough, at this, the great dark-favored man that sot at the head of the table, he fastened his eye upon me and said in a big threatening voice:

"'Who kick'd my dog?'

"By this time, my blood was up a little. What with the scare I had, and the stuff I'd been a-drinking, I felt a little desperate; and my eye was sot upon the man pretty bold as I said:

"'I was just reaching for my own liquor,'—(now, that warn't exactly true, I confess, for I was reaching for one of their own bottles)—'when the dog came in my way, and I just brushed him with my foot.'

"'Nobody shall kick my dog but myself,' said he, more fierce than ever; and looking as if he meant kicking! That made me sort o' wolfish, and just then, something put the old story of Lumley and the rattlesnake fresh into my head; and, I couldn't help myself—but I gin him for answer as nice an imitation of a snake's rattle—you know how well I kin do it, my friends—as ever he heerd in his born days.

"Lord! you should have seen the stir and heard the racket. Every fellow was on his feet in a minnit, and before I could dodge, the great dark-featured man, he rose up, and seized my jug by the handle, and whirled it furious about his head, and then he sent it at me, with such a curse, and such a cry, that I thought all the house a-tumbling to pieces. Like a great wind, they all rushed by me, men and dogs, and nigger, throwing me down in the door-way, and going over me as ef I was nothing in the way. Whether it was the jug that hit me, or them rushing over, and trampling me down, I can't say; but there I lay, pretty much stunned and stupified; not knowing anything for a long time;—and when I opened my eyes, and could look around me, there I was with Bram stooping over me and trying to raise me from the ground."

"*Dat's* true!" said Bram, laying special emphasis on *dat's* (that's) and shaking his head significantly. Ephraim continued:

"The strangers were all gone in the twinkling of an eye,—they had swept the platters,—carried off every thing clean,—carried off tables and chairs, bottles and cups, plates and dishes, dinner and drink, pots and ovens, and had even put out the fire; sence, when Bram waked up, there was not a sign of it to be seen. My jug was broke all to pieces, and lying beside me at the door, and not a drop of liquor to be had. What they didn't drink, they wasted, the spiteful divels, when they broke the jug over my head."

Such was Ephraim's story, grown into a faith with many, of the Haunted Forest and House near Izard's Camp. In Ephraim's presence, Bram does not venture to deny a syllable of the story. He only professes to have seen nothing of it, except the full jug when they arrived at the house, and the broken and empty vessel when he awoke from his sleep. In Ephraim's absence, however, he does not scruple to express his doubts wholly of the ghostly visitors and the strange liquor. His notion is, that Ephraim got drunk upon the "*bald-face*" (whiskey) and dreamed the rest. His only subject of difficulty is that the jug should have been broken. He denies, for himself, that he took a drop too much—considering the state of his stomach.—We must resume our journey hereafter.

(1852)

Selections from
SLAVE
NARRATIVES
and
DIARIES

MARY CHESNUT

Mary Chesnut's Civil War

June 2, 1862. A battle is said to be raging around Richmond.[1] I am at the Prestons'. J.C. has gone to Richmond.

J.C. went off suddenly to Richmond, on business of the military department.

It is always his luck to arrive in the nick of time and be present at a great battle.

Molly heard yesterday that one of her children was ill. Her mother, the best woman in the world, is given nothing else to do but take charge of Molly's children. Lige, Molly's husband, does not amount to much as an anxious parent. So Molly went off by the next train. She is to come back or stay as she pleases, for though I cannot well do without her, she would be a nuisance if she were dissatisfied. Everything depends upon the health of that child, I daresay.

Mrs. Bartow and Dr. Berrien—we had a pleasant drive. She was hard on the chivalry.

An old maumer on a plantation—South Carolina side of the Savannah—whining pathetically: "Massa Buckra. Enty, you see! we own Massa gone—obeshee gone. Everyting gone. Ain't lef' we so much as leetle dog to sic on Yankee if he come."

Scene—Dr. Berrien and Mary on the sofa between the windows—Mrs. Bartow and Mrs. Preston near the table.

"Have some Beauregard cakes with your raspberries?"

"There is fame for you—a cake named for a general."

"Can anyone separate the idea of Nesselrode from Nesselrode pudding?"

Wade Hampton shot in the foot and Johnston Pettigrew killed!

Telegraph says Lee and Davis both on the field.[2] Enemy being repulsed.

Telegraph operator: "Madam, our men are fighting."

1. The battle of Seven Pines (Fair Oaks), fought just five miles from Richmond on May 31 and June 1.

2. Pettigrew was wounded and captured, but not killed. On June 1, Robert E. Lee assumed field command of the Army of Northern Va. for the first time.

"Of course they are—what else is there for them to do now but fight?"

"But, Madam, the news is encouraging."

Each army burying its dead. That looks like a drawn battle.

We haunt the bulletin board.

In Saturday's *Mercury* there was a vindication of Ripley. And to do plainly, a map of all the coast and its defense were given, as not the very cleverest spy in the world without help from our headquarters could have given them to the enemy. General Ripley has now gone to Richmond. No doubt he has with him his aides Kirkland and Lowndes.[1]

Back to lodgers—Mem is ill. Her daughter Isabel warns me not to mention the battle raging around Richmond—young Cohen is in it.

She tells me her cousin Edwin DeLeon is sent by Mr. Davis on a mission to England.[2]

Mrs. Preston anxious and unhappy about her sons. John is with General Huger at Richmond. Willie in the swamps on our coast with his company.

Robert Barnwell has gone back to the hospital. Oh, that we had given our thousand dollars to the hospital and not to the gunboat.

"Stonewall Jackson's movement," the *Herald* says, "does them no harm North: it is bringing out volunteers there in great numbers." And a Philadelphia paper abused us so fervently—I felt all the blood in me run to my head with rage.

Allen Green said, "Johnston Pettigrew was rash, I suspect."

"Could you not find a better word to use? You are speaking of a hero dead upon the field of battle."

Then he began to qualify his rash expression and to praise him. He repeated Charles Lee's insult to Washington—"That rascally virtue discretion, of which your excellency possesses so much."[3]

Edwin DeLeon writes, "If we can only hold on till July!"

"Till he gets to England," says Mem significantly. Is that it?

June 3, 1862. Dr. John Cheves making infernal machines in Charleston to blow the

1. Capt. William Lennox Kirkland and Capt. Rawlins Lowndes, the twenty-four-year-old son of Charles Tidyman and Sabina (Huger) Lowndes.

2. Serving as U.S. consul general in Egypt when the war began, David Camden DeLeon's brother Edwin returned home with an Arabian horse, which he gave to Jefferson Davis.

3. Gen. Charles Lee, second in command of the Continental Army, called an unauthorized retreat at the battle of Monmouth in June 1778, and was censured by Washington. Lee demanded an apology in insulting terms and was court-martialed for disobedience and disrespect. Convicted and suspended from command, he attempted to vindicate himself in a newspaper campaign so offensive to Washington that one of the commander in chief's aides fought a duel with him.

Yankees up. Pretty name they have—those machines.[1]

Yeadon will be worse than ever. The adopted son whom the council would not promote—he has been killed.[2]

My horses, the overseer says, are too poor to send over. There was corn enough on the place for two years, they said in January. Now in June they write that it will not last until the new crop comes in. Somebody is having a good time on the plantation—if it be not my poor horses.

Molly will tell me all when she comes back—and more.

Mr. Venable made an aide to Gen. Robert E. Lee. He is at Vicksburg. He writes, "When the fight is over here, I will be glad to go to Virginia." He writes in capital spirits. I notice army men all do.

Dr. Berrien said he found Fort Sumter like a gun just cleaned and loaded, leaning against the wall, ready for the fall.

At Fort Johnson he could not so much as find out who was in command there.

Miss Bay handed me a *Courier* and said, with an air of surprise, "There is no attack upon the council in it."

This ever-blooming elderly Bay blossom I answered, "Council indeed! And a life-or-death struggle going on at Richmond. Where will your *Courier* be if Richmond falls?"

I gave her a race last night. I am glad it did not kill her. We walked home together. Suddenly I remembered Mrs. Bartow's adventure—and I fled, leaving her to keep up as best she might.

Mrs. Bartow and Dr. Berrien met Tradewell[3] dreadfully drunk the night before. They tried to evade him, but he would not let them escape. He was insolent and aggressive. He got in front of them and blocked the way. Dr. Berrien raised his stick, but Tradewell drew a pistol. So did Dr. Berrien. Mrs. Bartow threw her arms around her brother &c&c&c&c.

Telegrams from Richmond, ordering troops from Charleston. Cannot be sent, for they sre attacking Charleston, too—doubtless for this very reason, to prevent reinforcements from being sent from there.

Sat down at my window—beautiful moonlight. Tried hard for pleasant thoughts.

A man began to play on the flute, with piano accompaniment. First "Ever of Thee I am Fondly Dreaming," then "Long, Long, Weary Day." At first I found it but a complement to the beautiful scene, and it was soothing to my wrought-up nerves.

---

1. To protect Charleston Harbor from Union ships, the doctor, a brother of Langdon Cheves, Jr., was supervising construction of "submarine batteries"—underwater torpedo mines that could be detonated from shore.

2. A corporal in Hampton's Legion, Richard Yeadon, Jr. had been adopted by his uncle only a few months before his death at Seven Pines.

3. Probably James D. Tradewell, a Columbia attorney.

But von Weber's last waltz was too much. Suddenly I broke down. Heavens, what a bitter cry. Such a flood of tears. The wonder is, there was any of me left.

I see in Richmond the women go in their carriages for the wounded, carry them home, and nurse them. One man was too weak to hold his musket. She took it from him, put it on her shoulder, and helped the poor wounded fellow along.

If ever there was a man who could control every expression of his emotion, who can play stoic or an Indian chief, it is Colonel Chesnut. But one day when he came from the council he had to own a breakdown (or nearly). He was awfully ashamed of his weakness. There was a letter from Mrs. Gaillard, asking him to help her, and he tried to read it to the council. She wanted a permit to go on to her son, who was wounded in Virginia. He could not control his voice—and there was not a dry eye there.

Suddenly one man called out, "God bless the woman!"

Lewis Young, Johnston Pettigrew's A.D.C., says he left his chief mortally wounded on the battlefield. Left him?

Just before he went to Italy to take a hand there in their war for freedom and self-government—I met him one day at Mrs. Frank Hampton's.[1] Mr. Pettigrew, Mr. Preston, and myself were the only people who dined there that day. Mr. Preston announced the engagement of the beautiful Miss W[2] to Hugh Rose. I was too annoyed to speak. In his very quick, excited way, Johnston Pettigrew asked, "Why do you say that?"

"Well, it seemed to startle you, but it is so. I have never heard it, but I saw it. In London a month or so ago, I entered Mrs. Williams's[3] drawing room—they were seated on a sofa opposite the door—"

"That amounts to nothing."

"No, not in itself, but they looked so foolish and so happy. I have noticed newly engaged people always look that way."

"But they are not?"

"I am very sorry."

"You? Why?"

"Because when I see a splendid creature like that unmarried, I think what a deal of happiness some fellow is losing."

Johnston Pettigrew was white and red in quick succession during the turn of the conversation. He was in a rage of indignation and disgust.

"I think this kind of talk a liberty with the young lady's name—and an impertinence *in us*."

Mrs. Hampton said to Mrs. Preston afterward, "They say he is in love with Miss

---

1. The pronouns refer to Pettigrew, "In no other Southerner did romantic ideals show to greater advantage than in James Johnston Pettigrew, a young lawyer of Charleston." Clement Eaton, *Freedom of Thought in the Old South* (1941) p. 54.

2. Mary (Withers) Kirkland.

3. M.B.C.'s sister Kate.

W himself."

"Do they? Well! I hope he will stand fire under the enemy's guns better than he did a little *fun* today."

"Fun?"

I met him soon after, in the corridor of the Congaree House. I had just read that first pamphlet of his, against the slave trade.[1] And I stopped and told him how good I thought it was.

He showed his pleasure as frankly as he had shown his displeasure the day before.

I fancy him—left dying! I wonder what they feel—those who are deserted and left to die of their wounds on the battlefield. Hard lines.

Once long ago, I went with a family in dire distress—grief for the death of a promising eldest son—to Sullivan's Island. In April we expected to find it a desert island. We counted without Fort Moultrie and U.S. troops stationed there.

As we crossed the bay in the ferryboat, opposite to us sat Captain Vogdes and Lieutenant Silvey, not [that] we knew their names then—we only saw they were U.S. officers. And they evidently recognized the fact that on our side of the deck sat an astonishingly beautiful woman. For Miss W was a beauty. So great as to take one by surprise on first sight. Here was a new comet that the astronomers had not foretold. A beautiful girl had arisen, and there were evident perturbations in the official planetary system.

They came singly—and together. There was boating, bands of music, walks upon the beach. The solitary desert island was a delusion and a snare.

Agreeable men, clever and cultivated men, seem to spring up from the sands of the sea—among them, Johnston Pettigrew we have just accounted for. Captain, now General, Vogdes is repaying our kind hospitality by hammering away like a cooper somewhere on the outside of this poor, damaged, unhooped Confederacy.

Trescot, the very cleverest writer we have, is sulking, not in his tent like Achilles—far from it. I am sure he is in some very comfortable house.

John McCrady—where is he? He was so good-looking, so clever, we predicted a brilliant future for him. They told us he was scientific, and from the depth of our ignorance we appreciated that. Perhaps, like Professor LeConte at the niter bureau, he is doing some great work which makes a tremendous noise in the world of itself but does not mention its creator's name as it fulminates against the enemy. Lieutenant Cooper has risen in rank. Lieutenant Silvey, somebody said, was paralyzed &c&c&c.

Mrs. Pickens said, alluding to that savage attack upon the five ladies lolling in their landaus:

"Why not? General Washington attended the assembly balls and wanted everything done that could be done to amuse his soldiers and comfort and refresh them, given them new strength for the fray, when they came home for a short visit."

1. In an essay published in *De Bow's Review* (Aug.-Sept. 1858), Pettigrew argued that proposals to reopen the slave trade ignored the "vast difference between a system of civilized and a system of barbarian slavery." The essay appeared as a pamphlet the same year.

Comfort. Free schools are not everything. See this spelling.

Yankee epistles found in camp show how illiterate they can be, with all their boasted schools. Fredericksburg is spelled "Fretrexbug," medicine, "met-son," "to my *sweat* brother," &c&c.

"Well," said Mem, "Lieutenant Chesnut's horse bolts with him, but right into the heart of the enemy. No excuse like that man in the Crimea to make excuses that his horse bolted and took him out of the fight. Remember the sneer, 'We will not do Colonel ___'s (I forgot whose) magnificent horsemanship the injustice to say we believe him.'"

Mem gave me this scrap—one of her Jews is in it.

Isabel says when there is a battle and her brothers come out all right, Mem takes up on her Hebrew Bible and sings that glorious hymn of her namesake Miriam: "Sing ye to the Lord, for He hath triumphed, &c&c&c."

Mem is proud of her high lineage. She tells some great stories. Some man was terribly angry with his son, who had a weakness for some beautiful Jewess, swore at all Jews, and used bad language freely. Being high church and all that, he read the service for them on Sunday.

Son: "I do not want to hear anything from Isaiah or Solomon or Moses and the prophets—or Matthew, Mark, Luke, or John."

"Silence, sir—with your ribaldry."

"But, my father—you know they are only 'damned old Jews' anyhow."

Now, for the first time in my life, no book can interest me. But life is so real, so utterly earnest—fiction is so flat, comparatively. Nothing but what is going on in this distracted world of ours can arrest my attention for ten minutes at a time.

Wigfall's program—that is, *if* he had been president:

"Every afternoon, business hours over, I would walk down and stand on the pavement before the Spotswood. I would talk with all comers. How else is one to keep abreast of public opinion? It is the place to hear what all the world is saying."

It was suggested that the *Examiner* enlightened our president as to what his enemies were saying.

"No, no—that is not my idea at all. No one-sided affair. Every side. What everybody is saying. Vox populi vox dei. One might as well be in a balloon as shut up in that Brockenbrough house. Now, who dares tell the president the truth? Everybody is afraid of him."

Somebody sniggered and said, "The truth is coming in now, like the Yankee Army from Bulls Run—on horseback, on foot, by land, and by water. The very fowls of the air were bringing it."

There is the "reliable man on horseback." The president must encounter him in his rides. He has always the best of bad news in his saddlebags.

June 4, 1862. Battles near Richmond.

Bombardment of Charleston. Beauregard said to be fighting his way out—or in.[1]

---

1. Beauregard was retreating south from Corinth toward Tupelo, Miss., while McClellan's army remained only a few miles from Richmond. In S.C., Federal troops sporadically shelled Stono and other islands just below Charleston.

Mrs. Gibson is here at Dr. Gibbes's. Tears are always in her eyes. Her eldest son is Willie Preston's lieutenant. They are down the coast. She owns that she has no hope at all. She was a Miss Ayre of Philadelphia. Says: "We may look for Burnside now—our troops which held him down to his iron flotilla have been withdrawn. They are three to one against us now, and they have hardly begun to put out their strength. In numbers, I mean. We have come to the end of our tether. Except we wait for the yearly crop of boys, as they grow up to the requisite age."

She would make despondent the most sanguine person alive.

They have sent for Captain Ingraham, from Charleston. In this hour of our sorest need, they want him for a court-martial. One would think that could wait. So it was with Captain Hollins.[1] They telegraphed for him. He answered that his presence was absolutely essential at New Orleans. In a few moments a peremptory reply from the secretary of the navy.

"Come on at once."

When he arrived at Richmond, they met him with the news that New Orleans had fallen. In his excitement he rushed into the executive office. And he said outright, without any reserve, "I believe if I had been there in my proper place this might not have happened." Jeff Davis buried his face in his hands.

Now, remember, I write down all that I hear, and the next day, if I hear that it is not so, then I write down the contradiction, too.

Captain Slocum[2] has not been killed. Nor has his wife been "riven her hair." Though no doubt the pearly drops of anxiety are still in her eyes. More beautiful to the *oversoul* than the glistening solitaire in each ear.

"As a general rule," says Mrs. Gibson, "government people are sanguine, but the son of one high functionary whispered to Mary G as he handed her into the cars, 'Richmond is bound to go up.' Do you know, only one doctor in Richmond will take pay from wounded soldiers. Oh, the idea now is that we are to be starved out. Shut us in—prolong the agony. It can then have but one end."

In her rage she says, "The baboon's commissary general."

"Who is the baboon? Lincoln?"

"Oh, yes. One gets very bitter, with one's eldest son under his guns. His best friends say the Yankee president is just the ugliest, most uncouth—the nastiest jokes—&c&c."

Governor Pickens has been telegraphed for men for Stonewall. Frémont[3] may flank him. Down here we sleep securely, with the serenest faith that Stonewall is to flank everybody and never to be flanked himself.

Mrs. Preston and I whisper. Mrs. McCord scorns whispers. She speaks out. She

1. Capt. George Nicholas Hollins, commander of the Confederate Mississippi River fleet.
2. Probably Cuthbert H. Slocum, a New Orleans merchant wounded at Shiloh while serving as a quartermaster.
3. Maj. Gen. John Charles Frémont, the western explorer and Republican presidential candidate of 1856.

says: "There are our soldiers. Since the world began, there were never better, but God does not deign to send us a general worthy of them. I do not mean drill sergeants or military old maids who will not fight until everything is just so. The real ammunition of our war is faith in ourselves and enthusiasm in our cause. West Point sits down on enthusiasm—laughs it to scorn. It wants discipline.

"And now comes a new danger. These blockade-runners. They are filling their pockets, and they gird and sneer at the *fools who fight*. Don't you see? This Stonewall—how he fires the soldiers' hearts! He will be our leader—maybe—after all. They say he does not care how many are killed. His business is to save the country and not the army. He fights to win—God bless him—and he wins. If they do not want to be killed, they can stay at home. They say he leaves sick and wounded to be cared for by those whose business it is to do so. His business is war. They say he wants to hoist the black flag—have a short, sharp, decisive war and end it! Then he is a Christian soldier."

"Let us drop all talk of the merciful Christ just now."

"They say Stonewall comes down upon them like a house afire," said Miss Mary Stark.

Mrs. McCord continued, "The great Napoleon knew all about the *business* of war. He left nothing to chance and worthless understaffers. He knew every regiment, its exact numbers. Its officers, down to the least sergeant and corporal.

"Now, ask a general here for some captain or major in his command—he stares at you. He has lived up in Wigfall's balloon—high up in the air, too high up for his business."

Miriam's Mrs. McCord V.[1] The lady was more Confederate than the Confederation. She railed at that ape Lincoln—to whom she owed her devastated plantations. Lincoln's hordes—his rascals—his traitors &c&c.

And yet "spy" was whispered here and there, under the breath.

"Why?" "You see, one of the party wore green goggles and an enormous straw flat [hat] flapping over her face. 'Disguised,' they said. She was queer looking. No wonder they had hard thoughts of her. Then, you know—we are all crazy with suspicion, wartimes."

Miriam became acquainted with her in this way: She had a house to rent in town— and Mrs. McC. V. came to rent it. "Your maison garnie," she said, but she was too fluent and pointed out to Mem the duty of every woman to remain at her post to succor the ill and the wounded, to cheer, support, and stimulate the fainting soldier, &c&c. Mem knew she was leaving her house because she was afraid to stay. She suppressed her weakness and began to talk highfalutin back to Mrs. McC. V. That it was her duty to be near her son, who was with the Army of the Potomac &c. Here poor Mem laughed aloud—and then she cried a little.

"Many a true word spoken in jest," she said. As she saw Mem hesitate, Mrs. McC. V. offered to pay—monthly, weekly, in advance. Mem need not look to Mr. McC. V. When Mrs. McC. V. borrowed money from him, she gave him her note as she did any other man, and he dealt with her in like manner. She thought women who left their

1. Wilhelmina (McCord) Vernon, a journalist and secretary of the Richmond Ladies Defense Association, died in May 1862.

husbands and sons forfeited them to those who stayed and nursed them.

At this, Dr. Cohen,[1] whose wife had left the city, showed signs of life.

"No, sir. No, this is not for you. I have a splendid husband already and three more, ready to take his place in case of accident." Dr. Cohen leaned back, showing signs of relief.

She then related the only personal conflict she had ever engaged in.

"At my friend Fillmore's (ex-president) we met some Connecticut Yankees. On Mr. Fillmore's account I was civil. One day at Saratoga a bright-eyed Indian child inquired if they knew of her brother who was at the South. The poor ignorant Indian thought the "South" was a village.

The Connecticut Yankee said to the Indian girl: "Don't let that woman touch you. She is a nigger stealer. She whips negroes for the fun of it when she is at home."

"I struck a heroic attitude. 'Back, slanderers!—at your peril.'"

The Connecticutter did not back, however. Not a bit of it. She continued to warn the Indian child to beware of Mrs. McC. V. She even addressed the lady as a "nigger stealer."

Thereupon the much incensed Southron lost all self-control.

"I fell aboard of her and pommelled her soundly. Up rushed the husband of the creature. Coattails pigeoning in the air as he flew and fluttered—'Do you think this lady is a slave, that you beat her?'

"My hand was in, so I boxed his ears soundly. And I can tell you, the pigeon tails flew away faster than they came."

Mem protested that she used Mrs. McC. V.'s very words. Furthermore, the lady combatant averred that Governor Cobb, who was a spectator of the combat, pronounced it the neatest little fight and the most complete victory he ever saw.

Here someone said, "Was your acquaintance then put in the guardhouse?" Another interrupted, "Did you rent her your house?"

"I was completely cowed. I dared not refuse to rent her my house. That is, then—face-to-face—so I shilly-shallied—and after she left, one of my sisters-in-law asked me, 'To whom does she refer you?' 'Nobody. I was afraid to ask. I have too great a respect for my ears to rouse this boxer.'"

However, some male member of the family got Mem out of it. Mem said: "I sneaked out as best I might! Then it came out that the vigilance committee had its eyes on her—&c&c&c."

The lady, however, soon procured a house—which was closed hermetically from the time she and her party moved into it. Mrs. McC. V. was seen flitting here and there with a man in uniform. She also wrote innumerable letters of the most extravagantly patriotic type, which were always mailed in the open and aboveboard manner by the person in goggles. Of course, they were instantly pounced upon by the sagacious vigilance committee—opened and read.

The ostensible cause of the sojourn of these people in Charleston was to nurse at the hospitals.

One day the landlord received a note from Mrs. McC. V., saying she had gone for a few days to see her husband, who she heard was in Richmond; she had not seen him

1. Miriam Cohen's brother-in-law, Dr. Phillip Melvin Cohen of Charleston.

for fifteen months. She would be back at once. Indeed, her friend was, as the French would say, "faisant ses couches" in the house at that time and so could not leave it. The lady who was confined could not be told that her husband was killed. This was no time for grieving, so she was made to believe he had been taken prisoner.

The confiding landlord spoke of this letter from the brilliant woman to whom he had rented a house.

"Why! Your house is empty, wide open—deserted!"

So Mem screamed, "No payments—biannually, quarterly, monthly, weekly, daily, or in advance—in point of fact, no pay at all! Forgive me, I am a Jew. When people let themselves be cheated, I laugh."

So the landlord sorrowfully went to see for himself. He found on the front steps a congregation of old oyster women in tears and milkmen in arms, swearing like mad. Bread cart left in the lurch—perfect and impartial—pay-nobody style.

In Richmond again, Mem ran across her quondam would-be tenant. She held her tongue, for the lady was a "lionne." She had embroidered Mrs. Davis a point appliqué collar. ("Point appliqué means lace and not embroidery," interrupts one of the company.) "Oh! don't bother about nonessentials. I am not half-through," persisted Mem. "She was seen in the president's carriage. She was the president herself of all western associations—at the head of gunboat fairs, making speeches, instituting bazaars."

Miriam held her peace but watched and waited. Every day she expected to hear the magnificent lady was "over the border and awa'" wi' Jock of Hazeldean[1]—or anybody of the other side.

"When, lo—the poor soul was struck down with fever. And it was death at last with whom she made her flitting."

"Oh, Mem—what a shame! to have made us laugh like that at the poor thing—we feel so ill-used. Who could have expected such an ending? It was a farce—and all at once the tragedy sweeps in."

"I was ready for a catastrophic screaming farce—and you throw death in our faces."

"Well, in these climes and these times, that's the way it all ends. Very unexpected things come about. Now, these Yankees. They were depicted to us—held up to us in all the colors of the rainbow—marked cowards. And now, in their armies, you know, they are not acting so *very* cowardly, you know?"

"Yes, we know."

"Do you know," said a little girl, "that all the people would have it Mrs. McC. V. was a man in disguise—but Uncle H said he knew that was not true."

"Since the poor woman is dead, not another word."

June 5, 1862. Beauregard retreating—and his rear guard cut off. If Beauregard's veterans will not stand, why should we expect our newly levied reserves to do it?

Landing on John's Island and James Island—those awful Yankees![2]

1. A reference to the last two lines of Sir Walter Scott's ballad "Jock o' Hazeldean," which first appeared in Alexander Campbell, *Albyn's Anthology* (1816-18).

2. On June 2, Federal troops moved across John's Island and landed on James Island in preparation for an attack on Charleston, ten miles away.

Someone said we had recovered Johnston Pettigrew's body.

The Yankee general who is besieging Savannah announces his orders are to take Savannah in two weeks' time—and then proceeds to erase Charleston from the face of the earth.

A man named Albert Luria, whose true name was Moses—I can understand why he changed his name: to Moses and the prophets he means no disrespect. It is the modern Moses he did not want to be thought the tribe of.

This Luria was killed in the battle of June 1st. *Last* summer a bomb fell in the *very thick* of his company. He picked it up and threw it into the water. A bomb—put your hand on a bomb! Think of that—those of ye who love your life. The company sent the bomb to his father. Inscribed on it was "Albert Luria—bravest where all are brave." Small Isaac Hayne[1] did the same thing at Fort Moultrie.

We discussed clever women who help their husbands politically. Some men hate every man who says a good word of or to their wives. They can't be helped. Just as well. These lady politicians—if they are young and pretty—always get themselves a "little bit" talked about. Does anything pay for that? Besides, the most charitable person will think they must be a trifle too kind, to make such devoted adherents.

"I am writing to Mrs. Davis," said Mrs. Gibson.

"Dear mama," cried Mary, "do tell her how funny Columbia people are. How she will laugh!"

Mrs. Gibson frowned her down severely and tried to make an aside sign toward me.

"Oh, you need not fear me—I am only one of the 'exigencies of the war.' This is not my home. I am one of the floating population, like yourselves."

Mrs. Gibson turned upon me and said with grave dignity of manner, "I am sure I have seen nothing to laugh at in Columbia. How could I? I have been out of Dr. Gibbes's house but once, and then only to drive. It seems a charming place."

Mary turned her back to her mother and made a significant grimace to me. . . .[2]

Reading de Créquy—but the slightest noise brings me at a bound to the window.

"There he goes, newly done up—spic and span. New rig, new hat, new alpaca coat. Old India-rubber face. I know one could squeeze it into all manner of expressions."

"How can you?"

"His face resembles the India-rubber dolls that can be done that way."

Wilmot DeSaussure telegraphs for sandbags, cannon powder, and flatboats. Powder sent—the other things not ready.

Those rude Yankees. They will not wait until we are properly prepared to receive them.

We take it easy. We love the dolce far niente. We are the true Lotos Eaters.

We cannot get accustomed to be hurried about things.

This race have brains enough, they are not active-minded. Those old revolutionary

1. The son of Attorney General Isaac Hayne.

2. Omitted is an appeal for volunteers by J. C., addressed "To the Soldiers of South Carolina not yet in Confederate Service."

characters—Middletons, Lowndes, Rutledges,[1] Marions, Sumters—they came direct from active-minded forefathers, or they would not have been here. But two or three generations of gentlemen planters—how changed the blood became! Of late all of the active-minded men who spring to the front in our government were the immediate descendants of Scotch, or Scotch Irish. Calhoun, McDuffie,[2] Cheves. Petigru, who Huguenotted his name but could not tie up his Irish.

Our planters are nice fellows but slow to move. No—impulsive but hard to keep moving. They are wonderful for a spurt—put out all their strength and then like to rest.

Hammond's father was a Yankee. And Orr—well, he is the Rudolph Hapsburg of his race.

Last winter, how Mr. Venable worried to have pontoons made for those very rivers—and not gunboats that the Yankees were sure to take.

June 6, 1862. Paul Hayne, the poet, has taken rooms here.[3]

J.C. came and offered to buy me a pair of horses. He says I need more exercise in the open air.

"Come now, are you providing me with the means to beat a rapid retreat? I am pretty badly equipped for marching."

Our commissary here, being *a man*, telegraphs to General DeSaussure to know of what kind of cloth sandbags ought to be made.

A woman by this time would have had half Columbia sewing night and day with their machines and the other half sending them off.

"The other half filling them with sand."

"But," said J.C., without a smile, "they will not be filled with sand until they get to the coast. There is sand enough there."

After all! Johnston Pettigrew and Lomax are alive and in a Yankee prison.[4] So says the N.Y. *Herald*.

What fun for Johnston Pettigrew to read his own splendid obituary.

"Look out!" I hear from Mem's window. "There goes 'Insensible to Fear.'"

"They called Johnston Pettigrew eccentric, crack-brained, &c&c. Why?"

Because he was so much in earnest. He did not waste time haranguing "Kentucky resolutions," "states rights," "cotton is king"—&c&c. That fatuous style left the talkers [looking] imbecile when the time for action came and the time for talk was over.

1. Henry Middleton was president of the Continental Congress and his son Arthur signed the Declaration of Independence. Rawlins Lowndes succeeded John Rutledge as president of S.C. in 1778. (Later state executives were known as "governor.") Rutledge and his brother Edward served in the Continental Congress. A signer of the Declaration, Edward also helped draft the Constitution.

2. The father of Wade Hampton III's second wife, George McDuffie served as a U.S. congressman, governor of S.C., and U.S. senator before his death in 1851.

3. Paul Hamilton Hayne of S.C., one of the most popular Southern poets and critics, was the author of *Poems* (1855) and *Avolio, A Legend of the Island of Cos* (1860).

4. Although Pettigrew was alive, Col. Tennent Lomax, commanding the Third Ala. at Seven Pines, had been killed.

Someone boldly declared: If we ever have a man who will simply state the business in hand, go direct to the point at issue, and not try to enlighten the universal world by a long speech about everything else, he will be our leader. Can no man be found to spare us Madison, Jefferson, Monroe? Was Wigfall caricaturing all this when he began with Christopher Columbus? He is capable of it. You see, when Gabriel blows his horn, elect Americans will be found on a platform *speaking*.

Glory be to God, as my Irish Margaret said as an opening to all discourse—
Glory be to Him now—because they are washing the windows of Trinity Church.
Hitherto Mr. Shand has used the college chapel. During the communion service he puts the bread and wine, the consecrated body and blood, on the steps of the stage, where the students walked up and down! I am not the high church, but I felt shocked.
"Desecration! He is a good old man. I wish he would not do it! But we are going back to a genuine church."
Mrs. Rose Greenhow is in Richmond. One-half of these ungrateful Confederates say Seward sent her. J.C. says the Confederacy owes her a debt they never can pay. She warned them at Manassas. And so they got Joe Johnston and his paladins to appear upon the stage in the very nick of time. In Washington they said Lord Napier[1] left her a legacy *to* the British legation. And they accepted the gift. Unlike the British nation, who would not accept Emma Hamilton and her daughter Horatio—though they were willed to the nation by Lord Nelson.

Dreadful scene on the cars. Godard Bailey had heard that Mr. C was appointed one of the new brigadiers.
So, calling J.C. by name, he asked to be appointed one of his staff. Somebody asked J.C. who Godard Bailey was. Another man got up and told the story of that Floyd business—bonds &c&c—and denounced Godard Bailey bitterly, using the very ugliest and most exasperating epithets. Mr. Bailey drew his pistol. J.C. put his hand on it and forcibly prevented his shooting the man who had so gratuitously insulted him. Anne Sabb, his wife, said coolly, "Everybody knew Mr. Bailey came into the Confederacy under a cloud."[2]

One of our boarders here at lodgers is a German woman. She has been very ill. Dr. Fair attended her. She is still very feeble. Mem says that Dr. Fair advised her today to try and speak English—German was a very heavy language for one as weak as she was. "A very difficult language to speak," he said, turning to Mem. "She had better try French until she gains some strength—if she does not understand English. And the woman meekly responded, 'My own tongue is lighter for me.'"

Yeadon down on Mr. Barnwell, who said publishing his private conversation upholding Mr. Davis "was ill timed."

1. Lord Francis Napier, career diplomat and later governor of India, was the British envoy to Washington between 1857 and 1859.
2. In Dec. 1860, Godard Bailey, then a clerk in the Interior Department, confessed to the theft of 870,000 dollars in Indian bonds held in trust by the U.S. government. Bailey had used the bonds to prop up a firm of military contractors with which his wife's cousin, Secretary of War John B. Floyd, had dealt extensively. Both men were indicted but had their cases dismissed.

Now says Yeadon in his newspaper, "How can you think a vindication of Mr. Davis wrong at any time?"

He has him there.

And now a heavy blow! Joe Johnston, the staff upon [which] we leaned so heavily—his shoulder blade has been broken in battle.[1]

Someone said of Godard Bailey and the Floyd fuss: "Bailey is wonderfully clever and a very pleasant companion. I know, poor fellow, that he is a man to spend money and to waste it. Not one to make it. Or to *take it*."

Mem fresh from the hospital, where she went with a beautiful Jewess friend. Rachel we will call her (be it her name or not) was put to feed a very weak patient. Mem noticed what a handsome fellow he was, and how quiet and clean. She fancied by those tokens that he was a gentleman.

In performance of her duties, the lovely young nurse leaned kindly over him and held the cup to his lips. When that ceremony was over and she had wiped his mouth, to her horror she felt a pair of by no means weak arms around her neck and a kiss upon her lips—which she thought strong indeed. She did not say a word. She made no complaint. She slipped away from the hospital and hereafter she will in her hospital work fire at long range no matter how weak and weary, sick and sore, the patients may be.

"And," said Mem, "I thought he was a gentleman."

"Well, a gentleman is a man after all—and she ought not to have put those red lips of hers so near &c&c&c."

Joe Johnston has two ribs broken beside the shoulder-blade disaster. And now, pray, what are we to do? Who will take command until he gets well?

When the ironclads attack Drewry's Bluff, then Richmond must go—so say Mrs. Gibson's letters.

At Georgetown, Captain Ward commanded a battery which could have riddled with ease the old hulks sent to capture Georgetown, but Major Emanuel forbade him to fire upon them.

June 7, 1862. Captain Ward was so surprised, so exasperated, so mortified, tears of rage came into his eyes.

Commissary Jones told Mrs. McCord, "Each sandbag cost fifty-five cents." She answered, "You had but to put two lines in the morning paper, and every woman in Columbia would have been there with her needle and scissors—and they would have cost you nothing."

Cheves McCord's battery on the coast has three guns and one hundred men. If this battery should be captured, John's Island and James Island would be open to the

1. Johnston was severely wounded on the first day of Seven Pines.

enemy—and so Charleston exposed utterly.

Mrs. McCord spent the morning with me. She knew Mrs. Pickens before her marriage. At the White Sulphur several years ago Governor Pickens brought the beautiful belle Lucy Holcombe to see her. Lucy the fair was not slow and low-voiced and languid then. She was bright and fluttering. Unfortunately Mrs. McCord directed her conversation to Mr. Pickens. As they left the room, Miss Lucy Holcombe, who was not accustomed to play second fiddle or to be overlooked, was on her high horse and gave Mrs. McCord a Parthian shot.

"I came here supposing you were my friend, Mrs. Wilhelmina McCord, who is the editress of a New Orleans newspaper."

So a sidelight thrown on Mem's dark problem—Mrs. McC. V. was no man in disguise but a friend of Mrs. Governor Pickens.

Apricots, apricots. I am ill, so my friends shower apricots on me. And I am not too ill to eat them—far from it.

Mercury reduced to a half-sheet. Mrs. McCord stopped her paper when it published a map of the coast defenses in defense of Ripley. By the way, it was a false report. General Ripley is not dead. He has been given a command in Longstreet's division.

Wade Hampton writes to Mary McDuffie that Chickahominy[1] was not as decided a victory as he could have wished.

Fort Pillow and Memphis given up.[2] Next? And next?
Provost marshal in Richmond orders everyone to furnish a bed for a wounded soldier. If they are not given, they will be taken.

June 9, 1862. Bratton, who married Miss Means, taken prisoner. Beverly Means killed, his mother-in-law a few days ago found *stone dead* in her bed. Misfortunes enough for one family, surely.[3]

When we read of the battles in India, in Italy, in the Crimea—what did we care? Only an interesting topic like any other to look for in the paper.

Now you hear of a battle with a thrill and a shudder. It has come home to us. Half the people that we know in the world are under the enemy's guns.

A telegram comes to you. And you leave it on your lap. You are pale with fright. You handle it, or dread to touch it, as you would a rattlesnake—worse—worse. A snake would only strike you. How many, many, this scrap of paper may tell you, have gone to their death.

1. Seven Pines.
2. Left indefensible by Beauregard's evacuation of Corinth on May 30, Fort Pillow and Memphis on the Mississippi were surrendered to the Union in the first week of June.
3. Col. John Bratton of the Sixth S.C. Regiment, whose mother and not his wife was a member of the Means family, had been captured at Seven Pines, where his brother-in-law, Sgt. Maj. Beverly William Means of the same unit, was killed.

When you meet people, sad and sorrowful is the greeting; they press your hand, tears stand in their eyes or roll down their cheeks, as they happen to have more or less self-control. They have brothers, fathers, or sons—as the case may be—in battle. And this thing now seems never to stop. We have no breathing time given us. It cannot be so at the North, for the papers say gentlemen do not go in the ranks there. They are officers or clerks of departments, &c&c&c. Then, we see so many foreign regiments among our prisoners. Germans—Irish—Scotch. The proportion of trouble is awfully against us. Every company on the field is filled with our nearest and dearest—rank and file, common soldiers.

Miriam's story today:
A woman she knew heard her son was killed—had hardly taken in the horror of it, when they came to say it was all a mistake—mistake of name. She fell on her knees with a shout of joy. "Praise the Lord, oh, my soul!" she cried in her wild delight. The household were totally upset. The swing back of the pendulum from the scene of weeping and wailing of a few moments before was very exciting. In the midst of this hubbub, the hearse drove up with the poor boy in his metallic coffin.

Does anybody wonder so many women die? Grief and constant anxiety kill nearly as many women as men die on the battlefield. Miriam's friend is at the point of death with brain fever; the sudden changes from joy to grief were more than she could bear.

Story from New Orleans:
As some Yankees passed two boys playing in the street, one of the boys threw a handful of burnt cotton at them, saying, "I kept this for you." The other, not to be outdone, spit at the Yankees: "And *I* kept *this* for you." The Yankees marked the house. A corporal's guard came—Madame affably conversing with a friend. In vain the friend, who was a mere morning caller, protested he was not the master of the house. He was marched off to prison.

Now the Mississippi is virtually open to the Yankees. Beauregard has evacuated Corinth.

Henry Nott was killed at Shiloh. Mrs. Auzé wrote to tell us.
She had no hope. To be conquered and ruined was always her fate, strive as she might—and now she knew it would be her country through which she would be made to feel. She had had more than most women endure—and the battle of life she had tried to fight with courage, endurance, faith. We all knew that—&c. Long years ago, when she was young, her lover died. She was to have been married, but fever came instead. Afterward she married. Then her husband died, then her only son. When New Orleans fell, her only daughter was there, and Mrs. Auzé went for her—Butler to the contrary notwithstanding—and brought her back with her.
Well may she say that she has bravely borne her burden until now.

Stonewall said, in his quaint way, "I like strong drink—so I never touch it."
May heaven, who sent him to help us, save him from all harm!

How Mr. Moise[1] got his money out of New Orleans. He went to a station with his two sons, who are still small boys. When he got there the carriage that he expected was not to be seen. He had no money about him, for he knew he would be searched. Some friend called out, "I will lend you my horse, but then you will be obliged to leave the children." This offer was accepted, and as he rode off, one of the boys called out, "Papa, here is your tobacco, which you have forgot." He turned back, and his son handed him a roll of tobacco which he had held openly in his hand all the time. Mr. Moise took it, galloped off, waving his hat to them. In that roll of tobacco was encased twenty-five thousand dollars.

At the church door Mr. Preston joined me. Mary McDuffie was ill, he said. And a child of Mrs. Frank Hampton was dying.

"And now, Madame, go home, and thank God on your knees that you have no children to break your heart. Mrs. Preston and I spent the first ten years of our married life in mortal agony over ill and dying children."

"I won't do anything of the kind. Those lovely girls I see around you now—they make your happiness. They are something to thank God for—far more than anything I *have not*."

"They are nice. I do not see how I could live without them now."

Mrs. McCord has a Frenchman in her hospital so dissatisfied she thinks he is dangerous. She has taken possession of the college buildings for her hospital. "Gifts are various."[2] After my failure, illnesses, and fainting fits in Richmond, I have deemed it wise to do my hospital work from the outside. I felt humiliated at having to make this confession of weakness to Mrs. McCord.

The Paul Haynes are here, but not a member of the family have shown themselves so far. Paul Hayne himself came into the drawing room to speak to me.

J.C. traced Stonewall's triumphal career on the map. He has defeated Frémont and taken all of his cannon. Now he is after Shields.[3] The language of the telegram is vague—"Stonewall has taken *plenty* of prisoners." Plenty, no doubt of it—enough and to spare. We can't feed our own soldiers. How are we to feed prisoners?

A small fray at the Chickahominy. They tried to cross and did not make it out. They lost forty men—we lost two.

They denounced Toombs in some Georgia paper which I saw today, for planting a full crop of cotton. They say he ought to plant provisions for the soldiers.

And now the *Guardian* must try its hand after the fashion of the *Mercury*. It calls Federal attention to Columbia in denouncing governor and council for not fortifying

1. Born in Charleston, Edwin Warren Moise abandoned his medical practice and moved to New Orleans where he became a lawyer, state legislator, U.S. district attorney, and, at the beginning of the war, judge of the state supreme court.

2. An allusion to Alexander Pope, *An Essay on Man* (1734), epistle 4, lines 67-68.

3. Jackson brought his brilliant Valley campaign to a successful conclusion by defeating Frémont at Cross Keys on June 8 and James Shields at Port Republic on the ninth.

it. It demonstrates how easily it could be taken and shows what a rich prize it would prove if it fall into Yankee possession. We have all noticed—as soon as our newspapers point out some weak point which needs protection and have gratified their spleen by abusing men in power for not doing their duty in fortifying such a place—the Yankees quietly go there and seize the defenseless spot so indicated to them.

And now every man is in Virginia and the eastern part of South Carolina in revolt because old men and boys are ordered out as reserve corps—and worst of all, sacred property, that is, negroes, seized and sent to work on the fortifications along the coastline. We are in a fine condition to fortify Columbia.

June 10, 1862. General Gregg writes that Chickahominy was a victory *manqué* because Joe Johnston received a disabling wound and G.W. Smith[1] was ill. The subordinates in command had not been made acquainted with the plan of battle.

Letter from John Chesnut. He says it must be all a mistake about Hampton's wound, for he saw [him] in the field to the very last—that is, until late that night.

Hampton writes to Mary McDuffie that the ball was extracted from his foot on the field and that he was in the saddle all day. But that when he tried to take his boot off at night, his foot was so inflamed and swollen the boot had to be cut away—and the wound more troublesome than he had expected.

Mrs. Preston sent her carriage to take us to Mrs. Herbemont's. Mary Gibson calls her Mrs. Bergamot. Miss Bay came down—ever blooming, in a cap so formidable I could but laugh. It was covered with a bristling row of white satin spikes. She coyly refused to enter Mrs. Preston's carriage—"put foot into it," to use her own words—but she allowed herself to be overpersuaded.

Mrs. McCord makes a frightful list of what her hospital needs. She has J.C.'s ear, and he does all he can for her. No wonder she is so devoted to him. Her complaints are never without cause, so he gives heed at once.

And I am so ill. Mr. Ben Taylor said to Dr. Trezevant: "Surely she is too ill to be going about. She ought to be in bed."

"She is very feeble—very nervous, as you say—but then, she is living on nervous excitement. If you shut her up she would die at once."

A prostration of the heart, I have. Sometimes it beats so feebly I am sure it has stopped altogether. Then they say I have fainted, but I never lose consciousness.

Mr. Preston and I were talking of negroes and cows. A negro, no matter how sensible he is on any other subject, can never be convinced that there is any necessity to feed a cow. "Turn 'em out, let 'em grass—grass good 'nouf for cow."

---

1. Maj. Gen. Gustavus Woodson Smith, a veteran of the U.S. Army, briefly took command from the wounded Johnston at Seven Pines.

Famous news from Richmond—not so good from the coast.

Mrs. Izard said, quoting I forgot who, "If West Point could give brains as well as training!"

Smith is under arrest for disobedience of orders—Pemberton's orders. This is the third general Pemberton has displaced within a few weeks. Ripley, Mercer, and Smith.[1]

Another boat escaped to the Yankee fleet. Whatever the Charleston press fails to communicate daily to the Yankees, a boat openly puts out to sea and tells the latest news.

Mrs. McCord again—she is as little afraid of personal responsibility as the Jacksons—Andrew or Stonewall. She wishes to remedy this state of things.

"Routine work—visiting nurses consult head nurse before they dare act. Head nurse must see the steward, and the steward must speak to the doctors. All this complicated machinery takes time. They consult among themselves and waste time. The poor wounded soldier consults nobody and dies, meanwhile."

I see one new light breaking in upon the black question.

Even my Molly speaks scornfully when she alludes to "them white people." She says there is salt enough on the plantation. Master had the [salt] sent to the coast, three days' journey—"but we don't git enough. There is plenty of bread—and all the people has fine fat hogs, but you see our people n'usen to salt as much as they choose—and now they will grumble."

When I told J.C. that Molly was full of airs since her late trip home, he made answer. "Tell her to go the devil—she or anybody else on the plantation who is dissatisfied. Let them go. It is bother enough to feed and clothe them now."

It was a blow. When he went over to the plantation, he came back charmed with their loyalty to him—their affection for him &c&c&c.

June 11, 1862. Sixteen more Yankee regiments have landed on James Island. Eason[2] writes, "They have twice the energy and enterprise of our people."

Is answered: "Wait awhile. Let them alone until climate and mosquitoes and sand flies and dealing with negroes take it all out of them."

No doubt this is told of Pemberton because he is a Yankee born.

He has stopped the work of obstructing the harbor—and he has them busy making rat holes in the middle of the city, for men to hide in. Why? No one knows. All the cannon is on the battery—no casemates there for men to retire into.

Crimination and recrimination. Everybody's hand against everybody else. Pemberton said to have no heart in this business, so the city cannot be defended.

Stonewall is a regular brick! going all the time—winning his way wherever he goes.

1. Brig. Gen William Duncan Smith relieved Hugh Weedon Mercer as commander of S.C.'s First Military District on June 6. Although Pemberton repeatedly ordered Smith to move decisively against the Federal forces on James Island, Smith was never placed under arrest.

2. Probably J. M. Eason, a privateer and contractor for the Confederate Ordnance Department.

Governor Pickens called to see me. His wife is in great trouble—anxiety, uncertainty. Her brother and her brothers-in-law are either killed or taken prisoners.

Mrs. Herbemont said last night that Mrs. Pickens calls his former wives No. 1, No. 2.

Parody of the matchmaking mother.

June 4, 6, 9, 11, 1862.[1]
> Have husbands now to each affixed,
> The rest have still to hunt for one,
> Except the second girl alone
> Who has no earthly chance in five—
> Till leap year gives her to counter mine.

Splendid little boy of Paul Hayne's says he is a colonel—pulls out his commission, given him by Governor Pickens, who is his cousin.

"Need not show us that," says Miriam Cohen. "All good Carolinians are entitled to take the rank of colonel if they have property enough. In Alabama, if the boat takes a hundred bales from a man's plantation, he is a colonel. Before the war it required from three hundred to a thousand bales to make him a general."

Miss Mary Stark proudly declares, "I never knew a Yankee in my life."

Molly all in tears because I asked her if she were going to turn against me.

No, she would follow me to the ends of the earth—that is, she would if it warn't for her children. But this is the reason she was out. Jonathan is her father, and he is driver, headman of the colored people (she never says "negroes"—the only "nigger" is the devil—that's her idea). Overseer and Claiborne, head of the plows, connive together to cheat master "outin everything. Marster—the best marster the lord ever send." So much lying, cheating, on a plantation—no wonder she came back outer sorts. "Overseer's wife gitten so fat on yo' substance she can't git through the little gate—have to open the wagon gate for her. Sometimes of Sundays two hams is put on their table—de 'oman sho' to die of fat."

So Molly and I are reconciled, and she is as good and as attentive as ever. All the same, she was awfully stuck up when she first came back.

Tom Taylor says Wade Hampton did not leave the field on account of his wound. "What heroism!"

"No, what luck. He is the luckiest man alive. He'll never be killed. He was shot in the temple. That did not kill him! His soldiers believe in his luck."

Tom Taylor has a glorious beard still—but so far no commission.

General Scott on Southern soldiers. He says we have élan, courage, woodcraft, consummate horsemanship, endurance of pain equal to the Indians, but that we will not submit to discipline. We will not take care of things or husband our resources.

---

1. M.B. C. wrote "May" but obviously intended "June."

Where we are, there is waste and destruction. If it could all be done by one wild desperate dash, we would do it. But he does not think we can stand the long blank months between the acts—waiting! We can bear pain without a murmur, but we will not submit to be bored, &c&c&c.

Now for the other side. They can wait. They can bear discipline. They can endure forever—losses in battle nothing to them, resources in men and materials of war inexhaustible. And *if they see fit* they will fight to the bitter end.

Nice prospect for us—as comforting as the old man's croak at Mulberry, "Bad times, worse coming."

Old Mr. Chesnut says, "We could not have kept slavery here a day, but the powerful government of the U.S.A. protected it for us."

"They will wear you out," said General Scott. Now Seward says, "We will starve you out."

So nobody is allowed to go out of this huge stockade, and they will not even take their prisoners away—leave them here to help eat us out, says our poetical friend.

"We are like scorpions girt by fire—&c&c&c."[1]

"Not fair play."

"Far from it."

"Everything fair in love and war."

"This is war."

"Well! We must bear the ills—as we brag of the good of our hot Southern blood."

"Misery is everywhere suffered on this terrestrial globe."

"Stop that. Tell us something new. Who denies that?" says John Green snappishly.

Mrs. McCord says, "In the hospital the better born—that is, those born in the purple, the gentry, those who are accustomed to a life of luxury—they are better patients. They endure in silence. They are hardier, stronger, tougher—less liable to break down than the sons of the soil."

"Why is that?"

"The something in man that is more than the body."

The soldier boy for me.

> He who from battle runs away
> May pray and sing, sing and pray.
> Natheless Alcaeus—how so e'er
> Dulcet his song and warm his prayer
> And true his vows of love may be
> He ne'er shall run away with *Me*.

I know how it feels to die—I have felt it again and again.

For instance. Someone calls out, "Albert Sidney Johnston is killed." My heart stands still. I feel no more. I am for so many seconds, so many minutes—I know not

---

1. A reference to Byron's *The Giaour: A Fragment of a Turkish Tale* (1813), lines 422-23, 433-34.

how long—I am utterly without sensation of any kind—dead. And then there is that great throb, that keen agony of physical pain—the works are wound up again, the ticking of the clock begins anew, and I take up the burden of life once more. Someday it will stop too long, or my feeble heart will be too worn out to make that awakening jar, and all will be over. I know not—think when the end comes that there will be any difference except the miracle of the new wind up, throb. And now good news is just as bad—"Hurrah—Stonewall has saved us!" Pleasure that is almost pain—my way of feeling it!

Miriam's Luria—and the coincidences of his life. Luria (born Moses) and the hero of the bombshell.

His mother was at a hotel in Charleston. Kind hearted Anna DeLeon Moses went for her sister-in-law, gave up her own chamber to her, that her child might be born in the comfort and privacy of a home. Only our people are given to such excessive hospitality. So little Luria was born in Anna DeLeon's chamber. After Chickahominy, when this man was mortally wounded—again Anna, who is now living in Richmond, found him, and again she brought him home—her house being crowded to the doorsteps. Again she gave up her chambers to him—and as he was born in her room, so he died.

June 12, 1862. Yesterday I was reading Madame de Créquy. Someone came in. "Oh! At old Creaky still. Oh! how can you at such a time!! &c&c&c. A battle raging on James Island."

Willie Preston writes, "Never you fear. We will hold James Island—our men fight so well."

J.C. was not so hopeful. He said we had supinely let them possess themselves of the best places from which to bombard and assail us. Pemberton, Pemberton—alas!

Dr. Trezevant told me something he had just heard from young Thornwell.[1]

Butler of Hampton's Legion found himself unsupported when he saw the others hold back. He said, in his coolest manner, "Then, Palmetto boys, we will do it ourselves." And the Yankees were driven out.

Mr. Preston says we will not fight on equal terms until our press is muzzled—as Seward muzzles theirs.

New England's Butler, best known to us as Beast Butler, is famous or infamous now. His amazing order to his soldier and comments on it are in everybody's mouth. We hardly expected from Massachusetts behavior to shame a Comanche.

One happy moment in Mrs. Preston's life. I watched her face today as she read the morning papers. Willie's battery is lauded to the skies. Every paper gave him a paragraph of praise.

There was a cry of amazement and horror at the breakfast table! Followed by

---

1. James Henley Thornwell, Jr., whose father was a noted S.C. clergyman.

indignant denials of the fact.

The fact announced was this. No noted public character, no highly placed politician, could do anything so wrong as to disgrace him in this state.

"What if he goes contrary to all the prejudices of the people?"

"No. Mr. Petigru, he is as much respected as ever. Maybe his astounding pluck has raised him in the estimation of the people he flouts and contradicts in their tenderest points, but we meant moral turpitude."

"Mr. Calhoun was as pure a man, &c&c, and he was our idol."

"Oh, yes—but we are now talking of a member not quite as clever or as good as Mr. Calhoun."

"We will not call names."

"No necessity for that. State facts—and the names will attach themselves instantly in every mind."

Mr. Preston was indignant and eloquent in defense of the state.

Mrs. Preston's voice was heard in her low, distinct, tones: "Henry Junius Nott[1] said that. I have often heard him say moral obliquity was not an obstacle to a man's rise in public affairs in America."

"Did you ever see a man cut for any offense whatever?"

"Yes—cheating at cards, cowardice."

"No, not cowardice. Somebody always took his part—or the church did."

"I have seen two men only in all my life who were sent to Conventry thoroughly and deliberately—one a fine young officer in all his bravery of naval costume, traveling with a rich old harridan, at her expense, &c&c&c."

I asked why no one spoke to him—and they gave me no answer but a smile or a shrug of the shoulder. That was at Saratoga. In Washington I saw Mr. Sickles sitting alone on the benches of the Congress—House of Representatives, you know. He was as left to himself as if he had smallpox. There he sat—unfriended, melancholy, slow, solitary, sad of visage.

"What had the poor man done?"

"Killed Phil Barton Key."

"No, no. That was all right, they said. It was because he condoned his wife's profligacy and took her back."

They say, according to the Scripture rule, he had no right to cast a stone at her.

Chorus: "He had a perfect right to shoot down Key at sight. And the jury acquitted him."

"Unsavory subject," said Mr. P, with a sniff of disgust. "But there are Crawford,[2] Judge O'Neall,[3] Governor Perry, Mr. Petigru. They openly condemn this war—but no hand is lifted to turn them aside from any public praise or honor."

"We know they are honest. They have a right to their opinion."

---

1. Probably Josiah Clark Nott's brother, a noted lawyer and writer who died in a shipwreck off the N.C. coast in 1837.

2. The pen name used by George S. Bryan, one of S.C.'s leading Unionists, during the nullification debates.

3. As a member of the S.C. Court of Appeals in the 1830s, Judge John Belton O'Neall had opposed nullification. Although he served as chief justice of the state from 1859 until his death in 1863, O'Neall did not participate in the secession controversy and the disputes of the war years.

"In times of war, few people have been so considerate."

"They think us wrong—they do not take sides against us—&c&c&c."

"We are awfully magnanimous—that's our weak point."

"Now, listen—here it all is in a nutshell. Men may be dishonest, immoral, cruel, black with every crime. Take care how you say so unless you are a crack shot and willing to risk your life in defense of your words. For us, soon as one defamatory word is [uttered], pistols come at once to the fore. That is South Carolina ethics."

"Takes a woman to talk wildly."

"If you have stout hearts and good family connections, you can do pretty much as you please. Old Washington, our George of Mount Vernon, and Alexander Hamilton—the Federalists, pure and simple—they thought democratic republics no great things."

"Surely you know condoning vice in high places is not peculiar to democracies."

"Let the lives of great men alone. Burr was so much worse than Hamilton, whom he killed."

"Hamilton, now—the way he put the blame on that poor woman.[1] He was worse than our father Adam. Eve was his wife—'The woman tempted me.'"

"Surely no man with the instincts of a gentleman would have written that defense of himself."

"And his wife—how she must have hung her proud head for him."

"And yet Hamilton was nearer a gentleman than most men this side of the water."

Listen to Hamlet. This is his opinion of mankind at large and himself in particular, given with much violence to Ophelia:

"I am indifferent honest. And yet I could accuse me of such things—that it were better my mother had not borne me: I am very proud, revengeful, ambitious—&c&c—What should such fellows as I do, crawling between earth and heaven. We are arrant knaves all; believe none of us."

"Shut the door on him—that he may play the fool nowhere but in's own house." Eh?

"I'll give this plague for thy dowry." (Politicians?) "Be thou chaste as ice, pure as snow. Thou shall not escape calumny—"[2]

Paul Hayne says the governor has telegraphed the president to remove Pemberton. He added that Colonel Chesnut thought we surrendered when we gave up Cole's Island.[3]

It seems the governor has asked for Beauregard in Pemberton's place.

These governors of states must be a great nuisance to the War Department.

South Carolina was at Beauregard's feet after Fort Sumter. Since Shiloh she has gotten up and looks askance, rather, when his name is mentioned.

And without Price or Beauregard, who takes charge of the western forces?

1. In 1797, a disappointed office seeker published allegation that Secretary of the Treasury Alexander Hamilton had used government money to purchase the silence of his mistress, Mrs. James Reynolds, and her husband. Hamilton countered by publishing his correspondence with the couple, implying that the pair had consciously set out to blackmail him and proving that they had failed.

2. Paraphrased from *Hamlet,* act 3, scene 1.

3. The island, which protected a naval access to Charleston, was abandoned on March 27, over the objections of Governor Pickens.

Beauregard has just lost his wife. She was Mrs. Slidell's sister. Beauregard's true name is Toutant. He took this fine one from some place he owned.[1] Just now they say he is horribly depressed. In a sort of green melancholy.

And yet this is [his] second experience of wives who die.

"Can we hold out if England and France hold off?" cries Mem.

"No—our time has come."

"For shame—faint heart." Oratorically: "Our people are brave, our cause just, our spirit and our patient endurance beyond reproach, but—"

"I'll tell you what we wanted was a republic, strong, young, vigorous. What we did was to give [up], and we put in power, whenever we could, effete incapables. Worn-out old *U.S.A.* public servants."

Here came in Mary Cantey's strident voice: "I may not have any logic, any sense— I give it up. My woman's instinct tells me, all the same, slavery's turn has come. If we don't do it, they will."

What an actor Mr. Preston would have made! He has a regular genius that way. Then his wonderful voice. What a Coriolanus he would be!

After all this—tried to read *Uncle Tom*. Could not. Too sickening. A man send his little son to beat a human being tied to a tree? It is bad as Squeers beating Smike in the hack.[2] Flesh and blood revolts. You must skip that—it is too bad—or the pulling out of eyeballs in *Lear*.

Back to lodgers:

An old lady opposite giggled all the time. She was in a muslin print gown and diamonds.

I felt uncomfortable and wondered if there was anything amiss with me. I dressed in the dusk of the evening. Generally I hold Molly responsible that I shall not be a figure of fun. This afternoon she was not at home.

Maybe the old lady is always so. Some women are born with a constitutional titter, and it holds on till they die.

Mr. Preston's story of Joe Johnston as a boy.

A party of boys at Abingdon out on a spree—more boys than horses. So Joe Johnston rode behind John Preston, who is his cousin; while going over the mountains, tried to change horses and get behind a servant who was in charge of them all. Servant's horse kicked up, threw Joe Johnston, and broke his leg—a bone showed itself.

"Hello, boys! Come here and look—the confounded bone has come clear through," called out Joe coolly.

They had to carry him on their shoulders, relieving guard. As one party grew tired, another took him up. They knew he must suffer fearfully, but *he never said so*. He was

---

1. Caroline (Deslonde) Beauregard was ill in New Orleans, as M. B. C. has reported, but she did not die until the spring of 1864. Toutant was added to the Beauregard family name as the result of a seventeenth-century marriage settlement.

2. Dickens, *Nicholas Nickleby,* chapter 13.

as cool and quiet after his hurt as before. He was pretty roughly handled, but they could not help it.

His father was in a towering rage because his son's leg was to be set by a country doctor and it might be crooked in the process. At Chickahominy, brave but unlucky Joe had already eleven wounds.

June 13, 1862. Decca's wedding—which happened last year. We were all lying on the bed or sofas near it taking it coolly as to undress. Mrs. Singleton had the floor.

They were engaged before they went up to Charlottesville. Alexander the great was on Gregg's staff—and Gregg was not hard on him. She was the worst in-love girl I ever saw.

Letters came while we were at the hospital, from Alex, urging her to let him marry her at once. In wartimes human events, life especially, was very uncertain.

For several days consecutively she cried without ceasing. Then she consented. The rooms were all crowded, so Decca and I slept together in the same room. There were so many lady nurses at the hospital. It was arranged by letter that the marriage should take place. Then a luncheon at her grandfather Minor's, and then she was to depart with Alex for a few days at Richmond. That was to be their brief slice of honeymoon.

The day came. The wedding breakfast was ready. So was the bride, in all her bridal array. No Alex! No bridegroom—alas, such is the uncertainty of a soldier's life.

The bride said nothing, but she wept like a water nymph.

At dinner she plucked up heart, and at my earnest request she was about to join us. And then the cry, "The bridegroom cometh." He brought his best man and other friends. We had a jolly dinner. "Circumstances over which he had no control had kept him away."

His father sat next to Decca and talked to her all the time as if she were married. It was a piece of absent-mindedness on his part, pure and simple, but it was very trying. And the girl had had a good deal to stand that morning—you can well understand.

Chorus: "To be ready to be married—and the man not to come! The most awful thing of *all* we can imagine."

Immediately after dinner the belated bridegroom proposed a walk. So they walked up the mountain—for a very short walk indeed. Decca upon her return said to me: "Send for Robert Barnwell. I mean to be married today."

"Impossible—no spare room in the house. No getting away from here. The trains all gone—&c&c. Don't you know, this hospital place [is] crammed to the ceiling."

"Alex says I promised to marry him today. It is not his fault he could not come before." I shook my head.

"I don't care," said the positive little thing. "I promised Alex to marry him today, and I will. Send for the Rev. Robert Barnwell."

"Jack[1] and John Darby called him the Proud Prelate."

"Oh, don't interrupt—"

We found Robert, after a world of trouble, and the bride, lovely in Swiss muslin,

1. John Preston, Jr.

was married.

Then I proposed they should take another walk. Then I went to one of my sister nurses and begged her to take me in for the night, as I wished to resign my room to Mr. and Mrs. Haskell. When the bride came from her walk, she asked, "Where are they going to put me?" That was all. At daylight next day they took the train for Richmond, and the small allowance of honeymoon permitted in wartime.

Beauregard's telegram. He cannot leave the Army of the West. His health is bad. No doubt the sea breezes would restore him, but he cannot come now.

Such a lovely name—Gustave Toutant de Beauregard. But Jackson and Johnson and Smith and Jones will do—and *Lee*—short and sweet.

Ransom Spann,[1] another displaced man, came to see me—stayed several hours. All these wealthy young planters raised companies—often entirely at their own expense. Now the government, to induce the men to reenlist for the [duration?], gives them leave to choose their own captains &c. As a general rule the former captain is thrown out. He will not go down to the ranks of his own company. And he comes home to hunt another place with a commission attached. It is really very hard. These men have worked for more than a year to discipline and drill a company any man might be proud of. Then the strict martinet goes by the board. They elect a captain—a good fellow, one of themselves, one [who] will not be too strict with them.

Ransom Spann says in any case he goes straight back to the army. That sort of rough life in the open air agrees with him. He was never so well and hearty in his life.

And if the worst comes—if we fail! He has selected his vocation. He will be a highway robber—he knows the swamps.

"And there will be no danger of runaway negroes there!"

"No—that terror of swamps will be over. I am too old and too lazy to work. I mean to harry the new inhabitants who will come to replace us."

"Every day," says Miriam, "they come here in shoals—*men*—to say we cannot hold Richmond, we cannot hold Charleston, much longer. Wretched beasts—why do you come here? Why don't you stay there, then, and fight? Don't you see that you own yourselves cowards by coming away in the very face of a battle? If you are not liars as to the danger, you are cowards to run away from it," roars the practical Miriam, growing more furious at each word. These Jeremiahs laugh. They think she means the others—not present company.

While Ransom Spann was here, Franklin J. Moses, father of Governor Pickens's secretary, came to see Miriam Cohen. The elder Moses' eyes are similar to Beast Butler's. They are what are commonly called badly crossed. That is the reason he is mostly neutral—he sees both ends of the way at once. Again, another Moses last night, said to be the fiancé of Isabel Cohen. A fair-haired Jew. Miss Bay, like a venerable bluejay, kept hopping in and out of her room to watch Isabel and her lover. What could they be to Miss Bay? That amused me.

What the Middletons told me of Pemberton:

He goes about, saying his mistakes are now made plain to him. He sees that he

---

1. A planter from Sumter District.

ought not to have given up Cole's Island. Our men had the worst of it on James Island. But he told them there was nothing for them to do but fight to the death. He had no way of getting them off, in case of defeat.

Tom Huger resigned his place in the U.S. Navy and come to us. The *Iroquois* was his ship in the old navy. They say as he stood in the rigging, after he was shot in the leg, his ship leading the attack upon the *Iroquois* &c&c, his old crew in the *Iroquois* cheered him. And when his body was borne in, the Federals took off their caps, in respect for his gallant conduct. When he was dying, Meta Huger said to him: "An officer wants to see you. He is one of the enemy."

"Let him come in. I have no enemies now."

But when he heard the man's name:

"No, no. I do not want to see a Southern man who is now in Lincoln's navy."

The officers of the U.S.N. attended his funeral.

Paul Hayne began with Carlyle, which led to Emerson. We were having a good time with Longfellow when Miss Bay interrupted. Whenever we are fairly underway, somebody is sure to come and turn the conversation to——rubbish.

Miss Bay, in honor of the presence of Paul Hayne, poet, produced this. . . .[1]

June 14, 1862. Drop a tear for Turner Ashby.[2] The hero of the Valley. They say he is killed!

All things are against us. Memphis gone—Mississippi fleet annihilated.

And we hear it all, as stolidly apathetic as if it were a story of the English war against China which happened a year or so ago.

Mrs. McCord gives her whole soul to the hospital. "The saddest confusion prevails still," she says. Insufficient medical aid. Good nurses needed. Those she hires eat and drink the things provided for the sick and wounded.

She is the woman to put it straight, with her good common sense, her great administrative ability, and her indomitable will.

As Mrs. McCord went away, Rev. Mrs. Young came.

She wants rooms here. She laid her hand on my arm and said impressively: "You know I must have a room to myself. No third person must come between me and my God."

"Stupid that I am," said the irrepressible Miriam, after she left, "I thought she wanted to be alone for her bath—until she uttered the unexpected word we Jews fear to take in vain."

Gave the poor German woman the bouquet Mrs. McCord brought me. The German in her gratitude kissed both of my hands—queer sensation, a woman kissing your hand.

1. Miss Bay's poem, and comment thereon, deleted.
2. Ashby, the businessman and farmer from Va. who, despite his lack of military experience, became Stonewall Jackson's legendary cavalry commander, died in a minor action on June 6, 1862.

The sons of Mrs. John Julius Pringle have come. They were left at school at the North. A young Huger is with them. They seem to have had adventures enough. Walked, waded, rowed in boats, if boats they could find—swam rivers when boats there were none. Brave lads. One can but admire their pluck and energy. Mrs. Fisher of Philadelphia, née Middleton,[1] gave them money to make the attempt to get home.

Matilda Middleton was hard on my friend—"Do not name him, Mrs. C. I have no patience with any man who remains two years in the enemies' country—and his own country invaded."

While the Middletons were here, our venerable Bay blossom flew in and out— popped in, popped out upon the most preposterous errands. We could hear her ask of all passers in the corridor, "Who are they?" Alas, in this house nobody could tell her.

Finally she came for Mr. C and Paul Hayne to be witness to her will.

"I drew it myself. I am a lawyer's daughter."

Mr. C said, "It is all wrong."

"What does it matter?" she said. "There is nobody to contend for my estate. I have no heirs."

"And very few of us will have any estate to contend for, I fear, before long."

June 16, 1862. Felt suddenly ill in church. As I tried to slip by Mr. Preston unperceived, he looked up, and in his deepest tragic tones: "Shall I go with you?"

"No," I snapped, in a sharp treble.

After service they came to see why I had forsaken them. The heat was so oppressive I should certainly have fainted.

Now, they say, we are to have fighting on James Island. Pemberton has given Evans command there for five days.

Stuart's cavalry have rushed through McClellan's lines and burned five of his transports.[2]

Jackson has been reinforced by 16,000 men. And they hope the enemy will be drawn from around Richmond, and the Valley be the seat of war.

John Chesnut is in Whiting's brigade, which has been sent to Stonewall. Mem's son is with the Boykin Rangers—company A No.1, we call it. And she has persistently wept ever since she heard the news. It is no child's play, she says, when you are with Stonewall. He don't play at soldiering. He don't take care of his men at all. He only goes to kill the Yankees.

Somebody rushed in to tell us. Wade Hampton, who came home (wounded) last night, says: "France has recognized us. Now, that is a sure thing."

Louis Napoleon does not stop at trifles. He never botches his work; he is thorough. The coup d'état, par exemple. So we hope [he] will not help us with a half-hand.

And now, not a word of all this true. Wade Hampton is here, shot in the foot, but he knows no more about France than he does of the man in the moon. Wet blanket he is just now. Johnston badly wounded—Lee is king of spades. They are all once more

1. Elizabeth Izard (Middleton) Fisher, an aunt of Susan Matilda Middleton, was the wife of Joshua Francis Fisher, a publicist, historian, and humanitarian reformer.
2. Stuart completed his daring three-day reconnaissance operation around McClellan on June 15.

digging for dear life. Unless we can reinforce Stonewall, the game is up. Our chiefs contrive to dampen and destroy the enthusiasm of all who go near them. So much entrenching and falling back destroys the morale of any army.

This everlasting retreating, it kills the hearts of the men. Then we are scant of powder, &c&c&c.

J.C. is awfully proud of LeConte's powder manufacturing here. LeConte knows how to do it. J.C. provides him the means to carry out his plans.

Ripley, Pemberton, &c—why don't they put us in the hands of some Southern man who would rather die than *[page ends with incomplete sentence]*

The Hampton girls[1] have asked their father's friends Mr. and Mrs. Rose and Mr. and Mrs. Alfred Huger to stay with them at Millwood. Spend the summer, at any rate.

Anecdote of Mrs. Huger, née Rutledge. She was proud of her exquisite figure. And the fashion of the day enabled them to appear in next to nothing. Pink stockinet and a book muslin classically cut gown—nothing more.

It was by this liberal display of herself as nature made her that put the final stroke to Jérôme Napoleon. But I have wandered off to Miss Patterson.[2]

Mr. Venable don't mince matters. "If we do not [strike] a blow—a blow that will be felt—it will be soon all up with us. The Southwest will be lost to us. We cannot afford to shilly-shally much longer.

"Thousands are enlisting on the other side in New Orleans. Butler holds out inducements. To be sure, they are principally foreigners who want to escape starvation.

"Tennessee we may count as gone, since we abandoned her at Corinth, Fort Pillow, and Memphis. A man must be sent there—or it is all gone."

In my heart I feel "all is gone" now.

"You call a spade by that name, it seems, and not an agricultural instrument."

"They call Mars Robert 'Ole Spade Lee,' he keeps them digging so."

"General Lee is a noble Virginian. Respect something in this world. Caesar—call him Old Spade Caesar. As a soldier he was as much above suspicion as he required his wife to be, as—as Caesar's wife, you know. If I remember Caesar's *Commentaries*, he owns up to a lot of entrenching. You let Mars Robert alone. He knows what he is about."

"Tell us of the Creole way of taking the fall of New Orleans."

"Men, women, children ran around distracted, screaming, chattering, gesticulating. There was no head, no order—all was mere confusion and despair." Then he defended Lovell valiantly, for we charged with all our chivalry.

"Lovell had only 25 hundred regulars to follow him when he left New Orleans. The

---

1. The unmarried sisters of Wade Hampton III—Mary Fisher, Caroline Louisa, Ann, and Kate—who ranged in age from twenty-nine to thirty-eight.

2. In 1803, while visiting the U. S. on an unauthorized leave from the French navy, Jérôme Bonaparte, Napoleon's youngest brother, married Elizabeth Patterson, daughter of a Baltimore merchant. When he tried to return to France, Bonaparte found that his wife was forbidden to land anywhere on the Continent and that he faced a court-martial for desertion. The charge was dropped when he agreed to renounce his wife and child.

crack regiments of New Orleans remained. Butler captured twenty thousand men capable of bearing arms. And now they are spading for Butler at Fort Jackson. Many of the wealthiest citizens are there in their shirtsleeves, spade in hand."

"Don't you think they wish they were with Lovell?" cried the girls.

"It is possible they do."

"Tell us of the womenfolk—how did they take it?"

"They are an excitable race. As I was standing on the levee, a daintily dressed lady picked her way, parasol in hand, toward me. She accosted me with great politeness, and her face was as placid and unmoved as in antebellum days. Her first question: 'Will you be so kind as to tell me? What is the last general order?'

"No order that I know of, Madame. General Disorder prevails now."

"'Ah, I see. And why are those persons flying and yelling so noisily, and racing in the streets in that unseemly way?'

"They are looking for a shell to burst over their heads at any moment."

"'Ah!' Then—with a curtsy of dignity and grace—she waved her parasol and departed, but stopped to arrange her parasol at a proper angle to protect her face from the sun. There was no vulgar haste in her movements. She tripped away as gracefully as she came. I had failed to discompose her by my fearful revelations. That was the one self-possessed soul (that I know of) then in New Orleans.

"Another woman drew near to me, so overheated and out of breath she had barely time to say she had run miles of squares in her crazy terror and bewilderment when a sudden shower came up. In a second she was cool and calm. She forgot all the questions she came to ask.

"'My bonnet—I must save it at any sacrifice'—so turned her dress over her head and went off, forgetting her country's troubles and screaming for a cab."

At Secessionville we went to drive the Yankees out, and we were surprised ourselves.

We lost one hundred, the Yankees 400. They lost more men than we had in the engagement.[1]

Fair shooting, that! As they say in the West, "We whipped our weight in wildcats." And some to spare.

Henry King was killed. He died as a brave man would like to die. From all accounts they say he had not found this world (or his life in it) a bed of roses.

Timrod and Paul Hayne were discussing this battle tonight with eager excitement. "Oh," said Mrs. Bartow, "I hope each of them will give us a poem on it."

Went to see Mrs. Burroughs[2] at the old DeSaussure house. She has such a sweet face, such soft, kind, beautiful dark gray eyes. Such eyes are a poem; no wonder she had a long love story. We sat in the piazza twelve o'clock of a June day, the glorious Southern sun shining his very hottest. But we were in a dense shade. Magnolias in full

---

1. On June 16, an outnumbered force of 500 Confederates stopped the Federal drive up James Island at the hamlet of Secessionville. The Union suffered 683 casualties; the Confederates, 204.

2. Eliza Gibbes (DeSaussure) Burroughs, widow of Henry K. Burroughs.

bloom—ivy, vines of I know not what. And roses in profusion closed us in. It was a living wall of every[thing] beautiful and sweet. I have been thinking of it ever since. In all this flower garden of a Columbia, this is the most delicious corner I have been in yet.

Isabella awaited me at home. Mrs. McMahon was distinctly giving our old maid to understand that she must go. She could not afford to rent so large a room to a single person.

Whispered Isabella, "The cruelty of it! Don't she see how the spinster is doing her best still? It is not her fault that she is not double. Look at the false hair, the rouge, &c&c. What more can a woman do? And to be taunted with her failure!"

Dr. Tennent proved himself a crack shot at Secessionville. They handed him rifles loaded, in rapid succession. And at the point he aimed were found thirty dead men. Scotchmen—for the regiment of Federals at Secessionville were Scotch. And madly intoxicated. They had poured out whiskey for them like water. "With Tarintosh I fear no evil. With Usquabaugh I'll fan the Devil," says Scotch Burns.[1]

Got from the Prestons' French library *Fanny*, with a brilliant preface by Jules Janin.[2] Now, then, I have come to the worst. There can be no worse book than *Fanny*.

The lover is jealous of the husband. The woman is for polyandry rule of life. She cheats both and refuses to break with either. But to criticize it, one must be as shameless as the book itself. Of course, it is clever to the last degree, or it would be kicked into the gutter. It is not nastier or coarser than Mrs. Stowe, but then, it is not written in the interests of philanthropy.

De Créquy on de Genlis. . . .[3]

Decca Singleton, now Mrs. Haskell of a year's standing, has a daughter. Mary Manning[4]—at the top of her voice:

"*Little* Decca Singleton has a daughter. I don't believe a word of it!"

Mr. Preston said of — : "I felt so mortified. It must have been my gray hairs. She came down, she said, as soon as she saw my card. She did not make up for me. I know what that means. It means I am an older man than I thought myself. My dear friend— taken au naturel, she is sallow and freckled. And so careless in her dress. She had a rough, dried yellow gown. Some of the buttons were missing, and she held it together

---

1. Slightly misquoted from Robert Burns, "Tam o' Shanter": "Inspiring bold John Barleycorn! / What dangers thou canst make us scorn!/ Wi' tippenny, we fear nae evil; / Wi' usquebae, we'll face the devil!"

2. Ernest-Aimé Feydeau, *Fanny,* 2nd edition (1858). Jules-Gabriel Janin was a celebrated mid-nineteenth century literary critic.

3. Translated passages omitted. Stéphanie Félicité du Crest de Saint-Aubin, comtesse de Genlis (1746-1830), wrote popular novels and educational tracts, tutored Louis Philippe, and furnished Napoleon with letters on literature and politics.

4. Probably Mary (Cantey) Manning, a second cousin of J. C. Her husband, Brown Manning of Clarendon District, was John Manning's younger brother.

with her hand, but I stayed two hours because, after all, she is so interesting, charming, fascinating."

Mr. Chesnut gave quite otherwise in his account of his reception by her. "Her complexion is the loveliest thing I ever saw, quite a dazzling pink and white. Her gown was miraculous—white muslin and pink ribbons in knots all about and a train yards long—her beautiful hair was crepe and done up in the most intricate style. She was stiff as a stone—did 'grande dame' for me. It was an awful bore. I only stayed a few minutes."

"Oh! oh!" said Mr. Preston. "Which of us did she mean to flatter? For me she had her hair à la chinois—with the two tails of plaits hanging down behind. She has a noble brow. I did not [mind?] its being bared. I am humiliated. I am an old man—and she has found it out.'

"Another visit she sat on the goggle board[1] and bounced up and down between every sentence. All that was not goggle was giggle. She does not put on her dignity with me—I don't mind. She is awfully clever."

"You mean her eyes are beautifully blue."

"Why not? To have such eyes is the cleverest thing a woman can do."

I like them like Maintzey's, with the dark charm, you know—"rubbed in with a dirty finger." The perfection of all eyes.

We had an unexpected dinner party today. First Wade Hampton came and Mary McDuffie. Then Mr. and Mrs. Rose. I remember that the late Colonel Hampton[2] once said to me a thing I thought odd at the time. "Mr. James Rose" (and I forget now who was the other) "are the only two people on this side of the water who know how to give a state dinner."

Mr. and Mrs. James Rose. If anybody wishes to describe old Carolina at its best, let them try their hands at painting these two people.

Wade Hampton still limps a little, but he is rapidly recovering. Here is what he said—and he has fought so well that he is listened to:

"If we mean to play at war as we play a game of chess—West Point tactics prevailing—we are sure to lose the game. They have every advantage. They can lose pawns ad infinitum—to the end of time—and never feel it. We will be throwing away all that we had hoped so much from. Southern hot-headed dash, reckless gallantry, spirit of adventure—readiness to lead forlorn hopes—&c&c."

He says England is sending troops to Canada. And that she has refused to give up the *Emily St. Pierre* and that she has demanded the *Bermuda*. There is a rumor that Lord Lyons has demanded his passports.[3]

1. A bouncing board still found sometimes on Charleston piazzas.
2. Wade Hampton II.
3. In early June, Lord Lyons asked for and received permission to return to England for consultation with his government. Though his action caused speculation about a possible change in British policy, none was forthcoming. The number of British troops in Canada remained constant and restrained negotiations proceeded over the fate of the *Emily St. Pierre*, a Confederate blockade-runner whose crew had risen against their Federal captors and escaped to England.

Mrs. Rose is Miss Sarah Parker's aunt. Somehow it came out when I was not in the room—but those girls tell me everything. It seems Miss Sarah Parker said, "The reason I cannot bear Mrs. Chesnut is that she laughs at everything and at everybody."

If she saw me now, she would give me credit for some pretty hearty crying as well as laughing.

It was a mortifying thing to hear of oneself, all the same.

Mr. Preston came in and announced that Mr. Chesnut was in town. He had just seen Mr. Alfred Huger, who came up on the Charleston train with him. Then Mrs. McCord came and offered to take me back to Mrs. McMahon's to look him up. I found my room locked up. Laurence said his master had gone to look for me at the Prestons'.

Mrs. McCord proposed we should further hunt up my errant husband.

At the door we met Governor Pickens, who showed us telegrams from the president of the most important nature. The governor added, "And I have one from Jeems Chesnut, but I hear he has followed it so closely, coming on its heels, as it were, that I need not show you that one."

"You don't look interested at the sound of your husband's name?"

"Is that his name?"

"What does she mean?" to Mrs. McCord.

"I suppose she thought it was James."

"My advice to you is to find him, for Mrs. Pickens says he was last seen in the company of two very handsome women. And now you may call him any name you please."

It was not a case of Evangeline[1]—and both on the same errand, we soon met. The two beautiful dames Governor Pickens threw in my teeth were Sanders from Rafton Creek, almost neighbors. They only live fifteen miles from Camden.

Sandy Brown[2] and Grayson (the poet and friend of Mr. Petigru) are at it shovel and tongs. Sandy Brown is the man who stabbed William Izard Bull[3] in a brawl.

At Mrs. Preston's it was a feast of apricots. They break them in half, pile them up on a dish, and eat them as you do peaches, with cream and sugar.

By way of pleasant remark to Wade Hampton:

"Oh, general! The next battle will give you a chance to be major general."

"I was very foolish to give up my Legion," he answered gloomily.

"Promotion don't really annoy many people."

---

1. In Henry Wadsworth Longfellow's, *Evangeline: A Tale of Acadie*, (1847), a young woman searches for her fiancé, who had mysteriously disappeared on their wedding day. When she finds him on his deathbed, the shock of the discovery kills her.

2. Alexander Henry Brown was a member of the secession convention and provost marshal of Charleston who specialized in admiralty law. A former U.S. congressman, William John Grayson combined an ardent defense of slavery with opposition to secession. He wrote *The Hireling and the Slave* (1854) and *James Louis Petigru: A Biographical Sketch* (1866), which appeared posthumously.

3. Like Brown, William Izard Bull, Sr., a wealthy planter and longtime state legislator, lived in St. Andrew's Parish.

Mary Gibson says her father writes to them that they may go back. He thinks now that the Confederates can hold Richmond.

Gloria in excelsis!

Another personal defeat. Little Kate: "Oh, Cousin Mary, why don't you cultivate heart? They say at Kirkwood that you had better let your brains alone awhile and cultivate heart."

She had evidently caught up a phrase and repeated it again and again for my benefit. So that is the way they talk of me!

The only good of loving anyone with your whole heart is to give that person the power to hurt you. To hear those people complained of my want of heart! How it hurt.

And now, see how I am improving my mind. De Créquy, *Cousine Bette*, and last of all *Fanny*.

The merry brown hares are leaping—&c&c. How that thing seized me by the throat!

Free England—upon whose soil a slave has only to set his foot and the shackles fall off. And yet the rhymes of Kingsley touched a chord which vibrated, because this thing fitted into a slave state of things so well.

The possibilities of slavery the same everywhere.

(1905, 1949, 1981)

FREDERICK DOUGLASS

Narrative of the Life of Frederick Douglass:
An American Slave

I lived in Master Hugh's family about seven years. During this time, I succeeded in learning to read and write. In accomplishing this, I was compelled to resort to various stratagems. I had no regular teacher. My mistress, who had kindly commenced to instruct me, had, in compliance with the advice and direction of her husband, not only ceased to instruct, but had set her face against my being instructed by any one else. It is due, however, to my mistress to say of her, that she did not adopt this course of treatment immediately. She at first lacked the depravity indispensable to shutting me up in mental darkness. It was at least necessary for her to have some training in the exercise of irresponsible power, to make her equal to the task of treating me as though I were a brute.

My mistress was, as I have said, a kind and tender-hearted woman; and in the simplicity of her soul she commenced, when I first went to live with her, to treat me as she supposed one human being ought to treat another. In entering upon the duties of a slaveholder, she did not seem to perceive that I sustained to her the relation of a mere chattel, and that for her to treat me as a human being was not only wrong, but dangerously so. Slavery proved as injurious to her as it did to me. When I went there, she was a pious, warm, and tender-hearted woman. There was no sorrow or suffering for which she had not a tear. She had bread for the hungry, clothes for the naked, and comfort for every mourner that came within her reach. Slavery soon proved its ability to divest her of these heavenly qualities. Under its influence, the tender heart became stone, and the lamblike disposition gave way to one of tiger-like fierceness. The first step in her downward course was in her ceasing to instruct me. She now commenced to practise her husband's precepts. She finally became even more violent in her opposition than her husband himself. She was not satisfied with simply doing as well as he had commanded; she seemed anxious to do better. Nothing seemed to make her more angry than to see me with a newspaper. She seemed to think that here lay the danger. I have had her rush at me with a face made all up of fury, and snatch from me a newspaper, in a manner that fully revealed her apprehension. She was an apt woman; and a little experience soon demonstrated, to her satisfaction, that education and slavery were incompatible with each other.

From this time I was most narrowly watched. If I was in a separate room any considerable length of time, I was sure to be suspected of having a book, and was at once called to give an account of myself. All this, however, was too late. The first step had been taken. Mistress, in teaching me the alphabet, had given me the *inch*, and no precaution could prevent me from taking the *ell*.

The plan which I adopted, and the one by which I was most successful, was that of making friends of all the little white boys whom I met in the street. As many of these as I could, I converted into teachers. With their kindly aid, obtained at different times and in different places, I finally succeeded in learning to read. When I was sent of errands, I always took my book with me, and by going one part of my errand quickly, I found time to get a lesson before my return. I used also to carry bread with me, enough of which was always in the house, and to which I was always welcome; for I was much better off in this regard than many of the poor white children in our neighborhood. This bread I used to bestow upon the hungry little urchins, who, in return, would give me that more valuable bread of knowledge. I am strongly tempted to give the names of two or three of those little boys, as a testimonial of the gratitude and affection I bear them; but prudence forbids;–not that it would injure me, but it might embarrass them; for it is almost an unpardonable offence to teach slaves to read in this Christian country. It is enough to say of the dear little fellows, that they lived on Philpot Street, very near Durgin and Bailey's ship-yard. I used to talk this matter of slavery over with them. I would sometimes say to them, I wished I could be as free as they would be when they got to be men. "You will be free as soon as you are twenty-one, *but I am a slave for life!* Have not I as good a right to be free as you have?" These words used to trouble them; they would express for me the liveliest sympathy, and console me with the hope that something would occur by which I might be free.

I was now about twelve years old, and the thought of being *a slave for life* began to bear heavily upon my heart. Just about this time, I got hold of a book entitled "The Columbian Orator." Every opportunity I got, I used to read this book. Among much of other interesting matter, I found in it a dialogue between a master and his slave. The slave was represented as having run away from his master three times. The dialogue represented the conversation which took place between them, when the slave was retaken the third time. In this dialogue, the whole argument in behalf of slavery was brought forward by the master, all of which was disposed of by the slave. The slave was made to say some very smart as well as impressive things in reply to his master– things which had the desired though unexpected effect; for the conversation resulted in the voluntary emancipation of the slave on the part of the master.

In the same book, I met with one of Sheridan's mighty speeches on and in behalf of Catholic emancipation. These were choice documents to me. I read them over and over again with unabated interest. They gave tongue to interesting thoughts of my own soul, which had frequently flashed through my mind, and died away for want of utterance. The moral which I gained from the dialogue was the power of truth over the conscience of even a slaveholder. What I got from Sheridan was a bold denunciation of slavery, and a powerful vindication of human rights. The reading of these documents enabled me to utter my thoughts, and to meet the arguments brought forward to sustain slavery; but while they relieved me of one difficulty, they brought on another even more painful than the one of which I was relieved. The more I read, the more I was led to abhor and detest my enslavers. I could regard them in no other light than a band of successful robbers, who had left their homes, and gone to Africa, and stolen us from our homes, and in a strange land reduced us to slavery. I loathed them as being the meanest as well as the most wicked of men. As I read and contemplated the subject, behold! that very discontentment which Master Hugh had predicted would follow my learning to read had already come, to torment and sting my soul to unutterable anguish. As I writhed under it, I would at times feel that learning to read had been a curse rather than a blessing. It had given me a view of my wretched condition, without the remedy. It opened my eyes to the horrible pit, but to no ladder upon which to get out. In moments of agony, I envied my fellow-slaves for their stupidity. I have often wished myself a beast. I preferred the condition of the meanest reptile to my own. Any thing, no matter what, to get rid of thinking! It was this everlasting thinking of my condition that tormented me. There was no getting rid of it. It was pressed upon me by every object within sight or hearing, animate or inanimate. The silver trump of freedom had roused my soul to eternal wakefulness. Freedom now appeared, to disappear no more forever. It was heard in every sound, and seen in every thing. It was ever present to torment me with a sense of my wretched condition. I saw nothing without seeing it, I heard nothing without hearing it, and felt nothing without feeling it. It looked from every star, it smiled in every calm, breathed in every wind, and moved in every storm.

I often found myself regretting my own existence, and wishing myself dead; and but for the hope of being free, I have no doubt but that I should have killed myself, or done something for which I should have been killed. While in this state of mind, I was eager to hear any one speak of slavery. I was a ready listener. Every little while, I could hear something about the abolitionists. It was some time before I found what the word meant. It was always used in such connections as to make it an interesting word to me. If a slave ran away and succeeded in getting clear, or if a slave killed his master, set fire to barn, or did any thing very wrong in the mind of a slaveholder, it was spoken of as the fruit of *abolition*. Hearing the word in this connection very often, I set about learning what it meant. The dictionary afforded me little or no help. I found it was "the act of abolishing;" but then I did not know what was to be abolished. Here I was perplexed. I did not dare to ask any one about its meaning, for I was satisfied that it was something they wanted me to know very little about. After a patient waiting, I got one of our city papers, containing an account of the number of petitions from the north, praying for the abolition of slavery in the District of Columbia, and of the slave trade between the States. From this time I understood the words *abolition* and *abolitionist*, and always drew near when that word was spoken, expecting to hear something of importance to myself and fellow-slaves. The light broke in upon me by degrees. I went one day down on the wharf of Mr. Waters; and seeing two Irishmen unloading a scow of stone, I went, unasked, and helped them. When we had finished, one of them came to me and asked me if I were a slave. I told him I was. He asked, "Are ye a slave for life?" I told him that I was. The good Irishman seemed to be deeply affected by the statement. He said to the other that it was a pity so fine a little fellow as myself should be a slave for life. He said it was a shame to hold me. They both advised me to run away to the north; that I should find friends there, and that I should be free. I pretended not to be interested in what they said, and treated them as I did not understand them; for I feared they might be treacherous. White men have been known to encourage slaves to escape, and then, to get the reward, catch them and return them to their masters. I was afraid that these seemingly good men might use me so; but I nevertheless remembered their advice, and from that time I resolved to run away. I looked forward to a time at which it would be safe for me to escape. I was too young to think of doing so immediately; besides, I wished to learn how to write, as I might have occasion to write my own pass. I consoled myself with the hope that I should one day find a good chance. Meanwhile, I would learn to write.

The idea as to how I might learn to write was suggested to me by being in Durgin and Bailey's ship-yard, and frequently seeing the ship carpenters, after hewing, and getting a piece of timber ready for use, write on the timber the name of that part of the ship for which it was intended. When a piece of timber was intended for the larboard side, it would be marked thus—"L." When a piece was for the starboard side, it would be marked thus—"S." A piece for the larboard side forward would be marked thus —"L. F. " When a piece was for starboard side forward, it would be marked thus— "S. F. " For larboard aft, it would be marked thus—"L. A. " For starboard aft, it would be marked thus—"S. A. " I soon learned the names of these letters, and for what they were intended when placed upon a piece of timber in the ship-yard. I immediately commenced copying them, and in a short time was able to make the four letters named. After that, when I met with any boy who I knew could write, I would tell him I could write as well as he. The next word would be, "I don't believe you. Let me see you try it. " I would then make the letters which I had been so fortunate as to learn, and ask him to beat that. In this way I got a good many lessons in writing, which it is quite possible I should never have gotten in any other way. During this time, my copy-book was the board fence, brick wall, and pavement; my pen and ink was a lump of chalk. With these, I learned mainly how to write. I then commenced and continued copying the Italics in Webster's Spelling Book, until I could make them all without looking on the book. By this time, my little Master Thomas had gone to school, and learned how to write, and had written over a number of copy-books. These had been brought home, and shown to some of our near neighbors, and then laid aside. My mistress used to go to class meeting at the Wilk Street meetinghouse every Monday afternoon, and leave me to take care of the house. When left thus, I used to spend the time in writing in the spaces left in Master Thomas's copy-book, copying what he had written. I continued to do this until I could write a hand very similar to that of Master Thomas. Thus, after a long, tedious effort for years, I finally succeeded in learning how to write.

In a very short time after I went to live at Baltimore, my old master's youngest son Richard died; and in about three years and six months after his death, my old master, Captain Anthony, died, leaving only his son, Andrew, and daughter, Lucretia, to share his estate. He died while on a visit to see his daughter at Hillsborough. Cut off thus unexpectedly, he left no will as to the disposal of his property. It was therefore necessary to have a valuation of the property, that it might be equally divided between Mrs. Lucretia and Master Andrew. I was immediately sent for, to be valued with the other property. Here again my feelings rose up in detestation of slavery. I had now a new conception of my degraded condition. Prior to this, I had become, if not insensible to my lot, at least partly so. I left Baltimore with a young heart overborne with sadness, and a soul full of apprehension. I took passage with Captain Rowe, in the schooner Wild Cat, and, after a sail of about twenty-four hours, I found myself near the place of my birth. I had now been absent from it almost, if not quite, five years. I, however, remembered the place very well. I was only about five years old when I left it, to go and live with my old master on Colonel Lloyd's plantation; so that I was now between ten and eleven years old.

We were all ranked together at the valuation. Men and women, old and young, married and single, were ranked with horses, sheep, and swine. There were horses and men, cattle and women, pigs and children, all holding the same rank in the scale of being, and were all subjected to the same narrow examination. Silvery-headed age and sprightly youth, maids and matrons, had to undergo the same indelicate inspection. At this moment, I saw more clearly than ever the brutalizing effects of slavery upon both slave and slaveholder.

After the valuation, then came the division. I have no language to express the high excitement and deep anxiety which were felt among us poor slaves during this time. Our fate for life was now to be decided. We had no more voice in that decision than the brutes among whom we were ranked. A single word from the white men was enough–against all our wishes, prayers, and entreaties—to sunder forever the dearest friends, dearest kindred, and strongest ties known to human beings. In addition to the pain of separation, there was the horrid dread of falling into the hands of Master Andrew. He was known to us all as being a most cruel wretch, —a common drunkard, who had, by his reckless mismanagement and profligate dissipation, already wasted a large portion of his father's property. We all felt that we might as well be sold at once to the Georgia traders, as to pass into his hands; for we knew that that would be our inevitable condition, —a condition held by us all in the utmost horror and dread.

I suffered more anxiety than most of my fellow-slaves. I had known what it was to be kindly treated; they had known nothing of the kind. They had seen little or nothing of the world. They were in very deed men and women of sorrow, and acquainted with grief. Their backs had been made familiar with the bloody lash, so that they had become callous; mine was yet tender; for while at Baltimore I got few whippings, and few slaves could boast of a kinder master and mistress than myself; and the thought of passing out of their hands into those of Master Andrew—a man who, but a few days before, to give me a sample of his bloody disposition, took my little brother by the throat, threw him on the ground, and with the heel of his boot stamped upon his head till the blood gushed from his nose and ears—was well calculated to make me anxious as to my fate. After he had committed this savage outrage upon my brother, he turned to me, and said that was the way he meant to serve me one of these days, —meaning, I suppose, when I came into his possession.

Thanks to a kind Providence, I fell to the portion of Mrs. Lucretia, and was sent immediately back to Baltimore, to live again in the family of Master Hugh. Their joy at my return equalled their sorrow at my departure. It was a glad day to me. I had escaped a fate worse than lion's jaws. I was absent from Baltimore, for the purpose of valuation and division, just about one month, and it seemed to have been six.

Very soon after my return to Baltimore, my mistress, Lucretia, died, leaving her husband and one child, Amanda; and in a very short time after her death, Master Andrew died. Now all the property of my old master, slaves included, was in the hands of strangers, —strangers who had had nothing to do with accumulating it. Not a slave was left free. All remained slaves, from the youngest to the oldest. If any one thing in my experience, more than another, served to deepen my conviction of the infernal character of slavery, and to fill me with unutterable loathing of slaveholders, it was their base ingratitude to my poor old grandmother. She had served my old master faithfully from youth to old age. She had been the source of all his wealth; she had peopled his plantation with slaves; she had become a great grandmother in his service. She had rocked him in infancy, attended him in childhood, served him through life, and at his death wiped from his icy brow the cold death-sweat, and closed his eyes forever. She was nevertheless left a slave—a slave for life—a slave in the hands of strangers; and in their hands she saw her children, her grandchildren, and her great-grandchildren, divided, like so many sheep, without being gratified with the small privilege of a single word, as to their or her own destiny. And, to cap the climax of their base ingratitude and fiendish barbarity, my grandmother, who was now very old, having outlived my old master and all his children, having seen the beginning and end of all of them, and her present owners finding she was of but little value, her frame already racked with the pains of old age, and complete helplessness fast stealing over her once active limbs, they took her to the woods, built her a little hut, put up a little mud-chimney, and then made her welcome to the privilege of supporting herself there in perfect loneliness; thus virtually turning her out to die! If my poor old grandmother now lives, she lives to suffer in utter loneliness; she lives to remember and mourn over the loss of children, the loss of grandchildren, and the loss of great-grandchildren. They are, in the language of the slave's poet, Whittier, —

> "Gone, gone, sold and gone
> To the rice swamp dank and lone,
> Where the slave-whip ceaseless swings,
> Where the noisome insect stings,
> Where the fever-demon strews
> Poison with the falling dews,
> Where the sickly sunbeams glare
> Through the hot and misty air:—
>> Gone, gone, sold and gone
>> To the rice swamp dank and lone,
>> From Virginia hills and waters—
>> Woe is me, my stolen daughters!"

The hearth is desolate. The children, the unconscious children, who once sang and danced in her presence, are gone. She gropes her way, in the darkness of age, for a drink of water. Instead of the voices of her children, she hears by day the moans of the dove, and by night the screams of the hideous owl. All is gloom. The grave is at the door. And now, when weighed down by the pains and aches of old age, when the head inclines to the feet, when the beginning and ending of human existence meet, and helpless infancy and painful old age combine together—at this time, this most needful time, the time for the exercise of that tenderness and affection which children only can exercise towards a declining parent—my poor old grandmother, the devoted mother of twelve children, is left all alone, in yonder little hut, before a few dim embers. She stands—she sits—she staggers—she falls—she groans—she dies—and there are none of her children or grandchildren present, to wipe from her wrinkled brow the cold sweat of death, or to place beneath the sod her fallen remains. Will not a righteous God visit for these things?

In about two years after the death of Mrs. Lucretia, Master Thomas married his second wife. Her name was Rowena Hamilton. She was the eldest daughter of Mr. William Hamilton. Master now lived in St. Michael's. Not long after his marriage, a misunderstanding took place between himself and Master Hugh; and as a means of punishing his brother, he took me from him to live with himself at St. Michael's. Here I underwent another most painful separation. It, however, was not so severe as the one I dreaded at the division of property; for, during this interval, a great change had taken place in Master Hugh and his once kind and affectionate wife. The influence of brandy upon him, and of slavery upon her, had effected a disastrous change in the characters of both; so that, as far as they were concerned, I thought I had little to lose by the change. But it was not to them that I was attached. It was to those little Baltimore boys that I felt the strongest attachment. I had received many good lessons from them, and was still receiving them, and the thought of leaving them was painful indeed. I was leaving, too, without the hope of ever being allowed to return. Master Thomas had said he would never let me return again. The barrier betwixt himself and brother he considered impassable.

I then had to regret that I did not at least make the attempt to carry out my resolution to run away; for the chances of success are tenfold greater from the city than from the country.

I sailed from Baltimore for St. Michael's in the sloop Amanda, Captain Edward Dodson. On my passage, I paid particular attention to the direction which the steamboats took to go to Philadelphia. I found, instead of going down, on reaching North Point they went up the bay, in a north-easterly direction. I deemed this knowledge of the utmost importance. My determination to run away was again revived. I resolved to wait only so long as the offering of a favorable opportunity. When that came, I was determined to be off.

I have now reached a period of my life when I can give dates. I left Baltimore, and went to live with Master Thomas Auld, at St. Michael's, in March, 1832. It was now more than seven years since I lived with him in the family of my old master, on

Colonel Lloyd's plantation. We of course were now almost entire strangers to each other. He was to me a new master, and I to him a new slave. I was ignorant of his temper and disposition; he was equally so of mine. A very short time, however, brought us into full acquaintance with each other. I was made acquainted with his wife not less than with himself. They were well matched, being equally mean and cruel. I was now, for the first time during the space of more than seven years, made to feel the painful gnawings of hunger—a something which I had not experienced before since I left Colonel Lloyd's plantation. It went hard enough with me then, when I could look back to no period at which I had enjoyed a sufficiency. It was tenfold harder after living in Master Hugh's family, where I had always had enough to eat, and of that which was good. I have said Master Thomas was a mean man. He was so. Not to give a slave enough to eat, is regarded as the most aggravated development of meanness even among slaveholders. The rule is, no matter how coarse the food, only let there be enough of it. This is the theory; and in the part of Maryland from which I came, it is the general practice, —though there are many exceptions. Master Thomas gave us enough of neither coarse nor fine food. There were four slaves of us in the kitchen– my sister Eliza, my aunt Priscilla, Henny, and myself; and we were allowed less than a half of a bushel of corn-meal per week, and very little else, either in the shape of meat or vegetables. It was not enough for us to subsist upon. We were therefore reduced to the wretched necessity of living at the expense of our neighbors. This we did by begging and stealing, whichever came handy in the time of need, the one being considered as legitimate as the other. A great many times have we poor creatures been nearly perishing with hunger, when food in abundance lay mouldering in the safe and smoke-house, and our pious mistress was aware of the fact; and yet that mistress and her husband would kneel every morning, and pray that God would bless them in basket and store!

Bad as all slaveholders are, we seldom meet one destitute of every element of character commanding respect. My master was one of this rare sort. I do not know of one single noble act ever performed by him. The leading trait in his character was meanness; and if there were any other element in his nature, it was made subject to this. He was mean; and, like most other mean men, he lacked the ability to conceal his meanness. Captain Auld was not born a slaveholder. He had been a poor man, master only of a Bay craft. He came into possession of all his slaves by marriage; and of all men, adopted slaveholders are the worst. He was cruel, but cowardly. He commanded without firmness. In the enforcement of his rules, he was at times rigid, and at times lax. At times, he spoke to his slaves with the firmness of Napoleon and the fury of a demon; at other times, he might well be mistaken for an inquirer who had lost his way. He did nothing of himself. He might have passed for a lion, but for his ears. In all things noble which he attempted, his own meanness shone most conspicuous. His airs, words, and actions, were the airs, words, and actions of born slaveholders, and, being assumed, were awkward enough. He was not even a good imitator. He possessed all the disposition to deceive, but wanted the power. Having no resources within himself, he was compelled to be the copyist of many, and being such, he was forever the victim of inconsistency; and of consequence he was an object of contempt, and was held as such even by his slaves. The luxury of having slaves of his own to wait upon him was something new and unprepared for. He was a slaveholder without the ability to hold slaves. He found himself incapable of managing his slaves either by force, fear, or fraud. We seldom called him "master;" we generally called him "Captain Auld, " and were hardly disposed to title him at all. I doubt not that our conduct had much to do with making him appear awkward, and of consequence fretful. Our want of reverence for him must have perplexed him greatly. He wished to have us call him master, but lacked the firmness necessary to command us to do so. His wife used to insist upon calling him so, but to no purpose. In August, 1832, my master attended a Methodist camp-meeting held in the Bay-side, Talbot county, and there experienced religion. I indulged a faint hope that his conversion would lead him to emancipate his slaves, and that, if he did not do this, it would, at any rate, make him more kind and humane. I was disappointed in both these respects. It neither made him to be humane to his slaves, nor to emancipate them. If it had any effect on his character, it made him more cruel and hateful in all his ways; for I believe him to have been a much worse man after his conversion than before. Prior to his conversion, he relied upon his own depravity to shield and sustain him in his savage barbarity; but after his conversion, he found religious sanction and support for his slaveholding cruelty. He made the greatest pretensions to piety. His house was the house of prayer. He prayed morning, noon, and night. He very soon distinguished himself among his brethren, and was soon made a class-leader and exhorter. His activity in revivals was great, and he proved himself an instrument in the hands of the church in converting many souls. His house was the preachers' home. They used to take great pleasure in coming there to put up; for while he starved us, he stuffed them. We have had three or four preachers there at a time. The names of those who used to come most frequently while I lived there, were Mr. Storks, Mr. Ewery, Mr. Humphry, and Mr. Hickey. I have also seen Mr. George Cookman at our house. We slaves loved Mr. Cookman. We believed him to be a good man. We thought him instrumental in getting Mr. Samuel Harrison, a very rich slaveholder, to emancipate his slaves; and by some means got the impression that he was laboring to effect the emancipation of all the slaves. When he was at our house, we were sure to be called in to prayers. When the others were there, we were sometimes called in and sometimes not. Mr. Cookman took more notice of us than either of the other ministers. He could not come among us without betraying his sympathy for us, and, stupid as we were, we had the sagacity to see it.

While I lived with my master in St. Michael's, there was a white young man, a Mr. Wilson, who proposed to keep a Sabbath school for the instruction of such slaves as might be disposed to learn to read the New Testament. We met but three times, when Mr. West and Mr. Fairbanks, both class-leaders, with many others, came upon us with sticks and other missiles, drove us off, and forbade us to meet again. Thus ended our little Sabbath school in the pious town of St. Michael's.

I have said my master found religious sanction for his cruelty. As an example, I will state one of many facts going to prove the charge. I have seen him tie up a lame young woman, and whip her with a heavy cowskin upon her naked shoulders, causing the warm red blood to drip; and, in justification of the bloody deed, he would quote this passage of the Scripture—"He that knoweth his master's will, and doeth it not, shall be beaten with many stripes. "

Master would keep this lacerated young woman tied up in this horrid situation four or five hours at a time. I have known him to tie her up early in the morning, and whip her before breakfast; leave her, go to his store, return at dinner, and whip her again, cutting her in the places already made raw with his cruel lash. The secret of master's cruelty toward "Henny" is found in the fact of her being almost helpless. When quite a child, she fell into the fire, and burned herself horribly. Her hands were so burnt that she never got the use of them. She could do very little but bear heavy burdens. She was to master a bill of expense; and as he was a mean man, she was a constant offence to him. He seemed desirous of getting the poor girl out of existence. He gave her away once to his sister; but, being a poor gift, she was not disposed to keep her. . Finally, my benevolent master, to use his own words, "set her adrift to take care of herself. " Here was a recently-converted man, holding on upon the mother, and at the same time turning out her helpless child, to starve and die! Master Thomas was one of the many pious slaveholders who hold slaves for the very charitable purpose of taking care of them.

My master and myself had quite a number of differences. He found me unsuitable to his purpose. My city life, he said, had had a very pernicious effect upon me. It had almost ruined me for every good purpose, and fitted me for every thing which was bad. One of my greatest faults was that of letting his horse run away, and go down to his father-in-law's farm, which was about five miles from St. Michael's. I would then have to go after it. My reason for this kind of carelessness, or carefulness, was, that I could always get something to eat when I went there. Master William Hamilton, my master's father-in-law, always gave his slaves enough to eat. I never left there hungry, no matter how great the need of my speedy return. Master Thomas at length said he would stand it no longer. I had lived with him nine months, during which time he had given me a number of severe whippings, all to no good purpose. He resolved to put me out, as he said, to be broken; and, for this purpose, he let me for one year to a man named Edward Covey. Mr. Covey was a poor man, a farm-renter. He rented the place upon which he lived, as also the hands with which he tilled it. Mr. Covey had acquired a very high reputation for breaking young slaves, and this reputation was of immense value to him. It enabled him to get his farm tilled with much less expense to himself than he could have had it done without such a reputation. Some slaveholders thought it not much loss to allow Mr. Covey to have their slaves one year, for the sake of the training to which they were subjected, without any other compensation. He could hire young help with great ease, in consequence of this reputation. Added to the natural good qualities of Mr. Covey, he was a professor of religion—a pious soul—a member and a class-leader in the Methodist church. All of this added weight to his reputation as a "nigger-breaker. " I was aware of all the facts, having been made acquainted with them by a young man who had lived there. I nevertheless made the change gladly; for I was sure of getting enough to eat, which is not the smallest consideration to a hungry man.

I left Master Thomas's house, and went to live with Mr. Covey, on the 1st of January, 1833. I was now, for the first time in my life, a field hand. In my new employment, I found myself even more awkward than a country boy appeared to be in a large city. I had been at my new home but one week before Mr. Covey gave me a very severe whipping, cutting my back, causing the blood to run, and raising ridges on my flesh as large as my little finger. The details of this affair are as follows: Mr. Covey sent me, very early in the morning of one of our coldest days in the month of January, to the woods, to get a load of wood. He gave me a team of unbroken oxen. He told me which was the in-hand ox, and which the off-hand one. He then tied the end of a large rope around the horns of the in-hand ox, and gave me the other end of it, and told me, if the oxen started to run, that I must hold on upon the rope. I had never driven oxen before, and of course I was very awkward. I, however, succeeded in getting to the edge of the woods with little difficulty; but I had got a very few rods into the woods, when the oxen took fright, and started full tilt, carrying the cart against trees, and over stumps, in the most frightful manner. I expected every moment that my brains would be dashed out against the trees. After running thus for a considerable distance, they finally upset the cart, dashing it with great force against a tree, and threw themselves into a dense thicket. How I escaped death, I do not know. There I was, entirely alone, in a thick wood, in a place new to me. My cart was upset and shattered, my oxen were entangled among the young trees, and there was none to help me. After a long spell of effort, I succeeded in getting my cart righted, my oxen disentangled, and again yoked to the cart. I now proceeded with my team to the place where I had, the day before, been chopping wood, and loaded my cart pretty heavily, thinking in this way to tame my oxen. I then proceeded on my way home. I had now consumed one half of the day. I got out of the woods safely, and now felt out of danger. I stopped my oxen to open the woods gate; and just as I did so, before I could get hold of my ox-rope, the oxen again started, rushed through the gate, catching it between the wheel and the body of the cart, tearing it to pieces, and coming within a few inches of crushing me against the gate-post. Thus twice, in one short day, I escaped death by the merest chance. On my return, I told Mr. Covey what had happened, and how it happened. He ordered me to return to the woods again immediately. I did so, and he followed on after me. Just as I got into the woods, he came up and told me to stop my cart, and that he would teach me how to trifle away my time, and break gates. He then went to a large gum-tree, and with his axe cut three large switches, and, after trimming them up neatly with his pocketknife, he ordered me to take off my clothes. I made him no answer, but stood with my clothes on. He repeated his order. I still made him no answer, nor did I move to strip myself. Upon this he rushed at me with the fierceness of a tiger, tore off my clothes, and lashed me till he had worn out his switches, cutting me so savagely as to leave the marks visible for a long time after. This whipping was the first of a number just like it, and for similar offences.

I lived with Mr. Covey one year. During the first six months, of that year, scarce a week passed without his whipping me. I was seldom free from a sore back. My awkwardness was almost always his excuse for whipping me. We were worked fully up to the point of endurance. Long before day we were up, our horses fed, and by the first approach of day we were off to the field with our hoes and ploughing teams. Mr.

Covey gave us enough to eat, but scarce time to eat it. We were often less than five minutes taking our meals. We were often in the field from the first approach of day till its last lingering ray had left us; and at saving-fodder time, midnight often caught us in the field binding blades.

Covey would be out with us. The way he used to stand it, was this. He would spend the most of his afternoons in bed. He would then come out fresh in the evening, ready to urge us on with his words, example, and frequently with the whip. Mr. Covey was one of the few slaveholders who could and did work with his hands. He was a hard-working man. He knew by himself just what a man or a boy could do. There was no deceiving him. His work went on in his absence almost as well as in his presence; and he had the faculty of making us feel that he was ever present with us. This he did by surprising us. He seldom approached the spot where we were at work openly, if he could do it secretly. He always aimed at taking us by surprise. Such was his cunning, that we used to call him among ourselves, "the snake." When we were at work in the cornfield, he would sometimes crawl on his hands and knees to avoid detection, and all at once he would rise nearly in our midst, and scream out, "Ha, ha! Come, come! Dash on, dash on!" This being his mode of attack, it was never safe to stop a single minute. His comings were like a thief in the night. He appeared to us as being ever at hand. He was under every tree, behind every stump, in every bush, and at every window, on the plantation. He would sometimes mount his horse, as if bound to St. Michael's, a distance of seven miles, and in half an hour afterwards you would see him coiled up in the corner of the wood-fence, watching every motion of the slaves. He would, for this purpose, leave his horse tied up in the woods. Again, he would sometimes walk up to us, and give us orders as though he was upon the point of starting on a long journey, turn his back upon us, and make as though he was going to the house to get ready; and, before he would get half way thither, he would turn short and crawl into a fence-corner, or behind some tree, and there watch us till the going down of the sun.

Mr. Covey's *forte* consisted in his power to deceive. His life was devoted to planning and perpetrating the grossest deceptions. Every thing he possessed in the shape of learning or religion, he made conform to his disposition to deceive. He seemed to think himself equal to deceiving the Almighty. He would make a short prayer in the morning, and a long prayer at night; and, strange as it may seem, few men would at times appear more devotional than he. The exercises of his family devotions were always commenced with singing; and, as he was a very poor singer himself, the duty of raising the hymn generally came upon me. He would read his hymn, and nod at me to commence. I would at times do so; at others, I would not. My non-compliance would almost always produce much confusion. To show himself independent of me, he would start and stagger through with his hymn in the most discordant manner. In this state of mind, he prayed with more than ordinary spirit. Poor man! such was his disposition, and success at deceiving, I do verily believe that he sometimes deceived himself into the solemn belief, that he was a sincere worshipper of the most high God; and this, too, at a time when he may be said to have been guilty of compelling his woman slave to commit the sin of adultery. The facts in the case are these: Mr. Covey was a poor man; he was just commencing in life; he was only able to buy one slave;

and, shocking as is the fact, he bought her, as he said, for a *breeder*. This woman was named Caroline. Mr. Covey bought her from Mr. Thomas Lowe, about six miles from St. Michael's. She was a large, able-bodied woman, about twenty years old. She had already given birth to one child, which proved her to be just what he wanted. After buying her, he hired a married man of Mr. Samuel Harrison, to live with him one year; and him he used to fasten up with her every night! The result was, that, at the end of the year, the miserable woman gave birth to twins. At this result Mr. Covey seemed to be highly pleased, both with the man and the wretched woman. Such was his joy, and that of his wife, that nothing they could do for Caroline during her confinement was too good, or too hard, to be done. The children were regarded as being quite an addition to his wealth.

If at any one time of my life more than another, I was made to drink the bitterest dregs of slavery, that time was during the first six months of my stay with Mr. Covey. We were worked in all weathers. It was never too hot or too cold; it could never rain, blow, hail, or snow, too hard for us to work in the field. Work, work, work, was scarcely more the order of the day than of the night. The longest days were too short for him, and the shortest nights too long for him. I was somewhat unmanageable when I first went there, but a few months of this discipline tamed me. Mr. Covey succeeded in breaking me. I was broken in body, soul, and spirit. My natural elasticity was crushed, my intellect languished, the disposition to read departed, the cheerful spark that lingered about my eye died; the dark night of slavery closed in upon me; and behold a man transformed into a brute!

Sunday was my only leisure time. I spent this in a sort of beast-like stupor, between sleep and wake, under some large tree. At times I would rise up, a flash of energetic freedom would dart through my soul, accompanied with a faint beam of hope, that flickered for a moment, and then vanished. I sank down again, mourning over my wretched condition. I was sometimes prompted to take my life, and that of Covey, but was prevented by a combination of hope and fear. My sufferings on this plantation seem now like a dream rather than a stern reality.

Our house stood within a few rods of the Chesapeake Bay, whose broad bosom was ever white with sails from every quarter of the habitable globe. Those beautiful vessels, robed in purest white, so delightful to the eye of freemen, were to me so many shrouded ghosts, to terrify and torment me with thoughts of my wretched condition. I have often, in the deep stillness of a summer's Sabbath, stood all alone upon the lofty banks of that noble bay, and traced, with saddened heart and tearful eye, the countless number of sails moving off to the mighty ocean. The sight of these always affected me powerfully. My thoughts would compel utterance; and there, with no audience but the Almighty, I would pour out my soul's complaint, in my rude way, with an apostrophe to the moving multitude of ships:—

"You are loosed from your moorings, and are free; I am fast in my chains, and am a slave! You move merrily before the gentle gale, and I sadly before the bloody whip! You are freedom's swift-winged angels, that fly round the world; I am confined in bands of iron! O that I were free! O, that I were on one of your gallant decks, and under your protecting wing! Alas! betwixt me and you, the turbid waters roll. Go on, go on. O that I could also go! Could I but swim! If I could fly! O, why was I born a man, of whom to make a brute! The glad ship is gone; she hides in the dim distance. I am left in the hottest hell of unending slavery. O God, save me! God, deliver me! Let me be free! Is there any God! Why am I a slave! I will run away. I will not stand it. Get caught, or get clear, I'll try it. I had as well die with ague as the fever. I have only one life to lose. I had as well be killed running as die standing. Only think of it; one hundred miles straight north, and I am free! Try it? Yes! God helping me, I will. It cannot be that I shall live and die a slave. I will take to the water. This very bay shall yet bear me into freedom. The steamboats steered in a north-east course from North Point. I will do the same; and when I get to the head of the bay, I will turn my canoe adrift, and walk straight through Delaware into Pennsylvania. When I get there, I shall not be required to have a pass; I can travel without being disturbed. Let but the first opportunity offer, and come what will, I am off. Meanwhile, I will try to bear up under the yoke. I am not the only slave in the world. Why should I fret? I can bear as much as any of them. Besides, I am but a boy, and all boys are bound to some one. It may be that my misery in slavery will only increase my happiness when I get free. There is a better day coming."

Thus I used to think, and thus I used to speak to myself; goaded almost to madness at one moment, and the next reconciling myself to my wretched lot.

I have already intimated that my condition was much worse, during the first six months of my stay at Mr. Covey's, than in the last six. The circumstances leading to the change in Mr. Covey's course toward me form an epoch in my humble history. You have seen how a man was made a slave; you shall see how a slave was made a man. On one of the hottest days of the month of August, 1833, Bill Smith, William Hughes, a slave named Eli, and myself were engaged in fanning wheat. Hughes was clearing the fanned wheat from before the fan. Eli was turning, Smith was feeding, and I was carrying wheat to the fan. The work was simple, requiring strength rather than intellect; yet, to one entirely unused to such work, it came very hard. About three o'clock of that day, I broke down; my strength failed me; I was seized with a violent aching of the head, attended with extreme dizziness; I trembled in every limb. Finding what was coming, I nerved myself up, feeling it would never do to stop work. I stood as long as I could stagger to the hopper with grain. When I could stand no longer, I fell, and felt as if held down by an immense weight. The fan of course stopped; every one had his own work to do; and no one could do the work of the other, and have his own go on at the same time.

Mr. Covey was at the house, about one hundred yards from the treading-yard where we were fanning. On hearing the fan stop, he left immediately, and came to the spot where we were. He hastily inquired what the matter was. Bill answered that I was sick, and there was no one to bring wheat to the fan. I had by this time crawled away under the side of the post and rail-fence by which the yard was enclosed, hoping to find relief by getting out of the sun. He then asked where I was. He was told by one of the hands. He came to the spot, and, after looking at me awhile, asked me what was the matter. I told him as well as I could, for I scarce had the strength to speak. He then gave me a savage kick in the side, and told me to get up. I tried to do so, but fell back in the attempt. He gave me another kick, and again told me to rise. I again tried, and succeeded in gaining my feet; but, stooping to get the tub with which I was feeding the fan, I again staggered and fell. While down in this situation, Mr. Covey took up the hickory slat with which Hughes had been striking off the half-bushel measure, and with it gave me a heavy blow upon the head, making a large wound, and the blood ran freely; and with this again told me to get up. I made no effort to comply, having now made up my mind to let him do his worst. In a short time after receiving this blow, my head grew better. Mr. Covey had now left me to my fate. At this moment I resolved, for the first time, to go to my master, enter a complaint, and ask his protection. In order to do this, I must that afternoon walk seven miles; and this, under the circumstances, was truly a severe undertaking. I was exceedingly feeble; made so as much by the kicks and blows which I received, as by the severe fit of sickness to which I had been subjected. I, however, watched my chance, while Covey was looking in an opposite direction, and started for St. Michael's. I succeeded in getting a considerable distance on my way to the woods, when Covey discovered me, and called after me to come back, threatening what he would do if I did not come. I disregarded both his calls and his threats, and made my way to the woods as fast as my feeble state would allow; and thinking I might be overhauled by him if I kept the road, I walked through the woods, keeping far enough from the road to avoid detection, and near enough to prevent losing my way. I had not gone far before my little strength again failed me. I could go no farther. I fell down, and lay for a considerable time. The blood was yet oozing from the wound on my head. For a time I thought I should bleed to death; and think now that I should have done so, but the blood so matted my hair as to stop the wound. After lying there about three quarters of an hour, I nerved myself up again, and started on my way, through bogs and briers, barefooted and bareheaded, tearing my feet sometimes at nearly every step; and after a journey of about seven miles, occupying some five hours to perform it, I arrived at master's store. I then presented an appearance enough to affect any but a heart of iron. From the crown of my head to my feet, I was covered with blood. My hair was all clotted with dust and blood; my shirt was stiff with blood. My legs and feet were torn in sundry places with briers and thorns, and were also covered with blood. I suppose I looked like a man who had escaped a den of wild beasts, and barely escaped them. In this state I appeared before my master, humbly entreating him to interpose his authority for my protection. I told him all the circumstances as well as I could, and it seemed, as I spoke, at times to affect him. He would then walk the floor, and seek to justify Covey by saying he expected I deserved it. He asked me what I wanted. I told him, to let me get a new home; that as sure as I lived with Mr. Covey again, I should live with but to die with him; that Covey would surely kill me; he was in a fair way for it. Master Thomas ridiculed the idea that there was any danger of Mr. Covey's killing me, and said that he knew Mr. Covey; that he was a good man, and that he could not think of taking me from him; that, should he do so, he would lose the whole year's wages; that I belonged to Mr. Covey for one year, and that I must go back to him, come what might; and that I must not trouble him with any more stories, or that he would himself *get hold of me.* After threatening me thus, he gave me a very large dose of salts, telling me that I might remain in St. Michael's that night, (it being quite late,) but that I must be off back to Mr. Covey's early in the morning; and that if I did not, he would *get hold of me,* which meant that he would whip me. I remained all night, and, according to his orders, I started off to Covey's in the morning, (Saturday morning,) wearied in body and broken in spirit. I got no supper that night, or breakfast that morning. I reached Covey's about nine o'clock; and just as I was getting over the fence that divided Mrs. Kemp's fields from ours, out ran Covey with his cowskin, to give me another whipping. Before he could reach me, I succeeded in getting to the cornfield; and as the corn was very high, it afforded me the means of hiding. He seemed very angry, and searched for me a long time. My behavior was altogether unaccountable. He finally gave up the chase, thinking, I suppose, that I must come home for something to eat; he would give himself no further trouble in looking for me. I spent that day mostly in the woods, having the alternative before me, –to go home and be whipped to death, or stay in the woods and be starved to death. That night, I fell in with Sandy Jenkins, a slave with whom I was somewhat acquainted. Sandy had a free wife who lived about four miles from Mr. Covey's; and it being Saturday, he was on his way to see her. I told him my circumstances, and he very kindly invited me to go home with him. I went home with him, and talked this whole matter over, and got his advice as to what course it was best for me to pursue. I found Sandy an old adviser. He told me, with great solemnity, I must go back to Covey; but that before I went, I must go with him into another part of the woods, where there was a certain *root*, which, if I would take some of it with me, carrying it *always on my right side,* would render it impossible for Mr. Covey, or any other white man, to whip me. He said he had carried it for years; and since he had done so, he had never received a blow, and never expected to while he carried it. I at first rejected the idea, that the simple carrying of a root in my pocket would have any such effect as he had said, and was not disposed to take it; but Sandy impressed the necessity with much earnestness, telling me it could do no harm, if it did no good. To please him, I at length took the root, and, according to his direction, carried it upon my right side. This was Sunday morning. I immediately started for home; and upon entering the yard gate, out came Mr. Covey on his way to meeting. He spoke to me very kindly, bade me drive the pigs from a lot near by, and passed on towards the church. Now, this singular conduct of Mr. Covey really made me begin to think that there was something in the *root* which Sandy had given me; and had it been on any other day than Sunday, I could have attributed the conduct to no other cause than the influence of that root; and as it was, I was half inclined to think the *root* to be something more than I at first had taken it to be. All went well till Monday morning. On this morning the virtue of the *root* was fully tested. Long before daylight, I was called to go and rub, curry, and feed, the horses. I obeyed, and was glad to obey. But whilst thus engaged, whilst in the act of throwing down some blades from the loft, Mr. Covey entered the stable with a long rope; and just as I was half out of the loft, he caught hold of my legs, and was about tying me. As soon as I found what he was up to, I gave a sudden spring, and as I did so, he holding to my legs, I was brought sprawling on the stable floor. Mr. Covey seemed now to think he had me, and could do what he pleased; but at this moment—from whence came the spirit I don't know– I resolved to fight; and, suiting my action to the resolution, I seized Covey hard by the throat; and as I did so, I rose. He held on to me, and I to him. My resistance was so entirely unexpected, that Covey seemed taken all aback. He trembled like a leaf. This gave me assurance, and I held him uneasy, causing the blood to run where I touched him with the ends of my fingers. Mr. Covey soon called out to Hughes for help. Hughes came, and, while Covey held me, attempted to tie my right hand. While was in the act of doing so, I watched my chance, and gave him a heavy kick close under the ribs. This kick fairly sickened Hughes, so that he left me in the hands of Mr. Covey. This kick had the effect of not only weakening Hughes, but Covey also. When he saw Hughes bending over with pain, his courage quailed. He asked me if I meant to persist in my resistance. I told him I did, come what might; that he had used me like a brute for six months, and that I was determined to be used so no longer. With that, he strove to drag me to a stick that was lying just out of the stable door. He meant to knock me down. But just as he was leaning over to get the stick, I seized him with both hands by his collar, and brought him by a sudden snatch to the ground. By this time, Bill came. Covey called upon him for assistance. Bill wanted to know what he could do. Covey said, "Take hold of him, take hold of him!" Bill said his master hired him out to work, and not to help to whip me; so he left Covey and myself to fight our own battle out. We were at it for nearly two hours. Covey at length let me go, puffing and blowing at a great rate, saying that if I had not resisted, he would not have whipped me half so much. The truth was, that he had not whipped me at all. I considered him as getting the worst end of the bargain; for he had drawn no blood from me, but I had from him. The whole six months afterwards, that I spent with Mr. Covey, he never laid the weight of his finger upon me in anger. He would occasionally say, he didn't want to get hold me again. "No, " thought I, "you need not; for you will come off worse than you did before. "

This battle with Mr. Covey was the turning-point in my career as a slave. It rekindled the few expiring embers of freedom, and revived within me a sense of my own manhood. It recalled the departed self-confidence, and inspired me again with a determination to be free. The gratification afforded by the triumph was a full compensation for whatever else might follow, even death itself. He only can understand the deep satisfaction which I experienced, who has himself repelled by force the bloody arm of slavery. I felt as I never felt before. It was a glorious resurrection, from the tomb of slavery, to the heaven of freedom. My long-crushed spirit rose, cowardice departed, bold defiance took its place; and I now resolved that, however long I might remain a slave in form, the day had passed forever when I could be a slave in fact. I did not hesitate to let it be known of me, that the white man who expected to succeed in whipping, must also succeed in killing me.

From this time I was never again what might be called fairly whipped, though I remained a slave four years afterwards. I had several fights, but was never whipped.

It was for a long time a matter of surprise to me why Mr. Covey did not immediately have me taken by the constable to the whipping-post, and there regularly whipped for the crime of raising my hand against a white man in defence of myself. And the only explanation I can now think of does not entirely satisfy me; but such as it is, I will give it. Mr. Covey enjoyed the most unbounded reputation for being a first-rate overseer and negro-breaker. It was of considerable importance to him. That reputation was at stake; and had he sent me—a boy about sixteen years old—to the public whipping-post, his reputation would have been lost; so, to save his reputation, he suffered me to go unpunished.

My term of actual service to Mr. Edward Covey ended on Christmas day, 1833. The days between Christmas and New Year's day are allowed as holidays; and, accordingly, we were not required to perform any labor, more than to feed and take care of the stock. This time we regarded as our own, by the grace of our masters; and we therefore used or abused it nearly as we pleased. Those of us who had families at a distance, were generally allowed to spend the whole six days in their society. This time, however, was spent in various ways. The staid, sober, thinking and industrious ones of our number would employ themselves in making corn-brooms, mats, horse-collars, and baskets; and another class of us would spend the time in hunting opossums, hares, and coons. But by far the larger part engaged in such sports and merriments as playing ball, wrestling, running foot-races, fiddling, dancing, and drinking whisky; and this latter mode of spending the time was by far the most agreeable to the feelings of our masters. A slave who would work during the holidays was considered by our masters as scarcely deserving them. He was regarded as one who rejected the favor of his master. It was deemed a disgrace not to get drunk at Christmas; and he was regarded as lazy indeed, who had not provided himself with the necessary means, during the year, to get whisky enough to last him through Christmas.

From what I know of the effect of these holidays upon the slave, I believe them to be among the most effective means in the hands of the slaveholder in keeping down the spirit of insurrection. Were the slaveholders at once to abandon this practice, I have not the slightest doubt it would lead to an immediate insurrection among the slaves. These holidays serve as conductors, or safety-valves, to carry off the rebellious spirit of enslaved humanity. But for these, the slave would be forced up to the wildest desperation; and woe betide the slaveholder, the day he ventures to remove or hinder the operation of those conductors! I warn him that, in such an event, a spirit will go forth in their midst, more to be dreaded than the most appalling earthquake.

The holidays are part and parcel of the gross fraud, wrong, and inhumanity of slavery. They are professedly a custom established by the benevolence of the slaveholders; but I undertake to say, it is the result of selfishness, and one of the grossest frauds committed upon the down-trodden slave. They do not give the slaves this time because they would not like to have their work during its continuance, but because they know it would be unsafe to deprive them of it. This will be seen by the fact, that the slaveholders like to have their slaves spend those days just in such a manner as to make them as glad of their ending as of their beginning. Their object seems to be, to disgust their slaves with freedom, by plunging them into the lowest depths of dissipation. For instance, the slaveholders not only like to see the slave drink of his own accord, but will adopt various plans to make him drunk. One plan is, to make bets on their slaves, as to who can drink the most whisky without getting drunk; and in this way they succeed in getting whole multitudes to drink to excess. Thus, when the slave asks for virtuous freedom, the cunning slaveholder, knowing his ignorance, cheats him with a dose of vicious dissipation, artfully labelled with the name of liberty. The most of us used to drink it down, and the result was just what might be supposed: many of us were led to think that there was little to choose between liberty and slavery. We felt, and very properly too, that we had almost as well be slaves to man as to rum. So, when the holidays ended, we staggered up from the filth of our wallowing, took a long breath, and marched to the field, —feeling, upon the whole, rather glad to go, from what our master had deceived us into a belief was freedom, back to the arms of slavery.

I have said that this mode of treatment is a part of the whole system of fraud and inhumanity of slavery. It is so. The mode here adopted to disgust the slave with freedom, by allowing him to see only the abuse of it, is carried out in other things. For instance, a slave loves molasses; he steals some. His master, in many cases, goes off to town, and buys a large quantity; he returns, takes his whip, and commands the slave to eat the molasses, until the poor fellow is made sick at the very mention of it. The same mode is sometimes adopted to make the slaves refrain from asking for more food than their regular allowance. A slave runs through his allowance, and applies for more. His master is enraged at him; but, not willing to send him off without food, gives him more than is necessary, and compels him to eat it within a given time. Then, if he complains that he cannot eat it, he is said to be satisfied neither full nor fasting, and is whipped for being hard to please! I have an abundance of such illustrations of the same principle, drawn from my own observation, but think the cases I have cited sufficient. The practice is a very common one.

On the first of January, 1834, I left Mr. Covey, and went to live with Mr. William Freeland, who lived about three miles from St. Michael's. I soon found Mr. Freeland a very different man from Mr. Covey. Though not rich, he was what would be called an educated southern gentleman. Mr. Covey, as I have shown, was a well-trained negro-breaker and slave-driver. The former (slaveholder though he was) seemed to possess some regard for honor, some reverence for justice, and some respect for humanity. The latter seemed totally insensible to all such sentiments. Mr. Freeland had many of the faults peculiar to slaveholders, such as being very passionate and fretful; but I must do him the justice to say, that he was exceedingly free from those degrading vices to which Mr. Covey was constantly addicted. The one was open and frank, and we always knew where to find him. The other was a most artful deceiver, and could be understood only by such as were skilful enough to detect his cunningly-devised frauds. Another advantage I gained in my new master was, he made no pretensions to, or profession of, religion; and this, in my opinion, was truly a great advantage. I assert most unhesitatingly, that the religion of the south is a mere covering for the most horrid crimes, —a justifier of the most appalling barbarity, — a sanctifier of the most hateful frauds, —and a dark shelter under which the darkest, foulest, grossest, and most infernal deeds of slaveholders find the strongest protection. Were I to be again reduced to the chains of slavery, next to that enslavement, I should regard being the slave of religious master the greatest calamity that could befall me. For of all slaveholders with whom I have ever met, religious slaveholders are the worst. I have ever found them the meanest and basest, the most cruel and cowardly, of all others. It was my unhappy lot not only to belong to a religious slaveholder, but to live in a community of such religionists. Very near Mr. Freeland lived the Rev. Daniel Weeden, and in the same neighborhood lived the Rev. Rigby Hopkins. These were members and ministers in the Reformed Methodist Church. Mr. Weeden owned, among others, a woman slave, whose name I have forgotten. This woman's back, for weeks, was kept literally raw, made so by the lash of this merciless, *religious* wretch. He used to hire hands. His maxim was, Behave well or behave ill, it is the duty of a master occasionally to whip a slave, to remind him of his master's authority. Such was his theory, and such his practice.

Mr. Hopkins was even worse than Mr. Weeden. His chief boast was his ability to manage slaves. The peculiar feature of his government was that of whipping slaves in advance of deserving it. He always managed to have one or more of his slaves to whip every Monday morning. He did this to alarm their fears, and strike terror into those who escaped. His plan was to whip for the smallest offences, to prevent the commission of large ones. Mr. Hopkins could always find some excuse for whipping a slave. It would astonish one, unaccustomed to a slaveholding life, to see with what wonderful ease a slaveholder can find things, of which to make occasion to whip a slave. A mere look, word, or motion, —a mistake, accident, or want of power, —are all matters for which a slave may be whipped at any time. Does a slave look dissatisfied? It is said, he has the devil in him, and it must be whipped out. Does he speak loudly when spoken to by his master? Then he is getting high-minded, and should be taken down a button-hole lower. Does he forget to pull off his hat at the approach of a white person? Then he is wanting in reverence, and should be whipped for it. Does he ever venture to vindicate his conduct, when censured for it? Then he is guilty of impudence, —one of the greatest crimes of which a slave can be guilty. Does he ever venture to suggest a different mode of doing things from that pointed out by his master? He is indeed presumptuous, and getting above himself; and nothing less than a flogging will do for him. Does he, while ploughing, break a plough, —or, while hoeing, break a hoe? It is owing to his carelessness, and for it a slave must always be whipped. Mr. Hopkins could always find something of this sort to justify the use of the lash, and he seldom failed to embrace such opportunities. There was not a man in the whole county, with whom the slaves who had the getting of their own home, would not prefer to live, rather than with this Rev. Mr. Hopkins. And yet there was not a man any where round, who made higher professions of religion, or was more active in revivals, —more attentive to the class, love-feast, prayer and preaching meetings, or more devotional in his family, —that prayed earlier, later, louder, and longer, —than this same reverend slave-driver, Rigby Hopkins.

But to return to Mr. Freeland, and to my experience while in his employment. He, like Mr. Covey, gave us enough to eat; but, unlike Mr. Covey, he also gave us sufficient time to take our meals. He worked us hard, but always between sunrise and sunset. He required a good deal of work to be done, but gave us good tools with which to work. His farm was large, but he employed hands enough to work it, and with ease, compared with many of his neighbors. My treatment, while in his employment, was heavenly, compared with what I experienced at the hands of Mr. Edward Covey.

Mr. Freeland was himself the owner of but two slaves. Their names were Henry Harris and John Harris. The rest of his hands he hired. These consisted of myself, Sandy Jenkins,[1] and Handy Caldwell. Henry and John were quite intelligent, and in

1. This is the same man who gave me the roots to prevent my being whipped by Mr. Covey. He was "a clever soul." We used frequently to talk about the fight with Covey, and as often as we did so, he would claim my success as the result of the roots which he gave me. This superstition is very common among the more ignorant slaves. A slave seldom dies but that is death is attributed to trickery.

a very little while after I went there, I succeeded in creating in them a strong desire to learn how to read. This desire soon sprang up in the others also. They very soon mustered up some old spelling-books and nothing would do but that I must keep a Sabbath school. I agreed to do so, and accordingly devoted my Sundays to teaching these my loved fellow-slaves how to read. Neither of them knew his letters when I went there. Some of the slaves of the neighboring farms found what was going on, and also availed themselves of this little opportunity to learn to read. It was understood, among all who came, that there must be as little display about it as possible. It was necessary to keep our religious masters at St. Michael's unacquainted with the fact, that, instead of spending the Sabbath in wrestling, boxing, and drinking whisky, we were trying to learn how to read the will of God; for they had much rather see us engaged in those degrading sports, than to see us behaving like intellectual, moral, and accountable beings. My blood boils as I think of the bloody manner in which Messrs. Wright Fairbanks and Garrison West, both class-leaders, in connection with many others, rushed in upon us with sticks and stones, and broke up our virtuous little Sabbath school, at St. Michael's—all calling themselves Christians! Humble followers of the Lord Jesus Christ! But I am again digressing.

I held my Sabbath school at the house of a free colored man, whose name I deem it imprudent to mention; for should it be known, it might embarrass him greatly, though the crime of holding the school was committed ten years ago. I had at one time over forty scholars, and those of the right sort, ardently desiring to learn. They were of all ages, though mostly men and women. I look back to those Sundays with an amount of pleasure not to be expressed. They were great days to my soul. The work of instructing my dear fellow-slaves was the sweetest engagement with which I was ever blessed. We loved each other, and to leave them at the close of the Sabbath was a severe cross indeed. When I think that these precious souls are to-day shut up in the prison-house of slavery, my feelings overcome me, and I am almost ready to ask, "Does a righteous God govern the universe? and for what does he hold the thunders in his right hand, if not to smite the oppressor, and deliver the spoiled out of the hand of the spoiler?" These dear souls came not to Sabbath school because it was popular to do so, nor did I teach them because it was reputable to be thus engaged. Every moment they spent in that school, they were liable to be taken up, and given thirty-nine lashes. They came because they wished to learn. Their minds had been starved by their cruel masters. They had been shut up in mental darkness. I taught them, because it was the delight of my soul to be doing something that looked like bettering the condition of my race. I kept up my school nearly the whole year I lived with Mr. Freeland; and, beside my Sabbath school, I devoted three evenings in the week, during the winter, to teaching the slaves at home. And I have the happiness to know, that several of those who came to Sabbath school learned how to read; and that one, at least, is now free through my agency.

The year passed off smoothly. It seemed only about half as long as the year which preceded it. I went through it without receiving a single blow. I will give Mr. Freeland the credit of being the best master I ever had, *till I became my own master*. For the ease with which I passed the year, I was, however, somewhat indebted to the society of my fellow-slaves. They were noble souls; they not only possessed loving hearts, but brave ones. We were linked and interlinked with each other. I loved them with a love stronger than any thing I have experienced since. It is sometimes said that we slaves do not love and confide in each other. In answer to this assertion, I can say, I never loved any or confided in any people more than my fellow-slaves, and especially those with whom I lived at Mr. Freeland's. I believe we would have died for each other. We never undertook to do any thing, of any importance, without a mutual consultation. We never moved separately. We were one; and as much so by our tempers and dispositions, as by the mutual hardships to which we were necessarily subjected by our condition as slaves.

At the close of the year 1834, Mr. Freeland again hired me of my master, for the year 1835. But, by this time, I began to want to live *upon free land* as well as *with Freeland;* and I was no longer content, therefore, to live with him or any other slaveholder. I began, with the commencement of the year, to prepare myself for a final struggle, which should decide my fate one way or the other. My tendency was upward. I was fast approaching manhood, and year after year had passed, and I was still a slave. These thoughts roused me—I must do something. I therefore resolved that 1835 should not pass without witnessing an attempt, on my part, to secure my liberty. But I was not willing to cherish this determination alone. My fellow-slaves were dear to me. I was anxious to have them participate with me in this, my life-giving determination. I therefore, though with great prudence, commenced early to ascertain their views and feelings in regard to their condition, and to imbue their minds with thoughts of freedom. I bent myself to devising ways and means for our escape, and meanwhile strove, on all fitting occasions, to impress them with the gross fraud and inhumanity of slavery. I went first to Henry, next to John, then to the others. I found, in them all, warm hearts and noble spirits. They were ready to hear, and ready to act when a feasible plan should be proposed. This was what I wanted. I talked to them of our want of manhood, if we submitted to enslavement without at least one noble effort to be free. We met often, and consulted frequently, and told our hopes and fears, recounted the difficulties, real and imagined, which we should be called on to meet. At times we were almost disposed to give up, and try to content ourselves with our wretched lot; at others, we were firm and unbending in our determination to go. Whenever we suggested any plan, there was shrinking—the odds were fearful. Our path was beset with the greatest obstacles; and if we succeeded in gaining the end of it, our right to be free was yet questionable—we were yet liable to be returned to bondage. We could see no spot, this side of the ocean, where we could be free. We knew nothing about Canada. Our knowledge of the north did not extend farther than New York; and to go there, and be forever harassed with the frightful liability of being returned to slavery—with the certainty of being treated tenfold worse than before—the thought was truly a horrible one, and one which it was not easy to overcome. The case sometimes stood thus: At every gate through which we were to pass, we saw a watchman—at every ferry a guard—on every bridge a sentinel—and in every wood a patrol. We were hemmed in upon every side. Here were the difficulties, real or imagined—the good to be sought, and the evil to be shunned. On the one hand, there stood slavery, a stern reality, glaring frightfully upon us—its robes already crimsoned with the blood of millions, and even now feasting itself greedily upon our own flesh.

On the other hand, away back in the dim distance, under the flickering light of the north star, behind some craggy hill or snow-covered mountain, stood a doubtful freedom—half frozen—beckoning us to come and share its hospitality. This in itself was sometimes enough to stagger us; but when we permitted ourselves to survey the road, we were frequently appalled. Upon either side we saw grim death, assuming the most horrid shapes. Now it was starvation, causing us to eat our own flesh;—now we were contending with the waves, and were drowned;—now we were overtaken, and torn to pieces by the fangs of the terrible bloodhound. We were stung by scorpions, chased by wild beasts, bitten by snakes, and finally, after having nearly reached the desired spot, —after swimming rivers, encountering wild beasts, sleeping in the woods, suffering hunger and nakedness, —we were overtaken by our pursuers, and, in our resistance, we were shot dead upon the spot! I say, this picture sometimes appalled us, and made us

"rather bear those ills we had,
Than fly to others, that we knew not of. "

In coming to a fixed determination to run away, we did more than Patrick Henry, when he resolved upon liberty or death. With us it was a doubtful liberty at most, and almost certain death if we failed. For my part, I should prefer death to hopeless bondage.

Sandy, one of our number, gave up the notion, but still encouraged us. Our company then consisted of Henry Harris, John Harris, Henry Bailey, Charles Roberts, and myself. Henry Bailey was my uncle, and belonged to my master. Charles married my aunt: he belong to my master's father-in-law, Mr. William Hamilton.

The plan we finally concluded upon was, to get a large canoe belonging to Mr. Hamilton, and upon the Saturday night previous to Easter holidays, paddle directly up the Chesapeake Bay. On our arrival at the head of the bay, a distance of seventy or eighty miles from where we lived, it was our purpose to turn our canoe adrift, and follow the guidance of the north star till we got beyond the limits of Maryland. Our reason for taking the water route was, that we were less liable to be suspected as runaways; we hoped to be regarded as fishermen; whereas, if we should take the land route, we should be subjected to interruptions of almost every kind. Any one having a white face, and being so disposed, could stop us, and subject us to examination.

The week before our intended start, I wrote several protections, one for each of us. As well as I can remember, they were in the following words, to wit:—

"This is to certify that I, the undersigned, have given the bearer, my servant, full liberty to go to Baltimore, and spend the Easter holidays. Written with mine own hand, &c., 1835.

"William Hamilton,

"Near St. Michael's, in Talbot county, Maryland. "

We were not going to Baltimore; but, in going up the bay, we went toward Baltimore, and these protections were only intended to protect us while on the bay.

As the time drew near for our departure, our anxiety became more and more intense. It was truly a matter of life and death with us. The strength of our determination was about to be fully tested. At this time, I was very active in explaining every difficulty, removing every doubt, dispelling every fear, and inspiring all with the firmness indispensable to success in our undertaking; assuring them that half was gained the instant we made the move; we had talked long enough; we were now ready to move; if not now, we never should be; and if we did not intend to move now, we had as well fold our arms, sit down, and acknowledge ourselves fit only to be slaves. This, none of us were prepared to acknowledge. Every man stood firm; and at our last meeting, we pledged ourselves afresh, in the most solemn manner, that, at the time appointed, we would certainly start in the pursuit of freedom. This was in the middle of the week, at the end of which we were to be off. We went, as usual, to our several fields of labor, but with bosoms highly agitated with thoughts of our truly hazardous undertaking. We tried to conceal our feelings as much as possible; and I think we succeeded very well.

After a painful waiting, the Saturday morning, whose night was to witness our departure, came. I hailed it with joy, bring what of sadness it might. Friday night was a sleepless one for me. I probably felt more anxious than the rest, because I was, by common consent, at the head of the whole affair. The responsibility of success or failure lay heavily upon me. The glory of the one, and the confusion of the other, were alike mine. The first two hours of that morning were such as I never experienced before, and hope never to again. Early in the morning, we went, as usual, to the field. We were spreading manure; and all at once, while thus engaged, I was overwhelmed with an indescribable feeling, in the fulness of which I turned to Sandy, who was near by, and said, "We are betrayed!" "Well, " said he, "that thought has this moment struck me. " We said no more. I was never more certain of any thing.

The horn was blown as usual, and we went up from the field to the house for breakfast. I went for the form, more than for want of any thing to eat that morning. Just as I got to the house, in looking out at the lane gate, I saw four white men, with two colored men. The white men were on horseback, and the colored ones were walking behind, as if tied. I watched them a few moments till they got up to our lane gate. Here they halted, and tied the colored men to the gate-post. I was not yet certain as to what the matter was. In a few moments, in rode Mr. Hamilton, with a speed betokening great excitement. He came to the door, and inquired if Master William was in. He was told he was at the barn. Mr. Hamilton, without dismounting, rode up to the barn with extraordinary speed. In a few moments, he and Mr. Freeland returned to the house. By this time, the three constables rode up, and in great haste dismounted, tied their horses, and met Master William and Mr. Hamilton returning from the barn; and after talking awhile, they all walked up to the kitchen door. There was no one in the kitchen but myself and John. Henry and Sandy were up at the barn. Mr. Freeland put his head in at the door, and called me by name, saying, there were some gentlemen at the door who wished to see me. I stepped to the door, and inquired what they wanted. They at once seized me, and, without giving me any satisfaction, tied me—lashing my hands closely together. I insisted upon knowing what the matter was. They at length said, that they had learned I had been in a "scrape, " and that I was to be examined before my master; and if their information proved false, I should not be hurt.

In a few moments, they succeeded in tying John. They then turned to Henry, who had by this time returned, and commanded him to cross his hands. "I won't!" said

Henry, in a firm tone, indicating his readiness to meet the consequences of his refusal. "Won't you?" said Tom Graham, the constable. "No, I won't!" said Henry, in a still stronger tone. With this, two of the constables pulled out their shining pistols, and swore, by their Creator, that they would make him cross his hands or kill him. Each cocked his pistol, and, with fingers on the trigger, walked up to Henry, saying, at the same time, if he did not cross his hands, they would blow his damned heart out. "Shoot me, shoot me!" said Henry; "you can't kill me but once. Shoot, shoot, —and be damned! *I won't be tied!*" this he said in a tone of loud defiance; and at the same time, with a motion as quick as lightning, he with one single stroke dashed the pistols from the hand of each constable. As he did this, all hands fell upon him, and, after beating him some time, they finally overpowered him, and got him tied.

During the scuffle, I managed, I know not how, to get my pass out, and, without being discovered, put it into the fire. We were all now tied; and just as we were to leave for Easton jail, Betsy Freeland, mother of William Freeland, came to the door with her hands full of biscuits, and divided them between Henry and John. She then delivered herself of a speech, to the following effect:—addressing herself to me, she said, *"You devil! You yellow devil!* it was you that put it into the heads of Henry and John to run away. But for you, you long-legged mulatto devil! Henry nor John would never have thought of such a thing. " I made no reply, and was immediately hurried off towards St. Michael's. Just a moment previous to the scuffle with Henry, Mr. Hamilton suggested the propriety of making a search for the protections which he had understood Frederick had written for himself and the rest. But, just at the moment he was about carrying his proposal into effect, his aid was needed in helping to tie Henry; and the excitement attending the scuffle caused them either to forget, or to deem it unsafe, under the circumstances, to search. So we were not yet convicted of the intention to run away.

When we got about half way to St. Michael's, while the constables having us in charge were looking ahead, Henry inquired of me what he should do with his pass. I told him to eat it with his biscuit, and own nothing; and we passed the word around, *"Own nothing;"* and *"Own nothing!"* said we all. Our confidence in each other was unshaken. We were resolved to succeed or fail together, after the calamity had befallen us as much as before. We were now prepared for any thing. We were to be dragged that morning fifteen miles behind horses, and then to be placed in the Easton jail. When we reached St. Michael's, we underwent a sort of examination. We all denied that we ever intended to run away. We did this more to bring out the evidence against us, than from any hope of getting clear of being sold; for, as I have said, we were ready for that. The fact was, we cared but little where we went, so we went together. Our greatest concern was about separation. We dreaded that more than any thing this side of death. We found the evidence against us to be the testimony of one person; our master would not tell who it was; but we came to a unanimous decision among ourselves as to who their informant was. We were sent off to the jail at Easton. When we got there, we were delivered up to the sheriff, Mr. Joseph Graham, and by him placed in jail. Henry, John, and myself were placed in one room together— Charles, and Henry Bailey, in another. Their object in separating us was to hinder concert.

We had been in jail scarcely twenty minutes, when a swarm of slave traders, and agents for slave traders, flocked into jail to look at us, and to ascertain if we were for sale. Such a set of beings I never saw before! I felt myself surrounded by so many fiends from perdition. A band of pirates never looked more like their father, the devil. They laughed and grinned over us, saying, "Ah, my boys! we have got you, haven't we?" And after taunting us in various ways, they one by one went into an examination of us, with intent to ascertain our value. They would impudently ask us if we would not like to have them for our masters. We would make them no answer, and leave them to find out as best they could. Then they would curse and swear at us, telling us that they could take the devil out of us in a very little while, if we were only in their hands.

While in jail, we found ourselves in much more comfortable quarters than we expected when we went there. We did not get much to eat, nor that which was very good; but we had a good clean room, from the windows of which we could see what was going on in the street, which was very much better than though we had been placed in one of the dark, damp cells. Upon the whole, we got along very well, so far as the jail and its keeper were concerned. Immediately after the holidays were over, contrary to all our expectations, Mr. Hamilton and Mr. Freeland came up to Easton, and took Charles, the two Henrys, and John, out of jail, and carried them home, leaving me alone. I regarded this separation as a final one. It caused me more pain than any thing else in the whole transaction. I was ready for any thing rather than separation. I supposed that they had consulted together, and had decided that, as I was the whole cause of the intention of the others to run away, it was hard to make the innocent suffer with the guilty; and that they had, therefore, concluded to take the others home, and sell me, as a warning to the others that remained. It is due to the noble Henry to say, he seemed almost as reluctant at leaving the prison as at leaving home to come to the prison. But we knew we should, in all probability, be separated, if we were sold; and since he was in their hands, he concluded to go peaceably home.

I was now left to my fate. I was all alone, and within the walls of a stone prison. But a few days before, and I was full of hope. I expected to have been safe in a land of freedom; but now I was covered with gloom, sunk down to the utmost despair. I thought the possibility of freedom was gone. I was kept in this way about one week, at the end of which, Captain Auld, my master, to my surprise and utter astonishment, came up, and took me out, with the intention of sending me, with a gentleman of his acquaintance, into Alabama. But, from some cause or other, he did not send me to Alabama, but concluded to send me back to Baltimore, to live again with his brother Hugh, and to learn a trade.

Thus, after an absence of three years and one month, I was once more permitted to return to my old home at Baltimore. My master sent me away, because there existed against me a very great prejudice in the community, and he feared I might be killed.

In a few weeks after I went to Baltimore, Master Hugh hired me to Mr. William Gardner, an extensive ship-builder, on Fell's Point. I was put there to learn how to calk. It, however, proved a very unfavorable place for the accomplishment of this object. Mr. Gardner was engaged that spring in building two large man-of-war brigs, professedly for the Mexican government. The vessels were to be launched in the July of that year, and in failure thereof, Mr. Gardner was to lose a considerable sum; so that when I entered, all was hurry. There was no time to learn any thing. Every man had to do that which he knew how to do. In entering the shipyard, my orders from Mr. Gardner were, to do whatever the carpenters commanded me to do. This was placing me at the beck and call of about seventy-five men. I was to regard all these as masters. Their word was to be my law. My situation was a most trying one. At times I needed a dozen pair of hands. I was called a dozen ways in the space of a single minute. Three or four voices would strike my ear at the same moment. It was–"Fred., come help me to cant this timber here. "—"Fred., come carry this timber yonder. "—"Fred., bring that roller here. "—"Fred., go get a fresh can of water." —"Fred., come help saw off the end of this timber. "—"Fred., go quick, and get the crowbar. "—"Fred., hold on the end of this fall. "—"Fred., go to the blacksmith's shop, and get a new punch. "— "Hurra, Fred.! run and bring me a cold chisel. "—"I say, Fred., bear a hand, and get up a fire as quick as lightning under that steam-box. "—"Hallo, nigger! come, turn this grindstone. "—"Come, come! move, move! and *bowse* this timber forward. "— "I say, darky, blast your eyes, why don't you heat up some pitch?"—"Halloo! halloo! halloo!" (Three voices at the same time.) "Come here!—Go there!—Hold on where you are! Damn you, if you move, I'll knock your brains out!"

This was my school for eight months; and I might have remained there longer, but for a most horrid fight I had with four of the white apprentices, in which my left eye was nearly knocked out, and I was horribly mangled in other respects. The facts in the case were these. Until a very little while after I went there, white and black ship-carpenters worked side by side, and no one seemed to see any impropriety in it. All hands seemed to be very well satisfied. Many of the black carpenters were freemen. Things seemed to be going on very well. All at once, the white carpenters knocked off, and said they would not work with free colored workmen. Their reason for this, as alleged, was, that if free colored carpenters were encouraged, they would soon take the trade into their own hands, and poor white men would be thrown out of employment. They therefore felt called upon at once to put a stop to it. And, taking advantage of Mr. Gardner's necessities, they broke off, swearing they would work no longer, unless he would discharge his black carpenters. Now, though this did not extend to me in form, it did reach me in fact. My fellow-apprentices very soon began to feel it degrading to them to work with me. They began to put on airs, and talk about the "niggers" taking the country, saying we all ought to be killed; and, being encouraged by the journeymen, they commenced making my condition as hard as they could, by hectoring me around, and sometimes striking me. I, of course, kept the vow I made after the fight with Mr. Covey, and struck back again, regardless of consequences; and while I kept them from combining, I succeeded very well; for I could whip the whole of them, taking them separately. They, however, at length combined, and came upon me, armed with sticks, stones, and heavy handspikes. One came in front with a half brick. There was one at each side of me, and one behind me. While I was attending to those in front, and on either side, the one behind ran up with the handspike, and struck me a heavy blow upon the head. It stunned me. I fell, and with this they all ran upon me, and fell to beating me with their fists. I let them lay on for a while, gathering strength. In an instant, I gave a sudden surge, and rose to my hands and knees. Just as I did that, one of their number gave me, with his heavy boot, a powerful kick in the left eye. My eyeball seemed to have burst. When they saw my eye closed, and badly swollen, they left me. With this I seized the handspike, and for a time pursued them. But here the carpenters interfered, and I thought I might as well give it up. It was impossible to stand my hand against so many. All this took place in sight of not less than fifty white ship-carpenters, and not one interposed a friendly word; but some cried, "Kill the damned nigger! Kill him! kill him! He struck a white person. " I found my only chance for life was in flight. I succeeded in getting away without an additional blow, and barely so; for to strike a white man is death by Lynch law, —and that was the law in Mr. Gardner's ship-yard; nor is there much of any other out of Mr. Gardner's ship-yard.

I went directly home, and told the story of my wrongs to Master Hugh; and I am happy to say of him, irreligious as he was, his conduct was heavenly, compared with that of his brother Thomas under similar circumstances. He listened attentively to my narration of the circumstances leading to the savage outrage, and gave many proofs of his strong indignation at it. The heart of my once overkind mistress was again melted into pity. My puffed-out eye and blood-covered face moved her to tears. She took a chair by me, washed the blood from my face, and, with a mother's tenderness, bound up my head, covering the wounded eye with a lean piece of fresh beef. It was almost compensation for my suffering to witness, once more, a manifestation of kindness from this, my once affectionate old mistress. Master Hugh was very much enraged. He gave expression to his feelings by pouring out curses upon the heads of those who did the deed. As soon as I got a little the better of my bruises, he took me with him to Esquire Watson's, on Bond Street, to see what could be done about the matter. Mr. Watson inquired who saw the assault committed. Master Hugh told him it was done in Mr. Gardner's ship-yard, at midday, where there were a large company of men at work. "As to that, " he said, "the deed was done, and there was no question as to who did it. " His answer was, he could do nothing in the case, unless some white man would come forward and testify. He could issue no warrant on my word. If I had been killed in the presence of a thousand colored people, their testimony combined would have been insufficient to have arrested one of the murderers. Master Hugh, for once, was compelled to say this state of things was too bad. Of course, it was impossible to get any white man to volunteer his testimony in my behalf, and against the white young men. Even those who may have sympathized with me were not prepared to do this. It required a degree of courage unknown to them to do so; for just at that time, the slightest manifestation of humanity toward a colored person was denounced as abolitionism, and that name subjected its bearer to frightful liabilities. The watch-words of the bloody-minded in that region, and in those days, were, "Damn the abolitionists!" and "Damn the niggers!" There was nothing done, and probably nothing would have been done if I had been killed. Such was, and such remains, the state of things in the Christian city of Baltimore.

Master Hugh, finding he could get no redress, refused to let me go back again to Mr. Gardner. He kept me himself, and his wife dressed my wound till I was again restored to health. He then took me into the ship-yard of which he was foreman, in the employment of Mr. Walter Price. There I was immediately set to calking, and very soon learned the art of using my mallet and irons. In the course of one year from the time I left Mr. Gardner's, I was able to command the highest wages given to the most experienced calkers. I was now of some importance to my master. I was bringing him from six to seven dollars per week. I sometimes brought him nine dollars per week: my wages were a dollar and a half a day. After learning how to calk, I sought my own employment, made my own contracts, and collected the money which I earned. My pathway became much more smooth than before; my condition was now much more comfortable. When I could get no calking to do, I did nothing. During these leisure times, those old notions about freedom would steal over me again. When in Mr. Gardner's employment, I was kept in such a perpetual whirl of excitement, I could think of nothing, scarcely, but my life; and in thinking of my life, I almost forgot my liberty. I have observed this in my experience of slavery, —that whenever my condition was improved, instead of its increasing my contentment, it only increased my desire to be free, and set me to thinking of plans to gain my freedom. I have found that, to make a contented slave, it is necessary to make a thoughtless one. It is necessary to darken his moral and mental vision, and, as far as possible, to annihilate the power of reason. He must be able to detect no inconsistencies in slavery; he must be made to feel that slavery is right; and he can be brought to that only when he ceases to be a man.

I was not getting, as I have said, one dollar and fifty cents per day. I contracted for it; I earned it; it was paid to me; it was rightfully my own; yet, upon each returning Saturday night, I was compelled to deliver every cent of that money to Master Hugh. And why? Not because he earned it, —not because he had any hand in earning it, — not because I owed it to him, —nor because he possessed the slightest shadow of a right to it; but solely because he had the power to compel me to give it up. The right of the grim-visaged pirate upon the high seas is exactly the same.

(1845)

HARRIET A. JACOBS
(Linda Brent)

Incidents in the Life of a Slave Girl

A Perilous Passage in the Slave Girl's Life

After my lover went away, Dr. Flint contrived a new plan. He seemed to have an idea that my fear of my mistress was his greatest obstacle. In the blandest tones, he told me that he was going to build a small house for me, in a secluded place, four miles away from the town. I shuddered; but I was constrained to listen, while he talked of his intention to give me a home of my own, and to make a lady of me. Hitherto, I had escaped my dreaded fate, by being in the midst of people. My grandmother had already had high words with my master about me. She had told him pretty plainly what she thought of his character, and there was considerable gossip in the neighborhood about our affairs, to which the open-mouthed jealousy of Mrs. Flint contributed not a little. When my master said he was going to build a house for me, and that he could do it with little trouble and expense, I was in hopes something would happen to frustrate his scheme; but I soon heard that the house was actually begun. I vowed before my Maker that I would never enter it. I had rather toil on the plantation from dawn till dark; I had rather live and die in jail, than drag on, from day to day, through such a living death. I was determined that the master, whom I so hated and loathed, who had blighted the prospects of my youth, and made my life a desert, should not, after my long struggle with him, succeed at last in trampling his victim under his feet. I would do any thing, every thing, for the sake of defeating him. What *could* I do? I thought and thought, till I became desperate, and made a plunge into the abyss.

And now, reader, I come to a period in my unhappy life, which I would gladly forget if I could. The remembrance fills me with sorrow and shame. It pains me to tell you of it; but I have promised to tell you the truth, and I will do it honestly, let it cost me what it may. I will not try to screen myself behind the plea of compulsion from a master; for it was not so. Neither can I plead ignorance or thoughtlessness. For years, my master had done his utmost to pollute my mind with foul images, and to destroy the pure principles inculcated by my grandmother, and the good mistress of my childhood. The influences of slavery had had the same effect on me that they had on other young girls; they had made me prematurely knowing, concerning the evil ways of the world. I knew what I did, and I did it with deliberate calculation.

But, O, ye happy women, whose purity has been sheltered from childhood, who have been free to choose the objects of your affection, whose homes are protected by law, do not judge the poor desolate slave girl too severely! If slavery had been abolished, I, also, could have married the man of my choice; I could have had a home shielded by the laws; and I should have been spared the painful task of confessing what I am now about to relate; but all my prospects had been blighted by slavery. I wanted to keep myself pure; and, under the most adverse circumstances, I tried hard to preserve my self-respect; but I was struggling alone in the powerful grasp of the demon Slavery; and the monster proved too strong for me. I felt as if I was forsaken by God and man; as if all my efforts must be frustrated; and I became reckless in my despair.

I have told you that Dr. Flint's persecutions and his wife's jealousy had given rise to some gossip in the neighborhood. Among others, it chanced that a white unmarried gentleman had obtained some knowledge of the circumstances in which I was placed. He knew my grandmother, and often spoke to me in the street. He became interested in me, and asked questions about my master, which I answered in part. He expressed a great deal of sympathy, and a wish to aid me. He constantly sought opportunities to see me, and wrote to me frequently. I was a poor slave girl, only fifteen years old.

So much attention from a superior person was, of course, flattering; for human nature is the same in all. I also felt grateful for his sympathy, and encouraged by his kind words. It seemed to me a great thing to have such a friend. By degrees, a more tender feeling crept into my heart. He was an educated and eloquent gentleman; too eloquent, alas, for the poor slave girl who trusted in him. Of course I saw whither all this was tending. I knew the impassable gulf between us; but to be an object of interest to a man who is not married, and who is not her master, is agreeable to the pride and feelings of a slave, if her miserable situation has left her any pride or sentiment. It seems less degrading to give one's self, than to submit to compulsion. There is something akin to freedom in having a lover who has no control over you, except that which he gains by kindness and attachment. A master may treat you as rudely as he pleases, and you dare not speak; moreover, the wrong does not seem so great with an unmarried man, as with one who has a wife to be made unhappy. There may be sophistry in all this; but the condition of a slave confuses all principles of morality, and, in fact, renders the practice of them impossible.

When I found that my master had actually begun to build the lonely cottage, other feelings mixed with those I have described. Revenge, and calculations of interest, were added to flattered vanity and sincere gratitude for kindness. I knew nothing would enrage Dr. Flint so much as to know that I favored another; and it was something to triumph over my tyrant even in that small way. I thought he would revenge himself by selling me, and I was sure my friend, Mr. Sands, would buy me. He was a man of more generosity and feeling than my master, and I thought my freedom could be easily obtained from him. The crisis of my fate now came so near that I was desperate. I shuddered to think of being the mother of children that should be owned by my old tyrant. I knew that as soon as a new fancy took him, his victims were sold far off to get rid of them; especially if they had children. I had seen several women sold, with his babies at the breast. He never allowed his offspring by slaves to remain long in sight of himself and his wife. Of a man who was not my master I could ask to have my children well supported; and in this case, I felt confident I should obtain the boon. I also felt quite sure that they would be made free. With all these thoughts revolving in my mind, and seeing no other way of escaping the doom I so much dreaded, I made a headlong plunge. Pity me, and pardon me, O virtuous reader! You never knew what it is to be a slave; to be entirely unprotected by law or custom; to have the laws reduce you to the condition of a chattel, entirely subject to the will of another. You never exhausted your ingenuity in avoiding the snares, and eluding the power of a hated tyrant; you never shuddered at the sound of his footsteps, and trembled within hearing of his voice. I know I did wrong. No one can feel it more sensibly than I do. The painful and humiliating memory will haunt me to my dying day. Still, in looking back, calmly, on the events of my life, I feel that the slave woman ought not to be judged by the same standard as others

The months passed on. I had many unhappy hours. I secretly mourned over the sorrow I was bringing on my grandmother, who had so tried to shield me from harm. I knew that I was the greatest comfort of her old age, and that it was a source of pride to her that I had not degraded myself, like most of the slaves. I wanted to confess to her that I was no longer worthy of her love; but I could not utter the dreaded words.

As for Dr. Flint, I had a feeling of satisfaction and triumph in the thought of telling *him*. From time to time he told me of his intended arrangements, and I was silent. At last, he came and told me the cottage was completed, and ordered me to go to it. I told him I would never enter it. He said, "I have heard enough of such talk as that. You shall go, if you are carried by force; and you shall remain there."

I replied, "I will never go there. In a few months I shall be a mother."

He stood and looked at me in dumb amazement, and left the house without a word. I thought I should be happy in my triumph over him. But now that the truth was out, and my relatives would hear of it, I felt wretched. Humble as were their circumstances, they had pride in my good character. Now, how could I look them in the face? My self-respect was gone! I had resolved that I would be virtuous, though I was a slave. I had said, "Let the storm beat! I will brave it till I die." And now, how humiliated I felt!

I went to my grandmother. My lips moved to make confession, but the words stuck in my throat. I sat down in the shade of a tree at her door and began to sew. I think she saw something unusual was the matter with me. The mother of slaves is very watchful. She knows there is no security for her children. After they have entered their teens she lives in daily expectation of trouble. This leads to many questions. If the girl is of a sensitive nature, timidity keeps her from answering truthfully, and this well-meant course has a tendency to drive her from maternal counsels. Presently, in came my mistress, like a mad woman, and accused me concerning her husband. My grandmother, whose suspicions had been previously awakened, believed what she said. She exclaimed, "O Linda! has it come to this? I had rather see you dead than to see you as you now are. You are a disgrace to your dead mother." She tore from my fingers my mother's wedding ring and her silver thimble. "Go away!" she exclaimed, "and never come to my house, again." Her reproaches fell so hot and heavy, that they left me no chance to answer. Bitter tears, such as the eyes never shed but once, were my only answer. I rose from my seat, but fell back again, sobbing. She did not speak to me; but the tears were running down her furrowed cheeks, and they scorched me like fire. She has always been so kind to me! *So* kind! How I longed to throw myself at her feet, and tell her all the truth! But she had ordered me to go, and never to come there again. After a few minutes, I mustered strength, and started to obey her. With what feelings did I now close that little gate, which I used to open with such an eager hand in my childhood! It closed upon me with a sound I never heard before.

Where could I go! I was afraid to return to my master's. I walked on recklessly, not caring where I went, or what would become of me. When I had gone four or five miles, fatigue compelled me to stop. I sat down on the stump of an old tree. The stars were shining through the boughs above me. How they mocked me, with their bright, calm light! The hours passed by, and as I sat there alone a chilliness and deadly sickness came over me. I sank on the ground. My mind was full of horrid thoughts. I prayed to die; but the prayer was not answered. At last, with great effort I roused myself, and walked some distance further, to the house of a woman who had been a friend of my mother. When I told her why I was there, she spoke soothingly to me; but I could not be comforted. I thought I could bear my shame if I could only be reconciled to my grandmother. I longed to open my heart to her. I thought if she could know the real state of the case, and all I had been bearing for years, she would perhaps judge me less harshly. My friend advised me to send for her. I did so; but days of agonizing suspense passed before she came. Had she utterly forsaken me? No. She came at last. I knelt before her, and told her the things that had poisoned my life; how long I had been persecuted; that I saw no way of escape; and in an hour of extremity I had become desperate. She listened in silence. I told her I would bear any thing and do any thing, if in time I had hopes of obtaining her forgiveness. I begged of her to pity me, for my dead mother's sake. And she did pity me. She did not say, "I forgive you;" but she looked at me lovingly, with her eyes full of tears. She laid her old hand gently on my head, and murmured, "Poor child! Poor child!"

The New Tie to Life

I returned to my good grandmother's house. She had an interview with Mr. Sands. When she asked him why he could not have left her one ewe lamb, —whether there were not plenty of slaves who did not care about character, —he made no answer; but he spoke kind and encouraging words. He promised to care for my child, and to buy me, be the conditions what they might.

I had not seen Dr. Flint for five days. I had never seen him since I made the avowal to him. He talked of the disgrace I had brought on myself; how I had sinned against my master, and mortified my old grandmother. He intimated that if I had accepted his proposals, he, as a physician, could have saved me from exposure. He even condescended to pity me. Could he have offered wormwood more bitter? He, whose persecutions had been the cause of my sin!

"Linda, " said he, "though you have been criminal towards me, I feel for you, and

I can pardon you if you obey my wishes. Tell me whether the fellow you wanted to marry is the father of your child. If you deceive me, you shall feel the fires of hell."

I did not feel as proud as I had done. My strongest weapon with him was gone. I was lowered in my own estimation, and had resolved to bear his abuse in silence. But when he spoke contemptuously of the lover who had always treated me honorably; when I remembered that but for *him* I might have been a virtuous, free, and happy wife, I lost my patience. "I have sinned against God and myself, " I replied; "but not against you."

He clinched his teeth, and muttered, "Curse you!" He came towards me, with ill-suppressed rage, and exclaimed, "You obstinate girl! I could grind your bones to powder! You have thrown yourself away on some worthless rascal. You are weak-minded, and have been easily persuaded by those who don't care a straw for you. The future will settle accounts between us. You are blinded now; but hereafter you will be convinced that your master was your best friend. My lenity towards you is proof of it. I might have punished you in many ways. I might have had you whipped till you fell dead under the lash. But I wanted you to live; I would have bettered your condition. Others cannot do it. You are my slave. Your mistress, disgusted by your conduct, forbids you to return to the house; therefore I leave you here for the present; but I shall see you often. I will call tomorrow."

He came with frowning brows, that showed a dissatisfied state of mind. After asking about my health, he inquired whether my board was paid, and who visited me. He then went on to say that he had neglected his duty; that as a physician there were certain things that he ought to have explained to me. Then followed talk such as would have made the most shameless blush. He ordered me to stand up before him. I obeyed. "I command you, " said he, "to tell me whether the father of your child is white or black." I hesitated. "Answer me this instant!" he exclaimed. I did not answer. He sprang upon me like a wolf, and grabbed my arm as if he would have broken it. "Do you love him?" said he, in a hissing tone.

"I am thankful that I do not despise him, " I replied.

He raised his hand to strike me; but it fell again. I don't know what arrested the blow. He sat down, with lips tightly compressed. At last he spoke. "I came here, " said he, "to make you a friendly proposition; but your ingratitude chafes me beyond endurance. You turn aside all my good intentions towards you. I don't know what it is that keeps me from killing you." Again he rose, as if he had a mind to strike me.

But he resumed. "On one condition I will forgive your insolence and crime. You must henceforth have no communication of any kind with the father of your child. You must not ask any thing from him, or receive any thing from him. I will take care of you and your child. You had better promise this at once, and not wait till you are deserted by him. This is the last act of mercy I shall show towards you."

I said something about being unwilling to have my child supported by a man who had cursed it and me also. He rejoined, that a woman who had sunk to my level had no right to expect any thing else. He asked, for the last time, would I accept his kindness? I answered that I would not.

"Very well, " said he; "then take the consequences of your wayward course. Never look to me for help. You are my slave, and shall always be my slave. I will never sell you, that you may depend upon."

Hope died away in my heart as he closed the door after him. I had calculated that in his rage he would sell me to a slave-trader; and I knew the father of my child was on the watch to buy me.

About this time my uncle Phillip was expected to return from a voyage. The day before his departure I had officiated as bridesmaid to a young friend. My heart was then ill at ease, but my smiling countenance did not betray it. Only a year had passed, but what fearful changes it had wrought! My heart had grown gray in misery. Lives that flash in sunshine, and lives that are born in tears, receive their hue from circumstances. None of us know what a year may bring forth.

I felt no joy when they told me my uncle had come. He wanted to see me, though he knew what had happened. I shrank from him at first; but at last consented that he should come to my room. He received me as he always had done. O, how my heart smote me when I felt his tears on my burning cheeks! The words of my grandmother came to my mind, –"Perhaps your mother and father are taken from the evil days to come." My disappointed heart could now praise God that it was so. But why, thought I, did my relatives ever cherish hopes for me? What was there to save me from the usual fate of slave girls? Many more beautiful and more intelligent than I had experienced a similar fate, or a far worse one. How could they hope that I should escape?

My uncle's stay was short, and I was not sorry for it. I was too ill in mind and body to enjoy my friends as I had done. For some weeks I was unable to leave my bed. I could not have any doctor but my master, and I would not have him sent for. At last, alarmed by my increasing illness, they sent for him. I was very weak and nervous; and as soon as he entered the room, I began to scream. They told him my state was very critical. He had no wish to hasten me out of the world, and he withdrew.

When my babe was born, they said it was premature. It weighed only four pounds; but God let it live. I heard the doctor say I could not survive till morning. I had often prayed for death; but now I did not want to die, unless my child could die too. Many weeks passed before I was able to leave my bed. I was a mere wreck of my former self. For a year there was scarcely a day when I was free from chills and fever. My babe was also sickly. His little limbs were often racked with pain. Dr. Flint continued his visits, to look after my health; and he did not fail to remind me that my child was an addition to his stock of slaves.

I felt too feeble to dispute with him, and listened to his remarks in silence. His visits were less frequent; but his busy spirit could not remain quiet. He employed my brother in his office, and he was made the medium of frequent notes and messages to me. William was a bright lad, and of much use to the doctor. He had learned to put up medicines, to leech, cup, and bleed. He had taught himself to read and spell. I was proud of my brother; and the old doctor suspected as much. One day, when I had not seen him for several weeks, I heard his steps approaching the door. I dreaded the encounter, and hid myself. He inquired for me, of course; but I was nowhere to be found. He went to his office, and despatched William with a note. The color mounted to my brother's face when he gave it to me; and he said, "Don't you hate me, Linda, for bringing you these things?" I told him I could not blame him; he was a slave, and obliged to obey his master's will. The note ordered me to come to his office. I went. He demanded to know where I was when he called. I told him I was at home. He flew into a passion, and said he knew better. Then he launched out upon his usual themes, –my crimes against him, and my ingratitude for his forbearance. The laws were laid down to me anew, and I was dismissed. I felt humiliated that my brother should stand by, and listen to such language as would be addressed only to a slave. Poor boy! He was powerless to defend me; but I saw the tears, which he vainly strove to keep back. This manifestation of feeling irritated the doctor. William could do nothing to please him. One morning he did not arrive at the office so early as usual; and that circumstance afforded his master an opportunity to vent his spleen. He was put in jail. The next day my brother sent a trader to the doctor, with a request to be sold. His master was greatly incensed at what he called his insolence. He said he had put him there to reflect upon his bad conduct, and he certainly was not giving any evidence of repentance. For two days he harassed himself to find somebody to do his office work; but every thing went wrong without William. He was released, and ordered to take his old stand, with many threats, if he was not careful about his future behavior.

As the months passed on, my boy improved in health. When he was a year old, they called him beautiful. The little vine was taking deep root in my existence, though its clinging fondness excited a mixture of love and pain. When I was most sorely oppressed I found a solace in his smiles. I loved to watch his infant slumbers; but always there was a dark cloud over my enjoyment. I could never forget that he was a slave. Sometimes I wished that he might die in infancy. God tried me. My darling became very ill. The bright eyes grew dull, and the little feet and hands were so icy cold that I thought death had already touched them. I had prayed for his death, but never so earnestly as I now prayed for his life; and my prayer was heard. Alas, what mockery it is for a slave mother to try to pray back her dying child to life! Death is better than slavery. It was a sad thought that I had no name to give my child. His father caressed him and treated him kindly, whenever he had a chance to see him. He was not unwilling that he should bear his name; but he had no legal claim to it; and if I had bestowed it upon him, my master would have regarded it as a new crime, a new piece of insolence, and would perhaps, revenge it on the boy. O, the serpent of Slavery has many and poisonous fangs!

Fear of Insurrection

Not far from this time Nat Turner's insurrection broke out; and the news threw our town into great commotion. Strange that they should be alarmed, when their slaves were so "contented and happy"! But so it was.

It was always the custom to have a muster every year. On that occasion every white man shouldered his musket. The citizens and the so-called country gentlemen wore military uniforms. The poor whites took their places in the ranks in every-day dress, some without shoes, some without hats. This grand occasion had already passed; and when the slaves were told there was to be another muster, they were surprised and rejoiced. Poor creatures! They thought it was going to be a holiday. I was informed of the true state of affairs, and imparted it to the few I could trust. Most gladly would I have proclaimed it to every slave; but I dared not. All could not be relied on. Mighty is the power of the torturing lash.

By sunrise, people were pouring in from every quarter within twenty miles of the town. I knew the houses were to be searched; and I expected it would be done by country bullies and the poor whites. I knew nothing annoyed them so much as to see colored people living in comfort and respectability; so I made arrangements for them with especial care. I arranged every thing in my grandmother's house as neatly as possible. I put white quilts on the beds, and decorated some of the rooms with flowers. When all was arranged, I sat down at the window to watch. Far as my eye could reach, it rested on a motley crowd of soldiers. Drums and fifes were discoursing martial music. The men were divided into companies of sixteen, each headed by a captain. Orders were given, and the wild scouts rushed in every direction, wherever a colored face was to be found.

It was a grand opportunity for the low whites, who had no negroes of their own to scourge. They exulted in such a chance to exercise a little brief authority, and show their subserviency to the slaveholders; not reflecting that the power which trampled on the colored people also kept themselves in poverty, ignorance, and moral degradation. Those who never witnessed such scenes can hardly believe what I know was inflicted at this time on innocent men, women, and children, against whom there was not the slightest ground for suspicion. Colored people and slaves who lived in remote parts of the town suffered in an especial manner. In some cases the searchers scattered powder and shot among their clothes, and then sent other parties to find them, and bring them forward as proof that they were plotting insurrection. Every where men, women, and children were whipped till the blood stood in puddles at their feet. Some received five hundred lashes; others were tied hands and feet, and tortured with a bucking paddle, which blisters the skin terribly. The dwellings of the colored people, unless they happened to be protected by some influential white person, who was nigh at hand, were robbed of clothing and every thing else the marauders thought worth carrying away. All day long these unfeeling wretches went round, like a troop of demons, terrifying and tormenting the helpless. At night, they formed themselves into patrol bands, and went wherever they chose among the colored people, acting out their brutal will. Many women hid themselves in woods and swamps, to keep out of their way. If any of the husbands or fathers told of these outrages, they were tied up to the public whipping post, and cruelly scourged for telling lies about white men. The consternation was universal. No two people that had the slightest tinge of color in their faces dared to be seen talking together.

I entertained no positive fears about our household, because we were in the midst of white families who would protect us. We were ready to receive the soldiers whenever they came. It was not long before we heard the tramp of feet and the sound of voices. The door was rudely pushed open; and in they tumbled, like a pack of hungry wolves. They snatched at every thing within their reach. Every box, trunk, closet, and corner underwent a thorough examination. A box in one of the drawers containing some silver change was eagerly pounced upon. When I stepped forward to take it from them, one of the soldiers turned and said angrily, "What d'ye foller us fur? D'ye s'pose white folks is come to steal?"

I replied, "You have come to search; but you have searched that box, and I will take it, if you please."

At that moment I saw a white gentleman who was friendly to us; and I called to him, and asked him to have the goodness to come in and stay till the search was over. He readily complied. His entrance into the house brought in the captain of the company, whose business it was to guard the outside of the house, and see that none of the inmates left it. This officer was Mr. Litch, the wealthy slaveholder whom I mentioned, in the account of neighboring planters, as being notorious for his cruelty. He felt above soiling his hands with the search. He merely gave orders; and, if a bit of writing was discovered, it was carried to him by his ignorant followers, who were unable to read.

My grandmother had a large trunk of bedding and table cloths. When that was opened, there was a great shout of surprise; and one exlaimed, "Where'd the damned niggers git all dis sheet an' table clarf?"

My grandmother, emboldened by the presence of our white protector, said, "You may be sure we didn't pilfer 'em from *your* houses."

"Look here, mammy, "said a grim-looking fellow without any coat, "you seem to feel mighty gran' 'cause you got all them 'ere fixens. White folks oughter have 'em all."

His remarks were interrupted by a chorus of voices shouting, "We's got 'em! We's got 'em! Dis 'ere yaller gal's got letters!"

There was a general rush for the supposed letter, which, upon examination, proved to be some verses written to me by a friend. In packing away my things, I had overlooked them. When their captain informed them of their contents, they seemed much disappointed. He inquired of me who wrote them. I told him it was one of my friends. "Can you read them?" he asked. When I told him I could, he swore, and raved, and tore the paper into bits. "Bring me all your letters!" said he, in a commanding tone. I told him I had none. "Don't be afraid, " he continued, in an insinuating way. "Bring them all to me. Nobody shall do you any harm." Seeing I did not move to obey him, his pleasant tone changed to oaths and threats. "Who writes to you? half free niggers?" inquired he. I replied, "O, no; most of my letters are from white people. Some request me to burn them after they are read, and some I destroy without reading."

An exlamation of surprise from some of the company put a stop to our conversation. Some silver spoons which ornamented an old-fashioned buffet had just been discovered. My grandmother was in the habit of preserving fruit for many ladies in the town, and of preparing suppers for parties;consequently she had many jars of preserves. The closet that contained these was next invaded, and the contents tasted. One of them, who was helping himself freely, tapped his neighbor on the shoulder, and said, "Wal done! Don't wonder de niggers want to kill all de white folks, when dey live on 'sarves" [meaning preserves]. I stretched out my hand to take the jar, saying, "You were not sent here to search for sweetmeats."

"And what *were* we sent for?" said the captain, bristling up to me. I evaded the question.

The search of the house was completed, and nothing found to condemn us. They next proceeded to the garden, and knocked about every bush and vine, with no better success. The captain called his men together, and, after a short consultation, the order to march was given. As they passed out of the gate, the captain turned back, and pronounced a malediction on the house. He said it ought to be burned to the ground, and each of its inmates receive thirty-nine lashes. We came out of this affair very fortunately; not losing any thing except some wearing apparel.

Towards evening the turbulence increased. The soldiers, stimulated by drink, committed still greater cruelties. Shrieks and shouts continually rent the air. Not daring to go to the door, I peeped under the window curtain. I saw a mob dragging along a number of colored people, each white man, with his musket upraised, threatening instant death if they did not stop their shrieks. Among the prisoners was a respectable old colored minister. They had found a few parcels of shot in his house, which his wife had for years used to balance her scale. For this they were going to shoot him on Court House Green. What a spectacle was that for a civilized country! A rabble, staggering under intoxication, assuming to be the administrators of justice!

The better class of the community exerted their influence to save the innocent, persecuted people; and in several instances they succeeded, by keeping them shut up in jail till the excitement abated. At last the white citizens found that their own property was not safe from the lawless rabble they had summoned to protect them. They rallied the drunken swarm, drove them back into the country, and set a guard over the town.

The next day, the town patrols were commissioned to search colored people that lived out of the city; and the most shocking outrages were committed with perfect impunity. Every day for a fortnight, if I looked out, I saw horsemen with some poor panting negro tied to their saddles, and compelled by the lash to keep up with their speed, till they arrived at the jail yard. Those who had been whipped too unmercifully to walk were washed with brine, tossed into a cart, and carried to jail. One black man, who had not fortitude to endure such scourging, promised to give information about the conspiracy. But it turned out that he knew nothing at all. He had not even heard the name of Nat Turner. The poor fellow had, however, made up a story, which augmented his own sufferings and those of the colored people.

The day patrol continued for some weeks, and at sundown a night guard was substituted. Nothing at all was proved against the colored people, bond or free. The wrath of the slaveholders was somewhat appeased by the capture of Nat Turner. The imprisoned were released. The slaves were sent to their masters, and the free were permitted to return to their ravaged homes. Visiting was strictly forbidden on the plantations. The slaves begged the privilege of again meeting at their little church in the woods, with their burying ground around it. It was built by the colored people, and they had no higher happiness than to meet there and sing hymns together, and pour out their hearts in spontaneous prayer. Their request was denied, and the church was demolished. They were permitted to attend the white churches, a certain portion of the galleries being appropriated to their use. There, when every body else had partaken of the communion, and benediction had been pronounced, the minister said, "Come down, now, my colored friends, " They obeyed the summons, and partook of the bread and wine, in commemoration of the meek and lowly Jesus, who said, "God is your Father, and all ye are brethren. "

The Church and Slavery

After the alarm caused by Nat Turner's insurrection had subsided, the slave - holders came to the conclusion that it would be well to give the slaves enough of religious instruction to keep them from murdering their masters. The Episcopal clergyman offered to hold a separate service on Sundays for their benefit. His colored members were very few, and also very respectable, –a fact which I presume had some weight with him. The difficulty was to decide on a suitable place for them to worship. The Methodist and Baptist churches admitted them in the afternoon; but their carpets and cushions were not so costly as those at the Episcopal church. It was at last decided that they should meet at the house of a free colored man, who was a member.

I was invited to attend, because I could read. Sunday evening came, and, trusting to the cover of night, I ventured out. I rarely ventured out by daylight, for I always went with fear, expecting at every turn to encounter Dr. Flint, who was sure to turn me back, or order me to his office to inquire where I got my bonnet, or some other article of dress. When the Rev. Mr. Pike came, there were some twenty persons present. The reverend gentleman knelt in prayer, then seated himself, and requested all present, who could read, to open their books, while he gave out the portions he wished them to repeat or respond to.

His text was, "Servants, be obedient to them that are your masters according to the flesh, with fear and trembling, in singleness of your heart, as unto Christ."

Pious Mr. Pike brushed up his hair till it stood upright, and, in deep, solemn tones, began: "Hearken, ye servants! Give strict heed unto my words. You are rebellious sinners. Your hearts are filled with all manner of evil. 'Tis the devil who tempts you. God is angry with you, and will surely punish you, if you don't forsake your wicked ways. You that live in town are eye-servants behind your master's back. Instead of serving your masters faithfully, which is pleasing in the sight of your heavenly Master, you are idle, and shirk your work. God sees you. You tell lies. God hears you. Instead of being engaged in worshipping him, you are hidden away somewhere, feasting on your master's substance; tossing coffee-grounds with some wicked fortuneteller, or cutting cards with another old hag. Your masters may not find you out, but God sees you, and will punish you. O, the depravity of your hearts! When your master's work is done, are you quietly together, thinking of the goodness of God to such sinful creatures? No; you are quarrelling, and tying up little bags of roots to bury under the door-steps to poison each other with. God sees you. You men steal away to every grog shop to sell your master's corn, that you may buy rum to drink. God sees you. You sneak into the back streets, or among the bushes, to pitch coppers. Although your masters may not find you out, God sees you; and he will punish you. You must forsake your sinful ways, and be faithful servants. Obey your old master and your young master–your old mistress and your young mistress. If you disobey your earthly master, you offend your heavenly Master. You must obey God's commandments. When you go from here, don't stop at the corners of the streets to talk, but go directly home, and let your master and mistress see that you have come."

The benediction was pronounced. We went home, highly amused at brother Pike's gospel teaching, and we determined to hear him again. I went the next Sabbath evening, and heard pretty much a repetition of the last discourse. At the close of the meeting, Mr. Pike informed us that he found it very inconvenient to meet at the friend's house, and he should be glad to see us, every Sunday evening, at his own kitchen.

I went home with the feeling that I had heard the Reverend Mr. Pike for the last time. Some of his members repaired to his house, and found that the kitchen sported two tallow candles; the first time, I am sure, since its present occupant owned it, for the servants never had anything but pine knots. It was so long before the reverend gentleman descended from his comfortable parlor that the slaves left, and went to enjoy a Methodist shout. They never seem so happy as when shouting and singing at religious meetings. Many of them are sincere, and nearer to the gate of heaven than sanctimonious Mr. Pike, and other long-faced Christians, who see wounded Samaritans, and pass by on the other side.

The slaves generally compose their own songs and hymns; and they do not trouble their heads much about the measure. They often sing the following verses:

"Old Satan is one busy ole man;
    He rolls dem blocks all in my way;
But Jesus is my bosom friend;
    He rolls dem blocks away.

"If had died when I was young,
    Den how my stam'ring tongue would have sung;
But I am ole, and now I stand
    A narrow chance for to tread dat heavenly land."

I well remember one occasion when I attended a Methodist class meeting. I went with a burdened spirit, and happened to sit next a poor, bereaved mother, whose heart was still heavier than mine. The class leader was the town constable–a man who bought and sold slaves, who whipped his brethren and sisters of the church at the public whipping post, in jail or out of jail. He was ready to perform that Christian office any where for fifty cents. This white-faced, black-hearted brother came near us, and said to the stricken woman, "Sister, can't you tell us how the Lord deals with your soul? Do you love him as you did formerly?"

She rose to her feet, and said, in piteous tones, "My Lord and Master, help me! My load is more than I can bear. God has hid himself from me, and I am left in darkness and misery." Then, striking her breast, she continued, "I can't tell you what is in here! They've got all my children. Last week they took the last one. God only knows where they've sold her. They let me have her sixteen years, and then— O! O! Pray for her brothers and sisters! I've got nothing to live for now. God make my time short!"

She sat down, quivering in every limb. I saw that constable class leader become crimson in the face with suppressed laughter, while he held up his handkerchief, that those who were weeping for the poor woman's calamity might not see his merriment. Then, with assumed gravity, he said to the bereaved mother, "Sister, pray to the Lord that every dispensation of his divine will may be sanctified to the good of your poor needy soul!"

The congregation struck up a hymn, and sung as though they were as free as the birds that warbled round us, –

> "Ole Satan thought he had a mighty aim'
> He missed my soul, and caught my sins.
> Cry Amen, cry Amen, cry Amen to God!
>
> "He took my sins upon his back;
> Went muttering and grumbling down to hell.
> Cry Amen, cry Amen, cry Amen to God!
>
> "Ole Satan's church is here below.
> Up to God's free church I hope to go.
> Cry Amen, cry Amen, cry Amen to God!"

Precious are such moments to the poor slaves. If you were to hear them at such times, you might think they were happy. But can that hour of singing and shouting sustain them through the dreary week, toiling without wages, under constant dread of the lash?

The Episcopal clergyman, who, ever since my earliest recollection, had been a sort of god among the slaveholders, concluded, as his family was large, that he must go where was money was more abundant. A very different clergyman took his place. The change was very agreeable to the colored people, who said, "God has sent us a good man this time." They loved him, and their children followed him for a smile or a kind word. Even the slaveholders felt his influence. He brought to the rectory five slaves. His wife taught them to read and write, and to be useful to her and themselves. As soon as he was settled, he turned his attention to the needy slaves around him. He urged upon his parishioners the duty of having a meeting expressly for them every Sunday, with a sermon adapted to their comprehension. After much argument and importunity, it was finally agreed that they might occupy the gallery of the church on Sunday evenings. Many colored people, hitherto unaccustomed to attend church, now gladly went to hear the gospel preached. The sermons were simple, and they understood them. Moreover, it was the first time they had ever been addressed as human beings. It was not long before his white parishioners began to be dissatisfied. He was accused of preaching better sermons to the negroes than he did to them. He honestly confessed that he bestowed more pains upon those sermons than upon any others; for the slaves were reared in such ignorance that it was a difficult task to adapt himself to their comprehension. Dissensions arose in the parish. Some wanted he should preach to them in the evening, and to the slaves in the afternoon. In the midst of these disputings his wife died, after a very short illness. Her slaves gathered round her dying bed in great sorrow. She said, "I have tried to do you good and promote your happiness; and if I have failed, it has not been for want of interest in your welfare. Do not weep for me; but prepare for the new duties that lie before you. I leave you all free. May we meet in a better world." Her liberated slaves were sent away, with funds to establish them comfortably. The colored people will long bless the memory of that truly Christian woman. Soon after her death her husband preached his farewell sermon, and many tears were shed at his departure.

Several years after, he passed through our town and preached to his former congregation. In his afternoon sermon he addressed the colored people. "My friends," said he, "it affords me great happiness to have an opportunity of speaking to you again. For two years I have been striving to do something for the colored people of my own parish; but nothing is yet accomplished. I have not even preached a sermon to them. Try to live according to the word of God, my friends. Your skin is darker than mine; but God judges men by their hearts, not by the color of their skins." This was a strange doctrine from a southern pulpit. It was very offensive to slaveholders. They said he and his wife had made fools of their slaves, and that he preached like a fool to the negroes.

I knew an old black man, whose piety and childlike trust in God were beautiful to witness. At fifty-three years old he joined the Baptist church. He had a most earnest desire to learn to read. He thought he should know how to serve God better if he could only read the Bible. He came to me, and begged me to teach him. He said he could not pay me, for he had no money; but he would bring me nice fruit when the season for it came. I asked him if he didn't know it was contrary to law; and that slaves were whipped and imprisoned for teaching each other to read. This brought the tears into his eyes. "Don't be troubled, uncle Fred," said I. "I have no thoughts of refusing to teach you. I only told you of the law, that you might know the danger, and be on your guard." He thought he could plan to come three times a week without its being suspected. I selected a quiet nook, where no intruder was likely to penetrate, and there I taught him his A, B, C. Considering his age, his progress was astonishing. As soon as he could spell in two syllables he wanted to spell out words in the Bible. The happy smile that illuminated his face put joy into my heart. After spelling out a few words, he paused, and said, "Honey, it 'pears when I can read dis good book I shall be nearer to God. White man is got all de sense. He can larn easy. It ain't easy for ole black man like me. I only wants to read dis book, dat I may know how to live; den I hab no fear 'bout dying."

I tried to encourage him by speaking of the rapid progress he had made. "Hab patience, child, " he replied. "I larns slow."

I had no need of patience. His gratitude, and the happiness I imparted, were more than a recompense for all my trouble.

At the end of six months he had read through the New Testament, and could find any text in it. One day, when he had recited unusually well, I said, "Uncle Fred, how do you manage to get your lessons so well?"

"Lord bress you chile, " he replied. "You nebber gibs me a lesson dat I don't pray to God to help me to understan' what I spells and what I reads. And he *does* help me, chile. Bress his holy name!"

There are thousands, who, like good uncle Fred, are thirsting for the water of life; but the law forbids it, and the churches withhold it. They send the Bible to heathen abroad, and neglect the heathen at home. I am glad that missionaries go out to the dark corners of the earth; but I ask them not to overlook the dark corners at home. Talk to American slaveholders as you talk to savages in Africa. Tell *them* it is wrong to traffic in men. Tell them it is sinful to sell their own children, and atrocious to violate their own daughters. Tell them that all men are brethren, and that man has no right to shut out the light of knowledge from his brother. Tell them they are answerable to God for sealing up the Fountain of Life from souls that are thirsting for it.

There are men who would gladly undertake such missionary work as this; but, alas! their number is small. They are hated by the south, and would be driven from its soil, or dragged to prison to die, as others have been before them. The field is ripe for the harvest, and awaits the reapers. Perhaps the great grandchildren of uncle Fred may have freely imparted to them the divine treasures, which he sought by stealth, at the risk of the prison and the scourge.

Are doctors of divinity blind, or are they hypocrites? I suppose some are the one, and some the other; but I think if they felt the interest in the poor and lowly, that they ought to feel, they would not be so *easily* blinded. A clergyman who goes to the south, for the first time, has usually some feeling, however vague, that slavery is wrong. The slaveholder suspects this, and plays his game accordingly. He makes himself as agreeable as possible; talks on theology, and other kindred topics. The reverend gentleman is asked to invoke a blessing on a table loaded with luxuries. After dinner he walks round the premises, and sees the beautiful groves and flowering vines, and the comfortable huts of favored household slaves. The southerner invites him to talk with these slaves. He asks them if they want to be free, and they say, "O, no, massa." This is sufficient to satisfy him. He comes home to publish a "South-Side View of Slavery, " and to complain of the exaggerations of abolitionists. He assures people that he has been to the south, and seen slavery for himself; that it is a beautiful "patriarchal institution;" that the slaves don't want their freedom; that they have hallelujah meetings, and other religious privileges.

What does *he* know of the half-starved wretches toiling from dawn till dark on the plantations? of mothers shrieking for their children, torn from their arms by slave traders? of young girls dragged down into moral filth? of pools of blood around the whipping post? of hounds trained to tear human flesh? of men screwed into cotton gins to die? The slaveholder showed him none of these things, and the slaves dared not tell of them if he had asked them.

There is a great difference between Christianity and religion at the south. If a man goes to the communion table, and pays money into the treasury of the church, no matter if it be the price of blood, he is called religious. If a pastor has offspring by a woman not his wife, the church dismisses him, if she is a white woman; but if she is colored, it does not hinder his continuing to be their good shepherd.

When I was told Dr. Flint had joined the Episcopal church, I was much surprised. I supposed that religion had a purifying effect of the character of men; but the worst persecutions I endured from him were after he was a communicant. The conversation of the doctor, the day after he had been confirmed, certainly gave *me* no indication that he had "renounced the devil and all his works." In answer to some of his usual talk, I reminded him that he had just joined the church. "Yes, Linda, " said he. "It was proper for me to do so. I am getting in years, and my position in society requires it, and it puts an end to all the damned slang. You would do well to join the church, too, Linda."

"There are sinners enough in it already, " rejoined I. "If I could be allowed to live like a Christian, I should be glad."

"You can do what I require; and if you are faithful to me, you will be as virtuous as my wife, " he replied.

I answered that the Bible didn't say so.

His voice became hoarse with rage. "How dare you preach to me about your infernal Bible!" he exclaimed. "What right have you, who are my negro, to talk to me about what you would like, and what you wouldn't like? I am your master, and you shall obey me."

No wonder the slaves sing, –

"Ole Satan's church is here below;
     Up to God's free church I hope to go."

(1861)

JOHN S. MOSBY

Mosby's War Reminiscences

Soon after the outbreak of war in the spring of 1861 the First Regiment of Virginia Cavalry was organized with J. E. B. Stuart as colonel. He was then just twenty-eight years of age, a native of Virginia and a graduate of West Point. As lieutenant of cavalry he had had some experience in Indian warfare in the West in which he had been wounded; and in the raid of John Brown on the United States arsenal at Harper's Ferry had acted as aide to Colonel (afterwards General) Robert E. Lee.

The First Virginia Cavalry was attached to the command of General Joseph E. Johnston in the Shenandoah valley and assigned to the duty of watching Patterson, who had crossed the Potomac and was threatening the Southern army, then at Winchester. I was a private in a company of cavalry called the Washington Mounted Rifles, which was commanded by Capt. William E. Jones, an officer who some years before had retired from the United States army, and gave the company the name of his old regiment. Jones was a graduate of West Point and had been a comrade of Stonewall Jackson's while there. He has often entertained me in his tent at night with anecdotes of that eccentric genius. No man in the South was better qualified to mould the wild element he controlled into soldiers. His authority was exercised mildly but firmly, and to the lessons of duty and obedience he taught me I acknowledge that I am largely indebted for whatever success I may afterwards have had as a commander.

I first saw Stuart in the month of July, 1861, at a village called Bunker Hill on the pike leading from Winchester to Martinsburg, where Patterson was camped. His regiment was stationed there to observe the movements of the Union army. His personal appearance bore the stamp of his military character, the fire, the dash, the energy and physical endurance that seemed able to defy all natural laws. Simultaneously with the movement of McDowell against Beauregard, began Patterson's demonstration to keep Johnston at Winchester. It was, however, too feeble to have any effect except to neutralize his own forces. The plan of the Southern generals was to avoid a battle in the valley and concentrate their armies at Manassas. The duty was assigned to Stuart's cavalry of masking the march of Johnston to Manassas and at the same time watching Patterson. General Scott had ordered him to feel the enemy strongly and not to allow him to escape to Manassas to reinforce Beauregard. Patterson replied in the most confident tone that he was holding Johnston.

After the battle had been won by the Confederates, in reply to Scott's criticism upon him for not having engaged them, Patterson comforted him with the assurance that if he had done so, Scott would have had to mourn the defeat of two armies instead of one. The records show that at that time Patterson had about 18,000 men and Johnston about 10,000.

On the 15th of July, Patterson advanced and drove us with artillery from our camp at Bunker Hill. Stuart had none to reply with. All of us thought a battle at Winchester was imminent. Patterson had one regiment of the regular besides some volunteer cavalry from Philadelphia, but made no use of them. He never sent his cavalry outside his infantry lines, and their only service was to add to the pomp and circumstance of war on reviews and parades. He stayed one day at Bunker Hill, and then, thinking he had done enough in driving us away, turned off squarely to the left and marched down to Charlestown. He had not been in twelve miles of our army, and this was the way he executed General Scott's order to feel it strongly.

Stuart still hung so close on his flanks that he occasionally let a shell drop among us. As soon as the movement to Charlestown was developed, Johnston received intelligence of it through Stuart. He saw then that Patterson did not intend an attack, and got ready to join Beauregard. The Union general went into camp at Charlestown while the Confederate folded his tent like the Arab and quietly stole away. Stuart spread a curtain of cavalry between the opposing armies which so effectually concealed the movement of Johnston, that Patterson never suspected it until it had been accomplished. The telegraphic correspondence at that time between Generals Scott and Patterson now reads like an extract from the transactions of the Pickwick Club.

On July 13th, Scott telegraphs to Patterson: "Make demonstrations to detain Johnston in the valley." July 14th, Patterson replies: "Will advance to-morrow. Unless I can rout shall be careful not to set him in full retreat toward Strasburg." He seemed to be afraid of frightening Johnston so much that he would run away. Again, Scott telegraphs to Patterson: "Do not let the enemy amuse and delay you with a small force in front whilst he reinforces the junction with his main body." This shows that General Scott, who was in Washington, had the sagacity to discern what we were likely to do.

On July 18th, General Scott says to him: "I have been certainly expecting you to beat the enemy. If not, to hear that you had felt him strongly, or, at least, had occupied him by threats and demonstrations." At that time Patterson was twenty miles distant from Johnston and never got any closer. This was all the feeling he did. On the same day Patterson replies: "The enemy has stolen no march on me. I have kept him actively employed, and by threats and reconnoissances in force caused him to be reinforced." At that time, Johnston was marching to Manassas, and Stuart's cavalry were watching the smoke as it curled from the Union camps at Charlestown.

Again, on July 18th, in order to make General Scott feel perfectly secure, Patterson tells him: "I have succeeded, in accordance with the wishes of the General-in-Chief, in keeping Johnston's force at Winchester. A reconnoissance in force on Tuesday caused him to be largely reinforced from Strasburg." And on July 21st, when the junction of the two armies had been effected, and the great battle was raging at Manassas, he telegraphs to Scott: "Johnston left Millwood yesterday to operate on McDowell's right and to turn through Loudoun on me."

As Patterson was haunted by the idea that Johnston was after him, although he had marched in an opposite direction, he concluded to retreat to Harper's Ferry. The success of Johnston's strategy in eluding Patterson and cheating him into the belief that he was still in the valley, is due to the vigilance of Stuart and his activity and skill in the management of cavalry. The Northern General never discovered how badly he had been fooled until the day of the battle, when he was too far away to give any assistance. But Stuart was not satisfied with the work he had done. After the infantry had been transferred to the railroad east of the Blue Ridge, he left a single company as a veil in front of Patterson and joined the army at Manassas on the evening before the battle. We had been almost continuously in the saddle for a week, and I have a vivid remembrance of the faces of the men—bronzed with sun and dust from the long march. The two armies were in such close contact that all knew there would be a battle on the morrow. Patterson was safe in the valley.

When he was before the committee on the Conduct of the War to give his reasons for not advancing on Johnston at Winchester, he filed a paper containing the following statement: "Among the regiments there was one of Kentucky riflemen armed with heavy bowie knives; they refused to take more than one round of cartridges. They proposed to place themselves in the bushes for assault." Of course, no prudent commander would lead men where they would be disembowelled by an enemy hidden in the bushes. Perhaps General Patterson was imitating the example of Othello, and trying to captivate Congressmen, as the Moor did the ear of Desdemona, with tales of

> The cannibals that do each other eat;
> The anthropophagi, and men whose heads
> Do grow beneath their shoulders.

On the night before the battle, the raw troops were excited by every noise, and the picket firing was incessant. We slept soundly in our bivouac in the pines, and early in the morning were awakened by the reveille that called us to arms. As the sun rose, the rattle of musketry began along Bull Run, and soon from one end of the line to the other there was a continuous roar of small arms and artillery.

War loses a great deal of its romance after a soldier has seen his first battle. I have a more vivid recollection of the first than the last one I was in. It is a classical maxim that it is sweet and becoming to die for one's country; but whoever has seen the horrors of a battle-field feels that it is far sweeter to live for it. The Confederate generals had expected a battle on our right; as a fact, our left wing was turned, and the battle was mostly fought by Johnston's troops, who, having come up the day before, had been held in reserve. Stuart's regiment having just arrived, had not been sent on the outposts, and hence is in no way responsible for the surprise. In the crisis of the battle, when Jackson with his brigade was standing like a stone wall against the advancing host, he called for Stuart's cavalry to support him. Stuart sent one squadron to

Jackson's right, under the Major, who did nothing (I was with him), while with six companies he came up on Jackson's left, just in time to charge and rout the Ellsworth Zouaves. Their general, in his report, says that he was never able to rally them during the fight.

This cavalry charge had an important effect upon the fortunes of the day, as it delayed the enemy, and gave time for troops to come to the relief of Jackson, who was then hard pressed by superior numbers. Stuart afterward, with a battery of artillery, led the turning movement that caused the rout, and associated the stream of Bull Run with the most memorable panic in history. Shortly after the battle, all the cavalry of the army was organized into a brigade, with Stuart in command. Jones was also promoted to be colonel of the regiment, and Fitz Lee became lieutenant-colonel. From this time until the army evacuated Manassas, in the spring of 1862, the cavalry was almost exclusively engaged in outpost duty. McClellan kept close to the fortifications around Washington while he was organizing the army of the Potomac, and his cavalry rarely ventured beyond his infantry pickets. No field was open for brilliant exploits; but the discipline and experience of a life on the outpost soon converted the Confederate volunteers into veterans.

Without intending any disparagement, I may say that the habits and education of Northern men had not been such as to adapt them readily to the cavalry service, without a process of drilling; while, on the contrary, the Southern youth, who, like the ancient Persians, had been taught from his cradle "to ride, to shoot, and speak the truth," leaped into his saddle, almost a cavalryman from his birth. The Cossacks, who came from their native wilds on the Don to break the power of Napoleon, had no other training in war than the habits of nomadic life; and in the same school were bred the Parthian horsemen who drove to despair the legions of Crassus and Antony.

I must also say that the Confederate authorities made but slight use of the advantage they enjoyed in the early periods of the war, for creating a fine body of cavalry; and that little wisdom was shown in the use of what they did have. It would have been far better military policy, during the first winter of the war, to have saved the cavalry as McClellan did, either to lead the advance or cover the retreat in the spring campaign. It was largely consumed in work which the infantry might have done, without imposing much additional hardships on them, as the proportion of cavalry was so small. When the Southern army retired, in March, 1862, three-fourths of the horses had been broken down by the hard work of the winter, and the men had been furloughed to go home for fresh ones. The Confederate government did not furnish horses for the cavalry, but paid the men forty cents a day for the use of them. This vicious policy was the source of continual depletion of the cavalry. Stuart's old regiment,—the First Virginia Cavalry,—of which I was adjutant, with at least 800 men on its muster rolls, did not have 150 for duty on the morning we broke up winter quarters on Bull Run. If the cavalry brigade had been cantoned on the border in the rich counties of Fauquier and Loudoun, the ranks would have been full, and their granaries would not have been left as forage for the enemy. The Confederate army fell back leisurely from the front of Washington, and rested some weeks on the Rappahannock, waiting the development of McClellan's plans. Stuart's cavalry was the rearguard. Sumner pushed forward with a division along the Orange and Alexandria railroad, to make a demonstration and cover McClellan's operations in another direction. He rather overdid the thing. On reaching our picket line on Cedar Run, he made a grand display by deploying his whole force in an open field. I happened to be on the picket line that day, and told Col. Jones that it was only a feint to deceive us. We retired, and the enemy occupied our camping-ground that night.

The next morning Stuart was at Bealeton station; and our skirmishers were engaged with the enemy, who was advancing towards the Rappahannock. My own regiment had just taken position on the railroad, when I rode up to Stuart, with whom I had become pretty well acquainted. Since we had left the line of Bull Run, I had several times returned on scouts for him. He said to me,"I want to find out whether this is McClellan's army or only a feint." I replied,"I will go and find out for you." I immediately started towards the rear of the enemy's column with two or three men, and reached a point some distance behind it about the time they were shelling our cavalry they had driven over the river. I saw that the enemy was only making a demonstration, and rode nearly all night to get back to Stuart. When I got to the river, we came very near being shot by our own pickets, who mistook us for the enemy. I found Stuart with Gen. Ewell, anxiously waiting to hear from me, or for the enemy to cross the river.

I have not been so fortunate as to have a poet to do for me on this occasion what Longfellow did for the midnight ride of Paul Revere. There was a drizzling rain and a dense fog; it was impossible to see what the enemy were doing. I remember Stuart's joy and surprise when I told him that they were falling back from the river. In the rapture of the moment he told me that I could get any reward I wanted for what I had done. The only reward I asked was the opportunity to do the same thing again. In ten minutes the cavalry had crossed the river and was capturing prisoners. Nothing had been left before us but a screen of cavalry, which was quickly brushed away. It now became evident that McClellen would move down the Potomac and operate against Richmond from a new base and on another line. This was the first cavalry reconnaissance that had ever been made to the rear of the enemy, and was considered as something remarkable at that time; at a later period they were very common. Soon after this, Stuart's cavalry was transferred from the line of the Rappahannock with the rest of Johnston's army, to confront McClellan on the Peninsula. I dined with Gen. Lee at his headquarters, near Petersburg, about six weeks before the surrender. He told me then that he had been opposed to Gen. Johnston's withdrawing to the Peninsula, and had written to him while he was on the Rapidan, advising him to move back towards the Potomac. He thought that if he had done this, McClellan would have been recalled to the defence of Washington. He further said that, instead of falling back from Yorktown to Richmond, Gen. Johnston should have made a stand with his whole army, instead of a part of it, on the narrow isthmus at Williamsburg.

Just before we reached Williamsburg, news came of the passage of the conscription law, which preserved all the regimental organizations as they were. The men were held in the ranks, but allowed to elect their company officers; and these in turn elected field officers. It is hard to reconcile democracy with military principles; and, consequently, many of the best officers were dropped. Such was the fate of my colonel. The staff officers, not being elected, were supposed to hold over without reappointment. I immediately handed my resignation as adjutant to the new colo-nel,—Fitz Lee,—*who accepted it.*

The conscription law at first produced some dissatisfaction among the men, as most of them had served twelve months without a furlough; but this soon subsided. All acquiesced in what was regarded as imperious necessity. The loss of our positions in the First Virginia Cavalry resulted in a benefit both to Jones and myself. Through the influence of Stonewall Jackson, Jones was made a brigadier-general, and soon after the death of Ashby was given the command of his brigade. Stuart invited me to come to his headquarters and act as a scout for him. In this way I began my career as a partisan, which now, when I recall it through the mist of years, seems as unreal as the lives of the Paladins.

I wish it to be understood that a scout is not a spy who goes in disguise, but a soldier in arms and uniform who reconnoitres either inside or outside an enemy's line. Such a life is full of adventure, excitement, and romance. Stuart was not only an educated, but a heaven-born soldier, whose natural genius had not been stifled by red tape and the narrow rules of the schools.

The history of the war furnishes no better type of the American soldier; as a chief of cavalry he is without a peer. He cared little for formulas, and knew when to follow and when to disregard precedents. He was the first to see that the European methods of employing cavalry were not adapted to the conditions of modern war. His inventive genius discovered new ways of making cavalry useful, that had never been dreamed of by the regular professors of the science. I will now give some illustrations of his originality and the fertility of his resources. When McClellan was lying in the swamps of the Chickahominy, the infantry lines of the two armies were so close together that cavalry operations in their front were impracticable. One morning, when Stuart's headquarters were near Richmond, he invited me to breakfast with him, and at the table asked me to take two or three men and find out whether McClellan was fortifying on the Totopotomoy Creek. I had been inactive for some time, and this was just the opportunity I wanted. I started, but was diverted from the route I had been directed to go by there being a flag of truce on the road. I did not want to return without accomplishing something, so I turned north and made a wide detour by Hanover Court House. Although I was then engaged in the business of breaking idols, I had not lost all reverence for antiquity. I stopped a while to muse in the old brick building where Patrick Henry made his first speech at the bar, and pleaded the cause of the people against the parsons. In order to understand the enterprise on which I was going, a geographical description of the country and situation of the armies is necessary. The battle of Fair Oaks or Seven Pines had been fought, and the army of the Potomac was lying on the Peninsula between the James and Pamunkey rivers, and astraddle of the Chickahominy, which meanders between them and finally empties into the James. McClellan's right wing rested on the Pamunkey, with his base at the White House and his line of supply by the York River Railroad. His left extended to within a few miles of the James. The Totopotomoy Creek flows into the Pamunkey. I got down in the enemy's lines on the Totopotomoy and ascertained that six or eight miles of McClellan's front was a mere shroud of cavalry pickets that covered his line of communication with his depot at the White House. Of course, as he had no infantry on his right there would be no fortifications there. The idea immediately occurred to me that here was a grand opportunity for Stuart to strike a blow. It is now clear why General Lee wanted to get information about the enemy's fortifying the Totopotomoy.

About three weeks after that he called Jackson from the valley, who struck McClellan on this very ground. I was chased away from there and came out just behind a regiment of Union cavalry going on a scout. They very little thought that I was coming back so soon. I hastened to Stuart's headquarters to give him the information. Everybody there was in high glee. News had just come of Jackson's victories over Fremont and Shields: Cross Keyes and Port Republic had been inscribed on his banners. It was a hot day in June, and Stuart was sitting under the shade of a tree, and I lay down on the grass to tell him what I had learned. After giving him the information, I remarked, that as the cavalry was idle, he could find on the Pamunkey something for them to do. A blow on this weak point would greatly alarm McClellan for the safety of his supplies, and compel him to detach heavily from his front to guard them. After I got through, he said to me, "Write down what you have told me." I went to his adjutant's office and wrote it down hurriedly; but, not attaching much importance to it, did not sign the writing. When I brought the paper to Stuart he had his horse ready to mount. He called my attention to the omission, and I went back and signed it. He started off at a gallop with a single courier to General Lee's headquarters. He returned that afternoon, and orders were immediately issued for a part of the cavalry to get ready to march.

General Lee's instructions to Stuart, directing, or rather authorizing, the expedition, are dated June 11, which shows how soon he started after my return, which was on the 10th. With about 1200 cavalry and two pieces of artillery, on the morning of June 12, Stuart left Richmond, moving in a northerly direction, to create the impression that he was going to reinforce Jackson. That night we bivouacked within a few miles of Hanover Court House. During his absence his adjutant was left in charge of his headquarters. I was present when he started. The adjutant asked him how long he would be gone. Stuart's answer was, "It may be for years, and it may be forever." Taking leave of his staff had suggested the parting from Erin and Kathleen Mavourneen.

There were many surmises as to his destination; but I never doubted for a moment where we were going. Early the next morning Stuart sent me on in advance with a few men to Hanover Court House, and I then saw that my idea of a raid on McClellan's lines was about to be realized. When we got within a few hundred yards of the village, a squadron of cavalry was discovered there, and I sent a man back to inform Stuart of it, so that he might send a regiment round to cut off their retreat. He ordered the First Virginia Cavalry to go; but the enemy, suspecting that there was a stronger force than they could see, withdrew too soon to be caught.

The column then pushed rapidly towards the camp of Union cavalry at Old Church. At that place Captain Royall was stationed with two squadrons of the 5th U. S. regular cavalry. There was a running fight of several miles with the pickets, and finally we met Captain Royall, who came out with his whole command to reinforce the outpost. He had no suspicion of the number he was attacking, and as soon as he came in sight, Stuart ordered the front squadron of the 9th Virginia cavalry to charge. Royall was wounded and routed. On our side, Captain Latane was killed. We could not stay to give him even the hasty burial that the hero received who died on the ramparts of Corunna. This was left for female hands to do. The scene has been preserved on canvas by a Virginia artist. As Royall's command had been scattered, we soon had possession of his camp, and were feasting on the good things we found in it. Nearly everybody forgot—many never knew—the danger we were in. A mile or so on our left was an impassable river—not more than six miles to the right were McClellan's headquarters, with Fitz John Porter's corps and the reserve division of cavalry camped near us. Here was the turning-point of the expedition. Stuart was as jolly as anybody; but his head was always level in critical moments—even in the midst of fun. There was a short conference between him and the Lees, who were the colonels of the two Virginia regiments. I was sitting on my horse, buckling on a pistol I had just captured, within a few feet of them and heard all that passed. Stuart was for pushing on to the York River Railroad, which was still nine miles off. Lee, of the 9th (son of General R. E. Lee), was in favor of it, but Fitz Lee was opposed. Stuart had no idea of turning back, and determined to go on and strike McClellan in his rear. In the conception and execution of this bold enterprise he showed the genius and the intrepid spirit that took the plunge of the Rubicon.

Just as he gave the command, "Forward!" he turned to me, and said, "Mosby, I want you to ride some distance ahead." I replied: "Very well. But you must give me a guide; I don't know the road." He then ordered two cavalrymen who were familiar with the country to go with me; and I started on towards Tunstall's station. I was on a slow horse; and I remember that I had not gone very far before Stuart sent one of his staff to tell me to go faster and increase the distance between us. It was important that we should reach the railroad before dark, or reinforcements could be sent there. So I went on with my two men at a trot.

Stuart's biographer, without so intending, has made a statement which if true would rob him of all the glory of the enterprise. He says that after reaching Old Church, Stuart kept on because it was safer than to go back by the route he had come. The road to Hanover Court House was open; and it would not have been possible for the enemy to have closed it against him for several hours. The fight with Royall was near his camp, and did not last five minutes; it took only a few minutes to destroy it. If he had intended to return by Hanover, he would have left pickets behind him to keep the way open. But he did nothing of the kind. He took no more account of his rear than Cortez did when he burned his ships, and marched to the capital of the Aztec kings. The route of the two squadrons of cavalry was, in itself, an insignificant result as compared with the magnitude of the preparation. At this point, he had simply broken through McClellan's picket line, but had not gained his rear. To have returned after doing this and no more, would have been very much like the labor of a mountain and the birth of a mouse. The fight and capture of Royall's camp at Old Church occurred about two o'clock P.M., on June 13. The nearest camps were three or four miles off. Major Williams reports that he came on the ground with 380 of the 6th cavalry at 3.30 P.M., about one hour after the rear of Stuart's cavalry had passed on towards Tunstall's. This one hour would of itself have been amply sufficient to allow Stuart's return unmolested before the arrival of that force. It will hardly be contended that 380 men of any cavalry the world ever saw could have stopped Stuart with 1200 men and two pieces of artillery. The 5th U. S. cavalry came on the ground about five o'clock; and Gen. Cook (who was Stuart's father-in-law), with the rest of his cavalry division, Warren's brigade of infantry, and a battery of artillery, reached there after dark. It is very difficult, therefore, to see what there was to prevent Stuart from returning if he had so desired. In all, there were two brigades of cavalry, one of infantry, and a battery of artillery sent in pursuit of him.

Gen. Emory, who led the advance, says that he followed on Stuart's track, and reached Tunstall's at two o'clock that night, where he found Gen. Reynolds, who had come up with a brigade of infantry on the cars about twelve o'clock. Reynolds says that our rear guard had left there about two hours before he arrived. At Tunstall's, Gen. Emory says he lost Stuart's trail, and set every squadron he had to hunting for it, and did not succeed in finding it until eight o'clock the next morning. As Stuart had left Tunstall's on the plain country road on which he had been marching all day, and on which Gen. Emory had followed him, it seems strange that 1200 cavalry, with two pieces of artillery, should have left no track behind them. Gen. Warren says that "*the moon was shining brightly, making any kind of movement for ourselves or the enemy as easy as in daylight.*"

General Cook, with the rest of the cavalry, and infantry, and artillery, arrived about 9 o'clock the next morning. General Emory then moved forward in pursuit with infantry, cavalry, and artillery. Warren says: "*It was impossible for the infantry to overtake him [Stuart], and as the cavalry did not move without us, it was impossible for them to overtake him.*" And Fitz John Porter regrets, "*That when General Cook did pursue he should have tied his legs with the infantry command.*" Perhaps General Cook was acting on the maxim that recommends us to build a bridge of gold for a retreating foe. But then it can hardly be said that Stuart was retreating. As there were six cavalry regiments—including all the regulars—on our track, with a battery of artillery, it is hard to see the use they had for infantry, except as a brake to keep them from going too fast. The pursuit was from beginning to end a comedy of errors. The infantry could not have expected to overtake us, whereas, if we had attempted to return by the same route we came, then they might have intercepted us by remaining where they were.

Stuart was reduced to the alternative of returning home by the road along the Pamunkey, or the one up James River. If he took the latter, then a slight extension of McClellan's left flank would have barred his way. It could hardly have been imagined that we were going down to capture Fort Monroe, or that Stuart's cavalry were amphibious animals that could cross the York and James rivers without pontoons. Only the cavalry on McClellan's right was in the pursuit. He had an abundance on his left to block our way, and they had twenty-four hours' notice of our coming. Now to return to my narrative of Stuart's march. As I was jogging along with my two companions, a mile or two ahead of the column, I came upon a well-filled sutler's wagon at a cross-roads, of which I took possession by right of discovery. At the same time, about a mile off to my left, I could see the masts of several vessels riding at anchor in the river. I sent one of the men back to tell Stuart to hurry on. The sutler was too rich a prize to abandon, so I left the other man in charge of him and his wagon and hurried on. Just as I turned a bend of the road, I came plump upon another sutler, and a cavalry vidette was by him. They were so shocked by the apparition that they surrendered as quietly as the coon did to Captain Scott. Tunstall's Station was now in full view a half a mile off. I was all alone. Just then a bugle sounded. I saw about a squadron of cavalry drawn up in line, near the railroad. I knew that the head of our column must be close by, and my horse was too tired to run, so I just drew my sabre and waved it in the air. They knew from this that support was near me. In a few seconds our advance guard under Lieutenant Robbins appeared in sight, and the squadron in front of me vanished from view. Robbins captured the depot with the guard without firing a shot. Stuart soon rode up. Just then a train of cars came in sight, and as we had no implements with which to pull up a rail, a number of logs were put on the track. When the engineer got near us, he saw that he was in a hornet's nest, and with a full head of steam dashed on under a heavy fire, knocked the logs off the track, and carried the news to the White House below. General Ingalls, who was in command of the depot there, says that he had received a telegram from General McClellan's headquarters, telling him of the attack on Royall's camp and warning him of danger. As soon then as the telegraph line was broken, which was about sunset on the 13th, it was notice to McClellan that we were in his rear and on his line of communications.

There was now but one route by which we could return, and that was up James River. Yet he made no signs of a movement to prevent it, and the only evidence that he knew of our presence is a telegram to Stanton on the next day—dated 11 A.M., June 14th, saying that a body of cavalry had passed around his right and that he had sent cavalry in pursuit to punish them. Before reaching Tunstall's, Stuart sent a squadron to burn the transports in the river and a wagon train that was loading from them. The small guard fled at the approach of our cavalry, while the schooners and wagons disappeared in smoke. As some evidence of the consternation produced by this sudden irruption, I will mention the fact, that after we left Old Church, a sergeant with twenty-five men of the United States regular cavalry followed on under a flag of truce and surrendered to our *rear-guard*. They supposed they were cut off and surrounded. The Jeff Davis legion was the rear-guard, and these were the only enemies they saw.

The despatch to Stanton shows the bewildered state of McClellan's mind. At the time he was writing it we were lying on the banks of the Chickahominy, building a bridge to cross on. To have caught us, it was not necessary to pursue at all; all that he had to do was to spread his wings. We halted at Tunstall's long enough for the column to close up. Our march was slow, the artillery horses had broken down, and we were encumbered with a large number of prisoners on foot, and of course we could march no faster than they did. After dark the column moved down through New Kent towards the Chickahominy. On the road were large encampments of army wagons. Many a sutler was ruined that night; with sad hearts they fell into line with the prisoners, and saw their wagons, with their contents, vanish in flames. The heavens were lurid with the light reflected from the burning trains, and our track was as brilliant as the tail of a comet.

The Count of Paris, who was on McClellan's staff, thus describes Stuart's march: "But night had come, and the fires kindled by his hand flashing above the forest were so many signals which drew the Federals on his track." Now, the Count of Paris evidently means that the glowing sky ought to have been a guide to the Federal generals as the pillar of fire was to Moses. As a fact, the only pursuers we saw were those who came after us to surrender under a flag of truce. Stuart halted three hours at Baltimore Store, only five miles from Tunstall's. At twelve o'clock he started again for a ford of the Chickahominy, which was eight miles distant, and reached it about daylight.

That summer night was a carnival of fun I can never forget. Nobody thought of danger or of sleep, when champagne bottles were bursting, and Rhine wine was flowing in copious streams. All had perfect confidence in their leader. In the riot among the sutlers' stores "grim-visaged war had smoothed his wrinkled front," and Mars resigned his sceptre to the jolly god. The discipline of soldiers for a while gave way to the wild revelry of the crew of Comus. During all of this time General Emory was a few miles off, at Tunstall's Station, hunting our tracks in the sand with a lighted candle. Stuart had expected to ford the Chickahominy; but when we got there, it was found overflowing from the recent rains, and impassable. Up to this point our progress had been as easy as the descent to Avernus; but now, to get over the river, *hic labor, hic opus est.* He was fortunate in having two guides, Christian and Frayser, who lived in the neighborhood, and knew all the roads and fords on the river. Christian knew of a bridge, or rather, where a bridge had been, about a mile below the ford, and the column was immediately headed for it. But it had been destroyed, and nothing was left but some of the piles standing in the water. He was again fortunate in having two men, Burke and Hagan, who knew something about bridge-building. Near by were the remains of an old warehouse, out of which they built a bridge. It was marvellous with what rapidity the structure grew; in a few hours it was finished—it seemed almost by magic. It was not as good a bridge as Cæsar threw over the Rhine, but it was good enough for our purpose. While the men were at work upon it, Stuart was lying down on the bank of the stream, in the gayest humor I ever saw him, laughing at the prank he had played on McClellan.

As I was a believer in the Napoleonic maxim of making war support war, I had foraged extensively during the night, and from the sutlers' stores spread a feast that Epicurus might have envied. During all the long hours that we lay on the bank of the river waiting for the bridge, no enemy appeared in sight. That was a mystery nobody could understand. There was some apprehension that McClellan was allowing us to cross over in order to entrap us in the forks of the Chickahominy. When, at last, about two o'clock, the cavalry, artillery, prisoners and captured horses and mules were all over, and fire had been set to the bridge, some of Rush's lancers came on a hill and took a farewell look at us. They came, and saw, and went away, taking as their only trophy a drunken Dutchman we had left on the road. General Emory received news of the crossing eight miles off at Baltimore Store. Our escape over the river was immediately reported to him. In his official report, he says that we crossed the Chickahominy at daylight and that we left faster than we came. Now, I am unable to see the evidence of any particular haste in the march: in fact, it seems to have been conducted very leisurely. About one o'clock P.M., on the 13th, we captured Royall's camp at Old Church; about sunset we reached Tunstall's, nine miles distant, and at daylight on the 14th got to a point on the Chickahominy twelve miles from there, where we stayed until noon. So if we had been pursued at the rate of a mile an hour, we would have been overtaken.

But the danger was not over when we were over the Chickahominy. We were still thirty-five miles from Richmond and in the rear of McClellan's army, which was five or six miles above us. It was necessary to pass through swamps where the horses sunk to their saddle girths, and when we emerged from these, we had to go for twenty miles on a road in full view of the enemy's gunboats on one side of us in the James River, and McClellan's army within a few miles on the other. Nothing would have been easier than for him to have thrown a division of infantry as well as cavalry across our path. Then nothing could have saved us except such a miracle as destroyed Pharaoh and his host. Stuart, apprehending a movement on McClellan's left, had sent a messenger early in the morning to General Lee requesting him to make a diversion in his favor. But we were out of danger before he had time to do it. After getting through the swamp the command halted in Charles City for several hours to give rest to the men and horses. Stuart then turned over the command to Fitz Lee, as we were then in comparative safety, and with two men rode on to General Lee's headquarters, which he reached about daybreak the next morning. During the night march I was in advance of the column, but saw nothing in the path except occasionally a negro who would dart across it going into the Union lines. Early in the morning, just as I got in sight of Richmond, I met Stuart returning to the command. Although he had been in the saddle two days and nights without sleep, he was as gay as a lark and showed no signs of weariness. He had a right to be proud; for he had performed a feat that to this day has no parallel in the annals of war. I said to him, "This will make you a major-general." He said, "No, I don't think I can be a major-general until we have 10,000 cavalry." But in six weeks he had that rank.

This expedition, in which Stuart had ridden around McClellan in a circle of a radius of ten miles, created almost as much astonishment in Richmond and even in Europe as if he had dropped from the clouds, and made him the hero of the army. It had an electric effect on the *morale* of the Confederate troops and excited their enthusiasm to a high pitch. Always after that the sight of Stuart on the field was like

> A blast of that dread horn
> On Fontarabian echoes borne.

McClellan attempts in his report to belittle it, by saying that in this affair Stuart's cavalry did nothing but gain a little *éclat;* but with more truth it might be said that by it he lost a good deal. His staff officer, the Count of Paris, says, in reference to these operations of our cavalry: "They had, in point of fact, created a great commotion, shaken the confidence of the North in McClellan, and made the first experiment in those great cavalry expeditions which subsequently played so novel and so important a part during the war."

At midnight, on June 14, at the very hour when we were marching along his left flank, McClellan telegraphed to Stanton, "All quiet in every direction; the stampede of last night has passed away." In his telegram six hours before, he had said that we ran away from an infantry force, at Tunstall's, that he had sent after us. The fact was that we left that place long before the infantry arrived there, and never heard of it until long after we left. Gen. Reynolds says he never saw us. The stampede that McClellan talks about was not in *our* ranks. The Count of Paris again says: "As soon as he [Stuart] was known to be at Tunstall's, McClellan had divined his purpose, and despatched Averill to intercept him."

I have made a diligent examination of the archives of the war, but have been unable to find any authority for this statement. The despatches of the general-in-chief, the corps, division, brigade, and regimental commanders, in reference to this *raid*, have all been published, besides the report of Col. Clitz, who was ordered to investigate the conduct of those who were charged with the pursuit. They all relate to the operations on McClellan's right, and there is perfect silence as to any attempt to intercept us on his left, or any order to do so. Averill, who was stationed with the cavalry on the left flank, is nowhere mentioned, and there is no report from him. After we crossed the Chickahominy we were in a *cul de sac*, formed by the junction of that river with the James. Yet we never saw an enemy in that vicinity, although they must or ought to have had twenty-four hours' notice that we were coming, as the army headquarters were connected with each corps by both telegraph lines and signal stations.

As McClellan was very much criticised for permitting Stuart to escape, if it had been due to the failure of Averill or any one else to execute his orders, he would have put the blame where it belonged. McClellan's conduct on this occasion has always been unaccountable to me, and the only explanation I have ever seen of it is in the report of Gen. Pleasanton, who soon after that became his chief of cavalry. Pleasanton says: "McClellan dreaded the rebel cavalry, and supposed that by placing his army on a peninsula, with a deep river on each side, he was safe from that arm of the enemy; but the humiliation on the Chickahominy, of having a few thousand of the enemy's cavalry ride completely around his army, and the ignominious retreat to Harrison's Landing, are additional instances in support of the maxim 'that a general who disregards the rules of war finds himself overwhelmed by the consequences of such neglect, when the crisis of battle follows.'"

At that time Pleasanton was commanding the 2d U. S. Cavalry. The telegraph line at Tunstall's was repaired soon after Reynolds arrived, on the night of the 13th; and it is impossible to believe that he and Ingalls did not inform the general-in-chief which way we had gone. Stuart then had no choice of routes, but was confined to the road up James River, or not to return at all. This raid is unique, and distinguished from all others on either side during the war, on account of the narrow limits in which the cavalry was compelled to operate. From the time when he broke through McClellan's line on his right until he had passed around him on his left Stuart was enclosed by three unfordable rivers, over one of which he had to build a bridge to cross. During the whole operation the cavalry never drew a sabre except at the first picket post they encountered. But it was something more than a mere raid on McClellan's communications; it was, in fact, a *reconnaissance* in force to ascertain the exact location of the different corps of his army, and the prelude to the great battles that began ten days afterwards, in which Jackson's flank was covered by Stuart's cavalry.

The seven days' battles were fought behind intrenchments, and in swamps which afforded no opportunity for the use of cavalry except in guarding the flanks of the infantry and the minor operations of outpost duty. When they were over, the cavalry had a short respite from labor. I never could rest inactive; and so I asked Stuart to let me take a party of men to northern Virginia.

Gen. Pope had then just assumed command of that department. He had a long line of communications to guard; and his scattered army corps offered fine opportunities for partisan war. The wiser policy of concentration had not then been adopted by the Federal generals. Stuart was recruiting his cavalry, and was not willing to spare any for detached service; but gave me a letter of introduction to Gen. Jackson, who had been sent up to Gordonsville to observe Pope. He sent him by me a copy of Napoleon's maxims, which had just been published in Richmond. Stuart wanted Jackson to furnish a detail of cavalry to go with me behind Pope, who had just published the fact to the world that he intended to leave his rear to take care of itself. With a single companion, and full of enthusiasm, I started on my mission to Jackson. I concluded to take the cars at Beaver Dam and go on in advance to his headquarters and wait there for my horse to be led on. I was sitting in the depot, and my companion hardly got out of sight, when a regiment of Union cavalry rode up, and put an attachment upon my person. They had ridden all night from Fredericksburg to capture the train which was due in a few minutes. I was chagrined, not only at being a prisoner, but because my cherished hopes were now disappointed. The regiment fronted into a line to wait for the cars; and they placed me in the front rank. I called to an officer, and protested against being put where I would be shot by the guard on the train. For some reason, the commanding officer gave orders to leave; perhaps it was because he was as much opposed to being shot as I was. The train soon afterwards arrived; and I do not think there were any soldiers on it. That night, I slept on the floor of the guard-house at Fredericksburg; on the next day the *cartel* for the exchange of prisoners was agreed on. My imprisonment lasted ten days; and I confess that I rather enjoyed my visit to Washington. I kept up my habits as a scout, and collected a large budget of information. The steamer on which I came back lay four days in Hampton Roads, and then proceeded up James River. When we first arrived there I noticed a large number of transports, with troops on board, lying near Newport News, and learned that they belonged to Burnside's corps just arrived from North Carolina. Here, now, was a problem for me to solve. Where were they going? to reinforce Pope or McClellan? I set about to find out. If they went to Pope it meant the withdrawal of McClellan. The captain of the steamer promised me to find out their destination. A few hours before we left, I observed them all coming down and passing out by Fort Monroe. When the captain returned from on shore, he told me that the transports were going up the Potomac. This settled the question; the Peninsula campaign was over.

(1887)

SOLOMON NORTHUP

Twelve Years a Slave

Edwin Epps, of whom much will be said during the remainder of this history, is a large, portly, heavy-bodied man with light hair, high cheek bones, and a Roman nose of extraordinary dimensions. He has blue eyes, a fair complexion, and is, I should say, full six feet high. He has the sharp, inquisitive expression of a jockey. His manners are repulsive and coarse, and his language gives speedy and unequivocal evidence that he has never enjoyed the advantages of an education. He has the faculty of saying most provoking things, in that respect even excelling old Peter Tanner. At the time I came into his possession, Edwin Epps was fond of the bottle, his "sprees" sometimes extending over the space of two whole weeks. Latterly, however, he had reformed his habits, and when I left him, was as strict a specimen of temperance as could be found on Bayou Bœuf. When "in his cups," Master Epps was a roystering, blustering, noisy fellow, whose chief delight was in dancing with his "niggers," or lashing them about the yard with his long whip, just for the pleasure of hearing them screech and scream, as the great welts were planted on their backs. When sober, he was silent, reserved and cunning, not beating us indiscriminately, as in his drunken moments, but sending the end of his rawhide to some tender spot of a lagging slave, with a sly dexterity peculiar to himself.

He had been a driver and overseer in his younger years, but at this time was in possession of a plantation on Bayou Huff Power, two and a half miles from Holmesville, eighteen from Marksville, and twelve from Cheneyville, Louisiana. It belonged to Joseph B. Roberts, his wife's uncle, and was leased by Epps. His principal business was raising cotton, and inasmuch as some may read this book who have never seen a cotton field, a description of the manner of its culture may not be out of place.

The ground is prepared by throwing up beds or ridges, with the plough—back-furrowing, it is called. Oxen and mules, the latter almost exclusively, are used in ploughing. The women as frequently as the men perform this labor, feeding, currying, and taking care of their teams, and in all respects doing the field and stable work, precisely as do the ploughboys of the North.

The beds, or ridges, are six feet wide, that is, from water furrow to water furrow. A plough drawn by one mule is then run along the top of the ridge or center of the bed, making the drill, into which a girl usually drops the seed, which she carries in a bag hung round her neck. Behind her comes a mule and harrow, covering up the seed, so that two mules, three slaves, a plough and harrow, are employed in planting a row of cotton. This is done in the months of March and April. Corn is planted in February. When there are no cold rains, the cotton usually makes its appearance in a week. In the course of eight or ten days afterwards the first hoeing is commenced. This is performed in part, also, by the aid of the plough and mule. The plough passes as near as possible to the cotton on both sides, throwing the furrow from it. Slaves follow with their hoes, cutting up the grass and cotton, leaving hills two feet and a half apart. This is called scraping cotton. In two weeks more commences the second hoeing. This time the furrow is thrown towards the cotton. Only one stalk, the largest, is now left standing in each hill. In another fortnight it is hoed the third time, throwing the furrow towards the cotton in the same manner as before, and killing all the grass between the rows. About the first of July, when it is a foot high or thereabouts, it is hoed the fourth and last time. Now the whole space between the rows is ploughed, leaving a deep water furrow in the center. During all these hoeings the overseer or driver follows the slaves on horseback with a whip, such as has been described. The fastest hoer takes the lead row. He is usually about a rod in advance of his companions. If one of them passes him, he is whipped, If one falls behind or is a moment idle, he is whipped. In fact, the lash is flying from morning until night, the whole day long. The hoeing season thus continues from April until July, a field having no sooner been finished once, than it is commenced again.

In the latter part of August begins the cotton picking season. At this time each slave is presented with a sack. A strap is fastened to it, which goes over the neck, holding the mouth of the sack breast high, while the bottom reaches nearly to the ground. Each one is also presented with a large basket that will hold about two barrels. This is to put the cotton in when the sack is filled. The baskets are carried to the field and placed at the beginning of the rows.

When a new hand, one unaccustomed to the business, is sent for the first time into the field, he is whipped up smartly, and made for that day to pick as fast as he can possibly. At night it is weighed, so that his capability in cotton picking is known. He must bring in the same weight each night following. If it falls short, it is considered evidence that he has been laggard, and a greater or less number of lashes is the penalty.

An ordinary day's work is two hundred pounds. A slave who is accustomed to picking, is punished, if he or she brings in a less quantity than that. There is a great difference among them as regards this kind of labor. Some of them seem to have a natural knack, or quickness, which enables them to pick with great celerity, and with both hands, while others, with whatever practice or industry, are utterly unable to come up to the ordinary standard. Such hands are taken from the cotton field and employed in other business. Patsey, of whom I shall have more to say, was known as the most remarkable cotton picker on Bayou Bœuf. She picked with both hands and with such surprising rapidity, that five hundred pounds a day was not unusual for her.

Each one is tasked, therefore, according to his picking abilities, none, however, to come short of two hundred weight. I, being unskillful always in that business, would have satisfied my master by bringing in the latter quantity, while on the other hand, Patsey would surely have been beaten if she failed to produce twice as much.

The cotton grows from five to seven feet high, each stalk having a great many branches, shooting out in all directions, and lapping each other above the water furrow.

There are few sights more pleasant to the eye, than a wide cotton field when it is in the bloom. It presents an appearance of purity, like an immaculate expanse of light, new-fallen snow.

Sometimes the slave picks down one side of a row, and back upon the other, but more usually, there is one on either side, gathering all that has blossomed, leaving the unopened bolls for a succeeding picking. When the sack is filled, it is emptied into the basket and trodden down. It is necessary to be extremely careful the first time going through the field, in order not to break the branches off the stalks. The cotton will not bloom upon a broken branch. Epps never failed to inflict the severest chastisement on the unlucky servant who, either carelessly or unavoidably, was guilty in the least degree in this respect.

The hands are required to be in the cotton field as soon as it is light in the morning, and, with the exception of ten or fifteen minutes, which is given them at noon to swallow their allowance of cold bacon, they are not permitted to be a moment idle until it is too dark to see, and when the moon is full, they often times labor till the middle of the night. They do not dare to stop even at dinner time, nor return to the quarters, however late it be, until the order to halt is given by the driver.

The day's work over in the field, the baskets are "toted," or in other words, carried to the gin-house, where the cotton is weighed. No matter how fatigued and weary he may be—no matter how much he longs for sleep and rest—a slave never approaches the gin-house with his basket of cotton but with fear. If it falls short in weight—if he has not performed the full task appointed him, he knows that he must suffer. And if he has exceeded it by ten or twenty pounds, in all probability his master will measure the next day's task accordingly. So, whether he has too little or too much, his approach to the gin-house is always with fear and trembling. Most frequently they have too little, and therefore it is they are not anxious to leave the field. After weighing, follow the whippings; and then the baskets are carried to the cotton house, and their contents stored away like hay, all hands being sent in to tramp it down. If the cotton is not dry, instead of taking it to the gin-house at once, it is laid upon platforms, two feet high, and some three times as wide, covered with boards or plank, with narrow walks running between them.

This done, the labor of the day is not yet ended, by any means. Each one must then attend to his respective chores. One feeds the mules, another the swine—another cuts the wood, and so forth; besides, the packing is all done by candle light. Finally, at a late hour, they reach the quarters, sleepy and overcome with the long day's toil. Then a fire must be kindled in the cabin, the corn ground in the small hand-mill, and supper, and dinner for the next day in the field, prepared. All that is allowed them is corn and bacon, which is given out at the corncrib and smoke-house every Sunday morning. Each one receives, as his weekly allowance, three and a half pounds of bacon, and corn enough to make a peck of meal. That is all—no tea, coffee, sugar, and with the exception of a very scanty sprinkling now and then, no salt. I can say, from ten years' residence with Master Epps, that no slave of his is ever likely to suffer from the gout, superinduced by excessive high living. Master Epps' hogs were fed on *shelled* corn— it was thrown out to his "niggers" in the ear. The former, he thought, would fatten faster by shelling, and soaking it in the water—the latter, perhaps, if treated in the same manner, might grow too fat to labor. Master Epps was a shrewd caluulator and knew how to manage his own animals, drunk or sober.

The corn mill stands in the yard beneath a shelter. It is like a common coffee mill, the hopper holding about six quarts. There was one privilege which Master Epps granted freely to every slave he had. They might grind their corn nightly, in such small quantities as their daily wants required, or they might grind the whole week's allowance at one time, on Sundays, just as they preferred. A very generous man was Master Epps!

I kept my corn in a small wooden box, the meal in a gourd; and, by the way, the gourd is one of the most convenient and necessary utensils on a plantation. Besides supplying the place of all kinds of crockery in a slave cabin, it is used for carrying water to the fields. Another, also, contains the dinner. It dispenses with the necessity of pails, dippers, basins, and such tin and wooden superfluities altogether.

When the corn is ground, and fire is made, the bacon is taken down from the nail on which it hangs, a slice cut off and thrown upon the coals to broil. The majority of slaves have no knife, much less a fork. They cut their bacon with the axe at the woodpile. The corn meal is mixed with a little water, placed in the fire, and baked. When it is "done brown," ashes are scraped off, and being placed upon a chip, which answers for a table, the tenant of the slave hut is ready to sit down upon the ground to supper. By this time it is usually midnight. The same fear of punishment with which they approach the gin-house, possesses them again on lying down to get a snatch of rest. It is the fear of oversleeping in the morning. Such an offence would certainly be attended with not less than twenty lashes. With a prayer that he may be on his feet and wide awake at the first sound of the horn, he sinks to his slumbers nightly.

The softest couches in the world are not to be found in the log mansion of the slave. The one whereon I reclined year after year, was a plank twelve inches wide and ten feet long. My pillow was a stick of wood. The bedding was a coarse blanket, and not a rag or shred beside. Moss might be used, were it not that it directly breeds a swarm of fleas.

The cabin is constructed of logs, without floor or window. The latter is altogether unnecessary, the crevices between the logs admitting suffient light. In stormy weather the rain drives through them, rendering it comfortless and extremely disagreeable. The rude door hangs on great wooden hinges. In one end is constructed an awkward fire-place.

An hour before day light the horn is blown. Then the slaves arouse, prepare their breakfast, fill a gourd with water, in another deposit their dinner of cold bacon and corn cake, and hurry to the field again. It is an offence invariably followed by a flogging, to be found at the quarters after daybreak. Then the fears and labors of another day begin: and until its close there is no such thing as rest. He fears he will be caught lagging through the day; he fears to approach the gin-house with his basket-load of cotton at night; he fears, when he lies down, that he will oversleep himself in the morning. Such is a true, faithful, unexaggerated picture and description of the slave's daily life, during the time of cotton-picking on the shores of Bayou Bœuf.

In the month of January, generally, the fourth and last picking is completed. Then commences the harvesting of corn. This is considered a secondary crop, and receives far less attention than the cotton. It is planted, as already mentioned, in February. Corn is grown in that region for the purpose of fattening hogs and feeding slaves; very little, if any, being sent to market. It is the white variety, the ear of great size, and the stalk growing to the height of eight, and often times ten feet. In August the leaves are stripped off, dried in the sun, bound in small bundles, and stored away as provender for the mules and oxen. After this the slaves go through the field, turning down the ear, for the purpose of keeping the rains from penetrating to the grain. It is left in this condition until after cotton-picking is over, whether earlier or later. Then the ears are separated from the stalks, and deposited in the corncrib with the husks on; otherwise, stripped of the husks, the weevil would destroy it. The stalks are left standing in the field.

The Carolina, or sweet potato, is also grown in that region to some extent. They are not fed, however, to hogs or cattle, and are considered but of small importance. They are preserved by placing them upon the surface of the ground, with a slight covering of earth or cornstalks. There is not a cellar on Bayou Bœuf. The ground is so low it would fill with water. Potatoes are worth from two to three "bits," or shillings a barrel; corn, except when there is an unusual scarity, can be purchased at the same rate.

As soon as the cotton and corn crops are secured, the stalks are pulled up, thrown into piles and burned. The ploughs are started at the same time, throwing up the beds again, preparatory to another planting. The soil, in the parishes of Rapides and Avoyelles, and throughout the whole country, so far as my observation extended, is of exceeding richness and fertility. It is a kind of marl, of a brown or reddish color. It does not require those invigorating composts necessary to more barren lands, and on the same field the same crop is grown for many successive years.

Ploughing, planting, picking cotton, gathering the corn, and pulling and burning stalks, occupies the whole of the four seasons of the year. Drawing and cutting wood, pressing cotton, fattening and killing hogs, are but incidental labors.

In the month of September or October, the hogs are run out of the swamps by dogs, and confined in pens. On a cold morning, generally about New Year's day, they are slaughtered. Each carcass is cut into six parts, and piled one above the other in salt, upon large tables in the smoke-house. In this condition it remains a fortnight, when it is hung up, and a fire built, and continued more than half the time during the remainder of the year. This thorough smoking is necessary to prevent the bacon from becoming infested with worms. In so warm a climate it is difficult to preserve it, and very many times myself and my companions have received our weekly allowance of three pounds and a half, when it was full of these disgusting vermin.

Although the swamps are overrun with cattle, they are never made the source of profit, to any considerable extent. The planter cuts his mark upon the ear, or brands his initials upon the side, and turns them into the swamps, to roam unrestricted within their almost limitless confines. They are the Spanish breed, small and spike-horned. I have known of droves being taken from Bayou Bœuf, but it is of very rare occurrence. The value of the best cows is about five dollars each. Two quarts at one milking, would be considered an unusual large quantity. They furnish little tallow, and that of a soft, inferior quality. Notwithstanding the great number of cows that throng the swamps, the planters are indebted to the North for their cheese and butter, which is purchased in the New-Orleans market. Salted beef is not an article of food either in the great house, or in the cabin.

Master Epps was accustomed to attend shooting matches for the purpose of obtaining what fresh beef he required. These sports occurred weekly at the neighboring village of Holmesville. Fat beeves are driven thither and shot at, a stipulated price being demanded for the privilege. The lucky marksman divides the flesh among his fellows, and in this manner the attending planters are supplied.

The great number of tame and untamed cattle which swarm the woods and swamps of Bayou Bœuf most probably suggested that appellation to the French, inasmuch as the term, translated, signifies the creek or river of the wild ox.

Garden products, such as cabbages, turnips and the like, are cultivated for the use of the master and his family. They have greens and vegetables at all times and seasons of the year. "The grass withereth and the flower fadeth" before the desolating winds of autumn in the chill northern latitudes, but perpetual verdure overspreads the hot lowlands, and flowers bloom in the heart of winter, in the region of Bayou Bœuf.

There are no meadows appropriated to the cultivation of the grasses. The leaves of the corn supply a sufficiency of food for the laboring cattle, while the rest provide for themselves all the year in the ever-growing pasture.

There are many other peculiarities of climate, habit, custom, and of the manner of living and laboring at the South, but the foregoing, it is supposed, will give the reader an insight and general idea of life on a cotton plantation in Louisiana. The mode of cultivating cane, and the process of sugar manufacturing, will be mentioned in another place.

On my arrival at Master Epps', in obedience to his order, the first business upon which I entered was the making of an axe-helve. The handles in use there are simply a round, straight stick. I made a crooked one, shaped like those to which I had been accustomed at the North. When finished, and presented to Epps, he looked at it with astonishment, unable to determine exactly what it was. He had never before seen such a handle, and when I explained its conveniences, he was forcibly struck with the novelty of the idea. He kept it in the house a long time, and when his friends called, was wont to exhibit it as a curiosity.

It was now the season of hoeing. I was first sent into the cornfield, and afterwards set to scraping cotton. In this employment I remained until hoeing time was nearly passed, when I began to experience the symptoms of approaching illness. I was attacked with chills, which were succeeded by a burning fever. I became weak and emaciated, and frequently so dizzy that it caused me to reel and stagger like a drunken man. Nevertheless, I was compelled to keep up my row. When in health I found little difficulty in keeping pace with my fellow-laborers, but now it seemed to be an utter impossibility. Often I fell behind, when the driver's lash was sure to greet my back, infusing into my sick and drooping body a little temporary energy. I continued to decline until at length the whip became entirely ineffectual. The sharpest sting of the rawhide could not arouse me. Finally, in September, when the busy season of cotton picking was at hand, I was unable to leave my cabin. Up to this time I had received no medicine, nor any attention from my master or mistress. The old cook visited me occasionally, preparing me corn-coffee, and sometimes boiling a bit of bacon, when I had grown too feeble to accomplish it myself.

When it was said that I would die, Master Epps, unwilling to bear the loss, which the death of an animal worth a thousand dollars would bring upon him, concluded to incur the expense of sending to Holmesville for Dr. Wines. He announced to Epps that it was the effect of the climate, and there was a probability of his losing me. He directed me to eat no meat, and to partake of no more food than was absolutely necessary to sustain life. Several weeks elapsed, during which time, under the scanty diet to which I was subjected, I had partially recovered. One morning, long before I was in a proper condition to labor, Epps appeared at the cabin door, and, presenting me with a sack, ordered me to the cotton field. At this time I had had no experience whatever in cotton picking. It was an awkward business indeed. While others used both hands, snatching the cotton and depositing it in the mouth of the sack, with a precision and dexterity that was incomprehensible to me, I had to seize the boll with one hand, and deliberately draw out the white, gushing blossom with the other.

Depositing the cotton in the sack, moreover, was a difficulty that demanded the exercise of both hands and eyes. I was compelled to pick it from the ground where it would fall, nearly as often as from the stalk where it had grown. I made havoc also with the branches, loaded with the yet unbroken bolls, the long, cumbersome sack swinging from side to side in a manner not allowable in the cotton field. After a most laborious day I arrived at the gin-house with my load. When the scale determined its weight to be only ninety-five pounds, not half the quantity required of the poorest picker, Epps threatened the severest flogging, but in consideration of my being a "raw hand," concluded to pardon me on that occasion. The following day; and many days succeeding, I returned at night with no better success—I was evidently not designed for that kind of labor. I had not the gift—the dexterous fingers and quick motion of Patsey, who could fly along one side of a row of cotton, stripping it of its undefiled and fleecy whiteness miraculously fast. Practice and whipping were alike unavailing, and Epps, satisfied of it at last, swore I was a disgrace—that I was not fit to associate with a cotton-picking "nigger"—that I could not pick enough in a day to pay the trouble of weighing it, and that I should go into the cotton field no more. I was now employed in cutting and hauling wood, drawing cotton from the field to the gin-house, and performed whatever other service was required. Suffice to say, I was never permitted to be idle.

It was rarely that a day passed by without one or more whippings. This occurred at the time the cotton was weighed, The delinquent, whose weight had fallen short, was taken out, stripped, made to lie upon the ground, face downwards, when he received a punishment proportioned to his offence. It is the literal, unvarnished truth, that the crack of the lash, and the shrieking of the slaves, can be heard from dark till bed time, on Epps' plantation, any day almost during the entire period of the cotton-picking season.

The number of lashes is graduated according to the nature of the case. Twenty-five are deemed a mere brush, inflicted, for instance, when a dry leaf or piece of boll is found in the cotton, or when a branch is broken in the field; fifty is the ordinary penalty following all delinquencies of the next higher grade; one hundred is called severe: it is the punishment inflicted for the serious offence of standing idle in the field; from one hundred and fifty to two hundred is bestowed upon him who quarrels with his cabin-mates, and five hundred, well laid on, besides the mangling of the dogs, perhaps, is certain to consign the poor, unpitied runaway to weeks of pain and agony.

During the two years Epps remained on the plantation at Bayou Huff Power, he was in the habit, as often as once in a fortnight at least, of coming home intoxicated from Holmesville. The shooting-matches almost invariably concluded with a de-bauch. At such times he was boisterous and half-crazy. Often he would break the dishes, chairs, and whatever furniture he could lay his hands on. When satisfied with his amusement in the house, he would seize the whip and walk forth into the yard. Then it behooved the slaves to be watchful and exceeding wary. The first one who came within reach felt the smart of his lash. Sometimes for hours he would keep them running in all directions, dodging around the corners of the cabins. Occasionally he would come upon one unawares, and if he succeeded in inflicting a fair, round blow, it was a feat that much delighted him. The younger children, and the aged, who had become inactive, suffered then. In the midst of the confusion he would slily take his stand behind a cabin, waiting with raised whip, to dash it into the first black face that peeped cautiously around the corner.

At other times he would come home in a less brutal humor. Then there must be a merry-making. Then all must move to the measure of a tune. Then Master Epps must needs regale his melodious ears with the music of a fiddle. Then did he become bouyant, elastic, gaily "tripping the light fantastic toe" around the piazza and all through the house.

Tibeats, at the time of my sale, had informed him I could play on the violin. He had received his information from Ford. Through the importunites of Mistress Epps, her husband had been induced to purchase me one during a visit to New-Orleans. Frequently I was called into the house to play before the family, mistress being passionately fond of music.

All of us would be assembled in the large room of the great house, whenever Epps came home in one of his dancing moods. No matter how worn out and tired we were, there must be a general dance. When properly stationed on the floor, I would strike up a tune.

"Dance, you d——d niggers, dance," Epps would shout.

Then there must be no halting or delay, no slow or languid movements; all must be brisk, and lively, and alert. "Up and down, heel and toe, and away we go," was the order of the hour. Epps' portly form mingled with those of his dusky slaves, moving rapidly through all the mazes of the dance.

Usually his whip was in his hand, ready to fall about the ears of the presumptuous thrall, who dared to rest a moment, or even stop to catch his breath. When he was himself exhausted, there would be a brief cessation, but it would be very brief. With a slash, and crack, and flourish of the whip, he would shout again, "Dance, niggers, dance," and away they would go once more, pell-mell, while I, spurred by an occasional sharp touch of the lash, sat in a corner, extracting from my violin a marvelous quick-stepping tune. The mistress often upbraided him, declaring she would return to her father's house at Cheneyville; nevertheless, there were times she could not restrain a burst of laughter, on witnessing his uproarious pranks. Frequently, we were thus detained until almost morning. Bent with excessive toil—actually suffering for a little refreshing rest, and feeling rather as if we could cast ourselves upon the earth and weep, many a night in the house of Edwin Epps have his unhappy slaves been made to dance and laugh.

Notwithstanding these deprivations in order to gratify the whim of an unreasonable master, we had to be in the field as soon as it was light, and during the day perform the ordinary and accustomed task. Such deprivations could not be urged at the scales in extenuation of any lack of weight, or in the cornfield for not hoeing with the usual rapidity. The whippings were just as severe as if we had gone forth in the morning, strengthened and invigorated by a night's repose. Indeed, after such frantic revels, he was always more sour and savage than before, punishing for slighter causes, and using the whip with increased and more vindictive energy.

Ten years I toiled for that man without reward. Ten years of my incessant labor has contributed to increase the bulk of his possessions. Ten years I was compelled to address him with down-cast eyes and uncovered head—in the attitude and language of a slave. I am indebted to him for nothing, save undeserved abuse and stripes.

Beyond the reach of his inhuman thong, and standing on the soil of the free State where I was born, thanks be to Heaven, I can raise my head once more among men. I can speak of the wrongs I have suffered, and of those who inflicted them, with upraised eyes. But I have no desire to speak of him or any other one otherwise than truthfully. Yet to speak truthfully of Edwin Epps would be to say—he is a man in whose heart the quality of kindness or of justice is not found. A rough, rude energy, united with an uncultivated mind and an avaricious spirit, are his prominent characteristics. He is known as a "nigger breaker," distinguished for his faculty of subduing the spirit of the slave, and priding himself upon his reputation in this respect, as a jockey boasts of his skill in managing a refractory horse. He looked upon a colored man, not as a human being, responsible to his Creator for the small talent entrusted to him, but as a "chattel personal," as mere live property, no better, except in value, than his mule or dog. When the evidence, clear and indisputable, was laid before him that I was a free man, and as much entitled to my liberty as he—when, on the day I left, he was informed that I had a wife and children, as dear to me as his own babes to him, he only raved and swore, denouncing the law that tore me from him, and declaring he would find out the man who had forwarded the letter that disclosed the place of my captivity, if there was any virtue or power in money, and would take his life. He thought of nothing but his loss, and cursed me for having been born free. He could have stood unmoved and seen the tongues of his poor slaves torn out by the roots—he could have seen them burned to ashes over a slow fire, or gnawed to death by dogs, if it only brought him profit. Such a hard, cruel, unjust man is Edwin Epps.

There was but one greater savage on Bayou Bœuf than he. Jim Burns' plantation was cultivated, as already mentioned, exclusively by women. That barbarian kept their backs so sore and raw, that they could not perform the customary labor demanded daily of the slave. He boasted of his cruelty, and through all the country round was accounted a more thorough-going, energetic man than even Epps. A brute himself, Jim Burns had not a particle of mercy for his subject brutes, and like a fool, whipped and scourged away the very strength upon which depended his amount of gain.

Epps remained on Huff Power two years, when, having accumulated a considerable sum of money, he expended it in the purchase of the plantation on the east bank of Bayou Bœuf, where he still continues to reside. He took possession of it in 1845, after the holidays were passed. He carried thither with him nine slaves, all of whom, except myself, and Susan, who has since died, remain there yet. He made no addition to this force, and for eight years the following were my companions in his quarters, viz: Abram, Wiley, Phebe, Bob, Henry, Edward, and Patsey. All these except Edward, born since, were purchased out of a drove by Epps during the time he was overseer for Archy B. Williams, whose plantation is situated on the shore of Red River, not far from Alexandria.

Abram was tall, standing a full head above any common man. He is sixty years of age, and was born in Tennessee. Twenty years ago, he was purchased by a trader, carried into South Carolina, and sold to James Buford, of Williamsburgh county, in that State. In his youth he was renowned for his great strength, but age and unremitting toil have somewhat shattered his powerful frame and enfeebled his mental faculties.

Wiley is forty-eight. He was born on the estate of William Tassle, and for many years took charge of that gentleman's ferry over the Big Black River, in South Carolina.

Phebe was a slave of Buford, Tassle's neighbor, and having married Wiley, he bought the latter, at her instigation. Buford was a kind master, sheriff of the county, and in those days a man of wealth.

Bob and Henry are Phebe's children, by a former husband, their father having been abandoned to give place to Wiley. That seductive youth had insinuated himself into Phebe's affections, and therefore the faithless spouse had gently kicked her first husband out of her cabin door. Edward had been born to them on Bayou Huff Power.

Patsey is twenty-three—also from Buford's plantation. She is in no wise connected with the others, but glories in the fact that she is the offspring of a "Guinea nigger," brought over to Cuba in a slave ship, and in the course of trade transferred to Buford, who was her mother's owner.

This, as I learned from them, is a genealogical account of my master's slaves. For years they had been together. Often they recalled the memories of other days, and sighed to retrace their steps to the old home in Carolina. Troubles came upon their master Buford, which brought far greater troubles upon them. He became involved in debt, and unable to bear up against his failing fortunes, was compelled to sell these, and others of his slaves. In a chain gang they had been driven from beyond the Mississippi to the plantation of Archy B. Williams. Edwin Epps, who, for a long while had been his driver and overseer, was about establishing himself in business on his own account, at the time of their arrival, and accepted them in payment of his wages.

Old Abram was a kind-hearted being—a sort of patriarch among us, fond of entertaining his younger brethren with grave and serious discourse. He was deeply versed in such philosophy as is taught in the cabin of the slave; but the great absorbing hobby of Uncle Abram was General Jackson, whom his young master in Tennessee had followed to the wars. He loved to wander back, in imagination, to the place where he was born, and to recount the scenes of his youth during those stirring times when the nation was in arms. He had been athletic, and more keen and powerful than the generality of his race, but now his eye had become dim, and his natural force abated. Very often, indeed, while discussing the best method of baking the hoe-cake, or expatiating at large upon the glory of Jackson, he would forget where he left his hat, or his hoe, or his basket; and then would the old man be laughed at, if Epps was absent, and whipped if he was present. So was he perplexed continually, and sighed to think that he was growing aged and going to decay. Philosophy and Jackson and forgetfulness had played the mischief with him, and it was evident that all of them combined were fast bringing down the gray hairs of Uncle Abram to the grave.

Aunt Phebe had been an excellent field hand, but latterly was put into the kitchen, where she remained, except occasionally, in a time of uncommon hurry. She was a sly old creature, and when not in the presence of her mistress or her master, was garrulous in the extreme.

Wiley, on the contrary, was silent. He performed his task without murmur or complaint, seldom indulging in the luxury of speech, except to utter a wish that he was away from Epps, and back once more in South Carolina.

Bob and Henry had reached the ages of twenty and twenty-three, and were distinguished for nothing extraordinary or unusual, while Edward, a lad of thirteen, not yet able to maintain his row in the corn or the cotton field, was kept in the great house, to wait on the little Eppses.

Patsey was slim and straight. She stood erect as the human form is capable of standing. There was an air of loftiness in her movement, that neither labor, nor weariness, nor punishment could destroy. Truly, Patsey was a splendid animal, and were it not that bondage had enshrouded her intellect in utter and everlasting darkness, would have been chief among ten thousand of her people. She could leap the highest fences, and a fleet hound it was indeed, that could outstrip her in a race. No horse could fling her from his back. She was a skillful teamster. She turned as true a furrow as the best, and at splitting rails there were none who could excel her. When the order to halt was heard at night, she would have her mules at the crib, unharnessed, fed and curried, before uncle Abram had found his hat. Not, however, for all or any of these, was she chiefly famous. Such lightning-like motion was in her fingers as no other fingers ever possessed, and therefore it was, that in cotton picking time, Patsey was queen of the field.

She had a genial and pleasant temper, and was faithful and obedient. Naturally, she was a joyous creature, a laughing, light-hearted girl, rejoicing in the mere sense of existence. Yet Patsey wept oftener, and suffered more, than any of her companions. She had been literally excoriated. Her back bore the scars of a thousand stripes; not because she was backward in her work, nor because she was of an unmindful and rebellious spirit, but because it had fallen to her lot to be the slave of a licentious master and a jealous mistress. She shrank before the lustful eye of the one, and was in danger even of her life at the hands of the other, and between the two, she was indeed accursed. In the great house, for days together, there were high and angry words, poutings and estrangement, whereof she was the innocent cause. Nothing delighted the mistress so much as to see her suffer, and more than once, when Epps had refused to sell her, has she tempted me with bribes to put her secretly to death, and bury her body in some lonely place in the margin of the swamp. Gladly would Patsey have appeased this unforgiving spirit, if it had been in her power, but not like Joseph, dared she escape from Master Epps, leaving her garment in his hand. Patsey walked under a cloud. If she uttered a word in opposition to her master's will, the lash was resorted to at once, to bring her to subjection; if she was not watchful when about her cabin, or when walking in the yard, a billet of wood, or a broken bottle perhaps, hurled from her mistress' hand, would smite her unexpectedly in the face. The enslaved victim of lust and hate, Patsey had no comfort of her life.

These were my companions and fellow-slaves, with whom I was accustomed to be driven to the field, and with whom it has been my lot to dwell for ten years in the log cabins of Edwin Epps. They, if living, are yet toiling on the banks of Bayou Bœuf, never destined to breathe, as I now do, the blessed air of liberty, nor to shake off the heavy shackles that enthrall them, until they shall lie down forever in the dust.

The first year of Epps' residence on the bayou, 1845, the caterpillars almost totally destroyed the cotton crop throughout that region. There was little to be done, so that the slaves were necessarily idle half the time. However, there came a rumor to Bayou Bœuf that wages were high, and laborers in great demand on the sugar plantations in St. Mary's parish. This parish is situated on the coast of the Gulf of Mexico, about one hundred and forty miles from Avoyelles. The Rio Teche, a considerable stream, flows through St. Mary's to the gulf.

It was determined by the planters, on the receipt of this intelligence, to make up a drove of slaves to be sent down to Tuckapaw in St. Mary's, for the purpose of hiring them out in the cane fields. Accordingly, in the month of September, there were one hundred and forty-seven collected at Holmesville, Abram, Bob and myself among the number. Of these about one-half were women. Epps, Alonson Pierce, Henry Toler, and Addison Roberts, were the white men, selected to accompany, and take charge of the drove. They had a two-horse carriage and two saddle horses for their use. A large wagon, drawn by four horses, and driven by John, a boy belonging to Mr. Roberts, carried the blankets and provisions.

About 2 o'clock in the afternoon, having been fed, preparations were made to depart. The duty assigned me was, to take charge of the blankets and provisions, and see that none were lost by the way. The carriage proceeded in advance, the wagon following; behind this slaves were arranged, while the two horsemen brought up the rear, and in this order the procession moved out of Holmesville.

That night we reached a Mr. McCrow's plantation, a distance of ten or fifteen miles, when we were ordered to halt. Large fires were built, and each one spreading his blanket on the ground, laid down upon it. The white men lodged in the great house. An hour before day we were aroused by the drivers coming among us, cracking their whips and ordering us to arise. Then the blankets were rolled up, and being severally delivered to me and deposited in the wagon, the procession set forth again.

The following night it rained violently. We were all drenched, our clothes saturated with mud and water. Reaching an open shed, formerly a gin-house, we found beneath it such shelter as it afforded. There was not room for all of us to lay down. There we remained, huddled together, through the night, continuing our march, as usual, in the morning. During the journey we were fed twice a day, boiling our bacon and baking our corn-cake at the fires in the same manner as in our huts. We passed through Lafayetteville, Mountsville, New-Town, to Centreville, where Bob and Uncle Abram were hired. Our number decreased as we advanced—nearly every sugar plantation requiring the services of one or more.

On our route we passed the Grand Coteau or prairie, a vast space of level, monotonous country, without a tree, except an occasional one which had been transplanted near some dilapidated dwelling. It was once thickly populated, and under cultivation, but for some cause had been abandoned. The business of the scattered inhabitants that now dwell upon it is principally raising cattle. Immense herds were feeding upon it as we passed. In the centre of the Grand Coteau one feels as if he were on the ocean, out of sight of land. As far as the eye can see, in all directions, it is but a ruined and deserted waste.

I was hired to Judge Turner, a distinguished man and extensive planter, whose large estate is situated on Bayou Salle, within a few miles of the gulf. Bayou Salle is a small stream flowing into the bay of Atchafalaya. For some days I was employed at Turner's in repairing his sugar house, when a cane knife was put into my hand, and with thirty or forty others, I was sent into the field. I found no such difficulty in learning the art of cutting cane that I had in picking cotton. It came to me naturally and intuitively, and in a short time I was able to keep up with the fastest knife. Before the cutting was over, however, Judge Turner transferred me from the field to the sugar house, to act there in the capacity of driver. From the time of the commencement of sugar making to the close, the grinding and boiling does not cease day or night. The whip was given me with directions to use it upon any one who was caught standing idle. If I failed to obey them to the letter, there was another one for my own back. In addition to this my duty was to call on and off the different gangs at the proper time. I had no regular periods of rest, and could never snatch but a few moments of sleep at a time.

It is the custom in Louisiana, as I presume it is in other slave States, to allow the slave to retain whatever compensation he may obtain for services performed on Sundays. In this way, only, are they able to provide themselves with any luxury or convenience whatever. When a slave, purchased, or kidnapped in the North, is transported to a cabin on Bayou Bœuf, he is furnished with neither knife, nor fork, nor dish, nor kettle, nor any other thing in the shape of crockery, or furniture of any nature or description. He is furnished with a blanket before he reaches there, and wrapping that around him, he can either stand up, or lie down upon the ground, or on a board, if his master has no use for it. He is at liberty to find a gourd in which to keep his meal, or he can eat his corn from the cob, just as he pleases. To ask the master for a knife, or skillet, or any small convenience of the kind, would be answered with a kick, or laughed at as a joke. Whatever necessary article of this nature is found in a cabin has been purchased with Sunday money. However injurious to the morals, it is certainly a blessing to the physical condition of the slave, to be permitted to break the Sabbath. Otherwise there would be no way to provide himself with any utensils, which seem to be indispensable to him who is compelled to be his own cook.

On cane plantations in sugar time, there is no distinction as to the days of the week. It is well understood that all hands must labor on the Sabbath, and it is equally well understood that those especially who are hired, as I was to Judge Turner, and others in succeeding years, shall receive remuneration for it. It is usual, also, in the most hurrying time of cotton-picking, to require the same extra service. From this source, slaves generally are afforded an opportunity of earning sufficient to purchase a knife, a kettle, tobacco and so forth. The females, discarding the latter luxury, are apt to expend their little revenue in the purchase of gaudy ribbons, wherewithal to deck their hair in the merry season of the holidays.

I remained in St. Mary's until the first of January, during which time my Sunday money amounted to ten dollars. I met with other good fortune, for which I was indebted to my violin, my constant companion, the source of profit, and soother of my sorrows during years of servitude. There was a grand party of whites assembled at Mr. Yarney's, in Centreville, a hamlet in the vicinity of Turner's plantation. I was employed to play for them, and so well pleased were the merry-makers with my performance, that a contribution was taken for my benefit, which amounted to seventeen dollars.

With this sum in possession, I was looked upon by my fellows as a millionaire. It afforded me great pleasure to look at it—to count it over and over again, day after day. Visions of cabin furniture, of water pails, of pocket knives, new shoes and coat and hats, floated through my fancy, and up through all rose the triumphant contemplation, that I was the wealthiest "nigger" on Bayou Bœuf.

Vessels run up the Rio Teche to Centreville. While there, I was bold enough one day to present myself before the captain of a steamer, and beg permission to hide myself among the freight. I was emboldened to risk the hazard of such a step, from overhearing a conversation, in the course of which I ascertained he was a native of the North. I did not relate to him the particulars of my history, but only expressed an ardent desire to escape from slavery to a free State. He pitied me, but said it would be impossible to avoid the vigilant custom house officers in New-Orleans, and that detection would subject him to punishment, and his vessel to confiscation. My earnest entreaties evidently excited his sympathies, and doubtless he would have yielded to them, could he have done so with any kind of safety. I was compelled to smother the sudden flame that lighted up my bosom with sweet hopes of liberation, and turn my steps once more towards the increasing darkness of despair.

Immediately after this event the drove assembled at Centreville, and several of the owners having arrived and collected the monies due for our services, we were driven back to Bayou Bœuf. It was on our return, while passing through a small village, that I caught sight of Tibeats, seated in the door of a dirty grocery, looking somewhat seedy and out of repair. Passion and poor whiskey, I doubt not, have ere this laid him on the shelf.

During our absence, I learned from Aunt Phebe and Patsey, that the latter had been getting deeper and deeper into trouble. The poor girl was truly an object of pity. "Old Hogjaw," the name by which Epps was called, when the slaves were by themselves, had beaten her more severely and frequently than ever. As surely as he came from Holmesville, elated with liquor—and it was often in those days—he would whip her, merely to gratify the mistress; would punish her to an extent almost beyond endurance, for an offence of which he himself was the sole and irresistible cause. In his sober moments he could not always be prevailed upon to indulge his wife's insatiable thirst for vengeance.

To be rid of Patsey—to place her beyond sight or reach, by sale, or death, or in any other manner, of late years, seemed to be the ruling thought and passion of my mistress. Patsey had been a favorite when a child, even in the great house. She had been petted and admired for her uncommon sprightliness and pleasant disposition. She had been fed many a time, so Uncle Abram said, even on biscuit and milk, when the madam, in her younger days, was wont to call her to the piazza, and fondle her as she would a playful kitten. But a sad change had come over the spirit of the woman. Now, only black and angry fiends ministered in the temple of her heart, until she could look on Patsey but with concentrated venom.

Mistress Epps was not naturally such an evil woman, after all. She was possessed of the devil, jealousy, it is true, but aside from that, there was much in her character to admire. Her father, Mr. Roberts, resided in Cheneyville, an influential and honorable man, and as much respected throughout the parish as any other citizen. She had been well educated at some institution this side the Mississippi; was beautiful, accomplished, and usually good-humored. She was kind to all of us but Patsey— frequently, in the absence of her husband, sending out to us some little dainty from her own table. In other situations—in a different society from that which exists on the shores of Bayou Bœuf, she would have been pronounced an elegant and fascinating woman. An ill wind it was that blew her into the arms of Epps.

He respected and loved his wife as much as a coarse nature like his is capable of loving, but supreme selfishness always overmastered conjugal affection.

> *He loved as well as baser natures can,*
> But a mean heart and soul were in that man.

He was ready to gratify any whim—to grant any request she made, provided it did not cost too much. Patsey was equal to any two of his slaves in the cotton field. He could not replace her with the same money she would bring. The idea of disposing of her, therefore, could not be entertained. The mistress did not regard her at all in that light. The pride of the haughty woman was aroused; the blood of the fiery southern boiled at the sight of Patsey, and nothing less than trampling out the life of the helpless bondwoman would satisfy her.

Sometimes the current of her wrath turned upon him whom she had just cause to hate. But the storm of angry words would pass over at length, and there would be a season of calm again. At such times Patsey trembled with fear, and cried as if her heart would break, for she knew from painful experience, that if mistress should work herself to the red-hot pitch of rage, Epps would quiet her at last with a promise that Patsey should be flogged—a promise he was sure to keep. Thus did pride, and jealousy, and vengeance war with avarice and brute-passion in the mansion of my master, filling it with daily tumult and contention. Thus, upon the head of Patsey— the simpleminded slave, in whose heart God had implanted the seeds of virtue—the force of all these domestic tempests spent itself at last.

During the summer succeeding my return from St. Mary's parish, I conceived a plan of providing myself with food, which, though simple, succeeded beyond expectation. It has been followed by many others in my condition, up and down the bayou, and of such benefit has it become that I am almost persuaded to look upon myself as a benefactor. That summer the worms got into the bacon. Nothing but ravenous hunger could induce us to swallow it. The weekly allowance of meal scarcely sufficed to satisfy us. It was customary with us, as it is with all in that region, where the allowance is exhausted before Saturday night, or is in such a state as to render it nauseous and disgusting, to hunt in the swamps for coon and opossum. This, however, must be done at night, after the day's work is accomplished. There are planters whose slaves, for months at a time, have no other meat than such as is obtained in this manner. No objections are made to hunting, inasmuch as it dispenses with drafts upon the smoke-house, and because every marauding coon that is killed is so much saved from the standing corn. They are hunted with dogs and clubs, slaves not being allowed the use of fire-arms.

The flesh of the coon is palatable, but verily there is nothing in all butcherdom so delicious as a roasted 'possum. They are a round, rather long-bodied, little animal, of a whitish color, with nose like a pig, and caudal extremity like a rat. They burrow among the roots and in the hollows of the gum tree, and are clumsy and slow of motion. They are deceitful and cunning creatures. On receiving the slightest tap of a stick, they will roll over on the ground and feign death. If the hunter leaves him, in pursuit of another, without first taking particular pains to break his neck, the chances are, on his return, he is not to be found. The little animal has outwitted the enemy— has "played 'possom"—and is off. But after a long and hard day's work, the weary slave feels little like going to the swamp for his supper, and half the time prefers throwing himself on the cabin floor without it. It is for the interest of the master that the servant should not suffer in health from starvation, and it is also for his interest that he should not become gross from over-feeding. In the estimation of the owner, a slave is the most serviceable when in rather a lean and lank condition, such a condition as the race-horse is in, when fitted for the course, and in that condition they are generally to be found on the sugar and cotton plantations along Red River.

My cabin was within a few rods of the bayou bank, and necessity being indeed the mother of invention, I resolved upon a mode of obtaining the requisite amount of food, without the trouble of resorting nightly to the woods. This was to construct a fish trap. Having, in my mind, conceived the manner in which it could be done, the next Sunday I set about putting it into practical execution. It may be impossible for me to convey to the reader a full and correct idea of its construction, but the following will serve as a general description:

A frame between two and three feet square is made, and of a greater or less height, according to the depth of water. Boards or slats are nailed on three sides of this frame, not so closely, however, as to prevent the water circulating freely through it. A door is fitted into the fourth side, in such manner that it will slide easily up and down in the groves cut in the two posts. A movable bottom is then so fitted that it can be raised to the top of the frame without difficulty. In the centre of the movable bottom an auger hole is bored, and into this one end of a handle or round stick is fastened on the under side so loosely that it will turn. The handle ascends from the centre of the movable bottom to the top of the frame, or as much higher as is desirable. Up and down this handle, in a great many places, are gimlet holes, through which small sticks are inserted, extending to opposite sides of the frame. So many of these small sticks are running out from the handle in all directions, that a fish of any considerable dimensions cannot pass through without hitting one of them. The frame is then placed in the water and made stationary.

The trap is "set" by sliding or drawing up the door, and kept in that position by another stick, one end of which rests in a notch on the inner side, the other end in a notch made in the handle, running up from the centre of the movable bottom. The trap is baited by rolling a handful of wet meal and cotton together until it becomes hard, and depositing it in the back part of the frame. A fish swimming through the upraised door toward the bait, necessarily strikes one of the small sticks turning the handle, which displacing the stick supporting the door, the latter falls, securing the fish within the frame. Taking hold of the top of the handle, the movable bottom is then drawn up to the surface of the water, and the fish taken out. There may have been other such traps in use before mine was constructed, but if there were I never happened to see one. Bayou Bœuf abounds in fish of large size and excellent quality, and after this time I was very rarely in want of one for myself, or for my comrades. Thus a mine was opened—a new resource was developed, hitherto unthought of by the enslaved children of Africa, who toil and hunger along the shores of that sluggish, but prolific stream.

About the time of which I am now writing, an event occurred in our immediate neighborhood, which made a deep impression upon me, and which shows the state of society existing there, and the manner in which affronts are oftentimes avenged. Directly opposite our quarters, on the other side of the bayou, was situated the plantation of Mr. Marshall. He belonged to a family among the most wealthy and aristocratic in the country. A gentleman from the vicinity of Natchez had been negotiating with him for the purchase of the estate. One day a messenger came in great haste to our plantation, saying that a bloody and fearful battle was going on at Marshall's—that blood had been spilled—and unless the combatants were forthwith separated, the result would be disastrous.

On repairing to Marshall's house, a scene presented itself that beggars description. On the floor of one of the rooms lay the ghastly corpse of the man from Natchez, while Marshall, enraged and covered with wounds and blood, was stalking back and forth, "breathing out threatenings and slaughter." A difficulty had arisen in the course of their negotiation, high words ensued, when drawing their weapons, the deadly strife began that ended so unfortunately. Marshall was never placed in confinement. A sort of trial or investigation was had at Marksville, when he was acquitted, and returned to his plantation, rather more respected, as I thought, than ever, from the fact that the blood of a fellow being was on his soul.

Epps interested himself in his behalf, accompanying him to Marksville, and on all occasions loudly justifying him, but his services in this respect did not afterwords deter a kinsman of this same Marshall from seeking his life also. A brawl occurred between them over a gambling-table, which terminated in a deadly feud. Riding up on horseback in front of the house one day, armed with pistols and bowie knife, Marshall challenged him to come forth and make a final settlement of the quarrel, or he would brand him as a coward, and shoot him like a dog the first opportunity. Not through cowardice, nor from any conscientious scruples, in my opinion, but through the influence of his wife, he was restrained from accepting the challenge of his enemy. A reconciliation, however, was effected afterward, since which time they have been on terms of the closest intimacy.

Such occurrences, which would bring upon the parties concerned in them merited and condign punishment in the Northern States, are frequent on the bayou, and pass without notice, and almost without comment. Every man carries his bowie knife, and when two fall out, they set to work hacking and thrusting at each other, more like savages than civilized and enlightened beings.

The existence of Slavery in its most cruel form among them, has a tendency to brutalize the humane and finer feelings of their nature. Daily witnesses of human suffering—listening to the agonizing screeches of the slave—beholding him writhing beneath the merciless lash—bitten and torn by dogs—dying without attention, and buried without shroud or coffin—it cannot otherwise be expected, than that they should become brutified and reckless of human life. It is true there are many kind-hearted and good men in the parish of Avoyelles—such men as William Ford—who can look with pity upon the sufferings of a slave, just as there are, over all the world, sensitive and sympathetic spirits, who cannot look with indifference upon the sufferings of any creature which the Almighty has endowed with life. It is not the fault of the slaveholder that he is cruel, so much as it is the fault of the system under which he lives. He cannot withstand the influence of habit and associations that surround him. Taught from earliest childhood, by all that he sees and hears, that the rod is for the slave's back, he will not be apt to change his opinions in maturer years.

There may be humane masters, as there certainly are inhuman ones—there may be slaves well-clothed, well-fed, and happy, as there surely are those half-clad, half-starved and miserable; nevertheless, the institution that tolerates such wrong and inhumanity as I have witnessed, is a cruel, unjust, and barbarous one. Men may write fictions portraying lowly life as it is, or as it is not—may expatiate with owlish gravity upon the bliss of ignorance—discourse flippantly from arm chairs of the pleasures of slave life; but let them toil with him in the field—sleep with him in the cabin—feed with him on husks; let them behold him scourged, hunted, trampled on, and they will come back with another story in their mouths. Let them know the *heart* of the poor slave—learn his secret thoughts—thoughts he dare not utter in the hearing of the white man; let them sit by him in the silent watches of the night—converse with him in trustful confidence, of "life, liberty, and the pursuit of happiness," and they will find that ninety-nine out of every hundred are intelligent enough to understand their situation, and to cherish in their bosoms the love of freedom, as passionately as themselves.

In consequence of my inability in cotton-picking, Epps was in the habit of hiring me out on sugar plantations during the season of cane-cutting and sugar-making. He received for my services a dollar a day, with the money supplying my place on his cotton plantation. Cutting cane was an employment that suited me, and for three successive years I held the lead row at Hawkins', leading a gang of from fifty to an hundred hands.

In an previous chapter the mode of cultivating cotton is described. This may be the proper place to speak of the manner of cultivating cane.

The ground is prepared in beds, the same as it is prepared for the reception of the cotton seed, except it is ploughed deeper. Drills are made in the same manner. Planting commences in January, and continues until April. It is necessary to plant a sugar field only once in three years. Three crops are taken before the seed or plant is exhausted.

Three gangs are employed in the operation. One draws the cane from the rick, or stack, cutting the top and flags from the stalk, leaving only that part which is sound and healthy. Each joint of the cane has an eye, like the eye of a potato, which sends forth a sprout when buried in the soil. Another gang lays the cane in the drill, placing two stalks side by side in such manner that joints will occur once in four or six inches. The third gang follows with hoes, drawing earth upon the stalks, and covering them to the depth of three inches.

In four weeks, at the farthest, the sprouts appear above the ground, and from this time forward grow with great rapidity. A sugar field is hoed three times, the same as cotton, save that a greater quantity of earth is drawn to the roots. By the first of August hoeing is usually over. About the middle of September, whatever is required for seed is cut and stacked in ricks, as they are termed. In October it is ready for the mill or sugar-house, and then the general cutting begins. The blade of a cane-knife is fifteen inches long, three inches wide in the middle, and tapering towards the point and handle. The blade is thin, and in order to be at all serviceable must be kept very sharp. Every third hand takes the lead of two others, one of whom is on each side of him. The lead hand, in the first place, with a blow of his knife shears the flags from the stalk. He next cuts off the top down as far as it is green. He must be careful to sever all the green from the ripe part, inasmuch as the juice of the former sours the molasses, and renders it unsalable. Then he severs the stalk at the root, and lays it directly behind him.

His right and left hand companions lay their stalks, when cut in the same manner, upon his. To every three hands there is a cart, which follows, and the stalks are thrown into it by the younger slaves, when it is drawn to the sugar-house and ground.

If the planter apprehends a frost, the cane is winrowed. Winrowing is the cutting of the stalks at an early period and throwing them lengthwise in the water furrow in such a manner that the tops will cover the butts of the stalks. They will remain in this condition three weeks or a month without souring, and secure from frost. When the proper time arrives, they are taken up, trimmed and carted to the sugar-house.

In the month of January the slaves enter the field again to prepare for another crop. The ground is now strewn with the tops, and flags cut from the past year's cane. On a dry day fire is set to this combustible refuse, which sweeps over the field, leaving it bare and clean, and ready for the hoes. The earth is loosened about the roots of the old stubble, and in process of time another crop springs up from the last year's seed. It is the same the year following; but the third year the seed has exhausted its strength, and the field must be ploughed and planted again. The second year the cane is sweeter and yields more than the first, and the third year more than the second.

During the three seasons I labored on Hawkins' plantation, I was employed a considerable portion of the time in the sugar-house. He is celebrated as the producer of the finest variety of white sugar. The following is a general description of his sugar-house and the process of manufacture:

> The mill is an immense brick building, standing on the shore of the bayou. Running out from the building is an open shed, at least an hundred feet in length and forty or fifty feet in width. The boiler in which the steam is generated is situated outside the main building; the machinery and engine rest on a brick pier, fifteen feet above the floor, within the body of the building. The machinery turns two great iron rollers, between two and three feet in diameter and six or eight feet in length. They are elevated above the brick pier, and roll in towards each other. An endless carrier, made of chain and wood, like leathern belts used in small mills, extends from the iron rollers out of the main building and through the entire length of the open shed. The carts in which the cane is brought from the field as fast as it is cut, are unloaded at the sides of the shed. All along the endless carrier are ranged slave children, whose business it is to place the cane upon it, when it is conveyed through the shed into the main building, where it falls between the rollers, is crushed, and drops upon another carrier that conveys it out of the main building in an opposite direction, depositing it in the top of a chimney upon a fire beneath, which consumes it. It is necessary to burn it in this manner, because otherwise it would soon fill the building, and more especially because it would soon sour and engender disease. The juice of the cane falls into a conductor underneath the iron rollers, and is carried into a reservoir. Pipes convey it from thence into five filterers, holding several hogsheads each. These filterers are filled with bone-black, a substance resembling pulverized charcoal. It is made of bones calcinated in close vessels, and is used for the purpose of decolorizing, by filtration, the cane juice before boiling. Through these five filterers it passes in succession, and then runs into a large reservoir

underneath the ground floor, from whence it is carried up, by means of a steam pump, into a clarifier made of sheet iron, where it is heated by steam until it boils. From the first clarifier it is carried in pipes to a second and a third, and thence into close iron pans, through which tubes pass, filled with steam. While in a boiling state it flows through three pans in succession, and is then carried in other pipes down to the coolers on the ground floor. Coolers are wooden boxes with sieve bottoms made of the finest wire. As soon as the syrup passes into the coolers, and is met by the air, it grains, and the molasses at once escapes through the sieves into a cistern below. It is then white or loaf sugar of the finest kind—clear, clean, and as white as snow. When cool, it is taken out, packed in hogsheads, and is ready for market. The molasses is then carried from the cistern into the upper story again, and by another process converted into brown sugar.

There are larger mills, and those constructed differently from the one thus imperfectly described, but none, perhaps, more celebrated than this anywhere on Bayou Bœuf. Lambert, of New-Orleans, is a partner of Hawkins. He is man of vast wealth, holding, as I have been told, an interest in over forty different sugar plantations in Louisiana.

The only respite from constant labor the slave has through the whole year, is during the Christmas holidays. Epps allowed us three—others allow four, five and six days, according to the measure of their generosity. It is the only time to which they look forward with any interest or pleasure. They are glad when night comes, not only because it brings them a few hours repose, but because it brings them one day nearer Christmas. It is hailed with equal delight by the old and the young; even Uncle Abram ceases to glorify Andrew Jackson, and Patsey forgets her many sorrows, amid the general hilarity of the holidays. It is the time of feasting, and frolicking, and fiddling—the carnival season with the children of bondage. They are the only days when they are allowed a little restricted liberty, and heartily indeed do they enjoy it.

It is the custom for one planter to give a "Christmas supper," inviting the slaves from neighboring plantations to join his own on the occasion; for instance, one year it is given by Epps, the next by Marshall, the next by Hawkins, and so on. Usually from three to five hundred are assembled, coming together on foot, in carts, on horseback, on mules, riding double and triple, sometimes a boy and girl, at others a girl and two boys, and at others again a boy, a girl and an old woman. Uncle Abram astride a mule, with Aunt Phebe and Patsey behind him, trotting towards a Christmas supper, would be no uncommon sight on Bayou Bœuf.

Then, too, "of all days i' the year," they array themselves in their best attire. The cotton coat has been washed clean, the stump of a tallow candle has been applied to the shoes, and if so fortunate as to possess a rimless or a crownless hat, it is placed jauntily on the head. They are welcomed with equal cordiality, however, if they come bare-headed and barefooted to the feast. As a general thing, the women wear handkerchiefs tied about their heads, but if chance has thrown in their way a fiery red ribbon, or a cast-off bonnet of their mistress' grandmother, it is sure to be worn on such occasions. Red—the deep blood red—is decidedly the favorite color among the enslaved damsels of my acquaintance. If a red ribbon does not encircle the neck, you will be certain to find all the hair of their wooly heads tied up with red strings of one sort or another.

The table is spread in the open air, and loaded with varieties of meat and piles of vegetables. Bacon and corn meal at such times are dispensed with. Sometimes the cooking is performed in the kitchen on the plantation, at others in the shade of wide branching trees. In the latter case, a ditch is dug in the ground, and wood laid in and burned until it is filled with glowing coals, over which chickens, ducks, turkeys, pigs, and not unfrequently the entire body of a wild ox, are roasted. They are furnished also with flour, of which biscuits are made, and often with peach and other preserves, with tarts, and every manner and description of pies, except the mince, that being an article of pastry as yet unknown among them. Only the slave who has lived all the years on his scanty allowance of meal and bacon, can appreciate such suppers. White people in great numbers assemble to witness the gastronomical enjoyments.

They seat themselves at the rustic table—the males on one side, the females on the other. The two between whom there may have been an exchange of tenderness, invariably manage to sit opposite; for the omnipresent Cupid disdains not to hurl his arrows into the simple hearts of slaves. Unalloyed and exulting happiness lights up the dark faces of them all. The ivory teeth, contrasting with their black complexions, exhibit two long, white streaks the whole extent of the table. All round the bountiful board a multitude of eyes roll in ecstacy. Giggling and laughter and the clattering of cutlery and crockery succeed. Cuffee's elbow hunches his neighbor's side, impelled by an involuntary impulse of delight; Nelly shakes her finger at Sambo and laughs, she knows not why, and so the fun and merriment flows on.

When the viands have disappeared, and the hungry maws of the children of toil are satisfied, then, next in the order of amusement, is the Christmas dance. My business on these gala days always was to play on the violin. The African race is a music-loving one, proverbially; and many there were among my fellowbondsmen whose organs of tune were strikingly developed, and who could thumb the banjo with dexterity; but at the expense of appearing egotistical, I must, nevertheless, declare, that I was considered the Ole Bull of Bayou Bœuf. My master often received letters, sometimes from a distance of ten miles, requesting him to send me to play at a ball or festival of the whites. He received his compensation, and usually I also returned with many picayunes jingling in my pockets—the extra contributions of those to whose delight I had administered. In this manner I became more acquainted than I otherwise would, up and down the bayou. The young men and maidens of Holmesville always knew there was to be a jollification somewhere, whenever Platt Epps was seen passing through the town with his fiddle in his hand. "Where are you going now, Platt?" and "What is coming off tonight, Platt?" would be interrogatories issuing from every door and window, and many a time when there was no special hurry, yielding to pressing importunities, Platt would draw his bow, and sitting astride his mule, perhaps, discourse musically to a crowd of delighted children, gathered around him in the street.

Alas! had it not been for my beloved violin, I scarcely can conceive how I could have endured the long years of bondage. It introduced me to great houses—relieved me of many days' labor in the field—supplied me with conveniences for my cabin—with pipes and tobacco, and extra pairs of shows, and oftentimes led me away from the presence of a hard master, to witness scenes of jollity and mirth. It was my companion—the friend of my bosom—triumphing loudly when I was joyful, and uttering its soft, melodious consolations when I was sad. Often, at midnight, when sleep had fled affrighted from the cabin, and my soul was disturbed and troubled with the contemplation of my fate, it would sing me a song of peace. On holy Sabbath days, when an hour or two of leisure was allowed, it would accompany me to some quiet place on the bayou bank, and, lifting up its voice, discourse kindly and pleasantly indeed. It heralded my name round the country—made me friends, who, otherwise would not have noticed me—gave me an honored seat at the yearly feasts, and secured the loudest and heartiest welcome of them all at the Christmas dance. The Christmas dance! Oh, ye pleasure-seeking sons and daughters of idleness, who move with measured step, listless and snail-like, through the slow-winding cotillon, if ye wish to look upon the celerity, if not the "poetry of motion"—upon genuine happiness, rampant and unrestrained—go down to Louisiana, and see the slaves dancing in the starlight of a Christmas night.

On that particular Christmas I have now in my mind, a description whereof will serve as a description of the day generally, Miss Lively and Mr. Sam, the first belonging to Stewart, the latter to Roberts, started the ball. It was well known that Sam cherished an ardent passion for Lively, as also did one of Marshall's and another of Carey's boys; for Lively was *lively* indeed, and a heart-breaking coquette withal. It was a victory for Sam Roberts, when, rising from the repast, she gave him her hand for the first "figure" in preference to either of his rivals. They were somewhat crest-fallen, and, shaking their heads angrily, rather intimated they would like to pitch into Mr. Sam and hurt him badly. But not an emotion of wrath ruffled the placid bosom of Samuel, as his legs flew like drumsticks down the outside and up the middle, by the side of his bewitching partner. The whole company cheered them vociferously, and, excited with the applause, they continued "tearing down" after all the others had become exhausted and halted a moment to recover breath. But Sam's superhuman exertions overcame him finally, leaving Lively alone, yet whirling like a top.

Thereupon one of Sam's rivals, Pete Marshall, dashed in, and, with might and main, leaped and shuffled and threw himself into every conceivable shape, as if determined to show Miss Lively and all the world that Sam Roberts was of no account.

Pete's affection, however, was greater than his discretion. Such violent exercise took the breath out of him directly, and he dropped like an empty bag. Then was the time for Harry Carey to try his hand; but Lively also soon out-winded him, amidst hurrahs and shouts, fully sustaining her well-earned reputation of being the "fastest gal" on the bayou.

One "set" off, another takes its place, he or she remaining the longest on the floor receiving the most uproarious commendation, and so the dancing continues until broad daylight. It does not cease with the sound of the fiddle, but in that case they set up a music peculiar to themselves. This is called "patting," accompanied with one of those unmeaning songs, composed rather for its adaptation to a certain tune or measure, than for the purpose of expressing any distinct idea. The patting is performed by striking the hands on the knees, then striking the hands together, then striking the right shoulder with one hand, the left with the other—all the while keeping time with the feet, and singing, perhaps, this song:

> *Harper's creek and roarin' ribber,*
> *Thar, my dear, we'll live forebber;*
> *Den we'll go to de Ingin nation,*
> *All I want is dis creation,*
> *Is pretty little wife and big plantation.*

Chorus:
> *Up dat oak and down dat ribber,*
> *Two overseers and one little nigger.*

Or, if these words are not adapted to the tune called for, it may be that "Old Hog Eye" *is*—a rather solemn and startling specimen of versification, not, however, to be appreciated unless heard at the South. It runneth as follows:

> *Who's been here since I've been gone?*
> *Pretty little gal wid a josey on.*
> > *Hog Eye!*
> > *Old Hog Eye,*
> > *And Hosey too!*

> *Never see de like since I was born,*
> *Here come a little gal wid a josey on.*
> > *Hog Eye!*
> > *Old Hog Eye,*
> > *And Hosey too!*

Or, may be the following, perhaps, equally nonsensical, but full of melody, nevertheless, as it flows from the negro's mouth:

> *Ebo Dick and Jurdan's Jo,*
> *Them two niggers stole my yo'*
> Chorus: *Hop Jim along,*
> > *Walk Jim along,*
> > *Talk Jim along, &c*

> *Old black Dan, as black as tar,*
> *He dam glad he was not dar.*
> > *Hop Jim along, &c.*

During the remaining holidays succeeding Christmas, they are provided with passes, and permitted to go where they please within a limited distance, or they may remain and labor on the plantation, in which case they are paid for it. It is very rarely, however, that the latter alternative is accepted. They may be seen at these times hurrying in all directions, as happy looking mortals as can be found on the face of the earth. They are different beings from what they are in the field; the temporary relaxation, the brief deliverance from fear, and from the lash, producing an entire metamorphosis in their appearance and demeanor. In visiting, riding, renewing old friendships, or, perchance reviving some old attachment, or pursuing whatever pleasure may suggest itself, the time is occupied. Such is "southern life as it is," *three days in the year,* as I found it—the other three hundred and sixty-two being days of weariness, and fear, and suffering, and unremitting labor.

Marriage is frequently contracted during the holidays, if such an institution may be said to exist among them. The only ceremony required before entering into that "holy estate," is to obtain the consent of the respective owners. It is usually encouraged by the masters of female slaves. Either party can have as many husbands or wives as the owner will permit, and either is at liberty to discard the other at pleasure. The law in relation to divorce, or to bigamy, and so forth, is not applicable to property, of course. If the wife does not belong on the same plantation with the husband, the latter is permitted to visit her on Saturday nights, if the distance is not too far. Uncle Abram's wife lived seven miles from Epps', on Bayou Huff Power. He had permission to visit her once a fortnight, but he was growing old, as has been said, and truth to say, had latterly well nigh forgotten her. Uncle Abram had no time to spare from his meditations on General Jackson—connubial dalliance being well enough for the young and thoughtless, but unbecoming a grave and solemn philosopher like himself.

(1853)

ALEXANDER H. STEPHENS

Recollections

from His Diary: *Kept When a Prisoner at Fort Warren, Boston Harbour, 1865; Giving Incidents and Reflections of His Prison Life and Some Letters and Reminiscences.*

June 14.—Another bright morning out. Rose at 6:30. Thermometer 72. This thermometer is to be a sort of pet with me, I expect. Read Jeremiah 30, and all of Lamentations. The wailing of Israel's poet over the subjugation, desolation, and ruin of his Zion, meet a sympathetic response in my breast over a like condition of my own dear Georgia. How truly is our condition set forth:

> Our inheritance is turned to strangers, our houses to aliens. We are orphans and fatherless, our mothers are as widows. Our necks are under persecution: we labour and have no rest. The elders have ceased from the gate, the young men from their music. The joy of our heart is ceased; our dance is turned into mourning. For this our heart is faint; for these things our eyes are dim.... For thus said the Lord; we have heard a voice of trembling, of fear and not of peace. Ask ye now, and see whether a man doth travail with child? Wherefore do I see every man with his hands on his loins, as a woman in travail, and all faces are turned into paleness?

How vividly return to my mind the feelings with which I went from a sick-bed to address a vast concourse of people at Dalton, in 1860; in that address, with all due reverence, I exclaimed: "O Jerusalem, Jerusalem, thou that killest the prophets and stonest them which are sent unto thee, how often would I have gathered thy children together, even as a hen gathereth her chickens under her wings, and ye would not." This speech was made in prophecy of impending ruin; amidst interruptions and attempts to prevent my counsels from having effect, I warned our people to stay these calamities while they might.

I see a statement in the New York *Tribune* that the President has granted unconditional pardon, accompanying it with a letter, to Hon. W. W. Boyce, of South Carolina. This I was glad to see, not from any encouragement I may be supposed to take that similar grant may be made me, but because I think well of Mr. Boyce; think he deserved what he is reported to have received, notwithstanding he was so much more reponsible for this war than I; notwithstanding his speech in Columbia,

November, 5, 1860, in which he is reported to have said:

> The question then is, what are we to do? In my opinion the South ought not to submit. If you intend to resist, the way to resist in earnest is to act—the way to avert revolution is to stem it in the face. The only policy for us is to take up arms as soon as we receive authentic intelligence of the election of Lincoln; it is for South Carolina, in the quickest manner and by the most direct means, to withdraw from the Union. Thus, we will not submit, whether the other Southern States will act with us or with our enemies.

At this time, my utmost exertions were in the other direction. His impulses, I doubt not, were prompted by apprehension of danger to the Constitutional Rights of his State from Mr. Lincoln's election. I have no question that this was the case with Governor Joe Brown, Governor (then Judge) Magrath, and great numbers of other leading men whose actions and counsels "precipitated" the war. I was "precipitated" by them against my judgment and protest, and am suffering in consequence. I rejoice to see that these men—Boyce, Brown, Magrath, Smith (Governor of Virginia) and Cobb, with thousands of others who followed like course—at large enjoying on parole their personal liberty. Such liberty would be to me a great boon also, but perhaps it is better for me to suffer, if so be some few must suffer to satisfy public vengeance. Isolated and almost alone in the world, a strange creature of destiny at best, with but few ties to life, why should not I be one of the victims? My fate may be a hard one, but it has been a hard one throughout life.

Walked my room and thought of home—of Linton; smoked my pipe, the meerschaum Girardey gave me. This has been a great source of comfort to me. How often I have thought of him, Camille Girardey of Augusta, Ga., when I have puffed that meerschaum in this dungeon. Walked out at 6.15. Saw Jackson and DuBose on the opposite bastion—too far to recognize them. Lieut. W. told me who they were. Saw General Ewell on his crutches. He was walking on parapet. I remarked that I thought Ewell had an artificial leg; wondered he did not use it. Lieut. W. replied that Ewell said he was waiting before getting an artificial leg to see if the authorities were going to hang him; if he was going to be hung, he did not care to go to the expense; intended to wait and make out on his crutches until that matter was decided. Ewell has a sense of humour.

We heard a cannon. Turning toward the point from which the sound came, we saw smoke near a small craft lying at the wharf of a little town, called Hull, near by. Lieut. W. said, "Oh, it's Dexter Follet's yacht." "Who is he?" asked I. "A young man of Boston, son of a rich father. He keeps this yacht to sail about as he likes. Carries a gun on board, and always fires it off upon landing or leaving, upon heaving or hoisting anchor." We saw the yacht pass on its way to Boston.

Geary brought tea, toast, and strawberries. I thought of Dick Johnston's extensive bed of strawberries and of what an abundance of berries he must have had this spring. All gone by this time, I suppose.

June 15.—Rose at 6.45. Was disturbed by dreams. Richmond was the scene. I seemed to be roaming amid ruins, looking for Mr. Baskerville's house; was on my way home, and had stopped to see after Henry and Anthony. The house—in my dream—had been burned, not a vestige remained of it, nor of other houses that had stood around it; Mrs. Stanard's and all were swept away by fire. I could find nobody I knew and could learn nothing about Henry and Anthony; could hear nothing of Nancy, their mother. Read Bible until 8.15. Geary brought breakfast: fresh fish, beefsteak, hot rolls, coffee, fried potatoes, and cornbread. The cornbread I ate. Breakfast good enough, but I had no appetite for it, due, perhaps, to its late coming. It is essential to my health for me to have breakfast as soon as I can get ready after rising. Half an hour is my usual time for dressing. I can fast an hour after rising, but beyond that I cannot go with impunity. I want my breakfast at this season at seven; for several days I had it at this hour, but since Sunday—Geary saying he could not get it so soon—8.15 is the hour fixed. This morning it did not reach me until 8.45, a half-hour past the time for which I arranged my rising and dressing.

The Boston *Post* says, "The health of A. H. Stephens is said to be precarious." A letter from Charleston, in the N. Y. *Herald,* gives an account of Governor Aikens's return from Washington. I did not know that he had been in custody. The New York *Times* reports Breckinridge and Trenholm [of the Confederate Cabinet] as safely arrived in Bermuda. I am almost certain that this cannot in part be true. Trenholm, I have reason to believe, has not even attempted to leave his State.

Dinner at 2.45: salmon, beef-heels, mutton, vegetables, and gooseberry pie—no uncertainty about it to-day; it was gooseberry the same as that of yesterday. Upon my inquiry, Geary said so; that settled it. Besides this, there was a saucer of cream and jelly. My diet now is much over the proper mark for me as it was too low before. The *juste milieu* is in everything the most difficult point to attain. Could I get meals served in half the quantity and variety, to say nothing of some reduction in quality, with corresponding reduction in cost, I should feel myself as well off as possible in respect of food.

5 P. M.—Walked the room, exercising the whole body as much as I could by swinging my arms and giving them all sorts of motions. This has been my habit for several days, particularly after extinction of lights. I have a notion to get a rubber ball to play with. That would afford better exercise than I can take otherwise. During my walk I thought a great deal about home. Am beginning to doubt whether any of my letters have reached their destination. It is certainly time I heard from Mr. Baskerville, if he was in Richmond and got my letter. How relieved I should be by only a few lines from Linton, giving assurance that he is well! Could I but have the assurance that he is bearing up under my imprisonment with firmness and without too great uneasiness, I could stand all that is before me without a murmur. Wrote to Dr. Berckmans, Augusta, Ga.

Took overcoat for my walk at Lieut. W.'s suggestion; he said it was rather raw out. Did not feel well; pain in the side. Rested under music-stand and returned before hour expired. Saw Confederate prisoners on opposite bastion. I have a pretty large fire of anthracite coal in the grate. The fire in that grate has not gone out since I have been here; it has been kept up, day and night. A grate of this coal put on at 7 p. m. will burn until 6 a. m.

June 16.—Before I got up, Geary brought in a wooden box on legs. I suppose that

I will not be stating a matter of indifference to those sympathizing friends for whom these entries are made, when I tell them that I *live* in this cell except during the hour of my daily walk on the grounds. Whatever functions of nature are performed in eating, drinking, sleeping, or otherwise, are performed herein. At my request Geary got the carpenter to make this commode; price $1.83. While on this point, I will add that Geary is very attentive to my room; keeps it well swept and dusted; and makes up the bed every morning, that is, beats up the straw and arranges the covering, which, besides the sheets, are the blankets and afghan I brought with me. He brings cool water as often as I desire it; it is cistern water, clear and pure, about 65° in temperature. I see in the papers an account of John Mitchel's arrest in New York. Mitchel is a rare character, an eccentric genius. I was sorry, not only on his account, but on account of the South and her cause, when I saw some weeks ago that he was in New York writing for the *News*. He is a man of too much violence of temper, too much extravagance, and too little discretion, to be identified, to its advantage, as a leading exponent of any cause.

When Smith O'Brien was in this country on a visit to Washington, he stopped with Mitchel who had a house there. I was on friendly relations with Mitchel. [Mitchel and O'Brien, as leaders of the "Young Ireland Rebellion," had been banished from Great Britain in the 'forties. Mitchel edited by turns several papers in this country, and during the war, the Richmond *Enquirer,* reputed organ of the Confederate administration.] At his invitation, I called to see O'Brien and was well pleased with this far-famed "patriot and rebel." His bearing, as well as his high intelligence and virtue, could not fail to impress any one coming in contact with him. I assumed the discharge of the office, very agreeable to myself, of introducing him to President Buchanan; Mr. Mitchel accompanied us. As we were returning to our carriage, speaking of Mitchel in his presence to O'Brien, I said that Mitchel's greatest difficulty lay in extravagance of feeling and expression; that he seemed to forget that there were three degrees of comparison in language; he dealt almost exclusively in superlatives.

O'Brien nodded assent with a smile, while Mitchel did not seem to dissent from the justness of the criticism. Afterward, while O'Brien was on a visit to me at Liberty Hall, on his tour through the South, Mitchel was often the subject of our conversation. O'Brien, it was evident, was devotedly attached to him personally, while deeply regretting some of his eccentricities and extravagances. I am truly sorry for Mitchel. He did a great deal in bringing on the war. He has suffered severely for it. A son of his, of great promise, bearing, I think, his father's name, fell in defending Fort Sumter. The father seems, by nature, one of those restless spirits born to stir up strife, and to become the sport, football, and victim of adverse fortunes.

I get no letters; hear nothing from my application to the President, see no allusion to it in any of the papers. It must have reached Washington before this, but perhaps it is filed away in some pigeon-hole to be taken up in its turn, which may not be for weeks or months. Who in that busy crowd cares for me? A man in prison is soon forgot, almost as completely as if he were in his grave. With the great active living mass, in their pursuits of business or pleasure, or borne down with their own afflictions, the world moves on as before. The daily papers are sought by the merchant, the banker, the ship-owner, the politician, and the devotee of fashion, to see the state of the markets, the prices of stocks, the arrivals and departures of all sorts of water-craft, the progress of reconstruction, the new concerts and other amusements, marriages, and deaths, and what not. But who in all this turmoil thinks of me? A brother, a few relatives and friends and faithful domestics and, perhaps, three devoted dogs, are, in creation's range, the only beings that think once of me in a week or a month. Read Jeremiah. I can exclaim with him:

> Oh that my head were waters, and mine eyes a fountain of tears, that I might weep for the slain of the daughter of my people!

I turn to Job; my Bible opened at this:

> If I did despise the cause of my manservant or of my maidservant, when they contended with me; If I have withheld the poor from their desire, or have caused the eyes of the widow to fail; Or have eaten my morsel myself alone, and the fatherless hath not eaten thereof; If I have seen any perish for want of clothing, or any poor without covering; If his loins have not blessed me and if he were not warmed with the flece of my sheep; If I have lifted up my hand against the fatherless, when I saw my help in the gate: Then let mine arm fall from my shoulder-blade, and mine arm be broken from the bone. If I rejoiced at the destruction of him that hated me, or lifted up myself when evil found him: Neither have I suffered my mouth to sin by wishing a curse to his soul. The stranger did not lodge in the street: but I opened my doors to the traveller.

Most truly can I repeat this, if I know myself. When has suffering humanity appealed to me for assistance or redress that was not rendered if in my power? When have the poor, even the unfortunate blacks, driven from their abodes in winter cold and snow, appealed to me that they did not receive food and shelter? When has the voice of distress, from high or low, ever reached my ears unheard or unrelieved, if relief was in my power? I do feel that I have laboured more during my feeble, suffering life for the comfort and happiness of others than for my own.

I have aided between thirty and forty young men, poor and indigent or without present means, to get an education; the number I do not exactly recollect. Many of these I took through a regular collegiate course, or offered them the means for such a course. My assistance of this character has not been confined to young men; orphan and indigent girls have received liberally of my bounty. I have spent many thousands of dollars for the accommodation and comfort of those recognized as my slaves by our law, over and above all returns they ever made to me. This was of my own earnings. I commenced life without a cent; indeed I was in debt for my own education: as I had been assisted when in need, so I ever afterward assisted those in like circumstances, as far as I could. In all my troubles and trials, and they have not been few or small, I never cherished malice against those from whom I had received wrong. Never did I "rejoice at the destruction of him that hated me or lifted up myself when evil found him."

Finished "Ferdinand and Isabella." Whether the great heroine and heroes are not glossed over too much by glowing rhetoric, giving the work somewhat the character of a romance, may be suspected. And whether the benefits of the consolidation of the separate kingdoms of Spain into one government, which is a leading idea, are not over estimated, may be more than suspected. Many evils, to which Prescott alludes as following the consolidation, may be traced to it. Whether the conquest of Granada, Navarre, and Naples, and the consolidation of the Spanish Empire which enabled it to assume such grandeur amongst the powers of Europe at the close of Ferdinand's life, contributed anything to the real happiness of the people of Aragon and Castile may be more than questioned. It certainly resulted in the loss of many of their liberties, and it is difficult to see how it added to their progress in civilization and refinement. Might not those anterior causes, which prompted such heroic exertions and grand exhibitions of virtue in the reign of Ferdinand and Isabella, have led to far higher results under different guidance, results which would not have been attended, and almost necessarily, with the consequences that ensued under the reign of Charles V., and which ultimately ended in the present state of things in Spain?

Prescott pays too little attention to the old constitutions of Castile and Aragon, particularly the latter. The most important principle of this constitution which had lasted for nearly two centuries, required unanimity in both branches of the Cortes, as well as the sanction of the crown, to give validity to any legislative act. Any member of either branch by simply interposing his veto could arrest action, a very remarkable fact. The workings of any system established on such a principle deserve thorough consideration. Prescott passes over it with little more than incidental mention. Yet under this system, Aragon had risen from almost barbarism to that high state of culture, civilization, and liberty which had produced a Mena, Villena, and Santil-lanna, literary lights not supassed by any in Spain since their day. In that state of vigorous development in all that ennobles nations and peoples, Ferdinand found her when her future became subject to his influence as her sovereign according to the well-settled principles of this time-honoured constitution. Had he more carefully studied and conformed to its principles, looking more to internal policy than external acquisition, how vastly different might be the condition of things in Spain to-day! The world needs full exposition of the workings of these ancient systems of Aragon and Castile, these early germs of representative government in Spain. Whatever else the reign of Ferdinand and Isabella did, it led to the overthrow of these systems of liberty and to the establishment of despotism in their stead. Had the Cortes been consulted, as it ought to have been under the old constitution, who can believe that Torquemada could ever have introduced the Inquisition into Castile? And how much more difficult and even impossible would it have been for this most iniquitous institution to get a foothold in Aragon if unanimity in each branch of the Cortes had been necessary.

I see in the New York *Times* a short notice referring to the nature of my confinement, state of health, etc. I am weary in spirit and sick at heart waiting for letters from home. I begin to fear the officers do not transmit my letters with much dispatch. I should certainly have heard from Mr. Hill at Washington City. [Joshua Hill, of Georgia; Member of Congress, 1857-61; Unionist throughout the war; U.S. Senator, 1868-73.] I cannot believe he would be neglectful or remiss in writing to me. Why has not Mr. Baskerville answered my letter? Why have not I received some reply from the President? These things set heavily upon me.

Read Prescott's "Conquest of Mexico," until Geary brought evening paper. I see a telegram from Washington in reference to my application. It has me intimating, as a reason for acceding to secession, a belief that there would be no war. I did no such thing, and intended no such thing. My opinion from the beginning was that there would be war and a bloody war.

Walked out with Lieut. W. The warmest evening yet on the parapet. Geary brought tea.

Sunday—Rose at seven. Read Psalms; this came in order:

By the rivers of Babylon, there we sat down; yea, we wept, when we remembered Zion. We hanged our harps upon the willows in the midst thereof. For there they that carried us away captive required of us a song; and they that wasted us required of us mirth, saying, "Sing us one of the songs of Zion." How shall we sing the Lord's song in a strange land? If I forget thee, O Jerusalem, let my right hand forget her cunning. If I do not remember thee, let my tongue cleave to the roof of my mouth; if I prefer not Jerusalem above my chief joy.

With "Georgia" for "Zion" and "Jerusalem," these words might be the outpourings of my own heart. I remembered Georgia in her desolation; thought of home, its sweet endearments, of my brother and his little ones.

In the Boston *Herald*, I see that James Johnson, of Columbus, has been appointed Provisional Governor of Georgia. I know him well. He was my classmate in college, and contested the highest distinction with me. No honours were awarded by the faculty: but Johnson, William Crawford (son of the once-candidate for President of the United States) and myself were selected to deliver three orations: salutatory in Latin to the audience, trustees, and faculty; valedictory to the same and the class; and a philosophical oration to the audience. "Salutatory," "Valedictory," "Philosophical Oration" were written on separate slips of paper and put in a hat held by Dr. Church; he called Crawford who stepped forward and drew "Valedictory"; Johnson drew "Oration." Of course, "Salutatory" was left to me. The faculty allowed me to make also an address in English to the audience. The valedictory by college usage was always assigned as first honour, the Latin salutatory as second, and the philosophical oration as third; but as the faculty were prohibited from conferring honours, they fell upon this expedient of arranging for Commencement. Had honours been assigned according to roll of merit or class standing, the first would have been mine. Johnson and Crawford, I think, stood equal, two marks only below me. Johnson, like myself, was poor. He taught school, raised means thus, and was admitted to the bar. He is, by nature, of vigorous mind, adapted to the law. He rose rapidly at the bar, and has long stood amongst the best in his section of the State; has had little to do with politics, was generally on the unpopular side of agitating questions; was elected to Congress once and served out his term with distinction, but had no inclination to return, or at least, did not return. His election was during the excitement over the settlement of 1850; he was a strong Union man and was elected on that issue; he has remained in retirement since, pursuing his profession. He was a strong Union man in 1860, but when the storm of secession lowered and no man could advocate the Union without subjecting himself to sneers and insults if nothing worse, he gave in and went with the crowd, as I was informed; even made a speech in favour of secession and voted a secession ticket. I have but little doubt that that speech and vote were against his better judgment. His greatest defect is want of firmness and decision; so great is it that it may be said to amount to timidity. He is a man, however, of strong sense and good principles. How he will succeed as Executive in restoring order and bringing Georgia into the Union at this trying time and on this trying basis is to be seen. He has my best wishes, personally and officially, but I envy him not his task. We have always been friends. There was at college a little estrangement but it was soon over. In politics, we have differed at times, but this never interfered with our personal relations. He was brought up a Clarke man, while I was brought up a Troup man. [The party divisions, Clarke and Troup, took their names form the Governors—Clarke (1819-23), and Troup (1823-27), the "Great States Rights Governor."] When Nullification became the issue, he went with that faction of the Clarke party which espoused this doctrine, while I went with that portion of the Troup party, led by Troup and Crawford, which repudiated Nullification but stood on the doctrine of States Rights as proclaimed in Milledgeville, Nov. 13, 1833. Johnson went for Van Buren and I for Harrison in 1840. In 1850 we both went for the Union. In 1855 he went with the American Party while on the issues of that day I was with the Democratic. In 1860 I sustained Douglas while, I think, he was for Bell, though he sympathized with the friends of Douglas and would gladly have seen him elected. I am not sure that he gave the secession speech and vote as above stated, but such were the current rumours, and I never heard them denied.

Walked out with Lieut. W. Saw ships going out to sea, and one beautiful steamboat moving toward the summer resort at Hull.

June 19.—Read Psalms. Newly impressed with this: "The fear of the Lord is the beginning of wisdom, a good understanding have all they that do His commandments." It recalled to my mind the words of Solomon that my father, when I was a small boy, often repeated to me and made me repeat to him: "Fear God and keep His commandments: for this is the whole duty of man."

8.15—Breakfast. All good; coffee not quite as good as usual, being not quite so hot; still, far above the average standard furnished in the best hotels that I was ever at. The coffee here is of most excellent quality. Coffee is one of three things of which I have long considered myself a judge; the other two are lizards and watches. I do not mean to say these are the only things I think myself capable of forming correct opinion upon; but they are three that I do claim, especially, to be a good judge of.

Read "Conquest of Mexico" until Geary, ever punctual, brought daily papers. Confirmation of yesterday's despatch about my application; and what purports to be an official report of the death of Federal prisoners at Andersonville, Georgia, during 1864. Upon this subject—treatment by Confederates of Federals in prison at Andersonville and other places and the great mortality amongst them—this remark may not be inappropriate: Their sufferings, and what is called the inhumanity of their treatment, were in great measure an unavoidable necessity. Confederates had not means to make their prisoners comfortable or to furnish suitable diet; they were pressed for their own subsistence; many of the necessaries of life, to say nothing of luxuries, were cut off from the soldiers and the body of the people; they were themselves subject to privations from which many not only suffered, but contracted disease and died; soldiers in the field were often on very short rations and of a very unwholesome quality. My nephew, Wm. A. Greer, of the Fourth Georgia Regulars, wrote me last winter from near Petersburg, Virginia, that he had had nothing to eat for twenty-four hours but two small biscuits. He was writing at night, and said he did not know when the troops would get any rations; he had eaten nothing but the biscuit since the morning before, and was sick from hunger. His was not a single instance. From every quarter, news reached me of the suffering of our soldiers for food.

At Andersonville, there were crowded together on a small piece of ground, enclosed by a stockade, upward of 30,000 prisoners. The space occupied by this large number was, I believe, about ten acres; in this small compass this large body of men had to live, exposed to sun, rain, and all sorts of weather. What could be expected, even with an abundance of substantial food, but disease and death to great numbers? But whose fault was this? Was it entirely chargeable to Confederate authorities? The Confederates were ever anxious to exchange prisoners of war. This, the Federals refused to do. The Confederates could not separate their prisoners, or provide a number of places so as to have fewer men crowded together. They had not the means. They had not men to spare to build prisons or stockades in which to secure their many prisoners. Nor had they sufficient force in the field to spare men from it for guard duty even if they had been provided with proper places in plenty for the safe confinement of prisoners. The Federals were well advised of the conditions. May not the suffering, disease, and death of thousands who fell victims in these miserable places be, in part, charged to the conduct of their own Government which they had served so well and in whose cause they so mournfully and pitifully fell?

When I heard of the conditions at Andersonville, my feelings were excited to the highest degree of commiseration—just as much as when the sufferings of the Confederates captured in Arkansas were detailed to me by some one who had passed, still living, but shattered forever in health, through the dread ordeal which was their lamentable lot. When I was satisfied of the inability of the Confederate Government to provide for its prisoners as humanity required, I wished them all (or at least all in such places as Andersonville) to be released and sent home on parole. My policy was for Mr. Davis to address them, setting forth the cause for which we were contending, the great principle of States Rights and Self-Government for which their ancestors had pledged life and honour in 1776; and that we viewed this war, waged against us with such fearful odds on their side, as altogether wrong, aggressive, and utterly at conflict with these great fundamental principles of American constitutional liberty; that though the fortune of battle had placed them in our hands; though their own officials refused such exchange as was usual in civilized warfare; yet, as we could not supply them with such quarters or food as humanity dictated, we, with that magnanimity which ever characterizes those who take up arms nerved with a full sense of the justice of their cause, released them on their parole of honour not to engage further in the struggle until duly exchanged. To this policy, objection was made that it was necessary to hold these prisoners as hostages for our own men in prison, who, if we dismissed them, would be killed. Confederates escaping from Camp Chase and other Northern prisons represented their treatment in these places to be as bad as any now described in exaggerated statements going the rounds about barbarities at Anderson-ville, Salisbury, Belle Isle, and Libby. There were barbarities, no doubt, and atrocities on both sides horrible enough, if brought to light, to unnerve the stoutest heart and to cause the most cruel and vindictive to sigh over human depravity. War is at best a savage business. Yea, it is worse; it transforms the noblest work of God, His image, into a devil incarnate. All the outrages on humanity, the cruelties, the vile exhibitions of the most malignant passions that have attended this late lamentable war, are not confined to our side. Even the asserted project for firing cities, poisoning reservoirs of water, and assassination, hellish as they are, have actual, not merely asserted, counterparts in the depopulation of Atlanta, the sacking and burning of Columbia, and the daring though unsuccessful attempt of Dahlgren on Richmond, in which general robbery, arson, and the assassination of Davis and his Cabinet were said to be combined objects. If the Confederates, or any of them, were demons, certainly all of the Federals were not angels.

Dinner: The first snap-beans I have seen this season; the potatoes were new; these and the beets carried my mind back home. I thought of Harry's garden and what a plentiful crop of all these things he must have had long before now. I ate sparingly and still thinking of scenes about Liberty Hall, and of Harry, I finished with a drink from the bottle of whisky he put in my trunk just before I took my last departure from my own room in my own dearly beloved home.

June 20.—At every reading of Scripture I find something fitting my condition. This morning: "How long will thou forget me, O Lord? Forever? How long shall mine enemy be exalted over me?"

SCENE IN PRISONER'S ROOM, 19TH OF JUNE

Prisoner intensely interested in a great battle by Cortes, as described by Prescott, with Cortes in the hottest of the fight, when the bugle-blast sounded notice that all lights must be put out. Instantly, prisoner blew out his candle, leaving himself in darkness and in perfect bewilderment as to the result of the battle. He paced his room. Over what regions of time and space did not his thoughts wander? Their flights no walls or bars or bolts could restrain! The treasured meerschaum, gift of Camille E. Girardey, of Augusta, lay upon the table. He picks it up, fills it with some of the weed he brought from home; holds the small end of the poker in the fire until it becomes red, then applies it to the weed. This expedient after the candle is out is usual; he can not resort to match or paper without violating orders, and what might be the consequences of such indiscretion, even in the small matter of lighting a pipe, he does not know. He feels himself subject to rules neither definite nor prescribed. He paces on, indulging his roaming thoughts. On, time also moves. He goes to the wall where hangs his watch; the crystal being broken, he can not wear it in his fob; takes it down, and by the glare from the full grate of anthracite coal all aglow, he sees with the aid of his glasses that an hour has rolled around since he dropped his book and put out his candle. Still not wearied, he lays his meerschaum on the table, and resumes his walk.

He goes to one of his windows facing southeast and looks out upon the heavens. The sky is clear, the stars shine brightly. Prisoner gazes upon them as upon old acquaintances; theirs are the only familiar faces, save the sun's and moon's, that he has seen for many days. His heart is somewhat comforted as he watches the heavenly hosts move on in their far-off nightly courses, just as when he watched them from his own front porch at home. Home, and that porch with its two settees! a thousand thoughts and images of the past rush upon him. There, so many pleasant starlit summer nights have been spent. The refreshing, cooling southern winds seldom failed there. There, the silvery sheen of moonlight on the grass was chequered with the deep shade of cedar, oak, hickory, and other trees. In his mind, as he stood by his prison window, not only images of inanimate things arose, but the well-known forms of persons beloved and dear; among these Linton's.

All around was still; nothing to be seen without save dark outlines of the granite wall; above, the bright luminaries twinkling and sparkling in the high, bending arch of the heavens. Nothing was to be heard save the heavy tread of the guard in his solitary beat on the stone pavement. Prisoner turned and resumed his rounds; on, on, he walks while his thoughts still roam afar. Again, he consults his watch and sees that another hour has passed. He sets the blower as a screen before his grate so as to shut off the heat, takes the end of his bunk and turns it so as to make the length range as nearly north and south as he can guess (this has been done by him ever since he has been here); then spreads before his chair, a newspaper (New York *Herald* as it chanced to be), four mats double on the stone floor, as is his custom, thus making a mat for his feet; he undresses and stretches himself on his bunk. Here, with soul devout, he endeavours through prayer to put himself in communion with God. To the Eternal, Prisoner in weakness and with full consciousness of his own frailty, commits himself, saying from the heart, "Thy will and not mine be done." With thoughts embracing the well-being of absent dear ones and all the world of mankind besides, wither friend or foe, he sinks into that sweet and long sleep from which he arose this morning.

I see in the papers that Erskine, of Atlanta, will probably be District Judge of the State; a good appointment. See several allusions to myself. No two agree, and not one except that in the Boston *Post* is true, and that may not be. It states that my voluminous document has been committed to Secretary Seward for his examination and report.

Took up the last volume of "Conquest of Mexico." But first and foremost, took a seat on my bunk and, with penknife in hand, went deliberately to work and cut all the leaves so as to have an open field for reading. Uncut leaves impede my progress in reading. Why any publisher should send forth a book with the leaves uncut, I cannot imagine. But so it is; they do it greatly to the annoyance of the reader. After getting through with this work, I resumed the narrative with as much eager interest as I ever felt in a novel.

Dinner was not brought until 3.30. All cold; seemed to be scraps. This all grew out of Geary's absence. The orderly substituting him, Massury, said Geary was gone to town. I asked no further questions; I concluded that in Geary's absence I had been forgotten temporarily, and that such fragments of dinner, some time over, as could be gathered together, were sent me. An incident occurred under my observation just before this dinner was brought, which I should like to mention here, but as these entries may fall into other hands than those for whom intended, and as my motives in mentioning it might be misconstrued, I think proper to let it pass without record.

6.15—Walked out with Lieut. W. He told me he had sent off all prisoners from this place, except 33 including Reagan and myself. DuBose and Jackson are still here. All here have applied for amnesty.

Massury brought the cup of tea with dry toast, sweet cakes, and strawberries. I miss Geary, however.

June 21.—The little incident and some other matters, all small but seemingly cognate to it, or something else kept me from sleeping much. I was awake nearly all night, my mind dwelling on the little incident, or the combination of incidents. I may hereafter feel free to give an explanation; but, at present, can say no more. I miss Geary. My slop bucket was not emptied and no fresh water was brought this morning. I made out the best I could, humming my usual unmusical chant. Read in Jeremiah and Psalms.

Finished "Conquest of Mexico." Nothing else I have read, purporting to be history, has struck me as being so marvellous. Few of the wildest romances are more wonderful than Cortes's life.

Lieut. Woodman called to let me know he was going up to Boston; I had requested him to give me notice; I wished him to take my watch and have the broken crystal replaced. I asked him to get me an almanac. This is the 21st of June, the summer solstice. To-day, the great Monarch of the Seasons stops his northward march. This is the day predicted by Mr. Davis in his speech at Richmond, on the report of the Commissioners from Hampton Roads Conference, as that by which the authorities at Washington would be suing those at Richmond for peace on their own terms as their masters. Instead, alas! our cause has collapsed, our Government is dispersed, our armies disbanded; members of the Cabinet and of the higher grades of generals are under arrest, while Mr. Davis lies in a dungeon, manacled, perhaps awaiting trial for treason. His condition awakens my deepest sympathy and commiseration. But when he made that speech in Richmond, brilliant though it was, I looked upon it as not much short of dementation. I then thought that, unless his policy was speedily and rapidly, changed by the summer solstice there would hardly be a vestige of the Confederacy left. I felt assured that there would be no change in his policy. I am, with him and thousands of others, a victim of the wreck.

The solstice is upon us. But as the sun this day stops his progress North, and turns Southward in his course, may it not be hoped that there will be some corresponding turn of fortune toward the States of the South? May it not be hoped that they have reached the solstice of their desolation, ruin, and woe? May it not be hoped that Mr. Davis has reached the solstice of his own troubles, grief, sufferings, and anguish, and that henceforth, brighter prospects may open up even for him as well as for all the rest of us?

Massury brought daily papers. Hon. H. C. Burnett was arrested yesterday at Willard's Hotel in Washington. He was Senator in the United States Congress from

Kentucky; remained there until after the Bull Run fight, July 1861; then left Washington, and later represented Kentucky in the Confederate Senate. I suppose he will in due time be pardoned and released. According to Washington letters, applications for pardon pour in like a flood from all quarters of the South. Too many entirely for careful disposition by detail. I think it would be well for the President to dispose of them in lump somehow. When the good Catholic father Ximenes, Archbishop of Toledo, found it impossible to administer baptism singly to thousands of applicants (rushing almost *en masse* for it upon the conversion of the Moors as effected by the conquest of Granada), he fell upon the expedient of using a mop, by which means water was rapidly sprinkled with a few twirls of the hand over the vast multitude, constituting no inconsiderable portion of a once mighty nation. Now, in this matter of the absolution or purification of the South, I think it would be well to adopt some means like unto the good old father's mop, some short method of accomplishing the object wholesale. A general and universal amnesty should be proclaimed. In the *Times* I see Hon. Reverdy Johnson's argument against the constitutionality of the Military Commission now sitting on trial of the conspirators in the assassination; the argument is long; I have laid it away for perusal.

I got very hungry before dinner was brought. Hunger is unusual with me here. I seldom think of dinner until it appears. To-day I concluded that the hour had passed, and that the new orderly was neglecting me again. My watch was gone and I could not even guess the time, for the sun had passed out of range of my window: I could see no shadow by which to judge. I decided to call up Massury. So I went to the window, where the guard is always walking to and fro, night and day, with musket and bayonet. I said, "Guard, I wish to see the orderly." The guard instantly cried out, "Corporal of the Guard! Post Number 24!" Presently he reported through the window that the corporal was at the Adjutant's office, and would be here directly. I threw myself on the bunk to wait patiently. After awhile, the corporal made his appearance at the same place with the inquiry, "What is wanting?" I told him I wanted the orderly. Presently, Massury appeared, not at the window but in the door, which he had unlocked. I asked, "What time is it?" He said, "Twenty minutes to three." I asked, "When will you bring dinner?" He replied "I was going after it at three, but will go now, if you wish it." I said, "I wish you would; I am hungry; but bring some cool fresh water first, if you please." He brought me water; had got it out of some standing vessel; it was not cool as that Geary brings. He then brought dinner: all cold, which caused me to think my suspicions as to time correct. But cold as it was, hunger gave sauce to it. I ate heartily, and finished with a drink from Harry's bottle. I wish Geary would come back. I miss him very much. He begins to look and feel to me like homefolks. He attends to me diligently and promptly. Massury says he expects Geary to-night.

I see by the Boston *Journal* that it is telegraphed from Washington to-day that General Lee and myself, according to report, are to be pardoned on condition of leaving the country. I shall never accept pardon on such conditions. Georgia is my country; within her limits I shall live, and at the old homestead I shall be buried. In no event will I ever by election become an exile from Georgia. Whether in prison or by the hands of the executioner, I prefer to die where some kind friends may take charge of and deposit my earthly remains in Georgia.

5.30—Lieut. W. brought my watch with new crystal. No charge. The workman, he said, on being informed whose watch it was, would make none. I feel truly obliged to this unknown friend. A shower postponed my evening walk. Geary returned at six. Very glad to see him.

6.30—Shower ceased. Lieut. W. came for walk. We went on the terreplein, but it was too wet; went up on parapet; but the grass, which is heavy set on it, was too wet. We stood on the bastion and enjoyed the fine southern breeze. Looked over the harbour and saw several showers passing around us. Boston was immersed in one, and the rays of the sinking sun, beyond the city and coming through the falling rain, not thick enough to shut them out, gave a beautiful appearance to glistening domes and steeples. We saw Confederate prisoners on the bastion nearest that on which we stood. One, Lieut. W. said, was Jackson. I could not recognize him. DuBose was not among them. Lieut. W. told me that a gentleman, named Nourse, in Boston, told him to tell me, if I wanted clothing, money, or anything else, to call on him and he would let me have it. I asked the Lieutenant to return my thanks and say that I stood in need of nothing yet; if I were kept here long, I might require assistance; at present, was getting along comfortably. We came down without having walked much; I took three or four turns on the stone pavement and then came in. Geary brought my tea, toast, and sweet cakes. He had also brought sea-water for my bath in the morning. I found my room neatly done up.

While on the bastion, I saw a row of men, about twenty, walking, two together. They were moving from the entrance to the inside of the fort and toward some underground apartments formed by a sort of mound near the water's edge. I asked if these were soldiers going to their quarters for the night. They looked dejected as they walked along. "No," said the Lieutenant. "They are the chain-gang, the criminals, deserters, etc. They are made to work on the fort. They are going to their quarters for the night." I felt sorry for the poor fellows, and thought of Jean Valjean.

June 22.—I barely got through Bible reading when breakfast was brought in by Geary; everything good. An incident took me back to Georgia. Geary in cleaning up yesterday carrried away all cups and saucers. His usual plan is to bring coffee hot in some vessel and pour it into a cup kept here; he washes this cup in the adjoining orderly and corporal's room, as it seems to be. Cups and saucers had accumulated; these he took back to the sutler's. When coffee was to be poured this morning, there was no cup. It was too far to the sutler's, so he served it in a tumbler. I found I could not drink it, good as it was. Then recurred to me a remark made last winter by Mrs. Lou Stevens that she couldn't drink tea out of anything but china. The philosophy I cannot explain, but the fact is, I could not drink coffee out of glass. I took it from a cream pot. I have long known that water drinks better out of a gourd than out of tin, and out of glass than earthenware. But why coffee should reverse this and taste better earthenware than glass, I do not understand. Perhaps it is nothing but association of the same sort that makes hock wines taste better in greenish glasses and claret in reddish or brownish ones; while the clear crystal ones seem best for sherry and Madeira. This trifling incident brought in its train many memories of home.

In the *Tribune*, an item in reference to myself contains more truth than many other notices not half so long. It has some truth in it. My singing I do not think so good as one might believe on reading this account. Then, I think, I am free from anything like "a proud and haughty air." There is nothing of that in my nature or bearing. I have ever endeavoured to be correct and courteous to all, superiors as well as inferiors; neither sycophantic to the one class nor haughty toward the other. The bearing, which springs from the principle of doing to others as I would have them under like circumstances do to me, and which in my estimation is the stamp of true gentility, or the mark of the true gentleman, has ever been my standard, and I hope has characterized my intercourse with mankind.

I see Hidell has reached Nashville and taken the amnesty oath. I am glad to hear even indirectly from him. See that Breckinridge and party reached Cuba. What has become of Benjamin? Trenholm, I see, is at Hilton Head under arrest to be sent to Fortress Monroe. Cobb, it is stated, is still in Macon. Crops, the report from Augusta says, are good in that part of the State. I hope this is true, and that the same good condition extends up to my place. See account of a horrible accident below Shreveport to a steamboat loaded with paroled Confederate prisoners. The boat snagged, sunk, and over two hundred lives were lost. Mrs. Seward died yesterday in Washington. This I regret, not only from sympathy with Mr. Seward in such a severe affliction, but from fear that it will delay action on my application, which, as the papers report, was submitted to him. General Dix has been ordered to Montreal on business. His absence from New York may delay letters for me.

I dreamed of Judge James Thomas last night. Linton and several others figured; Linton only incidently. I did not see him; knew he was present. The scene was his house. Strange I have had no dream about himself since I saw him; none in which he has distinctly figured; and yet he has occupied more of my waking thoughts than all other persons besides. It is four weeks to-day since my imprisonment here. It seems to me, if I had then known that I should not hear from Linton or home before this time, I should have been crushed. And how I would now feel but for the few lines received from Mr. Myers, affording such indirect information as they did, I do not know. That little missive, that short letter, gave me great relief, and the more from hope created that it was pioneer of others soon to follow from those on whom my thoughts were most intent. But "hope deferred maketh the heart sick." Sometimes I have apprehensions that friends at home are keeping from me news they think would cause me distress. How long, O how long, shall I be doomed to this suspense?

SOMEWHAT OF A FANCY SKETCH AND YET NOT ALTOGETHER FANCY:

[Cell at Fort Warren. Alexander H. Stephens, *prisoner.* R. M. Johnston, *visitant* through window of imagination.]

Visitant. Well, what do you think of public affairs now? Only what you have told me for the last four or five years? Has the "pessimus" point not yet been reached?

Prisoner. Hardly, or as Jenkins says in one of his decisions, "Scarcely. No, not yet." [Charles J. Jenkins, Judge of Supreme Court of Georgia.] Things are truly in evil state; still they may get worse before they get better; and wise men, while hoping for better, should be prepared for worse. Over two years ago, William F. Fluker asked me if I didn't think the darkest hour of our troubles upon us, that hour which precedes light and cheer. I told him, No, that so far from having reached the darkest hour—the hour before the dawn—we were not even in the night of the war, the sun was not gone down. Last year, after Atlanta fell, he asked if I did not think the darkest hour had come. I told him the sun had set; we were in the night of our woes, but far from the midnight. "Well," asked he, "what is to become of us?" I said, it was a painful reflection to me that our people were so unconscious of their pending doom, of the great desolation coming upon them before their darkest hour would be passed, and before that dawn of better times for which all were so anxiously looking, would greet their eyes. I am not prepared to say that our people have reached their darkest hour.

Visitant. Why, what can be worse? The States are subjugated, their governments overthrown, their whole social system and internal policy uprooted and demolished, and most of their public men in prison, as you are, or in exile. How can matters be worse?

Prisoner. In many ways: internal strife, insurrection, and wars between races, ending in the extermination of one of the two now constituting the South's population, would make conditions, bad as they are, infinitely worse.

Visitant. What, in your opinion, is to be the remedy or end?

Prisoner. It is one thing to see threatening evils and a different one to prescribe measures for ending them, or to prejudge the extent to which they may go.

You may remember what I said to Bishop Elliott last year when we dined with him at Mr. Stanard's. [Stephen Elliott, first Protestant Episcopal Bishop of Georgia.] I told him that in my judgment abolition was the moving spirit of the war in the North; I did not think the war, end when or how it might, would leave slavery as it found it; while I looked on the institution recognized amongst us by our laws (which, so far as the spirit of the law was concerned, was only subordination of an inferior to a superior race) as sanctioned by God, yet I thought great wrongs had been perpetrated under it; as with all human institutions in accordance with the sanction of the Creator, there were reciprocal duties and obligations; when these were faithfully performed on both sides, reciprocal and mutual benefits were the results: in our system, the superior race had looked too much to the benefits received from the relation, and too little to its obligations to the inferior, and the benefits to which that inferior was entitled; the moral and intellectual culture of the inferior race, to which it was entitled to the extent of its capacity and condition, had been greatly neglected: the Negro had been made to perform his part of the obligation while the white man had failed to fully perform his: this was, in my judgment, one of the great sins for which our people were brought to trial. The status of the Negro would not be left by war where war found it. But if the principles of President Lincoln's Emancipation Proclamation—the ultimate policy therein indicated of attempting to establish perfect political and social equality between the races—should be carried out to its final results, it would end in the extermination or the driving from the country of one or the other of the races. That policy, I regarded as against nature, against the ordinances of God; it never could be practically worked. This and much more on the same line I said to the bishop at that time; I repeat the views then expressed.

Stephen Elliott, first Protestant Episcopal Bishop of Georgia.

If the principles of the Radicals, who are determined on the levelling system of making the black man in the South equal politically and socially to the white, are to be carried out, I see no end to it all but the ultimate extermination of one or the other of the races, so unfortunately, to both in this view, interspersed with each other. Will events take this course? I cannot answer; that is why I cannot say whether we have reached the darkest hour in our troubles. There are other courses events might take which could possibly bring about a better state of things for both races than existed under our slave system, yet not better than might have been attained under it with wise and philanthropic legislation. The long night of darkness has no promising dawn as yet to my vision.

Visitant. I come to you for comfort as for four years past, but you give no more when war is over than when it began. How do you feel as to yourself? What will they do with you, do you suppose?

Prisoner. All opinions are speculative. I look on my present confinement as a great outrage. Six weeks ago to-day I was arrested at my own home and have been in custody ever since. For four, I have been in close confinement in this cell or dungeon or room, call it what you may, without any warrant or oath or any charge legally alleged against me. This is done by those who profess to be the guardians and defenders of the Constitution. Indeed, to add mockery and insult to wrong, if called on for the reason of their course toward me, I suppose they would declare that their object is to uphold the Constitution against an atrocious rebellion designed to overthrow it, with which I was connected. That is, they openly trample under foot the most sacred guarantees of the Constitution for the purpose of upholding it. What worse treason can there be in any free country than that which strikes a blow at the principles of its fundamental law? These constitute the life and soul of a free people. How any man can feel himself justified in violating my most sacred rights under the Constitution, if I am amenable to it, on the pretense of its being his sworn duty to support that Constitution, I cannot perceive. It is simply absurd and shameful! If, as alleged in the newspapers, I had violated the laws of the country, had desired to overthrow its Constitution; had committed an act of treason and had become connected with the most atrocious rebellion on earth; yet, I was quietly at my home; the charge could have been made and the arrest as prescribed by law, and I should have been entitled to all the rights of a speedy and public trial on presentment or indictment by a grand jury as set forth in that great charter of constitutional liberty which, it is said, I was endeavouring to upset and overthrow. But, instead, all these securities and rights thus guaranteed have been denied me, and by those who have the unblushing effrontry in this very denial to pretend that thereby they maintain the Constitution!

Visitant. The papers say you have applied for amnesty. Is that so?

Prisoner. Yes. I thought perhaps it was but proper for me to do so. My case was a peculiar one. The more I thought of it the more I was inclined to that view, and I finally wrote to the President, going fully into details, and asking amnesty if my case came within the purview of his tender; in case that were not granted, for release on parole until charges could legally be preferred, and if not this, then that my confinement be somewhat mitigated in rigour and restrictions. As to whether my letter shall be answered favourably in whole or in part, I have no idea. I try not to let myself dwell on the subject. I am anxious to have a reply one way or the other. If the response is entirely unfavourable, I shall ask speedy trial. Whether that will be granted, I don't know. There is nothing so depressing to me as the prospect of continued close confinement in this or any place, cut off virtually from free communication with home; cut off from all communication, free and full communication, I mean, with Linton, the light of my life. This is not much short of a living death.

Visitant. The papers say the President is going to pardon you on condition that you leave the country.

Prisoner. I will not accept pardon on those terms. I am willing to die if I cannot return to my home and be with Linton while our joint lives last. As for dreading trial for treason, or its consequences, I care but little. My conscience is void of offense toward God and man. I should feel no shame in being executed for anything I have done; and if I cannot be permitted to spend the balance of my days at home, with the dear ones there, on my farm, in my gardens, orchards, and vineyards, and amongst my books, then let me die, even on the gallows though it be. My greatest sufferings, for many years at least, have been since I came here. At first I was almost overwhelmed. They spring from being cut off from communication with Linton and the rest at a time above all others when I want to be with him and consult with him on public as well as private affairs. Exile would be but continuation of this. No, give me death in preference! let my last breath be of my own native air! My native land, my country, the only one that is country to me, is Georgia. The winds that sweep over her hills are my native air. There, I wish to live and there to die, and if I am not permitted to die there, I wish at least to die somewhere, whether in prison or on the gallows, within reach of some kind friends who may gather up my remains and commit them to that last resting-place which I have prepared for them in the walled enclosure at the old homestead.

Visitant. What do you think we all had better do in Georgia, take the oath or not?

Prisoner. Conform to the existing order, accept the issues of the war; take things as you find them, and do the best you can with them as they arise. There is nothing in the oath that any man ought to hesitate in swearing to now that the Confederacy has failed, except what relates to the Emancipation Proclamation and the laws of Congress on the subjects alluded to therein. [Oath of Allegiance to the United States, prescribed in Johnson's Amnesty Proclamation.] But these are the results of the war; conformity follows as a matter of course. Swearing conformity does not add to the obligation that most men would feel they had incurred in accepting the issues without the oath. Slavery is abolished. Let every good citizen abide by this fact. Let every one who has had slaves do the best he can with them, working to their future interest as well as to his own. Let every suggestion as to the best policy in regard to the relation hereafter to be maintained between the races be listened to, and the wisest and most judicious adopted. If one experiment fails, let another be tried, and let the future, with honest exertions on the part of all for the best, be left to take care of itself. In this way, "sufficient unto the day is the evil thereof." Let no evils be unnecessarily anticipated, but let all have firm faith in God that all things will work out right in the end, whether it be according to their liking or not.

Visitant. Have you as strong confidence as ever in Democratic institutions? Do not late events shake your old ideas?

Prisoner. Not in the least. I still have unshaken confidence in the people under the providence of God. They do not always do right. The late horrible war on both sides may be attributed to considerable extent to popular passions spurred to excess; but reaction will come sooner or later. I have strong hopes that, after this generation shall have passed away, if not before, a new order will arise, from which still further progress in civilization will be made and a still higher and grander career entered upon by the people of this continent. The people in their passion often vibrate from one extreme to another until they settle down at the right point. What will be the state of things in twenty-five years on questions now agitating the public mind and which have produced so much suffering, desolation, and ruin, no one can predict. If the people of the United States can be kept true to the principles of their Constitution, all will yet be well. That they will prove true when the passions of the times have passed away with this generation, I cannot permit myself to doubt. I retain my confidence and faith, unshaken and undiminished by anything that has happened yet, in the people and their capacity for self-government. I have never believed that progress and civilization can be affected by arms. Reason and Justice are the principles through which reformations are to be made and by which all real and true progress is to be effected. A worse ordeal than any they have experienced may be in store for this generation, and yet a grand future may await and award that generation coming after. What shall be the form of our resurrected society, we know not; but hope, sustained by reason, looks forward to one on a higher, better, and grander scale. To this end, at least, I look and hope—though my eyes shall never see it—provided the people—the white people, I mean—be always left to govern themselves and provided they do not surrender their power.

[Here, the *Visitant*, with countenance betokening deep thought, and without another word, vanished through the window.]

Took short walk, but was driven in by another shower. Lieut. W. gave the name of the gentleman who offered any assistance I might need in funds—Benjamin F. Nourse, of Boston; and of the man who put the crystal in my watch—Isaac H. Tower. I wish to remember both. Geary brought from the library a book I sent for—Cicero on the Gods, Fates, etc. Got another pound of candles; six in a pound. The first pound lasted four weeks; I have a piece long enough to burn to-night.

(1910)

BOOKER T. WASHINGTON

Up From Slavery:
An Autobiography

The Reconstruction Period

The years from 1867 to 1878 I think may be called the period of Reconstruction. This included the time that I spent as a student at Hampton and as a teacher in West Virginia. During the whole of the Reconstruction period two ideas were constantly agitating the minds of the coloured people, or, at least, the minds of a large part of the race. One of these was the craze for Greek and Latin learning, and the other was a desire to hold office.

It could not have been expected that a people who had spent generations in slavery, and before that generations in the darkest heathenism, could at first form any proper conception of what an education meant. In every part of the South, during the Reconstruction period, schools, both day and night, were filled to overflowing with people of all ages and conditions, some being as far along in age as sixty and seventy years. The ambition to secure an education was most praiseworthy and encouraging. The idea, however, was too prevalent that, as soon as one secured a little education, in some unexplainable way he would be free from most of the hardships of the world, and, at any rate, could live without manual labour. There was a further feeling that a knowledge, however little, of the Greek and Latin languages would make one a very superior human being, something bordering almost on the supernatural. I remember that the first coloured man whom I saw who knew something about foreign languages impressed me at that time as being a man of all others to be envied.

Naturally, most of our people who received some little education became teachers or preachers. While among these two classes there were many capable, earnest, godly men and women, still a large proportion took up teaching or preaching as an easy way to make a living. Many became teachers who could do little more than write their names. I remember there came into our neighborhood one of this class who was in search of a school to teach, and the question arose while he was there as to the shape of the earth and how he would teach the children concerning this subject. He explained his position in the matter by saying that he was prepared to teach that the earth was either flat or round, according to the preference of a majority of his patrons.

The ministry was the profession that suffered most—and still suffers, though there has been great improvement—on account of not only ignorant but in many cases immoral men who claimed that they were "called to preach." In the earlier days of freedom almost every coloured man who learned to read would receive "a call to preach" within a few days after he began reading. At my home in West Virginia the process of being called to the ministry was a very interesting one. Usually the "call" came when the individual was sitting in church. Without warning the one called would fall upon the floor as if struck by a bullet, and would lie there for hours, speechless and motionless. Then the news would spread all through the neighbourhood that this individual had received a "call." If he were inclined to resist the summons, he would fall or be made to fall a second or third time. In the end he always yielded to the call. While I wanted an education badly, I confess that in my youth I had a fear that when I had learned to read and write well I would receive one of these "calls"; but, for some reason, my call never came.

When we add the number of wholly ignorant men who preached or "exhorted" to that of those who possessed something of an education, it can be seen at a glance that the supply of ministers was large. In fact, some time ago I knew a certain church that had a total membership of about two hundred, and eighteen of that number were ministers. But, I repeat, in many communities in the South the character of the ministry is being improved, and I believe that within the next two or three decades a very large proportion of the unworthy ones will have disappeared. The "calls" to preach, I am glad to say, are not nearly so numerous now as they were formerly, and the calls to some industrial occupation are growing more numerous. The improvement that has taken place in the character of the teachers is even more marked than in the case of the ministers.

During the whole of the Reconstruction period our people throughout the South looked to the Federal Government for everything, very much as a child looks to its mother. This was not unnatural. The central government gave them freedom, and the whole Nation had been enriched for more than two centuries by the labour of the Negro. Even as a youth, and later in manhood, I had the feeling that it was cruelly wrong in the central government, at the beginning of our freedom, to fail to make some provision for the general education of our people in addition to what the states might do, so that the people would be the better prepared for the duties of citizenship.

It is easy to find fault, to remark what might have been done, and perhaps, after all, and under all the circumstances, those in charge of the conduct of affairs did the only thing that could be done at the time. Still, as I look back now over the entire period of our freedom, I cannot help feeling that it would have been wiser if some plan could have been put in operation which would have made the possession of a certain amount of education or property, or both, a test for the exercise of the franchise, and a way provided by which this test should be made to apply honestly and squarely to both the white and black races.

Though I was but little more than a youth during the period of Reconstruction, I had the feeling that mistakes were being made, and that things could not remain in the condition that they were in then very long. I felt that the Reconstruction policy, so far as it related to my race, was in a large measure on a false foundation, was artificial and forced. In many cases it seemed to me that the ignorance of my race was being used as a tool with which to help white men into office, and that there was an element in the North which wanted to punish the Southern white men by forcing the Negro into positions over the heads of the Southern whites. I felt that the Negro would be the one to suffer for this in the end. Besides, the general political agitation drew the attention of our people away from the more fundamental matters of perfecting themselves in the industries at their doors and in securing property.

The temptations to enter political life were so alluring that I came very near yielding to them at one time, but I was kept from doing so by the feeling that I would be helping in a more substantial way by assisting in the laying of the foundation of the race through a generous education of the hand, head, and heart. I saw coloured men who were members of the state legislatures, and county officers, who, in some cases, could not read or write, and whose morals were as weak as their education. Not long ago, when passing through the streets of a certain city in the South, I heard some brick-masons calling out, from the top of a two-story brick building on which they were working, for the "Governor" to "hurry up and bring up some more bricks." Several times I heard the command, "Hurry up, Governor!" "Hurry up, Governor!" My curiosity was aroused to such an extent that I made inquiry as to who the "Governor" was, and soon found that he was a coloured man who at one time had held the position of Lieutenant-Governor of his state.

But not all the coloured people who were in office during Reconstruction were unworthy of their positions, by any means. Some of them, like the late Senator B. K. Bruce, Governor Pinchback, and many others, were strong, upright, useful men. Neither were all the class designated as carpetbaggers dishonourable men. Some of them, like ex-Governor Bullock, of Georgia, were men of high character and usefulness.

Of course the coloured people, so largely without education, and wholly without experience in government, made tremendous mistakes, just as any people similarly situated would have done. Many of the Southern whites have a feeling that, if the Negro is permitted to exercise his political rights now to any degree, the mistakes of the Reconstruction period will repeat themselves. I do not think this would be true, because the Negro is a much stronger and wiser man than he was thirty-five years ago, and he is fast learning the lesson that he cannot afford to act in a manner that will alienate his Southern white neighbours from him. More and more I am convinced that the final solution of the political end of our race problem will be for each state that finds it necessary to change the law bearing upon the franchise to make the law apply with absolute honesty, and without opportunity for double dealing or evasion, to both races alike. Any other course, my daily observation in the South convinces me, will be unjust to the Negro, unjust to the white man, and unfair to the rest of the states in the Union, and will be, like slavery, a sin that at some time we shall have to pay for.

In the fall of 1878, after having taught school in Malden for two years, and after I had succeeded in preparing several of the young men and women, besides my two brothers, to enter the Hampton Institute, I decided to spend some months in study at Washington, D.C. I remained there for eight months. I derived a great deal of benefit from the studies which I pursued, and I came into contact with some strong men and women. At the institution I attended there was no industrial training given to the students, and I had an opportunity of comparing the influence of an institution with no industrial training with that of one like the Hampton Institute, that emphasized the industries. At this school I found the students, in most cases, had more money, were better dressed, wore the latest style of all manner of clothing, and in some cases were more brilliant mentally. At Hampton it was a standing rule that, while the institution would be responsible for securing some one to pay the tuition for the students, the men and women themselves must provide for their own board, books, clothing, and room wholly by work, or partly by work and partly in cash. At the institution at which I now was, I found that a large proportion of the students by some means had their personal expenses paid for them. At Hampton the student was constantly making the effort through the industries to help himself, and that very effort was of immense value in character-building. The students at the other school seemed to be less self-dependent. They seemed to give more attention to mere outward appearances. In a word, they did not appear to me to be beginning at the bottom, on a real, solid foundation, to the extent that they were at Hampton. They knew more about Latin and Greek when they left school, but they seemed to know less about life and its conditions as they would meet it at their homes. Having lived for a number of years in the midst of comfortable surroundings, they were not as much inclined as the Hampton students to go into the country districts of the South, where there was little of comfort, to take up work for our people, and they were more inclined to yield to the temptation to become hotel waiters and Pullman-car porters as their life-work.

During the time I was a student in Washington the city was crowded with coloured people, many of whom had recently come from the South. A large proportion of these people had been drawn to Washington because they felt that they could lead a life of ease there. Others had secured minor government positions, and still another large class was there in the hope of securing Federal positions. A number of coloured men—some of them very strong and brilliant—were in the House of Representatives at that time, and one, the Hon. B. K. Bruce, was in the Senate. All this tended to make Washington an attractive place for members of the coloured race. Then, too, they knew that at all times they could have the protection of the law in the District of Columbia. The public schools in Washington for coloured people were better then than they were elsewhere. I took great interest in studying the life of our people there closely at that time. I found that while among them there was a large element of substantial, worthy citizens, there was also a superficiality about the life of a large class that greatly alarmed me. I saw young coloured men who were not earning more than four dollars a week spend two dollars or more for a buggy on Sunday to ride up and down Pennsylvania Avenue in, in order that they might try to convince the world that they were worth thousands. I saw other young men who received seventy-five or one hundred dollars per month from the Government, who were in debt at the end of every month. I saw men who but a few months previous were members of Congress, then without employment and in poverty. Among a large class there seemed to be a dependence upon the Government for every conceivable thing. The members of this class had little ambition to create a position for themselves, but wanted the Federal officials to create one for them. How many times I wished then, and have often wished since, that by some power of magic I might remove the great bulk of these people into the country districts and plant them upon the soil, upon the solid and never deceptive foundation of Mother Nature, where all nations and races that have ever succeeded have gotten their start—a start that at first may be slow and toilsome, but one that nevertheless is real.

In Washington I saw girls whose mothers were earning their living by laundrying. These girls were taught by their mothers, in rather a crude way it is true, the industry of laundrying. Later, these girls entered the public schools and remained there perhaps six or eight years. When the public-school course was finally finished, they wanted more costly dresses, more costly hats and shoes. In a word, while their wants had been increased, their ability to supply their wants had not been increased in the same degree. On the other hand, their six or eight years of book education had weaned them away from the occupation of their mothers. The result of this was in too many cases that the girls went to the bad. I often thought how much wiser it would have been to give these girls the same amount of mental training—and I favour any kind of training, whether in the languages or mathematics, that gives strength and culture to the mind—but at the same time to give them the most thorough training in the latest and best methods of laundrying and other kindred occupations.

Black Race and Red Race

During the year that I spent in Washington, and for some little time before this, there had been considerable agitation in the state of West Virginia over the question of moving the capital of the state from Wheeling to some other central point. As a result of this, the Legislature designated three cities to be voted upon by the citizens of the state as the permanent seat of government. Among these cities was Charleston, only five miles from Malden, my home. At the close of my school year in Washington I was very pleasantly surprised to receive, from a committee of white people in Charleston, an invitation to canvass the state in the interests of that city. This invitation I accepted, and spent nearly three months in speaking in various parts of the state. Charleston was successful in winning the prize, and is now the permanent seat of government.

The reputation that I made as a speaker during this campaign induced a number of persons to make an earnest effort to get me to enter political life, but I refused, still believing that I could find other service which would prove of more permanent value to my race. Even then I had a strong feeling that what our people most needed was to get a foundation in education, industry, and property, and for this I felt that they could better afford to strive than for political preferment. As for my individual self, it appeared to me to be reasonably certain that I could succeed in political life, but I had a feeling that it would be a rather selfish kind of success—individual success at the cost of failing to do my duty in assisting in laying a foundation for the masses.

At this period in the progress of our race a very large proportion of the young men who went to school or to college did so with the expressed determination to prepare themselves to be great lawyers, or Congressmen, and many of the women planned to become music teachers; but I had a reasonably fixed idea, even at that early period in my life, that there was need for something to be done to prepare the way for successful lawyers, Congressmen, and music teachers.

I felt that the conditions were a good deal like those of an old coloured man, during the days of slavery, who wanted to learn how to play on the guitar. In his desire to take guitar lessons he applied to one of his young masters to teach him; but the young man, not having much faith in the ability of the slave to master the guitar at his age, sought to discourage him by telling him: "Uncle Jake, I will give you guitar lessons; but, Jake, I will have to charge you three dollars for the first lesson, two dollars for the second lesson, and one dollar for the third lesson. But I will charge you only twenty-five cents for the last lesson."

Uncle Jake answered: "All right, boss, I hires you on dem terms. But, boss! I wants yer to be sure an' give me dat las' lesson first."

Soon after my work in connection with the removal of the capital was finished, I received an invitation which gave me great joy and which at the same time was a very pleasant surprise. This was a letter from General Armstrong, inviting me to return to Hampton at the next Commencement to deliver what was called the "post-graduate address." This was an honour which I had not dreamed of receiving. With much care I prepared the best address that I was capable of. I chose for my subject "The Force That Wins."

As I returned to Hampton for the purpose of delivering this address, I went over much of the same ground—now, however, covered entirely by railroad—that I had traversed nearly six years before, when I first sought entrance into Hampton Institute as a student. Now I was able to ride the whole distance in the train. I was constantly contrasting this with my first journey to Hampton. I think I may say, without seeming egotism, that it is seldom that five years have wrought such a change in the life and aspirations of an individual.

At Hampton I received a warm welcome from teachers and students. I found that during my absence from Hampton the institute each year had been getting closer to the real needs and conditions of our people; that the industrial teaching, as well as that of the academic department, had greatly improved. The plan of the school was not modelled after that of any other institution then in existence, but every improvement was made under the magnificent leadership of General Armstrong solely with the view of meeting and helping the needs of our people as they presented themselves at the time. Too often, it seems to me, in missionary and educational work among undeveloped races, people yield to the temptation of doing that which was done a hundred years before, or is being done in other communities a thousand miles away. The temptation often is to run each individual through a certain educational mould, regardless of the condition of the subject or the end to be accomplished. This was not so at Hampton Institute.

The address which I delivered on Commencement Day seems to have pleased every one, and many kind and encouraging words were spoken to me regarding it. Soon after my return to my home in West Virginia, where I had planned to continue teaching, I was again surprised to receive a letter from General Armstrong, asking me to return to Hampton partly as a teacher and partly to pursue some supplementary studies. This was in the summer of 1879. Soon after I began my first teaching in West Virginia I had picked out four of the brightest and most promising of my pupils, in addition to my two brothers, to whom I have already referred, and had given them special attention, with the view of having them go to Hampton. They had gone there, and in each case the teachers had found them so well prepared that they entered advanced classes. This fact, it seems, led to my being called back to Hampton as a teacher. One of the young men that I sent to Hampton in this way is now Dr. Samuel E. Courtney, a successful physician in Boston, and a member of the School Board of that city.

About this time the experiment was being tried for the first time, by General Armstrong, of educating Indians at Hampton. Few people then had any confidence in the ability of the Indians to receive education and to profit by it. General Armstrong was anxious to try the experiment systematically on a large scale. He secured from the reservations in the Western states over one hundred wild and for the most part perfectly ignorant Indians, the greater proportion of whom were young men. The special work which the General desired me to do was to be a sort of "house father" to the Indian young men—that is, I was to live in the building with them and have the charge of their discipline, clothing, rooms, and so on. This was a very tempting offer, but I had become so much absorbed in my work in West Virginia that I dreaded to give it up. However, I tore myself away from it. I did not know how to refuse to perform any service that General Armstrong desired of me.

On going to Hampton, I took up my residence in a building with about seventy-five Indian youths. I was the only person in the building who was not a member of their race. At first I had a good deal of doubt about my ability to succeed. I knew that the average Indian felt himself above the white man, and, of course, he felt himself far above the Negro, largely on account of the fact of the Negro having submitted to slavery—a thing which the Indian would never do. The Indians, in the Indian Territory, owned a large number of slaves during the days of slavery. Aside from this, there was a general feeling that the attempt to educate and civilize the red men at Hampton would be a failure. All this made me proceed very cautiously, for I felt keenly the great responsibility. But I was determined to succeed. It was not long before I had the complete confidence of the Indians, and not only this, but I think I am safe in saying that I had their love and respect. I found that they responded to kind treatment and resented ill-treatment. They were about like any other human beings; that they were continually planning to do something that would add to my happiness and comfort. The things that they disliked most, I think, were to have their long hair cut, to give up wearing their blankets, and to cease smoking; but no white American ever thinks that any other race is wholly civilized until he wears the white man's clothes, eats the white man's food, speaks the white man's language, and professes the white man's religion.

When the difficulty of learning the English language was subtracted, I found that in the matter of learning trades and in mastering academic studies there was little difference between the coloured and Indian students. It was a constant delight to me to note the interest which the coloured students took in trying to help the Indians in every way possible. There were a few of the coloured students who felt that the

Indians ought not to be admitted to Hampton, but these were in the minority. Whenever they were asked to do so, the Negro students gladly took the Indians as room-mates, in order that they might teach them to speak English and to acquire civilized habits.

I have often wondered if there was a white institution in this country whose students would have welcomed the incoming of more than a hundred companions of another race in the cordial way that these black students at Hampton welcomed the red ones. How often I have wanted to say to white students that they lift themselves up in proportion as they help to lift others, and the more unfortunate the race, and the lower in the scale of civilization, the more does one raise one's self by giving the assistance.

This reminds me of a conversation which I once had with the Hon. Frederick Douglass. At one time Mr. Douglass was travelling in the state of Pennsylvania, and was forced, on account of his colour, to ride in the baggage-car, in spite of the fact that he had paid the same price for his passage that the other passengers had paid. When some of the white passengers went into the baggage-car to console Mr. Douglass, and one of them said to him: "I am sorry, Mr. Douglass, that you have been degraded in this manner," Mr. Douglass straightened himself up on the box upon which he was sitting, and replied: "They cannot degrade Frederick Douglass. The soul that is within me no man can degrade. I am not the one that is being degraded on account of this treatment, but those who are inflicting it upon me."

In one part of our country, where the law demands the separation of the races on the railroad trains, I saw at one time a rather amusing instance which showed how difficult it sometimes is to know where the black begins and the white ends.

There was a man who was well known in his community as a Negro, but who was so white that even an expert would have hard work to classify him as a black man. This man was riding in the part of the train set aside for the coloured passengers. When the train conductor reached him, he showed at once that he was perplexed. If the man was a Negro, the conductor did not want to send him into the white people's coach; at the same time, if he was a white man, the conductor did not want to insult him by asking him if he was a Negro. The official looked him over carefully, examining his hair, eyes, nose, and hands, but still seemed puzzled. Finally, to solve the difficulty, he stooped over and peeped at the man's feet. When I saw the conductor examining the feet of the man in question, I said to myself, "That will settle it"; and so it did, for the trainman promptly decided that the passenger was a Negro, and let him remain where he was. I congratulated myself that my race was fortunate in not losing one of its members.

My experience has been that the time to test a true gentleman is to observe him when he is in contact with individuals of a race that is less fortunate than his own. This is illustrated in no better way than by observing the conduct of the old-school type of Southern gentleman when he is in contact with his former slaves or their descendants.

An example of what I mean is shown in a story told of George Washington, who, meeting a coloured man in the road once, who politely lifted his hat, lifted his own in return. Some of his white friends who saw the incident criticised Washington for his action. In reply to their criticism George Washington said: "Do you suppose that

I am going to permit a poor, ignorant, coloured man to be more polite than I am?"

While I was in charge of the Indian boys at Hampton, I had one or two experiences which illustrate the curious workings of caste in America. One of the Indian boys was taken ill, and it became my duty to take him to Washington, deliver him over to the Secretary of the Interior, and get a receipt for him, in order that he might be returned to his Western reservation. At that time I was rather ignorant of the ways of the world. During my journey to Washington, on a steamboat, when the bell rang for dinner, I was careful to wait and not enter the dining room until after the greater part of the passengers had finished their meal. Then, with my charge, I went to the dining saloon. The man in charge politely informed me that the Indian could be served, but that I could not. I never could understand how he knew just where to draw the colour line, since the Indian and I were of about the same complexion. The steward, however, seemed to be an expert in this matter. I had been directed by the authorities at Hampton to stop at a certain hotel in Washington with my charge, but when I went to this hotel the clerk stated that he would be glad to receive the Indian into the house, but said that he could not accommodate me.

An illustration of something of this same feeling came under my observation afterward. I happened to find myself in a town in which so much excitement and indignation were being expressed that it seemed likely for a time that there would be a lynching. The occasion of the trouble was that a dark-skinned man had stopped at the local hotel. Investigation, however, developed the fact that this individual was a citizen of Morocco, and that while travelling in this country he spoke the English language. As soon as it was learned that he was not an American Negro, all the signs of indignation disappeared. The man who was the innocent cause of the excitement, though, found it prudent after that not to speak English.

At the end of my first year with the Indians there came another opening for me at Hampton, which, as I look back over my life now, seems to have come providentially, to help to prepare me for my work at Tuskegee later. General Armstrong had found out that there was quite a number of young coloured men and women who were intensely in earnest in wishing to get an education, but who were prevented from entering Hampton Institute because they were too poor to be able to pay any portion of the cost of their board, or even to supply themselves with books. He conceived the idea of starting a night-school in connection with the Institute, into which a limited number of the most promising of these young men and women would be received, on condition that they were to work for ten hours during the day, and attend school for two hours at night. They were to be paid something above the cost of their board for their work. The greater part of their earnings was to be reserved in the school's treasury as a fund to be drawn on to pay their board when they had become students in the day-school, after they had spent one or two years in the night-school. In this way they would obtain a start in their books and a knowledge of some trade or industry, in addition to the other far-reaching benefits of the institution.

General Armstrong asked me to take charge of the night-school, and I did so. At the beginning of this school there were about twelve strong, earnest men and women who entered the class. During the day the greater part of the young men worked in the school's sawmill, and the young women worked in the laundry. The work was not easy in either place, but in all my teaching I never taught pupils who gave me such genuine satisfaction as these did. They were good students, and mastered their work thoroughly. They were so much in earnest that only the ringing of the retiring-bell would make them stop studying, and often they would urge me to continue the lessons after the usual hour for going to bed had come.

These students showed so much earnestness, both in their hard work during the day, as well as in their application to their studies at night, that I gave them the name of "The Plucky Class"—a name which soon grew popular and spread throughout the institution. After a student had been in the night-school long enough to prove what was in him, I gave him a printed certificate which read something like this:—

"This is to certify that James Smith is a member of The Plucky Class of the Hampton Institute, and is in good and regular standing."

The students prized these certificates highly, and they added greatly to the popularity of the night-school. Within a few weeks this department had grown to such an extent that there were about twenty-five students in attendance. I have followed the course of many of these twenty-five men and women ever since then, and they are now holding important and useful positions in nearly every part of the South. The night-school at Hampton, which started with only twelve students, now numbers between three and four hundred, and is one of the permanent and most important features of the institution.

Early Days at Tuskegee

During the time that I had charge of the Indians and the night-school at Hampton, I pursued some studies myself, under the direction of the instructors there. One of these instructors was the Rev. Dr. H. B. Frissell, the present Principal of the Hampton Institute, General Armstrong's successor.

In May, 1881, near the close of my first year in teaching the night-school, in a way that I had not dared expect, the opportunity opened for me to begin my life-work. One night in the chapel, after the usual chapel exercises were over, General Armstrong referred to the fact that he had received a letter from some gentlemen in Alabama asking him to recommend some one to take charge of what was to be a normal school for the coloured people in the little town of Tuskegee in that state. These gentlemen seemed to take it for granted that no coloured man suitable for the position could be secured, and they were expecting the General to recommend a white man for the place. The next day General Armstrong sent for me to come to his office, and, much to my surprise, asked me if I thought I could fill the position in Alabama. I told him that I would be willing to try. Accordingly, he wrote to the people who had applied to him for the information, that he did not know of any white man to suggest, but if they would be willing to take a coloured man, he had one whom he could recommend. In this letter he gave them my name.

Several days passed before anything more was heard about the matter. Some time afterward, one Sunday evening during the chapel exercises, a messenger came in and handed the General a telegram. At the end of the exercises he read the telegram to the school. In substance, these were its words: "Booker T. Washington will suit us. Send him at once."

There was a great deal of joy expressed among the students and teachers, and I received very hearty congratulations. I began to get ready at once to go to Tuskegee. I went by way of my old home in West Virginia, where I remained for several days, after which I proceeded to Tuskegee. I found Tuskegee to be a town of about two thousand inhabitants, nearly one-half of whom were coloured. It was in what was known as the Black Belt of the South. In the county in which Tuskegee is situated the coloured people outnumbered the whites by about three to one. In some of the adjoining and near-by counties the proportion was not far from six coloured persons to one white.

I have often been asked to define the term "Black Belt." So far as I can learn, the term was first used to designate a part of the country which was distinguished by the colour of the soil. The part of the country possessing this thick, dark, and naturally rich soil was, of course, the part of the South where the slaves were most profitable, and consequently they were taken there in the largest numbers. Later, and especially since the war, the term seems to be used wholly in a political sense—that is, to designate the counties where the black people outnumber the white.

Before going to Tuskegee I had expected to find there a building and all the necessary apparatus ready for me to begin teaching. To my disappointment, I found nothing of the kind. I did find, though, that which no costly building and apparatus can supply—hundreds of hungry earnest souls who wanted to secure knowledge.

Tuskegee seemed an ideal place for the school. It was in the midst of the great bulk of the Negro population, and was rather secluded, being five miles from the main line of railroad, with which it was connected by a short line. During the days of slavery, and since, the town had been a centre for the education of the white people. This was an added advantage, for the reason that I found the white people possessing a degree of culture and education that is not surpassed by many localities. While the coloured people were ignorant, they had not, as a rule, degraded and weakened their bodies by vices such as are common to the lower class of people in the large cities. In general, I found the relations between the two races pleasant. For example, the largest, and I think at that time the only hardware store in the town was owned and operated jointly by a coloured man and a white man. This co-partnership continued until the death of the white partner.

I found that about a year previous to my going to Tuskegee some of the coloured people who had heard something of the work of education being done at Hampton had applied to the state Legislature, through their representatives, for a small appropriation to be used in starting a normal school in Tuskegee. This request the Legislature had complied with to the extent of granting an annual appropriation of two thousand dollars. I soon learned, however, that this money could be used only for the payment of the salaries of the instructors, and that there was no provision for securing land, buildings, or apparatus. The task before me did not seem a very encouraging one. It seemed much like making bricks without straw. The coloured people were overjoyed, and were constantly offering their services in any way in which they could be of assistance in getting the school started.

My first task was to find a place in which to open the school. After looking the town over with some care, the most suitable place that could be secured seemed to be a rather dilapidated shanty near the coloured Methodist church, together with the church itself as a sort of assembly room. Both the church and the shanty were in about as bad condition as was possible. I recall that during the first months of school that I taught in this building it was in such poor repair that, whenever it rained, one of the older students would very kindly leave his lessons and hold an umbrella over me while I heard the recitations of the others. I remember, also, that on more than one occasion my landlady held an umbrella over me while I ate breakfast.

At the time I went to Alabama the coloured people were taking considerable interest in politics, and they were very anxious that I should become one of them politically, in every respect. They seemed to have a little distrust of strangers in this regard. I recall that one man, who seemed to have been designated by the others to look after my political destiny, came to me on several occasions and said, with a good deal of earnestness: "We wants you to be sure to vote jes' like we votes. We can't read de newspapers very much, but we knows how to vote, an' we wants you to vote jes' like we votes." He added: "We watches de white man, and we keeps watching de white man till we finds out which way de white man's gwine to vote; an' when we finds out which way de white man's gwine to vote, den we votes 'xactly de other way. Den we knows we's right."

I am glad to add, however, that at the present time the disposition to vote against the white man merely because he is white is largely disappearing, and the race is learning to vote from principle, for what the voter considers to be for the best interests of both races.

I reached Tuskegee, as I have said, early in June, 1881. The first month I spent in finding accommodations for the school, and in travelling through Alabama, examining into the actual life of the people, especially in the country districts, and in getting the school advertised among the class of people that I wanted to have attend it. The most of my travelling was done over the country roads, with a mule and a cart or a mule and a buggy wagon for conveyance. I ate and slept with the people, in their little cabins. I saw their farms, their schools, their churches. Since, in the case of the most of these visits, there had been no notice given in advance that a stranger was expected, I had the advantage of seeing the real, everyday life of the people.

In the plantation districts I found that, as a rule, the whole family slept in one room, and that in addition to the immediate family there sometimes were relatives, or others not related to the family, who slept in the same room. On more than one occasion I went outside the house to get ready for bed, or to wait until the family had gone to bed. They usually contrived some kind of a place for me to sleep, either on the floor or in a special part of another's bed. Rarely was there any place provided in the cabin where one could bathe even the face and hands, but usually some provision was made for this outside the house, in the yard.

The common diet of the people was fat pork and corn bread. At times I have eaten in cabins where they had only corn bread and "black-eye peas" cooked in plain water. The people seemed to have no other idea than to live on this fat meat and corn bread— the meat, and the meal of which the bread was made, having been bought at a high price at a store in town, notwithstanding the fact that the land all about the cabin homes could easily have been made to produce nearly every kind of garden vegetable that is raised anywhere in the country. Their one object seemed to be to plant nothing but cotton; and in many cases cotton was planted up to the very door of the cabin.

In these cabin homes I often found sewing-machines which had been bought, or were being bought, on instalments, frequently at a cost of as much as sixty dollars, or showy clocks for which the occupants of the cabins had paid twelve or fourteen dollars. I remember that on one occasion when I went into one of these cabins for dinner, when I sat down to the table for a meal with the four members of the family, I noticed that, while there were five of us at the table, there was but one fork for the five of us to use. Naturally there was an awkward pause on my part. In the opposite corner of that same cabin was an organ for which the people told me they were paying sixty dollars in monthly instalments. One fork, and a sixty-dollar organ!

In most cases the sewing-machine was not used, the clocks were so worthless that they did not keep correct time—and if they had, in nine cases out of ten there would have been no one in the family who could have told the time of day—while the organ, of course, was rarely used for want of a person who could play upon it.

In the case to which I have referred, where the family sat down to the table for the meal at which I was their guest, I could see plainly that this was an awkward and unusual proceeding, and was done in my honour. In most cases, when the family got up in the morning, for example, the wife would put a piece of meat in a frying-pan and put a lump of dough in a "skillet," as they called it. These utensils would be placed on the fire and in ten or fifteen minutes breakfast would be ready. Frequently the husband would take his bread and meat in his hand and start for the field, eating as he walked. The mother would sit down in a corner and eat her breakfast, perhaps from a plate and perhaps directly from the "skillet" or frying-pan, while the children would eat their portion of the bread and meat while running about the yard. At certain seasons of the year, when meat was scarce, it was rarely that the children who were not old enough or strong enough to work in the fields would have the luxury of meat.

The breakfast over, and with practically no attention given to the house, the whole family would, as a general thing, proceed to the cotton-field. Every child that was large enough to carry a hoe was put to work, and the baby—for usually there was at least one baby—would be laid down at the end of the cotton row, so that its mother could give it a certain amount of attention when she had finished chopping her row. The noon meal and supper were taken in much the same way as the breakfast.

All the days of the family would be spent after much this same routine, except Saturday and Sunday. On Saturday the whole family would spend at least half a day, and often a whole day, in town. The idea in going to town was, I suppose, to do shopping, but all the shopping that the whole family had money for could have been attended to in ten minutes by one person. Still, the whole family remained in town for most of the day, spending the greater part of the time in standing on the streets, the women, too often, sitting about somewhere smoking or dipping snuff. Sunday was usually spent in going to some big meeting. With few exceptions, I found that the crops were mortgaged in the counties where I went, and that the most of the coloured farmers were in debt. The state had not been able to build schoolhouses in the country districts, and, as a rule, the schools were taught in churches or in log cabins. More than once, while on my journeys, I found that there was no provision made in the house used for school purposes for heating the building during the winter, and consequently a fire had to be built in the yard, and teacher and pupils passed in and out of the house as they got cold or warm. With few exceptions, I found the teachers in these country schools to be miserably poor in preparation for their work, and poor in moral character. The schools were in session from three to five months. There was practically no apparatus in the schoolhouses, except that occasionally there was a rough blackboard. I recall that one day I went into a schoolhouse—or rather into an abandoned log cabin that was being used as a schoolhouse—and found five pupils who were studying a lesson from one book. Two of these, on the front seat, were using the book between them; behind these were two others peeping over the shoulders of the first two, and behind the four was a fifth little fellow who was peeping over the shoulders of all four.

What I have said concerning the character of the schoolhouses and teachers will also apply quite accurately as a description of the church buildings and the ministers.

I met some very interesting characters during my travels. As illustrating the peculiar mental processes of the country people, I remember that I asked one coloured man, who was about sixty years old, to tell me something of his history. He said that he had been born in Virginia, and sold into Alabama in 1845. I asked him how many were sold at the same time. He said, "There were five of us; myself and brother and three mules."

In giving all these descriptions of what I saw during my month of travel in the country around Tuskegee, I wish my readers to keep in mind the fact that there were many encouraging exceptions to the conditions which I have described. I have stated in such plain words what I saw, mainly for the reason that later I want to emphasize the encouraging changes that have taken place in the community, not wholly by the work of the Tuskegee school, but by that of other institutions as well.

Teaching School in a Stable and a Hen-House

I confess that what I saw during my month of travel and investigation left me with a very heavy heart. The work to be done in order to lift these people up seemed almost beyond accomplishing. I was only one person, and it seemed to me that the little effort which I could put forth could go such a short distance toward bringing about results. I wondered if I could accomplish anything, and if it were worth while for me to try.

Of one thing I felt more strongly convinced than ever, after spending this month in seeing the actual life of the coloured people, and that was that, in order to lift them up, something must be done more than merely to imitate New England education as it then existed. I saw more clearly than ever the wisdom of the system which General

Armstrong had inaugurated at Hampton. To take the children of such people as I had been among for a month, and each day give them a few hours of mere book education, I felt would be almost a waste of time.

After consultation with the citizens of Tuskegee, I set July 4, 1881, as the day for the opening of the school in the little shanty and church which had been secured for its accommodation. The white people, as well as the coloured, were greatly interested in the starting of the new school, and the opening day was looked forward to with much earnest discussion. There were not a few white people in the vicinity of Tuskegee who looked with some disfavour upon the project. They questioned its value to the coloured people, and had a fear that it might result in bringing about trouble between the races. Some had the feeling that in proportion as the Negro received education, in the same proportion would his value decrease as an economic factor in the state. These people feared the result of education would be that the Negroes would leave the farms, and that it would be difficult to secure them for domestic service.

The white people who questioned the wisdom of starting this new school had in their minds pictures of what was called an educated Negro, with a high hat, imitation gold eye-glasses, a showy walking-stick, kid gloves, fancy boots, and what not—in a word, a man who was determined to live by his wits. It was difficult for these people to see how education would produce any other kind of a coloured man.

In the midst of all the difficulties which I encountered in getting the little school started, and since then through a period of nineteen years, there are two men among all the many friends of the school in Tuskegee upon whom I have depended constantly for advice and guidance; and the success of the undertaking is largely due to these men, from whom I have never sought anything in vain. I mention them simply as types. One is a white man and and ex-slaveholder, Mr. George W. Campbell; the other is a black man and an ex-slave, Mr. Lewis Adams. These were the men who wrote to General Armstrong for a teacher.

Mr. Campbell is a merchant and banker, and had had little experience in dealing with matters pertaining to education. Mr. Adams was a mechanic, and had learned the trades of shoemaking, harness-making, and tinsmithing during the days of slavery. He had never been to school a day in his life, but in some way he had learned to read and write while a slave. From the first, these two men saw clearly what my plan of education was, sympathized with me, and supported me in every effort. In the days which were darkest financially for the school, Mr. Campbell was never appealed to when he was not willing to extend all the aid in his power. I do not know two men, one an ex-slaveholder, one an ex-slave, whose advice and judgment I would feel more like following in everything which concerns the life and development of the school at Tuskegee than those of these two men.

I have always felt that Mr. Adams, in a large degree, derived his unusual power of mind from the training given his hands in the process of mastering well three trades during the days of slavery. If one goes to-day into any Southern town, and asks for the leading and most reliable coloured man in the community, I believe that in five cases out of ten he will be directed to a Negro who learned a trade during the days of slavery.

On the morning that the school opened, thirty students reported for admission. I was the only teacher. The students were about equally divided between the sexes. Most of them lived in Macon County, the county in which Tuskegee is situated, and of which it is the county-seat. A great many more students wanted to enter the school, but it had been decided to receive only those who were above fifteen years of age, and who had previously received some education. The greater part of the thirty were public-school teachers, and some of them were nearly forty years of age. With the teachers came some of their former pupils, and when they were examined it was amusing to note that in several cases the pupil entered a higher class than did his former teacher. It was also interesting to note how many big books some of them had studied, and how many high-sounding subjects some of them claimed to have mastered. The bigger the book and the longer the name of the subject, the prouder they felt of their accomplishment. Some had studied Latin, and one or two Greek. This they thought entitled them to special distinction.

In fact, one of the saddest things I saw during the month of travel which I have described was a young man, who had attended some high school, sitting down in a one-room cabin, with grease on his clothing, filth all around him, and weeds in the yard and garden, engaged in studying a French grammar.

The students who came first seemed to be fond of memorizing long and complicated "rules" in grammar and mathematics, but had little thought or knowledge of applying these rules to the everyday affairs of their life. One subject which they liked to talk about, and tell me that they had mastered, in arithmetic, was "banking and discount," but I soon found out that neither they nor almost any one in the neighbourhood in which they lived had ever had a bank account. In registering the names of the students, I found that amost every one of them had one or more middle initials. When I asked what the "J" stood for, in the name of John J. Jones, it was explained to me that this was a part of his "entitles." Most of the students wanted to get an education because they thought it would enable them to earn more money as school-teachers.

Notwithstanding what I have said about them in these respects, I have never seen a more earnest and willing company of young men and women than these students were. They were all willing to learn the right thing as soon as it was shown them what was right. I was determined to start them off on a solid and thorough foundation, so far as their books were concerned. I soon learned that most of them had the merest smattering of the high-sounding things that they had studied. While they could locate the Desert of Sahara or the capital of China on an artificial globe, I found out that the girls could not locate the proper places for the knives and forks on an actual dinner-table, or the places on which the bread and meat should be set.

I had to summon a good deal of courage to take a student who had been studying cube root and "banking and discount," and explain to him that the wisest thing for him to do first was thoroughly to master the multiplication table.

The number of pupils increased each week, until by the end of the first month there were nearly fifty. Many of them, however, said that, as they could remain only for two or three months, they wanted to enter a high class and get a diploma the first year if possible.

At the end of the first six weeks a new and rare face entered the school as a co-teacher. This was Miss Olivia A. Davidson, who later became my wife. Miss Davidson was born in Ohio, and received her preparatory education in the public schools of that state. When little more than a girl, she heard of the need of teachers in the South. She went to the state of Mississippi and began teaching there. Later she taught in the city of Memphis. While teaching in Mississippi, one of her pupils became ill with smallpox. Every one in the community was so frightened that no one would nurse the boy. Miss Davidson closed her school and remained by the bedside of the boy night and day until he recovered. While she was at her Ohio home on her vacation, the worst epidemic of yellow fever broke out in Memphis, Tenn., that perhaps has ever occurred in the South. When she heard of this, she at once telegraphed the Mayor of Memphis, offering her services as a yellow-fever nurse, although she had never had the disease.

Miss Davidson's experience in the South showed her that the people needed something more than mere book-learning. She heard of the Hampton system of education, and decided that this was what she wanted in order to prepare herself for better work in the South. The attention of Mrs. Mary Hemenway, of Boston, was attracted to her rare ability. Through Mrs. Hemenway's kindness and generosity, Miss Davidson, after graduating at Hampton, received an opportunity to complete a two years' course at the Massachusetts State Normal School at Framingham.

Before she went to Framingham, some one suggested to Miss Davidson that, since she was so very light in colour, she might find it more comfortable not to be known as a coloured woman in this school in Massachusetts. She at once replied that under no circumstances and for no considerations would she consent to deceive any one in regard to her racial identity.

Soon after her graduation from the Framingham institution, Miss Davidson came to Tuskegee, bringing into the school many valuable and fresh ideas as to the best methods of teaching, as well as a rare moral character and a life of unselfishness that I think has seldom been equalled. No single individual did more toward laying the foundations of the Tuskegee Institute so as to insure the successful work that has been done there than Olivia A. Davidson.

Miss Davidson and I began consulting as to the future of the school from the first. The students were making progress in learning books and in developing their minds; but it became apparent at once that, if we were to make any permanent impression upon those who had come to us for training, we must do something besides teach them mere books. The students had come from homes where they had had no opportunities for lessons which would teach them how to care for their bodies. With few exceptions, the homes in Tuskegee in which the students boarded were but little improvement upon those from which they had come. We wanted to teach the students how to bathe; how to care for their teeth and clothing. We wanted to teach them what to eat, and how to eat it properly, and how to care for their rooms. Aside from this, we wanted to give them such a practical knowledge of some one industry, together with the spirit of industry, thrift, and economy, that they would be sure of knowing how to make a living after they had left us. We wanted to teach them to study actual things instead of mere books alone.

We found that the most of our students came from the country districts, where agriculture in some form or other was the main dependence of the people. We learned that about eighty-five per cent of the coloured people in the Gulf states depended upon agriculture for their living. Since this was true, we wanted to be careful not to educate our students out of sympathy with agricultural life, so that they would be attracted from the country to the cities, and yield to the temptation of trying to live by their wits. We wanted to give them such an education as would fit a large proportion of them to be teachers, and at the same time cause them to return to the plantation districts and show the people there how to put new energy and new ideas into farming, as well as into the intellectual and moral and religious life of the people.

All these ideas and needs crowded themselves upon us with a seriousness that seemed well-nigh overwhelming. What were we to do? We had only the little old shanty and the abandoned church which the good coloured people of the town of Tuskegee had kindly loaned us for the accommodation of the classes. The number of students was increasing daily. The more we saw of them, and the more we travelled through the country districts, the more we saw that our efforts were reaching, to only a partial degree, the actual needs of the people whom we wanted to lift up through the medium of the students whom we should educate and send out as leaders.

The more we talked with the students, who were then coming to us from several parts of the state, the more we found that the chief ambition among a large proportion of them was to get an education so that they would not have to work any longer with their hands.

This is illustrated by a story told of a colored man in Alabama, who, one hot day in July, while he was at work in a cotton-field, suddenly stopped, and, looking toward the skies, said: "O Lawd, de cotton am so grassy, de work am so hard, and the sun am so hot dat I b'lieve dis darky am called to preach!"

About three months after the opening of the school, and at the time when we were in the greatest anxiety about our work, there came into the market for sale an old and abandoned plantation which was situated about a mile from the town of Tuskegee. The mansion house—or "big house," as it would have been called—which had been occupied by the owners during slavery, had been burned. After making a careful examination of this place, it seemed to be just the location that we wanted in order to make our work effective and permanent.

But how were we to get it? The price asked for it was very little—only five hundred dollars—but we had no money, and we were strangers in the town and had no credit. The owner of the land agreed to let us occupy the place if we could make a payment of two hundred and fifty dollars down, with the understanding that the remaining two hundred and fifty dollars must be paid within a year. Although five hundred dollars was cheap for the land, it was a large sum when one did not have any part of it.

In the midst of the difficulty I summoned a great deal of courage and wrote to my friend General J. F. B. Marshall, the Treasurer of the Hampton Institute, putting the situation before him and beseeching him to lend me the two hundred and fifty dollars on my own personal responsibility. Within a few days a reply came to the effect that he had no authority to lend me money belonging to the Hampton Institute, but that he would gladly lend me the amount needed from his own personal funds.

I confess that the securing of this money in this way was a great surprise to me, as well as a source of gratification. Up to that time I never had had in my possession so much money as one hundred dollars at a time, and the loan which I had asked General Marshall for seemed a tremendously large sum to me. The fact of my being responsible for the repaying of such a large amount of money weighed very heavily upon me.

I lost no time in getting ready to move the school on to the new farm. At the time we occupied the place there were standing upon it a cabin, formerly used as the dining room, an old kitchen, a stable, and an old hen-house. Within a few weeks we had all of these structures in use. The stable was repaired and used as a recitation-room, and very presently the hen-house was utilized for the same purpose.

I recall that one morning, when I told an old coloured man who lived near, and who sometimes helped me, that our school had grown so large that it would be necessary for us to use the hen-house for school purposes, and that I wanted him to help me give it a thorough cleaning out the next day, he replied, in the most earnest manner: "What you mean, boss? You sholy ain't gwine clean out de hen-house in de *day*-time?"

Nearly all the work of getting the new location ready for school purposes was done by the students after school was over in the afternoon. As soon as we got the cabins in condition to be used, I determined to clear up some land so that we could plant a crop. When I explained my plan to the young men, I noticed that they did not seem to take to it very kindly. It was hard for them to see the connection between clearing land and an education. Besides, many of them had been school-teachers, and they questioned whether or not clearing land would be in keeping with their dignity. In order to relieve them from any embarrassment, each afternoon after school I took my axe and led the way to the woods. When they saw that I was not afraid or ashamed to work, they began to assist with more enthusiasm. We kept at the work each afternoon, until we had cleared about twenty acres and had planted a crop.

In the meantime Miss Davidson was devising plans to repay the loan. Her first effort was made by holding festivals, or "suppers." She made a personal canvass among the white and coloured families in the town of Tuskegee, and got them to agree to give something, like a cake, a chicken, bread, or pies, that could be sold at the festival. Of course the coloured people were glad to give anything that they could spare, but I want to add that Miss Davidson did not apply to a single white family, so far as I now remember, that failed to donate something; and in many ways the white families showed their interest in the school.

Several of these festivals were held, and quite a little sum of money was raised. A canvass was also made among the people of both races for direct gifts of money, and most of those applied to gave small sums. It was often pathetic to note the gifts of the older coloured people, most of whom had spent their best days in slavery. Sometimes they would give five cents, sometimes twenty-five cents. Sometimes the contribution was a quilt, or a quantity of sugarcane. I recall one old coloured woman, who was about seventy years of age, who came to see me when we were raising money to pay for the farm. She hobbled into the room where I was, leaning on a cane. She was clad in rags; but they were clean. She said: "Mr. Washin'ton, God knows I spent de bes' days of my life in slavery. God knows I's ignorant an' poor; but," she added, "I knows what you an' Miss Davidson is tryin' to do. I knows you is tryin' to make better men an' better women for de coloured race. I ain't got no money, but I wants you to take dese six eggs, what I's been savin' up, an' I wants you to put dese six eggs into de eddication of dese boys an' gals."

Since the work at Tuskegee started, it has been my privilege to receive many gifts for the benefit of the institution, but never any, I think, that touched me so deeply as this one.

(1901)

ESSAYS,
LETTERS
and
SPEECHES

JOSEPH GLOVER BALDWIN

How the Times Served the Virginians. Virginians in a New Country. The Rise, Decline, and Fall of the Rag Empire.

The disposition to be proud and vain of one's country, and to boast of it, is a natural feeling indulged or not in respect to the pride, vanity, and boasting, according to the character of the native: but, with a Virginian, it is a passion. It inheres in him even as the flavor of a York river oyster in that bivalve, and no distance of deportation, and no trimmings of a gracious prosperity, and no pickling in the sharp acids of adversity, can destroy it. It is a part of the Virginia character—just as the flavor is a distinctive part of the oyster—"which cannot, save by annihilating, die." It is no use talking about it—the thing may be right, or wrong:—like Falstaff's victims at Gadshill, it is past praying for: it is a sort of cocoa grass that has got into the soil, and has so matted over it, and so *fibred* through it, as to have become a part of it; at least, there is no telling which is the grass and which is the soil; and certainly it is useless labor to try to root it out. You may destroy the soil, but you can't root out the grass.

Patriotism with a Virginian is a noun personal. It is the Virginian himself and something over. He loves Virginia *per se* and *propter se:* he loves her for herself and for himself—because *she is* Virginia and—everything else beside. He loves to talk about her: out of the abundance of the heart the mouth speaketh. It makes no odds where he goes, he carries Virginia with him: not in the entirety always—but the little spot he came from is Virginia—as Swedenborg says the smallest part of the brain is an abridgment of all of it. *"Cœlum non animum mutant qui trans mare currunt,"* was made for a Virginian. He never gets acclimated elsewhere; he never loses citizenship to the old Home. The right of expatriation is a pure abstraction to him. He may breathe in Alabama, but he lives in Virginia. His treasure is there, and his heart also. If he looks at the Delta of the Mississippi, it reminds him of James River "low grounds;" if he sees the vast prairies of Texas, it is a memorial of the meadows of the Valley. Richmond is the centre of attraction, the *depot* of all that is grand, great, good and glorious. "It is the Kentucky of a place," which the preacher described Heaven to be to the Kentucky congregation.

Those who came many years ago from the borough towns, especially from the vicinity of Williamsburg, exceed, in attachment to their birthplace, if possible, the *emigrés* from the metropolis. It is refreshing in these costermonger times, to hear them speak of it:—they remember it when the old burg was the seat of fashion, taste, refinement, hospitality, wealth, wit, and all social graces; when genius threw its spell over the public assemblages and illumined the halls of justice, and when beauty brightened the social hour with her unmatched and matchless brilliancy.

Then the spirited and gifted youths of the College of old William and Mary, some of them just giving out the first scintillations of the genius that afterwards shone refulgent in the forum and the senate, added to the attractions of a society gay, cultivated and refined beyond example—*even* in the Old Dominion. A hallowed charm seems to rest upon the venerable city, clothing its very dilapidation in a drapery of romance and of serene and classic interest: as if all the sweet and softened splendor which invests the "Midsummer Night's Dream" were poured in a flood of mellow and poetic radiance over the now quiet and half "deserted village." There is something in the shadow from the old college walls, cast by the moon upon the grass and sleeping on the sward, that throws a like shadow soft, sad and melancholy upon the heart of the returning pilgrim who saunters out to view again, by moonlight, his old *Alma Mater*—the nursing mother of such a list and such a line of statesmen and heroes.

There is nothing presumptuously forward in this Virginianism. The Virginian does not make broad his phylacteries and crow over the poor Carolinian and Tennesseeian. He does not reproach him with his misfortune of birthplace. No, he thinks the affliction is enough without the triumph. The franchise of having been born in Virginia, and the prerogative founded thereon, are too patent of honor and distinction to be arrogantly pretended. The bare mention is enough. He finds occasion to let the fact be known, and then the fact is fully able to protect and take care of itself. Like a ducal title, there is no need of saying more than to name it: modesty then is a becoming and expected virtue; forbearance to boast is true dignity.

The Virginian is a magnanimous man. He never throws up to a Yankee the fact of his birthplace. He feels on the subject as a man of delicacy feels in alluding to a rope in the presence of a person, one of whose brothers "stood upon nothing and kicked at the U.S.," or to a female indiscretion, where there had been scandal concerning the family. So far do they carry this refinement, that I have known one of my countrymen, on occasion of a Bostonian owning where he was born, generously protest that he had never heard of it before. As if honest confession half obliterated the shame of the fact. Yet he does not lack the grace to acknowledge worth or merit in another, wherever the native place of that other: for it is a common thing to hear them say of a neighbor, "he is a clever fellow, *though* he *did* come from New Jersey or even Connecticut."

In politics the Virginian is learned much beyond what is written—for they have heard a great deal of speaking on that prolific subject, especially by one or two Randolphs and any number of Barbours. They read the same papers here they read in Virginia—the *Richmond Enquirer* and the *Richmond Whig*. The Democrat stoutly asseverates a fact, and gives *the Enquirer* as his authority with an air that means to say, *that* settles it: while the Whig quoted Hampden Pleasants with the same confidence. But the faculty of personalizing everything which the exceeding social turn of a Virginian gives him, rarely allowed a reference to the paper, *eo nomine;* but made him refer to the editor: as "Ritchie said" so and so, or "Hampden Pleasants said" this or that. When two of opposite politics got together, it was amusing, if you had nothing else to do that day, to hear the discussion. I never knew a debate that did not start *ab urbe condita*. They not only went back to first principles, but also to first times; nor did I ever hear a discussion in which old John Adams and Thomas Jefferson did not figure—as if an interminable dispute had been going on for so many generations between those disputatious personages; as if the quarrel had begun before time, but was not to end with it. But the strangest part of it to me was, that the dispute seemed to be going on without poor Adams having any defence or champion; and never waxed hotter than when both parties agreed in denouncing the man of Braintree as the worst of public sinners and the vilest of political heretics. They both agreed on one thing, and that was to refer the matter to the Resolutions of 1798-99; which said Resolutions, like Goldsmith's "Good Natured Man," arbitrating between Mr. and Mrs. Croaker, seemed so impartial that they agreed with both parties on every occasion.

Nor do I recollect of hearing any question debated that did not resolve itself into a question of constitution—strict construction, &c.,—the constitution being a thing of that curious virtue that its chief excellency consisted in not allowing the government to do any thing; or in being a regular prize fighter that knocked all laws and legislators into a cocked hat, except those of the objector's party.

Frequent reference was reciprocally made to "gorgons, hydras, and chimeras dire," to black cockades, blue lights, Essex juntos, the Reign of Terror, and some other mystic entities—but who or what these monsters were, I never could distinctly learn; and was surprised, on looking into the history of the country, to find that, by some strange oversight, no allusion was made to them.

Great is the Virginian's reverence of great men, that is to say, of great Virginians. This reverence is not Unitarian. He is a Polytheist. He believes in a multitude of Virginia Gods. As the Romans of every province and village had their tutelary or other divinities, besides having divers national gods, so the Virginian of every county has his great man, the like of whom cannot be found in the new country he has exiled himself to. This sentiment of veneration for talent, especially for speaking talent,—this amiable propensity to lionize men, is not peculiar to any class of Virginians among us: it abides in all. I was amused to hear "old Culpepper," as we call him (by nickname derived from the county he came from), declaiming in favor of the Union. "What, gentlemen," said the old man, with a sonorous swell—"what, burst up this glorious Union! and who, if *this* Union is torn up, could write another? Nobody except Henry Clay and J— S. B—, of Culpepper—and may be *they* wouldn't—and what then would you do for another?"

The greatest compliment a Virginian can ever pay to a speaker, is to say that he reminds him of a Col. Broadhorn or a Captain Smith, who represented some royal-named county some forty years or less in the Virginian House of Delegates; and of whom, the auditor, of course, has heard, as he made several speeches in the capitol at Richmond. But the force of the compliment is somewhat broken, by a long narrative, in which the personal reminiscences of the speaker go back to sundry sketches of the Virginia statesman's efforts, and recapitulations of his sayings, interspersed *par parenthèse,* with many valuable notes illustrative of his pedigree and performances; the whole of which, given with great historical fidelity of detail, leaves nothing to be wished for except the point, or rather, two points, the gist and the period.

It is not to be denied that Virginia is the land of orators, heroes and statesmen; and that, directly or indirectly, she has exerted an influence upon the national councils nearly as great as all the rest of the States combined. It is wonderful that a State of its size and population should have turned out such an unprecedented quantum of talent, and of talent as various in kind as prodigious in amount. She has reason to be proud; and the other States so largely in her debt (for, from Cape May to Puget's Sound she has colonized the other States and the territories with her surplus talent) ought to allow her the harmless privilege of a little bragging. In the showy talent of oratory has she especially shone. To accomplish her in this art the State has been turned into a debating society, and while she has been *talking* for the benefit of the nation, as she thought, the other, and, by nature, less favored States, have been *doing* for their own. Consequently, what she has gained in reputation, she has lost in wealth and *material aids*. Certainly the Virginia character has been less distinguished for its practical than its ornamental trains, and for its business qualities than for its speculative temper. *Cui bono* and utilitarianism, at least until latterly, were not favorite or congenial inquiries and subjects of attention to the Virginia politician. What the Virginian was upon his native soil, that he was abroad; indeed, it may be said that the *amor patriæ,* strengthened by absence, made him more of a conservative abroad than he would have been if he had staid at home; for most of them here would not, had they been consulted, have changed either of the old constitutions.

It is far, however, from my purpose to treat of such themes. I only glance at them to show their influence on the character as it was developed on a new theatre.

Eminently social and hospitable, kind, humane and generous is a Virginian, at home or abroad. They are so by nature and habit. These qualities and their exercise develop and strengthen other virtues. By reason of these social traits, they necessarily become well mannered, honorable, spirited, and careful of reputation, desirous of pleasing, and skilled in the accomplishments which please. Their insular position and sparse population, mostly rural, and easy but not affluent fortunes kept them from the artificial refinements and the strong temptations which corrupt so much of the society of the old world and some portions of the new. There was no character more attractive than that of a young Virginian, fifteen years ago, of intelligence, of good family, education and breeding.

It was of the instinct of a Virginian to seek society: he belongs to the gregarious, not to the solitary division of animals; and society can only be kept up by grub and gab—something to eat, and, if not something to talk about, talk. Accordingly they came accomplished already in the knowledge and the talent for these important duties.

A Virginian could always get up a good dinner. He could also do his share—a full hand's work—in disposing of one after it was got up. The qualifications for hostmanship were signal—the old Udaller himself, assisted by Claud Halrco, could not do up the thing in better style, or with a heartier relish, or a more cordial hospitality. In *petite* manners—the little attentions of the table, the filling up of the chinks of the conversation with small fugitive observations, the supplying the hooks and eyes that *kept* the discourse together, the genial good humor, which, like that of the family of the good Vicar, made up in laughter what was wanting in wit—in these, and in the science of getting up and in getting through a picnic or chowder party, or fish fry, the Virginian, like Eclipse, was first, and there was no second. Great was he too at mixing an apple toddy, or mint julep, where ice could be got for love or money; and not deficient, by any means, when it came to his turn to do honor to his own fabrics. It was in this department, that he not only shone but *out*shone, not merely all others but himself. Here he was at home indeed. His elocution, his matter, his learning, his education, were of the first order. He could discourse of every thing around him with an accuracy and a fulness which would have put Coleridge's or Mrs. Ellis's table talk to the blush. Every dish was a text, horticulture, hunting, poultry, fishing—(Isaac Walton or Daniel Webster would have been charmed and instructed to hear him discourse piscatory-wise,)—a slight divergence in favor of foxchasing and a detour towards a horse-race now and then, and continual parentheses of recommendation of particular dishes or glasses—Oh! I tell you if ever there was an interesting man it was he. Others might be agreeable, but he was fascinating, irresistible, not-to-be-done-without.

In the fulness of time the new era had set in—the era of the second great experiment of independence: the experiment, namely, of credit without capital, and enterprise without honesty. The Age of Brass had succeeded the Arcadian period when men got rich by saving a part of their earnings, and lived at their own cost and in ignorance of the new plan of making fortunes on the profits of what they owned. A new theory, not found in the works on political economy, was broached. It was found out that the prejudice in favor of the metals (brass excluded) was an absurd superstition; and that, in reality, any thing else, which the parties interested in giving it currency chose, might serve as a representative of value and medium for exchange of property; and as gold and silver had served for a great number of years as representatives, the republican doctrine of rotation in office required they should give way. Accordingly it was decided that Rags, a very familiar character, and very popular and easy of access, should take their place. Rags belonged to the school of progress. He was representative of the then Young America. His administration was not tame. It was *very* spirited. It was based on the Bonapartist idea of keeping the imagination of the people excited. The leading fiscal idea of his system was to *democratize* capital, and to make, for all purposes of trade, credit and enjoyment of wealth, the man that had *no* money a little richer, if anything, than the man that had a million. The principle of success and basis of operation, though inexplicable in the hurry of the time, is plain enough now: it was faith. Let the public believe that a smutted rag is money, it is money: in other words, it was a sort of financial biology, which made, at night, the thing conjured for, the thing that was seen, so far as the patient was concerned, while the fit was on him—except that now a man does not do his trading when under the mesmeric influence: in the flush times he did.

This country was just settling up. Marvellous accounts had gone forth of the fertility of its virgin lands; and the productions of the soil were commanding a price remunerating to slave labor as it had never been remunerated before. Emigrants came flocking in from all quarters of the Union, especially from the slaveholding States.

The new country seemed to be a reservoir, and every road leading to it a vagrant stream of enterprise and adventure. Money, or what passed for money, was the only cheap thing to be had. Every crossroad and every avocation presented an opening,— through which a fortune was seen by the adventurer in near perspective. Credit was a thing of course. To refuse it—if the thing was ever done—were an insult for which a bowie-knife were not a too summary or exemplary a means of redress. The State banks were issuing their bills by the sheet, like a patent steam printing-press *its* issues; and no other showing was asked of the applicant for the loan than an authentication of his great distress for money. Finance, even in its most exclusive quarter, had thus already got, in this wonderful revolution, to work upon the principles of the charity hospital. If an overseer grew tired of supervising a plantation and felt a call to the mercantile life, even if he omitted the compendious method of buying out a merchant wholesale, stock, house and good will, and laying down, at once, his bullwhip for the yard-stick—all he had to do was to go on to New-York, and present himself in Pearl-street with a letter avouching his citizenship, and a clean shirt, and he was regularly given a through ticket to speedy bankruptcy.

Under this stimulating process prices rose like smoke. Lots in obscure villages were held at city prices; lands, bought at the minimum cost of government, were sold at from thirty to forty dollars per acre, and considered dirt cheap at that. In short, the country had got to be a full ante-type of California, in all except the gold. Society was wholly unorganized: there was no retraining public opinion: the law was well-nigh powerless—and religion scarcely was heard of except as furnishing the oaths and *technics* of profanity. The world saw a fair experiment of what it would have been, if the fiat had never been pronounced which decreed subsistence as the price of labor.

Money, got without work, by those unaccustomed to it, turned the heads of its possessors, and they spent it with a recklessness like that with which they gained it. The pursuits of industry neglected, riot and coarse debauchery filled up the vacant hours. "Where the carcass is, there will the eagles be gathered together;" and the eagles that flocked to the Southwest, were of the same sort as the *black eagles* the Duke of Saxe-Weimar saw on his celebrated journey to the Natural Bridge. "The cankers of a long peace and a calm world"—there were no Mexican wars and filibuster expeditions in those days—gathered in the villages and cities by scores.

Even the little boys caught the taint of the general infection of morals; and I knew one of them—Jim Ellett by name—to give a man ten dollars to hold him up to bet at the table of a faro-bank. James was a fast youth; and I sincerely hope he may not fulfil his early promise, and some day be *assisted up still higher.*

The groceries—*vulgice* doggeries—were in full blast in those days, no village having less than a half-dozen all busy all the time: gaming and horse-racing were polite and well patronized amusements. I knew a Judge to adjourn two courts (or court twice) to attend a horse-race, at which he officiated judicially and ministerially, and with more appropriateness than in the judicial chair. Occasionally the scene was diversified by a murder or two, which though perpetrated from behind a corner, or behind the back of the deceased, whenever the accused *chose* to stand his trial, was always found to have been committed in self-defence, securing the homicide an honorable acquittal *at the hands of his peers.*

The old rules of business and the calculations of prudence were alike disregarded, and profligacy, in all the departments of the *crimen falsi*, held riotous carnival. Larceny grew not only respectable, but genteel, and ruffled it in all the pomp of purple and fine linen. Swindling was raised to the dignity of the fine arts. Felony came forth from its covert, put on more seemly habiliments, and took its seat with unabashed front in the upper places of the synagogue. Before the first circles of the patrons of this brilliant and dashing villainy, Blunt Honesty felt as abashed as poor Halbert Glendinning by the courtly refinement and supercilious airs of Sir Piercie Shafton.

Public office represented, by its incumbents, the state of public morals with some approach to accuracy. Out of sixty-six receivers of public money in the new States, sixty-two were discovered to be defaulters; and the agent, sent to look into the affairs of a peccant office-holder in the South-West, reported him *minus* some tens of thousands, but advised the government to retain him, for a reason one of Æsop's fables illustrates: the agent ingeniously surmising that the appointee succeeding would do his stealing without any regard to the proficiency already made by his predecessor; while the present incumbent would probably consider, in mercy to the treasury, that he *had* done *something* of the pious duty of providing for his household.

There was no petit larceny: there was all the difference between stealing by the small and the "operations" manipulated, that there is between a single assassination and an hundred thousand men killed in an opium war. The placeman robbed with the gorgeous magnificence of a Governor-General of Bengal.

The man of straw, not worth the buttons on his shirt, with a sublime audacity, bought lands and negroes, and provided times and terms of payment which a Wall-street capitalist would have to re-cast his arrangements to meet.

Oh, Paul Clifford and Augustus Tomlinson, philosophers of the road, practical and theoretical! if ye had lived to see those times, how great an improvement on your ruder scheme of distribution would these gentle arts have seemed; arts whereby, without risk, or loss of character, or the vulgar barbarism of personal violence, the same beneficial results flowed with no greater injury to the superstitions of moral education!

With the change of times and the imagination of wealth easily acquired came a change in the thoughts and habits of the people. "Old times were changed—old manners gone." Visions of affluence, such as crowded Dr. Samuel Johnson's mind, when advertising a sale of Thrale's Brewery, and casting a soft sheep's eye towards Thrale's widow, thronged upon the popular fancy. Avarice and hope joined partnership. It was strange how the reptile arts of humanity, as at a faro table, warmed into life beneath their heat. The *cacoethes accrescendi* became epidemic. It seized upon the universal community. The pulpits even were not safe from its insidious invasion. What men anxiously desire they willingly believe; and all believed a good time was coming—nay, had come.

"Commerce was king"—and Rags, Tag and Bobtail his cabinet council. Rags was treasurer. Banks, chartered on a specie basis, did a very flourishing business on the promissory notes of the individual stockholders ingeniously substituted in lieu of cash. They issued ten for one, the *one* being fictitious. They generously loaned all the directors could not use themselves, and were not choice whether Bardolph was the endorser for Falstaff, or Falstaff borrowed on his own proper credit, or the funds advanced him by Shallow. The stampede towards the golden temple became general: the delusion prevailed far and wide that this thing was not a burlesque on commerce and finance. Even the directors of the banks began to have their doubts whether the intended swindle was not a failure. Like Lord Clive, when reproached for extortion to the extent of some millions in Bengal, they exclaimed, after the bubble burst, "When they thought of what they had got, and what they might have got, they were astounded at their own moderation."

The old capitalists for a while stood out. With the Tory conservatism of cash in hand, worked for, they couldn't reconcile their old notions to the new regime. They looked for the thing's ending, and *then* their time. But the stampede still kept on. Paper fortunes still multiplied—houses and lands changed hands—real estate see-sawed up as morals went down on the other end of the plank—men of straw, corpulent with bank bills, strutted past them on 'Change. They began, too, to think there might be something in this new thing. Peeping cautiously, like hedge-hogs out of their holes, they saw the stream of wealth and adventurers passing by—then, looking carefully around, they inched themselves half way out—then, sallying forth and snatching up a morsel, ran back, until, at last, grown more bold, *they* ran out too with their hoarded store, in full chase with the other unclean beasts of adventure. They never got back again. Jonah's gourd withered one night, and next morning the vermin that had nestled under its broad shade were left unprotected, a prey to the swift retribution that came upon them. They were left naked, or only clothed themselves with cursing (the Specie Circular on the United States Bank) as with a garment. To drop the figure: Shylock himself couldn't live in those times, so reversed was every thing. Shaving paper and loaning money at a usury of fifty per cent, was for the first time since the Jews left Jerusalem, a breaking business to the operator.

The condition of society may be imagined:—vulgarity—ignorance—fussy and arrogant pretension—unmitigated rowdyism—bullying insolence, if they did not rule the hour, *seemed* to wield unchecked dominion. The workings of these choice spirits were patent upon the face of society; and the modest, unobtrusive, retiring men of worth and character (for there were many, perhaps a large majority of such) were almost lost sight of in the hurly-burly of those strange and shifting scenes.

Even in the professions were the same characteristics visible. Men dropped down into their places as from the clouds. Nobody knew who or what they were, except as they claimed, or as a surface view of their characters indicated. Instead of taking to the highway and magnanimously calling upon the wayfarer to stand and deliver, or to the fashionable larceny or credit without prospect or design of paying, some unscrupulous horse-doctor would set up his sign as "Physician and Surgeon," and draw his lancet on you, or fire at random a box of his pills into your bowels, with a vague chance of hitting some disease unknown to him, but with a better prospect of killing the patient, whom or whose administrator he charged some ten dollars a trial for his markmanship.

A superannuated justice or constable in one of the old States was metamorphosed into a lawyer; and though he knew not the distinction between a *fee tail* and a *female*, would undertake to construe, off-hand, a will involving all the subtleties of *uses and trusts.*

But this state of things could not last for ever: society cannot always stand on its head with its heels in the air.

The Jupiter Tonans of the White House saw the monster of a free credit prowling about like beast of apocalyptic vision, and marked him for his prey. Gathering all his bolts in his sinewy grasp, and standing back on his heels, and waving his wiry arm, he let them all fly, hard and swift upon all the hydra's heads. Then came a crash, as "if the ribs of nature broke," and a scattering, like the bursting of a thousand magazines, and a smell of brimstone, as if Pandemonium had opened a window next to earth for ventilation,—and all was silent. The beast never stirred in his tracks. To get down from the clouds to level ground, the Specie Circular was issued without warning, and the splendid lie of a false credit burst into fragments. It came in the midst of the dance and the frolic—as Tam O'Shanter came to disturb the infernal glee of the warlocks, and to disperse the rioters. Its effect was like that of a general creditor's bill in the chancery court, and a marshalling of all the assets of the trades-people. Gen. Jackson was no fairy; but he did some very pretty fairy work, in converting the bank bills back again into rags and oak-leaves. Men worth a million were insolvent for two millions: promising young cities marched back again into the wilderness. The ambitious town plat was re-annexed to the plantation, like a country girl taken home from the city. The frolic was ended, and what headaches, and feverish limbs the next morning! The retreat from Moscow was performed over again, and "Devil take the hindmost" was the tune to which the soldiers of fortune marched. The only question was as to the means of escape, and the nearest and best route to Texas. The sheriff was as busy as a militia adjutant on review day; and the lawyers were mere wreckers, earning salvage. Where are ye now my ruffling gallants? Where now the braw cloths and watch chains and rings and fine horses? Alas! for ye—they are glimmering among the things that were—the wonder of an hour! They live only in memory, as unsubstantial as the promissory notes ye gave for them. When it came to be tested, the whole matter was found to be hollow and fallacious. Like a sum ciphered out through a long column, the first figure an error, the whole, and all the parts were wrong, throughout the entire calculation.

Such is a charcoal sketch of the interesting region—now inferior to none in resources, and the character of its population—during the FLUSH TIMES; a period constituting an episode in the commercial history of the world—the reign of humbug, and wholesale insanity, just overthrown in time to save the whole country from ruin. But while it lasted, many of our countrymen came into the South-West in time to get "a benefit." The *auri sacra fames* is a catching disease. Many Virginians had lived too fast for their fortunes, and naturally desired to recuperate: many others, with a competency, longed for wealth; and others again, with wealth, yearned—the common frailty—for still more. Perhaps some friend or relative, who had come out, wrote back flattering accounts of the El Dorado, and fired with dissatisfaction those who were doing well enough at home, by the report of his real or imagined success; for who that ever moved off, was not "doing well" in the new country, himself or friends being chroniclers?

Superior to many of the settlers in elegance of manners and general intelligence, it was the weakness of the Virginian to imagine he was superior too in the essential art of being able to hold his hand and make his way in a new country, and especially *such* a country, and at *such* a time. What a mistake that was! The times were out of joint. It was hard to say whether it were more dangerous to stand still or to move. If the emigrant stood still, he was consumed, by no slow degrees, by expenses: if he moved, ten to one he went off in a galloping consumption, by a ruinous investment. Expenses then—necessary articles about three times as high, and extra articles still more extra-priced—were a different thing in the new country from what they were in the old. In the old country, a jolly Virginian, starting the business of free living on a capital of a plantation, and fifty or sixty negroes, might reasonably calculate, if no ill luck befell him, by the aid of a usurer, and the occasional sale of a negro or two, to hold out without declared insolvency, until a green old age. His estate melted like an estate in chancery, under the gradual thaw of expenses; but in this fast country, it went by the sheer cost of living—some *poker* loses included—like the fortune of the confectioner in California, who failed for one hundred thousand dollars in the six months keeping of a candy-shop. But all the habits of his life, his taste, his associations, his education—every thing—the trustingness of his disposition—his want of business qualifications—his sanguine temper—all that was Virginian in him, made him the prey, if not of imposture, at least of unfortunate speculations. Where the keenest jockey often was bit, what chance had *he?* About the same that the verdant Moses had with the venerable old gentleman, his father's friend, at the fair, when he traded the Vicar's pony for the green spectacles. But how could he believe it? How *could* he believe that that stuttering, grammarless Georgian, who had never heard of the resolutions of '98, could beat him in a land trade? "Have no money dealings with my father," said the friendly Martha to Lord Nigel, "for, idiot though he seems, he will make an ass of thee." What a pity some monitor, equally wise and equally successful with old Trapbois' daughter, had not been at the elbow of every Virginian! "Twad frae monie a blunder free'd him—an' foolish notion."

If he made a bad bargain, how could he expect to get rid of it? *He* knew nothing of the elaborate machinery of ingenious chicane,—such as feigning bankruptcy—fraudulent conveyances—making over to his wife—running property—and had never heard of such tricks of trade as sending out coffins to the graveyard, with negroes inside, carried off by sudden spells of imaginary disease, to be "resurrected," in due time, grinning, on the banks of the Brazos.

The new philosophy, too, had commended itself to his speculative temper. He readily caught at the idea of a new spirit of the age having set in, which rejected the saws of Poor Richard as being as much out of date as his almanacs. He was already, by the great rise of property, compared to his condition under the old-time prices, rich; and what were a few thousands of debt, which two or three crops would pay off, compared to the value of his estate? (He never thought that the value of property might come down, while the debt was a fixed fact.) He lived freely, for it was a liberal time, and liberal fashions were in vogue, and it was not for a Virginian to be behind others in hospitality and liberality. He required credit and security, and, of course, had to stand security in return. When the crash came, and no "accommodations" could be had, except in a few instances, and in those on the most ruinous terms, he fell an easy victim. They broke by neighborhoods. They usually endorsed for each other, and when one fell—like the child's play of putting bricks on end at equal distances, and dropping the first in the line against the second, which fell against the third, and so on to the last—all fell; each got broke as security, and yet few or none were able to pay their own debts! So powerless of protection were they in those times, that the witty H. G. used to say they reminded him of an oyster, both shells torn off, lying on the beach, with the sea-gulls screaming over them; the only question being, *which* should "gobble them up."

There was one consolation—if the Virginian involved himself like a fool, he suffered himself to be sold out like a gentleman. When his card house of visionary projects came tumbling about his ears, the next question was, the one Webster plagiarised—"Where am I to go?" Those who had fathers, uncles, aunts, or other like dernier resorts, in Virginia, limped back with feathers moulted and crestfallen, to the old stamping ground, carrying the returned Californian's fortune of ten thousand dollars—six bits in money, and the balance in experience. Those who were in the condition of the prodigal, (barring the father, the calf—the fatted one I mean—and the fiddle,) had to turn their accomplishments to account; and many of them, having lost all by eating and drinking, sought the retributive justice from meat and drink, which might, at least, support them in poverty. Accordingly, they kept tavern, and made a barter of hospitality, a business, the only disagreeable part of which was receiving the money, and the only one I know of for which a man can eat and drink himself into qualification. And while I confess I never knew a Virginian, out of the State, to keep a bad tavern, I never knew one to draw a solvent breath from the time he opened house, until death or the sheriff closed it.

Others again got to be, not exactly overseers, but some nameless thing, the duties of which were nearly analogous, for some more fortunate Virginian, who had escaped the wreck, and who had got his former boon companion to live with him on board, or other wages, in some such relation that the friend was not often found at table at the dinings given to the neighbors, and had got to be called Mr. Flournoy instead of Bob, and slept in an out-house in the yard, and only read the *Enquirer* of nights and Sundays.

Some of the younger scions that had been transplanted early, and stripped of their foliage at a tender age, had been turned into birches for the corrective discipline of youth. Yes; many, who had received academical or collegiate educations, disregarding the allurements of the highway—turning from the gala-day exercise of ditching—scorning the effeminate relaxation of splitting rails—heroically led the Forlorn Hope of the battle of life, the corps of pedagogues of country schools—*academies,* I beg pardon for *not* saying; for, under the Virginia economy, every cross-road log-cabin, where boys were flogged from B-a-k-e-r to Constantinople, grew into the dignity of a sort of runt college; and the teacher vainly endeavored to hide the meanness of the calling beneath the sonorous *sobriquet* of Professor. "Were there no wars?" Had *all* the oysters been opened? Where was the regular army? Could not interest procure service as a deck-hand on a steamboat? Did no stage-driver, with a contract for running at night, through the prairies in mid-winter, want help, at board wages, and sweet lying in the loft, when off duty, thrown in? What right had the Dutch Jews to monopolize *all* the peddling? "To such vile uses may we come at last, Horatio." The subject grows melancholy. I had a friend on whom this catastrophe descended. Tom Edmundson was a buck of the first head—gay, witty, dashing, vain, proud, handsome and volatile, and, withal, a dandy and lady's man to the last intent in particular. He had graduated at the University, and had just settled with his guardian, and received his patrimony of ten thousand dollars in money. Being a young gentleman of enterprise, he sought the alluring fields of South-Western adventure, and found them in this State. Before he well knew the condition of his exchequer, he had made a permanent investment of one-half of his fortune in cigars, champagne, trinkets, buggies, horses, and current expenses, including some small losses at poker, which game he patronized merely for amusement; and found that it diverted him a good deal, but diverted his cash much more. He invested the balance, on private information kindly given him, in "*Choctaw Floats;*" a most lucrative investment it would have turned out, but for the facts: 1. That the Indians never had any title; 2. The white men who kindly interposed to act as guardians for the Indians did not have the Indian title; and 3dly, the land, left subject to entry, if the "Floats" had been good, was not worth entering. "These imperfections off its head," I know of no fancy stock I would prefer to a "Choctaw Float." "Brief, brave and glorious" was "Tom's young career." When Thomas found, as he did shortly, that he had bought five thousand dollars' worth of moonshine, and had no title to it, he honestly informed his landlord of the state of his "fiscality," and that worthy kindly consented to take a new buggy, at half price, in payment of the old balance. The horse, a nick-tailed trotter, Tom had raffled off; but omitting to require cash, the process of collection resulted in his getting the price of one chance—the winner of the horse magnanimously paying his subscription. The rest either had gambling offsets, or else were not prepared just at any one particular, given moment, to pay up, though always ready, generally and in a general way.

Unlike his namesake, Tom and his landlady were not—for a sufficient reason—very gracious; and so, the only common bond, Tom's money, being gone, Tom received "notice to quit" in regular form.

In the hurly-burly of the times, I had lost sight of Tom for a considerable period. One day, as I was travelling over the hills in Greene, by a cross-road, leading me near a country mill, I stopped to get water at a spring at the bottom of a hill. Clambering up the hill, after remounting, the summit of it brought me to a view, on the other side, through the bushes, of a log country school-house, the door being wide open, and who did I see but Tom Edmundson, dressed as fine as ever, sitting back in an arm-chair, one thumb in his waistcoat armhole, the other hand brandishing a long switch, or rather pole. As I approached a little nearer, I heard him speak out: "Sir—Thomas Jefferson, of Virginia, was the author of the Declaration of Independence—mind that. I thought everybody knew that—even the Georgians." Just then he saw me coming through the bushes and entering the path that led by the door. Suddenly he broke from the chair of state, and the door was slammed to, and I heard some one of the boys, as I passed the door, say—"Tell him he can't come in—the master's sick." This is the last I ever saw of Tom. I understand he afterwards moved to Louisiana, where he married a rich French widow, having first, however, to fight a duel with one of her sons, whose opposition couldn't be appeased, until some such expiatory sacrifice to the manes of his worthy father was attempted; which failing, he made rather a *lame* apology for his zealous indiscretion—the poor fellow could make no other—for Tom had unfortunately fixed him for visiting his mother on crutches the balance of his life.

One thing I will say for the Virginians—I never knew one of them, under any pressure, extemporize a profession. The sentiment of reverence for the mysteries of medicine and law was too large for a deliberate quackery; as to the pulpit, a man might as well do his starving without the hypocrisy.

But others were not so nice. I have known them to rush, when the wolf was after them, from the counting-house or the plantation, into a doctor's shop or a law office, as if those places were the sanctuaries from the avenger; some pretending to be doctors that did not know a liver from a gizzard, administering medicine by the guess, without knowing enough of pharmacy to tell whether the stuff exhibited in the big-bellied blue, red and green bottles at the show-windows of the apothecaries' shops, was given by the drop or the half-pint.

Divers others left, but what became of them, I never knew any more than they know what becomes of the sora after frost.

Many were the instances of suffering; of pitiable misfortune, involving and crushing whole families; of pride abased; of honorable sensibilities wounded; of the provision for old age destroyed; of the hopes of manhood overcast: of independence dissipated, and the poor victim without help, or hope, or sympathy, forced to petty shifts for a bare subsistence, and a ground-scuffle, for what in happier days, he threw away. But there were too many examples of this sort for the expenditure of a useless compassion; just as the surgeon, after a battle, grows case-hardened, from an excess of objects of pity.

My memory, however, fixes itself on one honored exception, the noblest of the noble, the best of the good. Old Major Willis Wormley had come in long before the *new era*. He belonged to the old school of Virginians. Nothing could have torn him from the Virginia he loved, as Jacopi Foscari, Venice, but the marrying of his eldest daughter, Mary, to a gentleman of Alabama. The Major was something between, or made of about equal parts, of Uncle Toby and Mr. Pickwick, with a slight flavor of Mr. Micawber. He was the soul of kindness, disinterestedness and hospitality. Love to every thing that had life in it burned like a flame in his large and benignant soul; it flowed over in his countenance, and glowed through every feature, and moved every muscle in the frame it animated. The Major lived freely, was rather corpulent, and had not a lean thing on his plantations; the negroes; the dogs; the horses; the cattle; the very chickens, wore an air of corpulent complacency, and bustled about with a good-humored rotundity. There was more laughing, singing and whistling at "Hollywood," than would have set up a dozen Irish fairs. The Major's wife had, from a long life of affection, and the practice of the same pursuits, and the indulgence of the same feelings and tastes, got so much like him, that she seemed a feminine and modest edition of himself. Four daughters were all that remained in the family—two had been married off—and they had no son. The girls ranged from sixteen to twenty-two, fine, hearty, whole-souled, wholesome, cheerful lasses, with constitutions to last, and a flow of spirits like mountain springs—not beauties, but good housewife girls, whose open countenances, and neat figures, and rosy cheeks, and laughing eyes, and frank and cordial manners, made them, at home, abroad, on horseback or on foot, at the piano or discoursing on the old English books, or Washington Irving's Sketch Book, a favorite in the family ever since it was written, as entertaining and as well calculated to fix solid impressions on the heart, as any four girls in the country. The only difficulty was, they were so much alike, that you were put to fault which to fall in love with. They were all good housewives, or women, rather. But Mrs. Wormley, or Aunt Wormley, as we called her, was as far ahead of any other woman in that way, as could be found this side of the Virginia border. If there as any thing good in the culinary line that she couldn't make, I should like to know it. The Major lived on the main stage road, and if any decently dressed man ever passed the house after sundown, he escaped by accident. The Major knew everybody, and everybody near him knew the Major. The stage coach couldn't stop long, but in the hot summer days, about noon, as the driver tooted his horn at the top of the red hill, two negro boys stood opposite the door, with trays of the finest fruit, and a pitcher of cider for the refreshment of the wayfarers. The Major himself being on the look-out, with his hands over his eyes, bowing—as he only could bow—vaguely into the coach, and looking wistfully, to find among the passengers an acquaintance whom he could prevail upon to get out and stay a week with him. There wasn't a poor neighbor to whom the Major had not been as good as an insurer, without premium, for his stock, or for his crop; and from the way he rendered the service, you would think he was the party obliged—as he was.

This is not, in any country I have ever been in, a money-making business; and the Major though he always made good crops, must have broke at it long ago, but for the fortunate death of a few Aunts, after whom the girls were named, who, paying their several debts of nature, left the Major the means to pay his less serious, but still weighty obligations.

The Major—for a wonder, being a Virginian—had no partisan politics. He could not have. His heart could not hold anything that implied a warfare upon the thoughts or feelings of others. He voted all the time for his friend, that is, the candidate living nearest to him, regretting, generally, that he did not have another vote for the other man.

It would have done a Comanche Indian's heart good to see all the family together—grand-children and all—of a winter evening, with a guest or two, to excite sociability a little—not company enough to embarrass the manifestations of affection. Such a concordance—as if all hearts were attuned to the same feeling—the old lady knitting in the corner—the old man smoking his pipe opposite—both of their fine faces radiating in the pauses of the laugh, the jest, or the caress, the infinite satisfaction within.

It was enough to convert an abolitionist, to see the old Major when he came home from a long journey of two days to the county town; the negroes running in a string to the buggy; this one to hold the horse, that one to help the old man out, and the others to inquire how he was; and to observe the benignity with which—the kissing of the girls and the old lady hardly over—he distributed a piece of calico here, a plug of tobacco there, or a card of *town* ginger-bread to the little snow-balls that grinned around him; what was given being but a small part of the gift, divested of the kind, cheerful, rollicking way the old fellow had of giving it.

The Major had given out his autograph (as had almost everybody else) as endorser on three several bills of exchange, of even tenor and date, and all maturing at or about the same time. His friend's friend failed to pay as he or his firm agreed, the friend himself did no better, and the Major, before he knew anything at all of his danger, found a writ served upon him, and was told by his friend that he was dead broke, and all he could give him was his sympathy; the which, the Major as gratefully received as if it was a legal tender and would pay the debt. The Major's friends advised him he could get clear of it; that notice of protest not having been sent to the Major's post-office, released him; but the Major wouldn't hear of such a defence, he said *his* understanding was, that he was to pay the debt if his friend didn't; and to slip out of it by a quibble, was little better than pleading the gambling act. Besides, what would the lawyers say? And what would be said by his old friends in Virginia, when it reached their ears, that he had plead want of notice, to get clear of a debt, when everybody knew it was the same thing as if he had got notice. And if this defence were good at law, it would not be in equity; and if they took it into chancery, it mattered not what became of the case, the property would all go, and he never could expect to see the last of it. No, no; he would pay it, and had as well set about it at once.

The rumor of the Major's condition spread far and wide. It reached old N. D., "an angel," whom the Major had "entertained," and one of the few that ever travelled that road. He came, post haste, to see into the affair; saw the creditor; made him, upon threat of defence, agree to take half the amount, and discharge the Major; advanced the money, and took the Major's negroes—except the houseservants—and put them on his Mississippi plantation to work out the debt.

The Major's heart pained him at the thought of the negroes going off; he couldn't witness it; though he consoled himself with the idea of the discipline and exercise being good for the health of sundry of them who had contracted sedentary diseases.

The Major turned his house into a tavern—that is, changed its name—put up a sign, and three weeks afterwards, you couldn't have told that anything had happened. The family were as happy as ever—the Major never having put on airs of arrogance in prosperity, felt no humiliation in adversity; the girls were as cheerful, as bustling, and as light-hearted as ever, and seemed to think of the duties of hostesses as mere bagatelles, to enliven the time. The old Major was as profluent of anecdotes as ever, and never grew tired of telling the same ones to every new guest; and yet, the Major's anecdotes were all of Virginia growth, and not one of them under the legal age of twenty-one. If the Major had worked his negroes as he had those anecdotes, he would have been able to pay off the bills of exchange without any difficulty.

The old lady and the girls laughed at the anecdotes, though they must have heard them at least a thousand times, and knew them by heart; for the Major told them without the variations; and the other friends of the Major laughed too; indeed, with such an air of thorough benevolence, and in such a truly social spirit did the old fellow proceed "the tale to unfold," that a Cassius-like rascal that wouldn't laugh, whether he saw anything to laugh at or not, ought to have been sent to the Penitentiary for life— half of the time to be spent in solitary confinement.

(1853)

GEORGE WASHINGTON CABLE

Creole Slave Songs

The Quadroons

The patois in which these songs are found is common, with broad local variations, wherever the black man and the French language are met in the mainland or island regions that border the Gulf and the Caribbean Sea. It approaches probably nearer to good French in Louisiana than anywhere in the Antilles. Yet it is not merely bad or broken French; it is the natural result from the effort of a savage people to take up the language of an old and highly refined civilization, and is much more than a jargon. The humble condition and great numbers of the slave-caste promoted this evolution of an African-Creole dialect. The facile character of the French master-caste, made more so by the languorous climate of the Gulf, easily tolerated and often conde-scended to use the new tongue. It chimed well with the fierce notions of caste to have one language for the master and another for the slave, and at the same time it was convenient that the servile speech should belong to and draw its existence chiefly from the master's. Its growth entirely by ear where there were so many more African ears than French tongues, and when those tongues had so many Gallic archaisms which they were glad to give away and get rid of, resulted in a broad grotesqueness all its own.

We had better not go aside to study it here. Books have been written on the subject. They may be thin, but they stand for years of labor. A Creole lady writes me almost as I write this, "It takes a whole life to speak such a language in form." Mr. Thomas of Trinidad has given a complete grammar of it as spoken there. M. Marbot has versified some fifty of La Fontaine's fables in the tongue. Père Gaux has made a catechism in, and M. Turiault a complete grammatical work on, the Martinique variety. Dr. Armand Mercier, a Louisiana Creole, and Professor James A. Harrison, an Anglo-Louisianian, have written valuable papers on the dialect as spoken on the Mississippi delta. Mr. John Bigelow has done the same for the tongue as heard in Hayti. It is an amusing study. Certain tribes of Africa had no knowledge of the *v* and *z* sounds. The sprightly Franc-Congos, for all their chatter, could hardly master even this African-Creole dialect so as to make their wants intelligible. The Louisiana negro's *r*'s were ever being lost or mislaid. He changed *dormir* to *dromi'*. His master's children called the little fiddler-crab *Tourlourou*; he simplified the articulations to *Troolooloo*. Wherever the *r* added to a syllable's quantity, he either shifted it or dropped it overboard. *Po'té ça? Non!* not if he could avoid it. It was the same with many other sounds. For example, final *le*; a thing so needless—he couldn't be burdened with it; *li pas capab'!* He found himself profitably understood when he called his master *aimab' et nob'*, and thought it not well to be *trop sensib'* about a trifling *l* or two. The French *u* was vinegar to his teeth. He substituted *i* or *ei* before a consonant and *oo* before a vowel, or dropped it altogether; for *une*, he said *eine*; for *puis, p'is*; *absolument* he made *assoliment*; *tu* was nearly always *to*; a *mulâtresse* was a *milatraisse*. In the West Indies he changed *s* into *ch* or *tch*, making *songer chongé*, and *suite tchooite*; while in Louisiana he reversed the process and turned *ch* into *ç*— *c'erc'é* for *cherchez* or *chercher*.

He misconstrued the liaisons of correct French, and omitted limiting adjectives where he conveniently could, or retained only their final sound carried over and prefixed to the noun: *nhomme—zanimaux—zherbes—zaffaires*. He made odd substitutions of one word for another. For the verb to go he oftener than otherwise used a word that better signified his slavish pretense of alacrity, the verb to run: *mo courri,—mo* always, never *je,—mo courri, to courri, li courri*; always seizing whatever form of a verb was handiest and holding to it without change; *no courri, vo courri, yé courri*. Sometimes the plural was *no zôtt*—we others—*courri, vo zôtt courri, yé zôtt courri; no zôtt courri dans bois*—we are going to the woods. His auxiliary verb in imperfect and pluperfect tenses was not to have, but to be in the past participial form *été*, but shortened to one syllable. I have gone, thou hadst gone: *mo 'té courri, to 'té courri*.

There is an affluence of bitter meaning hidden under these apparently nonsensical lines.

> Milatraisse courri dans bal,
> Cocodrie po'té fanal,
> Trouloulou! C'est pas zaffaire à tou,
> C'est pas zaffaire à tou, Trouloulou!

It mocks the helpless lot of three types of human life in old Louisiana whose fate was truly deplorable. *Milatraisse* was, in Creole song, the generic term for all that class, famous wherever New Orleans was famous in those days when all foot-passengers by night picked their way through the mud by the rays of a hand-lantern—the freed or free-born quadroon or mulatto woman. *Cocodrie* (Spanish, *cocodrilla*, the crocodile or alligator) was the nickname for the unmixed black man; while *trouloulou* was applied to the free male quadroon, who could find admittance to the quadroon balls only in the capacity, in those days distinctly menial, of musician—fiddler. Now sing it!

> "Yellow girl goes to the ball;
> Nigger lights her to the hall.
> > Fiddler man!
> Now, what is that to you?
> Say, what is that to you,
> > Fiddler man?"

It was much to him; but it might as well have been little. What could he do? As they say, "*Ravette zamein tini raison divant poule*" ("Cockroach can never justify himself to the hungry chicken"). He could only let his black half-brother celebrate on Congo Plains the mingled humor and outrage of it in satirical songs of double meaning. They readily passed unchallenged among the numerous nonsense rhymes—that often rhymed lamely or not at all—which beguiled the hours afield or the moonlight gatherings in the "quarters," as well as served to fit the wild chants of some of their dances. Here is one whose characteristics tempt us to suppose it a calinda, and whose humor consists only in a childish play on words.

QUAND MO 'TE

Quand mo 'te dans grand chimin
Mo contré noin vié papa
Prise tobac jambette à couteau,
Taffia doux passé sirop.

Mo mandé quel heure li yé,
Li dit moin midi passé
Prise tobac jambette à couteau,
Taffia doux passé sirop.

Mo mandé mouchoi' tabac,
Li don moin mouchoi Madras.

There is another nonsense song that may or may not have been a dance. Its movement has the true wriggle. The dances were many; there were some popular in the West Indies that seem to have remained comparatively unknown in Louisiana: the *belair, bèlè,* or *béla*; the *cosaque*; the *biguine*. The *guiouba* was probably the famed *juba* of Georgia and the Carolinas.

NEG' PAS CAPA' MARCHÉ

Neg pas capa' marché sans mais dans poche,
   c'est pou volé poule.
Millate pas capa' marché sans la corde danse poche,
   c'est pou volé choual.
Blanc pas capa' marché sans la'zen dans poche,
   c'est pou volé filles.

The Love-Song

Among the songs which seem to have been sung for their own sake, and not for the dance, are certain sentimental ones of slow movement, tinged with that faint and gentle melancholy that every one of Southern experience has noticed in the glance of the African slave's eye; a sentiment ready to be turned, at any instant that may demand the change, into a droll, self-abasing humor. They have thus a special charm that has kept for them a place even in the regard of the Creole of to-day. How many ten thousands of black or tawny nurse "mammies," with heads wrapped in stiffly starched Madras kerchief turbans, and holding *'tit mait'e* or *'tit maitresse* to their bosoms, have made the infants' lullabies these gently sad strains of disappointed love or regretted youth, will never be known. Now and then the song would find its way through some master's growing child of musical ear, into the drawing-room; and it is from a Creole drawing-room in the Rue Esplanade that we draw the following, so familiar to all Creole ears and rendered with many variations of text and measure.

AH! SUZETTE

Ah! Suzette, Suzette to vé pas chère.
Ah! Suzette, chère amie, to pas laimein moin.

M'allé haut montagne zamie,
M'allé coupé canne zamie,
M'allé fé l'a'zent, chère amie,
Pou' po'té donne toi.

Ah! Suzette, Suzette to vé pas chère.
Ah! Suzette, chère amie, to pas laimein moin.

Mo courri dans bois, zamie,
Pou' toué zozo, zamie,
Pou'... fé l'a'zent, chère amie,
Pou' mo baille Suzette.

Ah! Suzette, Suzette to vé pas chère.
Ah! Suzette, chère amie, to pas laimein moin.

One may very safely suppose this song to have sprung from the poetic invention of some free black far away in the Gulf. A Louisiana slave would hardly have thought it possible to earn money for himself in the sugar-cane fields. The mention of mountains points back to St. Domingo.

It is strange to note in all this African-Creole lyric product how rarely its producers seem to have recognized the myriad charms of nature. The landscape, the seasons, the sun, moon, stars, the clouds, the storm, the peace that follows, the forest's solemn depths, the vast prairie, birds, insects, the breeze, the flowers—they are passed in silence. Was it because of the soul-destroying weight of bondage? Did the slave feel so painfully that the beauties of the natural earth were not for him? Was it because the overseer's eye was on him that his was not lifted upon them? It may have been—in part. But another truth goes with these. His songs were not often contemplative. They voiced not outward nature, but the inner emotions and passions of a nearly naked serpent-worshiper, and these looked not to the surrounding scene for sympathy; the surrounding scene belonged to his master. But love was his, and toil, and anger, and superstition, and malady. Sleep was his balm, food his reënforcement, the dance his pleasure, rum his longed-for nepenthe, and death the road back to Africa. These were his themes, and furnished the few scant figures of his verse.

The moment we meet the offspring of his contemplative thought, as we do in his apothegms and riddles, we find a change, and any or every object in sight, great or trivial, comely or homely, is wrought into the web of his traditional wit and wisdom. "Vo mié, savon, passé godron," he says, to teach a lesson of gentle forbearance ("Soap is worth more than tar"). And then, to point the opposite truth,—"Pas marré so chien avé saucisse" ("Don't chain your dog with links of sausage"). "Qui zamein 'tendé souris fé so nid dan zoré ç'at?" ("Who ever heard of mouse making nest in cat's ear?") And so, too, when love was his theme, apart from the madness of the dance—when his note fell to soft cooings the verse became pastoral. So it was in the song last quoted. And so, too, in this very African bit, whose air I have not:

> "Si to té tit zozo,
> Et mo-même, mo té fizi,
> Mo sré tchoué toé—boum!
> Ah! tchère bizou
> D'acazou,
> Mo laimein ou
> Comme cochon laimein la bou!"

Shall we translate literally?

> "If you were a little bird
> And myself, I were a gun,
> I would shoot you—boum!
> Ah! dear jewel
> Of mahogany,
> I love you
> As the hog loves mud."

One of the best of these Creole love-songs—one that the famed Gottschalk, himself a New Orleans Creole of pure blood, made use of—is the tender lament of one who sees the girl of his heart's choice the victim of chagrin in beholding a female rival wearing those vestments of extra quality that could only be the favors which both women had coveted from the hand of some one in the proud master-caste whence alone such favors could come. "Calalou," says the song, "has an embroidered petticoat, and Lolotte, or Zizi," as it is often sung, "has a—heartache." Calalou, here, I take to be a derisive nickname. Originally it is the term for a West Indian dish, a noted ragout. It must be intended to apply here to the quadroon women who swarmed into New Orleans in 1809 as refugees from Cuba, Guadeloupe, and other islands where the war against Napoleon exposed them to Spanish and British aggression. It was with this great influx of persons neither savage nor enlightened, neither white nor black, neither slave nor truly free, that the famous quadroon caste arose and flourished. If Calalou, in the verse, was one of these quadroon fair ones, the song is its own explanation.

POV' PITI MOMZEL ZIZI

Pov' piti Momzel Zizi,
Pov' piti Momzel Zizi,
Li gagin bo-bo, bo-bo
Dans so piti kèr à li.
Pov' piti Momzel Zizi,
Pov' piti Momzel Zizi,
Li gagin bo-bo, bo-bo
Dans so piti kèr à li.

Calalon poté madrasse
Li poté jipon garni;
Calalon poté madrasse
Li poté jipon garni!

Pov' piti Momzel Zizi,
Pov' piti Momzel Zizi,
Li gagin bo-bo, bo-bo
Dans so piti kèr à li.
Pov' piti Momzel Zizi,
Pov' piti Momzel Zizi,
Li gagin bo-bo, bo-bo
Dans so piti kèr à li.

D'amour quand poté la chaine.
Adieu, courri tout bonhèr;
D'amour quand poté la chaine.
Adieu, courri tout bonhèr!

Pov' piti Momzel Zizi,
Pov' piti Momzel Zizi,
Li gagin bo-bo, bo-bo
Dans so piti kèr à li.
Pov' piti Momzel Zizi,
Pov' piti Momzel Zizi,
Li gagin bo-bo, bo-bo
Li gagnin bo-bo, bo-bo…
Li gagnin bo-bo… dans kèr à li.

"Poor little Miss Zizi!" is what it means—"She has pain, pain in her little heart."
"À li" is simply the Creole possessive form; "corps à moin" would signify simply
myself. Calalou is wearing a Madras turban; she has on an embroidered petticoat;
[they tell their story and] Zizi has achings in her heart. And the second stanza
moralizes: "When you wear the chain of love"—maybe we can make it rhyme:

"When love's chains upon thee lie
Bid all happiness good-bye."

Poor little Zizi! say we also. Triumphant Calalou! We see that even her sort of freedom had its tawdry victories at the expense of the slave. A poor freedom it was, indeed: To have f. m. c. or f. w. c. tacked in small letters upon one's name perforce and by law, that all might know that the bearer was not a real freeman or freewoman, but only a free man (or woman) of color,—a title that could not be indicated by capital initials; to be the unlawful mates of luxurious bachelors, and take their pay in muslins, embroideries, prunella, and good living, taking with them the loathing of honest women and the salacious derision of the blackamoor; to be the sister, mother, father, or brother, of Calalou; to fall heir to property by sufferance, not by law; to be taxed for public education and not allowed to give that education to one's own children; to be shut out of all occupations that the master class could reconcile with the vague title of gentleman; to live in the knowledge that the law pronounced "death or imprisonment at hard labor for life" against whoever should be guilty of "writing, printing, publishing, or distributing anything having a tendency to create discontent among the free colored population": that it threatened death against whosoever should utter such things in private conversation; and that it decreed expulsion from the State to Calalou and all her kin of any age or condition if only they had come in across its bounds since 1807. In the enjoyment of such, ghastly freedom as this the flesh-pots of Egypt sometimes made the mouth water and provoked the tongue to sing its regrets for a past that seemed better than the present.

BON D'JE

> Dans tan mo té zène
> Mo zamein zonglé, bon Djé!
> A ç'tair m'apé vini vié,
> M'apé zonglé, bon Djé!
> M'apé zonglé bon tan qui passé,
> M'apé zonglé bon tan qui passé,
> M'apé zonglé bon tan qui passé.
>
> Dans tan mo té nesclave
> Mo servis mo maite, bon Djé!
> A ç'tair mo besoin repos,
> Mosers ton moune, bon Djé!
> M'apé zonglé bon tan qui passé,
> M'apé zonglé bon tan qui passé,
> M'apé zonglé bon tan qui passé.

Word for word we should have to render it,—"In times when I was young I never pondered—indulged in reverie, took on care," an archaic French word, *zongler*, still in use among the Acadians also in Louisiana; "mo zamein zonglé, bon D'jé"—"good Lord!" "*Açtair*" is "à cette heure"—"at this hour," that is, "now—these days." "These days I am getting old—I am pondering, good Lord!" etc. Some time in the future, it may be, some Creole will give us translations of these things, worthy to be called so. Meantime suffer this:

> "In the days of my youth not a dream had I, good Lord!
> These times I am growing old, full of dreams am I, good Lord!

I have dreams of those good times gone by! *(ter)*

When I was a slave, one boss had I, good Lord!
These times when I'm needing rest all hands serve I, good Lord!
I have dreams," etc.

The Lay and the Dirge

There were other strains of misery, the cry or the vagabond laugh and song of the friendless orphan for whom no asylum door would open, but who found harbor and food in the fields and wildwood and the forbidden places of the wicked town. When that Creole whom we hope for does come with his good translations, correcting the hundred and one errors that may be in these pages, we must ask him if he knows the air to this:

> "Pitis sans popa, pitis sans moman,
> Qui ça 'ou' zaut' fé pou' gagnein l'a'zanc,[1]
> > No courri l'aut' bord pou' cercé patt ç'at'[2]
> > No tournein bayou pou' péç'é patassa;[3]
> > Et v'là comm' ça no té fé nou' l'a'zan.

> "Pitis sans popa, pitis sans moman,
> Qui ça 'ou' zaut' fé, etc.
> > No courri dans bois fouillé latanié,[4]
> > No vend' so racin' pou' fou'bi' planç'é;
> > Et v'là, comm' ça, etc.

> "Pitis sans popa, etc.
> > Pou' fé di thé n'a fouillé sassaf'as
> > Pou' fé di l'enc' no po'té grain' sougras;[5]
> > Et v'là, etc.

> "Pitis sans popa, etc.
> > No courri dans bois ramassé cancos;[6]
> > Avé' nou' la caze no trappé zozos;[7]
> > Et v'là, etc.

> "Pitis sans popa, etc.
> > No courri à soir c'ez Mom'selle Maroto,
> > Dans la rie St. Ann ou no té zoué loto;
> > Et v'là," etc.

1. L'argent—money.
2. "We go to the other side" [of the river] "to get cats' paws," a delicious little blue swamp berry.
3. The perch. The little sunfish or "pumpkin seed," miscalled through the southwest.
4. Dwarf palmetto, whose root is used by the Creoles as a scrubbing-brush.
5. Pokeberries.
6. *Cancos,* Indian name for a wild purple berry.
7. Oiseaux, birds.

"Little ones without father, little ones without mother,
What do you to keep soul and body together?
    The river we cross for wild berries to search;
    We follow the bayou a-fishing for perch;
    And that's how we keep soul and body together.

"Little ones without, etc.
    Palmetto we dig from the swamp's bristling stores
    And sell its stout roots for scrubbing the floors;
    And that's how, etc.

"Little ones, etc.
    The sassafras root we dig up; it makes tea;
    For ink the ripe pokeberry clusters bring we;
    And that's how, etc.

"Little ones, etc.
    We go to the woods *cancos* berries to fetch,
    And in our trap cages the nonpareils[1] catch;
    And that's how, etc.

"Little ones, etc.
    At evening we visit Mom'selle Maroto,
    In St. Ann's street, to gamble awhile at keno;
    And that's how we keep soul and body together."

Here was companionship with nature—the companionship of the vagabond. We need not doubt that these little orphan vagrants could have sung for us the song, from which in an earlier article we have already quoted a line or two of Cayetano's circus, probably the most welcome intruder that ever shared with the man Friday and his song-dancing fellows and sweet-hearts the green, tough sod of Congo Square.

"C'est Miché Cayétane,
   Qui sorti la Havane
Avec so chouals[2] et so macacs.[3]
Li gagnein ein nhomme qui dancé dans sac;
Li gagnein qui dancé si yé la main;
Li gagnein zaut', à choual, qui boir' di vin;
Li gagnein oussi ein zein, zoli mom'selle,
Qui monté choual sans bride et sans selle!
Pou' di' tou' ça mo pas capab';
Mé mo souvien ein qui 'valé sab'!
Yé n'en oussi tou' sort' bétail.
Yé pas montré pou la négrail';
Gniapas là dotchians dos-brilé,[4]

1. The nonpareil, pape, or painted bunting, is the favorite victim of the youthful bird-trappers.
2. Chevals—chevaux.
3. Macaques.
4. "Gniapas là dotchians dos-brilé," "Il n'y pas là des *dotchians* avec les dos brulés." The *dotchian dos-brulé* is the white trash with sunburnt back, the result of working in the fields. It is an expression of supreme contempt for the *petits blancs*—low whites—to contrast them with the *gros madames et gros michies.*

Pou' fé tapaze et pou' hirlé;
Cé gros madame et gros miché,
Qui ménein là tous pitits yé,
   'Oir Miché Cayétane,
   Qui 'rivé la Havane
Avec so chouals et so macacs."

    Should the Louisiana Creole negro undertake to render his song to us in English, it would not be exactly the African-English of any other State in the Union. Much less would it resemble the gross dialects of the English-torturing negroes of Jamaica, or Barbadoes, or the Sea Islands of Carolina. If we may venture—

"Dass Cap'm Cayetano,
   W'at comin' fum Havano,[1]
Wid 'is monkey' an' 'is nag'!
An' one man w'at dance in bag,
An' mans dance on dey han'—cut shine'
An' gallop hoss sem time drink wine!
An' b'u'ful young missy dah beside,
Ridin' 'dout air sadd' aw brid'e;[2]
To tell h-all dat—he cann' be tole.
Man teck a sword an' swall' 'im whole!
Beas'es?[3] ev'y sawt o' figgah!
Dat show ain't fo' no common niggah!
Dey don' got deh no po' white cuss'—
Sunbu'nt back!—to holla an' fuss.
Dass ladies fine, and gennymuns gran'.
Fetchin' dey chilluns dah—all han'!
   Fo' see Cayetano,
   W'at come fum Havano
Wid 'is monkey' an' 'is nag'!"

    A remarkable peculiarity of these African Creole songs of every sort is that almost without exception they appear to have originated in the masculine mind, and to be the expressions of the masculine heart. Untrained as birds, their males made the songs. We come now, however, to the only exception I have any knowledge of, a song expressive of feminine sentiment, the capitulation of some belle Layotte to the tender enticement of a Creole-born chief or *candjo*. The pleading tone of the singer's defense against those who laugh at her pretty chagrin is—it seems to me—touching.

CRIOLE CANDJO

In zou' in zène in Criole Candjo,
Belle passé blanc dandan là yo,
Li té tout tans apé dire,
"Vini, zami, pou' nous rire."

---

    1. To turn final *a* into *o* for the purpose of rhyme is the special delight of the singing negro. I used to hear as part of a moonlight game.
    2. Riding without e'er a saddle or bridle.
    3. Beasts—wild animals.

Non, miché, m'pas oulé rire, moin.
Non, miché, m'pas oulé rire.
Non, miché, m'pas oulé rire, moin.
Non, miché, m'pas oulé rire.

Mo courri dans youn bois voisin;
Mais Criole là prend même ci min
Et tous tans li m'apé dire,
"Vini, zami, pou' nous rire."

Non, miché, m'pas oulé rire, moin.
Non, miché, m'pas oulé rire.
Non, miché, m'pas oulé rire, moin.
Non, miché, m'pas oulé rire.

Mais li té tant cicané moi,
Pou' li té quitté moin youn fois
Mo té 'blizé pou li dire,
Oui, miché, mo oulé rire.
        Oui miché, etc.

Zaut tous qu'ap'es rire moin là bas,
Si zaut té conné Candjo là,
Qui belle façon li pou' rire,
Djé pini moin! zaut s'ré dire,
        Oui, miché, etc.

One day one young Creole candio,
Mo' fineh dan sho nuf white beau,
        Kip all de time meckin' free—
        "Swithawt, meck merrie wid me."
"Naw, sah, I dawn't want meck merrie, me.
Naw, sah, I dawn't want meck merrie."

I go teck walk in wood close by;
But Creole tek' sem road, and try
        All time, all time, to meck free—
        "Swithawt, meck merrie wid me."
"Naw, sah, I dawn't want meck merrie, me.
Naw, sah, I dawn't want meck merrie."

But him slide roun' an' roun' dis chile,
Tell, jis' fo' sheck 'im off lill while,
        Me, I was bleedze fo' say, "Shoo!
        If I'll meck merrie wid you?
O, yass, I ziss leave meck merrie me;
Yass, seh, I ziss leave meck merrie."

You-alls w'at laugh at me so well,
I wish you'd knowed dat Creole swell,
        Wid all 'is swit, smilin' trick'.

'Pon my soul! you'd done say, quick,
"O, yass, I ziss leave meck merrie me;
Yass, seh, I ziss leave meck merrie."

But we began this chapter in order to speak of songs that bear more distinctly than anything yet quoted the features of the true lay or historical narrative song, commemorating pointedly and in detail some important episode in the history of the community.

It is interesting to contrast the solemnity with which these events are treated when their heroes were black, and the broad buffoonery of the song when the affair it celebrates was one that mainly concerned the masters. Hear, for example, through all the savage simplicity of the following rhymeless lines, the melancholy note that rises and falls but never intermits. The song is said to be very old, dating from the last century. It is still sung, but the Creole gentleman who procured it for me from a former slave was not able to transcribe or remember the air.

LUBIN

Tremblant-terr'[1] vini 'branlé moulin;
Tonnerr' chiel[2] tombé bourlé[3] moulin;
　　Tou' moun[4] dans moulin là péri.
Temoins vini qui vend'[5] Libin.
Yé dit Libin metté di fé.
Yé hissé saffaud[6] pou' so la tête.[7]
　　Saïda! m'allé mourri, Saïda!
Mo zamis di comm' ça: "Libin,
Faut to donn' Zilié to bitin."[8]
Cofaire[9] mo sré donnein Zilié?
Pou' moin Zilié zamein lavé;[10]
Zilié zamein 'passé[11] pou moin.
　　Saïda! m'allé mourri, Saïda!

An earthquake came and shook the mill;
The heavens' thunders fell and burned it;
Every soul in the mill perished.
Witnesses came who betrayed Lubin.
They said he set the mill on fire.
They raised a scaffold to take off his head.
　　Saïda! I am going to die!

1. Tremblant de terre—earthquake.
2. Ciel.
3. Brulée.
4. Tout le monde.
5. Vendaient—sold, betrayed.
6. Echafaud.
7. So la tetê: Creole possessive form for *his head*.
8. Butin: literally plunder, but used, as the word plunder is by the negro, for personal property.
9. Porquoi faire.
10. Washed (clothes).
11. Ironed.

My friends speak in this way: "Lubin,
You ought to give Julia your plunder."
Why should I give it to Julia?
For me Julia never washed clothes;
Julia never ironed for me.
      Saïda! I am going to die!

Or notice again the stately tone of lamentation over the fate of a famous negro insurrectionist, as sung by old Madeleine of St. Bernard parish to the same Creole friend already mentioned, who kindly wrote down the lines on the spot for this collection. They are fragmentary, extorted by littles from the shattered memory of the ancient crone. Their allusion to the Cabildo places their origin in the days when that old colonial council administered Spanish rule over the province.

OUARRÂ ST. MALO

Aïe! zein zens, vini fé ouarrâ
Pou' pôv' St. Malo dans l'embas!
Yé ç'assé li avec yé chien,
Yé tiré li ein coup d'fizi,

Yé halé li la cyprier,
So bras yé 'tassé[1] par derrier,
Yé 'tassé so la main divant;
Yé 'marré[2] li apé queue choual,
Yé trainein li zouqu'à la ville.
Divant michés là dans Cabil'e
Yé quisé[3] li li fé complot
Pou' coupé cou à tout ye blancs.
Yé 'mandé li qui so compères;
Pôv' St. Malo pas di' a-rien!
Zize[4] là li lir' so la sentence
Et pis[5] li fé dressé potence.
Ye halé choual—ç'arette parti—
Pôv St. Malo resté pendi!
Eine hèr soleil deza levée.
Quand yé pend li si la levée.
Yé laissé so corps balancé
Pou' carancro gagnein manzé.

1. Attachée.
2. Amarré, an archaism, common to negroes and Acadians: moored, for fastened.
3. Accusée.
4. Juge.
5. Puis.

THE DIRGE OF ST. MALO

Alas! young men, come, make lament
For poor St. Malo in distress!
They chased, they hunted him with dogs,
They fired at him with a gun,

They hauled him from the cypress swamp.
His arms they tied behind his back,
They tied his hands in front of him;
They tied him to a horse's tail,
They dragged him up into the town.
Before those grand Cabildo men
They charged that he had made a plot
To cut the throats of all the whites.
They asked him who his comrades were;
Poor St. Malo said not a word!
The judge his sentence read to him,
And then they raised the gallows-tree.
They drew the horse—the cart moved off—
And left St. Malo hanging there.
The sun was up an hour high
When on the Levee he was hung;
They left his body swinging there,
For carrion crows to feed upon.

It would be curious, did the limits of these pages allow, to turn from such an outcry of wild mourning as this, and contrast with it the clownish flippancy with which the great events are sung, upon whose issue from time to time the fate of the whole land—society, government, the fireside, the lives of thousands—hung in agonies of suspense. At the same time it could not escape notice how completely in each case, while how differently in the two, the African has smitten his image into every line: in the one sort, the white, uprolled eyes and low wail of the savage captive, who dares not lift the cry of mourning high enough for the jealous ear of the master; in the other, the antic form, the grimacing face, the brazen laugh, and self-abasing confessions of the buffoon, almost within the whisk of the public jailer's lash. I have before me two songs of dates almost fifty years apart. The one celebrates the invasion of Louisiana by the British under Admiral Cochrane and General Pakenham in 1814; the other, the capture and occupation of New Orleans by Commodore Farragut and General Butler in 1862.

It was on the morning of the twenty-third of December, 1814, that the British columns, landing from a fleet of barges and hurrying along the narrow bank of a small canal in a swamp forest, gained a position in the open plain on the banks of the Mississippi only six miles below New Orleans, and with no defenses to oppose them between their vantage-ground and the city. The surprise was so complete that, though they issued from the woods an hour before noon, it was nearly three hours before the news reached the town. But at nightfall General Jackson fell upon them and fought in the dark the engagement which the song commemorates, the indecisive battle of Chalmette.

The singer ends thus:

> "Fizi z'Anglé yé fé bim! bim!
> Carabin Kaintock yé fé zim! zim!
> Mo di' moin, sauvé to la peau!
> Mo zété corps au bord do l'eau;
> Quand mo rivé li té fé clair.
> Madàm' li prend' ein coup d'colère;
> Li fé donn' moin ein quat' piquié
> Passequé mo pas sivi mouchié;
> Mais moin, mo vo mié quat' piquié
> Passé ein coup d'fizi z'Anglé!"

> "The English muskets went bim! bim!
> Kentucky rifles went zim! zim!
> I said to myself, save your skin!
> I scampered along the water's edge;
> When I got back it was day-break.
> Mistress flew into a passion;
> She had me whipped at the 'four stakes,'
> Because I didn't stay with master;
> But the 'four stakes' for me is better than
> A musket shot from an Englishman."

The story of Farragut's victory and Butler's advent in April, 1862, is sung with the still lighter heart of one in whose day the "quartre piquets" was no longer a feature of the calaboose. Its refrain is:

> "An-hé!
> Qui ça qui rivé?
> C'est Ferraguitt et p'i Botlair,
> Qui rivé."

The story is long and silly, much in the humor of

> "Hark! hark!
> The dogs do bark."

We will lay it on the table.

The Voodoos

The dance and song entered into the negro worship. That worship was as dark and horrid as bestialized savagery could make the adoration of serpents. So revolting was it, and so morally hideous, that even in the West Indian French possessions a hundred years ago, with the slave-trade in full blast and the West Indian planter and slave what they were, the orgies of the Voodoos were forbidden. Yet both there and in Louisiana they were practiced.

The Aradas, St. Méry tells us, introduced them. They brought them from their homes beyond the Slave Coast, one of the most dreadfully benighted regions of all Africa. He makes the word Vaudaux. In Louisiana it is written Voudou and Voodoo, and is often changed on the negro's lips to Hoodoo. It is the name of an imaginary being of vast supernatural powers residing in the form of a harmless snake. This spiritual influence or potentate is the recognized antagonist and opposite of Obi, the great African manitou or deity, or him whom the Congoes vaguely generalize as Zombi. In Louisiana, as I have been told by that learned Creole scholar the late Alexander Dimitry, Voodoo bore as a title of greater solemnity the additional name of Maignan, and that even in the Calinda dance, which he had witnessed innumerable times, was sometimes heard, at the height of its frenzy, the invocation—

"Aïe! Aïe!
Voodoo Magnan!"

The worship of Voodoo is paid to a snake kept in a box. The worshipers are not merely a sect, but in some rude, savage way also an order. A man and woman chosen from their own number to be the oracles of the serpent deity are called the king and queen. The queen is the more important of the two, and even in the present dilapidated state of the worship in Louisiana, where the king's office has almost or quite disappeared, the queen is still a person of great note.

She reigns as long as she continues to live. She comes to power not by inheritance, but by election or its barbarous equivalent. Chosen for such qualities as would give her a natural supremacy, personal attractions among the rest, and ruling over superstitious fears and desires of every fierce and ignoble sort, she wields no trivial influence. I once saw, in her extreme old age, the famed Marie Laveau. Her dwelling was in the quadroon quarter of New Orleans, but a step or two from Congo Square, a small adobe cabin just off the sidewalk, scarcely higher than its close board fence, whose batten gate yielded to the touch and revealed the crazy doors and windows spread wide to the warm air, and one or two tawny faces within, whose expressions was divided between a pretense of contemptuous inattention and a frowning resentment of the intrusion. In the center of a small room whose ancient cypress floor was worn with scrubbing and sprinkled with crumbs of soft brick—a Creole affectation of superior cleanliness—sat, quaking with feebleness in an ill-looking old rocking-chair, her body bowed, and her wild, grey witch's tresses hanging about her shriveled, yellow neck, the queen of the Voodoos. Three generations of her children were within the faint beckon of her helpless, waggling wrist and fingers. They said she was over a hundred years old, and there was nothing to cast doubt upon the statement. She had shrunken away from her skin; it was like a turtle's. Yet withal one could hardly help but see that the face, now so withered, had once been handsome and commanding. There was still a faint shadow of the departed beauty on her forehead, the spark of an old fire in the sunken, glistening eyes, and a vestige of imperiousness in the fine, slightly aquiline nose, and even about her silent, woe-begone mouth. Her grandson stood by, an uninteresting quadroon between forty and fifty years old, looking strong, empty-minded, and trivial enough; but his mother, her daughter, was also present, a woman of some seventy years, and a most striking and majestic figure. In features, stature, and bearing she was regal. One had but to look on her, impute her brillian-cies—too untamable and severe to be called charms or graces—to her mother, and remember what New Orleans was long years ago, to understand how the name of Marie Laveau should have driven itself inextricably into the traditions of the town and the times. Had this visit been postponed a few months it would have been too late. Marie Laveau is dead; Malvina Latour is queen. As she appeared presiding over a Voodoo ceremony on the night of the 23d of June, 1884, she is described as a bright mulattress of about forty-eight, of "extremely handsome figure," dignified bearing, and a face indicative of a comparatively high order of intelligence. She wore a neat blue, white-dotted calico gown, and a "brilliant *tignon* (turban) gracefully tied."

It is pleasant to say that this worship, in Louisiana, at least, and in comparison with what it once was, has grown to be a rather trivial affair. The practice of its midnight forest rites seemed to sink into inanition along with Marie Laveau. It long ago diminished in frequency to once a year, the chosen night always being the Eve of St. John. For several years past even these annual celebrations have been suspended; but in the summer of 1884 they were—let it be hoped, only for the once—resumed.

When the queen decides that such a celebration shall take place, she appoints a night for the gathering, and some remote, secluded spot in the forest for the rendezvous. Thither all the worshipers are summoned. St. Méry, careless of the power of the scene, draws in practical, unimaginative lines the picture of such a gathering in St. Domingo, in the times when the "*véritable Vaudaux*" had lost but little of the primitive African character. The worshipers are met, decked with kerchiefs more or less numerous, red being everywhere the predominating color. The king, abundantly adorned with them, wears one of pure red about his forehead as a diadem. A blue ornamental cord completes his insignia. The queen, in simple dress and wearing a red cord and a heavily decorated belt, is beside him near a rude altar. The silence of midnight is overhead, the gigantic forms and shadows and still, dank airs of the tropical forest close in around, and on the altar, in a small box ornamented with little tinkling bells, lies, unseen, the living serpent. The worshipers have begun their devotions to it by presenting themselves before it in a body, and uttering professions of their fidelity and belief in its power. They cease, and now the royal pair, in tones of parental authority and protection, are extolling the great privilege of being a devotee, and inviting the faithful to consult the oracle. The crowd makes room, and a single petitioner draws near. He is the senior member of the order. His prayer is made. The king becomes deeply agitated by the presence within him of the spirit invoked. Suddenly he takes the box from the altar and sets it on the ground. The queen steps upon it and with convulsive movements utters the answers of the deity beneath her feet. Another and another suppliant, approaching in the order of seniority, present, singly, their petitions, and humbly or exultingly, according to the nature of the responses, which hangs on the fierce caprice of the priestess, accept these utterances and make way for the next, with his prayer of fear or covetousness, love, jealousy, petty spite or deadly malice. At length the last petitioner is answered. Now a circle is formed, the caged snake is restored to the altar, and the humble and multifarious oblations of the worshipers are received, to be devoted not only to the trivial expenses of this worship, but also to the relief of members of the order whose distresses call for such aid. Again, the royal ones are speaking, issuing orders for execution in the future, orders that have not always in view, mildly says St. Méry, good order and public tranquillity. Presently the ceremonies become more forbidding. They are taking a horrid oath, smearing their lips with the blood of some slaughtered animal, and swearing to suffer death rather than disclose any secret of the order, and to inflict death on any who may commit such treason. Now a new applicant for membership steps into their circle, there are a few trivial formalities, and the Voodoo dance begins. The postulant dances frantically in the middle of the ring, only pausing from time to time to receive heavy alcoholic draughts in great haste and return more wildly to his leapings and writhings until he falls in convulsions. He is lifted, restored, and presently conducted to the altar, takes his oath, and by a ceremonial stroke from one of the sovereigns is admitted a full participant in the privileges and obligations of the devilish freemasonry. But the dance goes on about the snake. The contortions of the upper part of the body, especially of the neck and shoulders, are such as threaten to dislocate them. The queen shakes the box and tinkles its bells, the rum-bottle gurgles, the chant alternates between king and chorus—

> "Eh! eh! Bomba, honc! honc![1]
> Canga bafio tay,
> Canga moon day lay,
> Canga do keelah,
> Canga li—"

There are swoonings and ravings, nervous tremblings beyond control, incessant writhings and turnings, tearing of garments, even biting of the flesh—every imaginable invention of the devil.

St. Méry tells us of another dance invented in the West Indies by a negro, analogous to the Voodoo dance, but more rapid, and in which dancers had been known to fall dead. This was the "Dance of Don Pedro." The best efforts of police had, in his day, only partially suppressed it. Did it ever reach Louisiana? Let us, at a venture, say no.

To what extent the Voodoo worship still obtains here would be difficult to say with certainty. The affair of June, 1884, as described by Messrs. Augustin and Whitney, eye-witnesses, was an orgy already grown horrid enough when they turned their backs upon it. It took place at a wild and lonely spot where the dismal cypress swamp behind New Orleans meets the waters of Lake Pontchartrain in a wilderness of cypress stumps and rushes. It would be hard to find in nature a more painfully desolate region. Here in a fisherman's cabin sat the Voodoo worshipers cross-legged on the floor about an Indian basket of herbs and some beans, some bits of bone, some oddly wrought bunches of feathers, and some saucers of small cakes. The queen presided, sitting on the only chair in the room. There was no king, no snake—at least none visible to the onlookers. Two drummers beat with their thumbs on gourds covered

1. "Hen, hen!" in St. Méry's spelling of it for French pronunciation. As he further describes the sound in a foot-note, it must have been a horrid grunt.

with sheepskin, and a white-wooled old man scraped that hideous combination of banjo and violin, whose head is covered with rattlesnake skin, and of which the Chinese are the makers and masters. There was singing—"*M'allé couri dans déser*" ("I am going into the wilderness"), a chant and refrain not worth the room they would take—and there was frenzy and a circling march, wild shouts, delirious gesticulations and posturings, drinking, and amongst other frightful nonsense the old trick of making fire blaze from the mouth by spraying alcohol from it upon the flame of a candle.

But whatever may be the quantity of the Voodoo *worship* left in Louisiana, its superstitions are many and are everywhere. Its charms are resorted to by the malicious, the jealous, the revengeful, or the avaricious, or held in terror, not by the timorous only, but by the strong, the courageous, the desperate. To find under his mattress an acorn hollowed out, stuffed with the hair of some dead person, pierced with four holes on four sides, and two small chicken feathers drawn through them so as to cross inside the acorn; or to discover on his door-sill at daybreak a little box containing a dough or waxen heart stuck full of pins; or to hear that his avowed foe or rival has been pouring cheap champagne in the four corners of Congo Square at midnight, when there was no moon, will strike more abject fear into the heart of many a stalwart negro or melancholy quadroon than to face a leveled revolver. And it is not only the colored man that holds to these practices and fears. Many a white Creole gives them full credence. What wonder, when African Creoles were the nurses of so nearly all of them? Many shrewd men and women, generally colored persons, drive a trade in these charms and in oracular directions for their use or evasion; many a Creole—white as well as other tints—female, too, as well as male—will pay a Voodoo "*monteure*" to "make a work," *i. e.*, to weave a spell, for the prospering of some scheme or wish too ignoble to by prayed for at any shrine inside the church. These milder incantations are performed within the witch's or wizard's own house, and are made up, for the most part, of a little pound cake, some lighted candle ends, a little syrup of sugar-cane, pins, knitting-needles, and a trifle of anisette. But fear naught; an Obi charm will enable you to smile defiance against all such mischief; or if you will but consent to be a magician, it is they, the Voodoos, one and all, who will hold you in absolute terror. Or, easier, a frizzly chicken! If you have on your premises a frizzly chicken, you can lie down and laugh—it is a checkmate!

A planter once found a Voodoo charm, or *ouanga* (wongah); this time it was a bit of cotton cloth folded about three cow-peas and some breast feathers of a barn-yard fowl, and covered with a tight wrapping of thread. When he proposed to take it to New Orleans his slaves were full of consternation. "Marse Ed, ef ye go on d'boat wid dat-ah, de boat'll sink wi' yer. Fore d'Lord, it will!" For some reason it did not. Here is a genuine Voodoo song, given me by Lafcadio Hearn, though what the words mean none could be more ignorant of than the present writer. They are rendered phonetically in French.

> Héron mandé, Héron mandé,
> Tigui li papa, Héron mandé,
> Tigui li papa, Héron mandé,

Héron mandé, Héron mandé,
Do sé dan go-do.

And another phrase: "Ah tingouai yé, Ah tingouai yé, Ah ouai ya, Ah ouai ya, Ah tingouai yé, Do sé dan go-do, Ah tingouai yé," etc.

Songs of Woods and Waters

A last page to the songs of the chase and of the boat. The circumstances that produced them have disappeared. There was a time, not so long ago, when traveling in Louisiana was done almost wholly by means of the paddle, the oar, or the "sweep." Every plantation had its river or bayou front, and every planter his boat and skilled crew of black oarsmen. The throb of their song measured the sweep of the oars, and as their bare or turbaned heads and shining bodies, naked to the waist, bowed forward and straightened back in ceaseless alternation, their strong voices chanted the praise of the silent, broad-hatted master who sat in the stern. Now and then a line was interjected in manly boast to their own brawn, and often the praise of the master softened off into tender laudations of the charms of some black or tawny Zilié, 'Zabette, or Zalli. From the treasures of the old chest already mentioned comes to my hand, from the last century most likely, on a ragged yellow sheet of paper, written with a green ink, one of these old songs. It would take up much room; I have made a close translation of its stanzas:

ROWERS' SONG

Sing, lads; our master bids us sing.
For master cry out loud and strong.
The water with the long oar strike.
Sing, lads, and let us haste along.

'Tis for our master we will sing.
We'll sing for our young mistresses.
And sweethearts we must not forget—
Zoé, Mérente, Zabelle, Louise.

Sing, fellows, for our own true loves.
My lottery prize! Zoé, my belle!
She's like a wild young doe, she knows
The way to jump and dance so well!

Black diamonds are her bright, black eyes,
Her teeth and lilies are alike.
Sing, fellows, for my true love, and
The water with the long oar strike.

See! see! the town! Hurrah! hurrah!
Master returns in pleasant mood.
He's going to treat his boys all 'round.
Hurrah! hurrah for master good!

From the same treasury comes a hunting song. Each stanza begins and ends with the loud refrain: *"Bomboula! bomboula!"* Some one who has studied African tongues may be able to say whether this word is one with Bamboula, the name of the dance and of the drum that dominates it. *Oula* seems to be an infinitive termination of many Congo verbs, and *boula*, De Lanzières says, means to beat. However, the dark hunters of a hundred years ago knew, and between their outcries of the loud, rumbling word sang, in this song, their mutual exhortation to rise, take guns, fill powder-horns, load up, call dogs, make haste and be off to the woods to find game for master's table and their own grosser *cuisine*; for the one, deer, squirrels, rabbits, birds; for the other, *chat oués* (raccoons), that make *"si bon gombo"* (such good gumbo!). "Don't fail to kill them, boys,—and the tigercats that eat men; and if we meet a bear, we'll vanquish him! Bomboula! bomboula!" The lines have a fine African ring in them, but—one mustn't print everything.

Another song, of wood and water both, though only the water is mentioned, I have direct from former Creole negro slaves. It is a runaway's song of defiance addressed to the high sheriff Fleuriau (Charles Jean Baptiste Fleuriau, Alguazil mayor), a Creole of the Cabildo a hundred and fifteen years ago. At least one can think so, for the name is not to be found elsewhere.

O Zénéral Florido!
C'est vrai yé pas capab' pran moin!
O Zénéral La Florido!
C'est vrai yé pas capab' pran moin!

O General Florido!
Indeed fo' true dey can't catch me!
O General La Fleuriau!
Indeed fo' true dey can't catch me!

Yen a ein counan si la mer
    C'est vrai, etc.   } *Bis.*

Dey got[1] one schooner out at sea
    Indeed fo' true, etc.   } *Bis.*

Sometimes the black man found it more convenient not to run away himself, but to make other articles of property seem to escape from custody. He ventured to forage on his own account, retaining his cabin as a base of operations, and seeking his adventures not so far from the hen-coop and pig-pen as rigid principles would have dictated. Now that he is free, he is willing to reveal these little pleasantries—as one of the bygones—to the eager historian. Much nocturnal prowling was done on the

---

1. "Dey got" is a vulgarism of Louisiana Creoles, white and colored, for "There is." It is a transfer into English of the French idiom *Il y a.*

waters of the deep, forest-darkened bayous, in *pirogues* (dug-outs). For secret signals to accomplices on shore they resorted to singing. What is so innocent as music! The words were in some African tongue. We have one of these songs from the negroes themselves, with their own translation and their own assurance that the translation is correct. The words have a very Congo-ish sound. The Congo tongue knows no *r*; but the fact is familiar that in America the negro interchanges the sounds of *r* and *l* as readily as does the Chinaman. We will use both an English and a French spelling.

DÉ ZAB

Day zab, day zab, day koonoo wi wi,
Day zab, day zab, day koonoo wi wi,
Koonoo wi wi wi wi,
Koonoo wi wi wi wi,
Koonoo wi wi wi momzah......
Momzah, momzah, momzah, momzah,
Rozah, rozah, rozah, a-a momzah.

Dé zab, dé zab, kounou ouaïe, ouaïe,
Dé zab, dé zab, kounou ouaïe, ouaïe,
Kounou ouaïe, ouaïe, ouaïe, ouaïe,
Kounou ouaïe, ouaïe, ouaïe, ouaïe,
Kounou ouaïe, ouaïe, ouaïe, momza......
Momza, momza, momza, momza,
Roza, roza, roza, et momza.

The whole chant consists of but six words besides a single conjunction. It means, its singers avowed, "Out from under the trees our boat moves into the open water— bring us large game and small game!" *Dé zab* sounds like *des arbs*, and they call it French, but the rest they claimed as good "Affykin." We cannot say. We are sappers and miners in this quest, not philologists. When they come on behind, if they ever think it worth their while to do so, the interpretation of this strange song may be not more difficult than that of the famous inscription discovered by Mr. Pickwick. But, as well as the present writer can know, all that have been given here are genuine antiques.

(1886)

GEORGE FITZHUGH

Southern Thought Again

When a public opinion is formed on a state of existing facts, and of anticipated results, and an entire change of facts and anticipations takes place, public opinion itself must also change.

Fifty years ago all christendom believed that if the negroes were emancipated, they would become more moral, intelligent, and industrious. The experiment of emancipation has been tried in every form, and on the large as well as the small scale.

Whether in South America or the West Indies, in our Southern or Northern States, in Liberia or Sierra Leone, the free negro is an idler and a nuisance. Besides, his emancipation has so diminished Southern tropical products, that the poor laboring whites cannot afford to purchase the common necessaries of life. Moreover, to obviate this great evil, we see France and England reviving the slave-trade, under new forms, and Cuba actively engaged in it, under its old form, rendered far more cruel, however, by the abortive attempts to suppress it.

Now, we say that, with the experience of the last fifty years, it is impossible for public opinion, in any part of christendom, to remain on the subject of negro slavery, what it was fifty years ago. Mistaken philanthropy has had full sway, and its entire failure must give rise to new doctrines on this subject.

These doctrines begin to be openly preached, and practiced on, too. The South leads opinion; she virtually proposes a renewal of the old slave trade. But the North and Europe are ahead of her in practice, for they are carrying on the trade, whilst she is only discussing its propriety. Yet, even in the British Parliament, regret is expressed for the great blunder of negro emancipation; and some speakers went on to palliate, if not to justify, the old slave-trade. One of them saying in debate, that only five per cent of the negroes died on the middle passage, whilst ten per cent of English troops sent to India perished on their way.

The latest accounts from Marautius show that she is flourishing. Because near two hundred thousand Asiatic slaves, or coolies, have been introduced into that single little colony within a few years past.

Abolitionism is dying out, because it is deprived of its old arguments and golden expectations, because it has done no good, and stands convicted before the world of infinite mischief.

The extreme pro-slavery men are the last to discover this state of facts; because a Northern sectional party is on the increase, they think abolition is increasing. But the origin and growth of that party has been all owing to the advance of pro-slavery doctrines at the South, and the consequent, seeming aggressions of the South. At the time of the ordinance of 1789, the South seemed willing to give up all share in the territories. Under the Missouri Compromise she claimed more; and now she claims equal right in all the territories with the North, and she is successfully maintaining her claim. She leads public opinion everywhere, because she is in advance of that new counter-current of opinion, that has set in everywhere, about slavery. Soon the Democratic party will be in a majority again at the North. The South will take some other advance step on the subject of slavery, and then a new Northern party will be formed to resist Southern aggression. But nature is sure in the long run to conquer, and nature is on the side of the South. Negro slavery is as indispensable to the North as to us. They begin to see it, and to feel it, too. The introduction of more negroes, and the extension of slave territory, are new doctrines with us. Give the North a little time, and she will eagerly adopt them. We are her slave colonies, and she will command the commerce of the world. In the conduct of France and England about coolies and apprentices, we have a foretaste of what the North will do. Those nations need slave colonies, and if Northern fanatics are tired of union with the South, France or England will be ready to unite with us on favorable terms.

The world sadly needs works on the general subject of slavery—on slavery in the abstract—a history and philosophy of the institution.

Though it has been through all time the most common condition of mankind, little is to be found in the literature of the world about it, except a few pages of Aristotle and our own crude suggestions.

The attempts to defend negro slavery as exceptional have been written with signal ability by the ablest men in the South. But it is vain to preach against the prejudices of mankind, especially where those prejudices have some foundation in truth. Negro slavery gave rise to abolition, (which never existed before) because, in its inception, it was attended with much that was odious and cruel, and continues so to be attended in Cuba and Brazil. There, slaves are still worked to death, and it requires large annual importations to keep up the supply.

The strongest argument against slavery, and all the prejudice against it, arise from the too great inferiority of race, which begets cruel and negligent treatment in the masters, who naturally feel little sympathy for ignorant, brutal savages. Inferiority of race is quite as good an argument against negro slavery as in its favor.

We, of the South, have most successfully shown that, as the negro advances in civilization, the master becomes attached to him; and that, eventually, this attachment secures to him kind treatment and an abundant supply of the necessaries of life. But the whole history of the institution shows, that, in giving up slavery in the abstract, we take the weakest position of defence that we could possibly select. We admit it to be wrong, and then attempt to defend it in that peculiar form which has always been most odious to mankind.

We set out to write something of a rambling essay, and, indeed, the subject of Southern Thought is so large and suggestive, that it is difficult to write otherwise.

The first great Southern thought will be to refute the political economy of the "let alone" Free Trade School, and adopt some more social, protective, and humanitarian, in its stead. *We* make no war on political economy in its large and extended sense, for we indulge in disquisitions ourselves on national and social wealth, and what will best promote social and national well-being; but only on that Adam Smith School, who encourage unlimited competition, beget a war of the wits, and propose to govern mankind by "letting them alone, and encouraging the strong, skillful, and rich, to oppress the weak and ignorant." The science of political economy, strictly under-stood, has but one principle, or at least one distinctive principle. This is variously expressed by the terms, "Pas trop gouverner," "Every man for himself," "Laissez-faire," "Demand will regulate supply," &c. It is this narrow and selfish philosophy which the South must refute; and, yet, which it is teaching in all its higher schools. It leads directly to the "No Government" doctrines of the abolitionists and socialists, and only involves slavery, in one common ruin, with all the other institutions of society.

Nothing is so directly adverse to slavery as a philosophy, which teaches that society succeeds best, when all are let alone to make their own way in the world. In truth, "Political Economy is the philosophy of universal liberty," and the outgrowth of that competitive society where the few wallow in luxury, and the unprotected masses, without masters to provide for them, are left to the grinding, unfeeling oppression of skill and capital, which starve them by the million. We must teach that slavery is necessary in all societies, as well to protect, as to govern the weak, poor, and ignorant. This is the opposite doctrine to that of the political economists.

Again: We should show that slave society, which is a series of subordinations, is consistent with christian morality—for fathers, masters, husbands, wives, children, and slaves, not being equals, rivals, competitors, and antagonists, best promote each others selfish interests when they do most for those above or beneath them. Within the precincts of the family, including slaves, the golden rule is a practical and wise guide of conduct. But in free society, where selfishness, rivalry, and competition are necessary to success, and almost to existence, this rule cannot be adopted in practice. It would reverse the whole action of such society, and make men martyrs to their virtues.

Here we may pause awhile, and consider that new system of ethical philosophy and of moral duties which slavery naturally suggests and gives rise to. Outside the Bible, the christian world has now no moral philosophy, except that selfish system, which teaches that each individual most promotes the good of others, and of the whole of society, by a continuous struggle for his own selfish good, by making good bargains, and by giving as little of his own labor as possible for as much as he can obtain of other peoples.

The scale of moral merit is nicely graduated, and he is universally considered most meritorious, who works least and gets best paid. The difference between honesty and dishonesty being, that the latter takes short cuts, whilst the former gets greater advantages, appropriates more of other people's labor, by deliberately bleeding all with whom it deals a little, than dishonesty does by grabbing at too much at once.

Lawyers, merchants, artists, mechanics, and professional and skillful men, of all kinds, are considered more honorable and meritorious than common laborers, because they work but little, and exchange a little of their light labor for the results of a great deal of common labor. All merit, in free society, consists in getting the advantage in dealing: all demerit and disgrace, in laboring more for others than they labor for you. This system is called by the French philosophers "exploitation," which means taking honest advantages. In the general, no other moral rule of conduct is practicable in free society, because separation of interests and competition arm men against each other, and keep up a continual social war of the wits. It is true, the doctrines of the Bible are as extensively known as those of the political economists, and those doctrines touch and mollify the hearts of men, and neutralize in some degree the poison of the selfish system.

We, of the South, can build up an ethical code, founded on the morality of the Bible, because human interests with us do not generally clash, but coincide. Without the family circle it is true competition and clashing interests exist, but slavery leaves few without the family, and the little competition that is left is among the rich and skillful, and serves to keep society progressive. It is enough that slavery will relieve the common laborers of the evils of competition, and the exactions of skill and capital.

We have thus attempted to show that Southern thought must build up an entire new system of ethical philosophy. The South must also originate a new political science, whose leading and distinctive principle will be, "the world is too little governed." Where government restraint and control and protection are most needed, modern politicians propose to have, and in practice have, no government. They express a holy horror of sumptuary laws, of Roman censors, of Jewish and Catholic Priests, and of all interference with the family. Ignorant fathers must riot in unrestrained despotism. They have "a right divine to govern wrong," and maltreat wives and children as much as they please. Modern, so called liberty, robs three-fourths of mankind, wives and children, of all rights, and subjects them to the despotism of brutal and ignorant fathers and husbands. The most important part of government is that which superintends and controls the action of the family, for society is composed of families; and if the parts be rotten, the whole cannot be sound. Slavery secures intelligent rulers, interested in the well-being of its subjects, and they never permit the maltreatment by slaves of their wives and children. Every mail teems with accounts of wife murders at the North, and yet we have never heard or read of a negro murdering his wife at the South. Nothing but the strong arm and inquisitorial superintendence of a master, can restrain their wife murderers; they need "more of government."

Southern thought will teach that protection and slavery must go hand in hand, for we cannot efficiently protect those whose conduct we cannot control. (Hence, the powers and obligations of husbands and fathers.) We can never be sure that our charities will not be misapplied, unless we can control their expenditure.

It is the duty of society to protect all its members, and it can only do so by subjecting each to that degree of government constraint or slavery, which will best advance the good of each and of the whole. Thus, ambition, or the love or power, properly directed, becomes the noblest of virtues, because power alone can enable us to be safely benevolent to the weak, poor, or criminal.

To protect the weak, we must first enslave them, and this slavery must be either political and legal, or social; the latter, including the condition of wives, apprentices, inmates of poor houses, idiots, lunatics, children, sailors, soldiers, and domestic slaves. Those latter classes cannot be governed, and also protected by mere law, and require masters of some kind, whose will and discretion shall stand as a law to them, who shall be entitled to their labor, and bound to provide for them. This social organization begets harmony and good will, instead of competition, rivalry, and war of the wits.

Slavery educates, refines, and moralizes the masses by separating them from each other, and bringing them into continual intercourse with masters of superior minds, information, and morality. The laboring class of Europe, associating with nothing above them, learn nothing but crime and immorality from each other, and are well described by Mr. Charles Dickens as "a heaving mass of poverty, ignorance, and crime." Slavery is necessary as an educational institution, and is worth ten times all the common schools of the North. Such common schools teach only uncommonly bad morals, and prepare their inmates to graduate in the penitentiary, as the statistics of crime at the North abundantly prove.

There certainly is in the human heart, under all circumstances, a love for all mankind, and a yearning desire to equalize human conditions. We are all philanthropists by force of nature, for we are social beings, tied to each other by invisible chords of sympathy. Nature, which makes us members or limbs of the being society, and affects us pleasantly or painfully, as any of those members or limbs, however distant from us, are affected, would teach us how to promote the well being of each and all, if we would but attend to her lessons. The slaveholder feels quite as sensibly the vibrations of the nervous system of humanitarian sympathy which makes society one being, as the abolitionist, the socialist, or the christian. They are all in pursuit of one object—the good of the whole—feeling that the good of each is indissolubly connected with the good of all. By observing and studying the habitudes of the bees and the ants, of flocking birds and gregarious animals, we must become satisfied that our social habits and sympathetic feelings are involuntary, a part of our nature, and necessary to our healthful and natural existence. This induces us to reject the social contract of Locke, which presupposes a state in which each human being has a separate independent existence; and also the philosophy of Adam Smith, which grew out of Locke's theory, and goes still further by insisting that "every man for himself" is the true doctrine of government.

Now, the question arises, how are man's social wants and habitudes to be satisfied, after rejecting the philosophy which dissociates him? How is that equality of social happiness and enjoyment to be attained which we all involuntarily desire? Has not nature, which made us social and gregarious, taught us ere this our best governmental policy? Has man no instincts, no divine promptings and directions; or is he accursed of God, and been left to grope and blunder in the dark for six thousand years, whilst other social animals have understood the science and practice of government from the first?

We, of the South, assume that man has all along instinctively understood and practiced that social and political government best suited to his nature, and that domestic slavery is, in the general, a natural and necessary part of that government, and that its absence is owing to a decaying and diseased state of society, or to something exceptional in local circumstances, as in desert, or mountainous, or new countries, where competition is no evil, because capital has no mastery over labor. But how does slavery equalize human conditions, whilst it vests with seemingly unlimited and despotic power a few, and subjects the many to all the ills or evils which that power may choose capriciously to inflict?

First: There is no such thing as despotic power in the moral world, for human beings act and re-act on each other, and affect each other's course of action, just as in the physical world all bodies, by the laws of gravitation, mutually attract and control each other's motions. The difference being, that in the moral world, the smaller and weaker bodies not only neutralize the despotism of the larger, but often control and rule them. The wife, the infant, the slave, by virtue of that nervous, social sympathy, which connects us together, by means of domestic and family affection, which shield and protect the weaker members of the household, and by that singular influence which compassion and pity for the helpless and dependent exercises most especially over the conduct of the strong, the brave, and the powerful, are in the general far more efficiently shielded from tyranny and ill treatment than they could be by the interposition of any human laws and penalties. Within the family circle it is impossible to interpose usefully many such laws and penalties; hence, Providence has abundantly supplied those checks to power which man in vain attempts to fabricate. "I am thy slave, deprives me of the power of a master!" All acknowledge and admire the truth and beauty of this sentiment, and thus tacitly admit the correctness of our theory.

But another step in the argument is necessary. This only proves that the despotic power of the master, the husband, and the father is no engine of tyranny, but usually and naturally a tie of affection, and a means of support and protection. Yet, it does nott prove that the condition of the inferiors is equally desirable with that of superiors.

The labors of life devolve on inferiors, its cares on superiors. Their obligations are mutual, and each in a broad sense equally slaves, for the superior is as much bound by law, natural feeling, self-interest, and custom, to take care of, govern, and provide for inferiors or dependents, as they to labor for him. Which is the happier condition, in general, none can determine.

Faith in God, which establishes and perpetuates the two conditions, should make us bow in humble submission to his will, and with reverential respect for his wisdom, benevolence, and justice, be ready to believe that in a naturally constituted society, high and low are equally happy.

We cannot dismiss this part of our subject without giving two extracts, the one from Shakespeare, the other from Virgil, portraying, as mere philosopher can never portray, those anguishing and corroding cares that oft afflict the breasts of kings; and masters, husbands, and fathers are but kings on a small scale.

King II.—

"How many thousand of my poorest subjects
Are at this hour asleep!—Sleep, gentle sleep,
Nature's soft nurse, how have I frighted thee,
That thou no more wilt weigh my eye-lids down,
And steep my senses in forgetfulness?
Why rather, sleep, liest thou in smoky cribs,
Upon uneasy pallets stretching thee,
And hush'd with buzzing night-flies to thy slumber;
Than in the perfum'd chambers of the great,
Under the canopies of costly state,
And lull'd with sounds of sweetest melody?
O thou dull god, why liest thou with the vile,
In loathsome beds; and leav'st the kingly couch,
A watch-case, or a common 'larum bell?
Wilt thou upon the high and giddy mast
Seal up the ship-boy's eyes, and rock his brains
In cradle of the rude imperious surge;
And in the visitation of the winds,
Who take the ruffian billows by the top,
Curling their monstrous heads, and hanging them
With deaf'ning clamors in the slippery clouds,
That, with the hurly, death itself awakes?
Can'st thou, O partial sleep! give thy repose
To the wet sea-boy in an hour so rude;
And, in the calmest and most stillest night,
With all appliances and means to boot,
Deny it to a king? Then, happy low, lie down!
Uneasy lies the head that wears a crown.
Second Part of King Henry IV., *Act* iii.

The passage we shall quote from Virgil describes a Queen in love, whose unrequited passion afflicts her with so much anguish and mortification, that she spends sleepless nights whilst all is profound peace and quiet around her. Her's are not the cares of the master for his family, or of the sovereign for his subjects; but, still, it is mental pain and anxiety, which the master and the sovereign continually feel, which follows them by day and by night, depriving them of appetite, and disturbing their rest; whilst moderate labor, under the superintendance and protection of a superior, is free from care, conduces to health, whets the appetite, and brings on profound and luxurious sleep. The anxious, wretched, sleepless Dido well represents the frequent condition of the master, whilst the profound repose around her, is but the sleep of wife, children, and slaves, freed from care by a master, of whose sleepless vigils they are all unconscious. At all events, the most fastidious reader will not object to an occasional oasis of poetry, 'mid the dreary waste of philosophical disquisition. In collating the passages which we have selected, one is at a loss which most to admire, the turbid passion of the English Bard, or the delicate tracery of the Latin Poet. Each is perfect in its kind, and perfectly adapted to the subject of the story:

"Nox erat et placidum carpebant fessa soporem
Corpora per terras, silvaeque et saeva quierant
Aequora, cum medio volvuntur sidera lapsu,
Cum tacet omnis ager, pecudes, pictaeque volucres,
Quaeque lacus late liquidos quaeque aspera dumis
Rura tenent, somno positae sub nocte silenti.
Lenibant curas et corda oblita laborum.
At non infelix animi Phoenissa neque umquam
Solvitur in somnos oculisve aut pectore noctem
Accipit."—Æneid, *Lib.* iv.

The cares of life are a full offset to the labors of life, and thus, and thus only, may human conditions be equalized.

But the free laborer has nightly care superadded to incessant daily toil, whilst his employer is exempted as well from the labor of life, as from most of its cares. The former is a slave, without the rights of a slave; the latter, a master, without the obligations of a master. What equality of condition can there be in free society?

Socially, slavery is quite as promotive of human happiness as it is morally and politically. "It is not good for man to be alone." His nature is social, and most of his happiness and enjoyment is reflected, and proceeds from his sympathy with the pleasures of others. Too small a family circle is injurious to happiness, as well because it circumscribes the pleasures of association, and prevents much interchange of ideas, as because it brings us nearer to that state of helplessness to which the solitary man is subjected. We cannot conceive of much pleasure or enjoyment in the life of a man and wife, with five or six infant children, living to themselves and cultivating their own lands. The sickness of either parent would render the situation of the whole family desperate. The healthy parent could not nurse the sick one, attend to the children, and to all domestic concerns, and also cultivate the land. The apprehension of this common event would suffice to mar enjoyment. But such a family, as we have described, would have scarcely any sources of social enjoyment at any time, for the constant drudgery of labor would confine them at home, and deprive them of the opportunity to acquire subjects for conversation, or ideas for interchange. Such a life is solitary and monotonous, begets cruel and despotic exercise of power on the part of the husband, who is not brought in contact with public opinion, negligence and slovenliness in the wife, and ignorance with the children. The boasted independence of such a life will not bear examination. The wife and six children are the slaves often of a cruel, capricious husband, who treats them badly, and provides for them insufficiently.

All this was obviated by the admirable slave institutions of the Romans, and other nations of antiquity. Society was divided into circles sufficiently large to insure against want, and to secure social enjoyment and intellectual improvement. These circles revolved around a common central head, thus securing order, concert and coöperation, and promoting kind and sympathetic feelings, instead of jealousy, rivalry, and competition. The Roman patrician had hundreds of followers, or clients, bound by hereditary ties to his house. For six hundred years, it is said, there never occurred an instance of faithlessness to the tie of patron and client. The nobleman never failed to protect, and the client never proved recreant to his duties when his patron needed his services. Next in the circle came the freedmen, who, although liberated from slavery, rarely forgot their allegiance to their late master—for they still needed his powerful protection. Lastly, were the slaves, who performed all common labor, but were relieved from the cares of life, and from the perils and privations of war. We can see in such society all the elements of social order, and of social happiness, and adequate *insurance* against casualties , sickness, injustice from without, and from hunger, nakedness, and poverty. Insurance is the business of government. Insurance is the object of society, and necessitates society. Modern free society neglects it, and foolishly says "the world is too much governed," thus forcing mankind to supply the deficiency of government, by thousands of forms of insurance, such as the Odd-Fellows, the Masons, the Sons of Temperance, Rappites, Mormons, Shakers, and Socialists of every hue; besides, the regular insurance companies, from fire and other casualties. Ancient slave society insured all its members, and so, in a great degree, does modern slave society—for master, mistress, and slaves, will never all be sick, or die at once, so that the weak and infirm are always secure of sufficient provision and attention.

Economically, slavery is necessary to bring about association of labor and division of expenses. Labor becomes far more efficient when many are associated together, and the expenses of living are greatly diminished when many families are united under a common government. The socialists are all aiming to attain these ends by an unnatural association, let them adopt the natural one, slavery, and they would show themselves wise and useful men.

We will cite a single example to illustrate our theory, that of farming. A single family, man, wife, and two or three children, under twenty-one years of age, cannot carry on farming profitably. Indeed, we believe their labors *on their own lands* would not support them, if mere grain producers, as well as slaves are usually supported. At least, where the family consisted of husband and wife and four or five young children, their labor would be inadequate to their support.

The expenses of small farms are proportionately much greater than those of large ones. To make and keep up an enclosure around a five acre field, of ordinary land, would cost more than the gross amount of slaes of crops. Farmers of fifty acres must have a wagon, a fan, granary, and many other things quite as costly as those on a farm of three hundred acres. The labor or expense of sending to mill, to the black-smith's shop, to stores, and to market, and the general labor of providing and superintending are as great on a small farm as on one of much larger size. Every day's experience of the world shows the great economy of carrying on business on a large scale. Mammoth steamships are taking the place of sail vessels, mammoth hotels of ordinary taverns, and railroads and omnibuses are supplanting common roads and carriages. Now, slavery, as an industrial institution, bears the same relation to independent, separate, free labor, that these modern improvements do to those which they have supplanted. But we have proof incontestible of the superior availability of slave labor in the fact, that the South, with a thin soil, is now producing a larger agricultural surplus than any other population of the same amount in the world, whilst the general comfort of its people, and its domestic consumption, exceed that of any other people.

We have thus attempted to show that Southern thought must inaugurate a new philosophy of ethics or morals, (in the restricted sense of the term morals,) because the present system resulting from the competition, and every-man-for-himself, theory of free society is selfish and anti-scriptural. That it must originate a new theory in politics, because the present system proposes to govern men by "letting them alone," and encouraging the strong, astute, and wealthy, to make a continual war of the wits and of capttal, upon the weak, poor, and ignorant.

That we must have a new social philosophy, because man is by nature helpless when alone, and social from taste, feeling, and necessity; and yet, political economy proposes to disintegrate society, and set every man up for himself.

And lastly, that we must have a new economic philosophy, because association of labor and division of expenses is the true secret of national and individual wealth, and that this is brought about by slavery, and prevented by free society. We know that after such society has lost its liberty, though still retaining its name, after a few have monopolized all capital, their power over the masses is greater than that of slave-owners. Then, association of labor and division of expenses is more perfect than in slave society. Then is (so called) free society more productive than slave society; but it is because slavery to capital has taken the place of domestic slavery. The employers profits become greater than those of the slaveholder, because he pays less wages to his laborers.

The Black Republicans and Abolitionists, with Sumner at the head, have displayed a degree of intellectual imbecility on the subject of the settlement of the public lands, that is absolutely marvellous and astounding, especially in a party, who, for thirty years, have done little else than study, write, speak, and agitate about sociological questions.

They boast that lands are dearer and labor cheaper at the North than the South. They say, (and say truly) if you introduce white labor into Kansas, lands will be more valuable than if it be settled by slaveholders. Now, is it possible that they are such simpletons as not to see that they are asserting that the white laborers of the North, as slaves to capital, get less wages than our slaves? Lands do not breed produce of themselves nothing valuable, and, if as common to all as air and water, would be as valueless as air and water. Their value is the amount which land monopoly enables the land owner to exact from the laborer. Where the laborer is allowed most of the proceeds of his labor, there lands are cheapest. Where he is allowed least, there lands are most valuable. Dogberry wished to be "written down an ass;" these men write themselves down asses twice in one sentence. Say they, "lands are dearer and labor cheaper at the North." If either proposition be true, their white laborers are more of slaves than our negroes. If it be true, as the abolitionists assert, that lands are dearer North than South, then our negroes are freer than their white laborers, for the price of land is the thermometer of liberty. But there is a vast deal more of knavery and hypocrisy than idiotcy about these men. They are deliberately planning the enslavement of white men. The most active and influential man among them was the first man in America to demonstrate that land monopoly occasioned the enslavement of the laboring classes, and that as population became denser, this slavery to capital became infinitely worse than domestic slavery. He says, "during the last five centuries there has been a complete, a disastrous revolution in the ordinary condition of the toiling millions of civilized Europe—a revolution which has depressed them from comfort to wretchedness, from careless ease to incessant anxiety, and struggle for the bare means of existence." Now, Mr. Greely, for it is his language we quote, well knows that five centuries ago, when the laborers of Europe lived "in comfort and careless ease," they were slaves. Besides, this same Mr. Greely said free immigrants were worth a thousand dollars a head at a time negroes sold for five hundred. That is, yankee employers could cruelly and unmercifully squeeze twice as much from the labor of the immigrant, as the more generous and humane Southerner from the negro. In other words, the white laborer is just half as free as the negro slave, for he works twice as much for other people, and half as much for himself. Mr. Greely is the most active man in sending white laborers to Kansas to enhance the price of lands there. He is doing so with the deliberate purpose of enslaving them. Others, such as Sumner, may put in the plea of idiotcy, for Sumner is a simpleton, but he, Mr. Greely, understands the subject, and has well expounded it in a controversy with Mr. Raymond, as the following extract will show:

> "Will any say, you are talking of *British* distresses: what do they prove as to *us?* Ah, sirs! the same general causes which have produced this fearful change in Europe are now at work here. Population is rapidly increasing; wealth is concentrating; the public lands are rapidly passing into private ownership, often by tens of thousands of acres to a single individual. And as our population becomes compact, and land costly as in England, the evils now experienced by the many in Europe, will gradually fasten upon their brethren here. Our political institutions may do something to mitigate this; but how much? The master-evil in the condition of the English and Irish is the monopoly by the few of the God-given elements of production, which are necessary to all. Abolish monarchy, titles of nobility, church establishment, national debt, and whatever else you please, so long as the land shall remain the exclusive property of a small and isolated class, competition for the use of it as active as now, and rents consequently as high, so long will nothing have been accomplished beyond clearing away some of the elementary obstacles of the real and essential reform.
>
> "But in our own country the footsteps of advancing destitution and abject dependence of the many, already sound ominously near. In our journals are advertisements to let out some hundreds of robust men from the immigrant alms-houses to work through the winter for their board, while tens of thousands in our city would gladly have been so disposed of from December to April. Nor is this lack of employment by any means confined to immigrants with those displaced by them. Thousands of American-born women are at this moment working long days in our city, for less than the cost of one good meal of vituals per day, say twenty-five cents; and it was but yesterday that a friend, living in the country, casually informed me that he could hire as much farm labor in winter as he wanted, for the laborer's own board, or for 37 1/2 cents per day without board. And these laborers are not foreigners, but the descendants of those who won our liberties on the battle-fields of the Revolution."

The South should daily remind the abolitionists that they, themselves, in effect, are continually asserting that the condition of our slaves is better than that of their free laborers—for if lands be dearer and labor cheaper with them, it only proves that their laborers, who cultivate the soil, get less of the proceeds of their labor than our slaves, and the land-owner more of those proceeds than our slaveholders.

But the abolitionists are mendacious and hypocritical, for it is not possible, constituted as the human mind is, that since the universal and disastrous failure of negro emancipation, they can hold the same opinions that they did thirty years ago, when they were sanguinely expecting the entire success of the emancipation experiment. Many were then sincere—all are now false and hypocritical.

(1857)

HENRY W. GRADY

The New South

"There was a South of slavery and secession—that South is dead. There is a South of union and freedom—that South, thank God, is living, breathing, growing every hour." These words, delivered from the immortal lips of Benjamin H. Hill, at Tammany Hall, in 1866, true then and truer now, I shall make my text to-night.

Mr. President and gentlemen : Let me express to you my appreciation of the kindness by which I am permitted to address you. I make this abrupt acknowledgment advisedly, for I feel that if, when I raise my provincial voice in this ancient and august presence, it could find courage for no more than the opening sentence, it would be well if in that sentence I had met in a rough sense my obligation as a guest, and had perished, so to speak, with courtesy on my lips and grace in my heart.

Permitted, through your kindness, to catch my second wind, let me say that I appreciate the significance of being the first Southerner to speak at this board, which bears the substance, if it surpasses the semblance, of original New England hospitality, and honors the sentiment that in turn honors you, but in which my personality is lost, and the compliment to my people made plain.

I bespeak the utmost stretch of your courtesy to-night. I am not troubled about those from whom I come. You remember the man whose wife sent him to a neighbor with a pitcher of milk, and who, tripping on the top step, fell with such casual interruptions as the landings afforded into the basement, and, while picking himself up, had the pleasure of hearing his wife call out, "John, did you break the pitcher?"

"No, I didn't," said John, "but I'll be dinged if I don't."

So, while those who call me from behind may inspire me with energy, if not with courage, I ask an indulgent hearing from you. I beg that you will bring your full faith in American fairness and frankness to judgment upon what I shall say. There was an old preacher once who told some boys of the Bible lesson he was going to read in the morning. The boys, finding the place, glued together the connecting pages. The next morning he read on the bottom of one page, "When Noah was one hundred and twenty years old he took unto himself a wife who was"—then turning the page—"140 cubits long, 40 cubits wide, built of gopher wood, and covered with pitch inside and out."

He was naturally puzzled at this. He read it again, verified it, and then said: "My friends, this is the first time I ever met this in the Bible, but I accept this as an evidence of the assertion that we are fearfully and wonderfully made." If I could get you to hold such faith to-night, I could proceed cheerfully to the task I otherwise approach with a sense of consecration.

Pardon me one word, Mr. President, spoken for the sole purpose of getting into the volumes that go out annually freighted with the rich eloquence of your speakers—the fact that the Cavalier as well as the Puritan was on the continent in its early days, and that he was "up and able to be about." I have read your books carefully, and I find no mention of this fact, which seems to me an important one for preserving a sort of historical equilibrium, if for nothing else.

Let me remind you that the Virginia Cavalier first challenged France on the continent—that Cavalier John Smith gave New England its very name, and was so pleased with the job that he has been handing his own name around ever since; and that while Myles Standish was cutting off men's ears for courting a girl without her parents' consent, and forbade men to kiss their wives on Sunday, the Cavalier was courting everything in sight, and that the Almighty had vouchsafed great increase to the Cavalier colonies, the huts in the wilderness being as full as the nests in the woods.

But having incorporated the Cavalier as a fact in your charming little books, I shall let him work out his own salvation, as he has always done, with engaging gallantry, and we will hold no controversy as to his merits. Why should we? Neither Puritan nor Cavalier long survived as such. The virtues and good traditions of both happily still live for the inspiration of their sons and the saving of the old fashion. But both Puritan and Cavalier were lost in the storm of the first Revolution, and the American citizen, supplanting both and stronger than either, took possession of the Republic bought by their common blood and fashioned to wisdom, and charged himself with teaching men government and establishing the voice of the people as the voice of God.

My friends, Dr. Talmage has told you that the typical American has yet to come. Let me tell you that he has already come. Great types, like valuable plants, are slow to flower and fruit. But from the union of these colonists, Puritans and Cavaliers, from the straightening of their purposes and the crossing of their blood, slow perfecting through a century, came he who stands as the first typical American, the first who comprehended within himself all the strength and gentleness, all the majesty and grace, of this Republic—Abraham Lincoln. He was the sum of Puritan and Cavalier, for in his ardent nature were fused the virtues of both, and in the depths of his great soul the faults of both were lost. He was greater than Puritan, greater than Cavalier, in that he was American, and that in his honest form were first gathered the vast and thrilling forces of his ideal government, charging it with such tremendous meaning and elevating it above human suffering, that martyrdom, though infamously aimed, came as a fitting crown to a life consecrated from the cradle to human liberty. Let us, each cherishing the traditions and honoring his fathers, build with reverent hands to the type of this simple but sublime life, in which all types are honored, and in our common glory as Americans there will be plenty and to spare for your forefathers and for mine.

Dr. Talmage has drawn for you, with a master's hand, the picture of your returning armies. He has told you how, in the pomp and circumstance of war, they came back to you, marching with proud and victorious tread, reading their glory in a nation's eyes! Will you bear with me while I tell you of another army that sought its home at the close of the late war?—an army that marched home in defeat and not in victory, in pathos and not in splendor, but in glory that equaled yours, and to hearts as loving as ever welcomed heroes home! Let me picture to you the footsore Confederate soldier, as, buttoning up in his faded gray jacket the parole which was to bear testimony to his children of his fidelity and faith, he turned his face southward from Appomattox in April, 1865. Think of him as, ragged, half-starved, heavy-hearted, enfeebled by want and wounds, having fought to exhaustion, he surrenders his gun, wrings the hands of his comrades in silence, and lifting his tear-stained and pallid face for the last time to the graves that dot old Virginia hills, pulls his gray cap over his brow and begins the slow and painful journey.

What does he find—let me ask you who went to your homes eager to find, in the welcome you had justly earned, full payment for four years' sacrifice—what does he find when, having followed the battle-stained cross against overwhelming odds, dreading death not half so much as surrender, he reaches the home he left so prosperous and beautiful? He finds his house in ruins, his farm devastated, his slaves free, his stock killed, his barns empty, his trade destroyed, his money worthless, his social system, feudal in its magnificence, swept away, his people without law or legal status, his comrades slain, and the burdens of others heavy on his shoulders. Crushed by defeat, his very traditions are gone; without money, credit, employment, material, or training; and besides all this, confronted with the gravest problem that ever met human intelligence—the establishment of a status for the vast body of his liberated slaves.

What does he do—this hero in gray with a heart of gold? Does he sit down in sullenness and despair? Not for a day. Surely God, who had stripped him of his prosperity, inspired him in his adversity. As ruin was never before so overwhelming, never was restoration swifter. The soldier stepped from the trenches into the furrow; horses that had charged federal guns marched before the plow, and fields that ran red with human blood in April were green with the harvest in June; women reared in luxury cut up their dresses and made breeches for their husbands, and, with a patience and heroism that fit women always as a garment, gave their hands to work. There was little bitterness in all this. Cheerfulness and frankness prevailed. "Bill Arp" struck the keynote when he said, "Well, I killed as many of them as they did of me, and now I'm going to work." So did the soldier returning home after defeat and roasting some corn on the roadside who made the remark to his comrades, "You may leave the South if you want to, but I'm going to Sandersville, kiss my wife, and raise a crop, and if the Yankees fool with me any more, I'll whip 'em again."

I want to say to General Sherman, who is considered an able man in our parts, though some people think he is a kind of careless man about fire, that from the ashes he left us in 1864 we have raised a brave and beautiful city; that somehow or other we have caught the sunshine in the bricks and mortar of our homes, and have builded therein not one ignoble prejudice or memory.

But what is the sum of our work? We have found out that in the summing up the free negro counts more than he did as a slave. We have planted the schoolhouse on the hilltop and made it free to white and black. We have sown towns and cities in the place of theories, and put business above politics. We have challenged your spinners in Massachusetts and your ironmakers in Pennsylvania. We have learned that the $400,000,000 annually received from our cotton crop will make us rich when the supplies that make it are home-raised. We have reduced the commercial rate of interest from 24 to 6 per cent, and are floating 4 per cent bonds. We have learned that one Northern immigrant is worth fifty foreigners, and have smoothed the path to Southward, wiped out the place where Mason and Dixon's line used to be, and hung out the latchstring to you and yours.

We have reached the point that marks perfect harmony in every household, when the husband confesses that the pies which his wife cooks are as good as those his mother used to bake; and we admit that the sun shines as brightly and the moon as softly as it did before the war. We have established thrift in city and country. We have fallen in love with work. We have restored comfort to homes from which culture and elegance never departed. We have let economy take root and spread among us as rank as the crab-grass which sprung from Sherman's cavalry camps, until we are ready to lay odds on the Georgia Yankee as he manufactures relics of the battlefield in a one-story shanty and squeezes pure olive oil out of his cotton seed, against any down-easter that ever swapped wooden nutmegs for flannel sausage in the valleys of Vermont. Above all, we know that we have achieved in these "piping times of peace" a fuller independence for the South than that which our fathers sought to win in the forum by their eloquence or compel in the field by their swords.

It is a rare privilege, sir, to have had part, however humble, in this work. Never was nobler duty confided to human hands than the uplifting and upbuilding of the prostrate and bleeding South—misguided, perhaps, but beautiful in her suffering, and honest, brave, and generous always. In the record of her social, industrial, and political illustration we await with confidence the verdict of the world.

But what of the negro? Have we solved the problem he presents or progressed in honor and equity toward solution? Let the record speak to the point. No section shows a more prosperous laboring population than the negroes of the South, none in fuller sympathy with the employing and land-owning class. He shares our school fund, has the fullest protection of our laws, and the friendship of our people. Self-interest, as well as honor, demand that he should have this. Our future, our very existence, depend upon our working out this problem in full and exact justice. We understand that when Lincoln signed the Emancipation Proclamation, your victory was assured, for he then committed you to the cause of human liberty, against which the arms of man cannot prevail—while those of our statesmen who trusted to make slavery the corner stone of the Confederacy doomed us to defeat as far as they could, committing us to a cause that reason could not defend or the sword maintain in sight of advancing civilization.

Had Mr. Toombs said, which he did not say, "that he would call the roll of his slaves at the foot of Bunker Hill," he would have been foolish, for he might have known that whenever slavery became entangled in war it must perish, and that the chattel in human flesh ended forever in New England when your fathers—not to be blamed for parting with what didn't pay—sold their slaves to our fathers—not to be praised for knowing a paying thing when they saw it. The relations of the Southern people with the negro are close and cordial. We remember with what fidelity for four years he guarded our defenseless women and children, whose husbands and fathers were fighting against his freedom. To his eternal credit be it said that whenever he struck a blow for his own liberty, he fought in open battle, and when at last he raised his black and humble hands that the shackles might be struck off, those hands were innocent of wrong against his helpless charges, and worthy to be taken in loving grasp by every man who honors loyalty and devotion. Ruffians have maltreated him, rascals have misled him, philanthropists established a bank for him, but the South, with the North, protests against injustice to this simple and sincere people.

To liberty and enfranchisement is as far as law can carry the negro. The rest must be left to conscience and common sense. It must be left to those among whom his lot is cast, with whom he is indissolubly connected, and whose prosperity depends upon their possessing his intelligent sympathy and confidence. Faith has been kept with him, in spite of calumnious assertions to the contrary by those who assume to speak for us or by frank opponents. Faith will be kept with him in the future, if the South holds her reason and integrity.

But have we kept faith with you? In the fullest sense, yes. When Lee surrendered— I don't say when Johnston surrendered, because I understand he still alludes to the time when he met General Sherman last as the time when he determined to abandon any further prosecution of the struggle—when Lee surrendered, I say, and Johnston quit, the South became, and has since been, loyal to this Union. We fought hard enough to know that we were whipped, and in perfect frankness accept as final the arbitrament of the sword to which we had appealed. The South found her jewel in the toad's head of defeat. The shackles that had held her in narrow limitations fell forever when the shackles of the negro slave were broken. Under the old régime the negroes were slaves to the South; the South was a slave to the system. The old plantation, with its simple police regulations and feudal habit, was the only type possible under slavery. Thus was gathered in the hands of a splendid and chivalric oligarchy the substance that should have been diffused among the people, as the rich blood, under certain artificial conditions, is gathered at the heart, filling that with affluent rapture, but leaving the body chill and colorless.

The old South rested everything on slavery and agriculture, unconscious that these could neither give nor maintain healthy growth. The new South presents a perfect democracy, the oligarchs leading in the popular movement; a social system compact and closely knitted, less splendid on the surface, but stronger at the core; a hundred farms for every plantation, fifty homes for every palace; and a diversified industry that meets the complex needs of this complex age.

The new South is enamored of her new work. Her soul is stirred with the breath of a new life. The light of a grander day is falling fair on her face. She is thrilling with the consciousness of growing power and prosperity. As she stands upright, full-statured and equal among the people of the earth, breathing the keen air and looking out upon the expanded horizon, she understands that her emancipation came because, through the inscrutable wisdom of God, her honest purpose was crossed and her brave armies were beaten.

This is said in no spirit of time-serving or apology. The South has nothing for which to apologize. She believes that the late struggle between the States was war and not rebellion, revolution and not conspiracy, and that her convictions were as honest as yours. I should be unjust to the dauntless spirit of the South and to my own convictions if I did not make this plain in this presence. The South has nothing to take back.

In my native town of Athens is a monument that crowns its central hill—a plain, white shaft. Deep cut into its shining side is a name dear to me above the names of men—that of a brave and simple man who died in brave and simple faith. Not for all the glories of New England, from Plymouth Rock all the way, would I exchange the heritage he left me in his soldier's death. To the foot of that shaft I shall send my children's children to reverence him who ennobled their name with his heroic blood. But, sir, speaking from the shadow of that memory which I honor as I do nothing else on earth, I say that the cause in which he suffered and for which he gave his life was adjudged by a higher and fuller wisdom than his or mine, and I am glad that the omniscient God held the balance of battle in His Almighty hand, and that human slavery was swept forever from American soil—that the American Union was saved from the wreck of war.

This message, Mr. President, comes to you from consecrated ground. Every foot of soil about the city in which I live is sacred as a battleground of the Republic. Every hill that invests it is hallowed to you by the blood of your brothers who died for your victory, and doubly hallowed to us by the blood of those who died hopeless, but undaunted, in defeat—sacred soil to all of us, rich with memories that make us purer and stronger and better, silent but stanch witnesses in its red desolation of the matchless valor of American hearts and the deathless glory of American arms, speaking an eloquent witness in its white peace and prosperity to the indissoluble union of American States and the imperishable brotherhood of the American people.

Now, what answer has New England to this message? Will she permit the prejudice of war to remain in the hearts of the conquerors, when it has died in the hearts of the conquered? Will she transmit this prejudice to the next generation, that in their hearts, which never felt the generous ardor of conflict, it may perpetuate itself? Will she withhold, save in strained courtesy, the hand which straight from his soldier's heart Grant offered to Lee at Appomattox? Will she make the vision of a restored and happy people, which gathered above the couch of your dying captain, filling his heart with grace, touching his lips with praise, and glorifying his path to the grave—will she make this vision, on which the last sigh of his expiring soul breathed a benediction, a cheat and delusion?

If she does, the South, never abject in asking for comradeship, must accept with dignity its refusal; but if she does not refuse to accept in frankness and sincerity this message of good will and friendship, then will the prophecy of Webster, delivered in this very society forty years ago amid tremendous applause, be verified in its fullest sense, when he said: "Standing hand to hand and clasping hands, we should remain united as we have been for sixty years, citizens of the same country, members of the same government, united, all united now and united forever. There have been difficulties, contentions, and controversies, but I tell you that in my judgment,—

"'Those opposed eyes,
Which like the meteors of a troubled heaven,
All of one nature, of one substance bred,
Did lately meet in th' intestine shock,
Shall now, in mutual well-beseeming ranks,
March all one way.'"

(1886)

JAMES HENRY HAMMOND

Letter to an English Abolitionist

Silver Bluff, [So. Ca.,]
January 28, 1845
To Thomas Clarkson, Esq.

Sir: I received, a short time ago, a letter from the Rev. Willoughby M. Dickinson, dated at your residence, "Playford Hall, near Ipswich, 26th November, 1844," in which was enclosed a copy of your Circular Letter, addressed to professing Christians in our Northern States, having no concern with Slavery, and to others there. I presume that Mr. Dickinson's letter was written with your knowledge, and the document enclosed with your consent and approbation. I therefore feel that there is no impropriety in my addressing my reply directly to yourself, especially as there is nothing in Mr. Dickinson's communication requiring serious notice. Having abundant leisure, it will be a recreation to devote a portion of it to an examination and free discussion of the question of Slavery as it exists in our Southern States: and since you have thrown down the gauntlet to me, I do not hesitate to take it up.

Familiar as you have been with the discussions of this subject in all its aspects, and under all the excitements it has occasioned for sixty years past, I may not be able to present much that will be new to you. Nor ought I to indulge the hope of materially affecting the opinions you have so long cherished, and so zealously promulgated. Still, time and experience have developed facts, constantly furnishing fresh tests to opinions formed sixty years since, and continually placing this great question in points of view, which could scarcely occur to the most consummate intellect even a quarter of a century ago: and which may not have occurred yet to those whose previous convictions, prejudices, and habits of thought, have thoroughly and permanently biased them to one fixed way of looking at the matter: while there are peculiarities in the operation of every social system, and special local as well as moral causes materially affecting it, which no one, placed at the distance you are from us, can fully comprehend or properly appreciate. Besides, it may be possibly, a novelty to you to encounter one who conscientiously believes the domestic Slavery of these

States to be not only an inexorable necessity for the present, but a moral and humane institution, productive of the greatest political and social advantages, and who is disposed, as I am, to defend it on these grounds.

I do not propose, however, to defend the African slave trade. That is no longer a question. Doubtless great evils arise from it as it has been, and is now conducted: unnecessary wars and cruel kidnapping in Africa: the most shocking barbarities in the middle passage: and perhaps a less humane system of Slavery in countries continually supplied with fresh laborers at a cheap rate. The evils of it, however, it may be fairly presumed, are greatly exaggerated. And if I might judge of the truth of transactions stated as occurring in this trade, by that of those reported as transpiring among us, I should not hesitate to say, that a large proportion of the stories in circulation are unfounded, and most of the remainder highly colored.

On the passage of the Act of Parliament prohibiting this trade to British subjects rests, what you esteem, the glory of your life. It required twenty years of arduous agitation, and the intervening extraordinary political events, to convince your countrymen, and among the rest your pious king, of the expediency of the measure: and it is but just to say, that no one individual rendered more essential service to the cause than you did. In reflecting on the subject, you cannot but often ask yourself: What, after all, has been accomplished; how much human suffering has been averted; how many human beings have been rescued from transatlantic Slavery? And on the answers you can give these questions, must in a great measure, I presume, depend on the happiness of your life. In framing them, how frequently must you be reminded of the remark Mr. Grosvenor, in one of the early debates upon the subject, which I believe you have yourself recorded, "that he had twenty objections to the abolition of the slave trade: the first was, *that it was impossible*—the rest he need not give."…

Experience having settled the point, that this trade *cannot be abolished by the use of force*, and that blockading squadrons serve only to make it more profitable and more cruel, I am surprised that the attempt is persisted in, unless it serves as a cloak to other purposes. It would be far better than it now is, for the African, if the trade was free from all restrictions, and left to the mitigation and decay which time and competition would surely bring about. If kidnapping, both secretly and by war made for the purpose, could be by any means prevented in Africa, the next greatest blessing you could bestow upon that country would be to transport its actual slaves in comfortable vessels across the Atlantic. Though they might be perpetual bondsmen, still they would emerge from darkness to light—from barbarism into civilization—from idolatry to Christianity—in short from death to life.

But let us leave the African slave-trade, which has so signally defeated the *philanthropy* of the world, and turn to American Slavery, to which you have now directed your attention, and against which a crusade has been preached as enthusiastic and ferocious as that of Peter the Hermit—destined, I believe, to be about as successful. And here let me say, there is a vast difference between the two, though you may not acknowledge it. The wisdom of ages has concurred in the justice and expediency of establishing rights by prescriptive use, however tortious in their origin they may have been. You would deem a man insane, whose keen sense of equity would lead him to denounce your right to the lands you hold, and which perhaps you inherited from a long line of ancestry, because your title was derived from a Saxon or Norman conqueror, and your lands were originally wrested by violence from the vanquished Britons. And so would the New-England abolitionist regard any one who would insist that he should restore his farm to the descendants of the slaughtered red men, to whom God had as clearly given it as he gave life and freedom to the kidnapped African. That time does not consecrate wrong, is a fallacy which all history exposes; and which the best and wisest men of all ages and professions of religious faith have practically denied. The means, therefore, whatever they may have been, by which the African race now in this country have been reduced to Slavery, cannot affect us, since they are our property, as your land is yours, by inheritance or purchase and prescriptive right. You will say that man cannot hold *property in man*. The answer is, that he can and *actually does* hold property in his fellow all the world over, in a variety of forms, and *has always done so*. I will show presently his authority for doing it.

If you were to ask me whether I am an advocate of Slavery in the abstract, I should probably answer, that I am not, according to my understanding of the question. I do not like to deal in abstractions. It seldom leads to any useful ends. There are few universal truths. I do not now remember any single moral truth universally acknowledged. We have no assurance that it is given to our finite understanding to comprehend abstract moral truth. Apart from revelation and the inspired writings, what ideas should we have even of God, salvation and immortality? Let the heathen answer. Justice itself is impalpable as an abstraction, and abstract liberty the merest phantasy that ever amused the imagination. This world was made for man, and man for the world as it is. We ourselves, our relations with one another and with all matter, are real, not ideal. I might say that I am no more in favor of Slavery in the abstract, than I am of poverty, disease, deformity, idiocy, or any other inequality in the condition of the human family; that I love perfection, and think I should enjoy a millennium such as God has promised. But what would that amount to? A pledge that I would join you to set about eradicating those apparently inevitable evils of our nature, in equalizing the condition of all mankind, consummating the perfection of our race, and introducing the millennium? By no means. To effect these things, belongs exclusively to a higher power. And it would be well for us to leave the Almighty to perfect his own works and fulfil his own covenants. Especially, as the history of the past shows how entirely futile all human efforts have proved, when made for the purpose of aiding Him in carrying out even his revealed designs, and how invariably he has accomplished them by unconscious instruments, and in the face of human expectation. Nay more, that every attempt which has been made by fallible man to extort from the world obedience to his "abstract" notions of right and wrong, has been invariably attended with calamities dire, and extended just in proportion to the breadth and vigor of the movement. On Slavery in the abstract, then, it would not be amiss to have as little as possible to say. Let us contemplate it as it is. And thus contemplating it, the first question we have to ask ourselves is, whether it is contrary to the will of God, as revealed to us in his Holy Scriptures—the only certain means given us to ascertain his will. If it is, then Slavery is a sin. And I admit at once that every man is bound to set his face against it, and to emancipate his slaves, should he hold any.

Let us open these Holy Scriptures. In the twentieth chapter of Exodus, seventeenth verse, I find the following words: "Thou shalt not covet thy neighbor's house, thou shalt not covet thy neighbor's wife, nor his man-servant, nor his maid-servant, nor his ox, nor his ass, nor anything that is thy neighbor's"—which is the tenth of those commandments that declare the essential principles of the great moral law delivered to Moses by God himself. Now discarding all technical and verbal quibbling as wholly unworthy to be used in interpreting the Word of God, what is the plain meaning, undoubted intent, and true spirit of this commandment? Does it not emphatically and explicitly forbid you to disturb your neighbor in the enjoyment of his property; and more especially of that which is here specifically mentioned as being lawfully, and by this commandment made sacredly his? Prominent in the catalogue stands his "man-servant and his maid-servant," who are thus distinctly *consecrated as his property*, and guaranteed to him for his exclusive benefit, in the most solemn manner. You attempt to avert the otherwise irresistible conclusion, that Slavery was thus ordained by God, by declaring that the word "slave" is not used here, and is not to be found in the Bible. And I have seen many learned dissertations on this point from abolition pens. It is well known that both the Hebrew and Greek words translated "servant" in the Scriptures, mean also, and most usually, "slave." The use of the one word, instead of the other, was a mere matter of taste with the translators of the Bible, as it has been with all the commentators and religious writers, the latter of whom have, I believe, for the most part, adopted the term "slave," or use both terms indiscriminately. If, then, these Hebrew and Greek words include the idea of both systems of servitude, the conditional and unconditional, they should, as the major includes the minor proposition, be always translated "slaves," unless the sense of the whole text forbids it. The real question, then is, what idea is intended to be conveyed by the words used in the commandment quoted? And it is clear to my mind, that as no limitation is affixed to them, and the express intention was to secure to mankind the peaceful enjoyment of every species of property, that the terms "men-servants and maid-servants" include all classes of servants, and establish a lawful, exclusive, and indefeasible interest equally in the "Hebrew brother who shall go out in the seventh year," and "the yearly hired servant," and "those purchased form the heathen round about," who were to be "bondmen forever," *as the property of their fellow-man*.

You cannot deny that there were among the Hebrews "bondmen forever." You cannot deny that God especially authorized his chosen people to purchase "bondmen forever" from the heathen, as recorded in the twenty-fifth chapter of Leviticus, and that they are there designated by the very Hebrew word used in the tenth commandment. Nor can you deny that a "BONDMAN FOREVER" is a "SLAVE;" yet you endeavor to hang an argument of immortal consequence upon the wretched subterfuge, that the precise word "slave" is not to be found in the *translation* of the Bible. As if the translators were canonical expounders of the Holy Scriptures, and *their words*, not *God's meaning*, must be regarded as his revelation.

It is vain to look to Christ or any of his Apostles to justify such blasphemous perversions of the word of God. Although Slavery in its most revolting form was everywhere visible around them, no visionary notions of piety or philanthropy ever tempted them to gainsay the LAW, even to mitigate the cruel severity of the existing system. On the contrary, regarding Slavery as an *established*, as well as *inevitable condition of the human society*, they never hinted at such a thing as its termination on earth, any more than that "the poor may cease out of the land," which God affirms to Moses shall never be: and they exhort "all servants under the yoke" to "count their masters as worthy of all honor:" "to obey them in all things according to the flesh; not with eye-service as men-pleasers, but in singleness of heart, fearing God;" "not only the good and gentle, but also the froward:" "for what glory is it if when ye are buffetted for your faults ye shall take it patiently? but if when ye do well and suffer for it ye take it patiently, this is acceptable of God." St. Paul actually apprehended a runaway slave, and sent him to his master! Instead of deriving from the Gospel any sanction for the work you have undertaken, it would be difficult to imagine sentiments and conduct more strikingly in contrast, than those of the Apostles and the abolitionists.

It is impossible, therefore, to suppose that Slavery is contrary to the will of God. It is equally absurd to say that American Slavery differs in form or principle from that of the chosen people. *We accept the Bible terms as the definition of our Slavery, and its precepts as the guide of our conduct.* We desire nothing more. Even the right to "buffet," which is esteemed so shocking, finds its express license in the gospel: 1 Peter ii. 20. Nay, what is more, God directs the Hebrews to "bore holes in the ears of their brothers" to *mark* them, when under certain circumstances they become *perpetual slaves*: Exodus xxi. 6.

I think, then, I may safely conclude, and I firmly believe, that American Slavery is not only not a sin, but especially commanded by God through Moses, and approved by Christ through his apostles. And here I might close its defence; for what God ordains, and Christ sanctifies, should surely command the respect and toleration of man. But I fear there has grown up in our time a transcendental religion, which is throwing even transcendental philosophy into the shade—a religion too pure and elevated for the Bible; which seeks to erect among men a higher standard of morals than the Almighty has revealed, or our Saviour preached; and which is probably destined to do more to impede the extension of God's kingdom on earth than all the infidels who have ever lived. Error is error. It is as dangerous to deviate to the right hand as the left. And when men, professing to be holy men, and who are by numbers so regarded, declare those things to be sinful which our Creator has expressly authorized and instituted, they do more to destroy his authority among mankind than the most wicked can effect, by proclaiming that to be innocent which he has forbidden. To this self-righteous and self-exalted class belong all the abolitionists whose writings I have read. With them it is no end of the argument to prove your propositions by the text of the Bible, interpreted according to its plain and palpable meaning, and as understood by all mankind for three thousand years before their time. They are more ingenious at construing and interpolating to accommodate it to their new-fangled and etherial code of morals, than ever were Voltaire and Hume in picking it to pieces, to free the world from what they considered a delusion. When the abolitionists proclaim "man-stealing" to be a sin, and show me that it is so written down by God, I admit them to be right, and shudder at the idea of such a crime. But when I show them that to hold "bondmen forever" is ordained by God, *they deny the Bible, and set up in its place a law of their own making*. I must then cease to reason with them on this branch of the question. Our religion differs as widely as our manners. The great judge in our day of final account must decide between us.

Turning from the consideration of slaveholding in its relations to man as an accountable being, let us examine it in its influence on his political and social state. Though, being foreigners to us, you are in no wise entitled to interfere with the civil institutions of this country, it has become quite common for your countrymen to decry Slavery as an enormous political evil to us, and even to declare that our Northern States ought to withdraw from the Confederacy rather than continue to be contaminated by it. The American abolitionists appear to concur fully in these sentiments, and a portion, at least, of them are incessantly threatening to dissolve the Union. Nor should I be at all surprised if they succeed. It would not be difficult, in my opinion, to conjecture which region, the North or South, would suffer most by such an event. For one, I should not object, by any means, to cast my lot in a confederacy of States whose citizens might all be slaveholders.

I endorse without reserve the much abused sentiment of Governor M'Duffie, that "Slavery is the corner-stone of our republican edifice;" while I repudiate, as ridiculously absurd, that much lauded but nowhere accredited dogma of Mr. Jefferson, that "all men are born equal." No society has ever yet existed, and I have already incidentally quoted the highest authority to show that none ever will exist, without a natural variety of classes. The most marked of these must, in a country like ours, be the rich and the poor, the educated and the ignorant. It will scarcely be disputed that the very poor have less leisure to prepare themselves for the proper discharge of public duties than the rich; and that the ignorant are wholly unfit for them at all. In all countries save ours, these two classes, or the poor rather, who are presumed to be necessarily ignorant, are by law expressly excluded from all participation in the management of public affairs. In a Republican Government this cannot be done. Universal suffrage, though not essential in theory, seems to be in fact a necessary appendage to a republican system. Where universal suffrage obtains, it is obvious that the government is in the hands of a numerical majority; and it is hardly necessary to say that in every part of the world more than half the people are ignorant and poor. Though no one can look upon poverty as a crime, and we do not here generally regard it as any objection to a man in his individual capacity, still it must be admitted that it is a wretched and insecure government which is administered by its most ignorant citizens, and those who have the least at stake under it. Though intelligence and wealth have great influence here, as everywhere, in keeping in check reckless and unenlightened numbers, yet it is evident to close observers, if not to all, that these are rapidly usurping all power in the non-slaveholding States, and threaten a fearful crisis in republican institutions there at no remote period. In the slaveholding States, however, nearly one-half of the whole population, and those the poorest and most ignorant, have no political influence whatever, because they are slaves. Of the other half, a large proportion are both educated and independent in their circumstances, while those who unfortunately are not so, being still elevated far above the mass, are higher toned and more deeply interested in preserving a stable and well ordered government, than the same class in any other country. Hence, Slavery is truly the "corner-stone" and foundation of every well-designed and durable "republican edifice."

With us every citizen is concerned in the maintenance of order, and in promoting honesty and industry among those of the lowest class who are our slaves; and our habitual vigilance renders standing armies, whether of soldiers or policemen, entirely unnecessary. Small guards in our cities, and occasional patrols in the country, ensure us a repose and security known no where else. You cannot be ignorant that, excepting the United States, there is no country in the world whose existing government would not be overturned in a month, but for its standing armies, maintained at an enormous and destructive cost to those whom they are destined to over-awe—so rampant and combative is the spirit of discontent wherever nominal free labor prevails, with its ostensive privileges and its dismal servitude. Nor will it be long before the "*free States*" of this Union will be compelled to introduce the same expensive machinery, to preserve order among their "free and equal" citizens. Already has Philadelphia organized a permanent battalion for this purpose; New-York, Boston and Cincinnati will soon follow her example; and then the smaller towns and densely populated counties. The intervention of their militia to repress violations of the peace is becoming a daily affair. A strong government, after some of the old fashions—though probably with a new name—sustained by the force of armed mercenaries, is the ultimate destiny of the non-slave-holding section of this confederacy, and one which may not be very distant.

It is a great mistake to suppose, as is generally done abroad, that in case of war slavery would be a source of weakness. It did not weaken Rome, nor Athens, nor Sparta, though their slaves were comparatively far more numerous than ours, of the same color for the most part with themselves, and large numbers of them familiar with the use of arms. I have no apprehension that our slaves would seize such an opportunity to revolt. The present generation of them, born among us, would never think of such a thing at any time, unless instigated to it by others. Against such instigations we are always on our guard. In time of war we should be more watchful and better prepared to put down insurrections than at any other periods. Should any foreign nation be so lost to every sentiment of civilized humanity, as to attempt to erect among us the standard of revolt, or to invade us with black troops, for the base and barbarous purpose of stirring up servile war, their efforts would be signally rebuked. Our slaves could not be easily seduced, nor would any thing delight them more than to assist in stripping Cuffee of his regimentals to put him in the cotton-field, which would be the fate of most black invaders, without any very prolix form of "apprenticeship." If, as I am satisfied would be the case, our slaves remained peaceful on our plantations, and cultivated them in time of war under the superintendence of a limited number of our citizens, it is obvious that we could put forth more strength in such an emergency, at less sacrifice, than any other people of the same numbers. And thus we should in every point of view, "out of this nettle danger, pluck the flower safety."

How far Slavery may be an advantage or disadvantage to those not owning slaves, yet united with us in political association, is a question for their sole consideration. It is true that our representation in Congress is increased by it. But so are our taxes; and the non slave-holding States, being the majority, divide among themselves far the greater portion of the amount levied by the Federal Government. And I doubt not that, when it comes to a close calculation, they will not be slow in finding out that the balance of profit arising from the connection is vastly in their favor.

In a social point of view the abolitionists pronounce Slavery to be a monstrous evil. If it was so, it would be our own peculiar concern, and superfluous benevolence in them to lament over it. Seeing their bitter hostility to us, they might leave us to cope with our own calamities. But they make war upon us out of excess of charity, and attempt to purify by covering us with calumny. You have read and assisted to circulate a great deal about affrays, duels and murders, occurring here, and all attributed to the terrible demoralization of Slavery. Not a single event of this sort takes place among us, but it is caught up by the abolitionists, and paraded over the world, with endless comments, variations and exaggerations. You should not take what reaches you as a mere sample, and infer that there is a vast deal more you never hear. You hear all, and more than all, the truth.

It is true that the point of honor is recognized throughout the slave region, and that disputes of certain classes are frequently referred for adjustment, to the "trial by combat." It would not be appropriate for me to enter, in this letter, into a defence of the practice of duelling, nor to maintain at length, that it does not tarnish the character of a people to acknowledge a standard of honor. Whatever evils may arise from it, however, they cannot be attributed to Slavery, since the same custom prevails both in France and England....Slavery has nothing to do with these things. Stability and peace are the first desires of every slave-holder, and the true tendency of the system. It could not possibly exist amid the eternal anarchy and civil broils of the ancient Spanish dominions in America. And for this very reason, domestic Slavery has ceased there. So far from encouraging strife, such scenes of riot and bloodshed, as have within the last few years disgraced our Northern cities, and as you have lately witnessed in Birmingham and Bristol and Wales, not only never have occurred, but I will venture to say, never will occur in our slave-holding States. The only thing that can create a mob (as you might call it) here, is the appearance of an abolitionist, whom the people assemble to chastise. And this is no more of a mob, than a rally of shepherds to chase a wolf out of their pastures would be one....

It is roundly asserted, that we are not so well educated nor so religious here as elsewhere. I will not go into tedious statistical statements on these subjects. Nor have I, to tell the truth, much confidence in the details of what are commonly set forth as statistics. As to education, you will probably admit that slave-holders should have more leisure for mental culture than most people. And I believe it is charged against them, that they are peculiarly fond of power, and ambitious of honors. If this be so, as all the power and honors of this country are won mainly by intellectual superiority, it might be fairly presumed, that slave-holders would not be neglectful of education. In proof of the accuracy of this presumption, I point you to the facts, that our Presidential chair has been occupied for forty-four out of fifty-six years, by slave-holders; that another has been recently elected to fill it for four more, over an opponent who was a slave-holder also; and that in the Federal Offices and both Houses of Congress, considerably more than a due proportion of those acknowledged to stand in the first rank are from the South. In this arena, the intellects of the free and slave States meet in full and fair competition. Nature must have been unusually bountiful to us, or we have been at least reasonably assiduous in the cultivation of such gifts as she has bestowed—unless indeed you refer our superiority to moral qualities, which

I am sure *you* will not. More wealthy we are not; nor would mere wealth avail in such rivalry.

The piety of the South is unobtrusive. We think it proves but little, though it is a confident thing for a man to claim that he stands higher in the estimation of his Creator, and is less a sinner than his neighbor. If vociferation is to carry the question of religion, the North, and probably the Scotch, have it. Our sects are few, harmonious, pretty much united among themselves, and pursue their avocations in humble peace. In fact, our professors of religion seem to think—whether correctly or not— that it is their duty "to do good in secret," and to carry their holy comforts to the heart of each individual, without reference to class *or color*, for his special enjoyment, and not with a view to exhibit their zeal before the world. So far as numbers are concerned, I believe our clergymen, when called on to make a showing, have never had occasion to blush, if comparisons were drawn between the free and slave States. And although our presses do not teem with controversial pamphlets, nor our pulpits shake with excommunicating thunders, the daily walk of our religious communicants furnishes, apparently, as little food for gossip as is to be found in most other regions. It may be regarded as a mark of our want of excitability—though that is a quality accredited to us in an eminent degree—that few of the remarkable religious *Isms* of the present day have taken root among us. We have been so irreverent as to laugh at Mormonism and Millerism, which have created such commotions farther North; and modern prophets have no honor in our country. Shakers, Rappists, Dunkers, Socialists, Fourrierists and the like, keep themselves afar off. Even Puseyism has not yet moved us. You may attribute this to our domestic Slavery if you choose. I believe you would do so justly. There is no material here for such characters to operate upon.

But your grand charge is, that licentiousness in intercourse between the sexes, is a prominent trial of our social system, and that it necessarily arises from Slavery. This is a favorite theme with the abolitionists, male and female. Folios have been written on it. It is a common observation, that there is no subject on which ladies of eminent virtue so much delight to dwell, and on which in especial learned old maids, like Miss Martineau, linger with such insatiable relish. They expose it in the slave States with the most minute observance and endless iteration. Miss Martineau, with peculiar gusto, relates a series of scandalous stories, which would have made Boccacio jealous of her pen, but which are so ridiculously false as to leave no doubt, that some wicked wag, knowing she would write a book, has furnished her materials—a game too often played on tourists in this country. The constant recurrence of the female abolitionists to this topic, and their bitterness in regard to it, cannot fail to suggest to even the most charitable mind, that

"Such rage without betrays the fires within."

Nor are their immaculate coadjutors of the other sex, though perhaps less specific in their charges, less violent in their denunciations. But recently in your Island, a clergyman has, at a public meeting, stigmatized the whole slave region as a "brothel." Do these people thus cast stones, being "without sin?" or do they only

"Compound for sins they are inclined to
By damning those they have no mind to."

Alas that David and Solomon should be allowed to repose in peace—that Leo should be almost canonized, and Luther more than sainted—that in our own day courtezans should be formally licensed in Paris, and tenements in London rented for years to women of the town for the benefit of the Church, with the knowledge of the Bishop—and the poor slave States of America alone pounced upon, and offered up as a holocaust on the altar of immaculateness, to atone for the abuse of natural instinct by all mankind; and if not actually consumed, at least exposed, anathematized and held up to scorn, by those who

"Write,
Or with a rival's or an eunuch's spite."

But I do not intend to admit that this charge is just or true. Without meaning to profess uncommon modesty, I will say that I wish the topic could be avoided. I am of opinion, and I doubt not every right-minded man will concur, that the public exposure and discussion of this vice, even to rebuke, invariably does more harm than good; and that if it cannot be checked by instilling pure and virtuous sentiments, it is far worse than useless to attempt to do it, by exhibiting its deformities. I may not, however, pass it over; nor ought I to feel any delicacy in examining a question, to which the slave-holder is invited and challenged by clergymen and virgins. So far from allowing, then, that licentiousness pervades this region, I broadly assert, and I refer to the records of our courts, to the public press, and to the knowledge of all who have ever lived here, that among our white population there are fewer cases of divorce, separation, crim. con., seduction, rape and bastardy, than among any other five millions of people on the civilized earth. And this fact I believe will be conceded by the abolitionists of this country themselves. I am almost willing to refer it to them and submit to their decision on it. I would not hesitate to do so, if I thought them capable of an impartial judgment on any matter where Slavery is in question. But it is said, that the licentiousness consists in the constant intercourse between white males and colored females. One of your heavy charges against us has been, that we regard and treat these people as brutes; you now charge us with habitually taking them to our bosoms. I will not comment on the inconsistency of these accusations. I will not deny that some intercourse of the sort does take place. Its character and extent, however, are grossly and atrociously exaggerated. No authority, divine or human, has yet been found sufficient to arrest all such irregularities among men. But it is a known fact, that they are perpetrated here, for the most part, in the cities. Very few mulattoes are reared on our plantations. In the cities, a large proportion of the inhabitants do not own slaves. A still larger proportion are natives of the North, or foreigners. They should share, and justly, too, an equal part in this sin with the slave-holders. Facts cannot be ascertained, or I doubt not, it would appear that they are the chief offenders. If the truth be otherwise, then persons from abroad have stronger prejudices against the African race than we have. Be this as it may, it is well known, that this intercourse is regarded in our society as highly disreputable. If carried on habitually, it seriously affects a man's standing, so far as it is known; and he who takes a colored mistress—with rare and extraordinary exceptions—loses caste at once. You will say that *one* exception should damn our whole country. How much less criminal is it to take a white mistress? In your eyes it should be at least an equal offence. Yet look around you at home, from the cottage to the throne, and count how many mistresses are kept in unblushing notoriety, without loss of caste. Such cases are nearly unknown here, and down even to the lowest walks of life, it is almost invariably fatal to a man's position and prospects to keep a mistress openly, whether white or black. What Miss Martineau relates of a young man's purchasing a colored concubine from a lady, and avowing his designs, is too absurd even for contradiction. No person would dare to allude to such a subject, in such a manner, to any decent female in this country.

After all, however, the number of the mixed breed, in proportion to that of the black, is infinitely small, and out of the towns next to nothing. And when it is considered that the African race has been among us for two hundred years, and that those of the mixed breed continually intermarry—often rearing large families—it is a decided proof of our continence, that so few comparatively are to be found. Our misfortunes are two-fold. From the prolific propagation of these mongrels among themselves, we are liable to be charged by tourists with delinquencies where none have been committed, while, where one has been, it cannot be concealed. Color marks indelibly the offence, and reveals it to every eye. Conceive that, even in your virtuous and polished country, if every bastard, through all the circles of your social system, was thus branded by nature and known to all, what shocking developments might there not be! How little indignation might your saints have to spare for the licentiousness of the slave region. But I have done with this disgusting topic. And I think I may justly conclude, after all the scandalous charges which tea-table gossip, and long-gowned hypocrisy have brought against the slave-holders, that a people whose men are proverbially brave, intellectual and hospitable, and whose women are unaffectedly chaste, devoted to domestic life, and happy in it, can neither be degraded nor demoralized, whatever their institutions may be. My decided opinion is, that our system of Slavery contributes largely to the development and culture of these high and noble qualities.

In an economical point of view—which I will not omit—Slavery presents some difficulties. As a general rule, I agree it must be admitted, that free labor is cheaper than slave labor. It is a fallacy to suppose that ours is *unpaid labor*. The slave himself must be paid for, and thus his labor is all purchased at once, and for no trifling sum. His price was, in the first place, paid mostly to your countrymen, and assisted in building up some of those colossal English fortunes, since illustrated by patents of nobility, and splendid piles of architecture, stained and cemented, if you like the expression, with the blood of kidnapped innocents; but loaded with no heavier curses than abolition and its begotten fanaticisms have brought upon your land—some of them fulfilled, some yet to be. But besides the first cost of the slave, he must be fed and clothed, well fed and well clothed, if not for humanity's sake, that he may do good work, retain health and life, and rear a family to supply his place. When old or sick, he is a clear expense, and so is the helpless portion of his family. No poor law provides for him when unable to work, or brings up his children for our service when we need them. These are all heavy charges on slave labor. Hence, in all countries where the denseness of the population has reduced it to a matter of perfect certainty, that labor can be obtained, whenever wanted, and the laborer be forced, by sheer necessity, to hire for the smallest pittance that will keep soul and body together, and rags upon his back while in actual employment—dependent at all other times on alms or poor rates—in all such countries it is found cheaper to pay this pittance, than to clothe, feed, nurse, support through childhood, and pension in old age, a race of slaves. Indeed, the advantage is so great as speedily to compensate for the loss of the value of the slave. And I have no hesitation in saying, that if I could cultivate my lands on these terms, I would, without a word, resign my slaves, provided they could be properly disposed of. But the question is, whether free or slave labor is cheapest to us in this country, at this time, situated as we are. And it is decided at once by the fact that we cannot avail ourselves of any other than slave labor. We neither have, nor can we procure, other labor to any extent, or on anything like the terms mentioned. We must, therefore, content ourselves with our dear labor, under the consoling reflection that what is lost to us, is gained to humanity; and that, inasmuch as our slaves costs us more than your free man costs you, by so much is he better off. You will promptly say, emancipate your slaves, and then you will have free labor on suitable terms. That might be if there were five hundred where there now is one, and the continent, from the Atlantic to the Pacific, was as densely populated as your Island. But until that comes to pass, no labor can be procured in America on the terms you have it.

While I thus freely admit that to the individual proprietor slave labor is dearer than free, I do not mean to admit as equally clear that it is dearer to the community and to the State. Though it is certain that the slave is a far greater consumer than your laborer, the year round, yet your pauper system is costly and wasteful. Supported by your community at large, it is not administered by your hired agents with that intwrested care and economy—not to speak of humanity—which mark the management of ours, by each proprietor, for his own non-effectives; and is both more expensive to those who pay, and less beneficial to those who receive its bounties. Besides this, Slavery is rapidly filling up our country with a hardy and healthy race, peculiarly adapted to our climate and productions, and conferring signal political and social advantages on us as a people, to which I have already referred.

I have yet to reply to the main ground on which you and your coadjutors rely for the overthrow of our system of Slavery. Failing in all your attempts to prove that it is sinful in its nature, immoral in its effects, a political evil, and profitless to those who maintain it, you appeal to the sympathies of mankind, and attempt to arouse the world against us by the most shocking charges of tyranny and cruelty. You begin by a vehement denunciation of "the irresponsible power of one man over his fellow men." The question of the responsibility of power is a vast one. It is the great political question of modern times. While nations divide off upon it and establish different fundamental systems of government. That "responsibility," to which one set of millions seems amply sufficient to check the government, to the support of which they devote their lives and fortunes, appears to another set of millions a mere mockery of restraint. And accordingly as the opinions of these millions differ, they honor each other with the epithets of "serfs" or "anarchists." It is ridiculous to introduce such an idea as this into the discussion of a mere domestic institution; but since you have introduced it, I deny that the power of the slave-holder in America is "irresponsible." He is responsible to God. He is responsible to the world—a responsibility which abolitionists do not intend to allow him to evade—and in acknowledgment of which, I write you this letter. He is responsible to the community in which he lives, and to the laws under which he enjoys his civil rights. Those laws do not permit him to kill, to maim, or to punish beyond certain limits, or to overtask, or to refuse to feed and clothe his slave. In short, they forbid him to be tyrannical or cruel. If any of these laws have grown obsolete, it is because they are so seldom violated, that they are forgotten. You have disinterred one of them, from a compilation by some Judge Stroud of Philadelphia, to stigmatize its inadequate penalties for killing, maiming, &c. Your object appears to be—you can have no other—to produce the impression, that it must be often violated on account of its insufficiency. You say as much, and that it marks our estimate of the slave. You forget to state that this law was enacted by *Englishmen*, and only indicates *their* opinion of the reparation due for these offences. Ours is proved by the fact, though perhaps unknown to Judge Stroud or yourself, that we have essentially altered this law; and the murder of a slave has for many years been punishable with death in this State. And so it is, I believe, in most or all the slave States. You seem well aware, however, that laws have been recently passed in all these States, making it penal to teach slaves to read. Do you know what occasioned their passage, and renders their stringent enforcement necessary? I can tell you. It was the abolition agitation. If the slave is not allowed to read his bible, the sin rests upon the abolitionists; for they stand prepared to furnish him with a key to it, which would make it, not a book of hope, and love, and peace, but of despair, hatred and blood; which would convert the reader, not into a Christian, but a demon. To preserve him from such a horrid destiny, it is a sacred duty which we owe to our slaves, not less than to ourselves, to interpose the most decisive means. If the Catholics deem it wrong to trust the bible to the hands of ignorance, shall we be excommunicated because we will not give it, and with it the corrupt and fatal commentaries of the abolitionists, to our slaves? Allow our slaves to read your writings, stimulating them to cut our throats! Can you believe us to be such unspeakable fools?...

Still, though a slaveholder, I freely acknowledge my obligations as a man; and that I am bound to treat humanely the fellow-creatures whom God has entrusted to my charge. I feel, therefore, somewhat sensitive under the accusation of cruelty, and disposed to defend myself and fellow-slaveholders against it. It is certainly the interest of all, and I am convinced that it is also the desire of every one of us, to treat our slaves with proper kindness. It is necessary to our deriving the greatest amount of profit from them. Of this we are all satisfied. And you snatch from us the only consolation we Americans could derive from the opprobrious imputation of being wholly devoted to making money, which your disinterested and gold-despising countrymen delight to cast upon us, when you nevertheless declare that we are ready to sacrifice it for the pleasure of being inhuman. You remember that Mr. Pitt could not get over the idea that self-interest would ensure kind treatment to slaves, until you told him your woful stories of the middle passage. Mr. Pitt was right in the first instance, and erred, under your tuition, in not perceiving the difference between a temporary and permanent ownership of them. Slaveholders are no more perfect than other men. They have passions. Some of them, as you may suppose, do not at all times restrain them. Neither do husbands, parents and friends. And in each of these relations, as serious suffering as frequently arises from uncontrolled passions, as ever does in that of master and slave, and with as little chance of indemnity. Yet you would not on that account break them up. I have no hesitation in saying that our slaveholders are kind masters, as men usually are kind husbands, parents and friends—as a general rule, kinder. A bad master—he who overworks his slaves, provides ill for them, or treats them with undue severity—loses the esteem and respect of his fellow-citizens to as great an extent as he would for the violation of any of his social and most of his moral obligations. What the most perfect plan of management would be, is a problem hard to solve. From the commencement of Slavery in this country, this subject has occupied the minds of all slaveholders, as much as the improvement of the general condition of mankind has those of the most ardent philanthropists; and the greatest progressive amelioration of the system has been effected. You yourself acknowledge that in the early part of your career you were exceedingly anxious for the *immediate* abolition of the slave trade, lest those engaged in it should so mitigate its evils as to destroy the force of your arguments and facts. The improvement you then *dreaded* has gone on steadily here, and would doubtless have taken place in the slave trade, but for the measures adopted to suppress it.

Of late years we have been not only annoyed, but greatly embarrassed in this matter, by the abolitionists. We have been compelled to curtail some privileges; we have been debarred from granting new ones. In the face of discussions which aim at loosening all ties between master and slave, we have in some measure to abandon our efforts to attach them to us, and control them through their affections and pride. We have to rely more and more on the power of fear. We must, in all our intercourse with them, assert and maintain strict mastery, and impress it on them that they are slaves. This is painful to us, and certainly no present advantage to them. But it is the direct consequence of the abolition agitation. We are determined to continue masters, and to do so we have to draw the rein tighter and tighter day by day to be assured that we hold them in complete check. How far this process will go on, depends wholly and solely on the abolitionists. When they desist, we can relax. We may not before. I do not mean by all this to say that we are in a state of actual alarm and fear of our slaves; but under existing circumstances we should be ineffably stupid not to increase our vigilance and strengthen our hands. You see some of the fruits of your labors. I speak freely and candidly—not as a colonist, who, though a slaveholder, has a master; but as a free white man, holding, under God, and resolved to hold, my fate in my own hands; and I assure you that my sentiments, and feelings, and determinations, are those of every slaveholder in this country.

The research and ingenuity of the abolitionists, aided by the invention of runaway slaves—in which faculty, so far as improvising falsehood goes, the African race is without a rival—have succeeded in shocking the world with a small number of pretended instances of our barbarity. The only wonder is, that considering the extent of our country, the variety of our population, its fluctuating character, and the publicity of all our transactions, the number of cases is so small. It speaks well for us. Yet of these, many are false, all highly colored, some occurring half a century, most of them many years ago; and no doubt a large proportion of them perpetrated by foreigners. With a few rare exceptions, the emigrant Scotch and English are the worst masters among us, and next to them our Northern fellow-citizens. Slaveholders born and bred here are always more humane to slaves, and those who have grown up to a large inheritance of them, the most so of any—showing clearly that the effect of the system is to foster kindly feelings. I do not mean so much to impute innate inhumanity to foreigners, as to show that they come here with false notions of the treatment usual and necessary for slaves, and that newly acquired power here, as everywhere else, is apt to be abused. I cannot enter into a detailed examination of the cases stated by the abolitionists. It would be disgusting, and of little avail. I know nothing of them. I have seen nothing like them, though born and bred here, and have rarely heard anything at all to be compared to them. Permit me to say that I think most of *your* facts must have been drawn from the West Indies, where undoubtedly slaves were treated much more harshly than with us. This was owing to a variety of causes, which might, if necessary, be stated. One was, that they had at first to deal more extensively with barbarians fresh from the wilds of Africa; another, and a leading one, the absenteeism of proprietors. Agents are always more unfeeling than owners, whether placed over West Indian or American slaves, or Irish tenantry. We feel this evil greatly even here. You describe the use of *thumb screws*, as one mode of punishment among us. I doubt if a thumb screw can be found in America. I never saw or heard of one in this country. Stocks are rarely used by private individuals, and confinement still more seldom, though both are common punishments for whites, all the world over. I think they should be more frequently resorted to with slaves, as substitutes for flogging, which I consider the most injurious and least efficacious mode of punishing them for serious offences. It is not degrading, and unless excessive, occasions little pain. You may be a little astonished, after all the flourishes that have been made about "cart whips," &c., when I say flogging is not the most degrading punishment in the world. It may be so to a white man in most countries, but how is it to the white boy? That necessary coadjutor of the schoolmaster, the "birch," is never thought to have rendered infamous the unfortunate victim of pedagogue ire; nor did Solomon in his wisdom dream that he was counselling parents to debase their offspring, when he exhorted them not to spoil the child by sparing the rod. Pardon me for recurring to the now exploded ethics of the Bible. Custom, which, you will perhaps agree, makes most things in this world good or evil, has removed all infamy from the punishment of the lash to the slave. Your blood boils at the recital of stripes inflicted on a man; and you think you should be frenzied to see you own child flogged. Yet see how completely this is ideal, arising from the fashions of society. You doubtless submitted to the rod yourself, in other years, when the smart was perhaps as severe as it would be now; and you have never been guilty of the folly of revenging yourself on the Preceptor, who, in the plenitude of his "irresponsible power," thought proper to chastise your son. So it is with the negro, and the negro father.

As to chains and irons, they are rarely used; never, I believe, except in cases of running away. You will admit that if we pretend to own slaves, they must not be permitted to abscond whenever they see fit; and that if nothing else will prevent it, these means must be resorted to. See the inhumanity necessarily arising from Slavery, you will exclaim. Are such restraints imposed on no other class of people, giving no more offence? Look to your army and navy. If your seamen, impressed from their peaceful occupations, and your soldiers, recruited at the gin-shops—both of them as much kidnapped as the most unsuspecting victim of the slave trade, and doomed to a far more wretched fate—if these men manifest a propensity to desert, the heaviest manacles are their mildest punishment. It is most commonly death, after summary trial. But armies and navies, you say, are indispensable, and must be kept up at every sacrifice. I answer, that they are no more indispensable than Slavery is to us—and to *you*; for you have enough of it in your country, though the form and name differ from ours.

Depend upon it that many things, and in regard to our slaves, most things which appear revolting at a distance, and to slight reflection, would, on a nearer view and impartial comparison with the customs and conduct of the rest of mankind, strike you in a very different light. Remember that on our estates we dispense with the whole machinery of public police and public courts of justice. Thus we try, decide, and execute the sentences, in thousands of cases, which in other countries would go into the courts. Hence, most of the acts of our alleged cruelty, which have any foundation in truth. Whether our patriarchal mode of administering justice is less humane than the Assizes, can only be determined by careful enquiry and comparison. But this is never done by the abolitionists. All our punishments are the outrages of "irresponsible power." If a man steals a pig in England, he is transported—torn from wife, children, parents, and sent to the antipodes, infamous, and an outcast forever, though probably he took from the superabundance of his neighbor to save the lives of his famishing little ones. If one of our well-fed negroes, merely for the sake of fresh meat, steals a pig, he gets perhaps forty stripes. If one of your cottagers breaks into another's house, he is hung for burglary. If a slave does the same here, a few lashes, or it may be, a few hours in the stocks, settles the matter. Are our courts or yours the most humane? If Slavery were not in question, you would doubtless say ours is mistaken lenity. Perhaps it often is; and slaves too lightly dealt with sometimes grow daring. Occasionally, though rarely, and almost always in consequence of excessive indulgence, an individual rebels. This is the highest crime he can commit. It is treason. It strikes at the root of our whole system. His life is justly forfeited, though it is never intentionally taken, unless after trial in our public courts. Sometimes, however, in capturing, or in self-defence, he is unfortunately killed. A legal investigation always follows. But, terminate as it may, the abolitionists raise a hue and cry, and another "shocking case" is held up to the indignation of the world by tender-hearted male and female philanthropists, who would have thought all right had the master's throat been cut, and would have triumphed in it.

I cannot go into a detailed comparison between the penalties inflicted on a slave in our patriarchal courts, and those of the Courts of Sessions, to which freemen are sentenced in all civilized nations; but I know well that if there is any fault in our criminal code, it is that of excessive mildness.

Perhaps a few general facts will best illustrate the treatment this race receives at our hands. It is acknowledged that it increases at least as rapidly as the white. I believe it is an established law, that population thrives in proportion to its comforts. But when it is considered that these people are not recruited by immigration from abroad, as the whites are, and that they are usually settled on our richest and least healthy lands, the fact of their equal comparative increase and greater longevity, outweighs a thousand abolition falsehoods, in favor of the leniency and providence of our management of them. It is also admitted that there are incomparably fewer cases of insanity and suicide among them than among the whites. The fact is, that among the slaves of the African race these things are almost wholy unknown. However, frequent suicide may be among those brought from Africa, I can say that in my time I cannot remember to have known or heard of a single instance of deliberate self-destruction, and but of one of suicide at all. As to insanity, I have seen but one permanent case of it, and that twenty years ago. It cannot be doubted that among three millions of people there must be some insane and some suicides; but I will venture to say that more cases of both occur annually among every hundred thousand of the population of Great Britain, than among all our slaves. Can it be possible, then, that they exist in that state of abject misery, goaded by constant injuries, outraged in their affections, and worn down with hardships, which the abolitionists depict, and so many ignorant and thoughtless persons religiously believe?

With regard to the separation of husbands and wives, parents and children, nothing can be more untrue than the inferences drawn from what is so constantly harped on by abolitionists. Some painful instances perhaps may occur. Very few that can be prevented. It is, and it always has been, and object of prime consideration with our slaveholders, to keep families together. Negroes are themselves both perverse and comparatively indifferent about this matter. It is a singular trait, that they almost invariably prefer forming connexions with slaves belonging to other masters, and at some distance. It is, therefore, impossible to prevent separations sometimes, by the removal of one owner, his death, or failure, and dispersion of his property. In all such cases, however, every reasonable effort is made to keep the parties together, if they desire it. And the negroes forming these connexions, knowing the chances of their premature dissolution, rarely complain more than we all do of the inevitable strokes of fate. Sometimes it happens that a negro prefers to give up his family rather than separate from his master. I have known such instances. As to wilfully selling off a husband, or wife, or child, I believe it is rarely, very rarely done, except when some offence has been committed demanding "transportation." At sales of estates, and even at Sheriff's sales, they are always, if possible, sold in families. On the whole, notwithstanding the migratory character of our population, I believe there are more families among our slaves, who have lived and died together without losing a single member from their circle, except by the process of nature, and in the enjoyment of constant, uninterrupted communion, than have flourished in the same space of time, and among the same number of civilized people in modern times. And to sum up all, if pleasure is correctly defined to be the absence of pain—which, so far as the great body of mankind is concerned, is undoubtedly its true definition—I believe our slaves are the happiest three millions of human beings on whom the sun shines. Into their Eden is coming Satan in the guise of an abolitionist.

As regards their religious condition, it is well known that a majority of the communicants of the Methodist and Baptist churches of the South are colored. Almost everywhere they have precisely the same opportunities of attending worship that the whites have, and, besides special occasions for themselves exclusively, which they prefer. In many places not so accessible to clergymen in ordinary, missionaries are sent, and mainly supported by their masters, for the particular benefit of the slaves. There are none I imagine who may not, if they like, hear the gospel preached at least once a month—most of them twice a month, and very many every week. In our thinly settled country the whites fare no better. But in addition to this, on plantations of any size, the slaves who have joined the church are formed into a class, at the head of which is placed one of their number, acting as deacon or leader, who is also sometimes a licensed preacher. This class assembles for religious exercises weekly, semi-weekly, or oftener, if the members choose. In some parts, also, Sunday schools for blacks are established, and Bible classes are orally instructed by discreet and pious persons. Now where will you find a laboring population possessed of greater religious advantages than these? Not in London, I am sure, where it is known that your churches, chapels, and religious meetinghouses, of all sorts, cannot contain one-half of the inhabitants.

I have admitted, without hesitation, what it would be untrue and profitless to deny, that slaveholders are responsible to the world for the humane treatment of the fellow-beings whom God has placed in their hands. I think it would be only fair for you to admit, what is equally undeniable, that every man in independent circumstances, all the world over, and every government, is to the same extent responsible to the whole human family, for the condition of the poor and laboring classes in their own country, and around them, wherever they may be placed, to whom God has denied the advantages he has given themselves. If so, it would naturally seem the duty of true humanity and rational philanthropy to devote their time and labor, their thoughts, writings and charity, first to the objects placed as it were under their own immediate charge. And it must be regarded as a clear evasion and skillful neglect of this cardinal duty, to pass from those whose destitute situation they can plainly see, minutely examine and efficiently relieve, to enquire after the condition of others in no way entrusted to their care, to exaggerate evils of which they cannot be cognizant, to expend all their sympathies and exhaust all their energies on these remote objects of their unnatural, not to say dangerous, benevolence; and finally, to calumniate, denounce, and endeavor to excite the indignation of the world against their unoffending fellow-creatures for not hastening, under their dictation, to redress wrongs which are stoutly and truthfully denied, while they themselves go but little farther in alleviating those chargeable on them than openly and unblushingly to acknowledge them. There may be indeed a sort of merit in doing so much as to make such an acknowledgment, but it must be very modest if it expects appreciation.

Now I affirm, that in Great Britain the poor and laboring classes of your own race and color, not only your fellow-beings, but your *fellow-citizens*, are more miserable and degraded, morally and physically, than our slaves; to be elevated to the actual condition of whom, would be to these, *your fellow-citizens*, a most glorious act of *emancipation*. And I also affirm, that the poor and laboring classes of our older free

States would not be in a much more enviable condition, but for our Slavery. One of their own Senators has declared in the U.S. Senate, "that the repeal of the Tariff would reduce New-England to a howling wilderness." And the American Tariff is neither more nor less than a system by which the slave States are plundered for the benefit of those States which do not tolerate Slavery.

To prove what I say of Great Britain to be true, I make the following extracts from the Reports of Commissioners appointed by Parliament, and published by order of the House of Commons. I can make but few and short ones. But similar quotations might be made to any extent, and I defy you to deny that these specimens exhibit the real condition of your operatives in every branch of your industry. There is of course a variety in their sufferings. But the same incredible amount of toil, frightful destitution, and utter want of morals, characterize the lot of every class of them.

Collieries.—"I wish to call the attention of the Board to the pits about Brampton. The seams are so thin that several of them have only two feet headway to all the working. They are worked altogether by boys from eight to twelve years of age, on all-fours, with a dog belt and chain. The passages being neither ironed nor wooded, and often an inch or two thick with mud. In Mr. Barnes' pit these poor boys have to drag the barrows with one hundred weight of coal or slack sixty times a day sixty yards, and the empty barrows back, without once straightening their backs, unless they choose to stand under the shaft, and run the risk of having their heads broken by a falling coal."—*Report on Mines*, 1842, p. 71. "In Shropshire the seams are no more than eighteen or twenty inches."—*Ibid.*, p. 67. "At the Booth pit," says Mr. Scriven, "I walked, rode, and crept eighteen hundred yards to one of the nearest faces."—*Ibid.* "Chokedamp, firedamp, wild fire, sulphur, and water, at all times menace instant death to the laborers in these mines." "Robert North, aged 16: Went into the pit at seven years of age, to fill up skips. I drew about twelve months. When I drew by the girdle and chain my skin was broken, and the blood ran down. I durst not say anything. If we said anything, the butty, and the reeve, who works under him, would take a stick and beat us."—*Ibid.* "The usual punishment for theft is to place the culprit's head between the legs of one of the biggest boys, and each boy in the pit—sometimes there are twenty—inflicts twelve lashes on the back and rump with a cat."—*Ibid.* "Instances occur in which children are taken into these mines to work as early as four years of age, sometimes at five, not unfrequently at six and seven, while from eight to nine is the ordinary age at which these employments commence."—*Ibid.* "The wages paid at these mines is from two dollars fifty cents to seven dollars fifty cents per month for laborers, according to age and ability, and out of this they must support themselves. They work twelve hours a day."—*Ibid.*

In Calico Printing.—"It is by no means uncommon in all the districts for children five or six years old to be kept at work fourteen to sixteen hours consecutively."— *Report on Children*, 1842, p. 59.

I could furnish extracts similar to these in regard to every branch of your manufactures, but I will not multiply them. Everybody knows that your operatives habitually labor from twelve to sixteen hours, men, women, and children, and the men occasionally twenty hours per day. In lace-making, says the last quoted report, children sometimes commence work at two years of age.

Destitution.—It is stated by your Commissioners that forty thousand persons in Liverpool, and fifteen thousand in Manchester, live in cellars; while twenty-two thousand in England pass the night in barns, tents, or the open air. "There have been found such occurrences as seven, eight, and ten persons in one cottage, I cannot say for one day, but for whole days, without a morsel of food. They have remained on their beds of straw for two successive days, under the impression that in a recumbent posture the pangs of hunger were less felt."—*Lord Brougham's Speech*, 11th July, 1842. A volume of frightful scenes might be quoted to corroborate the inferences to be necessarily drawn from the facts here stated. I will not add more, but pass on to the important enquiry as to

Morals and Education. "Elizabeth Barrett, aged 14: I always work without stockings, shoes, or trowsers. I wear nothing but a shift. I have to go up to the headings with the men. *They are all naked* there. I am got used to that." *Report on Mines.* "As to illicit sexual intercourse it seems to prevail universally, and from an early period of life." "The evidence might have been doubled, which attest the early commencement of sexual and promiscuous intercourse among boys and girls." "A lower condition of morals, in the fullest sense of the term, could not, I think, be found. I do not mean by this that there are many more prominent vices among them, but that moral feelings and sentiments do not exist. *They have no morals.*" "Their appearance, manners, and moral natures—so far as the word *moral* can be applied to them—are in accordance with their half-civilized condition."—*Report on Children.* "More than half a dozen instances occurred in Manchester, where a man, his wife, and his wife's grown-up sister, habitually occupied the same bed."—*Report on Sanitary Condition.* "Robert Crucilow, aged 16: I don't know anything of Moses—never heard of France. I don't know what America is. Never heard of Scotland or Ireland. Can't tell how many weeks there are in a year. There are twelve pence in a shilling, and twenty shillings in a pound. There are eight pints in a gallon of ale."—*Report on Mines.* "Ann Eggly, aged 18: I walk about and get fresh air on Sundays. I never go to church or chapel. I never heard of Christ at all."—*Ibid.* Others: "The Lord sent Adam and Eve on earth to save sinners." "I don't know who made the world; I never heard about God." "I don't know Jesus Christ—I never saw him—but I have seen Foster who prays about him." "Employer: You have expressed surprise at Thomas Mitchel's not hearing of God. I judge there are few colliers here about that have."—*Ibid.* I will quote no more. It is shocking beyond endurance to turn over your records, in which the condition of your laboring classes is but too faithfully depicted. Could our slaves but see it, they would join us in lynching the abolitionists, which, by the by, they would not now be loth to do. We never think of imposing on them such labor, either in amount or kind. We never put them to *any work*, under ten, more generally twelve years of age, and then the very lightest. Destitution is absolutely unknown—never did a slave starve in America; while in moral sentiments and feelings, in religious information, and even in general intelligence, they are infinitely the superiors of your operatives. When you look around you, how dare you talk to us before the world of Slavery? For the condition of your wretched laborers, you, and every Briton who is not one of them, are responsible before God and man. If you are really humane, philanthropic, and charitable, here are objects for you. Relieve them. Emancipate them. Raise them from the condition of brutes, to the level of human beings—of American slaves, at least. Do not for an instant suppose that the *name* of being freemen is the slightest comfort to them, situated as they are, or that the bombastic boast that "whoever touches British soil stands redeemed, regenerated, and disenthralled," can meet with anything but the ridicule and contempt of mankind, while that soil swarms, both on and under its surface, with the most abject and degraded wretches that ever bowed beneath the oppressor's yoke.

I have said that Slavery is an established and inevitable condition to human society. I do not speak of the *name*, but the *fact*. The Marquis of Normandy has lately declared your operatives to be "*in effect slaves*." Can it be denied? Probably, for such philanthropists as your abolitionists care nothing for facts. They deal in terms and fictions. It is the *word* "slavery" which shocks their tender sensibilities; and their imaginations associate it with "hydras and chimeras dire." The thing itself, in its most hideous reality, passes daily under their view unheeded—a familiar face, touching no chord of shame, sympathy or indignation. Yet so brutalizing is your iron bondage that the English operative is a bye-word through the world. When favoring fortune enables him to escape his prison house, both in Europe and America he is shunned. With all the skill which fourteen hours of daily labor from the tenderest age has ground into him, his discontent, which habit has made second nature, and his depraved propensities, running riot when freed from his wonted fetters prevent his employment whenever it is not a matter of necessity. If we derived no other benefit from African Slavery in the Southern States than that it deterred your *freedmen* from coming hither, I should regard it as an inestimable blessing.

And how unaccountable is that philanthropy, which closes its eyes upon such a state of things as you have at home, and turns its blurred vision to our affairs beyond the Atlantic, meddling with matters which no way concern them—presiding, as you have lately done, at meetings to denounce the "iniquity of our laws" and "the atrocity of our practices," and to sympathize with infamous wretches imprisoned here for violating decrees promulgated both by God and man? Is this doing the work of "your Father which is in heaven," or is it seeking only "that you may have glory of man?" Do you remember the denunciation of our Saviour, "Woe unto you, Scribes and Pharisees; hypocrites! for ye make clean the outside of the cup and platter, but within they are full of extortion and excess."

But after all, supposing that every thing you say of Slavery be true, and its abolition a matter of the last necessity, how do you expect to effect emancipation, and what do you calculate will be the result of its accomplishment? As to the means to be used, the abolitionists, I believe, affect to differ, a large proportion of them pretending that their sole purpose is to apply "moral suasion" to the slaveholders themselves. As a matter of curiosity, I should like to know what their idea of this "moral suasion" is. Their discourses—yours is no exception—are all tirades, the exordium, argument and peroration, turning on the epithets "tyrants," "thieves," "murderers," addressed to us. They revile us as "atrocious monsters," "violators of the laws of nature, God and man," our homes the abode of every iniquity, our land a "brothel." We retort, that they are "incendiaries" and "assassins." Delightful argument! Sweet, potent "moral suasion!" What slave has it freed—what proselyte can it ever make? But if your course was wholly different—if you distilled nectar from your lips, and discoursed sweetest music, could you reasonably indulge the hope of accomplishing your object by such means? Nay, supposing that we were all convinced, and thought of Slavery precisely as you do, at what era of "moral suasion" do you imagine you could prevail on us to give up a thousand millions of dollars in the value of our slaves, and a thousand millions of dollars more in the depreciation of our lands, in consequence of the want of laborers to cultivate them? Consider: were ever any people civilized or savage, persuaded by any argument, human or divine, to surrender voluntarily two thousand millions of dollars? Would you think of asking five millions of Englishmen to contribute, either at once or gradually, four hundred and fifty millions of pounds of sterling to the cause of philanthropy, even if the purpose to be accomplished was not of doubtful goodness? If you are prepared to undertake such a scheme, try it at home. Collect your fund—return us the money for our slaves, and do with them as you like. Be all the glory yours, fairly and honestly won. But you see the absurdity of such an idea. Away, then, with your pretended "moral suasion." You know it is mere nonsense. The abolitionists have no faith in it themselves. Those who expect to accomplish any thing count on means altogether different. They aim, first, to alarm us: that failing, to compel us by force to emancipate our slaves, at our own risk and cost. To these purposes they obviously direct all their energies. Our Northern liberty men endeavored to disseminate their destructive doctrine among our slaves, and excite them to insurrection. But we have put an end to that, and stricken terror into them. They dare not show their faces here. Then they declared they would dissolve the Union. Let them do it. The North would repent it far more than the South. We are not alamed at the idea. We are well content to give up the Union sooner than sacrifice two thousand millions of dollars, and with them all the rights we prize. You may take it for granted that it is impossible to persuade or alarm us into emancipation, or to making the first step towards it. Nothing, then, is left to try, but sheer force. If the abolitionists are prepared to expend their own treasure and shed their own blood as freely as they ask us to do ours, let them come. We do not court the conflict; but we will not and we cannot shrink from it. If they are not ready to go so far; if, as I expect, their philanthropy recoils from it; if they are looking only for *cheap* glory, let them turn their thoughts elsewhere, and leave us in peace. Be the sin, the danger and the evils of Slavery all our own. We compel, we ask none to share them with us....

But what do you calculate will be the result of emancipation, by whatever means accomplished? You will probably point me, by way of answer, to the West Indies—doubtless to Antigua, the great boast of abolition. Admitting that it has succeeded there—which I will do for the sake of the argument—do you know the reason of it? The true and only causes of whatever success has attended it in Antigua are, that the population was before crowded, and all or nearly all the arable land in cultivation. The emancipated negroes could not, many of them, get away if they desired; and knew not where to go, in case they did. They had, practically, no alternative but to remain on the spot; and remaining, they must work on the terms of the proprietors, or perish—the strong arm of the mother country forbidding all hope of seizing the land for themselves. The proprietors, well knowing that they could thus command labor for the merest necessities of life, which was much cheaper than maintaining the non-effective as well as effective slaves in a style which decency and interest, if not humanity, required, willingly accepted half their value, and at once realized far more than the interest on the other half in the diminution of their expenses, and the reduced comforts of the *freemen*. One of your most illustrious judges, who was also a profound and philosophical historian, has said "that villeinage was not abolished, but went into decay in England." This was the process. This has been the process wherever (the name of) villeinage or slavery has been successfully abandoned. Slavery, in fact, "went into decay" in Antigua. I have admitted that, under similar circumstances, it might profitably cease here—that is, profitably to the individual proprietors. Give me half the value of my slaves, and compel them to remain and labor on my plantation, at ten to eleven cents a day, as they do in Antigua, supporting themselves and families, and you shall have them tomorrow, and if you like dub them "free." Not to stickle, I would surrender them without price. No—I recall my words: My humanity revolts at the idea. I am attached to my slaves, and would not have act or part in reducing them to such a condition. I deny, however, that Antigua, as a community, is, or ever will be, as *prosperous* under present circumstances, as she was before abolition, though fully ripe for it. The fact is well known. The reason is that the African, if not a distinct, is an inferior race, and never will effect, as it never has effected, as much in any other condition as in that of Slavery.

I know of no other *slaveholder* who has visited the West Indies since Slavery was abolished, and published *his* views of it. All our facts and opinions come through the friends of the experiment, or at least those not opposed to it. Taking these, even without allowance, to be true as stated, I do not see where the abolitionists find cause for exultation. The tables of exports, which are the best evidences of the condition of a people, exhibit a woful falling off—excused, it is true, by unprecedented droughts and hurricanes, to which their free labor seems unaccountably more subject than slave labor used to be. I will not go into detail. It is well known that a large proportion of British legislation and expenditure, and that proportion still constantly increasing, is most anxiously devoted to repairing the monstrous error of emancipation. You are actually galvanizing your expiring colonies. The truth, deduced from all the facts, was thus pithily stated by the London Quarterly Review, as long ago as 1840: "None of the benefits anticipated by mistaken good intentions have been realized, while every evil wished for by knaves and foreseen by the wise has been painfully verified. The wild rashness of fanaticism has made the emancipation of the slaves equivalent to the loss of one-half of the West Indies, and yet put back the chance of negro civilization."…Such are the *real fruits* of your never-to-be-too-much-glorified abolition, and the valuable dividend of your twenty millions of pounds sterling invested therein.

If any farther proof was wanted of the utter and well-known, though not yet openly avowed, failure of West Indian emancipation, it would be furnished by the startling fact, that THE AFRICAN SLAVE TRADE HAS BEEN ACTUALLY REVIVED UNDER THE AUSPICES AND PROTECTION OF THE BRITISH GOVERN-MENT. Under the specious guise of "immigration," they are replenishing those Islands with slaves from the coast of Africa. Your colony of Sierra Leone, founded on that coast to prevent the slave trade, and peopled, by the bye, in the first instance, by negroes stolen from these States during the Revolutionary War, is the depot to which captives taken from slavers by your armed vessels are transported. I might say returned, since nearly half the Africans carried across the Atlantic are understood to be embarked in this vicinity. The wretched survivors, who are there set at liberty, are immediately seduced to "immigrate" to the West Indies. The business is systematically carried on by black "delegates," sent expressly from the West Indies, where, on arrival, the "immigrants" are *sold into Slavery* for twenty-one years, under conditions ridiculously trivial and wickedly void, since few or none will ever be able to derive any advantage from them. The whole prime of life thus passed in bondage, it is contemplated, and doubtless it will be carried into effect, to turn them out in their old age to shift for themselves, and to supply their places with fresh and vigorous "immigrants." Was ever a system of Slavery so barbarous devised before? Can you think of comparing it with ours? Even your own religious missionaries at Sierra Leone denounce it "as worse than the slave state in Africa." And your black delegates, fearful of the influence of these missionaries, as well as on account of the inadequate supply of captives, are now preparing to procure the able-bodied and comparatively industrious Kroomen of the interior, by *purchasing from their head-men* the privilege of inveigling them to the West India market! So ends the magnificent farce—perhaps I should say tragedy, of West India abolition! I will not harrow your feelings by asking you to review the labors of your life and tell me what you and your brother enthusiasts have accomplished for "injured Africa," but while agreeing with Lord Stowell, that "villeinage decayed," and admitting that Slavery might do so also, I think I am fully justified by passed and passing events in saying, as Mr. Grosvenor said of the slave trade, that its *abolition* is "impossible."

You are greatly mistaken, however, if you think that the consequences of emancipation here would be similar and no more injurious than those which followed from it in your little sea-girt West India Islands, where nearly all were blacks. The system of Slavery is not in "decay" with us. It flourishes in full and growing vigor. Our country is boundless in extent. Dotted here and there with villages and fields, it is, for the most part, covered with immense forests and swamps of almost unknown size. In such a country, with a people so restless as ours, communicating of course some of that spirit to their domestics, can you conceive that any thing short of the power of the master over the slave, could confine the African race, notoriously idle and improvident, to labor on our plantations? Break this bond, but for a day, and these plantations will be solitudes. The negro loves change, novelty and sensual excitements of all kinds, *when awake*. "Reason and order," of which Mr. Wilberforce said "liberty was the child," do not characterize him. Released from his present obligations, his first impulse would be to go somewhere. And here no natural boundaries would restrain him. At first they would all seek the towns, and rapidly accumulate in squalid groups upon their outskirts. Driven thence by the "armed police," which would immediately spring into existence, they would scatter in all directions. Some bodies of them might wander towards the "free" States, or to the Western wilderness, marking their tracks by their depredations and their corpses. Many would roam wild in our "big woods." Many more would seek the recesses of our swamps for secure covert. Few, very few of them, could be prevailed on to do a stroke of work, none to labor continuously, while a head of cattle, sheep or swine could be found in our ranges, or an ear of corn nodded in our abandoned fields. These exhausted, our folds and poultry yards, barns and store houses, would become their prey. Finally, our scattered dwellings would be plundered, perhaps fired, and the inmates murdered. How long do you suppose that we could bear these things? How long would it be before we should sleep with rifles at our bedsides, and never move without one in our hands. This work once begun, let the story of our British ancestors and the aborigines of this country tell the sequel. Far more rapid, however, would be the catastrophe. "Ere many moons went by," the African race would be exterminated, or reduced again to Slavery, their ranks recruited, after your example, by fresh "emigrants" from their fatherland.

Is timely preparation and gradual emancipation suggested to avert these horrible consequences? I thought your experience in the West Indies had, at least, done so much as to explode that idea. If it failed there, much more would it fail here, where the two races, approximating to equality in numbers, are daily and hourly in the closest contact. Give room for but a single spark of real jealousy to be kindled between them, and the explosion would be instantaneous and universal. It is the most fatal of all fallacies, to suppose that these two races can exist together, after any length of time, or any process of preparation, on terms at all approaching to equality. Of this, both of them are finally and fixedly convinced. They differ essentially, in all the leading traits which characterize the varieties of the human species, and color draws an indelible and insuperable line of separation between them. Every scheme founded upon the idea that they can remain together on the same soil, beyond the briefest period, in any other relation than precisely that which now subsists between them, is not only preposterous, but fraught with deepest danger. If there was no alternative but to try the "experiment" here, reason and humanity dictate that the sufferings of "gradualism" should be saved, and the catastrophe of "immediate abolition" enacted as rapidly as possible. Are you impatient for the performance to commence? Do you long to gloat over the scenes I have suggested, but could not hold the pen to portray? In your long life many such have passed under your review. You know that *they* are not "*impossible*." Can they be to your taste? Do you believe that in laboring to bring them about, the abolitionists are doing the will of God? No! God is not there. It is the work of Satan. The arch-fiend, under specious guises, has found his way into their souls, and with false appeals to philanthropy, and foul insinuations to ambition, instigates them to rush headlong to the accomplishment of his diabolical designs.

We live in a wonderful age. The events of the last three quarters of a century appear to have revolutionized the human mind. Enterprise and ambition are only limited in their purposes by the horizon of the imagination. It is the transcendental era. In philosophy, religion, government, science, arts, commerce, nothing that has been is to be allowed to be. Conservatism, in any form, is scoffed at. The slightest taint of it is fatal. Where will all this end? If you can tolerate one ancient maxim, let it be that the best criterion of the future is the past. That, if anything, will give a clue. And, looking back only through your time, what was the earliest feat of this same transcendentalism? The rays of the new moral Drummond Light were first concentrated to a focus at Paris, to illuminate the universe. In a twinkling it consumed the political, religious and social systems of France. It could not be extinguished there until literally drowned in blood. And then, from its ashes arose that supernatural man, who, for twenty years, kept affrighted Europe in convulsions. Since that time, its scattered beams, refracted by broader surfaces, have, nevertheless, continued to scathe wherever they have fallen. What political structure, what religious creed, but has felt the galvanic shock, and even now trembles to its foundations? Mankind, still horror-stricken by the catastrophe of France, have shrunk from rash experiments upon social systems. But they have been practicing in the East, around the Mediterranean, and through the West India Islands. And growing confident, a portion of them seem desperately bent on kindling the all-devouring flame in the bosom of our land. Let it once again blaze up to heaven, and another cycle of blood and devastation will dawn upon the world. For our own sake, and for the sake of those infatuated men who are madly driving on the conflagration; for the sake of human nature, we are called on to strain every nerve to arrest it. And be assured our efforts will be bounded only with our being. Nor do I doubt that five millions of people, brave, intelligent, united, and prepared to hazard every thing, will, in such a cause, with the blessing of God, sustain themselves. At all events, come what may, it is ours to meet it.

We are well aware of the light estimation in which the abolitionists, and those who are taught by them, profess to hold us. We have seen the attempt of a portion of the Free Church of Scotland to reject our alms, on the ground that we are "slave-drivers," after sending missionaries to solicit them.… . These people may exhaust their slang, and make black-guards of themselves, but they cannot defile us. And as for the suggestion to exclude slaveholders from your London clubs, we scout it. Many of us, indeed, do go to London, and we have seen your breed of gawky lords, both there and here, but it never entered into our conceptions to look on them as better than ourselves. The American slaveholders, collectively or individually, ask no favors of any man or race who tread the earth. In none of the attributes of men, mental or physical, do they acknowledge or fear superiority elsewhere. They stand in the broadest light of the knowledge, civilization and improvement of the age, as much favored of heaven as any of the sons of Adam. Exacting nothing undue, they yield nothing but justice and courtesy, even to royal blood. They cannot be flattered, duped, nor bullied out of their rights or their propriety. They smile with contempt at scurrility and vaporing beyond the seas, and they turn their backs upon it where it is "irresponsible;" but insolence that ventures to look them in the face, will never fail to be chastised.

I think I may trust you will not regard this letter as intrusive. I should never have entertained an idea of writing it, had you not opened the correspondence. If you think anything in it harsh, review your own—which I regret that I lost soon after it was received—and you will probably find that you have taken your revenge before hand. If you have not, transfer an equitable share of what you deem severe, to the account of the abolitionists at large. They have accumulated against the slaveholders a balance of invective, which, with all our efforts, we shall not be able to liquidate much short of the era in which your national debt will be paid. At all events, I have no desire to offend you personally, and, with the best wishes for your continued health, I have the honor to be,

Your obedient servant,
JAMES H. HAMMOND

PAUL HAMILTON HAYNE

Selected Letters to Sidney Lanier

"Copse Hill" Geo R Road;
September, 8th 1871

My Dear Lanier;

Thanks for your long and interesting letter. The details of your sickness I have read with great attention, and *frankly*, my dear fellow, I'm sorry to see that things are worse than I expected. *Not* that you ought to be discouraged; for Consumption is not a cureless disease, & moreover it is certain that, as yet, you cannot be properly said to have consumption.

Still, all your symptoms point to great feebleness of the lungs; & the muscular & nervous disorganization you mention, is significant & serious enough. Then, your *average* weight being near a hundred & fifty pounds, you only weigh a hundred & *twenty two* at present, (which, by the way, is *my* average *precisely*).

What *should* be done in view of these considerations?

I can only tell you what cured *me*, after I had become a mere shaking & rattling *skeleton*.

My Physician—an English Doctor, & an eccentric, whom some persons laughed at—informed me, that my chances of life were just represented by the biggest of big *Osts* [*sic*], in fact were absolutely *nil* & that I was a good patient to experiment upon.

"Experiment away!" said I, "what the deuce does it matter, since I'm booked for Charon's boat?" "Now," cried the Doctor, "I'll *kill*, or *cure* you!" Whereupon he took me in hand, and made me drink from 2 to 3 *strong milk punches* a day, (generally 3) and beginning with a 5th of a grain of *morphine*, pretty rapidly increased the dose to 1,—2,—3, & lastly 4 *grains*!!

Opium, quoth *Aësculapius*, is "absurdly miscomprehended by the Profession, both in America, & Europe. It is, rightly administered, a *great tissue* saver; & acts *indirectly* upon *diseased lungs*, in rendering the system impervious to *colds* &c.

"No opium eater ever dies of consumption; and it is a remarkable fact that in China, the *mandarins* who take *small specified doses of the drug daily*, arrive as a Class, at extreme old age!

"When, therefore, the consumptive patient comes to me, declaring that the other Doctors have given him up, I treat, and have often cured him, with *milk punch* and *morphine*. The taking of the *latter* may *generally* necessitate a *partial* subservience to the medicine *ever after*; but *that* is better than death, despite the howlings of Coleridge and De Quincey, who *abused* a great blessing, and were punished accordingly."—Thus far my Dr. In a *desperate* position, he resorted to a *desperate* remedy,—and in my case—*succeeded*!!! Should the *Leeches* begin to shake their heads over *your* Condition, follow my advice, *Lanier*, and at least *try* the course recommended.

—God grant you may get well, *without* it, however, & pursue your life course brilliantly & successfully to the end.

Well may you refer mournfully to Literature, above all, to Poetry, as the means of gaining one's bread!

Bitterly myself do I feel the degradation, when *forced* to manufacture verses for the *Market*. But with *debt*, & *starvation* staring a man in the face, he is driven to "little" expedients, & loses a portion of his squeamishness, (alack! that it *should* be so!) as time rolls on!

As regards *yourself*, I *can't* help believing that if *circumstances* drive you into *Literature, as a profession*, you will *unequivocally* succeed; & I could almost find it in my soul to rejoice if you had to become an author. "'*Tis thy vocation, Lucius*!"

You are going positively to N. York City. Would to Heaven I could spare the time & cash to accompany you! But Fate sternly sayeth, "*no!*" as She *always does* manage to say, whenever I specially desire to do something agreeable, & after mine own heart.

Think of it! *Lanier*, since 1866, I have never been more than 10 miles from my cottage home! I who *delight* in movement, travel, adventure!, & who *previous* to *that* period had been accustomed to rove from *Carolina* to *Canida* [*sic*], from Manhattan, to the *great West*!!

I ask of *Destiny,* "Stern *Mother*!, what sin hath thy son committed, that he should thus be "cabinned, cribbed, confined?"—But, the "oracles are dumb," and perforce I must *endure*.

'Tis harder than ever, when I read the poems *("Songs of the Sierras")* of the new celebrity *Joaquin Miller*, who despite his infernal name, is I assure you a *true Genius*, evincing the Strongest imagination, veined all over with the rich, ripe blood of youth & passion!

The fellow sings what he has *seen*, and *heard*, and *acted*, and so, there's a *reality* & *vim* about his tales, and metrical pictures, very striking & effective. The London *guilds* have gone mad over him, & in this Country some critics, (*women* critics especially) are trying their d——t to ruin him; but *Miller* has the true *afflatus*, & may refuse to be ruined—*artistically at least*.

—To return to New York! Shall I send you the letters of introduction *there*, or *at once* to *Marietta*? Have you time to inform me? "*Cambyses*" was mailed you in a very rough state, & you have made but little of the poem, I fear. Yet the legend is *striking*, and in the right hands would have come out gloriously.

God bless you *my friend*, & may the *Angel of Health*, re-visit you. She is an Angel *I* have not seen for a quarter of a century.

> Always Faithfully,
> Paul H Hayne
> PO Box 635, Augusta Geo

"Copse Hill," Ga. R Road
Thursday, 27th March (1873)

My Dear Poet;

Your note of the 12th inst—with its precious "MSS" enclosure, duly reached me, but I have had no leisure to reply until *now*.

Good news it is to hear you say, that your strength has *measureably* returned, and that henceforth you intend devoting much time and energy to *art*!

I think so highly Lanier! of your powers, especially of the *delicacy* and marvellous opulence of your *fancy*; and of your sense of *rhythmic harmonies*, and *verse-music*, *without* which the *greatest poems* seem harsh, and the *greatest poets uncouth* (if indeed great poems *are*, or great *poets* possible without this sense), that I hail the determination you express to *snub Law* for *Literature* with *real* delight!! And let me add, that *hereafter* I shall look for & shall *confidently* expect to hail brilliant artistic performances on *your part*!

If you *disappoint* me *"odd's! zooks! and boddikins!"* [*sic*]—but I'll manage to torment you in some fashion!

And now for the *"June Dreams in January"*:

Very attentively, and *half* a *dozen times* over, have I perused this poem, quite a remarkable composition in many respects.

Firstly, I stand *amazed* at the lavish imagery, and the rich overpowering Orientalism of the piece!

Why *Hafiz* might have written it, or *Firdusi*!—Only *one other* English speaking bard ever sang in *this* precise *style*, and that was Alex: Smith in his *"Life Drama,"* a production *enormously* overrated, no doubt, *at first*, but most unjustly depreciated *now*.

Your *"June Dreams"* belong to a section of the *"Arte Poetique,"* I have never myself affected, and *were* I to do so, heavens!*what* an ass I *would* appear in the eyes of the judicious!!

Don't conceive me as *depreciating* this Oriental magnificence of metaphor, this rapid, magical reproduction of rainbow-blue similes, and bright verbal ingenuities.

On the contrary, there are moods when such things both dazzle & charm me.

And in *such* a mood I read your last poem!

Let us come to *particulars*: (*1st Stanza:*) Your *friend's* objection to this, as "improper," (i.e.) "*Swinburnish*," & too voluptuous, is with due deference—perfectly *absurd*! I like the stanza because it opens the poem nobly, gives at once the *key-note*, and moreover, the personification is equally bold and clear.

2nd Stanza; 1st line reads *haltingly*, why don't you leave out, "*while th'intense hours* &c [*"*] with its needless *elision* and substitute the following—

"*Throb Beautiful! the fervid (fervent) hours exhaled &c &c*" The idea of the "*kisses* faint-blown from June's *finger-tips* up to *the Sun*," has a certain *prettiness*, but I can't help thinking it a little *artificial* too.

3rd Stanza: Altogether *lovely*!!—with its mellow picture of the "tender darkness," and "crushed day flowers" &c (By the way do you like to put so much stress & emphasis upon the last syllable of a word like *flower*? thus; (*flow-ér*) I *don't*!!

4th & 5th *Stanzas both fine*, very *fine*! *One* expression only I would alter, "And *short-breathed* winds &c."—'Tis horribly suggestive of the *asthma*, or *consumption*!! At *best*, it brings up *prosaic*, not *poetical* images; such as the figure of a burly tourist panting up a mountainside; or a fat *Adonis* like *Joseph Sedl[e]y* (*vide* "*Vanity Fair!*") on his knees panting & perspiring before some coquettish Becky *Sharp*! And *these stanzas*, (4*th* & 5th) are too beautiful to be marred even by a trifling *mal-apropos* phrase like the one I've pointed out.

6th Stanze: a *little* extravagant isn't it?

7th Stanza: The *first couplet exquisite*.

8th: The line beginning, "*Or clambering*" &c, affects my imagination with a peculiar feeling of *quaintness*, a remote, fantastic quaintness. As for the 9th & *concluding* verse, it is not merely the artistic appropriate winding up of a poem, sweet and ardent as the June marvels it describes, and the rich June atmosphere, which surrounds & interpenetrates every line—, but *in itself*, how musical, how suggestive, how *perfect*!!

Indeed, *such* a stanza might have arisen, (like the bubbling of fresh waters from some secluded fountain, flower-crowned), out of Edmund Spenser's *heart*, and been at once glorified by his divine imagination, in the days of his golden youth, before disappointment, & the "*hell it is in suing, long to bide*," had done their wild work upon his sweet, exalted nature!!

These lines have sunk into my memory, and are likely to remain there. They differ in *quality* of *tone* & *sentiment* from all the preceding verses, and still they *harmonize* with them!

In regard to the little story outlined in *blank* verse, I think it a rather happy conception, and see nothing to specially amend, or alter:

"Come *Name*, come *Fame*, and kiss my *Sweetheart's* feet!," I *like* exceedingly.

To wind up—in "*June Dreams*" you have happily embodied a quaint, fantastic, alluring, and richly fanciful topic,—;—there is the "*lush*," *juicy richness* of the season *itself* in it, and *all* thro it!!

Let me tell you as a somewhat *odd coincidence* that *just previous to* the arrival of your "*June Dreams*" I had myself completed a poem upon "*Midsummer in the South*," the general style whereof I *do* think or *hope* at least, you may be pleased with:

It opens *thus*:

"I love queen August's stately sway—,
And all her fragrant South Winds say,
With strange, mysterious meanings fraught,
Of half-articulated thought:—
Those winds in charge of gloom & gleam
Seem wandering thro a golden dream—,
The rare midsummer dream that lies
In humid depths of Nature's Eyes,
Weighing her languid forehead down,
Beneath a fair, but fiery crown;
Its witching rules o'er earth & skies,
Fills with divine amenities
The bland, blue spaces of air,
And smiles with looks of drowsy cheer,
Mid hollows of the brown-hued hills,
And in the tongues of tinkling rills,
A softer, homilier utterance finds,
Than that which haunts the lingering winds!

But I have no leisure to proceed. I'll send you extracts *another* time.
Ever (in haste) but Faithfully

                                        Paul H Hayne

P.S. Send me your photograph.

---

my address is PO Box, 635 Augusta Geo
"Copse Hill" Ga Central RR
(Saturday afternoon) March 29th 1873:

My Dear Lanier;

   I wrote you at some *length* yesterday, enclosing at the same time the "MSS" poem you had kindly given me the chance of reading *before* the general public could catch a glimpse *thereof.*
   I have frankly told you in what manner the poem affected me, pointing out here & there some trifling blemish, but upon *the whole* expressing *warm* admiration of as pretty a piece of rich, fanciful, *Oriental* composition, as ever came to my notice—not excepting *Alex Smith's gorgeous*, and really striking passages in the *"Life Drama."* (By the way, I have *never* ceased to wonder *how*, and *why* it was that *Smith*, whose *poetic youth* blossomed so *luxuriantly*, failed in every sense, to carry out its *superb promise*).

What in *your* *"June Dreams"* particularly charmed me, *was* or *is* the *lush*, juicy, overflowing richness & vitality of style & fancy, a species of half *sensuous,* and half *intellectual abandon* to the sweet *impulses of a poetic mood*, which was common with the un-artificial Elizabethan *Singers*, from Shakspeare, down to Phineas Fletcher, but which now-a-days, the *trim, careful* Muses are evidently afraid of &c &c.

When fairly published, send me *half a dozen printed copies* of your *"Dreams";* I shall have *good uses* for them! Enclosed, you'll find a rough copy of *"Midsummer in the South"*

Please read it *critically!*

You are the only man—*South*—now *living* to whom I would come in this way, asking counsel, and *free*—nay! the *freest* criticism! Perhaps by an exchange of *poems* (in *course* of composition) *thus*—we may mutually benefit one another. I know that your *hints* as to my *"Sunset in the Pine Barrens,"* were *pregnant* with *meaning*; as you'll perceive, when the poem entirely *re-written, because* of your suggestions—is sent you in its *last* form—printed!!

Write me *very soon*, & Believe me Always Fraternally & most Faithfully Yr's

Paul H Hayne

P.S. You write in a way not altogether satisfactory ab't *your health*. What do you mean, *(for example)*, by saying, that the *"moderate degree of strength"* you have attained, will be devoted chiefly to *"artistic labors,"* since *"it seems fated* that you are *not* to practice your profession of the *law"*? *Why* fated? Because while your physical *"strength"* admits of moderate *"art-labor,"* it is insufficient for the exacting duties of the Lawyer? Is *such* the *case*?

Address PO Box 635 *Augusta,* GA
"Copse Hill," Central Georgia R Road.
Friday 2nd May; (1873)

Dearly Beloved Poet;

I think, nay! I am all but *certain* that *yours* of the 11th ul*t* remains unacknowledged! The letter I mean, was despatched from Brunswick.

Thanks again, and heartfelt thanks too, for the trouble you vouchsafed to take with my *"Midsummer in the South"*—

'Tis encouraging to be informed, that taking that piece *as a whole*, you decidedly like it, and so feel disposed to rank the verses among my *best*.

Yet, *twice* has the poem been rejected, (albeit with *mellifous* excuses!), by certain Yankee Editors; *a fact* I mention in order that you may not yourself deem it singular that *"the Atlantic"* returned the MSS of your *"June Dream."*

Of about 8 carefully written poems of mine, sent to *Howells* during the past year, just *4* were accepted, and subsequently *published*. And verily, you must know, that such rejection by no means invariably signifies *inferiority, apropos* of the verses dismissed. Length, elaboration, has a great deal to do with it!

'Tis no *mere* excuse likewise, but a *fact* the *Edt's* are often *buried almost* under accumulated *loads* of *rhyme*; and that they *must decline* poetry even of a *high* order, when thus oppressed.

Recently I mailed to *"Scribner's"* two poems, one a *legend* of Scandinavia, the other a trifle of 5 stanzas, a brief lyric in fact! Holland *returns* the "legend," and (as a very special *distinction* I'm disposed to believe), accepts the *song*, at the same time, calling my attention to certain pencil marks upon the outside of my rejected *"copy."*

I look, and to my *amazement*, decipher the figures, 2,756(!!!) indicating that just that number of poems are now on hand, *unpublished*, and many *unexamined*, in the drawers of the *"sanctum"* bureau!!

Discouraging isn't it?—

And next, comes my good friend O. B. *Bunce*, (do you know him?) the present Ed: of *"Appleton's Journal,"* who in a half-despairing note, *begs*, & entreats me almost on his knees, metaphorically—to spare him for months to come; (i.e.) to forward him no more verses!!

Poetry—he cries, with a most plaintive outcry,—"will be my *death*, if things go on as they *threaten* to do! All verse-mongers are not reasonable, like yourself—" (that's *me*, you must know!) "On the contrary, here am I, up to the *neck already* in reams of metrical "MSS," flooded with a fresh tide of inspiration from these four well-known *literateurs*, the rejection of whose pieces, will bring on my devoted head, God knoweth how much abuse, & detraction!"—

And all this is the Gospel truth! We must sympathise a little with the Ed'ts, no less than with their *victims*(!!)

If I can dare to *advise*, I should tell you to put by for the nonce your longer poems—as far as the Magzns are concerned, and to elaborate with *immense* care a series of *short lyrics*, "Swallow flights of song" &c. Put all your richness of fancy, and all your gracious art into these efforts, and my word for it, they'll bring you substantial results both in *repute* and *greenbacks*!!

Try the experiment!!

I'm sorry to hear about your *health*, and the necessary abandonment of your profession; but still, *Art and Letters* may gain *thereby*!!

Have you any acquaintance with a young man, named Fred Williams, a Lawyer of Augusta? I ask, because he mailed me a *vol* of his verses 2 weeks agone, requesting my *"candid opinion"* in regard to "their merits or demerits!" As *kindly* as possible, I wrote and told him what I thought, viz, that his verses, (generally), were insufferably bad! Now, 'tis whispered in mine ear, that a *literary clique* in *Augusta* feel assured of my *narrow, mean,* and *envious* (!) temper!

I would fain put down a fiery genius; lest perchance—but you know what is meant!—

Again, they *persecute* me with copies, by mail, of a tale called *"Clifford Troup,"*

(Mrs. Westmoreland author), and then, when I criticise it, as a *worthless, & stupid production*, which it really *is*—I am threatened with intellectual and literary extinguishment!!—

—By God, Lanier! it is *disgusting*—this attempt to bully men like—yourself, (for ins:) and your humble servant—into bepuffing and beplastering every ambitious fool, whether, man or woman, of the South, who chooses to reach after literary honors!

I am sick of it, and if they bother me in the papers much longer, I'll wax savage—for once—; and speak the plain truth in tones *not* to be miscomprehended. What right have mere society-women, like *this*—what the devil's her name?—to come forward, but pshaw! "the game's not worth the *candle*" &c.

Basta! Basta!

In a fortnight's time, I start (DV), for the *North*; hope to visit Philadelphia, N York, Boston &c &c. You are going too, this season—but *when*? Write, & tell me!

> Ever Yr's sincerely
> Paul H Hayne

[P.S.] Return "*Violets*" when you are done with the piece! I know 'tis full of *artistic faults*; yet perhaps there be lines in it, you'll like well enou'!

THOMAS JEFFERSON

Notes on the State of Virginia

Query XVIII: Manners

It is difficult to determine on the standard by which the manners of a nation may be tried, whether *catholic,* or *particular.* It is more difficult for a native to bring to that standard the manners of his own nation, familiarized to him by habit. There must doubtless be an unhappy influence on the manners of our people produced by the existence of slavery among us. The whole commerce between master and slave is a perpetual exercise of the most boisterous passions, the most unremitting despotism on the one part, and degrading submissions on the other. Our children see this, and learn to imitate it; for man is an imitative animal. This quality is the germ of all education in him. From his cradle to his grave he is learning to do what he sees others do. If a parent could find no motive either in his philanthropy or his self-love, for restraining the intemperance of passion towards his slave, it should always be a sufficient one that his child is present. But generally it is not sufficient. The parent storms, the child looks on, catches the lineaments of wrath, puts on the same airs in the circle of smaller slaves, gives a loose to his worst of passions, and thus nursed, educated, and daily exercised in tyranny, cannot but be stamped by it with odious peculiarities. The man must be a prodigy who can retain his manners and morals undepraved by such circumstances. And with what execration should be the stateman be loaded, who permitting one half the citizens thus to trample on the rights of the other, transforms those into despots, and these into enemies, destroys the morals of the one part, and the amor patriæ of the other. For if a slave can have a country in this world, it must be any other in preference to that in which he is born to live and labour for another: in which he must lock up the faculties of his nature, contribute as far as depends on his individual endeavors to the evanishment of the human race, or entail his own miserable condition on the endless generations proceeding from him. With the morals of the people, their industry also is destroyed. For in a warm climate, no man will labour for himself who can make another labour for him. This is so true, that of the proprietors of slaves a very small proportion indeed are ever seen to labour. And can the liberties of a nation be thought secure when we have removed their only firm basis, a conviction in the minds of the people that these liberties are of the gift of God?

That they are not to be violated but with his wrath? Indeed I tremble for my country when I reflect that God is just: that his justice cannot sleep for ever: that considering numbers, nature and natural means only, a revolution of the wheel of fortune, an exchange of situation, is among possible events: that it may become probable by supernatural interference! The Almighty has no attribute which can take side with us in such a contest.—But it is impossible to be temperate and to pursue this subject through the various considerations of policy, of morals, of history natural and civil. We must be contented to hope they will force their way into every one's mind. I think a change already perceptible, since the origin of the present revolution. The spirit of the master is abating, that of the slave rising from the dust, his condition mollifying, the way I hope preparing, under the auspices of heaven, for a total emancipation, and that this is disposed, in the order of events, to be with the consent of the masters, rather than by their extirpation.

(1785)

To Edward Coles
Monticello, August 25, 1814

Dear Sir,—Your favour of July 31, was duly received and was read with peculiar pleasure. The sentiments breathed through the whole do honor to both the head and heart of the writer. Mine on the subject of slavery of negroes have long since been in possession of the public, and time has only served to give them stronger root. The love of justice, and the love of country plead equally the cause of these people, and it is a moral reproach to us that they should have pleaded it so long in vain, and should have produced not a single effort, nay I fear not much serious willingness to relieve them & ourselves from our present condition of moral & political reprobation. From those of the former generation who were in the fulness of age when I came into public life, which was while our controversy with England was on paper only, I soon saw that nothing was to be hoped. Nursed and educated in the daily habit of seeing the degraded condition, both bodily and mental, of those unfortunate beings, not reflecting that that degradation was very much the work of themselves & their fathers, few minds have yet doubted but that they were as legitimate subjects of property as their horses and cattle. The quiet and monotonous course of colonial life has been disturbed by no alarm, and little reflection on the value of liberty. And when alarm was taken at an enterprize on their own, it was not easy to carry them to the whole length of the principles which they invoked for themselves. In the first or second session of the Legislature after I became a member, I drew to this subject the attention of Col. Bland, one of the oldest, ablest & most respected members, and he undertook to move for certain moderate extensions of the protection of the laws to these people. I seconded his motion, and, as a younger member, was more spared in the debate; but he was denounced as an enemy of his country, & was treated with the grossest indecorum. From an early stage of our revolution other & more distant duties were assigned to me, so that from that time till my return from Europe in 1789, and I may say till I returned to reside at home in 1809, I had little opportunity of knowing the progress of public sentiment here on this subject. I had always hoped that the younger generation receiving their early impressions after the flame of liberty had been kindled in every breast & had become as it were the vital spirit of every American, that the generous temperament of youth, analogous to the motion of their blood, and above the suggestions of avarice, would have sympathized with oppression wherever found, and proved their love of liberty beyond their own share of it. But my intercourse with them since my return has not been sufficient to ascertain that they had made towards this point the progress I had hoped. Your solitary but welcome voice is the first which has brought this sound to my ear; and I have considered the general silence which prevails on this subject as indicating an apathy unfavorable to every hope. Yet the hour of emancipation is advancing, in the march of time. It will come, and whether brought on by the generous energy of our own minds; or by the bloody process of St Domingo, excited and conducted by the power of our present enemy, if once stationed permanently within our Country, and offering asylum & arms to the oppressed, is a leaf of our history not yet turned over. As to the method by which this difficult work is to be effected, if permitted to be done by ourselves, I have seen no proposition so expedient on the whole, as that as emancipation of those born after a given day, and of their education and expatriation after a given age. This would give time for a gradual extinction of that species of labour & substitution of another, and lessen the severity of the shock which an operation so fundamental cannot fail to produce. For men probably of any color, but of this color we know, brought from their infancy without necessity for thought or forecast, are by their habits rendered as incapable as children of taking care of themselves, and are extinguished promptly wherever industry is necessary for raising young. In the mean time they are pests in society by their idleness, and the depredations to which this leads them. Their amalgamation with the other color produces a degradation to which no lover of his country, no lover of excellence in the human character can innocently consent. I am sensible of the partialities with which you have looked towards me as the person who should undertake this salutary but arduous work. But this, my dear sir, is like bidding old Priam to buckle the armour of Hector "trementibus æquo humeris et inutile ferruncingi." No, I have overlived the generation and with which mutual labors & perils begat mutual confidence and influence. This enterprise is for the young; for those who can follow it up, and bear it through to its consummation. It shall have all my prayers, & these are the only weapons of an old man. But in the mean time are you right in abandoning this property, and your country with it? I think not. My opinion has ever been that, until more can be done for them, we should endeavor, with those whom fortune has thrown on our hands, to feed and clothe them well, protect them from all ill usage, require such reasonable labor only as is performed voluntarily by freemen, & be led by no repugnancies to abdicate them, and our duties to them. The laws do not permit us to turn them loose, if that were for their good: and to commute them for other property is to commit them to those whose usage of them we cannot control. I hope then, my dear sir, you will reconcile yourself to your country and its unfortunate condition; that you will not lessen its stock of sound disposition by withdrawing your portion from the mass. That, on the contrary you will come forward in the public councils, become the missionary of this doctrine truly christian; insinuate & inculcate it softly but steadily, through the medium of writing and conversation; associate others in your labors, and when the phalanx is formed, bring on and press the proposition perseveringly until its accomplishment. It is an encouraging observation that no good measure was ever proposed, which, if duly pursued, failed to prevail in the end. We have proof of this in the history of the endeavors in the English parliament to suppress that very trade which brought this evil on us. And you will be supported by the religious precept, "be not weary in well-doing." That your success may be as speedy & complete, as it will be of honorable & immortal consolation to yourself, I shall as fervently and sincerely pray as I assure you of my great friendship and respect.

Thomas Jefferson

To John Holmes
Monticello, April 22, 1820

I thank you, dear Sir, for the copy you have been so kind as to send me of the letter to your constituents on the Missouri question. It is a perfect justification to them. I had for a long time ceased to read newspapers, or pay any attention to public affairs, confident they were in good hands, and content to be a passenger in our bark to the shore from which I am not distant. But this momentous question, like a fire bell in the night, awakened and filled me with terror. I considered it at once as the knell of the Union. It is hushed, indeed, for the moment. But this is a reprieve only, not a final sentence. A geographical line, coinciding with a marked principle, moral and political, once conceived and held up to the angry passions of men, will never be obliterated; and every new irritation will mark it deeper and deeper. I can.say, with conscious truth, that there is not a man on earth who would sacrifice more than I would to relieve us from this heavy reproach, in any *practicable* way. The cession of that kind of property, for so it is misnamed, is a bagatelle which would not cost me a second thought, if, in that way, a general emancipation and *expatriation* could be effected; and gradually, and with due sacrifices, I think it might be. But as it is, we have the wolf by the ears, and we can neither hold him, nor safely let him go. Justice is in one scale, and self-preservation in the other. Of one thing I am certain, that as the passage of slaves from one State to another, would not make a slave of a single human being who would not be so without it, so their diffusion over a greater surface would make them individually happier, and proportionally facilitate the accomplishment of their emancipation, by dividing the burthen on a greater number of coadjutors. An abstinence too, from this act of power, would remove the jealousy excited by the undertaking of the Congress to regulate the condition of the different descriptions of men composing a State. This certainly is the exclusive right of every State, which nothing in the constitution has taken from them and given to the General Government. Could Congress, for example, say, that the non-freemen of Connecticut shall be freemen, or that they shall not emigrate into any other State?

I regret that I am now to die in the belief, that the useless sacrifice of themselves by the generation of 1776, to acquire self-government and happiness to their country, is to be thrown away by the unwise and unworthy passions of their sons, and that my only consolation is to be, that I live not to weep over it. If they would but dispassionately weigh the blessings they will throw away, against an abstract principle more likely to be effected by union than by scission, they would pause before they would perpetrate this act of suicide on themselves, and of treason against the hopes of the world. To yourself, as the faithful advocate of the Union, I tender the offering of my high esteem and respect.

Thomas Jefferson

To Albert Gallatin
Monticello, December 26, 1820

Dear Sir—'It is said to be an ill wind which blows favorably to no one.' My ill health has long suspended the too frequent troubles I have heretofore given you with my European correspondence. To this is added a stiffening wrist, the effect of age on an antient dislocation, which renders writing slow and painful, and disables me nearly from all correspondence, and may very possibly make this the last trouble I shall give you in that way.

Looking from our quarter of the world over the horizon of yours we imagine we see storms gathering which may again desolate the face of that country. So many revolutions going on, in different countries at the same time, such combinations of tyranny, and military preparations and movements to suppress them. England & France unsafe from internal conflict, Germany, on the first favorable occasion, ripe for insurrection, such a state of things, we suppose, must end in war, which needs a kindling spark in one spot only to spread over the whole. Your information can correct these views which are stated only to inform you of impressions here.

At home things are not well. The flood of paper money, as you well know, had produced an exaggeration of nominal prices and at the same time a facility of obtaining money, which not only encouraged speculations on fictitious capital, but seduced those of real capital, even in private life, to contract debts too freely. Had things continued in the same course, these might have been manageable. But the operations of the U.S. bank for the demolition of the state banks, obliged these suddenly to call in more than half of their paper, crushed all fictitious and doubtful capital, and reduced the prices of property and produce suddenly to 1/3 of what they had been. Wheat, for example, at the distance of two or three days from market, fell to and continues at from one third to half a dollar. Should it be stationary at this for a while, a very general revolution of property must take place. Something of the same character has taken place in our fiscal system. A little while back Congress seemed at a loss for objects whereupon to squander the supposed fathomless funds of our treasury. This short frenzy has been arrested by a deficit of 5 millions the last year, and of 7. millions this year. A loan was adopted for the former and is proposed for the latter, which threatens to saddle us with a perpetual debt. I hope a tax will be preferred, because it will awaken the attention of the people, and make reformation & economy the principles of the next election. The frequent recurrence of this chastening operation can alone restrain the propensity of governments to enlarge expence beyond income. The steady tenor of the courts of the US. to break down the constitutional barrier between the coordinate powers of the States, and of the Union, and formal opinion lately given by 5. lawyers of too much eminence to be neglected, give uneasiness. But nothing has ever presented so threatening an aspect as which is called the Missouri question. The Federalists compleatly put down, and despairing of ever rising again under the old division of whig and tory, devised a new one, of slave-holding, & non-slave-holding states, which, while it had a semblance of being Moral, was at the same time Geographical, and calculated to give them ascendancy by debauching their old opponents to a coalition with them. Moral the question certainly is not, because the removal of slaves from one state to another, no more than their removal from one country to another, would never make a slave of one human being who would not be so without it. Indeed if there were any morality in the question it is on the other side; because by spreading them over a larger surface, their happiness would be increased, & the burthen of their future liberation lightened by bringing a greater number of shoulders under it. However it served to throw dust into the eyes of the people, and to fanaticise them, while to the knowing ones it gave a geographical and preponderant line of the Patomac and Ohio, throwing 12. States to the North and East, & 10. to the South & West. With these therefore it is merely a question of power: but with this geographical minority it is a question of existence. For if Congress once goes out of the Constitution to arrogate a right of regulating the conditions of the inhabitants of the States, its majority may, and probably will next declare that the condition of men within the US. shall be that of freedom, in which case all the whites South of the Patomak and Ohio must evacuate their States; and most fortunate those who can do it first. And so far this crisis seems to be advancing. The Missouri constitution is recently rejected by the House of Representatives. What will be their next step is yet to be seen. If accepted on the condition that Missouri shall expunge from it the prohibition of free people of colour from emigration to their state, it will be expunged, and all will be quieted until the advance of some new state shall present the question again. If rejected unconditionally, Missouri assumes independent self-government, and Congress, after pouting awhile, must receive them on the footing of the original states. Should the Representative propose force, 1. the Senate will not concur. 2. were they to concur, there would be a secession of the members South of the line, & probably of the three North Western states, who, however inclined to the other side, would scarcely separate from those who would hold the Misisipi from it's mouth to it's source. What next? Conjecture itself is at a loss. But whatever it shall be you will hear from others and from the newspapers. And finally the whole will depend on Pensylvania. While she and Virginia hold together, the Atlantic states can never separate. Unfortunately in the present case she has become more fanaticised than any other state. However useful where you are, I wish you were with them. You might turn the scale there, which would turn it for the whole. Should this scission take place, one of it's most deplorable consequences would be its encouragement of the efforts of the European nations in the regeneration of their oppressive and Cannibal governments.

Amidst this prospect of evil, I am glad to see one good effect. It has brought the necessity of some plan of general emancipation & deportation more home to the minds of our people than it has ever been before. Insomuch, that our Governor has ventured to propose one to the legislature. This will probably not be acted on at this time. Nor would it be effectual; for while it proposes to devote to that object one third of the revenue of the State, it would not reach one tenth of the annual increase. My proposition would be that the holders should give up all born after a certain day, past, present, or to come, that these should be placed under the guardianship of the State, and sent at a proper age to S. Domingo. There they are willing to receive them, & the shortness of the passage brings the deportation within the possible means of taxation aided by charitable contributions. In this I think Europe, which has forced this evil on us, and the Eastern states who have been it's chief instruments of importation, would be bound to give largely. But the proceeds of the land office, if appropriated, would be quite sufficient. God bless you and preserve you multos años.

Thomas Jefferson

To Jared Sparks
Monticello, February 4, 1824

Dear Sir,—I duly received your favor of the 13th, and with it, the last number of the North American Review. This has anticipated the one I should receive in course, but have not yet received, under my subscription to the new series. The article on the African colonization of the people of color, to which you invite my attention I have read with great consideration. It is, indeed, a fine one, and will do much good. I learn from it more, too, than I had before known, of the degree of success and promise of that colony.

In the disposition of these unfortunate people, there are two rational objects to be distinctly kept in view. First. The establishment of a colony on the coast of Africa, which may introduce among the aborigines the arts of cultivated life, and the blessings of civilization and science. By doing this, we may make to them some retribution for the long course of injuries we have been committing on their population. And considering that these blessings will descend to the *"nati natorum, et qui nascentur ab illis,"* we shall in the long run have rendered them perhaps more good than evil. To fulfil this object, the colony of Sierra Leone promises well, and that of Mesurado adds to our prospect of success. Under this view, the colonization society is to be considered as a missionary society, having in view, however, objects more humane, more justifiable, and less aggressive on the peace of other nations, than the others of that appellation.

The subject object, and the most interesting to us, as coming home to our physical and moral characters, to our happiness and safety, is to provide an asylum to which we can, by degrees, send the whole of that population from among us, and establish them under our patronage and protection, as a separate, free and independent people, in some country and climate friendly to human life and happiness. That any place on the coast of Africa should answer the latter purpose, I have ever deemed entirely impossible. And without repeating the other arguments which have been urged by others, I will appeal to figures only, which admit no controversy. I shall speak in round numbers, not absolutely accurate, yet not so wide from truth as to vary the result materially. There are in the United States a million and a half of people of color in slavery. To send off the whole of these at once, nobody conceives to be practicable for us, or expedient for them. Let us take twenty-five years for its accomplishment, within which time they will be doubled. Their estimated value as property, in the first place, (for actual property has been lawfully vested in that form, and who can lawfully take it from the possessors?) at an average of two hundred dollars each, young and old, would amount to six hundred millions of dollars, which must be paid or lost by somebody. To this, add the cost of their transportation by land and sea to Mesurado, a year's provision of food and clothing, implements of husbandry and of their trades, which will amount to three hundred millions more, making thirty-six millions of dollars a year for twenty-five years, with the insurance of peace all that time, and it is impossible to look at the question a second time. I am aware that at the end of about sixteen years, a gradual detraction from this sum will commence, from the gradual diminution of breeders, and go on during the remaining nine years. Calculate this deduction, and it is still impossible to look at the enterprise a second time. I do not say this to induce an inference that the getting rid of them is forever impossible. For that is neither my opinion, nor my hope. But only that it cannot be done in this way. There is, I think, a way in which it can be done; that is, by emancipating the after-born, leaving them, on due compensation, with their mothers, until their services are worth their maintenance, and then putting them to industrious occupations, until a proper age for deportation. This was the result of my reflections on the subject five and forty years ago, and I have never been able to conceive any other practicable plan. It was sketched in the Notes on Virginia, under the fourteenth query. The estimated value of the new-born infant is so low, (say twelve dollars and fifty cents,) that it would probably be yielded by the owner gratis, and would thus reduce the six hundred millions of dollars, the first head of expense, to thirty-seven millions and a half; leaving only the expense of nourishment while with the mother, and of transportation. And from what fund are these expenses to be furnished? Why not from that of the lands which have been ceded by the very States now needing this relief? And ceded on no consideration, for the most part, but that of the general good of the whole. These cessions already constitute one fourth of the States of the Union. It may be said that these lands have been sold; are now the property of the citizens composing those States; and the money long ago received and expended. But an equivalent of lands in the territories since acquired, may be appropriated to that object, or so much, at least, as may be sufficient; and the object, although more important to the slave States, is highly so to the others also, if they were serious in their arguments on the Missouri question. The slave States, too, if more interested, would also contribute more by their gratuitous liberation, thus taking on themselves alone the first and heaviest item of expense.

In the plan sketched in the Notes on Virginia, no particular place of asylum was specified; because it was thought possible, that in the revolutionary state of America, then commenced, events might open to us some one within practicable distance. This has now happened. St. Domingo has become independent, and with a population of that color only; and if the public papers are to be credited, their Chief offers to pay their passage, to receive them as free citizens, and to provide them employment. This leaves, then, for the general confederacy, no expense but of nurture with the mother a few years, and would call, of course, for a very moderate appropriation of the vacant lands. Suppose the whole annual increase to be of sixty thousand effective births, fifty vessels, of four hundred tons burthen each, constantly employed in that short run, would carry off the increase of every year, and the old stock would die off in the ordinary course of nature, lessening from the commencement until its final disappearance. In this way no violation of private right is proposed. Voluntary surrenders would probably come in as fast as the means to be provided for their care would be competent to it. Looking at my own State only, and I presume not to speak for the others, I verily believe that this surrender of property would not amount to more, annually, than half our present direct taxes, to be continued fully about twenty or twenty-five years, and then gradually diminishing for as many more until their final extinction; and even this half tax would not be paid in cash, but by the delivery of an object which they have never yet known or counted as part of their property; and those not possessing the object will be called on for nothing. I do not go into all the details of the burthens and benefits of this operation. And who could estimate its blessed effects? I leave this to those who will live to see their accomplishment, and to enjoy a beatitude forbidden to my age. But I leave it with this admonition, to rise and be doing. A million and a half are within their control; but six millions, (which a majority of those now living will see them attain,) and one million of these fighting men, will say, "we will not go."

I am aware that this subject involves some constitutional scruples. But a liberal construction, justified by the object, may go far, and an amendment of the constitution, the whole length necessary. The separation of infants from their mothers, too, would produce some scruples of humanity. But this would be straining at a gnat, and swallowing a camel.

I am much pleased to see that you have taken up the subject of the duty on imported books. I hope a crusade will be kept up against it, until those in power shall become sensible of this stain on our legislation, and shall wipe it from their code, and from the remembrance of man, if possible.

I salute you with assurances of high respect and esteem.

                                                            Thomas Jefferson

THOMAS NELSON PAGE

The Old South: Essays Social and Political

In the selection of a theme for this occasion, I have, curious to relate, been somewhat embarrassed. Not that good subjects were not manifold, and material plentiful; but for me, on this occasion, when I am to address this audience, in this presence, there could be but one subject—the best.

I deem myself fortunate that I am permitted to address you on this spot; for this University, whose friend was George Washington and whose establisher was Robert E. Lee, impresses me as the spot on earth to which my discourse is most appropriate. Broad enough to realize the magnificent ideal of its first benefactor as a university where the youth of this whole country may meet and acquire the grand idea of this American Union, it is yet so distinctly free from the materialistic tendencies which of late are assailing kindred institutions and insiduously threatening even the existence of the Union itself, that it may be justly regarded as the citadel of that conservatism which, mated with immortal devotion to duty, may be termed the cardinal doctrine of the Southern civilization.

Something more than twenty years ago there fell upon the South a blow for which there is no parallel among the casualties which may happen to an individual, and which has rarely in history befallen nations. Under the euphemism of reconstruction an attempt was made after the war to destroy the South. She was dismembered, disfranchised, denationalized. The States which composed her were turned by her conquerors into military districts, and their governments were subverted to military tribunals. Virginia, that had given Washington, Jefferson, Henry, Nelson, the Lees, Madison, Marshall, and a host of others who had made the nation, became "District No. 1."

The South was believed to be no more. It was intended that she should be no more. But God in his providence had his great purpose for her and he called her forth. With the old spirit strong within her she renewed her youth like the eagles, fixed her gaze upon the sun, and once more spreading her strong pinions, lifted herself for another flight.

The outside world gazed astonished at her course, and said, this is not the Old

South, but a new civilization, a New South.

The phrase by imperative inference institutes invidious comparison with and implies censure of something else—of some other order—of a different civilization.

That order, that civilization, I propose to discuss briefly this evening; to, so far as may be in the narrow limits of an address, repel this censure; show that comparison is absurd, and that the New South is, in fact, simply the Old South with its energies directed into new lines.

The civilization which is known by this name was as unique as it was distinct. It combined elements of the three great civilizations which since the dawn of history have enlightened the world. It partook of the philosophic tone of the Grecian, of the dominant spirit of the Roman, and of the guardfulness of individual rights of the Saxon civilization. And over all brooded a softness and beauty, the joint product of Chivalry and Christianity.

This individuality began almost with the first permanent Anglo-Saxon settlement of this continent; for the existence of its distinguishing characteristics may be traced from the very beginning of the colonial period. The civilization flourished for two hundred and fifty years, and until its vitality, after four years of invasion and war, expired in the convulsive throes of reconstruction.

Its distinctiveness, like others of its characteristics, was referable to its origin, and to its subsequent environing conditions.

Its tendency was towards exclusiveness and conservatism. It tolerated no invasion of its rights. It admitted the jurisdiction of no other tribunal than itself. The result was not unnatural. The world, barred out, took its revenge, and the Old South stands to-day charged with sterility, with attempting to perpetuate human slavery, and with rebellion.

That there was shortcoming in certain directions may not be denied; but it was not what is charged.

If, when judged by the narrow standard of mere, common materialism, the Southern civilization fell short, yet there is another standard by which it measured the fullest stature: the sudden supremacy of the American people to-day is largely due to the Old South, and to its contemned civilization.

The difference between the Southern civilization and the Northern was the result of the difference between their origins and subsequent surroundings.

The Northern colonies of Great Britain in America were the asylums of religious zealots and revolutionists who at their first coming were bent less on the enlargement of their fortunes than on the freedom to exercise their religious convictions, however much the sudden transition from dependence and restriction to freedom and license may in a brief time have tempered their views of liberty and changed them into proscriptors of the most tyrannical type.

The Southern colonies, on the other hand, were from the first the product simply of a desire for adventure, for conquest and for wealth.

The Northern settlements were, it is true, founded under the law; but it was well understood that they contained an element which was not friendly to the government and that the latter was well satisfied to have the seas stretch between them. The Southern, on the other hand, came with the consent of the crown, the blessing of the

Church, and under the auspices and favor of men of high standing in the kingdom. They came with all the ceremonial of an elaborate civil government—with an executive, a council deputed by authorities at home, and formal and minute instructions and regulations.

The crown hoped to annex the unknown land lying between the El Dorado, which Spain had obtained amid the summer seas, and the unbounded claims of its hereditary enemy, France, to the North and West.

The Church, which viewed the independence of the Northern refugees as schism, if not heresy, gave to this enterprise its benison in the belief that "the adventurers for the plantations of Virginia were the most noble and worthy advancers of the standard of Christ among the Gentiles." The company organized and equipped successive expeditions in the hope of gain; and soldiers of fortune, and gentlemen in misfortune, threw in their lot in the certainty of adventure and the probability that they might better their condition.

Under such auspices the Southern colonies necessarily were rooted in the faith of the England from which they came—political, religious, and civil. Thus from the very beginning the spirit of the two sections was absolutely different, and their surrounding conditions were for a long time such as to keep them diverse.

The first governor of the colony of Virginia was a member of a gentle Huntingdonshire family, and he was succeeded in office by a long line of men, most of them of high degree. In the first ship-load of colonists there were "four carpenters, twelve laborers, and fifty-four gentlemen."

John Smith, the strongest soul that planted the British spirit upon this continent, and who was himself a soldier of fortune, cried out in the bitterness of his heart against such colonists; yet he came afterwards to note that these "gentlemen" cut down more trees in a day than the ordinary laborers.

With the controversy as to whether or not the inhabitants of the Southern colonies were generally the descendants of Cavaliers it is not necessary to deal. It makes no difference now to the race which established this Union whether its ancestors fought with the Norman conqueror on Seulac Hill or whether they were among the "villians" who followed the standards of Harold's earls. It may, however, be averred that the gentle blood and high connection which undoubtedly existed in a considerable degree exerted widely a strengthening and refining power, and were potent in their influence to elevate and sustain not only the families which claimed to be their immediate possessors, but through them the entire colonial body, social and politic.

I make a prouder claim than this: the inhabitants of these colonies were the strongest strains of many stocks—Saxon, Celt, and Teuton; Cavalier and Puritan.

The ship-loads of artisans and adventurers who came, caught in time the general spirit, and found in the new country possibilities never dreamed of in the old. Each man, whether gentle or simple, was compelled to assert himself in the land where personal force was of more worth than family position, however exalted; but having proved his personal title to individual respect, he was eager to approve likewise his claim to honorable lineage, which still was held at high value. The royal governors, with all the accompaniments of a vice-regal court, only so much modified as was necessary to suit the surroundings, kept before the people the similitude of royal state;

and generation after generation of large planters and thriving merchants, with broad grants acquired from the crown or by their own enterprise, as they rose, fell into the tendency of the age and perpetuated or augmented the spirit of the preceding generation.

With the Huguenot immigration came a new accession of the same spirit, intensified in some directions, if tempered in others.

As society grew more and more indulgent its demands became greater; the comforts of life became more readily obtainable in the colonies just at the time that civil and religious restrictions became more burdensome in the old country, and the stream of immigration began to flow more freely.

Slavery had become meantime a factor in the problem—potent at first for perhaps mitigated good, finally for immeasurable ill to all except the slaves themselves.

This class of labor was so perfectly suited to the low alluvial lands of the tide-water section that each generation found itself wealthier than that which had preceded it, and it was evident that the limits between the mountains and the coast would soon be too narrow for a race which had colonized under a charter that ran "up into the land to the farthest sea."

To this reason was added that thirst for adventure and that desire for glory which is a characteristic of the people, and in Virginia Spottswood and his Knights of the Golden Horseshoe set out to ride to the top of the Blue Ridge, which till then was the barricade beyond which no Saxon was known to have ventured, and from which it was supposed the Great Lakes might be visible. They found not "the unsalted seas," but one of the fairest valleys on earth stretched before them; and the Old Dominion suddenly expanded from a narrow province to a land from whose fecund womb commonwealths and peoples have sprung.

By a strange destiny, almost immediately succeeding this discovery, the vitality of the colony received an infusion of another element, which became in the sequel a strong part of that life which in its development made the "Southern civilization."

This element occupied the new valley and changed it from a hunting-ground to a garden. The first settler, it is said, came to it by an instinct as imperative as that which brought the dove back to the ark of safety. It was not the dove, however, which came when John Lewis settled in this valley; but an eagle, and in his eyry he reared a brood of young who have been ever ready to strike for the South. He had been forced to leave Ireland because he had slain his landlord, who was attempting to illegally evict him, and the curious epitaph on his tomb begins, "Here lies John Lewis, who slew the Irish Lord."

He was followed by the McDowells, Alexanders, Prestons, Grahams, Reids, McLaughlins, Moores, Wallaces, McCluers, Mathews, Woods, Campbells, Waddells, Greenlees, Bowyers, Andersons, Breckenridges, Paxtons, Houstons, Stuarts, Gambles, McCorkles, Wilsons, McNutts, and many others, whose descendants have held the highest offices in the land which their fortitude created, and who have ever thrown on the side of principle the courage, resolution, and loyalty with which they held out for liberty and Protestantism in the land from which they came.

It was a sturdy strain which had suddenly flung itself along the frontier, and its effect has been plainly discernible in the subsequent history of the Old South, running a somewhat sombre thread in the woof of its civilization, but giving it "a body" which perhaps it might otherwise not have possessed. A somewhat similar element, though springing from a different source, held the frontier in the other States. Its force was not towards the East, but towards the West; not towards the sea and the old country, but towards the mountains and the new; and to its energy was due the Western settlement, as to the other and the older class was due the Eastern.

As the latter had created and opened up the first tier of States along the sea-coast, so these new-comers now crossed the mountains, penetrated "the dark and bloody ground," and conquered the second tier, hewing out of primeval forests—and holding them alike against Indians, French and British—the States of Ohio, Kentucky, and Tennessee, and opening up for the first time the possibility of a great American continent.

They were not slave holders to a great extent; for they were frontiersmen, who mainly performed their own work; they were not generally connected with the old families of the Piedmont and Tidewater, for they had in large part entered the State by her northern boundary, or had been brought to take up land under "cabin rights," or had come across the mountain barrier and had cut their own way into the forests, and they traced their lineage to Caledonian stock; they were not bound to them by the ties of a common religion, for they repudiated the Anglican Church, with its hierarchy and "malignant doctrines," as that Church had repudiated them, and they worshipped God, according to their own consciences, "in a way agreeable to the principles of their education."

Thus, neither by interest, blood, nor religion, were they for a time connected with the original settlers of the Southern colonies; and yet they were distinctly and irrevocably an integral part of the South and of the Southern civilization,—as the waters of the Missouri and the upper Mississippi are said to flow side by side for a hundred miles, each distinguishable, yet both together mingling to make the majestic Father of Waters.

There was something potent in the Southern soil, which drew to it all who once rested on its bosom, without reference to race, or class, or station. Let men but once breathe the air of the South and generally they were thenceforth Southerners forever. So, having crossed the mountains, this race made Kentucky and Tennessee Southern States, and, against the allurements of their own interest and the appeals of the North, held them so, and infused a strong Southern element into the State of Ohio.

Steam had not been then invented, and the infinite forces of electricity were as yet unknown; yet, without these two great civilizers, the Southern spirit bore the ensign of the Anglo-Saxon across the mountains, seized the West, and created this American continent.

There is another work which the South may justly claim. As it pushed advance up first against the French confines and then beyond them, and made this country English, so it preserved the spirit of civil and religious liberty pure and undefiled, and established it as the guiding star of the American people forever.

I believe that the subordination of everything else to this principle is the key to the Southern character.

The first charter of Virginia, the leading Southern colony, "secured" to her people "the privileges, franchises, and immunities of native-born Englishmen forever," and they never forgot it nor permitted others to overlook it.

She had a Legislative Assembly as early as 1619, and the records show that it guarded with watchful vigilance against all encroachments those rights which, thanks to it, are to-day regarded as inalienable among all English-speaking races.

The Assembly was hardly established before it struck its first blow for constitutional liberty.

When the royal commissioners sent by James to investigate the "Seditious Parliament" came and demanded the records of the Assembly it refused to give them up; and when the clerk, under a bribe, surrendered them, the Assembly stood him in the pillory and cut off one of his ears. This did not save their charter; but in the sequel it turned out that the forfeiture of the charter was a great blessing.

As early as 1623-24 the General Assembly of the colony adopted resolutions defining and declaring the right of the colonists, and limiting the powers of the executive.

The governor was not "to lay any taxes or impositions upon the colony, their lands, or other way than by authority of the General Assembly, to be levied and employed as the General Assembly shall appoint." Moreover, the governor was not to withdraw the inhabitants from their labor for his service, and the Burgesses attending the General Assembly were to be privileged from arrest.

The colony of Maryland went farthest yet in the way of liberty, and, under the direction of Lord Baltimore, passed the famous Act of Toleration on the 2d of April, 1649, which first established the principle of freedom of conscience on the earth.

Thus early was the South striking for those great principles of liberty which are fundamental now mainly because of the spirit of our forefathers. It was not until some years after Virginia had declared herself that the issue was finally joined in England.

From this time the light of liberty flamed like a beacon. The colonies declared themselves devotedly loyal to the crown, but were more true to their own rights; and they frequently found themselves opposed to the government as vested in and manifested by the royal governor.

During the time of the Commonwealth the Southern colonies held by the crown, and became the asylum of many hard-pressed Cavaliers who found Cromwell's interest in them too urgent to permit them to remain at home. And Charles II himself was offered a crown by his loyal subjects in Virginia when he was a fugitive with a price set on his head.

So notorious was this fealty that the Great Protector was obliged to send a war fleet to Virginia to quell this spirit and to make terms of peace. The treaty is made as between independent powers.

The colonies were to obey the Commonwealth; but this submission was to be acknowledged a voluntary act, not forced nor constrained by a conquest upon the country. The people were "to enjoy such freedom and privileges as belong to free-born people in England." The continuance of their Representative Assembly was guaranteed. There was to be total indemnity. The colony was to have free trade, notwithstanding the Navigation Act. The General Assembly alone was to have the power to levy taxes; and there were other provisions securing those privileges and immunities which were claimed as the birthright of the race.

After Cromwell's death the General Assembly declared the supreme power to be "resident in" itself until such command or commission should come out of England as the General Assembly adjudged lawful. And when the king once more came into his own the General Assembly accepted his governor willingly, as did the colony of Maryland, but held firmly to the advantages it had secured during the interregnum.

The colony welcomed the followers of Cromwell in the hour of their adversity, and offered them as secure an asylum as it had done a few years before to the hard-pressed Cavaliers. Thus society came to be knit of the strongest elements of all parties and classes, who merged all factions into loyalty for their collective rights.

Then came the contest with Berkeley. Charles forgot the people who offered him a kingdom when he was an exile and a wanderer, and his representative neglected their rights.

England claimed the monopoly of the colonial trade, and imposed a heavy duty on their exports. Not content with this, the silly king gave away half of the settled portion of Virginia to two of his followers. The colony sent commissioners to protest, but before the trouble could be remedied Virginia, demanding self-government, flamed into revolution, with Nathaniel Bacon at its head.

We are told that the great revolution of 1688 established the liberties of the English people. The chief Southern colony of Great Britain had fought out its revolution twelve years before, and although the revolution failed disastrously for its participants, and it has come down in history as a rebellion, yet its ends were gained.

The troops of the fiery Bacon were beaten and scattered, those who were captured were hanged as insurrectionists, and the gallant leader himself died of fever contracted in the trenches, a fugitive and an outlaw, with a stigma so welded to his name that after two centuries he is known but as "Bacon the Rebel."

Judged by the narrow standard which makes success the sole test, Nathaniel Bacon was a rebel, and the uprising which he headed was a rebellion; but there are "rebellions" which are not rebellions, but great revolutions, and there are "rebels" who, however absolutely their immediate purposes may have failed, and however unjustly contemporary history may have recorded their actions, shall yet be known to posterity as patriots pure and lofty, whose motives and deeds shall evoke the admiration of all succeeding time.

Such was Nathaniel Bacon. They called him rebel and outlawed him; but he headed a revolution for the protection of the same rights, the same "privileges, franchises, and immunities," whose infringement caused another revolution just one hundred years later, the leader of whose armies was the rebel George Washington, the founder of this University.

The elder rebel failed of his purpose for the time, yet haply but for that stalwart blow struck at Jamestown for the rights of the colonists there had never been a Declaration of Independence, a Bunker Hill, a Yorktown, or the United States of America.

The spirit never receded. The opening up of lands, the increase of slaves, the extension of commerce, made the Southern colonies wealthier generation after generation, and their population filled the territory up to the mountains and then flowed over, as we have seen, into the unknown regions beyond; and generation after generation, as they grew stronger, they grew more self-contained, more independent, more assertive of their rights, more repellant of any invasion, more jealous of tyranny, more loving of liberty.

Against governors, councils, metropolitans, commissaries, and clergy, in the Burgesses and in the vestries, they fought the fight with steadfast courage and persistency.

The long contest between the vestries and the Church was only a different phase of this same spirit, and was in reality the same struggle between the colony and the government at home, transferred to a different theatre. The planters were churchmen; but they claimed the right to control the Church, and repudiated the right of the Church to control them. It was the sacred right of self-government for which they contended; and the first cry of "treason" was when the contest culminated in that celebrated Parsons case, in which the orator of the Revolution burst suddenly into fame.

"The gentleman has spoken treason," declared the counsel for the plaintiff; but it was the treason that was in all hearts, and was the first step of the young advocate in his ascent to a fame for oratory so transcending that the mind of a later and more prosaic generation fails to grasp its wondrousness, and there is nothing by which to measure it since the day when the Athenian orator thundered against the Macedonian tyrant.

The same principles which inspired the uprising of Bacon a century before, and had animated the continuous struggle since, swept the colonies into revolution now.

The Stamp Act of 1766 set the colonies into flame, and from this time to the outbreak of flagrant war, a decade later, the people stood with steadfast faces set against all encroachment; and when the time came for war the South sprang to arms. She did not enter upon the enterprise from ignorance of her danger, nor yet in recklessness.

The Southern planter sent his son to England to be educated, and many of the men who sat in the great conventions, or who subscribed the Declaration of Independence, had been themselves educated in England, and knew full well the magnitude of the hazard they were assuming in instituting with a handful of straggling colonies a revolution against a power which made Chatham the ruler of Europe, and which only a generation later tore the victorious eagles of Napoleon himself.

Thomas Nelson, Jr., the wealthiest man in the Colony of Virginia, had sat by Charles James Fox at Eton and knew England and her power. Others did also.

They know all this full well; and yet for the sake of those principles, of those rights and liberties, which they believed were theirs of right, and which they meant to transmit undiminished to their children, they gave up wealth and ease and security, blazoned on their standard the motto "Virginia for Constitutional Liberty," and launched undaunted on the sea of revolution.

There is an incident connected with the signing of the Declaration of Independence which illustrates at once the character of Southern planter and the point I am endeavoring to make.

You may have observed, in looking over the signers of the Declaration of Independence, that Charles Carroll of Maryland subscribed himself "Charles Carroll of Carrollton." Unless you know the story it would appear that simple arrogance prompted such a subscription. The facts, however, were these: It was a serious occasion, and a solemn act this group of men were performing, assembled to affix their names to this document, which was to be forever a barrier between them and Great Britain; it had not been so very long since the headsman's axe had fallen for a less overt treason than they were then publicly declaring, and if they failed they were likely to feel its weight or else to meet a yet more disgraceful death.

Benjamin Franklin had just replied to the remark, "We must all hang together," with his famous pleasantry, "Yes, or we shall all hang separately," when Carroll, perhaps the wealthiest man in Maryland, took the pen. As he signed his name, "Charles Carroll," and rose from his seat, some one said, "Carroll, you will get off easily; there are so many Charles Carrolls they will never know which one it is." Carroll walked back to the table, and, seizing the pen again, stooped and wrote under his name "of Carrollton."

They affixed their names to the Declaration, comprehending the peril they were braving, as well as they did the propositions which they were enunciating to the world, and they intended to shoulder all the responsibility of their act.

The South emerged from the Revolution mangled and torn, but free, and with the Anglo-Saxon spirit whetted by success and intensified. She emerged also with her character already established, and with those qualities permanently fixed which subsequently came to be known through their results as the Southern civilization.

Succeeding the Revolution came a period not very distinctly marked in the common idea of important steps, but full of hazard and equally replete with pregnant results—a period in which the loose and impotent Confederation became through the patriotism of the South this Union.

At last, the Constitution was somewhat of a compromise, and the powers not expressly delegated to Congress were reserved to each State in her sovereign capacity, and it was upon this basis simply that the Union was established.

It may throw light on the part that the South took in this to recall the fact that when the point was made that Virginia should relinquish her Northwestern territory, Virginia ceded to the country, without reservation, the territory stretching north to the Great Lakes and west to the Father of Waters. She granted it without consideration, and without grudging, as she had always given generously whenever she was called upon, and when she had stripped herself of her fairest domain, in retribution a third of the small part which she had retained was torn from her, without giving her even a voice to protest against it. There is no act of the Civil War, or of its offspring, the days of reconstruction, so arbitrary, so tyrannical, and so unjustifiable.

When the South emerged from the Revolutionary War, her character was definitely recognized as manifesting the qualities which combined to give her civilization the peculiar and strongly marked traits that have made it since distinctive among the English-speaking races. And in the succeeding years these traits became more and more prominent.

The guiding principle of the South had steadily been what may be termed public spirit; devotion to the rights and liberties of the citizen, the embodiment of which in a form of government was aptly termed the Commonwealth.

To this yielded even the aristocratic sentiment. The Southerner was attached to the British mode of inheritance, yet he did away with the law of primogeniture; he was devoted to the traditions of his Church, yet he declared for religious freedom, and not only disestablished the Church, but confiscated and made common the Church lands, and it is due to the South, to-day, that man is free to worship God according to his conscience wherever the true God is known and feared.

The South changed far less after its separation from Great Britain than did the North. Indeed, the change was during the entire *ante-bellum* period comparatively small when viewed beside the change in the other portion of the country.

It had been said that it was provincial. It certainly did not so consider itself, for it held a self-esteem and self-content as unquestioning and sublime as that which pervaded Rome; and wherever the provinces were, they were to the Southerner assuredly beyond the confines of the Southern States. Yet the naked fact is, that, assuming provincialism to be what it has been aptly defined to be, "localism, or being on one side and apart from the general movement of contemporary life," the South was provincial.

African slavery, which had proven ill-adapted to the needs and conditions of the North, and consequently had disappeared more because of this fact than because of the efforts of the Abolitionists, had proved perfectly suited to the needs of the South.

The negro flourished under the warm skies of the South, and the granaries and tobacco fields of Maryland and Virginia, the cotton fields of the Carolinas, Georgia, and Alabama, and the sugar plantations of the Mississippi States, bore ample testimony to his utility as a laborer. But the world was moving with quicker strides than the Southern planter knew, and slavery was banishing from his land all the elements of that life which was keeping stride with progress without. Thus, before the Southerner knew it, the temper of the time had changed, slavery was become a horror, and he himself was left behind and was in the opposition.

Changes came, but they did not affect the South—it remained as before or changed in less ratio; progress was made; the rest of the world fell into the universal movement; but the South advanced more slowly. It held by its old tenets when they were no longer tenable, by its ancient customs when, perhaps, they were no longer defensible. All interference from the outside was repelled as officious and inimical, and all intervention was instantly met with hostility and indignation. It believed itself the home of liberality when it was, in fact, necessarily intolerant;—of enlightenment, of progress, when it had been so far distanced that it knew not that the world had passed by.

The cause of this was African slavery, with which the South is taunted as if she alone had instituted it. For this she suffered; for this, at last, she was forced to fight and pour out her blood like water.

Slavery had forced the South into a position where she must fight or surrender her rights.

The fight on the part of the North was for the power to adapt the Constitution to its new doctrine, and yet to maintain the Union; on the part of the South, it was for the preservation of guaranteed constitutional rights.

Through the force of circumstances and under "an inexorable political necessity," the South found itself compelled to assume finally the defence of the system; but it was not responsible either for its origin or its continuance, and the very men who fought to prevent external interference with it had spent their lives endeavoring to solve the problem of its proper abolition.

The African slave trade, dating from about the year 1442 (although it did not flourish for a century or more), when it was begun by Anthony Gonzales, a Portuguese, was continued until the present century was well installed.

It was chartered and encouraged by Queen Elizabeth, and by her royal successors, against the protest of the Southern colonies, down to the time of the American Revolution. The first nation on the civilized globe to protest against it as monstrous was the Southern colony, Virginia. Twenty-three times her people protested to the crown in public acts of her Assembly.

One of the most scathing charges, brought by the writer of the Declaration of Independence against the crown, was that in which he arraigns the king of England for having "waged cruel war against human nature itself, violating its most sacred rights of life and liberty in the persons of a distant people who never offended him, captivating and carrying them into slavery in another hemisphere, or incurring a miserable death in their transportation thither.

"This piratical warfare, the opprobrium of infidel powers, is the warfare of the Christian king of Great Britain.

"Determined to keep open a market where men should be bought and sold, he has prostituted his negative for suppressing any legislative attempt to prohibit and restrain the execrable commerce," etc.

This clause was the product of Thomas Jefferson, a Southerner, and although it was stricken out in compliance with the wishes of two of the Southern colonies, yet substantially the same charge was made in the Constitution of Virginia, where in its preamble is set forth "the detestable and insupportable tyranny of the king of Great Britain, that he had prompted to rise in rebellion those very negroes whom by any inhuman use of his royal negative he had refused us permission to exclude by law."

If the South had at any previous time inclined to profit by the slave trade, it was only in common with the rest of Christendom—particularly with New England— when the most zealous and religious were participants in it; when the Duke of York, the future sovereign himself, was the head of the company chartered under the Great Seal of England, and when the queen-mother, the queen-consort, Prince Rubert, the Earl of Shaftsbury, and the leading men of the times were incorporators.

Even the godly John Newton was interested in the traffic.

In the South, however, long before Jefferson framed his famous arraignment of the king of Great Britain, protest on protest had been made against the iniquity, and all the ingenuity of those men who produced the Declaration of Independence and the Constitution of the United States had been exercised to bring it to an end.

The House of Burgesses often attempted to lay a duty of from £10 to £20 a head on the negro slaves, and against the veto of the crown they continued to levy duties, until the oppression by the crown culminated, and "The gentlemen of the House of Burgesses and the body of merchants assembled in the old capital of Virginia on the 2d June, 1770, resolved, among other things, that we will not import or bring into the colony, or cause to be imported or brought into the colony, either by sea or land, any slaves, or make sale of any upon commission, or purchase any slave or slaves that may be imported by others, after the 1st day of November next, unless the same have been twelve months on the continent."

On the 1st of April, 1772, the House of Burgesses addressed a hot petition to the crown, "imploring his Majesty's paternal assistance in averting a calamity of a most alarming nature." It proceeds: "The importation of slaves into the colonies from the coast of Africa hath long been considered as a trade of great inhumanity, and under its present encouragement we have too much reason to fear will endanger the very existence of your Majesty's American dominions. We are sensible that some of your Majesty's subjects of Great Britain may reap emoluments from this sort of traffic, but when we consider that it greatly retards the settlement of the colonies with more useful inhabitants, and may in time have the most destructive influence, we presume to hope that the interest of a few will be disregarded when placed in competition with the security and happiness of such number of your Majesty's dutiful and loyal servants. Deeply impressed with these sentiments, we most humbly beseech your Majesty to remove all those restraints on your Majesty's governors of the colony which inhibit their assenting to such laws as might check so very pernicious a commerce."

It was not until the following year that the Philadelphia petition to the Pennsylvania Assembly was gotten up, and it accords the credit to the Southern colony by asking similar action with that of "the province of Virginia, whose House of Burgesses have lately petitioned the king."

On the 5th of October, 1778, Virginia passed an act forbidding the further importation of slaves, *by land or water*, under a penalty of £1000 from the seller and £500 from the buyer, and freedom to the slave: thus giving to the world the first example of an attempt by legislative enactment to destroy the slave trade.

When the vote was taken in the Federal Congress on the resolution to postpone the prohibition of the trade to the year 1808, Virginia used all her influence to defeat the postponement, and it was carried by New Hampshire, Massachusetts, and Connecticut voting with Maryland, the Carolinas, and Georgia. John Adams, writing of a speech of James Otis in 1761, says: "Nor were the poor negroes forgotten. Not a Quaker in Philadelphia, nor *Mr. Jefferson of Virginia*, ever asserted the rights of negroes in stronger terms. Young as I was and ignorant as I was, I shuddered at the doctrine he taught."

The final prohibition of the slave trade by act of Congress was brought about through the influence of President Jefferson and by the active efforts of Virginians. And greatly to the labors of the representatives from Virginia was due the final extinction of the vile traffic through the act of Congress declaring it to be piracy, five years before Great Britain took similar action with regard to her subjects.

Such is the actual record of the much-vilified South relating to the African slave trade, taken from official records.

Now as to slavery itself. We have seen how it was brought upon the South without its fault, and was continued to be forced upon her against her protests. Let us for a moment investigate the facts connected with its continuance.

The gradual system of emancipation adopted at the North had undoubtedly led to many of the slaves being shipped off to the South and sold. When, therefore, after this "abolition," the movement, from being confined to the comparatively small band of liberators who were actuated by pure principle, extended to those who had been their persecutors, it aroused a suspicion at the South which blinded it to a just judgment of the case.

If the South maintained slavery unjustifiably, during its continuance, instead of its unnecessary horrors being, as is popularly believed, augmented by the natural brutality of the Southerner, the real facts are that the system was at the South perhaps fraught with less atrocity than it was whilst it continued at the North.

In the earliest period of the institution it was justified on the ground of the slaves being heathen, and a doubt was raised whether baptism would not operate to emancipate. At the South it was adjudicated that it did not so operate; but long prior to this act negroes were admitted to the Church. In the leading colony at the North baptism was at the time expressly prohibited. The necessary concomitants of slavery were wretched enough, and the continuance of the system proved the curse of the fair land where it flourished, but to the African himself it was a blessing; it gave his race the only civilization it has had since the dawn of history.

The statutory laws relating to slavery at the South are held up as proof of the brutality with which they were treated even under the law. But these laws were not more cruel than were the laws of England at the period when they were enacted; they were rarely put into practical execution; and, at least, Southerners never tolerated wholesale burning at the stake as a legal punishment, as was done in New York as late as 1741, when fourteen negroes were burnt at the stake on the flimsy testimony of a half-crazy servant girl; and as was done in Massachusetts as late as 1755, when a negro was burnt for murder.

In the cotton and sugar States, where the negroes were congregated in large numbers, and where a certain degree of absenteeism prevailed, there was naturally and necessarily more hardship.

African slavery was tolerated in Virginia and the Carolinas, but it received its first express legislative sanction from the Commonwealth of Massachusetts.

This Commonwealth, which has done so much to advance civilization, must bear the distinction of being the first American colony to proclaim slavery; to endorse the slave trade by legal sanction, and to build and equip the first slave-ship which sailed from an American port. Even the *Mayflower*, whose timbers one might have supposed would be regarded as sanctified by the holy fathers whose feet first touched Plymouth Rock, was, according to tradition, turned to a more secular use, and is reported by general tradition to have been subsequently employed as an African slaver. Whether this be true or not, the first American slaver was the Salem ship *The Desire*, which was built and equipped at Marblehead in 1636, and was the prototype of a long line of slavers, in which, through many decades, continuing long after slavery was abolished in New England, and after the Southern States were piling protest on protest and act on act to inhibit the slave trade, New England shippers, in violation of law, plied their hellish traffic between the African coast and the slave-holding countries.

Whatever may have been the horrors of African slavery in the South, it was in its worst form and under its most inhuman surroundings a mild and beneficent system, benevolent in its features and philanthropic in its characteristics, when compared with the slave trade itself. The horrors of "the middle passage," when human beings, often to the number of eight or nine hundred, were "piled almost in bulk on water-casks," or were packed between the hatches in a space where there was "not room for a man to sit unless inclining his head forward, their food half a pint of rice per day, with one pint of water," with "a blazing sun above, the boiling sea beneath, a withering air around," had never been equalled before, and in the providence of God will never be again.

It is not necessary to defend slavery, to defend the race which found it thrust upon it, contrary to what it deemed its rights, and which, after long and futile effort to rid itself of it, in accordance with what it held to be consistent at once with its rights and its security, refused to permit any outside interference. This was not primarily because it was wedded to slavery, but because it tolerated no invasion of its rights under any form of upon any pretext.

Vermont was the first State to lead off with emancipation in 1777. By the census of 1790 but seventeen slaves remained in the State. New Hampshire and Massachusetts failed to fix a statutory period; but the census of 1790 gives the former State 158 slaves, "and one or these was still reported in 1840."

Rhode Island and Connecticut about the same time adopted a gradual plan of emancipation. The latter State held 2759 slaves in 1790—too many to admit of immediate emancipation.

Pennsylvania had by the same census 3737 slaves, and, recognizing the peril of injecting such a number of freedmen into the body politic, provided in 1780, by an act said to have been drafted by Benjamin Franklin, that all slaves born after that time should be free when they attained the age of twenty-eight years. The census of 1840 showed sixty-four still held in slavery.

In New York, by an act passed in 1799, the future issue of slaves were set free—males at the age of twenty-eight and females at the age of twenty-five years. In 1790 there were 21,324 slaves in the State. In 1800, before the act of emancipation could take effect, this number had fallen off 981.

New Jersey in 1790 held 11,433 slaves. In 1804 her act of gradual emancipation was adopted. She had 674 slaves in 1840 and 236 in 1850.

This movement was largely owing in its inception to the efforts of the Quakers, who have devoted to peace those energies which others have given to war, and who have ever been moved by the spirit to take the initiative in all action which tends to the amelioration of the condition of the human race.

While this spirit of emancipation was passing over the North, the South, to whose action in asserting general freedom and universal civil equality was due the impulse, was stirring in the same direction. With her, however, the problem was far more difficult of solution, and although she addressed herself to it with energy and sincerity, she proved finally unequal to the task, and it was reserved, in the providence of an all-wise God, for the bitter scalpel of war to remove that which had served its purpose and was slowly sapping the life-blood of the South.

In the New England and Northern States, there were, by the census of 1790, less than 42,000 slaves: in Virginia alone, by the same census, there were 293,427 slaves—about seven times the number contained in all the others put together.

How were they to be freed with advantage to the slaves and security to the State?

John Randolph of Roanoke described the situation aptly when he said we were holding a wolf by the ears, and it was equally dangerous to let go and to hold on.

The problem was stupendous. But it was not despaired of. Many masters manumitted their slaves, the example being set by numbers of the same benevolent sect to which reference has been made. By the census of 1781 there were in Virginia 12,866 free negroes. Schemes of general emancipation of the slaves in Virginia had been proposed to the legislature by Jefferson in 1776; by William Craighead, and by Dr. William Thornton in 1785, whilst other schemes were proposed by St. George Tucker in 1796, by Thomas Jefferson Randolph in 1832, and by others from time to time. The vast body of slaves in the country, however, rendered it a matter so perilous as to prevent the schemes from ever being effectuated.

The most feasible plan appeared to be one that should lead to the colonization of the race in Africa; and the American Colonization Society was organized in Washington on the 1st of January, 1817, with Bushrod Washington president, and William H. Crawford, Henry Clay, John Taylor, and General John Mason, John Eager Howard, Samuel F. Smith, and John C. Herbert of Maryland, and Andrew Jackson of Tennessee among its vice-presidents.

Auxiliary societies were organized all over Virginia, John Marshall being the president of that established in Richmond, and ex-governors Pleasants and Tyler being vice-presidents. James Madison, James Monroe, and John Tyler all threw the weight of their great influence to carry out the purposes of the society and make it successful. Strange to say, every act on the part of the South leading towards liberation was viewed with suspicion by the Abolitionists of the North, and every step in that direction was opposed by them. Later a new and independent State organization was formed, called the Colonization Society of Virginia. Its president was John Marshall; its vice-presidents James Madison, James Monroe, James Pleasants, John Tyler, Hugh Nelson, and others; and its roll of membership embraced the most influential men in the State.

Everything was looking towards the gradual but final extinction of African slavery. It was prevented by the attitude of the Northern Abolitionists. Their furious onslaughts, accompanied by the illegal circulation of literature calculated to excite the negroes to revolt, and by the incursions of emissaries whose avowed object was the liberation of the slaves, but the effect of whose action was the instigation of the race to rise and fling off the yoke by rebellion and murder, chilled this feeling, the balance of political power came into question, and the temper of the South changed.

From this movement dates the unremittingly hostile attitude of the two sections towards each other. Before there had been antagonism; now there was open hostility. Before there had been conflicting rights, but they had been compromised and adjusted; from this time there was no compromise. The Northerner was a "miserable Yankee" and the Southerner was a "brutal slave-holder."

The two sections grew to be as absolutely separated as though a sea rolled between them. The antagonism increased steadily and became intensified. It extended far beyond the original cause, and finally became a factor in every problem, social and political, which existed in the whole land, affecting its results and often controlling its solution; forcing the two sections wider and wider apart, and eventually dividing them by an impassable gulf. Slavery, the prime cause, sank into insignificance in the multitudinous and potent differences which reared themselves between the two sections. It was employed simply as the battle-cry of the two opponents who stood arrayed against each other on a much broader question. The real fight was whether the conservative South should, with its doctrine of States rights, of original State sovereignty, rule the country according to a literal reading of the Constitution, or whether the North should govern according to a more liberal construction, adapted, as it claimed, by necessity to the new and more advanced conditions of the nation. Finally it culminated. After convulsions which would have long before destroyed a less stable nation, the explosion came.

The South, outraged at continual violation of the Constitution, declared that it would no longer act in unison with the North, and, after grave deliberation and hesitation, rendered proper by the magnitude of the step contemplated, the far Southern States exercised their sovereign right and dissolved their connection with the Union. Then came the President's call for troops, and finding themselves forced to secede or to make war upon their sister States, the border States withdrew.

The North made war upon the South, and, backed by the resources and the sentiment of the world, after four years compelled her to recede from her action.

Such in outline is the history of the South as it relates to slavery.

What has taken place since belongs partly to the New South and partly to the Old South.

The Old South made this people. One hundred years ago this nation, like Athene, sprang full panoplied from her brain.

It was the South that planned first the co-operation of the colonies, then their consolidation, and finally their establishment as free and independent States.

It was a Southerner, Henry, who first struck the note of independence. It was a Southerner, Nelson, who first moved, and the Convention of Virginia, a Southern colony, which first adopted the resolution "that the delegates appointed to represent this colony in General Congress be instructed to propose to that respectable body to declare the United Colonies free and independent States, absolved from all allegiance to or dependence on the crown or Parliament of Great Britain."

It was a Southern colony which first emblazoned on her standard the emblem of her principle, *Virginia for Constitutional Liberty.*

It was a Southerner who wrote the *Declaration of Independence.*

These acts created revolution, and a Southerner led the armies of the revolutionists to victory; and when victory had been won it was to Southern intellect and Southern patriotism which created the Federal Constitution, that was due the final consolidation of the separated and disjointed elements extended along the Atlantic coast into one grand union of republics known as the United States.

From this time the South was as prominent in the affairs of the nation as she had been when she stood, a rock of defence, between the encroachments of the crown and the liberties of the colonies.

Of the Presidents who had governed the United States up to the time of the Civil

War, the Old South had contributed Washington, Jefferson, Madison, Monroe, Jackson, Harrison, Tyler, Polk, and Taylor, and the cabinets had been filled with the representatives of the same civilization. In the only two wars which had ruffled the peaceful surface of the nation's course during this period the leading generals had been Southerners, and of the Chief Justices, John Marshall and Roger B. Taney had presided successively over the supreme bench of the United States from 1801, bringing to bear upon the decisions of that tribunal the force of their great minds, and the philosophic thought which is characteristic of the civilization of which they were such distinguished exponents.

Next to George Washington, John Marshall probably did more than any other one man to establish the principles on which this government is founded; for by his decisions he settled the mutual rights of the States on a firm and equitable basis, and determined forever those questions which might have strained the bonds of the young government.

To the South is due the fact that Louisiana is not now a French republic, and that the Mississippi rolls its whole length through the free land of the United States; to the South that the vast empire of Texas is not a hostile government; to the South is due the establishment of this Union in its integrity, and of the doctrines upon which it is maintained.

Thus in the council chamber and the camp, in the forum or on the field of battle, opposing invading armies or fighting for those principles which are ingrained in the very web and woof of our national life, the representatives of that contemned civilization always took the lead. In the great Civil War the two greatest men who stood for the Union, and to whom its preservation was due, were in large part the product of this civilization. Both Grant and Lincoln—the great general and the still greater President—spring from Southern loins.

Can the New South make a better showing than this, or trace its lineage to a stronger source?

But as grand as this exhibition of her genius, this is not her best history. The record of battles and of splendid deeds may serve to arrest admiration and to mark the course of events, as the constellations in the arch above us appear to the beholder nobler than the infinite multitude of the stars that fill the boundless reaches between; but the true record of the life of that civilization is deeper and worthier than this.

As the azure fields that stretch away through space are filled with stars which refuse their individual rays to the naked eye, yet are ever sending light through all the boundless realms of space, so under this brilliant exhibition of the South's public career lies the record of a life, of a civilization so pure, so noble, that the world to-day holds nothing equal to it.

After less than a generation it has become among friends and enemies the recognized field of romance.

Its chief attribute was conservatism. Others were courage, fidelity, purity, hospitality, magnanimity, honesty, and truth.

Whilst it proudly boasted itself democratic, it was distinctly and avowedly anti-radical—holding fast to those things which were proved, and standing with its conservatism a steadfast bulwark against all novelties and aggressions.

No dangerous isms flourished in that placid atmosphere; against that civilization innovations beat vainly as the waves lash themselves to spray against the steadfast shore.

Slavery itself, which proved the spring of woes unnumbered, and which clogged the wheels of progress and withdrew the South from sympathy with the outer world, christianized a race and was the automatic balance-wheel between labor and capital which prevented, on the one hand, the excessive accumulation of wealth, with its attendant perils, and on the other hand prevented the antithesis of the immense pauper class which work for less than the wage of the slave without any of his incidental compensations.

In the sea-island cotton and rice districts, and the sugar sections, it is true that there was a class which accumulated wealth and lived in a splendor unknown to the people of Virginia and of the interior portions of the cotton and sugar States; but the proportion of these to the entire population of the South who in the aggregate made up the Southern civilization is so small that it need scarcely be taken into account.

That the Southerner was courageous the whole world admits. His friends claim it; his foes know it. Probably never has such an army existed as that which followed Lee and Jackson from the time when, march-stained and battle-scarred, it flung itself across the swamps of the Chickahominy and stood a wall of fire between McClellan and the hard-pressed capital of the Confederate South.

It was not discipline, it was not *esprit de corps*; it was not traditional renown, it was not mere generalship which carried that army through. It was personal, individual courage and devotion to principle which welded it together and made it invincible, until it was almost extirpated.

The mills of battle and of grim starvation ground it into dust; yet even then there remained a valor which might well have inspired that famous legend which was one of the traditions of the conflict between the Church and its assailants in earlier ages, that after the destruction of their bodies their fierce and indomitable spirits continued the desperate struggle in the realms of air.

The tendency to hospitality was not local nor narrow; it was the characteristic of the entire people, and its concomitant was a generosity so general and so common in its application that it created the quality of magnanimity as a race characteristic.

It was these qualities to which the South was indebted for her controlling influence in the government of the country, throughout that long period which terminated only when the North abrogated the solemn compact which bound the two sections together.

No section of this country more absolutely, loyally, and heartily accepts the fact that slavery and secession can never again become practical questions in this land, than does that which a generation ago flung all its weight into the opposite scale. But to pretend that we did not have the legal, constitutional right to secede from the Union is to stultify ourselves in falsification of history.

If any portion of this nation doubt the South's devotion to the Union, let it attempt to impair the Union. If the South is ever to be once more the leader of this nation, she must cherish the traditional glory of her former station, and prove to the world that her revolution was not a rebellion, but was fought for a principle upon which she was established as her foundation-stone—the sacred right of self-government.

Government was the passion of the Southerner. Trained from his earliest youth by the care and mastery of slaves, and the charge of affairs which demanded the qualities of mastership, the control of men became habitual with him, and domination became an instinct. Consequently, the only fields which he regarded as desirable were those which afforded him the opportunity for its exercise.

Thus every young Southerner of good social connection who was too poor to live without work, or too ambitious to be contented with his plantation, devoted himself to the learned professions—the law being the most desirable as offering the best opportunity for forensic display, and being the surest stepping-stone to political preferment.

Being emotional and impulsive, the Southerner was as susceptible to the influences of rhetoric as was the Athenian, and public speaking was cultivated as always a necessary qualification for public position.

The South on this account became celebrated for its eloquence which, if somewhat fervid when judged by the severe standard of later criticism, was, when measured by its immediate effects, extraordinarily successful. It contributed to preserve through the decades preceding the war the supremacy of the slave-holding South, even against the rapidly growing aggressiveness of the North, with the sentiment of the modern world at its back.

It is not necessary to make reference to those orators who in the public halls of the nation, and in their native States, whenever questions of moment were agitated, evoked thunders of applause alike from rapturous friends and dazzled enemies. Their fame is now a part of the history of the country,

But in every circuit throughout the length and breadth of the South are handed down, even now, traditions of speakers who, by the impassioned eloquence of their appeals, carried juries against both law and evidence, or on the hustings, in political combat, swept away immense majorities by the irresistible impetuosity of their oratory.

That the Old South was honest, no sensible man who reads the history of that time can doubt, and no honest man will deny. Its whole course throughout its existence, whatever other criticism it may be subjected to, was one of honesty and of honor. Even under the perils of public life, which try men's souls, the personal integrity which was a fruit of the civilization in which it flourished was never doubted.

In confirmation of this proposition, appeal can be made with confidence to the history of the public men of the South. They were generally poor men, frequently reckless men, not infrequently insolvent men; but their bitterest enemies never aspersed their honesty.

There was not one of them who could not say, with Laurens of South Carolina, "I am a poor man—God knows I am a poor man; but your king is not rich enough to buy me!"

In this they were the representatives of their people. The faintest suspicion of delinquency in this respect would have blasted the chances of any man at the South, however powerful or however able he might have been, and have consigned him to everlasting infamy. Whatever assaults may be made on that civilization, its final defence is this: The men were honorable and the women pure. So highly were these qualities esteemed, that the aspersion of either was deemed sufficient cause to take life.

If it has appeared to modern civilization that life has not been held sufficiently sacred at the South, this may be urged in her defence: that a comparative statement, based on the statistics, does not show that homicide is, or has ever been more general at the South than at the North, when all classes are embraced in the statement; and if it has been tolerated among the upper classes under a form which has now happily passed away, it was in obedience to a sentiment which although grossly abused, had this much justification—that it placed honor above even life.

The principal element of weakness in the civilization of the Old South was that it was not productive in material wealth. The natural agricultural resources of the country were so great and so suited to the genius of the people that there were no manufactures to speak of.

The tendency of the civilization was the reduction of everything to principles, and not to disturb them by experiment. In this way there was an enormous waste. The physical resources of the country and the intellectual resources of its people were equally subject to this fault.

Whilst oratory flourished to a greater extent than under any other civilization which has existed since the invention of the printing-press, there was no Southern literature. Rather, there were no publishers and no public. There were critics who might have shone on the *Edinburgh Review*, and writers who might have made an Augustan literature; but the atmosphere was against them.

A Virginian farmer sat down and wrote the great Bill of Rights, the finest State paper ever penned on this continent; a Virginian was called on to draft a paper in the absence of another who was to have drawn it, and he wrote the Declaration of Independence. Another, a naval officer, laid down the laws of the winds and tides, and charted the pathless deep into highways, so that men come and go as securely as on dry land. There was genius enough, but the spirit of the time was against it. In the main the authors wrote for their diversion, and the effort was not repeated. The environments were not conducive to literary production, and it was not called into being. The harpers were present at the feast, but no one called for the song.

It was to this that the South owed her final defeat. It was for lack of a literature that she was left behind in the great race for outside support, and that in the supreme moment of her existence she found herself arraigned at the bar of the world without an advocate and without a defence.

Only study the course of the contest against the South and you cannot fail to see how she was conquered by the pen rather than by the sword; and how unavailing against the resources of the world, which the North commanded through the sympathy it had enlisted, was the valiance of that heroic army, which, if courage could have availed, had withstood the universe.

That Southern army was worn away as a blade is worn by use and yet retains its temper while but a fragment exists.

When the supreme moment came, the South had the world against her; the North had brought to its aid the sympathy of Christendom, and its force was as the gravitation of the earth—imperceptible, yet irresistible.

From their standpoint they were right, as we were right from ours. Slavery was a great barrier which kept out the light, and the North wrote of us in the main only what it believed.

If it was ignorant, it is our fault that it was not enlightened. We denied and fought, but we did not argue. Be this, however, our justification, that slavery did not admit of argument. Argument meant destruction.

The future historian of the Old South and of its civilization is yet to arise.

If in this audience to-night there by any young son of the South in whose veins there beats the blood of a soldier who perilled his life for that civilization which has been so inadequately outlined, and who, as he has heard from his mother's lips the story of his father's glorious sacrifice, has felt his pulses throb and his heart burn with noble aspiration, let him know that though he may never, like his father, be called upon to defend his principles with his life, yet he has before him a work not less noble, a career not less glorious: the true recording of that story, of that civilization whose history has never yet been written—the history of the Old South.

What nobler task can he set himself than this—to preserve from oblivion, or worse, from misrepresentation, a civilization which produced as its natural fruit Washington and Lee!

It is said that in all history there is no finer flight of human eloquence than that in which the Athenian orator aroused his countrymen by his appeal to the spirits of their sires who fell at Marathon. Shall not some one preserve the history of our fathers who fell in what they deemed a cause as sacred? Can any good come forth of a generation that believe that their fathers were traitors? I thank God that the sword of the South will nevermore be drawn except in defence of this Union; but I thank God equally that it is now without a stain. The time will come when the North as well as the South shall know that this Union is more secure because of the one heritage that our fathers have left us—the heritage of an untarnished sword.

If he shall feel the impulse stirring in his bosom to consecrate to this work the powers which have been nurtured at the nourishing breasts of this bountiful mother, there can be no fitter place for his sacrament than these hallowed walls—no better time than the present.

Within these sacred precincts three monuments meet his gaze. Each of them, by coincidence, is dedicated to the memory of one who had learnt by heart the lesson which that history teaches when rightly read,—the devotion of life to duty.

One of these was the leader of armies, the noblest character the South has produced, the great Lee; who, putting aside proffers of wealth and place and honor, gave himself to teaching the South the sublime beauty of devotion to duty—that lesson whose most admirable example was his own life. One was the surgeon, James M. Ambler, who refused to accept his life, and died amid the snows of the Lena Delta, pistol in hand, guarding the bodies of his dead comrades. Who does not remember the story of the young surgeon, kneeling amid the perpetual snows, pointing his dying comrades to Christ the crucified! The third, William E. Lynch, was a student, who while yet a lad put into action the same divine lesson, and to save a fellow-student plunged dauntless into the icy river and died, while yet a boy, a hero's death. All three speak to us this evening with sublime eloquence the heroic story of the Old South!

Here within these sacred walls, where the foremost soldier, the knightliest gentlemen, the noblest man of his race, taught his sublime lesson, and his pupils learned to put it into such divine practice, the heart cannot but feel that the true story of their life must be told, the song must be sung, through the ages.

Not far off repose the ashes of another great soldier, Stonewall Jackson, the representative of the element that settled this valley, as Lee was representative of that which settled the tide-water. He flashed across the sky, a sudden meteor, and expired with a fame for brilliancy second only to Napoleon.

Near by him, and side by side with his own only son, Stonewall Jackson's aide-de-damp, Colonel Alexander S. Pendleton, slain in battle at the age of twenty-three, lies one to whom I owe a personal debt which I desire to acknowledge publicly tonight: General William Nelson Pendleton, a soldier who doffed the cassock for the uniform, and who lived a warrior-priest, leading his men in peace as he had done in war, and like his old commander, the highest type of the Christian soldier.

Standing here beside the sacred ashes of the noblest exponent of that civilization, which I have attempted to outline, delivering my message from this University, his grandest monument, I hail the future historian of the Old South.

(1892)

WALTER HINES PAGE

The Last Hold
of the Southern Bully

Competent observers in almost every part of the South agree that crimes against white women by Negroes are becoming very much more frequent, that more frequent becomes the lynching of Negroes, and that this method of dealing with crime is tolerated and hence approved in an increasing number of communities. The race-clash, therefore, takes a somewhat new turn, and in this succession of crimes there is a singular conjunction of dangerous forces.

Most of the men who were masters and most who were slaves are dead. The men of each race that are now in active life have not the attitude to each other that their fathers had. There could be no more conclusive or startling evidence of such a change than the frequency of a social crime that was unknown and impossible in slavery, and that was very infrequent as long as the manners and traditions of slavery survived. This somewhat new race-clash, which is different from the old political race-clash, brings for the first time a grave social danger. Whatever race-conflicts might come, it had generally been taken for granted that we should be spared this one. For this kind of a crime may light all the inflammable material in the race-relation. To begin with, it is a social crime; and, if so ludicrously slight a social jar as whites and blacks riding in the same railway coach has in the past stirred anger, what shall be expected of this? Nothing else could so arouse all the white man's race-feeling, no other crime or combination of other crimes—not even murder and arson and massacre all together.

Moreover all round about such a point of race-contact, the social structure is exceedingly sensitive. In addition to the defensive attitude that any other civilized society has toward its women there is in the South the tradition of a "knightly" attitude toward them. Whatever part this old-fashioned gallantry may play or may ever have played between individual men and women, the tradition of it is indomitable. The veriest bully feels a sort of sanctity gather about him when he goes forth to defend or to avenge a women: the race tiger and the romantic tiger both leap to life.

Now as to the other crime thus provoked—the crime of lynching: since this in turn must be withstood and dealt with by local public sentiment and since it will thrive directly in proportion to the weakness of public sentiment in upholding law, let us see in what condition Southern public sentiment finds itself to deal with an outbreak of lawlessness. Here, too, the presence of both races must be remembered.

The wholesale bestowal of the ballot on the freedman while in all essential respects but one he was yet a slave, prevented the rise of a balanced public sentiment. What was by law a crime came to be regarded as political duty—the duty of self-defence. Public sentiment in the South was thrown still more out of plumb. There is proof of this in the fact that the old instinct of political leadership spent itself in the task of preventing Negro electoral equality, and it had little energy left for other tasks. Commonplace men whose equipment was an equipment of traditions became the natural public leaders, when no new life and no new thought had play, and rural Southern communities, even just now, have shown that they are the easy victims of such forces as the Farmers' Alliance and "Gideon's Band." It is sad to say that of the many honorable and useful Southern public men, there is not a single one who stands out to-day as a great leader of opinion or as a strong force in our national life. This could never have been said till now since the foundation of the government. Thus ill prepared, this public sentiment must now in the first place face this new social danger, and doubly ill-prepared it is called on to deal calmly and firmly with the spirit of revenge that this era of a new crime arouses. And during this generation of political race-conflict, as the old type of gentleman of the former time has receded into tradition, the qualities that were characteristic of him, growing rank on the lower slopes of life, have produced the bully, the race-bully, the romantic bully; and it is the brute of one race and the bully of the other that unite their forces against civilization, just where public sentiment is weakest.

On the side of the lower race, too, slavery, to speak mildly, did not promote good morals; and it was inevitable, that chastity should at the time of freedom be an almost unknown virtue among the Negroes. Since then, especially in recent years, according to the evidence of the leaders of the race, there has been as rapid an improvement as any wise moralist could expect—for he was not wise who expected a sudden change in morals, since morals are habits; and the lifting up of the women has gone on, to their infinite credit, against the double disadvantage of having the dissolute of both races of men to withstand. Now in proportion as chastity has become esteemed among Negroes, they feel the more keenly their former humiliation in morals, and this is a keener feeling, I imagine, than the humiliation of mere servitude. It is not unnatural for the Negro, sensitive to this inherited degradation, to ask, Why deal with the Negro so severely for a social crime against a white woman when similar if by law lesser crimes were, and perhaps are to a degree still, regarded as venial offences when committed by white men against Negro women? But I have said enough to hint at the many-sided dangers in the social relation of the races in the future, now that a new generation has come into activity—a generation one remove from the influence of slavery on the race-relation. Such is the social background of the crime itself that has given a new impulse to the lawless dealing with crime.

How the brute and the bully unite against civilization may be made clearer by a description of a particular town where a Negro was lynched. It is a pleasant county-town of comfortable homes and intelligent and kindly people, and the moral tone of individual conduct—the moral tone of the individuals as distinguished from the moral tone of public sentiment—is exceptionally firm. A school of more than local fame has so long been established that a stock remark to strangers is, "Our town, you know, is quite an educational centre." The older generation in particular have a social grace about them that you recall long afterwards with pleasure, and the people practise their old habit of hospitality. They go about their business, clothed with leisure as with a garment, like men on a perpetual holiday; but life is as easy as it is simple and cheerful, and there are neither very poor people nor very rich people there. They all belong to the churches, with hardly an exception but the keepers of the groggeries, and the most frequent little jars in the social life of the town are caused by the friction of the church-cliques or an argument about theology. Nearly half the population is of blacks, who live chiefly at one end of the town. Most of the younger Negroes are educated in a rudimentary way, many of them are prosperous, many more measured by their standard are fairly well-to-do, and the rest, half perhaps, lead the more or less wandering and irresponsible life of day-laborers. But they, too, are good-natured and generally law-abiding, in no way different from the usual black population of any Southern town where the whites predominate; and there has never been any serious race-friction. Cases of theft chiefly engage the court, now and then an assault, very rarely a murder.

But one day near the outskirts of the town a young Negro committed a crime against a white woman. The news quickly spread. Parties of men went forth and caught the criminal, for there is hardly a doubt but that the captive was the criminal although there was no formal proof of it. In spite of a threat to lynch him, he was brought to the jail by a circuitous route and locked up, and a double guard was placed there. But just before midnight a group of perhaps fifty men, at least the leaders of whom were armed, came to the jail and demanded the prisoner. The guards, willing to do their duty but weak, did not long withstand the determined threats of the mob. The negro was taken out and hanged and shot.

The next morning the people went about their business as usual. But a sort of terror spread among the Negroes, and a desperate suggestion was of course made to the criminally inclined. There was a feeling that a white man would have had a trial, and that the criminal was lynched not only because of the crime but because he was a Negro. The whites said little about the lynching. There was an evident desire not to discuss it. Some said, "No more than he deserved," but more wished that the law had been allowed to take its course. They talked much, however, about the crime, and with a sort of dazed indignation. It stirred the whole community to its depths. The report that was published in the papers was chiefly an expression of this indignation at the Negro, but it was an odd mixture of sensationalism and moral reflections on chastity. In a little while the whole matter seemed to be forgotten.

There is no doubt but the public sentiment in the town passively approved the lynching. No effort was made to discover the lynchers. Overcome by indignation, public sentiment was subdued. The mob that killed the criminal killed civic spirit as well. Yet if a week before the lynching or a week afterward, every man there had been asked his opinion singly, nine-tenths of them would have expressed disapproval of the lynching. But it is certain that another crime of the same kind would be avenged in the same way. As regards this crime, therefore, the law there has been permanently suspended. The strongest proof of the demoralization is that the public is unmindful of the consequences to itself of accepting lynching as a pardonable if not a proper substitute for law. It has not occurred to the community that though the rape was the beginning, the lynching was by no means the end of the matter. It has yielded to the insidious mastery of the bully, who seemed to the weak public spirit of the place, to have its own righteous indignation as his ally. Of course, a similar crime may be committed in any community. In other communities, too, a lynching has at some time occurred. But the ominous fact about this crime and this lynching (and about all like it) is the acquiescence of the public spirit of the town in lynching as a method of dealing with the crime. It was by this acquiescence that the community let its civic sentiment die.

To any man who has ever considered the tedious development of civil society— and to these men of this town when any other crime than this crime or murder committed by a Negro is considered—it is plain that mob-law denies its first principle, which is nothing else than this: that men instead of avenging their own wrongs consent to have justice dealt out by law. Thus only is it that justice has come to take in civilized life the place that revenge held in savage life. The fundamental mistake they make is in supposing that lynching for a particular crime will deter from that crime. This belies all history, for all revengeful dealing with crime has increased crime. Every lynching adds a desperate dash to the temper of the whole community, especially to the criminal temper. The preventive of crime—the only preventive that men have found—is the undelayed and certain and solemn punishment by law, sustained by a confident and unyielding body of public opinion.

The breaking-down place in their public sentiment is the place so accurately pointed out by Judge Bleckley—that acquiescence in mob-rule brings its terrible demoralization without reference to the character of the crime that provoked it. There is no escape from this conclusion. The building-up of institutions that fortify us against the vengeance-taking temper of the savage, which is yet in us at no great depth below civilization, is the *summum bonum* of human achievement; and that the maintenance of these institutions is our only safeguard against a return to vengeance is perhaps the single great human judgment that no conceivable experience of our race can ever make subject to revision.

The gravest significance of this whole matter, therefore, lies not in the first violation of law, nor in the crime of lynching, but in the danger that Southern public sentiment itself under the stress of this new and horrible phase of the race-problem will lose the true perspective of civilization. If this happens, the white will not lift the Negro; both will go down to the vengeance-taking level. This raises the old question whether after all if a social clash comes, Southern institutions will prove equal in the black districts to the task of maintaining themselves. Jefferson wrote in his Autobiography: "Nothing is more certainly written in the book of fate than that these people [the Negro slaves] are to be free; nor is it less certain that the two races, equally free, cannot live in the same government." Then after pleading for emancipation and deportation he declared that if the evil of slavery or of the Negroes' presence "is left to force itself on, human nature must shudder at the prospect held up." In fact civilization has already nearly gone out in certain low-lands where the Negro is dominant in morals and in numbers, and in every way except in politics. Of these regions we hear little; but whenever for any reason we decide to reclaim them we shall have a task of a new kind. Fortunately these places where the Negro lives almost apart from white civilization and almost beyond its influence are not yet extensive. But the fate that has befallen them must serve as a reminder of two cardinal principles that the experience of the two races in their unnatural living together has established; for these two principles have been established if no more: First, that the white man's surrounding and educating civilization is necessary to the elevation of the blacks or even to the maintenance of the level they have reached: the white man must save himself from Negro dominance, or both will sink. The next principle is that the yielding of public sentiment to the white bully will so dwarf and misdirect public sentiment that civilization itself will suffer an eclipse. Then the long shadow which has before given so many hints of it may at last unroll from its folds—barbarism. Consider the present condition of South Carolina where the bully has distorted and weakened public sentiment till it has fallen so low as to rejoice in its subjection. It has lost the true perspective of civilization and is of no help whatever to the moral force of the nation. It has, indeed, reached that grotesque level where the bully plays the part of a moral reformer.

Indeed it is as a sort of moral reformer, a dispenser of justic,e that the bully begins his career. To go back to the main matter in hand, let us see how insidiously under his influence vengeance comes to take the guise of justice and to break down the saner convictions even of strong and good men. The tone of some Southern newspapers bears witness to this in the comment that a lynching is a grave offence but that certain crimes require it. This gives up the case of civilization against the bully, for its throws away the only defence that civilization has against him—a confident and unconquerable reliance on law. It is only the worse that the men who make such comment are good men, mean to be good men; for it is only when good men yield that public sentiment decays.

Even a man of as great good sense as Major Charles H. Smith, of Georgia, a man of the most sterling personal qualities, sees in a lynching chiefly the deserved punishment of a brute. Deserved? Yes. But this does not touch the fringes of the question. Are men's deserts to be dealt out to them by mobs? Then the more righteous the mob, the fewer will be spared; and a really righteous mob, if it were not to encounter a stronger mob of a different mind, might go forth and clear the earth for the coming of the just. But it would meet another mob, and there would be as many mobs as men had impulses. There is nothing new in this: our ancestors spent many centuries thus; and thus to-day some of the African kinsmen of our colored people are engaged. History has usually called this barbarism.

Bishop Haygood, too, whose untiring labor to solve this same dark problem entitles him to the sincerest admiration, and I can speak of him only with the greatest respect—Bishop Haygood, who declares over and over again that mob-rule is anarchy, and does not mean to apologize for it, explains the burning of a brute who violated and murdered a child by saying that the mob suffered from "emotional insanity." Pray, what ails any mob? The question lies far back of this: for the community accepted and acquiesced in the mob's work. This the Bishop does not point out. He does not seem to see that herein lies the greatest danger of all—which is not the "emotional insanity" of the mob but the permanence of the insanity and imbecility of the public sentiment that accepts the mob instead of law.

And the bully distorts the incipient public sentiment even of the Negro himself. A correspondent, a Negro who has spent many years in teaching his race and is a man held in esteem where he lives, puts this question: "Why is it that a white man never was and never will be lynched for a similar crime against a Negro woman?" This goes to the heart of the lurking danger that lies in any race-conflict involving a social question. It may be meant as a cry for justice, but it will be heard as a cry for revenge. Because a Negro is lynched, a white man should not be lynched even for the same crime: each alike should be punished by law. But the Negro justly cries for justice in dealing with social crimes. Let it come, striking through all traditions of slavery, through race-hatreds, through the degrading attitude of men to women of their own race or of other races; let it come lifting men and levelling all artificial social standards to its equal dealing! He has not profited by democracy who flinches or hesitates. Let it come and work as inexorably as a law of nature! But men who know what social growths are, know that the standard of justice anywhere—especially touching any social institution—is a thing that has been slowly evolved and can be but slowly changed. The standard of justice that one race or one grade of society anywhere applies to another race or another social grade is not what the other race or other social grade would have; but the existing standard, high or low, can be changed in only two ways—by revenge (which will change it by making it lower), and by a firm tolerance and by time. The memory of slavery must become dimmer than it has become through one generation, and men must become milder and women stronger, before justice can anywhere come in our dealing with a social crime that cuts across a race-line or even across a social line. But its coming in Southern life will not be hastened by the Negro's reminding the white man of his own crimes. This will rip wide open all the healing seams that Time has sewed to cover up the social skeleton of slavery. The brute instinct will thrive on such a reminder, and the race cleavage will widen.

It is proper to remember and I most solemnly insist that it be not forgotten, that nowhere else has public sentiment such a strain on it, nowhere else has civilization such a burden, as in the South. No student of institutions can measure the weight of this burden, from the time that slavery began till now—a weight the heavier because both slavery and reconstruction misdirected civilization—no man can measure it who has not lived under it and studied it while it crushed him. It is the colossal and continuous misfortune of modern times, the furthest-reaching blunder, attended with a longer train of evils than any other, than any war or pestilence—the coming of the African to this continent at all; for which he alone of all the parties concerned is guiltless, and by which he only, hard as his lot is, has profited. Herein lies the trouble. If he had come to our shores as a conqueror we should have driven him back. With this kind of problem the dominant races of the world have long known how to deal. But we dragged him from the jungles and brought him against his wish. He is a conqueror none the less. What matter, for instance, who owns the land of certain low-lying parts of the South, or gathers tribute, or holds the little posts of honor there, so long as only Negroes live there, and set the slow pace of life, the low standard of living, the measure of receding morals? There they are the economic conquerors, and the world profits nothing by their conquest. With this kind of problem it is yet to be seen if we know how to deal. Even in slavery the Negro was an economic burden[1]— and a social burden of course. In freedom he is a social and a political and, to a degree, an economic burden still, and a burden he will be on thought and character, as far into the future as men can yet see—except them who are always seeing the dawn of the millennium.

And the Negro's own case is nothing less than pathetic. Consider him at his best. I cite the case of a manly and accomplished gentleman of the race. His life has no background. What we mean by ancestry is lacking to him; and not only is it lacking but its lack is proclaimed by his color and he is always reminded of it. Be he who he may and do he what he may, when the final personal test comes, he finds himself a man set apart, a marked man. There is a difference between the discrimination against him in one part of the country and in another part, but it is a difference in degree only. He is not anywhere in a fellowship of complete equipoise with men of the other race. Nor does this end it. The boundless sweep of opportunity which is the inheritance of every white citizen of the Republic falls to him curtailed, hemmed in, a mere pathway to a few permissible endeavors. A sublime reliance on the ultimate coming of justice may give him the philosophic temper. But his life will bring chiefly opportunities to cultivate it. And for his children what better? To those that solve great social problems with professional ease, I commend this remark that Mr. Lowell is said to have made: "I am glad that I was not born a Jew; but if I had been born a Jew, I should be prouder of that fact than of any other." You can find men who are glad that they were not born Negroes, but can you find a man who, if he had been born a Negro, would be prouder of that fact than of any other? When you have found many men of this mind, then this race-problem will, owing to some change in human nature, have become less tough; but till then, patience and tolerance.

1. See Mr. Frederick Law Olmsted's books, which seem strangely to have been forgotten in the mass of angry and useless literature that followed them—a literature, by the way, on which as much good brains was wasted as good blood was wasted on the battlefields it led to.

Now, as for the remedy, which is a remedy also for many other evils: Build up and vitalize the local public sentiment of the best men in the South. An energetic campaign should be made to strengthen it against acquiescence in lynch-law. Especially should those rapidly advancing communities whose industry has solved the race-problem and many other problems besides, make it known that they will not dally with this threat to their civilization and progress. If the business-man deal with the bully, he ought to make short work of him. Let it be proclaimed by boards of trade, by merchants, by bankers, by manufacturers, that they will not have industry and commerce hindered by lawlessness. All other machinery for strengthening public sentiment should be used. There are three thousand newspapers in the Southern States. If the editor of every paper, each in his own town (as not a few are now doing, especially in North Carolina), were to ask the men of influence and of character there whether under any circumstances or for any crime they ever approve of lynching, he would give expression to the real sentiment of his town; for a mob never represents the sentiment of a community until a community's spirit is utterly dead. In the State of Tennessee, for instance, where not long ago there was a lynching, there are more than two hundred papers of all classes. If every paper in the State had published the opinion of a hundred of the foremost men of character and influence in its community, they would have given expression to the disapproval of twenty thousand of the most influential citizens of the State, and this surely would have had a tonic effect on public sentiment and a deterring influence on criminals.

Then there are the ecclesiastical organizations. The preacher is in certain ways a greater power in most Southern communities than in any other part of the country. If the regular Conferences of the Methodists, the Associations of the Baptists, the Synods of the Presbyterians, as a part of their proceedings were to recite the hurt done to the character of every community by mob-violence and were to speak frankly what they all feel—this would have a strong influence, and it would encourage every preacher to be as bold in practical religion as he is valiant in theological argument.

But, most important of all, every political convention should recognize this evil and work for its abolition. If the platforms of the State conventions demand it, most of all if the county conventions demand it and require candidates for the shrievalty to declare boldly that they will resist mobs at the risk of their lives,—as several sheriffs have lately done with great bravery, and as the mayor of Roanoke, Virginia, did—public sentiment would soon actively shape itself into such condemnation of mob-violence that it would cease. Thus, through these organizations, and especially through the grand juries of every county whose sworn duty this is, the dazed and languid sentiment of any unfortunate community can be strengthened. It is the vast majority of good men, law-loving men who make up these organizations, and it is they that must defend themselves from the dangerous savagery of the smaller number who regard it as a manly thing to take the law into their own hands.

It is safe to say that there are not five men in every thousand in any county in all the black States who ever went with a mob or ever lynched a man. The appalling spectacle is therefore presented of a few men bringing great commonwealths into disrepute, holding back their development, and demoralizing their civilization. This is the simple truth; but the whole truth is more—the nine hundred and ninety-five law-abiding and law-loving men share in the guilt as they must share in its consequences, if they show themselves unable or unwilling to put an end to it. Acquiescence is surrender.

With the brute the law can deal; and there are most hopeful indications that the bully is doing his last violence to a civilization that he has so long cowed. He is an old acquaintance to those who know Southern life, this imitator of the faults and pretender to the traditions of that much-discussed worthy, "the old Southern gentleman." He had much to do with a war the penalty of which other men who had nothing to do with it have had to pay. With his oaths and "honor" he has strutted through all the quiet ways of Southern life, calling himself "the South," writing and speaking of "our people," and now he leads mobs to avenge "our women." The new spirit of industry should take him in hand. Commerce has no social illusions; it has the knack of rooting up vested social interests that stand in its way; and it has been left for commerce, by infusing its influence into the body of local public sentiment in the South, to rid us at last of this historic, red-handed, deformed, and swaggering villain.

(1893)

Selections from
TRAVEL ESSAYS
and
SOUTHERN LANDSCAPES

EDWARD KING

The Great South
Vicksburg and Natchez, Mississippi—
Society and Politics.
A Louisiana Parish Jury.

The journey along the Mississippi river from Napoleon, on the Arkansas shore, to Vicksburg, the largest town in the State of Mississippi, discloses naught save vast and gloomy stretches of forest and flat, of swamp and inlet, of broad current and green island, until Columbia, a pretty town on the Arkansas side, is passed. Below Columbia, the banks of the river are lined with cotton plantations for more than 150 miles.

Vicksburg, the tried and troubled hill-city, her crumbling bluffs still filled with historic memorials of one of the most desperate sieges and defences of modern times, rises in quite imposing fashion from the Mississippi's banks in a loop in the river, made by a long delta, which at high water is nearly submerged. The bluffs run back some distance to an elevated plateau. In the upper streets are many handsome residences. The Court-House has climbed to the summit of a fine series of terraces; here and there a pretty church serves as a land-mark; and the remains of the old fort from which "Whistling Dick," a famous Confederate gun was wont to sing defiance to the Federals, are still visible on a lofty eminence. From the grass-grown ramparts one can see "Grant's Cut-off" in the distance; overlook the principal avenue—Washington Street, well-lined with spacious shops and stores, and unhappily filled at all hours with lounging negroes; can see the broad current sweeping round the tongue of land on which the towns of De Soto and Delta stand, and the ferries plying to the landings of the railroad which cuts across North Louisiana to Shreveport; can see the almost perpendicular streets scaling the bluff from the water-side, and, down by the river, masses of elevators and warehouses, whence the white, stately packets come and go. There is evidence of growth; neat houses are scattered on hill and in valley in every direction; yet the visitor will find that money is scarce, credit is poor, and that every tradesman is badly discouraged.

The river is so intricate in its turnings that one is at first puzzled on seeing a steamboat passing, to know whether it is ascending or descending; at the end of the "loop," near the mouth of the Yazoo river, and at the point where Sherman made his entrance from the "Valley of Death," is the largest national cemetery in the country, in whose grassy plats repose the mortal remains of sixteen thousand soldiers. The view from the slopes of the cemetery, reached by many a detour through dusty cuts in the hills, is too flat to be grandiose, but ample enough to be inspiring. The wooded point; the cross-current setting around it; the wide sweep away toward the bend, are all charming. The old Scotch gardener and sexton told me that twelve thousand of the graves were marked "unknown." The original design contemplated the planting of the cemetery with tree-bordered avenues intended to resemble the aisles and nave of a cathedral. This was impracticable; but oaks have been planted throughout the ground, and the graves were covered with lovely blossoms. The section of Vicksburg between the cemetery and the town is not unlike the park of the Buttes Chaumont in Paris. Grapes grow wild in the adjacent valleys, and might readily be cultivated on the hill-sides. A simple marble shaft in the cemetery is destined to commemorate the spot where Grant held his famous interview with Pemberton.

Vicksburg has acquired a not altogether enviable notoriety as a town where shooting at sight is a popular method of vengeance, and, shortly before my second visit there, three murders were committed by men who deemed it manly to take the law into their own hands. There is still rather too much of this barbarism remaining in Mississippi, and it has not always the excuse of intoxication to palliate it. The Vicksburg method seems not to be the duel, but cold-blooded murder. The laws of the duello are pretty thoroughly expunged in Mississippi, although I was not a little amused to learn from Governor Ames that the ultra-Democratic people in those counties of the State bordering on Louisiana refused in any manner to aid the authorities in securing duelists who steal out from New Orleans to fight on Missis-sippi soil, on the ground that the "d—d Yankees want to do away with dueling so as to make their own heads safe." Mississippi is a sparsely settled State, and in some of the counties life is yet as rough as on the Southwestern frontier. But that open and deliberate murder should be encouraged in a city of fifteen thousand inhabitants, where there is good society, and where church and school flourish, is monstrous!

Vicksburg was once the scene of a terrible popular vengeance. A number of gamblers persisted in remaining in the town against the wishes of the citizens, and having shown fight and killed one or two townsmen, they were themselves lynched, and buried among the bluffs. The town gets its name from one of the oldest and most highly respected families in Mississippi,—the Vicks,—whose family mansion stands on a handsome eminence in the town of to-day. Colonel Vick, the present represen-tative of the family, is a specimen of the noble-looking men grown in the Mississippi valley,—six feet four in stature, erect and stately, with the charming courtesy of the old school. The picture which our artist has given of him does justice only to the fine, manly face; it cannot reproduce the form and the manner. Mississippi raises noble men, and they were wonderful soldiers, showing pluck, persistence, and grip. Nineteen lines of steam-packets ply between New Orleans and Vicksburg, and from Vicksburg up the Yazoo River. The scene in the elevators at the river-side, as in Memphis, is in the highest degree animated. Thousands of bales and barrels roll and tumble down the gangways which communicate with the boats, and the shouting is terrific. The railroad from Vicksburg to Jackson, the Mississippian capital, runs through the scene of some of the heaviest fighting of the war, crossing the Big Black river, and passing Edwards and other flourishing towns, set down between charming forests and rich cotton fields.

Sailing on through the submerged country from Vicksburg was sorrowful work; every one was depressed with imminent disaster. We passed into the great bend, or lake, where, on Hurricane Island, lie the plantations formerly owned by the Davis Brothers,—famous for their wealth. The broad acres once known as the property of Jefferson Davis are now in the hands of his ex-slave, who, by the way, is said to be a miracle of thrift and intelligence.

Negroes were toiling in the mud at some of the landings, building ineffectual dams, around which the current of the great river, sooner or later, remorselessly ran. The white men, splashing along the overflowed roads on horseback, looked grimly courageous, and gave their orders in a cool, collected manner. The whole land seemed one treacherous morass; the outlook was very discouraging.

We passed several rude villages on the eastern bank, which had been built by colonies of negroes, who had fled as the floods came upon them. These blacks gain a precarious livelihood by cutting wood and growing chickens for passing steamers; they depend on the captains of the boats for their supplies of cornmeal, molasses, pork and whiskey, and are sometimes reduced almost to starvation when their natural recklessness and improvidence have resulted in empty larders.

At one of these primitive settlements, known as "Waterproof" (it was by no means proof against the water, however), there were once two negro preachers who were extravagantly fond of whiskey. As each desired to maintain in the eyes of the other a reputation for strictest temperance, some secrecy in procuring the supplies of the coveted article was necessary, and each made the clerk of the "Great Republic" his confidant. Whenever the boat stopped at "Waterproof," the preachers were promptly on hand, each one obtaining of the clerk a private interview, and imploring him to bring, on the return trip, a good keg of whiskey, carefully enveloped, so that "dat udder nigger" should not know what it was. When the clerk complied, he received at the hands of the grateful preachers, thank-offerings of chickens and fat ducklings, and whenever he mischievously threatened to expose the reverend sinners, he would hear the frightened words:

"Fo' de Lord, you's gwine to ruin me!"

When the river destroys the land upon which the negroes have built a town, and tumbles their cabins and their little church into the current, they retire to the higher lands, a few miles back, or seek a new water-side location. They cultivate but little corn, and give much of their time to merry-makings, "meetings," mule races, and long journeys from one settlement to another. As we passed a little village where there were, perhaps, a hundred negroes, comfortably installed in weather-proof cabins, a passenger on the "Great Republic," who was a planter of the old *régime,* indulged in the following monologue:

"Thar's what they call free niggers. Thar's a change from a few years ago, sir. Them poor things thar are just idlin' away their time, I reckon; and you notice, they're mighty ragged and destitute lookin'. Thar's a d——d nigger a-ridin' a mule, as comfortable like as ye please. Not much like the old times, when they were all working quiet-like in the fields. Sundays yo'd seen 'em in their clean white clothes, singin' and shoutin' or may be doin' a bit of fishin', and at night, when the plantation bell rung, agoin' peaceful as lambs to quarters. Now it's all frolic. I reckon they'll starve. What kin they do alone, sir?"

"I hain't nothin' agin a free nigger," said a tall native of Mississippi bound for Texas, "but I don't want him to say a word to me. The world's big enough for us both, I reckon. We ain't made to live together under this new style o' things. Free niggers and me couldn't agree." And the two spat sympathetically.

The negroes in the valley cheered the "Great Republic" as she passed; the swart mothers, fondling their babes, looked up and waved their hands, and some of the men doffed their hats, unconsciously retaining the respectful manner which they had been forced to observe during the stern domination of slavery.

The western bank of the river below Vicksburg, even to the Gulf of Mexico, is within the bounds of Louisiana. The eastern bank, to a point nearly opposite the Red River, is in Mississippi. The characteristics of the river-side populations in both States are much the same. The negroes in many of the counties are largely in the majority, and hold responsible offices. One of the prominent citizens of Natchez, who was in former days a man of large wealth, owning several hundred negroes, was sitting on his verandah one day, when a negro with a book under his arm approached, and with the dignity befitting a state official, said to the Caucasian:

"I's de century-man, sah!"

He was the officer appointed to take the census for the county. He could not read well, and his chirography was painful, but he showed diligence and determination.

Grand Gulf, in Mississippi, is a pretty town, lying on romantic hills, whose bases are bathed by the great stream. A railway extends from Grand Gulf to Port Gibson, eight miles distant, and a thriving trade is done with the interior. The hills overhanging the river were advantageous positions for the Confederates in war time, and the Federal fleet of gun-boats shelled the town and its battery-crowned heights in 1862. Below Grand Gulf there are no towns of importance on either side of the river until Natchez, one of the loveliest of Southern towns, and without exception, the most beautiful in Mississippi, is reached.

Natchez, like Vicksburg, lies on a line of bluffs which rear their bold heads from the water in an imposing manner. He who sees only Natchez-under-the-Hill from a steamboat's deck gets an impression of a few prosaic houses huddled together not far from a wharf-boat, a road leading up a steep and high hill, and here and there masses of foliage. Let him wander ashore, and scale the cliff, and he will find himself in a quiet, unostentatious, beautifully shaded town, from which, so oppressive at first is the calm, he almost fancies

"Life and thought are gone away;"

but he finds cheeriest of people,—cheery, too, under heavy misfortunes,— and homes rich in refinement and half buried under the lustrous and voluptuous blossoms which the wonderful climate favors. Natchez has an impressive cathedral, a fine court-house, a handsome Masonic temple, and hosts of pretty houses. You walk beneath the shade of the China-tree and the water oak, the cedar and the laurimunda. Nowhere is there glare of sun on the pavement; nothing more clamorous than the galloping of a horse stirs the blood of the nine thousand inhabitants.

There were, before the war, great numbers of planters' residences in the suburbs,—beautiful houses, with colonnades and verandahs, with rich drawing and dining-rooms, furnished in heavy antique style, and gardens modeled after the finest in Europe. Many of these homes have been destroyed. We visited one or two whose owners have been fortunate enough to keep them. The lawns and gardens are luxurious. The Mississippian wealth of roses is inconceivable to him who has not visited such gardens as Brown's, in Natchez-under-the-Hill, and that of Mr. Shields, in the suburbs of the upper town. I remember no palace garden in Europe which impressed me so powerfully with the sense of richness and exquisite profusion of costly and delicate blooms as Brown's, at Natchez, which a wealthy Scotchman cultivated for a quarter of a century, and handed down to his family, with injunctions to maintain its splendor.

From the bluff above this indescribably charming spot one can overlook the plain of Concordia, in Louisiana, on the west side the broad, tranquil river, and catch the gleam of the lake among the mammoth trees.

There are still many wealthy families in Natchez, independent of the war and its abasements. Here and there a French name and tradition remind one that the town is of French origin, that D'Iberville founded it in 1700, and that Bienville once had a trading-post there among the Natchez Indians. There that tribe, fire-worshipers and noble savages, passed an innocent and Arcadian existence, keeping ever alight on their altars a fire in honor of the sun. But the white man came; the fire on the altars went out; the Indian was swept away. Gayarre, who has written well concerning these Southern Indian tribes, says the Natchez were the Athenians of Louisiana, as the Choctaws were the Bœotians. A hundred years after the Natchez had first seen the French, Fort Rosalie, on the bluff,—its site is still pointed out to the stranger,—was evacuated by the Spaniards, that the flag of the United States might be raised over it, and since 1803 Natchez has been an incorporated American city. It has no manufactures now; its trade depends entirely on cotton. No railroad reaches it, but a narrow-gauge, called the Natchez, Jackson and Columbus Road, has been begun. The adjoining counties furnish from five to twenty thousand bales of cotton annually, which are shipped to New Orleans for sale.

Natchez was out of debt when it was given over to the Republican Party, but has acquired quite a heavy indebtedness since. The negroes came into power there in 1867. The present Sheriff, the County Treasurer and Assessor, the majority of the magistrates, and all the officers managing county affairs, except one, are negroes. The Board of Aldermen has three negroes in it. There is the usual complaint among the Conservatives that money has been dishonestly and foolishly expended; but the government of the city seemed, on the whole, very satisfactory. About a thousand children are at school in the public schools, and four hundred of them,—the colored pupils,—have a handsome new schoolhouse, called the "Union," built expressly for them. Natchez had an excellent system of public schools before the war, and the "Natchez Institute," the original free-school, is still kept up. The Catholic institutions are numerous and thriving. A good many of the negroes, as in Louisiana, are Catholics.

One-half of the population of Natchez is black, and seems to live on terms of amity with the white half. White and black children play together in the streets, and one sometimes feels like asking "Why, if that be so, should they not go to school together?" But the people of Mississippi, like the people throughout the South, will not hear of mixed schools. The negroes are vociferously prominent as hackmen, wharfmen, and public servants generally; but they do not like to leave the town and settle down to hard work on the worn-out hills at the back of the city.

On the bluffs, some three miles from the town, is a national cemetery, beautifully planned and decorated, and between it and Natchez stands the dilapidated United States Marine Hospital, and the grass-grown ramparts of Fort McPherson mark the site of a beautiful mansion which was razed for military purposes. When its owner, a rich Frenchman, was offered compensation by the army officer superintending the work, he gruffly refused it, saying that he had enough still left to buy the United States Government.

The taxes in Natchez and vicinity are very oppressive, amounting to nearly six per cent. The State and county tax touches four per cent, and is based on full two-thirds the valuation. The railroad movement has, however, done something to increase these burdens.

Many of the Natchez planters own plantations on the Louisiana side of the river, but, of course, have no political influence there, and are dependent on the negroes for the local legislation necessary to secure them in their rights, and for measures to prevent inundation. I attended a session of a parish jury in Vidalia, opposite Natchez, and was surprised to find it almost entirely composed of blacks. The white planters with whom I conversed grumbled bitterly over their hard fate, and recounted thrilling stories of the exploits of carpet-baggers in their vicinity. From the tone of their conversation, it was easy to see that they believed these carpet-baggers had misled the negroes, who would otherwise have been well enough disposed.

The jury, whose office corresponds, so far as I could learn, very much to that of our county commissioners in the Northern States, comprised men of various grades of intelligence. One or two of the negroes were well dressed, and quiet and gentlemanly in their manners; the others were slouching, unkempt, suspicious in their demeanor, and evidently unfit for any public duty. The planters addressed them familiarly, stating their needs, and making hearty appeals to the common sense of the most intelligent of the number. As the inundation was rapidly invading all the neighboring lands,the negroes recognized the necessity of action.

At Vidalia, I also met one of the prominent negro members of the Louisiana Legislature, Mr. David Young, a coal black man. When I first saw him he was addressing a row of his fellow-citizens, who were seated upon a fence in that nerveless, unexpectant attitude so characteristic of the lowland negro. As an election was about to occur in Vidalia, he was endeavoring to impress on the colored voters the necessity of electing reform officers, and indulged in some general remarks on the importance of a purification of Louisiana politics. Brandishing his ballots, he warned the listeners to vote for honest representatives; whereupon one ragged negro said sullenly:

"I's done gwine to vote to suit myself. Dave Young nor no udder man ain't gwine to tell me nothin' 'bout my vote."

Mr. Young then proceeded to explain to them that Northern sentiment was beginning to rebel against the misrule at the South, and that the colored voters throughout the State must be "wise in time." The listeners shook their heads suspiciously, although evidently impressed with what they had heard. As we drew near, and entered into conversation, Mr. Young turned his attention to us, and expressed himself desirous of a fair government in the State for both whites and blacks. While he gave his views, in plain but well chosen language, I noticed that the other negroes listened intently, making whispered comments on his remarks.They were far from friendly toward Young, as he was a candidate for re-election to the Legislature against a white man who had a notoriously evil reputation as a carpet-bagger, yet who had obtained the firm support of a majority of the negroes in the parish.

"We do not object," said one planter to me, as we left Vidalia, "to the presence of the negro in the parish jury, we complain because nine out of ten who sit upon the jury are ignorant and have no property at all, and yet are permitted to judge of what is best for the interests of property-holders. We are often compelled to submit questions of vital importance to the judgment of irresponsible and suspicious fellows, who, because they are opposed to us politically, seem to think it their bounden duty to do nothing for our material well-being. But such men as Dave Young do some good. They are teaching the negroes a little prudence and moderation. I would rather have a nigger like David, than a white man like —" (mentioning the wicked carpet-bagger).

Life on Cotton Plantations.

During my stay in Natchez, one of the many gentlemen interested in cotton-planting on the west or Louisiana side of the river, invited me to accompany him on a tour of inspection. The rapidly-rising river threatened to inundate the lands on which hundreds of negroes had been expending weeks of patient care, and the planter felt it his duty to take a horseback ride over the trio of plantations under his charge; so we crossed the Mississippi, and rode twelve miles into the interior of Louisiana.

On the road, which led along the lovely banks of Lake Concordia, the planter chatted of some of the vexations by which he is daily beset, and spoke rather hopelessly of the labor problem. The condition of society, too, he thought very bad, and that it was an actual hindrance to the development of the section.

"Are the negroes," I asked him, "aggressive and insolent toward the white people?"

But as the planter was about to answer this question, we approached a ferry-boat or barge, in which we were to cross an arm of the lake to the island on which my friend's plantations were situated. An old negro man, much the worse for liquor, was preparing to monopolize the boat with his mule-team, but held back the mules, and touched his hat with drunken courtesy as we came up.

"Stand aside, uncle," said the planter firmly, but very politely; "we wish to cross at once, and there is not room for us all."

"Yas, sah; yas, Colonel," said the old man. "I's willin' to wait on you gemmen, 'cause you is gemmen; but ef yer was no count folks, I'd go for yer. Ride in, Colonel."

When we were some distance from the shore, the planter said:

"That old man made way for us simply out of deference to our social position. The negroes are courteous enough to us; it has been their habit so long that they cannot forget it. But they will kill our deer and steal our poultry and bacon, and we have no redress."

After an hour or two of journeying over rough roads we came to one of the plantations. A host of negroes were busily filling a breach in a dyke which the treacherous water might sweep away if rains came to swell the already ominous floods of the Mississippi. A pack of hounds came yelping to meet the planter; and the black women in the cabin courtesied obsequiously.

We crossed the field, bordered by noble cypresses and oaks, stopping now and then to watch the negroes as they carefully prepared the ground which an inundation might, in less than a day, reduce to a hopeless wilderness of mud. Entering the house of the overseer, we found that functionary smoking his pipe and reposing after a long ride over the plantation. He was a rough, hearty, good-natured man, accustomed to living alone and faring rudely. I asked him what he thought of the negro as a free laborer.

"He works well, mostly, sir. These yer Alabama niggers that's workin' on our plantations now do well on wages. They make some little improvements around their cabins, but mighty little, sir. Ef politics would only let 'em alone, they'd get along well enough, I reckon."

"Do the negroes on this plantation vote?"

"I reckon not (laughing). I don't want my niggers to have anything to do with politics. They can't vote as long as they stay with us, and these Alabama boys don't take no interest in the elections here."

"What do they receive as monthly wages?"

"From ten to sixteen dollars. It costs us about fifteen dollars per head to bring 'em from Alabama. These niggers likes wages better than shares. We keep a store here, and, Saturday nights, most of the money they have earned comes back to us in trade. They're fond o' whiskey and good things to eat."

"What is the routine of your work on a large plantation like this, and those adjoining it, throughout the year?"

"Wal, sir, I reckon that's a long story. We don't have much spare time, and mighty little amusement. Wal, sir, the first thing we do, sir, we begin early in January, a few weeks after the old crop is all gathered in, to repair fences and clean out all the ditches, sir. Then we pull down the old stalks, and start the ploughs to throw quadruple furrows in the fields. Then we throw out the 'middles.' "

"What are they?"

"Wal, sir, we throw out soil at the sides so as to leave a slope bed of fresh ground to plant on, and loose earth to cover it with. If the spring freshet breaks on to this yer prepared earth, we've got to begin over again, and that makes the season very late.

"Planting begins about the last of March, or very early in April. Piles of cotton seed are laid along some ways apart on the field, and then the niggers sow it along the beds, a ton of seed to eight acres. Then it is 'barred off'—covered up, that means.

"Ez soon as the cotton stalks begin to peep up, 'scraping' begins. The hands weed every row carefully, and don't leave any weakly plants. That, and looking after the caterpillars, keeps 'em busy till July. Caterpillars ain't the only danger we have to fight against. Thar's a hundred others. Cotton's a ticklish plant to raise. You've got to watch it mighty close, and then the worms and the weather will sometimes ruin the crop.

"Between July and September we keep the hands busy, getting out baskets, and setting things in order; then we pile in new help, and for the rest of the season, employ three times as many hands as thar's in the fields now. Up to Christmas it's picking and ginning, and it's right lively, you can be sure."

From the overseer's conversation I learned that cotton-picking is done quite as thoroughly under the system of free labor as in the days when slave-driving was permissible; but that the "niggers" require constant watching. On many plantations where the yield is abundant, it is difficult to concentrate labor enough at the proper time to get the cotton into the gin-house the same year that it is planted. I have seen cotton-fields still white with their creamy fleeces late in December, because the negroes were either too lazy or too busily engaged in their annual merry-making to gather the harvest. But on the large lowland plantations along the Mississippi, the crop is usually gathered early, and the picking is very thorough. I could not discover that there was any system of "forced labor" now in use, and I thought the overseer's statement, that a "good field-hand now-a-days would pick 250 pounds of cotton daily," was excellent testimony in favor of free labor. He added, however, that on many plantations the average hands would not pick more than 100 pounds per day.

The laborers were coming in from the field in a long picturesque procession. As it was spring-time many of them had been ploughing, and were mounted upon the backs of the stout mules which had been their companions all day. Some of the men were singing rude songs, others were shouting boisterously and scuffling as they went their way along the broad pathway bordered by giant cypresses and noble oaks. The boys tumbling and wriggling in the grass perpetually exploded into guffaws of contagious laughter. Many of the men were tall and finely formed. They had an intelligent look, and were evidently not so degraded as those born on the Louisiana lowlands. The overseer sat on the veranda of his house, now and then calling out a sharp command or a caution, the negroes looking up obsequiously and touching their hats as they heard his voice. When the mules were stabled the men came lounging back to the cabins, where the women were preparing their homely supper, and an hour afterward we heard the tinkle of banjos, the pattering of feet and uproarious laughter. The interiors of the negro cabins were of the rudest description. The wretched huts in which the workmen live seem to them quite comfortable, however. I saw no one who appeared discontented with his surroundings. Few of these laborers could read at all. Even those who had some knowledge of the alphabet did not seem to be improving it.

Late in the evening, as the planter, with his heavy cloak thrown about his shoulders, was reposing from the fatigues of a wearisome ride over the broad acres, a delegation of field-hands came to see him, all to ask favors of "de Cunnel,"—to get him to write a few letters, or to bring some tiny parcel from the town on his next visit to the plantation. The men came huddling in, bowing awkwardly, and stood with their caps in their hands as near the door as possible, as if ready to run on the slightest provocation. If I looked at them steadily, they burst into uneasy laughter and moved away, while the black women in the door-way and on the porch re-echoed the merriment. Meantime the planter listened to one after another of the delegation. Charles, a black boy, six feet tall, and with sinews strong as steel, stepped forward to the flickering light given by the candles and the burning logs in the fire-place.

"Cunnel, I wish you read me dat letter, please, sah."

The "Cunnel" read it, Charles meantime standing erect, with his great arms folded across his mighty chest and the massive column of his throat throbbing with scornful emotion. There was a strange, baffled expression in his face; a look of contempt for his own helplessness which was painful.

The letter was common-place enough, reproaching Charles for having left Alabama before liquidating the pressing claims of certain swarthy creditors. Having, after some trouble, deciphered the letter's meaning, the Colonel said, gently but coldly:

"Stand aside, Charles. Andy, who is the likeliest negro from Alabama now on the plantation?"

No answer for a minute. Andy stepped forward into the light, looking first into the fire-place, then at the deer's horns over the mantel, then at the shining revolver on the rough wooden table, while his immense lips worked nervously, as if endeavoring to draw in inspiration from the air.

"Did you hear me, Andy?"

"Cunnel, I's a studyin', sah."

After having studied some time, Andy darted out without a word, and presently returned with three hulking black giants, who huddled together in the same helpless way that the first arrivals did. They held their shapeless felt hats in their enormous hands, glancing from them into the faces of the white men; then exchanging significant looks with each other, burst into the regulation laugh.

"Did the colored politicians try to keep you from leaving Alabama to come here with me, boys?" inquired the Colonel.

Intense surprise on the part of the negroes.

"No, sah; reckon not, sah."

"Did you vote in Alabama?"

"Yas, Cunnel; yas, sah, always voted, sah."

"Can you do better here than in Alabama?"

After mature reflection, the trio responded in the affirmative.

"Would you care to vote here?"

Hesitatingly, "No, sah;" whereupon the three negroes were dismissed into the darkness.

The Alabama papers at the beginning of the current year reported that the colored laborers were leaving that State in troops of thousands. They were nearly all *en route* for the cotton plantations of Mississippi, and on the Louisiana bank of the Father of Waters. Central Alabama appeared at that time to be undergoing rapid depopulation for the benefit of the richer lands along the Mississippi bottom. It was estimated in the spring of 1874 that Alabama had already lost from $700,000 to $1,000,000 in her labor element alone. How long the influx of the freedmen into Mississippi and Louisiana from the South Atlantic States and from Alabama will continue is uncertain. In 1873 Georgia lost fully 20,000 of her able-bodied colored laborers, and gained but little in white immigration to balance it.

The women and children on the cotton plantations near the Mississippi river do not work in the fields as much as they used. Rude as are their surroundings in the little cabins which they now call their own, they are beginning to take an interest in their homes, and the children spend some time each year at school. The laborers on the plantations in Louisiana have sometimes been paid as high as thirty dollars per month, and furnished with a cabin, food, and a plot of ground for a garden; but this is exceptional.

While supper was being prepared the master of the plantation apologized for what he modestly called the homely fare which, he said, was all that he could set before us.

"We are so far from town here," he said, "that we can offer you only plantation fare—rough meat and eggs, with bacon, a loaf of baker's bread, and some bottles of claret which I brought from Vidalia."

I ventured to suggest that on the plantation he had every facility for a superb garden, and to wonder that the overseers did not employ some of the negroes to cultivate a plot of ground that its fruits might appear on the table.

"Oh,oh," laughed the overseer. "Make a garden here; reckon it would have to have a mighty high wall; the niggers would steal everything in it as fast as it was ripe."

But I suggested that if each of the negroes had a small garden, which he seemed to have ample time after hours to cultivate, he would not desire to steal.

The Colonel smiled gravely, and the overseer shook his head incredulously, adding:

"These is good niggers, but stealing is as natural as eating to them" and, with this remark, we were ushered into the supper-room, where two black servant girls ran nimbly about, bringing in plain but substantial fare, which our hard riding made thoroughly palatable.

There was no white lady on the plantation. The overseer and his two assistants were busy from dawn till dark, and when night threw its shadows over the great cypress-bordered aisles of the forest and the wide expanse of the fields, they dismissed the negroes about the store and the stables and retired to rest. But on the occasion of our visit we saw unusual activity. A violent storm arose while we were at supper, and the overseers mounted their horses and rode off in different directions to inspect the levées. Troops of negroes were dispatched in skiffs along the lake with hundreds of sacks, which they were instructed to fill with sand and place at weak points on the levées. All night they fought the slowly but steadily-rising waters, while my companion and I slept on a mattress on the floor of the overseer's room, undisturbed by anything save the sighing of the winds through the noble trees surrounding the house, and the clatter of rain upon the shingles.

With early morning back came the Colonel, pale and worn with a night of battle with the steadily-rising water, and, as he laid aside his heavy cloak, placed his revolver on the table, and sat down with a weary sigh, he said it was hardly worth trying to be a successful cotton-planter now-a-days; things human and things divine seemed to conspire to make it impossible to succeed. I thought of his sigh and of his helpless look a day or two afterward, when I was told that one thousand acres of his plantation had been flooded and badly injured by the offensive policy of a neighbor planter, who had cut the Colonel's levées to save his own.

With daylight also, although the rain was steadily falling, the plantation blossomed into activity. The overseers had arisen long before the dim streaks of the dawn were seen on the lowland horizon; had galloped over many a broad acre, but returned gloomily, announcing that the land was too wet to work that day. The negroes slouchingly disposed themselves about the store and the overseer's "mansion," keeping at a respectful distance from the kitchen, where sat the overseer himself, surrounded by his dogs. Nothing more dispiriting could be imagined than the atmosphere of this lowland plantation over which imminent disaster seemed breaking. From right and left came stories of trouble and affliction. Here and there a planter had made a good crop and had laid aside a little money, but the evidences of material prosperity were painfully few. The overseers, while doggedly persistent in working the plantations up to their full capacity, still seemed to have a grim sense of a fate which overhung the whole locality, and which would not permit consecutive years of prosperity and plenty.

There is still much on one of these remote and isolated plantations to recall the romance which surrounded them during the days of slavery. The tall and stalwart women, with their luxuriant wool carefully wrapped in gayly-colored handkerchiefs; the picturesque and tattered children, who have not the slightest particle of education, and who have not been reached even since the era of reconstruction, by the influences of schools and teachers; the groups of venerable darkeys, with their gray slouch hats and impossible garments, who chatter for hours together on the sunny side of some out-buildings, and the merry-makings at night, all recall a period which, the planter will tell you, with a mournful look, comprised the halcyon days of Louisiana.

The thing which struck me as most astonishing here, in the cotton-lands, as on the rice plantations of South Carolina, was the absolute subjection of the negro. Those with whom I talked would not directly express any idea. They gave a shuffling and grimacing assent to whatever was suggested; or, if they dissented, would beg to be excused from differing verbally, and seemed to be much distressed at being required to express their opinions openly. Of course, having the most absolute political liberty, because in that section they were so largely in the majority, numerically, that no intimidation could have been practiced, it seemed astonishing that they should be willing to forego the right to vote, and to willingly isolate themselves from their fellows. I could not discover that any of the negroes were making a definite progress, either manifested by a subscription to some newspaper or by a tendency to discussion; and, while the planter gave me the fullest and freest account of the social status of the negroes employed by him, he failed to mention any sign of a definite and intellectual growth. The only really encouraging sign in their social life was the tendency to create for themselves homes, and now and then to cultivate the land about them.

The rain continued to fall in torrents as we rode across the island along the muddy roads, under the great arches of the cypress-trees, on our return to Natchez. Here and there a few negroes were desperately striving afield, endeavoring to effect something in spite of the storm; but the planter shook his head gravely, and said that all agricultural operations must now be two months later than usual. The lack of concerted operations among the planters against the inroads of the floods, and the disastrous consequences of an incompetent labor system, were, to his thinking, effectual drawbacks to much material progress for a long time. In a previous chapter I have shown how the production of Concordia Parish has fallen off since slavery was abolished; and he could not give any encouragement to my hope that the wretched state of affairs would soon be changed.

At last we reached the arm of the lake where we expected to find our sable ferry-man, but the rain had washed the waters into quite a fury, and we could see neither ferry-man nor barge. Half-an-hour's hallooing at last brought the old man from his cabin on the opposite side, and another half hour brought him, dripping wet, with the gray wool of his beard glistening with rain-drops, to the shore on which we stood. He complained bitterly of his poverty, yet I was surprised to learn that each time the Colonel visited his plantation he paid this venerable boatman a dollar for his ride across the lake. Although I diligently endeavored to enter into conversation with the aged black man, he steadily avoided any reference to political topics, and assumed a look of blank amazement when I appealed to him for a direct opinion. But he was always civil, courteous to a degree not discoverable among people in his rank of life in the North. His character swayed and bent before any aggression, but did not break; it was as stubborn as elastic.

In the forest through which ran the road leading to the Colonel's plantation, we met a brown man mounted on a stout horse, and loaded down with a small armory of fire-arms, in addition to which he carried a long knife and a hatchet, evidently intended for dissecting some deer.

"Ha!" said the Colonel pleasantly, yet with a touch of annoyance in his voice; "so you are going poaching on my land again? There will soon be no deer left."

"Yas, Cunnel," said the fellow, impudently shifting his long rifle from his right to his left shoulder. "I reckon ef I see any deer I 's gwine to go for 'em, sho';" then, putting spurs to his steed, he galloped off.

There was no redress, and the Colonel was compelled to submit anew to the plundering of his preserves.

Driving homeward with my artist companion, the Colonel having left us to return to his fight with the levées, we were struck with the picturesque clusters of negro cabins by the wayside. Nowhere else in the agricultural regions of the South had we perceived such a tendency to an artistic grouping of buildings. Along the road, which was now so covered with water that we could hardly pick our way, a few uproarious negroes, with whiskey bottles protruding from their pockets, were picking their dubious way. As we approached they saluted us, touching their hats with sudden dignity. Everywhere in this lowland region we found the negro courteous more from habit than from desire. Even when he fell into the sullen silence which marks his supremest dissent, he was deferential and polite to a degree which made that silence all the more exasperating. I have never in my life seen a more gracious and civil personage than the weather-stained and tattered old negro who stood on a shelving bank by the lake-side, and carefully pointed out to us the best spots in the submerged road, as we drove through the little village of which he was an inhabitant.

The local river packets, which depend mainly upon the commerce of the cotton plantations between Vicksburg and New Orleans, are the only means which the planters possess of communication with the outer world. The arrivals of the "Robert E. Lee," or of the "Natchez," at the plantation landings, always furnish picturesque and interesting scenes. We had occasion to journey from Natchez to Vicksburg, departing from the former town late at night. The negro hackman who was to transport us from the upper town to Natchez-under-the-Hill for the moderate sum of three dollars, bade us remain quietly in our rooms until "de Lee whistled." So, toward midnight, hearing the three hoarse yells from the colossal steam-pipes of the Robert E. Lee, we were hurried down to the great wharf-boat, where we found a motley crowd of negro men and women, of sickly, ague-stricken, poor whites, and smartly-dressed planters, whose immaculate linen and rich garments betrayed but little of the poverty and anxiety now afflicting the whole section.

Presently, out of the gloom which shrouded the great river, a giant shape seemed slowly approaching, and while we were endeavoring to discover what it might be, flaring pine torches sent forth an intense light which disclosed the great packet, with her forward deck crowded with negro roustabouts, whose faces shone as the flame was reflected upon them. The tall pipes sent out sparks and smoke, and the river-monster, which seemed stealthily drawing near to us to devour us, winked its fiery eyes and sleepily drew up at the wharf, where, with infinite trouble, it was made fast with many stout ropes, while the mates screamed and cursed as only Mississippi boatmen can.

The cabin of one of these steamers presents quite a different aspect from those of the Northern packets which come from St. Louis and Cincinnati. The bar is a conspicuous object as one enters, and around it cluster eager groups busily discussing the latest phase of the Kellogg usurpation, or, in such times of depression and disaster as during my visit, lamenting their fate with a philosophic air doubtless somewhat enhanced by the soothing nature of the liquids imbibed.

As the traveler goes to register his name and purchase his ticket, the obliging clerk hands him the latest file of the New Orleans papers, of which hundreds of copies are given away at all the ports where the packets stop. No planter along the line thinks of buying a newspaper, but depends on the clerk of the steamer, who willingly furnishes him the news of the day.

About the card-tables men are busily absorbed in the intricacies of "poker" and "seven-up," and the talk is of cotton and of corn, of the rise and fall of the river, and reminiscences of adventures in forest and on stream during the "waw." On the "Robert E. Lee" I found a number of prominent young cotton-planters, all of whom were complaining of the effects of the inundation. Many of these planters were educated gentlemen, familiar with life at the North, and with the best society. None of them were especially bitter or partisan in their views; their material interests seemed to command their immediate attention, and they, as others throughout the cotton country of the South, complained of the seeming impossibility of reorganizing labor upon a fair and proper basis. All were unanimous in their testimony as to the superiority of free over slave labor, but all asserted that it was attended with so many drawbacks and vexations that they feared it would end in the promotion of much distress, and in the ruin of hundreds of planters. They, however, were by no means confronted with the worst aspects of the labor question, since labor was flowing to them, and not receding from them, as from the planters in Central Alabama, and in certain portions of Mississippi.

Mr. Robert Somers, in his excellent observations on the labor question, as viewed in Alabama, made during a journey throughout the Southern States in 1870–71, hits upon some truths with regard to the relations of the planter and freedman, in the following manner:

"What the planters are disposed to complain of is, that while they have lost their slaves, they have not got free laborers in any sense common either in the Northern States or in Europe. One cannot but think that the New England manufacturer and the Old England farmer must be equally astonished at a recital of the relations of land, capital and labor, as they exist on the cotton plantations of the Southern States. The wages of the negroes, if such a term can be applied to a mode of remuneration so unusual and anomalous, consist, as I have often indicated, of one-half the crop of corn and cotton, the only crops in reality produced.

"The negro on the semi-communistic basis thus established finds his own rations; but, as these are supplied to him by the planter or the planter's notes of credit on the merchants, and as much more sometimes as he thinks he needs by the merchants on his own credit, from the 1st of January onward throughout the year, in anticipation of crops which are not marketable until the end of December, he can lose nothing by the failures or deficient outcome of the crops, and is always sure of his subsistence. As a permanent economic relation, this would be startling anywhere betwixt any classes of men brought together in the business of life. Applied to agriculture, in any other part of the world, it would be deemed outrageously absurd, but this is only a part of the 'privileges' (a much more accurate term than 'wages') of the negro field-hand. In addition to half the crops, he has a free cottage of the kind he seems to like, and the windows of which he or his wife persistently nail up; he has abundance of wood from the planter's estate for fuel, and for building his corn-cribs and other out-houses, with teams to draw it from the forest. He is allowed to keep hogs and milch cows and young cattle, which roam and feed with the same right of pasture as the hogs and cattle of the planter, free of all charge. Though entitled to one-half the crops, he is not required to contribute any portion of the seed, nor is he called upon to pay any part of the taxes on the plantation. The only direct tax on the negroes is a poll tax." Mr. Somers declares that he found this tax "everywhere in arrear, and, in some places, in a helpless chaos of non-payment. Yet," he adds, "while thus freed from the burden of taxation, the negro has, up to this period of reconstruction, enjoyed the monopoly of representation; and has had all legislative and executive power moulded to his will by Governors, Senators and Deputies, who have been either his tools, or of whom he himself has been the dupe. For five years," he concludes, "the negroes have been kings, lords and commoners, and something more, in the Southern States."

"But to come back," continues Mr. Somers, "to the economic condition of the plantations, the negro field-hand, with his right of half-crop and privileges as described, who works with ordinary diligence, looking only to his own pocket, and gets his crops forward and gathered in due time, is at liberty to go to other plantations and pick cotton, in doing which he may make from two to two and a-half dollars a day. For every piece of work outside the crop that he does even on his own plantation, he must be paid a dollar a day. While the land owner is busy keeping account betwixt himself and his negro hands, ginning their cotton for them, doing all the marketing of produce and supplies, of which they have the lion's share, and has hardly a day he can call his own, the hands may be earning a dollar a day from him for work which is quite as much theirs as his. Yet the negroes with all their superabounding privilege on the cotton-field, make little of it. A ploughman or a herd in the Old World would not exchange his lot for theirs, as it stands and as it appears in all external circumstances."

I have quoted these excellent remarks, as they afford a glimpse into some of the causes of the discouragement which prevails among large numbers of cotton-planters.

Nothing can be more beautiful than the appearance of a cotton-field, extending over many hundreds of acres, when the snowy globes of wool are ready for picking, and the swart laborers, with sacks suspended from their shoulders, wander between the rows of plants, culling the fleeces. The cotton-plant is beautiful from the moment when the minute leaflets appear above the moist earth until the time when it is gathered in. In June, when it is in bloom and when the blossoms change their color day by day, a cotton plantation looks like an immense flower garden. In the morning the blooms of upland cotton are often of a pale straw color; at noon of a pure white; in the afternoon perhaps faint pink, and the next morning perfect pink. It is noticed, however, that the blossom of the sea-island cotton always remains a pale yellow. When the flowers fall away, and the young bolls begin to grow, the careful negroes watch for the insidious approach of the cotton-worms, terrible enemies to plantation prosperity. There are many kinds of these worms; they multiply with astonishing rapidity, and sometimes cut off the entire crop of whole districts. Their presence cannot be accounted for, although elaborate investigations into the cause of their appearance have been undertaken ever since 1800, when they first appeared in the South. There is a popular belief that they come at intervals of three years in the same districts, and that their greatest ravages occur after intervals of twenty-one years. Their appetites are exclusively confined to cotton, of which they devour both the long and the short staples greedily.

The planters build fires in the fields when they perceive that the insects are about to visit their crops, hoping to attract and destroy the moths which are the parents of the worms; but in many cases this proves insufficient. When the cotton-worm appears early in the season there are usually three broods. If the fires are built exactly at the time of the appearance of the first moths, then their speedy destruction, preventing the appearance of the second and third broods, aids in limiting the ravages; but the remedies are rarely undertaken in time. The ally of this vicious destroyer of the planter's fondest hopes is the boll-worm moth, a tawny creature who in the summer and autumn evenings hovers over the cotton-blooms and deposits a single egg in each flower. In three or four days this egg is hatched and out of it comes a worm who voraciously eats his way into the centre of the boll, and then, ere it falls to the ground, seeks another, in which he in like manner buries himself. In Central Alabama, in 1873, we were told that plantations were so devastated by worms that they seemed as if lightning had passed over them and scathed them. The bolls were, in many cases, cut down for entire acres as completely as if the reaper's sickle had been thrust into them.

During the picking season in the States of North and South Carolina, Georgia, Northern Florida, Louisiana, Alabama, and Mississippi, the southern half of Arkansas and the eastern half of Texas, plantation life is busy and merry. If the planter has made a good crop, he calls in multitudes of negroes from the surrounding country to help him pick. These laborers sometimes wander from plantation to plantation, like the hop-pickers in the West; but where labor is not scarce, an extra force for a few days is all that is required.

By the middle of October the season is at its height. Each person is expected to pick two or three hundred pounds of cotton daily, and as fast as the fleeces are picked they are carried either in wagons or in baskets, on the heads of negroes, to the gin-house. There, if the cotton is damp, it is dried in the sun, and then the fibre is separated from the seed, to which it is quite firmly attached.

Nothing can be simpler or more effective than the machinery of the ordinary Whitney cotton-gin. Its main cylinder, upon which is set a series of circular saws, is brought into contact with a mass of cotton separated from the cylinder by steel bars or gratings. The teeth of the saws, playing between these bars, catch the cotton and draw it through, leaving the seeds behind. Underneath the saws a set of stiff brushes, revolving on another cylinder moving in an opposite direction, brushes off from the saw-teeth the lint which was taken from the seed, and a revolving fan, producing a rapid current of air, throws the light lint to a convenient distance from the gin. The ginning of sea-island cotton is practiced in South Carolina and Georgia, and requires the use of two fluted rollers, commonly made of wood, but sometimes of vulcanized rubber or steel, placed parallel in a frame which keeps them almost in contact. These rollers revolve in opposite directions, and draw the cotton between them, while the seeds, owing to the lack of space, do not pass through.

Horse power is ordinarily used on small plantations in ginning cotton, while the great planters employ steam. But now a host of enterprising individuals have set up gin-houses in neighborhoods central to many plantations, and to them flock the many whites and blacks who cultivate one or two acres in cotton. The gins in these houses are usually run by steam, and many a man has made a small fortune in two or three years since the war by preparing the cotton brought to him from the country round about. Fires are frequent in these gin-houses, and sometimes the freedmen revenge themselves upon their ex-masters by sending their expensive machinery heavenward in a blaze. Such malice as this, however, is not common, although there are some instances of planters who have lost many thousands of dollars by the torch of the incendiary.

After the cotton leaves the gin it passes to the press, where it is packed into bales. On small plantations these presses are worked by hand or by horse power, while on the great and finer ones hydraulic presses are common. On well-ordered lands the picking is, of course, over before Christmas, and the planters and laborers alike give themselves up to the jollity of holidays; but, as I have already mentioned, the sight of acres of unpicked cotton in January and February in some parts of the South is not at all uncommon. It is the most effectual proof of the complete disorganization of the labor system.

One of the peculiar vexations which the planter suffers is the constant stealing of cotton by the negroes during picking time. They manage to abstract it in petty quantities; and after having accumulated a little stock, they take it, if they live in the vicinity of a city, to what is known as a "dead fall house," where a clever "fence," or receiver of stolen goods, buys unquestioningly whatever they bring. If they live in some remote section, they boldly carry the cotton to the local merchant, who receives it in barter, very likely before the eyes of the planter from whom it was stolen, and who knows that he has no practical redress. Most of the negroes on the plantation have not the strong sense of honor which should lead them to consider their employers' interests as their own, and many of the merchants encourage them in their thievish propensities.

Sixty-five miles below Natchez the Red river empties into the Mississippi. The recent improvements made by the General Government upon this river, under the direction of the Board of Engineers, in the removal of the raft of drift-wood, have given it new commercial possibilities. The raft, which was thirty miles long, had, for many years, rendered navigation north of Shreveport impossible. The river runs through one of the finest cotton regions in the country, and, in its ample and fertile valley, immense quantities of cotton and sugar, grain and tobacco will, in future, be produced. Not only Louisiana, but Arkansas and Texas, have been directly benefited by the improvement of the stream.

(1875)

FREDERICK LAW OLMSTED

The Cotton Kingdom:
A Traveller's Observations on Cotton and Slavery in the American Slave States

The city of Raleigh (old Sir Walter), the capital of North Carolina, is a pleasing town—the streets wide, and lined with trees, and many white wooden mansions, all having little court-yards of flowers and shrubbery around them. The State-house is, in every way, a noble building, constructed of brownish-gray granite, in Grecian style. It stands on an elevated position, near the centre of the city, in a square field, which is shaded by some tall old oaks, and could easily be made into an appropriate and beautiful little park; but which, with singular negligence, or more singular economy (while $500,000 has been spent upon the simple edifice), remains in a rude state of undressed nature, and is used as a hog-pasture. A trifle of the expense, employed with doubtful advantage, to give a smooth exterior face to the blocks of stone, if laid out in grading, smoothing, and dressing its ground base, would have added indescribably to the beauty of the edifice. An architect should always begin his work upon the ground.

It is hard to admire what is common; and it is, perhaps, asking too much of the citizens of Raleigh, that they should plant for ornament, or even cause to be retained about such institutions as their Lunatic Asylum, the beautiful evergreens that crowd about the town; but can any man walk from the Capitol oaks to the pine grove, a little beyond the Deaf and Dumb Institution, and say that he would not far rather have the latter than the former to curtain in his habitation? If he can in summer, let him try it again, as I did, in a soft winter's day, when the evergreens fill the air with a balsamic odour, and the green light comes quivering through them, and the foot falls silently upon the elastic carpet they have spread, deluding one with all the feelings of spring.

The country, for miles about Raleigh, is nearly all pine forest, unfertile, and so little cultivated, that it is a mystery how a town of 2,500 inhabitants can obtain sufficient supplies from it to exist.

The public-house at which I stayed was, however, not only well supplied, but was excellently well kept, for a house of its class, in all other respects. The landlord superintended his business personally, and was always attentive and obliging to his guests; and the servants were sufficiently numerous, intelligent, and well instructed.

Though I had no acquaintances in Raleigh, I remained, finding myself in such good quarters, several days. I think the house was called "The Burlinghame."

After this stay, rendered also partly necessary for the repair of damages to my clothing and baggage on the Weldon stage, I engaged a seat one day on the coach, advertised to leave at nine o'clock for Fayetteville. At half-past nine, tired of waiting for its departure, I told the agent, as it was not ready to start, I would walk on a bit, and let them pick me up. I found a rough road—for several miles a clayey surface and much water—and was obliged to pick my way a good deal through the woods on either side. Stopping frequently, when I came to cultivated land, to examine the soil and the appearance of the stubble of the maize—the only crop—in three different fields I made five measurements at random, of fifty feet each, and found the stalks had stood, on an average, five feet by two feet one inch apart, and that, generally, they were not over an inch in diameter at the butt. In one old-field, in process of clearing for new cultivation, I examined a most absurd little plough, with a share not more than six inches in depth, and eight in length on the sole, fastened by a socket to a stake, to which was fitted a short beam and stilts. It was drawn by one mule, and its work among the stumps could only be called scratching. A farmer told me that he considered twenty-five bushels of corn a large crop, and that he generally got only as much as fifteen. He said that no money was to be got by raising corn, and very few farmers here "made" any more than they needed for their own force. It cost too much to get it to market, and yet sometimes they had to buy corn at a dollar a bushel, and waggon it home from Raleigh, or further, enough not having been raised in the country for home consumption. Cotton was the only crop they got any money for. I, nevertheless, did not see a single cotton-field during the day. He said that the largest crop of corn that he knew of, reckoned to be fifty bushels to the acre, had been raised on some reclaimed swamp, while it was still so wet that horses would mire on it all the summer, and most of it had been tended entirely with hoes.

After walking a few miles, the country became more flat, and was covered with old forests of yellow pine, and, at nine miles south of Raleigh, there were occasionally young long-leaved pines; exceedingly beautiful they are while young, the colour being more agreeable than that of any other pine, and the leaves, or "straw," as its foliage is called here, long, graceful, and lustrous. As the tree gets older, it becomes of stiffer character and darker colour.

I do not think I passed, in ten miles, more than half a dozen homesteads, and of these but one was at all above the character of a hut or cabin. The same remarkable appearance of listlessness, which I had noticed so often in Virginia, characterized the men who stood leaning against the logs of the hovels. They blinked at me as I passed, as if unable to withdraw their hands from their pockets to shade their eyes. Every dwelling sent its pack of curs to meet me, and as often as they opened cry, a woman, with a pipe in her mouth, would come to the door and call them off; the men and boys blinking on in rest and silence.

A little after one o'clock I reached "Banks's," a plantation where the stage horses are changed, eleven miles from Raleigh. Here I waited nearly an hour, till the coach arrived, when, fresh horses having been put on, I took an outside seat.

"There ain't a man in North Car'lina could drive them horses up the hills without a whip," said the driver. "You ought to get yesef a whip, massa," said one of the negroes. "Durnation! Think I'm going to buy whips! the best whip in North Car'lina wouldn't last a week on this road." "Dat's a fac—dat ar is a fac; but look yeah, massa, ye let me hab yer stick, and I'll make a whip for ye; ye nebber can make Bawley go widout it, no how." The stick was a sapling rod, of which two or three lay on the coach top; the negro fastened a long leather thong to it. "Dah! ye can fetch old Bawley wi' dat." "Bawley" had been tackled in as the leader of the "spike team;" but, upon attempting to start, it was found that he couldn't be driven in that way at all, and the driver took him out and put him to the pole, within reach of the butt of his stick, and another horse was put on the lead.

One negro now took the leader by the head, and applied a stick lustily to his flanks; another, at the near wheeler, did the same; and the driver belaboured Bawley from the box. But as soon as they began to move forward, and the negro let go the leader's head, he would face about. After this had been repeated many times, a new plan of operations was arranged that proved successful. Leaving the two wheelers to the care of the negroes, the driver was enabled to give all his attention to the leader. When the wheelers started, of course he was struck by the pole, upon which he would turn tail and start for the stable. The negroes kept the wheelers from following him, and the driver with his stick, and another negro with the bough of a tree, thrashed his face; he would then turn again, and, being hit by the pole, start ahead. So, after ten minutes of fearful outcry, we got off.

"How far is it to Mrs. Barclay's?" a passenger had asked. "Thirteen miles," answered a negro; "but I tell 'ou, massa, dais a heap to be said and talk 'bout 'fore 'ou see Missy Barclay's wid dem hosses." There was, indeed.

"Bawley—*you!* Bawley—Bawley! wha' 'bout?—ah!"

"*Rock!* wha' you doin'?—(durned sick horse—an't fit to be in a stage, nohow)."

"Bawley! you! g'up!"

"Oh! you dod-rotted Bob—*Bob!*—(he don't draw a pound, and he an't a gwine to)—*you*, Bob!—(well, he can't stop, can he, as long as the wheelers keep movin'?) Bob! I'll break yer legs, you don't git out the way."

"Oh, Bawley!—(no business to put such a lame hoss into the stage.) Blamnation, Bawley! Now, if you stop, I'll kill you."

"Wha' 'bout, Rock? Dod burn that Rock! You stop if you dare! (I'll be durned to Hux if that 'ere hoss arn't all used up.)"

"You, *Bob!* get out de way, or I'll be — —."

"Oh! d'rot yer soul, Bawley—y're gwine to stop! G'up! G'up! *Rock!* You all-fired ole villain! Wha' 'bout? (If they jus' git to stoppin', all hell couldn't git the mails through to-night.)"

After about three miles of this, they did stop. The driver threw the reins down in despair. After looking at the wheels, and seeing that we were on a good piece of road, nothing unusual to hinder progress, he put his hands in his pockets, and sat quietly a minute, and then began, in a business-like manner, to swear, no longer confining himself to the peculiar idiomatic profanity of the country, but using real, outright, old-fashioned, uncompromising English oaths, as loud as he could yell. Then he stopped, and after another pause, began to talk quietly to the horses:

"You, Bob, you won't draw? Didn't you git enough last night?" (I jabbed my knife into his face twice when we got into that fix last night;" and the wounds on the horse's head showed that he spoke the truth.) "I swar, Bob, if I have to come down thar, I'll cut your throat."

He stopped again, and then sat down on the foot-board and began to beat the wheelers as hard and as rapidly as possible with the butt of his stick. They started, and, striking Bob with the pole, he jumped and turned round; but a happy stroke on "the raw" in his face brought him to his place; and the stick being applied just in time to the wheelers, he caught the pole and jumped ahead. We were off again.

"Turned over in that 'ere mire hold last night," said the driver. "Couldn't do anythin' with 'em—passengers camped out—thar's were they had their fire, under that tree; didn't get to Raleigh till nine o'clock this mornin'. That's the reason I wern't along after you any sooner—hadn't got my breakfast; that's the reason the hosses don't draw no better to-day, too, I s'pose. *You*, Rock!—*Bawley!*—Bob!"

After two miles more, the horses stopped once more. The driver now quietly took the leader off (he had never drawn at all), and tied him behind the coach. He then began beating the near wheeler, a passenger did the same to Bawley—both standing on the ground—while I threw off my overcoat and walked on. For a time I could occasionally hear the cry, "Bawl—Rock!" and I knew that the coach was moving again; gradually I outwalked the sound.

The road was a mere opening through a forest of the long-leafed pine; the trees from eight to eighteen inches in diameter, with straight trunks bare for nearly thirty feet and their evergreen foliage forming a dense dark canopy at that height, the surface of the ground undulating with long swells, occasionally low and wet. In the latter case, there was generally a mingling of deciduous trees and a watercourse crossing the road, with a thicket of shrubs. The soil sandy, with occasionally veins of clay; the latter more commonly in the low ground, or in the descent to it. Very little grass, herbage, or underwood; and the ground covered, except in the road, with the fallen pine-leaves. Every tree, on one, two, or three sides, was scarified for turpentine. In ten miles, I passed half a dozen cabins, one or two small clearings, in which corn had been planted, and one turpentine distillery, with a dozen sheds and cabins clustered about it.

In about an hour after I left the coach, the driver, mounted on Bob, overtook me; he was going to get fresh horses.

After dark, I had some difficulty in keeping the road, there being frequent forks, and my only guide the telegraph wire. I had to cross three or four brooks, which were now high, and had sometimes floated off the logs which, in this country are commonly placed, for the teamsters, along the side of the road, where it runs through water. I could generally jump from stump to stump; and, by wading a little at the edges in my staunch Scotch shooting-boots, get across dry-shod. Where, however, the water was too deep, I always found, by going up or down stream, a short way, a fallen trunk across it, by which I got over.

I met the driver returning with two fresh horses; and at length, before eight o'clock, reached a long one-story cabin, which I found to be Mrs. Barclay's. It was right cheerful and comforting to open the door, from the dark, damp, chilly night, into a large room, filled with blazing light from a great fire of turpentine pine, by which two stalwart men were reading newspapers, a door opening into a background of supper-table and kitchen, and a nice, stout, kindly-looking, Quaker-like old lady coming forward to welcome me.

As soon as I was warm, I was taken out to supper: seven preparations of swine's flesh, two of maize, wheat cakes, broiled quails, cold roast turkey, coffee, and tea.

My bed-room was a house by itself, the only connection between it and the main building being a platform, or gallery, in front. A great fire burned here also in a board fire-place; a stuffed easy-chair had been placed before it, and a tub of hot water, which I had not thought to ask for, to bathe my weary feet.

And this was a piny woods stage-house! But genius will find its development, no matter where its lot is cast; and there is as much genius for inn-keeping as for poetry. Mrs. Barclay is a Burns in her way, and with even more modesty; for, after twenty-four hours of the best entertainment that could be asked for, I was only charged one dollar. I paid two dollars for my stage-coach privileges—to wit, riding five miles and walking twenty-one.

At three o'clock in the morning, the three gentlemen that I had left ten miles back at four o'clock the previous day, were dragged, shivering in the stage-coach, to the door. They had had no meal since breakfasting at Raleigh; and one of them was now so tired that he could not eat, but dropt prone on the floor before the fire and slept the half-hour they were changing horses, or rather resting horses, for no relay was left.

I afterwards met one of the company in Fayetteville. Their night's adventure after I left them, and the continued cruelty to the horses, were most distressing. The driver once got off the box, and struck the poor, miserable, sick "Rock" with a rail, and actually knocked him down in the road. At another time, after having gotten fresh horses, when they, too, were "stalled," he took them out of the harness and turned them loose, and, refusing to give any answer to the inquiries of the passengers, looked about for a dry place, and laid down and went to sleep on the ground. One of the passengers had then walked on to Mrs. Barclay's, and obtained a pair of mules, with which the coach was finally brought to the house. The remainder kindled a fire, and tried to rest themselves by it. They were sixteen hours in coming thirty miles, suffering much from cold, and without food.

The next day I spent in visiting the turpentine and rosin works, piny-wood farms, etc., under the obliging guidance of Mrs. Barclay's son-in-law, and in the evening again took the coach. The horses were better than on the previous stage: upon my remarking this to the driver, he said that the reason was, that they took care of this team themselves (the drivers); on the last stage the horses were left to negroes, who would not feed them regularly, nor take any decent care of them. "Why, what do you think?" said he; "when I got to Banks's, this morning, I found my team hadn't been fed all day; they hadn't been rubbed nor cleaned, nary durned thing done to 'em, and thar the cussed darkey was, fast asleep. Reckon I didn't gin him a wakin' up!"

"You don't mean the horses that you drove up?"

"Yes, I do, and they hadn't a cussed thing to eat till they got back to Barclay's!"

"How was it possible for you to drive them back?"

"Why I don't suppose I could ha' done it if I'd had any passengers: (you *Suze!*)

shall lose a mail again to-night, if this mare don't travel better, (durn ye, yer ugly, I believe). She's a good mare—a heap of go in her, but it takes right smart of work to get it out. *Suze!"*

So we toiled on, with incessant shouting, and many strange piny-woods oaths, and horrid belabouring of the poor horses' backs, with the butt-end of a hickory whip-stalk, till I really thought their spinal columns must break. The country, the same undulating pine forest, the track tortuous among the trees, which frequently stood so close that it required some care to work between them. Often we made detours from the original road, to avoid a fallen tree, or a mire-hole, and all the time we were bouncing over protruding roots and small stumps. There was but little mud, the soil being sand, but now and then a deep slough. In one of these we found a waggon, heavily laden, stuck fast, and six mules and five negroes tugging at it. With our help it was got out of the way, and we passed on. Soon afterwards we met the return coach, apparently in a similar predicament; but one of the passengers, whom I questioned, replied: "No, not stalled, exactly, but somehow *the horses won't draw.* We have been more than three hours coming about four miles."

"How is it you have so many balky horses?" I asked the driver.

"The old man buys 'em up cheap, 'cause nobody else can do anything else with 'em."

"I should not think you could do much with them, either—except to kill them."

"Well, that's what the old man says he buys 'em for. He was blowing me up for losing the mail t'other night; I told him, says I, 'You have to a'most kill them horses, 'fore you can make 'em draw a bit,' says I. 'Kill 'em, damn 'em, kill 'em, then; that's what I buy 'em for,' says he. 'I buy 'em a purpose to kill; that's all they are good for, ain't it?' says he. 'Don't s'pose they're going to last for ever, do ye?' says he."

We stopped once, nearly half an hour, for some unexplained reason, before a house on the road. The door of the house was open, an enormous fire was burning in it, and, at the suggestion of the driver, I went in to warm myself. It was a large log-cabin, of two rooms, with beds in each room, and with an apartment overhead, to which access was had by a ladder. Among the inmates were two women; one of them sat in the chimney-corner smoking a pipe, and rocking a cradle; the other sat directly before the fire, and full ten feet distant. She was apparently young, but her face was as dry and impassive as a dead man's. She was doing nothing, and said but little; but, once in about a minute, would suddenly throw up her chin, and spit with perfect precision into the hottest embers of the fire. The furniture of the house was more scanty and rude than I ever saw before in any house, with women living in it, in the United States. Yet these people were not so poor but that they had a negro woman cutting and bringing wood for their fire.

It must be remembered that this is a long-settled country, having been occupied by Anglo-Saxons as early as any part of the Free States, and that it is the main road between the capital of North Carolina and its chief sea-port.

There is nothing that is more closely connected, both as cause and effect, with the prosperity and wealth of a country, than its means and modes of travelling, and of transportation of the necessities and luxuries of life. I saw this day, as I shall hereafter describe, three thousand barrels of resin, worth a dollar and a half a barrel in New

York, thrown away, a mere heap of useless offal, because it would cost more to transport it than it would be worth. There was a single waggon, with a ton or two of sugar, and flour, and tea, and axes, and cotton cloths, unable to move, with six mules, and five negroes at work upon it. Raleigh is a large distributing post-office, getting a very heavy mail from the North; here was all that is sent by one of its main radii, travelling one day two miles an hour, the next four miles, and on each occasion failing to connect with the conveyances which we pay to scatter further the intelligence and wealth transmitted by it. Barbarous is too mild a term to apply to the manner in which even this was done. The improvidence, if not the cruelty, no sensible barbarian could have been guilty of.

Afterwards, merely to satisfy my mind (for there is a satisfaction in seeing even scoundrelism consistently carried out, if attempted at all in a business), I called on the agent of the line at Fayetteville, stated the case, and asked if any part of what I had paid for my passage would be returned me, on account of the disappointment and delay which I had suffered from the inability of the proprietor to carry out his contract with me. The impudence of the suggestion, of course, only created amusement; and I was smilingly informed that the business was not so "lucky" that the proprietor could afford to pay back money that he had once got into his hands. What I had seen was regarded by no one, apparently, as at all unusual.

At one of the stations for changing horses, an old coloured man was taken into the coach. I ascertained from him that he was a blacksmith, and had been up the line to shoe the horses at the different stables. Probably he belonged (poor fellow!) to the man who bought horses to be killed in doing his work. After answering my inquiries, he lay down in the bottom of the coach, and slept until we reached Fayetteville. The next time we changed, the new driver inquired of the old one what passengers he had. "Only one gentleman, and old man Ned."

"Oh! is old man along—that's good—if we should turn over, or break down, or anything, reckon he could nigh about pray us up—he's right smart at prayin'."

"Well, I tell you, now, ole man can trot out as smart a prayer, when he's a mind to go in for't, as any man I ever heerd, durned if he can't."

The last ten miles we came over rapidly, smoothly, and quietly, by a plank-road, reaching Fayetteville about twelve, of a fine, clear, frosty night.

Entering the office or bar-room of the stage-house, at which I had been advised to stay while in Fayetteville, I found it occupied by a group of old soakers, among whom was one of perhaps sixteen years of age. This lad, without removing the cigar which he had in his mouth, went to the bar, whither I followed him, and, without saying a word, placed an empty tumbler before me.

"I don't wish anything to drink," said I; "I am cold and tired, and I would like to go to a room. I intend to stay here some days, and I should be glad if you could give me a private room with a fire in it."

"Room with a fire in it?" he inquired, as he handed me the registry-book.

"Yes; and I will thank you to have it made immediately, and let my baggage be taken up."

He closed the book, after I had written my name, and returned to his seat at the stove, leaving me standing, and immediately engaged in conversation, without paying attention to my request. I waited some time, during which a negro came into the room, and went out again. I then repeated my request, necessarily aloud, and in such a way as to be understood, not only by the boy, but by all the company. Immediately all conversation ceased, and every head was turned to look at me. The lad paused a moment, spit upon the stove, and then—

"Want a room to yourself?"

"Yes, if convenient."

No answer and no movement, all the company staring at me as if at a detected burglar.

"Perhaps you can't accommodate me?"

"Want a fire made in your room?"

"Why, yes, if convenient; but I should like to go to my room, at any rate; I am very tired."

After puffing and spitting for a moment, he rose and pulled a bell; then took his seat again. In about five minutes a negro came in, and during all this time there was silence.

"What'll you drink, Baker?" said the lad, rising and going to the bar, and taking no notice of the negro's entrance. A boozy man followed him, and made some reply; the lad turned out two glasses of spirits, added water to one, and drank it in a gulp.[1]

"Can this boy show me to my room?" I asked.

"Anybody in number eleven Peter?"

"Not as I knows on, sar."

"Take this man's baggage up there."

I followed the negro up to number eleven, which was a large back room in the upper story, with four beds in it.

"Peter?" said I, "I want a fire made here."

"Want a fire, sar?"

"Yes, I want you to make a fire."

"Want a fire, master, this time o' night?"

"Why, yes; I want a fire. Where are you going with the lamp?"

"Want a lamp, massa?"

"Want a lamp? Certainly, I do."

After about ten minutes, I heard a man splitting wood in the yard, and, in ten more, Peter brought in three sticks of green wood, and some chips; then, the little bed-lamp having burned out, he went into an adjoining room, where I heard him talking to some one, evidently awakened by his entrance to get a match; that failing, he went for another. By one o'clock, my fire was made.

"Peter," said I, "are you going to wait on me, while I stay here?"

"Yes, sar; I 'tends to dis room."

"Very well; take this, and, when I leave, I'll give you another, if you take good care of me. Now, I want you to get me some water."

"I'll get you some water in de morning, sar."

[1] The mother of this young man remonstrated with a friend of mine, for permitting his son to join a company of civil engineers, engaged, at the time, in surveying a route for a road—he would be subject to fatiguing labour, and so much exposure to the elements; and congratulated herself that her own child was engaged in such an easy and gentleman-like employment as that of hotel-clerk and bar keeper.

"I want some to-night—some water and some towels; don't you think you can get them for me?"

"I reckon so, massa, if you wants 'em. Want 'em 'fore you go to bed?"

"Yes; and get another lamp."

"Want a lamp?"

"Yes, of course."

"Won't the fire do you?"

"No; bring a lamp. That one won't burn without filling; you need not try it."

The water and the lamp came, after a long time.

In the morning, early, I was awakened by a knock at the door.

"Who's there?"

"Me, massa; I wants your boots to black."

I got up, opened the door, and returned to bed. Falling asleep, I was soon again awakened by Peter throwing down an armful of wood upon the floor. Slept again, and was again awakened, by Peter's throwing up the window, to empty out the contents of the wash bowl, etc. The room was filled with smoke of the fat light wood: Peter had already made a fire for me to dress by; but I again fell asleep, and, when I next awoke, the breakfast bell was ringing. Peter had gone off, and left the window and door open, and the fire had burned out. My boots had been taken away, and the bell-wire was broken. I dressed, and walking to the bar-room, asked the bar-keeper—a complaisant, full-grown man—for my boots. He did not know where they were, and rang the bell for Peter. Peter came, was reprimanded for his forgetfulness, and departed. Ten minutes elapsed, and he did not return. I again requested that he should be called; and this time he brought my boots. He had had to stop to black them; having, he said, been too busy to do it before breakfast.

The following evening, as it grew too cold to write in my room, I went down, and found Peter, and told him I wanted a fire again, and that he might get me a couple of candles. When he came up, he brought one of the little bed-lamps, with a capacity of oil for fifteen minutes' use. I sent him down again to the office, with a request to the proprietor that I might be furnished with candles. He returned, and reported that there were no candles in the house.

"Then, get me a larger lamp."

"Aint no larger lamps, nuther, sar;—none to spare."

"Then go out, and see if you can't buy me some candles somewhere."

"Aint no stores open, Sunday, massa, and I don't know where I can buy 'em."

"Then go down, and tell the bar-keeper, with my compliments, that I wish to write in my room, and I would be obliged to him if he would send me a light of some sort; something that will last longer, and give more light, than those little lamps."

"He won't give you none, massa—not if you hab a fire. Can't you see by da light of da fire? When a gentleman hab a fire in his room, dey don't count he wants no more light 'n dat."

"Well, make the fire, and I'll go down and see about it."

As I reached the foot of the stairs, the bell rang, and I went in to tea. The tea table was moderately well lighted with candles. I waited till the company had generally left it, and then said to one of the waiters—

"Here are two dimes: I want you to bring me, as soon as you can, two of these candles to number eleven; do you understand?"

"Yes, sar; I'll fetch 'em, sar."

And he did.

About eight o'clock, there was an alarm of fire. Going into the street, I was surprised to observe how leisurely the people were walking toward the house in flames, standing very prominently, as it did, upon a hill, at one end of the town. As I passed a church, the congregation was coming out; but very few quickened their step above a strolling pace. Arrived near the house, I was still more astonished to see how few, of the crowd assembled, were occupied in restraining the progress of the fire, or in saving the furniture, and at the prevailing stupidity, confusion, and want of system and concert of action in the labour for this purpose. A large majority of those engaged were negroes. As I returned toward the hotel, a gentleman, walking, with a lady, before me, on the side walk, accosted a negro whom he met:

"What! Moses! That you? Why were you not here sooner?"

"Why, Mass Richard, I was singing, an' I didn' her de bells and— I see twant in our ward, sar, and so I didn' see as dar was zactly 'casion for me to hurry myself to def. Ef eed a been in our ward, Mass Richard, I'd a rallied, you knows I would. Mose would ha rallied, ef eed a been in our ward—ha! ha! ha!—you knows it, Mass Richard!"

And he passed on, laughing comically, without further reproof.

Fayetteville.—The negroes employed in the turpentine business, to which during the last week I have been giving some examination, seem to me to be unusually intelligent and cheerful, decidedly more so than most of the white people inhabiting the turpentine forest. Among the latter there is a large number, I should think a majority, of entirely uneducated, poverty-stricken vagabonds. I mean by vagabonds, simply, people without habitual, definite occupation or reliable means of livelihood. They are poor, having almost no property but their own bodies; and the use of these, that is, their labour, they are not accustomed to hire out statedly and regularly, so as to obtain capital by wages, but only occasionally by the day or job, when driven to it by necessity. A family of these people will commonly hire, or "squat" and build, a little log cabin, so made that it is only a shelter from rain, the sides not being chinked, and having no more furniture or pretension to comfort than is commonly provided a criminal in the cell of a prison. They will cultivate a little corn, and possibly a few roods of potatoes, cow-peas, and coleworts. They will own a few swine, that find their living in the forest; and pretty certainly, also, a rifle and dogs; and the men, ostensibly, occupy most of their time in hunting. I am, mainly, repeating the statements of one of the turpentine distillers, but it was confirmed by others, and by my own observation, so far as it went.

A gentleman of Fayetteville told me that he had, several times, appraised, under oath, the whole household property of families of this class at less than $20. If they have need of money to purchase clothing, etc., they obtain it by selling their game or meal. If they have none of this to spare, or an insufficiency, they will work for a neighbouring farmer for a few days, and they usually get for their labour fifty cents a day, *finding themselves.* The farmers and distillers say, that they do not like to employ them, because they cannot be relied upon to finish what they undertake, or to work according to directions, and because, being white men, they cannot "drive" them. That is to say, their labour is even more inefficient and unmanageable than that of slaves.

That I have not formed an exaggerated estimate of the proportion of such a class, will appear to the reader more probable from the testimony of a pious colporteur, given before a public meeting in Charleston, in February, 1855. I quote from a Charleston paper's report. The colporteur had been stationed at —— county, N.C.: —"*The larger portion* of the inhabitants seemed to be totally given up to a species of mental hallucination, which carried them captive at its will. They nearly all believed implicitly in witchcraft , and attributed everything that happened, good or bad, to the agency of persons whom they supposed possessed of evil spirits."

The majority of what I have termed turpentine-farmers—meaning the small proprietors of the long-leafed pine forest land—are people but a grade superior, in character or condition, to these vagabonds. They have habitations more like houses— log cabins, commonly, sometimes chinked, oftener not—without windows of glass, but with a few pieces of substantial old-fashioned heir-loom furniture; a vegetable garden, in which, however, you will find no vegetable but what they call "collards" (colewort) for "greens;" fewer dogs, more swine, and larger clearings for maize, but no better crops than the poorer class. Their property is, nevertheless, often of considerable money value, consisting mainly of negroes, who, associating intimately with their masters, are of superior intelligence to the slaves of the wealthier classes.

Some of the larger proprietors, who are also often cotton planters, cultivating the richer low lands, are said to be gentlemen of good estate—intelligent, cultivated, and hospitable.

North Carolina has a proverbial reputation for the ignorance and torpidity of her people; being, in this respect, at the head of the Slave States. I do not find the reason of this in any innate quality of the popular mind; but, rather, in the circumstances under which it finds its development. Owing to the general poverty of the soil in the Eastern part of the State, and to the almost exclusive employment of slave labour on the soils productive of cotton; owing also, to the difficulty and expense of reaching market with bulky produce from the interior and western districts, population and wealth is more divided than in the other Atlantic States; industry is almost entirely rural, and there is but little communication or concert of action among the small and scattered proprietors of capital. For the same reason, the advantages of education are more difficult to be enjoyed, the distance at which families reside apart preventing children from coming together in such numbers as to give remunerative employment to a teacher. The teachers are, generally, totally unfitted for their business; young men, as a clergyman informed me, themselves not only unadvanced beyond the lowest knowledge of the elements of primary school learning, but often coarse, vulgar, and profane in their language and behaviour, who take up teaching as a temporary business, to supply the demand of a neighbourhood of people as ignorant and uncultivated as themselves.

The native white population of North Carolina is	550,267
The whole white population under 20 years, is	301,106
Leaving white adults over 20	249,161
Of these there are natives who cannot read and write	73,226[1]

Being more than one-fourth of the native white adults.

But the aspect of North Carolina with regard to slavery is, in some respects, less lamentable than that of Virginia. There is not only less bigotry upon the subject, and more freedom of conversation, but I saw here, in the institution, more of patriarchal character than in any other State. The slave more frequently appears as a family servant—a member of his master's family, interested with him in his fortune, good or bad. This is a result of the less concentration of wealth in families or individuals, occasioned by the circumstances I have described. Slavery thus loses much of its inhumanity. It is still questionable, however, if, as the subject race approaches civilization, the dominant race is not proportionately detained in its onward progress. One is forced often to question, too, in viewing slavery in this aspect, whether humanity and the accumulation of wealth, the prosperity of the master, and the happiness and improvement of the subject, are not in some degree incompatible.

These later observations are made after having twice again passed through the State, once in a leisurely way on horseback. In some of the Western and Northern central parts of the State, there is much more enterprise, thrift, and comfort than in the Eastern part, where I had my first impressions.

I left Fayetteville in a steamboat (advertised for 8 o'clock, left at 8.45) bound down Cape Fear River to Wilmington. A description of the river, with incidents of the passage, will serve to show the character of most of the navigable streams of the cotton States, flowing into the Atlantic and the Gulf, and of the manner of their navigation.

The water was eighteen feet above its lowest summer stages; the banks steep, thirty feet high from the present water surface—from fifty to one hundred feet apart—and covered with large trees and luxuriant vegetation; the course crooked; the current very rapid; the trees overhanging the banks, and frequently falling into the channel— making the navigation hazardous. The river is subject to very rapid rising. The master told me that he had sometimes left his boat aground at night, and, on returning in the morning, found it floating in twenty-five feet of water, over the same spot. The difference between the extremes of low stages and floods is as much as seventy feet. In summer, there are sometimes but eighteen inches of water on the bars; the boat I was in drew but fourteen inches, light. She was a stern-wheel craft—the boiler and engine (high pressure) being placed at opposite ends, to balance weights. Her burden was three hundred barrels, or sixty tons measurement. This is the character of most of the boats navigating the river—of which there are now twelve. Larger boats are almost useless in summer, from their liability to ground; and even the smaller ones, at low stages of water, carry no freight, but are employed to tow up "flats" or shallow barges. At this season of the year, however, the steamboats are loaded close to the water's edge.

The bulk of our freight was turpentine; and the close proximity of this to the furnaces suggested a danger fully equal to that from snags or grounding. On calling

[1]Official Census Report, pp. 309, 299, 317

the attention of a fellow-passenger to it, he told me that a friend of his was once awakened from sleep, while lying in a berth on one of these boats, by a sudden, confused sound. Thinking the boiler had burst, he drew the bed-clothing over his head, and laid quiet, to avoid breathing the steam; until, feeling the boat ground, he ran out, and discovered that she was on fire near the furnace. Having some valuable freight near by, which he was desirous to save, and seeing no immediate danger, though left alone on the boat, he snatched a bucket, and drawing water from alongside, applied it with such skill and rapidity as soon to quench the flames, and eventually to entirely extinguish the fire. Upon the return of the crew, a few repairs were made, steam was got up again, and the boat proceeded to her destination in safety. He afterwards ascertained that three hundred kegs of gunpowder were stowed beneath the dock that had been on fire—a circumstance which sufficiently accounted for the panic-flight of the crew.

Soon after leaving, we passed the Zephyr, wooding up: an hour later, our own boat was run to the bank, men jumped from her fore and aft, and fastened head and stern lines to the trees, and we also commenced wooding.

The trees had been cut away so as to leave a clear space to the top of the bank, which was some fifty feet from the boat, and moderately steep. Wood, cut, split, and piled in ranks, stood at the top of it, and a chute of plank, two feet wide and thirty long, conveyed it nearly to the water. The crew rushed to the wood-piles—master, passengers, and all, but the engineer and chambermaid, deserting the boat—and the wood was first passed down, as many as could, throwing into the chute, and others forming a line, and tossing it, from one to another, down the bank. From the water's edge it was passed, in the same way, to its place on board, with great rapidity—the crew exciting themselves with yells. They were all blacks, but one.

On a tree, near the top of the bank, a little box was nailed on which a piece of paper was tacked, with this inscription:

> **"Notice**
> to all persons takin wood from this
> landin pleas to leav a ticket payable to
> the subscriber, at $1,75 a cord as
> heretofore. Amos Sikes."

and the master—just before the wood was all on board—hastily filled a blank order (torn from a book, like a checkbook, leaving a memorandum of the amount, etc.) on the owner of the boat for payment, to Mr. Sikes, for two cords of pine-wood, at $1.75, and two cords of light-wood, at $2—and left it in the box. The wood used had been measured in the ranks with a rod, carried for the purpose, by the master, at the moment he reached the bank.

Before, with all possible haste, we had finished wooding, the Zephyr passed us; and, during the rest of the day, she kept out of our sight. As often as we met a steamboat, or passed any flats or rafts, our men were calling out to know how far ahead of us she was; and when the answer came back each time, in an increasing number of miles, they told us that our boat was more than usually sluggish, owing to an uncommonly heavy freight; but still, for some time, they were ready to make bets that we should get first to Wilmington.

Several times we were hailed from the shore, to take on a passenger, or some light freight; and these requests, as long as it was possible, were promptly complied with—the boat being run up, so as to rest her bow upon the bank, and then shouldered off by the men, as if she had been a skiff.

There were but three through-passengers, besides myself. Among them, was a glue-manufacturer, of Baltimore—getting orders from the turpentine-distillers,—and a turpentine-farmer and distiller. The glue-manufacturer said that, in his factory, they had formerly employed slaves; had since used Irishmen, and now employed Germans. Their operations were carried on night and day, and one gang of the men had to relieve another. The slaves they had employed never would be *on hand*, when the hour for relieving came. It was also necessary to be careful that certain operations should be performed at a certain time, and some judgment and watchfulness was necessary, to fix this time; the slaves never could be made to care enough for the matter, to be depended upon for discretion, in this respect; and great injury was frequently done in consequence. Some of the operations were disagreeable, and they would put one another up to thinking and saying that they ought not to be required to do such dirty work—and try to have their owners get them away from it.

Irishmen, he said, worked very well, and to a certain extent faithfully, and, for a time, they liked them very much; but they found that, in about a fortnight, an Irishman always thought he knew more than his master, and would exercise his discretion a little too much, as well as often directly disregard his orders. Irishmen were, he said, *"too* faithful"—that is, self-confident and officious.

At length, at a hurried time, they had employed one or two Germans. The Irishmen, of course, soon quarrelled with them, and threatened to leave, if they were kept. Whereupon, they were, themselves, all discharged, and a full crew of Germans, at much less wages, taken; and they proved excellent hands—steady, plodding, reliable, though they never pretended to know anything, and said nothing about what they could do. They were easily instructed, obeyed orders faithfully, and worked fairly for their wages, without boasting or grumbling.

The turpentine-distiller gave a good account of some of his men; but said he was sure they never performed half as much work as he himself could; and they sometimes would, of their own accord, do twice as much in a day, as could usually be got out of them. He employed a Scotchman at the "still," but he never would have white people at ordinary work, because he couldn't drive them. He added, with the utmost simplicity—and I do not think any one present saw, at the time, how much the remark expressed more than it was intended to—"I never can drive a white man, for I know I could never bear to be driven, myself, by anybody."

The other passenger was "a North of England man," as I suspected from the first words I heard from him—though he had been in this country for about twenty years. He was a mechanic, and employed several slaves; but testified strongly of the expensive character of their labour; and declared, without any reserve, that the system was ruinous in its effects upon the character and value of all classes of working men.

The country on the river-bank was nearly all wooded, with, occasionally, a field of corn, which, even in the low alluvial meadows, sometimes overflowed by the river, and enriched by its deposit, had evidently yielded but a very meagre crop—the stalks standing singly, at great distances, and very small. The greater part, even of these once rich low lands, that had been in cultivation, were now "turned out," and covered either with pines or broom-sedge and brushwood.

At some seventy or eighty miles, I should think, below Fayetteville, the banks became lower, and there was much swamp land, in which the ground was often covered with a confusion of logs and sawn lumber, mingled with other rubbish, left by floods of the river. The standing timber was very large, and many of the trees were hung with the long, waving drapery of the tylandria, or Spanish moss, which, as well as the mistletoe, I here first saw in profusion. There was also a thick network among the trees, of beautiful climbing plants. I observed some very large grape-vines, and many trees of greater size than I ever saw of their species before. I infer that this soil, properly reclaimed, and protected from floods of the river, might be most profitably used in the culture of the various half-tropical trees and shrubs, of whose fruits we now import so large and costly an amount. The fig, I have been informed, grows and bears luxuriantly at Wilmington, seldom or never suffering in its wood, though a crop of fruit may be occasionally injured by a severe late spring frost. The almond, doubtless, would succeed equally well, so also the olive; but of none of these is there the slightest commercial value produced in North Carolina, or in all our country.

In the evening we passed many boats and rafts, blazing with great fires, made upon a thick bed of clay, and their crews singing at their sweeps. Twenty miles above Wilmington, the shores became marshy, the river wide, and the woody screen that had hitherto, in a great degree, hid the nakedness of the land, was withdrawn, leaving open to view only broad, reedy savannahs, on either side.

We reached Wilmington, the port at the mouth of the river, at half-past nine. Taking a carriage, I was driven first to one hotel and afterwards to another. They were both so crowded with guests, and excessive business duties so prevented the clerks from being tolerably civil to me, that I feared if I remained in either of them I should have another Norfolk experience. While I was endeavoring to ascertain if there was a third public-house, in which I might, perhaps, obtain a private room, my eye fell upon an advertisement of a new railroad line of passage to Charleston. A boat, to take passengers to the railroad, was to start every night, from Wilmington, at ten o'clock. It was already something past ten; but being pretty sure that she would not get off punctually, and having a strong resisting impulse to being packed away in a close room, with any chance stranger the clerk of the house might choose to couple me with, I shouldered my baggage and ran for the wharves. At half-past ten I was looking at Wilmington over the stern of another little wheelbarrow-steamboat, pushing back up the river. When or how I was to be taken to Charleston, I had not yet been able to ascertain. The captain assured me it was all right, and demanded twenty dollars. Being in his power I gave it to him, and received in return a pocketful of tickets, guaranteeing the bearer passage from place to place; of not one of which places had I ever heard before, except Charleston.

The cabin was small, dirty, crowded, close, and smoky. Finding a warm spot in the deck, over the furnace, and to leeward of the chimney, I pillowed myself on my luggage and went to sleep.

The ringing of the boat's bell awoke me, after no great lapse of time, and I found we were in a small creek, heading southward. Presently we reached a wharf, near which stood a locomotive and train. A long, narrow plank having been run out, half a dozen white men, including myself, went on shore. Then followed as many negroes, who appeared to be a recent purchase of their owner. Owing, probably, to an unusually low tide, there was a steep ascent from the boat to the wharf, and I was amused to see the anxiety of this gentleman for the safe landing of his property, and especially to hear him curse them for their carelessness, as if their lives were of much greater value to him than to themselves. One was a woman. All carried over their shoulders some little baggage, probably all their personal effects, slung in a blanket; and one had a dog, whose safe landing caused him nearly as much anxiety as his own did *his* owner.

"Gib me da dog now," said the dog's owner, standing half way up the plank.

"Damn the dog," said the negro's owner; "give me your hand up here. Let go of the dog; d'ye hear! Let him take care of himself."

But the negro hugged the dog, and brought him safely on shore.

After a short delay the train started: the single passenger car was a fine one (made at Wilmington, Delaware), and just sufficiently warmed. I should have slept again if it had not been that two of the six inmates were drunk—one of them uproariously.

Passing through long stretches of cypress swamps, with occasional intervals of either pine-barrens, or clear water ponds, in about two hours we came, in the midst of the woods, to the end of the rails. In the vicinity could be seen a small tent, a shanty of loose boards, and a large, subdued fire, around which, upon the ground, a considerable number of men were stretched out asleep. This was the camp of the hands engaged in laying the rails, and who were thus daily extending the distance which the locomotive could run.

The conductor told me that there was here a break of about eighty miles in the rail, over which I should be transferred by a stage coach, which would come as soon as possible after the driver knew that the train had arrived. To inform him of this, the locomotive trumpeted loud and long.

The negro property, which had been brought up in a freight car, was immediately let out on the stoppage of the train. As it stepped on to the platform, the owner asked, "Are you all here?"

"Yes, massa, we is all heah," answered one. "Do dysef no harm, for we's all heah," added another, in an undertone.

The negroes immediately gathered some wood, and taking a brand from the railroad hands, made a fire for themselves; then, all but the woman, opening their bundles, wrapped themselves in their blankets and went to sleep. The woman, bareheaded, and very inadequately clothed as she was, stood for a long time alone, erect and statue-like, her head bowed, gazing in the fire. She had taken no part in the light chat of the others, and had given them no assistance in making the fire. Her dress too was not the usual plantation apparel. It was all sadly suggestive.

The principal other freight of the train was one hundred and twenty bales of Northern hay. It belonged, as the conductor told me, to a planter who lived some twenty miles beyond here, and who had bought it in Wilmington at a dollar and a half a hundred weight, to feed his mules. Including the steamboat and railroad freight, and all the labour of getting it to his stables, its entire cost to him would not be much less than two dollars a hundred, or at least four times as much as it would have cost to raise and make it in the interior of New York or New England. There are not only several forage crops which can be raised in South Carolina, that cannot be grown on account of the severity of the winter in the Free States, but, on a farm near Fayetteville, a few days before, I had seen a crop of natural grass growing in half-cultivated land, dead upon the ground; which, I think, would have made, if it had been cut and well treated in the summer, three tons of hay to the acre. The owner of the land said that there was no better hay than it would have made, but he hadn't had time to attend to it. He had as much as his hands could do of other work at the period of the year when it should have been made.

Probably the case was similar with the planter who had bought this Northern hay at a price four times that which it would have cost a Northern farmer to make it. He had preferred to employ his slaves at other business.

The inference must be, either that there was most improbably-foolish, bad management, or that the slaves were more profitably employed in cultivating cotton, than they could have been in cultivating maize, or other forage crops.

I put the case, some days afterwards, to an English merchant, who had had good opportunities, and made it a part of his business to study such matters.

"I have no doubt," said he, "that if hay cannot be obtained here, other valuable forage can, with less labour than anywhere at the North; and all the Southern agricultural journals sustain this opinion, and declare it to be purely bad management that neglects these crops, and devotes labour to cotton so exclusively. Probably, it is so—at the present cost of forage. Nevertheless, the fact is also true, as the planters assert, that they cannot afford to apply their labour to anything else but cotton. And yet, they complain that the price of cotton is so low that there is no profit in growing it, which is evidently false. You see that they prefer buying hay to raising it at, to say the least, three times what it costs your Northern farmers to raise it. Of course, if cotton could be grown in New York and Ohio, it could be afforded at one-third the cost it is here—say at three cents per pound. And that is my solution of the slavery question. Bring cotton down to three cents a pound, and there would be more abolitionists in South Carolina than in Massachusetts. If that can be brought about, in any way—and it is not impossible that we may live to see it, as our railways are extended in India, and the French enlarge their free-labour plantations in Algiers—there will be an end of slavery."

It was just one o'clock when the stage-coach came for us. There was but one passenger beside myself—a Philadelphia gentleman, going to Columbia. We proceeded very slowly for about three miles, across a swamp, upon a "corduroy road," then more rapidly, over rough ground, being tossed about in the coach most severely, for six or eight miles further. Besides the driver, there was on the box the agent or superintendent of the coach line, who now opened the doors, and we found ourselves before a log stable, in the midst of a forest of large pines. The driver took out a horse, and, mounting him, rode off, and we collected wood, splitting it with a hatchet that was carried on the coach, and, lighting it from the coach lamp, made a fire. It was very cold, ice half an inch thick, and a heavy hoar frost. We complained to the agent that there was no straw in the coach bottom, while there were large holes bored in it, that kept our feet excessively cold. He said there was no straw to be had in the country. They were obliged to bed their horses with pine leaves, which were damp, and would be of no service to us. The necessity for the holes he did not immediately explain, and we, in the exercise of our Yankee privilege, resolved that they were made with reference to the habit of expectoration, which we had observed in the car to be very general and excessive.

In about half an hour the driver of the new stage came to us on the horse that the first had ridden away. A new set of horses was brought out and attached to the coach, and we were driven on again. An hour later, the sun rose; we were still in pine-barrens, once in several miles passing through a clearing, with a log farm-house, and a few negro huts about it; often through cypress swamps, and long pools of water. At the end of ten miles we breakfasted, and changed horses and drivers at a steam saw-mill. A few miles further on, we were asked to get on the top of the coach, while it was driven through a swamp, in which the water was over the road, for a quarter of a mile, to such a depth that it covered the foot-board. The horses really groaned, as they pushed the thin ice away with their necks, and were very near swimming. The holes in the coach bottom, the agent now told us, were to allow the water that would here enter the body to flow out. At the end of these ten miles we changed again, at a cotton planter's house—a very neat, well-built house, having pine trees about it, but very poor, old, negro quarters.

Since the long ford, we had kept the top, the inside of the coach being wet, and I had been greatly pleased with the driving—the coachman, a steady-going sort of a fellow, saying but little to his horses, and doing what swearing he thought necessary in English; driving, too, with great judgment and skill. The coach was a fine, roomy, old-fashioned, fragrant, leathery affair, and the horses the best I had seen this side of Virginia. I could not resist expressing my pleasure with the whole establishment. The new team was admirable; four sleek, well-governed, eager, sorrel cobs, and the driver, a staid, bronzed-faced man, keeping them tight in hand, drove quietly and neatly, his whip in the socket. After about fifteen minutes, during which he had been engaged in hushing down their too great impetuosity, he took out a large silver hunting-watch, and asked what time it was.

"Quarter past eleven," said the agent.

"Twelve minutes past," said the Philadelphian.

"Well, fourteen, only, I am," said the agent.

"Thirteen," said I.

"Just thirteen, I am," said the driver, slipping back his watch to its place, and then, to the agent, "ha'an't touched a hand of her since I left old Lancaster."

Suddenly guessing the meaning of what had been for some time astonishing me—
"You are from the North?" I asked.

"Yes, sir."

"And you, too, Mr. Agent?"

"Yes, sir."

"And the coach, and the cattle, and all?"

"All from Pennsylvania."

"How long have you been here?"

"We have been here about a fortnight, stocking the road. We commenced regular trips yesterday. You are the first passenger through, sir."

It was, in fact, merely a transfer from one of the old National Road lines, complete. After a little further conversation, I asked, "How do you like the country, here?"

"Very nice country," said the agent.

"It's the cussedest poor country God ever created," napped out the driver.

"You have to keep your horses on ——"

"*Shucks!* [1] damn it."

The character of the scenery was novel to me, the surface very flat, the soil a fine-grained, silvery white sand, shaded by a continuous forest of large pines, which had shed their lower branches, so that we could see from the coach-top, to the distance of a quarter of a mile, everything upon the ground. In the swamps, which were frequent and extensive, and on their borders, the pines gave place to cypresses, with great pedestal trunks, and protuberant roots, throwing up an awkward dwarf progeny of shrub, cypress, and curious bulbous-like stumps, called "cypress-knees." Mingled with these were a few of our common deciduous trees, the white-shafted sycamore, the gray beech, and the shrubby blackjack oak, with broad leaves, brown and dead, yet glossy, and reflecting the sunbeams. Somewhat rarely, the red cedar, and more frequently than any other except the cypress, the beautiful American holly. Added to these, there was often a thick undergrowth of evergreen shrubs. Vines and creepers of various kinds grew to the tops of the tallest trees and dangled beneath and between their branches, in intricate net-work. The tylandria hung in festoons, sometimes several feet in length, and often completely clothed the trunks, and every branch of the trees in the low ground. It is like a fringe of tangled hair, of a light gray pearly colour, and sometimes produces exquisite effects when slightly veiling the dark green, purple, and scarlet of the cedar, and the holly with their berries. The mistletoe also grew in large, vivid, green tufts, on the ends of the branches of the oldest and largest trees. A small fine and wiry dead grass, hardly perceptible, even in the most open ground, from the coach-tops, was the only sign of herbage. Large black buzzards were constantly in sight, sailing slowly, high above the treetops. Flocks of larks, quails, and robins were common, as were also doves, swiftly flying in small companies. The redheaded woodpecker could at any time be heard hammering the old tree-trunks, and would sometimes show himself, after his rat-tat, cocking his head archly, and listening to hear if the worm moved under the bark. The drivers told me that they had on previous days, as they went over the road, seen deer, turkeys, and wild hogs.

At every tenth mile, or thereabout, we changed horses; and, generally, were allowed half an hour to stroll in the neighbourhood of the stable—the agent observing that we could reach the end of the staging some hours before the cars should leave to take us further; and, as there were no good accommodations for sleeping there, we would pass the time quite as pleasantly on the road. We dined at "Marion County House," a pleasant little village (and the only village we saw during the day), with a

[1] Husks of maize.

fine pine-grove, a broad street, a court-house, a church or two, a school-house, and a dozen or twenty dwellings. Towards night, we crossed the Great Pedee of the maps, the *Big Pedee* of the natives, in a flat boat. A large quantity of cotton, in bales, was upon the bank, ready for loading into a steamboat—when one should arrive—for Charleston.

The country was very thinly peopled; lone houses often being several miles apart. The large majority of the dwellings were of logs, and even those of the white people were often without glass windows. In the better class of cabins, the roof is usually built with a curve, so as to project eight or ten feet beyond the log-wall; and a part of this space, exterior to the logs, is enclosed with boards, making an additional small room—the remainder forms an open porch. The whole cabin is often elevated on four corner-posts, two or three feet from the ground, so that the air may circulate under it. The fire-place is built at the end of the house, of sticks and clay, and the chimney is carried up outside, and often detached from the log-walls; but the roof is extended at the gable, until in a line with its outer side. The porch has a railing in front, and a wide shelf at the end, on which a bucket of water, a gourd, and hand-basin, are usually placed. There are chairs, or benches, in the porch, and you often see women sitting at work in it, as in Germany.

The logs are usually hewn but little; and, of course, as they are laid up, there will be wide interstices between them—which are increased by subsequent shrinking. These, very commonly, are not "chinked," or filled up in any way; nor is the wall lined on the inside. Through the chinks, as you pass along the road, you may often see all that is going on in the house; and, at night, the light of the fire shines brightly out on all sides.

Cabins, of this class, would almost always be flanked by two or three negro huts. The cabins of the poor whites, much the largest in number, were of a meaner sort— being mere square pens of logs, roofed over, provided with a chimney, and usually with a shed of boards, supported by rough posts, before the door.

Occasionally, where, near the banks of a water-course, the silvery sand was darkened by a considerable intermixture of mould, there would be a large plantation, with negro-quarters, and a cotton press and gin-house. We passed half a dozen of these, perhaps, during the day. Where the owners resided in them, they would have comfortable-looking residences, not unlike the better class of New England farm-houses. On the largest, however, there was no residence for the owner, at all, only a small cottage, or whitewashed cabin, for the overseer. The negro-cabins, here, were the smallest I had seen—I thought not more than twelve feet square, inside. They stood in two rows, with a wide street between them. They were built of logs, with no windows—no opening at all, except the doorway, with a chimney of sticks and mud; with no trees about them, no porches, or shades, of any kind. Except for the chimney—the purpose of which I should not readily have guessed if I had seen one of them in New England—I should have conjectured that it had been built for a powder-house, or perhaps an ice-house—never for an animal to sleep in.

We stopped, for some time, on this plantation, near where some thirty men and women were at work, repairing the road. The women were in majority, and were engaged at exactly the same labour as the men; driving the carts, loading them with dirt, and dumping them upon the road; cutting down trees, and drawing wood by hand, to lay across the miry places; hoeing, and shoveling. They were dressed in coarse gray gowns, generally very much burned, and very dirty; which, for greater convenience of working in the mud, were reefed up with a cord drawn tightly around the body, a little above the hips—the spare amount of skirt bagging out between this and the waist-proper. On their legs were loose leggings, or pieces of blanket or bagging wrapped about, and lashed with thongs; and they wore very heavy shoes. Most of them had handkerchiefs, only, tied around their heads, some wore men's caps, or old slouched hats, and several were bareheaded.

The overseer rode about among them, on a horse, carrying in his hand a raw-hide whip, constantly directing and encouraging them; but, as my companion and I, both, several times noticed, as often as he visited one end of the line of operations, the hands at the other end would discontinue their labour, until he turned to ride towards them again. Clumsy, awkward, gross, elephantine in all their movements; pouting, grinning, and leering at us; sly, sensual, and shameless, in all their expressions and demeanour; I never before had witnessed, I thought, anything more revolting than the whole scene.

At length, the overseer dismounted from his horse, and, giving him to a boy to take to the stables, got upon the coach, and rode with us several miles. From the conversation I had with him, as well as from what I saw of his conduct in the field, I judged that he was an uncommonly fit man for his duties; at least ordinarily amiable in disposition, and not passionate; but deliberate, watchful, and efficient. I thought he would be not only a good economist, but a firm and considerate officer or master.

If these women, and their children after them, were always naturally and necessarily to remain of the character and capacity stamped on their faces—as is probably the opinion of their owner, in common with most wealthy South Carolina planters—I don't know that they could be much less miserably situated, or guided more for their own good and that of the world, than they were. They were fat enough, and didn't look as if they were at all overworked, or harassed by cares, or oppressed by a consciousness of their degradation. If that is all—as some think.

Afterwards, while we were changing at a house near a crossing of roads, strolling off in the woods for a short distance, I came upon two small white-topped waggons, each with a pair of horses feeding at its pole; near them was a full camp fire, with a bake-kettle and coffee-pot, some blankets and a chest upon the ground, and an old negro sitting with his head bowed down over a meal sack, while a negro boy was combing his wool with a common horse-card. "Good evening, uncle," said I, approaching them. "Good evening, sar," he answered, without looking up.

"Where are you going?"

"Well, we ain't gwine nower, master; we's peddlin' tobacco roun."

"Where did you come from?"

"From Rockingham County, Norf Car'lina, master."

"How long have you been coming from there?"

"'Twill be seven weeks, to-morrow, sar, sin we leff home."

"Have you most sold out?"

"We had a hundred and seventy-five boxes in both waggons, and we's sold all but sixty. Want to buy some tobacco, master?" (Looking up.)

"No, thank you; I am only waiting here, while the coach changes. How much tobacco is there in a box?"

"Seventy-five pound."

"Are these the boxes?"

"No, them is our provision boxes, master. Show de gemman some of der tobacco, dah." (To the boy.)

A couple of negroes here passed along near us; the old man hailed them:

"Ho dah, boys! Doan you want to buy some backey?"

"No." (Decidedly.)

"Well, I'm sorry for it." (Reproachfully.)

"Are you bound homeward, now?" I asked.

"No, master; wish me was; got to sell all our backey fuss; you don't want none, master, does you? Doan you tink it pretty fair tobacco, sar? Juss try it: it's right sweet, reckon you'll find."

"I don't wish any, thank you; I never use it. Is your master with you?"

"No, sar; he's gone across to Marion, to-day."

"Do you like to be travelling about, in this way?"

"Yes, master; I likes it very well."

"Better than staying at home, eh?"

"Well, I likes my country better dan dis; must say dat, master; likes my country better dan dis. I'se a free nigger in my country, master."

"Oh, you are a free man, are you! North Carolina is a better country than this, for free men, I suppose."

"Yes, master, I likes my country de best; I gets five dollar a month for dat boy." (Hastily, to change the subject.)

"He is your son, is he?"

"Yes, sar; he drives dat waggon, I drives dis; and I haant seen him fore, master, for six weeks, till dis mornin'."

"How were you separated?"

"We separated six weeks ago, sar, and we agreed to meet here, last night. We didn', dough, till dis mornin'."

The old man's tone softened, and he regarded his son with earnestness.

" 'Pears, dough, we was bofe heah, last night; but I couldn't find um till dis mornin'. Dis mornin some niggers tole me dar war a nigger camped off yander in de wood; and I knew 'twas him, and I went an' found him right off."

"And what wages do you get for yourself?"

"Ten dollars a month, master."

"That's pretty good wages."

"Yes, master, any nigger can get good wages if he's a mind to be industrious, no matter wedder he's slave or free."

"So you don't like this country as well as North Carolina?"

"No, master. Fac is, master, 'pears like wite folks doan' ginnerally like niggers in dis country; day doan' ginerally talk so to niggers like as do in my country; de niggers ain't so happy heah; 'pears like de wite folks was kind o' different, somehow. I doan' like dis country so well; my country suits me very well."

"Well, I've been thinking, myself, the niggers did not look so well here as they did in North Carolina and Virginia; they are not so well clothed, and they don't appear so bright as they do there."

"Well, master, Sundays dey is mighty well clothed, dis country; 'pears like dere an't nobody looks better Sundays dan dey do. But Lord! workin' days, seems like dey haden no close dey could keep on 'um at all, master. Dey is a'mos' naked, wen deys at work, some on 'em. Why, master, up in our country, de wite folks—why, some on 'em has ten or twelve niggers; dey doan' hev no real big plantation, like dey has heah, but some on 'em has ten or twelve niggers, may be, and dey juss lives and talks along wid 'em; and dey treats 'um most as if dem was dar own chile. Dey doan' keep no niggers dey can't treat so; dey won't keep 'em, won't be bodered wid 'em. If dey gets a nigger and he doan behave himself, day won't keep him; dey juss tell him, sar, he must look up anudder master, and if he doan' find hisself one, I tell 'ou, when de trader cum along, dey sells him, and he totes him away. Dey allers sell off all de bad niggers out of our country; dat's de way all de bad nigger and all dem no-account nigger keep a cumin' down heah; dat's de way on't, master."

"Yes, that's the way of it, I suppose; these big plantations are not just the best thing for niggers, I see that plainly."

"Master, you wan't raise in dis country, was 'ou?"

"No; I came from the North."

"I tort so, sar; I knew 'ou wan't one of dis country people; 'peared like 'ou was one o' my country people, way 'ou talks; and I loves dem kine of people. Won't you take some whisky, sar? Heah, you boy! bring dat jug of whisky dah, out o' my waggon; in dah,—in dat box under dem foddar."

"No, don't trouble yourself, I am very much obliged to you; but I don't like to drink whisky."

"Like to have you drink some, master, if you'd like it. You's right welcome to it. 'Pears like I knew you was one of my country people. Ever been in Greensboro,' master? dat's in Guilford."

"No, I never was there. I came from New York, further North than your country."

"New York, did 'ou, master? I heerd New York was what dey calls a Free State; all de niggers free dah."

"Yes, that is so."

"Not no slaves at all; well, I expec dat's a good ting, for all de niggers to be free. Greensboro' is a right comely town; tain't like dese heah Souf Car'lina towns."

"I have heard it spoken of as a beautiful town, and there are some fine people there."

"Yes, dere's Mr.—, I knows him—he's a mightly good man."

"Do you know Mr.—?"

"O yes, sar, he's a mighty fine man, he is, master; ain't no better kind of man dan him."

"Well, I must go, or the coach will be kept waiting for me. Good-bye to you."

"Far'well, master, far'well; 'pears like it's done me good to see a man dat's cum out of my country again. Far'well, master."

We took supper at a neat log-cabin, standing a short distance off the road, with a beautiful evergreen oak, the first I had observed, in front of it. There was no glass in the windows, but drapery of white muslin restrained the currents of air, and during the day would let in sufficient light, while a blazing wood-fire both warmed and lighted the room by night. A rifle and powder-horn hung near the fire-place, and the master of the house, a fine, hearty, companionable fellow, said that he had lately shot three deer, and that there were plenty of cats, and foxes, as well as turkeys, hares, squirrels, and other small game in the vicinity. It was a perfectly charming little backwoods farm-house—good wife, supper, and all; but one disagreeable blot darkened the otherwise most agreeable picture of rustic civilization—we were waited upon at the table by two excessively dirty, slovenly-dressed, negro girls. In the rear of the cabin were two hovels, each lighted by large fires, and apparently crowded with other slaves belonging to the family.

Between nine and ten at night, we reached the end of the completed railroad, coming up in search for that we had left the previous night. There was another camp and fire of the workmen, and in a little white frame-house we found a company of engineers. There were two trains and locomotives on the track, and a gang of negroes was loading cotton into one of them.

I strolled off until I reached an opening in the woods, in which was a cotton-field and some negro-cabins, and beyond it large girdled trees, among which were two negroes with dogs, barking, yelping, hacking, shouting, and whistling, after 'coons and 'possums. Returning to the railroad, I found a comfortable, warm passenger-car, and, wrapped in my blanket, went to sleep. At midnight I was awakened by loud laughter, and, looking out, saw that the gang of negroes had made a fire, and were enjoying a right merry repast. Suddenly, one raised such a sound as I never heard before; a long, loud, musical shout, rising and falling, and breaking into falsetto, his voice ringing through the woods in the clear, frosty night air, like a bugle-call. As he finished, the melody was caught up by another, and then another, and then by several in chorus. When there was silence again, one of them cried out, as if bursting with amusement: "Did yer see de dog?—when I began eeohing, he turn roun, an' look me straight into der face; ha! ha! ha!" and the whole party broke into the loudest peals of laughter, as if it was the very best joke they had ever heard.

After a few minutes I could hear one urging the rest to come to work again, and soon he stepped towards the cotton bales, saying, "Come, brederen, come; let's go at it; come now, eoho! roll away! eeoho-eeoho-weeioho-i!"—and the rest taking it up as before, in a few moments they all had their shoulders to a bale of cotton and were rolling it up the embankment.

About half-past three, I was awakened again by the whistle of the locomotive, answering, I suppose, the horn of a stage-coach, which in a few minutes drove up, bringing a mail. A negro man and woman who had been sleeping near me, replenished the fire; two other passengers came in, and we started.

In the woods I saw a negro by a fire, while it was still night, shaving shingles very industriously. He did not even stop to look at the train. No doubt he was a slave, working by task, and of his own accord at night, that he might have the more daylight for his own purposes.

The negroes enjoy fine blazing fires in the open air, and make them at every opportunity. The train on this road was provided with a man and maid-servant to attend to the fire and wait on the passengers—a very good arrangement, by the way, yet to be adopted on our own long passenger trains. When we arrived at a junction where we were to change cars, as soon as all the passengers had left the train, they also left; but instead of going into the station-house with us, they immediately collected some pine branches and chips, and getting a brand from the locomotive, made a fire upon the ground, and seated themselves by it. Other negroes soon began to join them, and as they approached were called to: "Doan' yer cum widout som' wood! Doan' yer cum widout som' wood!" and every one had to make his contribution. At another place, near a cotton plantation, I found a woman collecting pine leaves into heaps, to be carted to the cattle-pens. She, too, had a fire near her. "What are you doing with a fire, aunty?" "Oh, jus' to warm my hans wen dey gits cold, massa." The weather was then almost uncomfortably warm.

We were running during the forenoon, for a hundred miles, or more, in a southerly direction, on nearly a straight course, through about the middle of the State of South Carolina. The greater part of this distance, the flat, sandy pine barrens continued, scarcely a foot of grading, for many miles at a time, having been required in the construction of the railroad. As the swamps, which were still frequent, were crossed on piles and tressel-work, the roads must have been built very cheaply—the land damages being nothing. We passed from the track of one company to that of another, several times during the day—the speed was from fifteen to twenty miles an hour with long stoppages at the stations. A conductor said they could easily run forty miles, and had done it, including stoppages; but they were forbidden now to make fast time, from the injury it did the road—the superstructure being much more shaken and liable to displacement in these light sands than on our Northern roads. The locomotives that I saw were all made in Philadelphia; the cars were all from the Hartford, Conn., and Worcester, Mass., manufactories, and invariably, elegant and comfortable. The roads seemed to be doing a heavy freighting business with cotton. We passed at the turn-outs half a dozen trains, with nearly a thousand bales on each, but the number of passengers was always small. A slave country can never, it is evident, furnish a passenger traffic of much value. A majority of the passenger trains, which I saw used in the South, were not paying for the fuel and wages expended in running them.

For an hour or two we got above the sandy zone, and into the second, middle, or "wave" region of the State. The surface here was extremely undulating, gracefully swelling and dipping in bluffs and dells—the soil a mellow brown loam, with some indications of fertility, especially in the valleys. Yet most of the ground was occupied by pine woods (probably old-field pines, on exhausted cotton-fields). For a few miles, on a gently sloping surface of the same sort of soil, there were some enormously large cotton-fields.

I saw women working again, in large gangs with men. In one case they were distributing manure—ditch scrapings it appeared to be—and the mode of operation was this: the manure had been already carted into heaps upon the ground; a number of the women were carrying it in from the heap in baskets, on their heads, and one in her apron, and spreading it with their hands between the ridges on which the cotton grew last year; the rest followed with great, long-handled, heavy, clumsy hoes, and pulled down the ridges over the manure, and so made new ridges for the next planting. I asked a young planter who continued with me a good part of the day, why they did not use ploughs. He said this was rather rough land, and a plough wouldn't work in it very well. It was light soil, and smooth enough for a parade ground. The fact is, in certain parts of South Carolina, a plough is yet an almost unknown instrument of tillage.

About noon we turned east, on a track running direct to Charleston. Pine barrens continued alternating with swamp, with some cotton and corn fields on the edges of the latter. A few of the pines were "boxed" for turpentine; and I understood that one or two companies from North Carolina had been operating here for several years. Plantations were not very often seen along the road through the sand; but stations, at which cotton was stored and loading, were comparatively frequent.

At one of the stations an empty car had been attached to the train; I had gone into it, and was standing at one end of it, when an elderly countryman with a young woman and three little children entered and took seats at the other. The old man took out a roll of deerskin, in which were bank-bills, and some small change.

"How much did he say 'twould be?" he inquired.

"Seventy cents."

"For both on us?"

"For each on us."

"Both on us, I reckon."

"Reckon it's each."

"I've got jess seventy-five cents in hard money."

"Give it to him, and tell him it's all yer got; reckon he'll let us go."

At this I moved to attract their attention; the old man started, and looked towards me for a moment, and said no more. I soon afterwards walked out on the platform, passing him, and the conductor came in, and collected their fare; I then returned, and stood near them, looking out of the window of the door. The old man had a good-humoured, thin, withered, very brown face, and there was a speaking twinkle in his eye. He was dressed in clothes much of the Quaker cut—a broad-brimmed, low hat; white cotton shirt, open in front, and without cravat, showing his hairy breast; a long-skirted, snuff-coloured coat, of very coarse homespun; short trousers, of brown drilling; red woollen stockings, and heavy cow-hide shoes. He presently asked the time of the day; I gave it to him, and we continued in conversation, as follows:—

"Right cold weather."

"Yes."

"G'wine to Branchville?"

"I am going beyond there—to Charleston."

"Ah—come from Hamburg this mornin'?"

"No—from beyond there."

"Did ye?—where 'd you come from?"

"From Wilmington."

"How long yer ben comin'?"

"I left Wilmington night before last, about ten o'clock. I have been ever since on the road."

"Reckon yer a night-bird."

"What?"

"Reckon you are a night-bird—what we calls a night-hawk; keeps a goin' at night, you know."

"Yes—I've been going most of two nights."

"Reckon so; kinder red your eyes is. Live in Charleston, do ye?"

"No, I live in New York."

"New York—that's a good ways, yet, ain't it?"

"Yes."

"Reckon yer arter a chicken, up here."

"No."

"Ah, ha—reckon ye are."

The young woman laughed, lifted her shoulder, and looked out of the window.

"Reckon ye'll get somebody's chicken."

"I'm afraid not."

The young woman laughed again, and tossed her head.

"Oh, reckon ye will—ah, ha! But yer mustn't mind my fun."

"Not at all, not at all. Where did *you* come from?"

"Up here to —; g'wine hum; g'wine to stop down here, next deeper. How do you go, w'en you get to Charleston?"

"I am going on to New Orleans."

"Is New York beyond New Orleans?"

"Beyond New Orleans? Oh, no."

"In New Orleans, is't?"

"What?"

"New York is somewhere in New Orleans, ain't it?"

"No; it's the other way—beyond Wilmington."

"Oh! Been pretty cold thar?"

"Yes; there was a foot and a half of snow there, last week, I hear."

"Lord o'massy! why! have to feed all the cattle!—whew!—ha!—whew!— don't wonner ye com' away."

"You are a farmer."

"Yes."

"Well, I am a farmer, too."

"Be ye—to New York?"

"Yes; how much land have you got?"

"A hundred and twenty-five acres; how much have you?"

"Just about the same. What's you land worth, here?"

"Some on't—what we call swamp-land—kinder low and wet like, you know— that's worth five dollars an acre; and mainly it's worth a dollar and a half or two dollars—that's takin' a common trac' of upland. What's yours worth?"

"A hundred and fifty to two hundred dollars."

"What!"

"A hundred and fifty to two hundred."

"Dollars?"

"Yes."

"Not an acre?"

"Yes."

"Good Lord! yer might as well buy niggers to onst. Do you work any niggers?"

"No."

"May be they don't have niggers—that is, slaves—to New York."

"No, we do not. It's against the law."

"Yes, I heerd 'twas, some place. How do yer get yer work done?"

"I hire white men—Irishmen, generally."

"Do they work good?"

"Yes, better than negroes, I think, and don't cost nearly as much."

"What do yer have to give'em?"

"Eight or nine dollars a month, and board, for common hands, by the year."

"Hi, Lordy! and they work up right smart, do they? Why, yer can't get any kind of good nigger less'n twelve dollars a month."

"And board?"

"And board 'em? yes; and clothe, and blank, and shoe 'em, too."

He owned no negroes himself and did not hire any.

"They," his family, "made their own crap." They raised maize, and sweet potatoes, and cow-peas. He reckoned, in general, they made about three barrels of maize to the acre; sometimes, as much as five. He described to me, as a novelty, a plough, with a "sort of a wing, like, on one side," that pushed off, and turned over a slice of the ground; from which it appeared that he had, until recently, never seen a mould-board; the common ploughs of this country being constructed on the same principles as those of the Chinese, and only rooting the ground, like a hog or a mole—not cleaving and turning. He had never heard of working a plough with more than one horse. He was frank and good-natured; embarrassed his daughter by coarse jokes about herself and her babies, and asked me if I would not go home with him, and when I declined, pressed me to come and see them when I returned. That I might do so, he gave me directions how to get to his farm; observing that I must start pretty early in the day—because it would not be safe for a stranger to try to cross the swamp after dark. The moment the train began to check its speed, before stopping at the place at which he was to leave, he said to his daughter, "Come, gal! quick now; gather up yer young ones!" and stepped out, pulling her after him, on to the platform. As they walked off, I noticed that he strode ahead, like an Indian or a gipsy man, and she carried in her arms two of the children and a bundle, while the third child held to her skirts.

A party of fashionably-dressed people took the train for Charleston, two families, apparently, returning from a visit to their plantations. They came to the station in handsome coaches. Some minutes before the rest, there entered the car, in which I was then again alone, and reclining on a bench in the corner, an old nurse, with a baby, and two young negro women, having care of half a dozen children, mostly girls, from three to fifteen years of age. As they closed the door, the negro girls seemed to resume a conversation, or quarrel. Their language was loud and obscene, such as I never heard before from any but the most depraved and beastly women of the streets. Upon observing me, they dropped their voices, but not with any appearance of shame, and continued their altercation, until their mistress entered. The white children, in the mean time, had listened, without any appearance of wonder or annoyance. The moment the ladies opened the door, they became silent.

Plantation, February, I left town yesterday morning, on horseback, with a letter in my pocket to Mr. X., under whose roof I am now writing. The weather was fine, and, indeed, since I left Virginia, the weather for out-of-door purposes has been as fine as can be imagined. The exercise of walking or of riding warms one, at any time between sunrise and sunset, sufficiently to allow an overcoat to be dispensed with, while the air is yet brisk and stimulating. The public-houses are overcrowded with Northerners, who congratulate themselves on having escaped the severe cold, of which they hear from home.

All, however, who know the country, out of the large towns, say that they have suffered more from cold here than ever at the North; because, except at a few first-class hotels, and in the better sort of mansions and plantation residences, any provision for keeping houses warm is so entirely neglected. It is, indeed, too cool to sit quietly, even at midday, out of sunshine, and at night it is often frosty. As a general rule, with such exceptions as I have indicated, it will be full two hours after one has asked for a fire in his room before the servants can be got to make it. The expedient of closing a door or window to exclude a draught of cold air seems really to be unknown to the negroes. From the time I left Richmond, until I arrived at Charleston, I never but once knew a servant to close the door on leaving a room, unless he was requested at the moment to do so.

The public-houses of the smaller towns, and the country houses generally, are so loosely built, and so rarely have unbroken glass windows, that to sit by a fire, and to avoid remaining in a draught at the same time, is not to be expected.

As the number of Northerners, and especially of invalids, who come hither in winter, is every year increasing, more comfortable accommodations along the line of travel must soon be provided; if not by native, then by Northern enterprise. Some of the hotels in Florida, indeed, are already, I understand, under the management of Northerners; and this winter, cooks and waiters have been procured for them from the North. I observe, also, that one of them advertises that meats and vegetables are received by every steamer from New York.

Whenever comfortable quarters, and means of conveyance are extensively provided, at not immoderately great expense, there must be a great migration here every winter. The climate and the scenery, as well as the society of the more wealthy planters' families, are attractive, not to invalids alone, but even more to men and women who are able to enjoy invigorating recreations. Nowhere in the world could a man, with a sound body and a quiet conscience, live more pleasantly, at least as a guest, it seems to me, than here where I am. I was awakened this morning by a servant making a fire in my chamber. Opening the window, I found a clear, brisk air, but without frost—the mercury standing at 35° F. There was not a sign of winter, except that a few cypress trees, hung with seed attached to pretty pendulous tassels, were leafless. A grove which surrounded the house was all in dark verdure; there were green oranges on trees nearer the window; the buds were swelling on a jessamine-vine, and a number of camelia-japonicas were in full bloom; one of them, at least seven feet high, and a large compact shrub, must have had several hundred blossoms on it. Sparrows were chirping, doves cooing, and a mocking-bird whistling loudly. I walked to the stable, and saw clean and neatly-dressed negroes grooming thorough-bred horses, which pawed the ground, and tossed their heads, and drew deep inspirations, and danced as they were led out, in exuberance of animal spirits; and I felt as they did. We drove ten miles to church, in the forenoon, with the carriage-top thrown back, and with our overcoats laid aside; nevertheless, when we returned, and came in to the house, we found a crackling wood fire, as comfortable as it was cheerful. Two lads, the sons of my host, had returned the night before from a "marooning party," with a boat-load of venison, wild fowl, and fish; and at dinner this evening there were delicacies which are to be had in perfection, it is said, nowhere else than on this coast. The woods and waters around us abound, not only with game, but with most interesting subjects of observation to the naturalist and the artist. Every-thing encourages cheerfulness, and invites to healthful life.

Now to think how people are baking in their oven-houses at home, or waddling out in the deep snow or mud, or across the frozen ruts, wrapped up to a Falstaffian rotundity in flannels and furs, one can but wonder that those, who have means, stay there, any more than these stay here in summer; and that my host would no more think of doing than the wild-goose.

But I must tell how I got here and what I saw by the way.

A narrow belt of cleared land—"vacant lots"—only separated the town from the pine-forest—that great broad forest which extends uninterruptedly, and merely dotted with a few small corn and cotton fields, from Delaware to Louisiana.

Having some doubt about the road, I asked a direction of a man on horseback, who overtook and was passing me. In reply, he said it was a straight road, and we should go in company for a mile or two. He inquired if I was a stranger; and, when he heard that I was from the North, and now first visiting the South, he remarked that there was "no better place for me to go than that for which I had inquired. Mr. X. was a very fine man—rich, got a splendid plantation, lived well, had plenty of company always, and there were a number of other show plantations near his. He reckoned I would visit some of them."

I asked what he meant by "show plantations." "Plantations belonging to rich people," he said, "where they had everything fixed up nice. There were several places that had that name; their owners always went out and lived on them part of the year, and kept a kind of open house, and were always ready to receive company. He reckoned I might go and stay a month round on them kind of places on —— river, and it would not cost me a cent. They always had a great many Northerners going to see them, those gentlemen had. Almost every Northerner that came here was invited right out to visit some of them; and in summer, a good many of them went to the North themselves."

(It was not till long afterwards, long after the above paragraph was first printed, that I fully comprehended the significance of the statement, that on the show plantations it would not cost me a cent.)

During the forenoon my road continued broad and straight, and I was told that it was the chief outlet and thoroughfare of a very extensive agricultural district. There was very little land in cultivation within sight of the road, however; not a mile of it fenced, in twenty, and the only houses were log-cabins. The soil varied from a coarse, clean yellow sand, to a dark, brown, sandy loam. There were indications that much of the land had, at some time, been under cultivation—had been worn out, and deserted.

Long teams of mules, driven by negroes, toiled slowly toward the town, with loads or rice or cotton. A stage-coach, with six horses to drag it through the heavy road, covered me, as it passed, with dust; and once or twice, I met a stylish carriage with fashionably-clad gentlemen and ladies and primly-liveried negro-servants; but much the greatest traffic of the road was done by small one-horse carts, driven by white men, or women.

These carts, all but their wheels, which come from the North, look as if they were made by their owners, in the woods, with no better tools than axes and jack-knives. Very little iron is used in their construction; the different parts being held together by wooden pins, and lashings of hide. The harness is made chiefly of ropes and undressed hide; but there is always a high-peaked riding-saddle, in which the driver prefers to sit, rather than on his cart. Once, I met a woman riding in this way, with a load of children in the cart behind her. From the axle-tree often hung a gourd, or an iron kettle. One man carried a rifle on his pommel. Sometimes, these carts would contain a single bale of cotton, more commonly, an assorted cargo of maize, sweet potatoes, poultry, game, hides, and peltry, with, always, some bundles of corn-leaves, to be fed to the horse. Women and children were often passengers, or travelled on foot, in company with the carts, which were usually furnished with a low tilt. Many of them, I found, had been two or three days on the road, bringing down a little crop to market; whole families coming with it, to get reclothed with the proceeds.

The men with the carts were generally slight, with high cheekbones and sunken eyes, and were of less than the usual stature of the Anglo-Saxon race. They were dressed in long-skirted homespun coats, wore slouched hats, and heavy boots, outside their trousers. As they met me, they usually bowed, and often offered a remark upon the weather, or the roads; in a bold, but not uncourteous manner—showing themselves to be, at least, in one respect, better off than the majority of European peasants, whose educated servility of character rarely fails to manifest itself, when they meet a well-dressed stranger.

The household markets of most of the Southern towns seem to be mainly supplied by the poor country people, who, driving in this style, bring all sorts of produce to exchange for such small stores and articles of apparel as they must need obtain from the shops. Sometimes, owing to the great extent of the back country from which the supplies are gathered, they are offered in great abundance and variety: at other times, from the want of regular market-men, there will be a scarcity, and prices will be very high.

A stranger cannot but express surprise and amusement at the appearance and manners of these country traffickers in the market-place. The "wild Irish" hardly differ more from the English gentry than these rustics from the better class of planters and towns-people, with whom the traveller more commonly comes in contact. Their language even is almost incomprehensible, and seems exceedingly droll, to a Northern man. I have found it quite impossible to report it. I shall not soon forget the figure of a little old white woman, wearing a man's hat, smoking a pipe, driving a little black bull with reins; sitting herself bolt upright, upon the axle-tree of a little truck, on which she was returning from market. I was riding with a gentleman of the town at the time, and, as she bowed to him with an expression of ineffable self-satisfaction, I asked if he knew her. He had known her for twenty years, he said, and until lately she had always come into town about once a week, on foot, bringing fowls, eggs, potatoes, or herbs, for sale in a basket. The bull she had probably picked up astray, when a calf, and reared and broken it herself; and the cart and harness she had made herself; but he did not think anybody in the land felt richer than she did now, or prouder of her establishment.

In the afternoon, I left the main road, and, towards night, reached a much more cultivated district. The forest of pines still extended uninterruptedly on one side of the way, but on the other was a continued succession of very large fields, of rich dark soil—evidently reclaimed swap-land—which had been cultivated the previous year, in Sea Island cotton. Beyond them, a flat surface of still lower land, with a silver thread of water curling through it, extended, Holland-like, to the horizon. Usually at as great a distance as a quarter of a mile from the road, and from half a mile to a mile apart, were the residences of the planters—white houses, with groves of evergreen trees about them; and between these and the road were little villages of slave-cabins.

My directions not having been sufficiently explicit, I rode in, by a private lane, to one of these. It consisted of some thirty neatly-whitewashed cottages, with a broad avenue planted with Pride-of-China trees between them.

The cottages were framed buildings, boarded on the outside with shingle roofs and brick chimneys; they stood fifty feet apart, with gardens and pig-yards, enclosed by palings, between them. At one, which was evidently the "sick house," or hospital, there were several negroes of both sexes, wrapped in blankets and reclining on the door steps or on the ground, basking in the sunshine. Some of them looked ill, but all were chatting and laughing as I rode up to make an inquiry. I learned that it was not the plantation I was intending to visit, and received a direction, as usual, so indistinct and incorrect that it led me wrong.

At another plantation which I soon afterwards reached, I found the "settlement" arranged in the same way, the cabins only being of a slightly different form. In the middle of one row was a well-house, and opposite it, on the other row, was a mill-house, with stones, at which the negroes grind their corn. It is a kind of pestle and mortar; and I was informed afterwards that the negroes prefer to take their allowance of corn and crack it for themselves, rather than to receive meal, because they think the mill-ground meal does not make as sweet bread.

At the head of the settlement, in a garden looking down the street, was an overseer's house, and here the road divided, running each way at right angles; on one side to barns and a landing on the river, on the other toward the mansion of the proprietor. A negro boy opened the gate of the latter, and I entered.

On either side, at fifty feet distant, were rows of old live-oak trees, their branches and twigs slightly hung with a delicate fringe of gray moss, and their dark, shining, green foliage, meeting and intermingling naturally but densely overhead. The sunlight streamed through, and played aslant the lustrous leaves, and fluttering pendulous moss; the arch was low and broad; the trunks were huge and gnarled, and there was a heavy groining of strong, rough, knotty, branches. I stopped my horse and held my breath; I thought of old Kit North's rhapsody on trees; and it was no rhapsody—it was all here, and real: "Light, shade, shelter, coolness, freshness, music, dew, and dreams dropping through their umbrageous twilight—dropping direct, soft, sweet, soothing, and restorative from heaven."

Alas! No angels; only little black babies, toddling about with an older child or two to watch them, occupied the aisle. At the upper end was the owner's mansion, with a circular court-yard around it, and an irregular plantation of great trees; one of the oaks, as I afterwards learned, seven feet in diameter of trunk, and covering with its branches a circle of one hundred and twenty feet in diameter. As I approached it, a smart servant came out to take my horse. I obtained from him a direction to the residence of the gentleman I was searching for, and rode away, glad that I had stumbled into so charming a place.

After riding a few miles further I reached my destination.

Mr. X. has two plantations on the river, besides a large tract of poor pine forest land, extending some miles back upon the upland, and reaching above the malarious region. In the upper part of this pine land is a house, occupied by his overseer during the malarious season, when it is dangerous for any but negroes to remain during the night in the vicinity of the swamps or rice-fields. Even those few who have been born in the region, and have grown up subject to the malaria, are said to be generally weakly and short-lived. The negroes do not enjoy as good health on the rice plantations as elsewhere; and the greater difficulty with which their lives are preserved, through infancy especially, shows that the subtle poison of the miasma is not innocuous to them; but Mr. X. boasts a steady increase of his negro stock, of five per cent per annum, which is better than is averaged on the plantations of the interior.

The plantation which contains Mr. X.'s winter residence has but a small extent of rice land, the greater part of it being reclaimed upland swamp soil, suitable for the culture of Sea Island cotton. The other plantation contains over five hundred acres of rice-land, fitted for irrigation; the remainder is unusually fertile reclaimed upland swamp, and some hundred acres of it are cultivated for maize and Sea Island cotton.

There is a "negro settlement" on each; but both plantations, although a mile or two apart, are worked together as one, under one overseer—the hands being drafted from one to another as their labour is required. Somewhat over seven hundred acres are at the present time under the plough in the two plantations: the whole number of negroes is two hundred, and they are reckoned to be equal to about one hundred prime hands—an unusual strength for that number of all classes. The overseer lives, in winter, near the settlement of the larger plantation, Mr. X. near that of the smaller.

It is an old family estate, inherited by Mr. X.'s wife, who, with her children, were born and brought up upon it in close intimacy with the negroes, a large proportion of whom were also included in her inheritance, or have been since born upon the estate. Mr. X. himself is a New England farmer's son, and has been a successful merchant and manufacturer.

The patriarchal institution should be seen here under its most favourable aspects; not only from the ties of long family association, common traditions, common memories, and, if ever, common interests, between the slaves and their rulers, but, also, from the practical talent for organization and administration, gained among the rugged fields, the complicated looms, and the exact and comprehensive counting-houses of New England, which directs the labour.

The house-servants are more intelligent, understand and perform their duties better, and are more appropriately dressed, than any I have seen before. The labour required of them is light, and they are treated with much more consideration for their health and comfort than is usually given to that of free domestics. They live in brick cabins, adjoining the house and stables, and one of these, into which I have looked, is neatly and comfortably furnished. Several of the house-servants, as is usual, are mulattoes, and good-looking. The mulattoes are generally preferred for in-door occupations. Slaves brought up to house-work dread to be employed at field labour; and those accustomed to the comparatively unconstrained life of the negro settlement, detest the close control and careful movements required of the house-servants. It is a punishment for a lazy field-hand, to employ him in menial duties at the house, as it is to set a sneaking sailor to do the work of a cabin-servant; and it is equally a punishment to a neglectful house-servant, to banish him to the field-gangs. All the household economy is, of course, carried on in a style appropriate to a wealthy gentleman's residence—not more so, nor less so, that I observe, than in an establishment of a similar grade at the North.

It is a custom with Mr. X., when on the estate, to look each day at all the work going on, inspect the buildings, boats, embankments, and sluice-ways, and examine the sick. Yesterday I accompanied him in one of these daily rounds.

After a ride of several miles through the woods, in the rear of the plantations we came to his largest negro-settlement. There was a street, or common, two hundred feet wide, on which the cabins of the negroes fronted. Each cabin was a framed building, the walls boarded and whitewashed on the outside, lathed and plastered within, the roof shingled; forty-two feet long, twenty-one feet wide, divided into two family tenements, each twenty-one by twenty-one; each tenement divided into three rooms—one, the common household apartment, twenty-one by ten; each of the others (bedrooms), ten by ten. There was a brick fire-place in the middle of the long side of each living room, the chimneys rising in one, in the middle of the roof. Besides these rooms, each tenement had a cock-loft, entered by steps from the household room. Each tenement is occupied, on an average, by five persons. There were in them closets, with locks and keys, and a varying quantity of rude furniture. Each cabin stood two hundred feet from the next, and the street in front of them being two hundred feet wide, they were just that distance apart each way. The people were nearly all absent at work, and had locked their outer doors, taking the keys with them. Each cabin has a front and back door, and each room a window, closed by a wooden shutter, swinging outward, on hinges. Between each tenement and the next house, is a small piece of ground, inclosed with palings, in which are coops of fowl with chickens, hovels for nests, and for sows with pig. There were a great many fowls in the street. The negroes' swine are allowed to run in the woods, each owner having his own distinguished by a peculiar mark. In the rear of the years were gardens—a half-acre to each family. Internally the cabins appeared dirty and disordered, which was rather a pleasant indication that their home-life was not interfered with, though I found certain police regulations were enforced.

The cabin nearest the overseer's house was used as a nursery. Having driven up to this, Mr. X. inquired first of an old nurse how the children were; whether there had been any births since his last visit; spoke to two convalescent young mothers, who were lounging on the floor of the portico, with the children, and then asked if there were any sick people.

"Nobody, oney dat boy, Sam, sar."

"What Sam is that?

"Dat little Sam, sar; Tom's Sue's Sam, sar."

"What's the matter with him?'

"Don' 'spec dere's noting much de matter wid him now, sar. He came in S'dy complainin' he had de stomach-ache, an' I gin him some ile, sar; 'spec he mus' be well, dis time, but he din go out dis morning'."

"Well, I'll see to him.

Mr. X. went to Tom's Sue's cabin, looked at the boy, and, concluding that he was well, though he lay abed, and pretended to cry with pain, ordered him to go out to work. Then, meeting the overseer, who was just riding away, on some business of the plantation, he remained some time in conversation with him, while I occupied myself in making a sketch of the nursery and street of the settlement in my note-book. On the verandah and the steps of the nursery, there were twenty-seven children, most of them infants, that had been left there by their mothers, while they were working their tasks in the fields. They probably make a visit to them once or twice during the day, to nurse them, and receive them to take to their cabins, or where they like, when they have finished their tasks—generally in the middle of the afternoon. The older children were fed with porridge, by the general nurse. A number of girls, eight or ten years old, were occupied in holding and tending the youngest infants. Those a little older—the crawlers—were in the pen, and those big enough to toddle were playing on the steps, or before the house. Some of these, with two or three bigger ones, were singing and dancing about a fire that they had made on the ground. They were not at all disturbed or interrupted in their amusement by the presence of their owner and myself. At twelve years of age, the children are first put to regular field-work; until then no labour is required of them, except, perhaps, occasionally they are charged with some light kind of duty, such as frightening birds from corn. When first sent to the field, one quarter of an able-bodied hand's day's work is ordinarily allotted to them, as their task.

From the settlement, we drove to the "mill"—not a flouring mill, though I believe there is a run of stones in it—but a monster barn, with more extensive and better machinery for threshing and storing rice, driven by a steam-engine, than I have ever seen used for grain before. Adjoining the mill-house were shops and sheds, in which blacksmiths, carpenters, and other mechanics—all slaves, belonging to Mr. X.— were at work. He called my attention to the excellence of their workmanship, and said that they exercised as much ingenuity and skill as the ordinary mechanics that he was used to employ in New England. He pointed out to me some carpenter's work, a part of which had been executed by a New England mechanic, and a part by one of his own hands, which indicated that the latter was much the better workman.

I was gratified by this, for I had been so often told, in Virginia, by gentlemen anxious to convince me that the negro was incapable of being educated or improved to a condition in which it would be safe to trust him with himself—that no negro-mechanic could ever be taught, or induced to work carefully or nicely—that I had begun to believe it might be so.

We were attended through the mill-house by a respectable-looking, orderly, and quiet-mannered mulatto, who was called, by his master, "the watchman." His duties, however, as they were described to me, were those of a steward or intendant. He carried, by a strap at his waist, a very large number of keys, and had charge of all the stores of provisions, tools, and materials of the plantations, as well as of all their produce before it was shipped to market. He weighed and measured out all the rations of the slaves and the cattle; superintended the mechanics, and made and repaired, as was necessary, all the machinery, including the steam-engine.

In all these departments, his authority was superior to that of the overseer. The overseer received his private allowance of family provisions from him, as did also the head-servant at the mansion, who was his brother. His responsibility was much greater than that of the overseer; and Mr. X. said he would trust him with much more than he would any overseer he had ever known.

Anxious to learn how this trustworthiness and intelligence, so unusual in a slave, had been developed or ascertained, I inquired of his history which was briefly as follows.

Being the son of a favourite house-servant, he had been, as a child, associated with the white family, and received by chance something of the early education of the white children. When old enough, he had been employed, for some years, as a waiter; but, at his own request, was eventually allowed to learn the blacksmith's trade, in the plantation shop. Showing ingenuity and talent, he was afterwards employed to make and repair the plantation cotton-gins. Finally, his owner took him to a steam-engine builder, and paid $500 to have him instructed as a machinist. After he had become a skillful workman, he obtained employment as an engineer; and for some years continued in this occupation, and was allowed to spend his wages for himself. Finding, however, that he was acquiring dissipated habits, and wasting his earnings, Mr. X. eventually brought him, much against his inclinations, back to the plantations. Being allowed peculiar privileges, and given duties wholly flattering to his self-respect, he soon became contented; and, of course, was able to be extremely valuable to his owner.

I have seen another slave-engineer. The gentleman who employed him told me that he was a man of talent, and of great worth of character. He had desired to make him free, but his owner, who was a member of the Board of Brokers, and of Dr.—'s Church, in New York, believed that Providence designed the negro race for slavery, and refused to sell him for that purpose. He thought it better that he (his owner) should continue to receive two hundred dollars a year for his services, while he continued able to work, because then, as he said, he should feel responsible that he did not starve, or come upon the public for a support, in his old age. The man himself, having light and agreeable duties, well provided for, furnished with plenty of spending money by his employer, patronized and flattered by the white people, honoured and looked up to by those of his own colour, was rather indifferent in the matter; or even, perhaps, preferred to remain a slave, to being transported for life to Africa.

The watchman was a fine-looking fellow; as we were returning from church, on Sunday, he had passed us, well dressed and well mounted, and as he raised his hat, to salute us, there was nothing in his manner or appearance, except his colour, to distinguish him from a gentleman of good breeding and fortune.

When we were leaving the house, to go to church, on Sunday, after all the white family had entered their carriages, or mounted their horses, the head house-servant also mounted a horse—as he did so, slipping a coin into the hands of the boy who had been holding him. Afterwards, we passed a family of negroes, in a light waggon, the oldest among them driving the horse. On my inquiring if the slaves were allowed to take horses to drive to church, I was informed that in each of these three cases, the horses belonged to the negroes who were driving or riding them. The old man was infirm, and Mr. X. had given him a horse, to enable him to move about. He was probably employed to look after the cattle at pasture, or at something in which it was necessary, for his usefulness, that he should have a horse; I say this, because I afterwards found, in similar cases on other plantations, that it was so. But the watchman and the house servant had bought their horses with money. The watchman was believed to own three horses; and, to account for his wealth, Mr. X.'s son told me that his father considered him a very valuable servant, and frequently encouraged his good behaviour with handsome gratuities. He receives, probably, considerably higher wages, in fact (in the form of presents), than the white overseer. He knew his father gave him two hundred dollars at once, a short time ago. The watchman has a private house, and, no doubt, lives in considerable luxury.

Will it be said, "therefore, Slavery is neither necessarily degrading nor inhumane?" On the other hand, so far as it is not, there is no apology for it. It is possible, though not probable, that this fine fellow, if he had been born a free man, would be no better employed than he is here; but in that case, where is the advantage? Certainly not in the economy of the arrangement. And if he were self-dependent, if, especially, he had to provide for the present and future of those he loved, and was able to do so, would he not necessarily live as a happier, stronger, better, and more respectable man?

After passing through tool-rooms, corn-rooms, mule-stables, store-rooms, and a large garden, in which vegetables to be distributed among the negroes, as well as for the family, are grown, we walked to the rice-land. It is divided by embankments into fields of about twenty acres each, but varying somewhat in size, according to the course of the river. The arrangements are such that each field may be flooded independently of the rest, and they are subdivided by open ditches into rectangular plats of a quarter acre each. We first proceeded to where twenty or thirty women and girls were engaged in raking together, in heaps and winrows, the stubble and rubbish left on the field after the last crop, and burning it. The main object of this operation is to kill all the seeds of weeds, or of rice, on the ground. Ordinarily it is done by tasks—a certain number of the small divisions of the field being given to each hand to burn in a day; but owing to a more than usual amount of rain having fallen lately, and some other causes, making the work harder in some places than others, the women were now working by the day, under the direction of a "driver," a negro man, who walked about among them, taking care that they left nothing unburned. Mr. X. inspected the ground they had gone over, to see whether the driver had done his duty. It had been sufficiently well burned, but not more than a quarter as much ground had been gone over, he said, as was usually burned in task-work,—and he thought they had been very lazy, and reprimanded them. The driver made some little apology, but the women offered no reply, keeping steadily and, it seemed, sullenly, on at their work.

In the next field, twenty men, or boys, for none of them looked as if they were full-grown, were ploughing, each with a single mule, and a light, New York-made plough. The soil was friable, the ploughing easy, and the mules proceeded at a smart pace; the furrows were straight, regular, and well turned. Their task was nominally an acre and a quarter a day; somewhat less actually, as the measure includes the space occupied by the ditches, which are two to three feet wide, running around each quarter of an acre. The ploughing gang was superintended by a driver, who was provided with a watch; and while we were looking at them he called out that it was twelve o'clock. The mules were immediately taken from the ploughs, and the plough-boys mounting them, leapt the ditches, and cantered off to the stables, to feed them. One or two were ordered to take their ploughs to the blacksmith, for repairs.

The ploughmen got their dinner at this time: those not using horses do not usually dine till they have finished their tasks; but this, I believe, is optional with them. They commence work, I was told, at sunrise, and at about eight o'clock have breakfast brought to them in the field, each hand having left a bucket with the cook for that purpose. All who are working in connection, leave their work together, and gather about a fire, where they generally spend about half an hour. The provisions furnished consist mainly of meal, rice, and vegetables, with salt and molasses, and occasionally bacon, fish, and coffee. The allowance is a peck of meal, or an equivalent quantity of rice per week, to each working hand, old or young, besides small stores. Mr. X. says that he has lately given a less amount of meat than is now usual on plantations, having observed that the general health of the negroes is not as good as formerly, when no meat at all was customarily given them. (The general impression among planters is, that the negroes work much better for being supplied with three or four pounds of bacon a week.)

Leaving the rice-land, we went next to some of the upland fields, where we found several other gangs of negroes at work; one entirely of men engaged in ditching; another of women, and another of boys and girls, "listing" an old corn-field with hoes. All of them were working by tasks, and were overlooked by negro drivers. They all laboured with greater rapidity and cheerfulness than any slaves I have before seen; and the women struck their hoes as if they were strong, and well able to engage in muscular labour. The expression of their faces was generally repulsive, and their *ensemble* anything but agreeable. The dress of most was uncouth and cumbrous, dirty and ragged; reefed up, as I have once before described, at the hips, so as to show their heavy legs, wrapped round with a piece of old blanket, in lieu of leggings or stockings. Most of them worked with bare arms, but wore strong shoes on their feet, and handkerchiefs on their heads; some of them were smoking, and each gang had a fire burning on the ground, near where they were at work, by which to light their pipes and warm their breakfast. Mr. X. said this was always their custom, even in summer. To each gang a boy or girl was also attached, whose business it was to bring water for them to drink, and to go for anything required by the driver. The drivers would frequently call back a hand to go over again some piece of his or her task that had not been worked to his satisfaction, and were constantly calling to one or another, with a harsh and peremptory voice, to strike harder, or hoe deeper, and otherwise taking care that the work was well done. Mr. X. asked if Little Sam ("Tom's Sue's Sam") worked yet with the "three-quarter" hands, and learning that he did, ordered him to be put with the full hands, observing that though rather short, he was strong and stout, and, being twenty years old, well able to do a man's work.

The field-hands are all divided into four classes, according to their physical capacities. The children beginning as "quarter-hands," advancing to "half-hands," and then to "three-quarter hands;" and, finally, when mature, and able-bodied, healthy, and strong, to "full hands." As they decline in strength, from age, sickness, or other cause, they retrograde in the scale, and proportionately less labour is required of them. Many, of course, of naturally weak frame, never are put among the full hands. Finally, the aged are left out at the annual classification, and no more regular field-work is required of them, although they are generally provided with some light, sedentary occupation. I saw one old woman picking "tailings" of rice out of a heap of chaff, an occupation at which she was probably not earning her salt. Mr. X. told me she was a native African, having been brought when a girl from the Guinea coast. She spoke almost unintelligibly; but after some other conversation, in which I had not been able to understand a word she said, he jokingly proposed to send her back to Africa. She expressed her preference to remain where she was, very emphatically. "Why?" She did not answer readily, but being pressed, threw up her palsied hands, and said furiously, "I lubs 'ou, mas'r, oh, I lubs 'ou. I don't want go 'way from 'ou."

The field-hands are nearly always worked in gangs, the strength of a gang varying according to the work that engages it; usually it numbers twenty or more, and is directed by a driver. As on most large plantations, whether of rice or cotton, in Eastern Georgia and South Carolina, nearly all ordinary and regular work is performed *by tasks:* that is to say, each hand has his labour for the day marked out before him, and can take his own time to do it in. For instance, in making drains in light, clean meadow land, each man or woman of the full hands is required to dig one thousand cubic feet; in swamp-land that is being prepared for rice culture, where there are not many stumps, the task for a ditcher is five hundred feet: while in a very strong cypress swamp, only two hundred feet is required; in hoeing rice, a certain number of rows, equal to one-half or two-thirds of an acre, according to the condition of the land; in sowing rice (strewing in drills), two acres; in reaping rice (if it stands well), three-quarters of an acre; or, sometimes a gang will be required to reap, tie in sheaves, and carry to the stack-yard the produce of a certain area, commonly equal to one fourth the number of acres that there are hands working together. Hoeing cotton, corn, or potatoes; one half to one acre. Threshing; five to six hundred sheaves. In ploughing rice-land (light, clean, mellow soil) with a yoke of oxen, one acre a day, including the ground lost in and near the drains—the oxen being changed at noon. A cooper, also, for instance, is required to make barrels at the rate of eighteen a week. Drawing staves, 500 a day. Hoop poles, 120. Squaring timber, 100 ft. Laying worm-fence, 50 panels per hand. Post and rail do., posts set 2-1/2 to 3 ft. deep, 9 ft. apart, nine or ten panels per hand. In getting fuel from the woods, (pine, to be cut and split,) one cord is the task for the day. In "mauling rails," the taskman selecting the trees (pine) that he judges will split easiest, one hundred a day, ends not sharpened.

These are the tasks for first-class able-bodied men; they are lessened by one quarter for three quarter hands, and proportionately for the lighter classes. In allotting the tasks, the drivers are expected to put the weaker hands where (if there is any choice in the appearance of the ground, as where certain rows in hoeing corn would be less weedy than others,) they will be favoured.

These tasks certainly would not be considered excessively hard, by a Northern labourer; and, in point of fact, the more industrious and active hands finish them often by two o'clock. I saw one or two leaving the field soon after one o'clock, several about two; and between three and four, I met a dozen women and several men coming home to their cabins, having finished their day's work.

Under this "Organization of Labour," most of the slaves work rapidly and well. In nearly all ordinary work, custom has settled the extent of the task, and it is difficult to increase it. The driver who marks it out, has to remain on the ground until it is finished, and has no interest in overmeasuring it; and if it should be systematically increased very much, there is danger of a general stampede to the "swamp"—a danger the slave can always hold before his master's cupidity. In fact, it is looked upon *in this region* as a proscriptive right of the negroes to have this incitement to diligence offered them; and the man who denied it, or who attempted to lessen it, would, it is said, suffer in his reputation, as well as experience much annoyance from the obstinate "rascality" of his negroes. Notwithstanding this, I have heard a man assert, boastingly, that he made his negroes habitually perform double the customary tasks. Thus we get a glimpse again of the black side. If he is allowed the power to do this, what may not a man do?

It is the driver's duty to make the tasked hands do their work well. If, in their haste to finish it, they neglect to do it properly, he "sets them back," so that carelessness will hinder more than it will hasten the completion of their tasks.

In the selection of drivers, regard seems to be had to size and strength—at least, nearly all the drivers I have seen are tall and strong men—but a great deal of judgment, requiring greater capacity of mind than the ordinary slave is often supposed to be possessed of, is certainly needed in them. A good driver is very valuable and usually holds office for life. His authority is not limited to the direction of labour in the field, but extends to the general deportment of the negroes. He is made to do the duties of policeman, and even of police magistrate. It is his duty, for instance, on Mr. X.'s estate, to keep order in the settlement; and, if two persons, men or women, are fighting, it is his duty to immediately separate them, and then to "whip them both."

Before any field of work is entered upon by a gang, the driver who is to superintend them has to measure and stake off the tasks. To do this at all accurately, in irregular-shaped fields, must require considerable powers of calculation. A driver, with a boy to set the stakes, I was told, would accurately lay out forty acres a day, in half-acre tasks. The only instrument used is a five-foot measuring rod. When the gang comes to the field, he points out to each person his or her duty for the day, and then walks about among them, looking out that each proceeds properly. If, after a hard day's labour, he sees that the gang has been overtasked, owing to a miscalculation of the difficulty of the work, he may excuse the completion of the tasks; but he is not allowed to extend them. In the case of uncompleted tasks, the body of the gang begin new tasks the next day, and only a sufficient number are detailed from it to complete, during the day, the unfinished tasks of the day before. The relation of the driver to the working hands seems to be similar to that of the boatswain to the seamen in the navy, or of the sergeant to the privates in the army.

Having generally had long experience on the plantation, the advice of the drivers is commonly taken in nearly all the administration, and frequently they are, *de facto*, the managers. Orders on important points of the plantation economy, I have heard given by the proprietor directly to them, without the overseer's being consulted or informed of them; and it is often left with them to decide when and how long to flow the rice-grounds—the proprietor and overseer deferring to their more experienced judgment. Where the drivers are discreet, experienced, and trusty, the overseer is frequently employed merely as a matter of form, to comply with the laws requiring the superintendence or presence of a white man among every body of slaves; and his duty is rather to inspect and report than to govern. Mr. X. considers his overseer an uncommonly efficient and faithful one, but he would not employ him, even during the summer, when he is absent for several months, if the law did not require it. He has sometimes left his plantation in the care of one of the drivers for a considerable length of time, after having discharged an overseer; and he thinks it has then been quite as well conducted as ever. His overseer consults the drivers on all important points, and is governed by their advice.

Mr. X. said, that though overseers sometimes punished the negroes severely, and otherwise ill-treated them, it is their more common fault to indulge them foolishly in their disposition to idleness, or in other ways to curry favour with them, so they may not inform the proprietor of their own misconduct or neglect. He has his overseer bound to certain rules, by written contract; and it is stipulated that he can discharge him at any moment, without remuneration for his loss of time and inconvenience, if he should at any time be dissatisfied with him. One of the rules is, that he shall never punish a negro with his own hands, and that corporeal punishment, when necessary, shall be inflicted by the drivers. The advantage of this is, that it secures time for deliberation, and prevents punishment being made in sudden passion. His drivers are not allowed to carry their whips with them in the field; so that if the overseer wishes a hand punished, it is necessary to call a driver; and the driver has then to go to his cabin, which is, perhaps, a mile or two distant, to get his whip, before it can be applied.

I asked how often the necessity of punishment occurred?

"Sometimes, perhaps, not once for two or three weeks; then it will seem as if the devil had got into them all, and there is a good deal of it."

As the negroes finish the labour required of them by Mr. X., at three or four o'clock in the afternoon, they can employ the remainder of the day in labouring for themselves, if they choose. Each family has a half-acre of land allotted to it, for a garden; besides which, there is a large vegetable garden, cultivated by a gardener for the plantation, from which they are supplied, to a greater or lesser extent. They are at liberty to sell whatever they choose from the products of their own garden, and to make what they can by keeping swine and fowls. Mr. X.'s family have no other supply of poultry and eggs than what is obtained by purchase from his own negroes; they frequently, also, purchase game from them. The only restriction upon their traffic is a "liquor law." They are not allowed to buy or sell ardent spirits. This prohibition, like liquor laws elsewhere, unfortunately, cannot be enforced; and, of late years, grog-shops, at which stolen goods are bought from the slaves, and poisonous liquors—chiefly the worst whisky, much watered and made stupefying by an infusion of tobacco—are clandestinely sold to them, have become an established evil, and the planters find themselves powerless to cope with it. They have, here, lately organized an association for this purpose, and have brought several offenders to trial; but, as it is a penitentiary offence, the culprit spares no pains or expense to avoid conviction—and it is almost impossible, in a community of which so large a proportion is poor and degraded, to have a jury sufficiently honest and intelligent to permit the law to be executed.

A remarkable illustration of this evil has lately occurred. A planter, discovering that a considerably quantity of cotton had been stolen from him, informed the patrol of the neighboring planters of it. A stratagem was made use of, to detect the thief, and, what was of much more importance—there being no question but that this was a slave—to discover for whom the thief worked. A lot of cotton was prepared, by mixing hair with it, and put in a tempting place. A negro was seen to take it, and was followed by scouts to a grog-shop, several miles distant, where he sold it—its real value being nearly ten dollars—for ten cents, taking his pay in liquor. The man was arrested, and, the theft being made to appear, by the hair, before a justice, obtained bail in $2,000, to answer at the higher court. Some of the best legal counsel of the State has been engaged, to obtain, if possible, his conviction.

This difficulty in the management of slaves is a great and very rapidly increasing one. Everywhere that I have been, I have found the planters provoked and angry about it. A swarm of Jews, within the last ten years, has settled in nearly every Southern town, many of them men of no character, opening cheap clothing and trinket shops; ruining, or driving out of business, many of the old retailers, and engaging in an unlawful trade with the simple negroes, which is found very profitable.[1]

1. *From the Charleston Standard, Nov. 23rd,* 1854.—"This abominable practice of trading with slaves is not only taking our produce from us, but injuring our slave property. It is true the owner of slaves may lock, watch, and whip, as much as he pleases—the negroes will steal and trade as long as white persons hold out to them temptations to steal and bring to them. Three-fourths of the persons who are guilty, you can get no fine from; and, if they have some property, all they have to do is confess a judgment to a friend, go to jail, and swear out. It is no uncommon thing for a man to be convicted of offences against the State, and against the persons and property of individuals, and pay the fines, costs, and damages, by swearing out of jail, and then go and commit similar offences. The State, or the party injured, has the cost of all these prosecutions and suits to pay, besides the trouble of attending Court: the guilty is convicted, the injured prosecutor punished."

The law which prevents the reception of the evidence of a negro in courts, here strikes back, with a most annoying force, upon the dominant power itself. In the mischief thus arising, we see a striking illustration of the danger which stands before the South, whenever its prosperity shall invite extensive immigration, and lead what would otherwise be a healthy competition to flow through its channels of industry.

This injury to slave property, from grog-shops, furnishes the grand argument for the Maine Law at the South.[1]

Mr. X. remarks that his arrangements allow his servants no excuse for dealing with these fellows. He has a rule to purchase everything they desire to sell, and to give them a high price for it himself. Eggs constitute a circulating medium on the plantation. Their par value is considered to be twelve for a dime, at which they may always be exchanged for cash, or left on deposit, without interest, at his kitchen.

Whatever he takes of them he cannot use in his own family, or has not occasion to give to others of his servants, is sent to town to be resold. The negroes do not commonly take money for the articles he has of them, but the value of them is put to their credit, and a regular account kept with them. He has a store, usually well supplied with articles that they most want, which are purchased in large quantities, and sold to them at wholesale prices; thus giving them a great advantage in dealing with him rather than with the grog-shops. His slaves are sometimes his creditors to large amounts; at the present time he says he owes them about five hundred dollars. A woman has charge of the store, and when there is anything called for that she cannot supply, it is usually ordered, by the next conveyance, of his factors in town.

The ascertained practicability of thus dealing with slaves, together with the obvious advantages of the method of working them by tasks, which I have described, seem to me to indicate that it is not so impracticable as is generally supposed, if only it was desired by those having the power, to rapidly extinguish Slavery, and while

1. *From an Address to the people of Georgia, by a Committee of the State Temperance Society, prior to the election of* 1855.—"We propose to turn the 2,200 *foreign* grog-shop keepers, in Georgia, out of office, and ask them to help us. They (the Know-Nothings) reply, 'We have no time for that now—we are trying to turn *foreigners* out of office; and when we call upon the Democratic party for aid, they excuse themselves, upon the ground that they have work enough to do in keeping these foreigners in office."
From the Penfield (Ga.) Temperance Banner, Sept, 29th, 1855
"OUR SLAVE POPULATION
"We take the following from the *Savannah Journal and Courier,* and would ask every candid reader if the evils referred to ought not to be corrected. How shall it be done?
" 'By reference to the recent homicide of a negro, in another column, some facts will be seen suggestive of a state of things, in this part of our population, which should not exist, and which cannot endure without danger, both to them and to us. The collision, which terminated thus fatally, occurred at an hour past midnight—at a time when none but the evil-disposed are stirring, unless driven by necessity; and yet, at that hour, those negroes and others, as many as chose, were passing about the country, with ample opportunity to commit any act which might happen to enter their heads. In fact, they did engage, in the public highway in a broil terminating in homicide. It is not difficult to imagine that their evil passions might have taken a very different direction, with as little danger of meeting control or obstacle.
" 'But it is shown, too, that to the impunity thus given them by the darkness of midnight, was added the incitement to crime drawn from the abuse of liquor. They had just left one of those resorts where the negro is supplied with the most villainously-poisonous compounds, fit only to excite him to deeds of blood and violence. The part that this had in the slaughter of Saturday night ,we are enabled only to imagine; but experience would teach us that its share was by no means small. Indeed, we have the declaration of the slayer, that the blow, by which he was exasperated so as to return it by the fatal stab, was inflicted by a bottle of brandy! In this fact, we fear, is a clue to the whole history of the transaction.'
"Here, evidently, are considerations deserving the grave notice of, not only those who own negroes, but for all others who live in a society where they are held."

doing so, to educate the negro for taking care of himself, in freedom. Let, for instance, any slave be provided with all things he will demand, as far as practicable, and charge him for them at certain prices—honest, market prices for his necessities, higher prices for harmless luxuries, and excessive, but not absolutely prohibitory, prices for everything likely to do him harm. Credit him, at a fixed price, for every day's work he does, and for all above a certain easily accomplished task in a day, at an increased price, so that his reward will be in an increasing ratio to his perseverance. Let the prices of provisions be so proportioned to the price of task-work, that it will be about as easy as it is now for him to obtain a bare subsistence. When he has no food and shelter due to him, let him be confined in solitude, or otherwise punished, until he asks for opportunity to earn exemption from punishment by labour.

When he desires to marry, and can persuade any woman to marry him, let the two be dealt with as in partnership. Thus, a young man or young woman will be attractive somewhat in proportion to his or her reputation for industry and providence. Thus industry and providence will become fashionable. Oblige them to purchase food for their children, and let them have the benefit of their children's labour, and they will be careful to teach their children to avoid waste, and to honour labour. Let those who have not gained credit while hale and young, sufficient to support themselves in comfort when prevented by age or infirmity from further labour, be supported by a tax upon all the negroes of the plantation, or of a community. Improvidence, and pretence of inability to labour, will then be disgraceful.

When any man has a balance to his credit equal to his value as a slave, let that constitute him a free man. It will be optional with him and his employer whether he shall continue longer in the relation of a servant. If desirable for both that he should, it is probable that he will; for unless he is honest, prudent, industrious, and discreet, he will not have acquired the means of purchasing his freedom.

If he is so, he will remain where he is, unless he is more wanted elsewhere; a fact that will be established by his being called away by higher wages, or the prospect of greater ease and comfort elsewhere. If he is so drawn off, it is better for all parties concerned that he should go. Better for his old master; for he would not refuse him sufficient wages to induce him to stay, unless he could get the work he wanted him to do done cheaper than he would justly do it. Poor wages would certainly, in the long run, buy poor work; fair wages, fair work.

Of course there will be exceptional cases, but they will always operate as cautions for the future, not only to the parties suffering, but to all who observe them. And be sure they will not be suffered, among ignorant people, to be lost. This is the beneficient function of gossip, with which wise and broad-working minds have nothing to do, this not being benefitted by the iteration of the lessons of life.

Married persons, of course, can only become free together. In the appraisement of their value, let that of their young children be included, so that they cannot be parted from them; but with regard to children old enough to earn something more than their living, let it be optional what they do for them.

Such a system would simply combine the commendable elements of the emancipation law of Cuba,[1] and those of the reformatory punishment system, now in

---

[1] In Cuba every slave has the privilege of emancipating himself, by paying a price which does not depend upon the selfish exactions of the masters; but it is either a fixed price, or else is fixed, in each case, by

successful operation in some of the British penal colonies, with a few practical modifications. Further modifications would, doubtless, be needed, which any man who has had much practical experience in dealing with slaves might readily suggest. Much might be learned from the experience of the system pursued in the penal colonies, some account of which may be seen in the report of the Prisoners' Aid Society of New York, for 1854, or in a previous little work of my own. I have here only desired to suggest, apropos to my friend's experience, the practicability of providing the negroes an education in essential social morality, while they are drawing towards personal freedom; a desideratum with those who do not consider Slavery a purely and eternally desirable thing for both slave and slave-master, which the present system is calculated, as far as possible, in every direction to oppose.

Education in theology and letters could be easily combined with such a plan as I have hinted at; or, if a State should wish to encourage the improvement of its negro constituent—as, in the progress of enlightenment and Christianity, may be hoped to eventually occur—a simple provision of the law, making a certain standard of proficiency the condition of political freedom, would probably create a natural demand for education, which commerce, under its inexorable higher laws, would be obliged to satisfy.

I do not think, after all I have heard to favour it, that there is any good reason to consider the negro, naturally and essentially, the moral inferior of the white; or, that if he is so, it is in those elements of character which should for ever prevent us from trusting him with equal social munities with ourselves.

So far as I have observed, slaves show themselves worthy of trust most, where their masters are most considerate and liberal towards them. Far more so, for instance, on the small farms of North Carolina than on the plantations of Virginia and South Carolina. Mr. X.'s slaves are permitted to purchase fire-arms and ammunition, and to keep them in their cabins; and his wife and daughters reside with him, among them, the doors of the house never locked, or windows closed, perfectly defenceless, and miles distant from any other white family.

Another evidence that negroes, even in slavery, when trusted, may prove wonderfully reliable, I will subjoin, in a letter written by Mr. Alexander Smets, of Savannah, to a friend in New York, in 1853. It is hardly necessary to say, that the "servants" spoken of were negroes, and the "suspicious characters," providentially removed, were whites. The letter was not written for publication:—

> The epidemic which spread destruction and desolation through our city, and many other places in most of the Southern States, was, with the exception of that of 1820, the most deadly that was ever known here. Its appearance being sudden, the inhabitants were seized with a panic, which caused an immediate *sauve qui peut* seldom witnessed before. I left, or rather fled, for the sake of my daughters, to Sparta, Hancock county. They were dreadfully frightened.
>
> Of a population of fifteen thousand, six thousand, who could not get away, remained, nearly all of whom were more or less seized with the prevailing disease. The negroes, with very few exceptions, escaped.

disinterested appraisers. The consequence is, that emancipations are constantly going on, and the free people of colour are becoming enlightened, cultivated, and wealthy. In no part of the United States do they occupy the high social position which they may enjoy in Cuba.

Amidst the desolation and gloom pervading the deserted streets, there was a feature that showed our slaves in a favourable light. There were entire blocks of houses, which were either entirely deserted—the owners in many instances having, in their flight, forgotten to lock them up—or left in charge of the servants. A finer opportunity for plunder could not be desired by thieves; and yet the city was remarkable, during the time, for order and quietness. There were scarcely any robberies committed, and as regards fires, so common in the winter, none! Every householder, whose premises had escaped the fury of the late terrific storm, found them in the same condition he had left them. Had not the yellow fever scared away or killed those suspicious characters, whose existence is a problem, and who prowl about every city, I fear that our city might have been laid waste. Of the whole board of directors of five banks, three or four remained, and these at one time were sick. Several of the clerks were left, each in the possession of a single one. For several weeks it was difficult to get anything to eat; the bakers were either sick or dead. The markets closed, no countryman dared venture himself into the city with the usual supplies for the table, and the packets had discontinued their trips. I shall stop, otherwise I could fill a volume with the occurrences and incidents of the dismal period of the epidemic.

On most of the large rice plantations which I have seen in this vicinity, there is a small chapel, which the negroes call their prayer-house. The owner of one of these told me that, having furnished the prayer-house with seats having a back-rail, his negroes petitioned him to remove it, because it did not leave them *room enough to pray.* It was explained to me that it is their custom, in social worship, to work themselves up to a great pitch of excitement, in which they yell and cry aloud, and finally, shriek and leap up, clapping their hands and dancing, as it is done at heathen festivals. The back-rail they found to seriously impede this exercise.

Mr. X. told me that he had endeavoured, but with little success, to prevent this shouting and jumping of the negroes at their meetings on his plantation, from a conviction that there was not the slightest element of religious sentiment in it. He considered it to be engaged in more as an exciting amusement than from any really religious impulse. In the town churches, except, perhaps, those managed and conducted almost exclusively by negroes, the slaves are said to commonly engage in religious exercises in a sober and decorous manner; yet, a member of a Presbyterian church in a Southern city told me, that he had seen the negroes in his own house of worship, during "a season of revival," leqp from their seats, throw their arms wildly in the air, shout vehemently and unintelligibly, cry, groan, rend their clothes, and fall into cataleptic trances.

On almost every large plantation, and in every neighbourhood of small ones, there is one man who has come to be considered the head or pastor of the local church. The office among the negroes, as among all other people, confers a certain importance and power. A part of the reverence attaching to the duties is given to the person; vanity and self-confidence are cultivated, and a higher ambition aroused than can usually enter the mind of a slave. The self-respect of the preacher is also often increased by the consideration in which he is held by his master, as well as by his fellows; thus, the preachers generally have an air of superiority to other negroes; they acquire a remarkable memory of words, phrases, and forms; a curious sort of poetic talent is developed, and a habit is obtained of rhapsodizing and exciting furious emotions, to a great degree spurious and temporary, in themselves and others, through the imagination. I was introduced, the other day, to a preacher, who was represented to be quite distinguished among them. I took his hand, respectfully, and said I was happy to meet him. He seemed to take this for a joke, and laughed heartily. He was a "driver," and my friend said—

"He drives the negroes at the cotton all the week, and Sundays he drives them at the Gospel—don't you, Ned?"

He commenced to reply in some scriptural phrase, soberly; but before he could say three words, began to laugh again, and reeled off like a drunken man—entirely overcome with merriment. He recovered himself in a moment, and returned to us.

"They say he preaches very powerfully, too."

"Yes, massa! 'kordin' to der grace—*yah! yah!*"

And he staggered off again, with the peculiar hearty negro guffaw. My friend's tone was, I supposed, slightly humorous, but I was grave, and really meant to treat him respectfully, wishing to draw him into conversation; but he had got the impression that I intended to make fun of him, and generously assuming a merry humour, I found it impossible to get a serious reply.

A majority of the public houses of worship at the South are small, rude structures of logs, or rough boards, built by the united labour or contributions of the people of a large neighbourhood or district of country, and are used as places of assembly for all public purposes. Few of them have any regular clergymen, but preachers of different denominations go from one to another, sometimes in a defined rotation, or "circuit," so that they may be expected at each of their stations at regular intervals. A late report of the Southern Aid Society states that hardly one-fifth of the preachers are regularly educated for their business, and that "you would starve a host of them if you debarred them from seeking additional support for their families by worldly occupation."

In one presbytery of the Presbyterian Church, which is, perhaps, the richest, and includes the most educated body of people of all the Southern Churches, there are twenty-one ministers whose wages are not over two hundred and fifty dollars each. The proportion of ministers, of all sorts, to people, is estimated at one to thirteen hundred. (In the Free States it is estimated at one to nine hundred.) The report of this Society also states, that "within the limits of the United States religious destitution lies comparatively at the South and South-west; and that from the first settlement of the country the North has preserved a decided religious superiority over the South, especially in three important particulars: in ample supply of Christian institutions; extensive supply of Christian truth; and thorough Christian regimen, both in the Church and in the community." It is added that, "while the South-western States have always needed a stronger arm of the Christian ministry to raise them up toward a Christian equality with their Northern brethren, their supply in this respect has always been decidedly inferior." The reason of this is the same with that which explains the general ignorance of the people of the South: The effect of Slavery in preventing social association of the whites, and in encouraging vagabond and improvident habits of life among the poor.

The two largest denominations of Christians at the South are the Methodists and

Baptists—the last having a numerical superiority. There are some subdivisions of each, and of the Baptists, especially, the nature of which I do not understand. Two grand divisions of the Baptists are known as the Hard Shells and the Soft Shells. There is an intense rivalry and jealousy among these various sects and sub-sects, and the controversy between them is carried on with a bitterness and persistence exceeding anything which I have known at the North, and in a manner which curiously indicates how the terms Christianity, piety, etc., are misapplied to partisanship and conditions of the imagination.

A general want of essential reverence of character seems to be evidenced in the frequent familiar and public use of expressions of rare reverence, and in high-coloured descriptions of personal feelings and sentiments, which, if actual, can only be among a man's dearest, most interior and secret, stillest, and most uncommunicable experiences. Men talk in public places, in the churches, and in bar-rooms, in the stage-coach, and at the fireside, of their personal communions with the Deity, and of the mutations of their harmony with His Spirit, just as they do about their family and business matters. The familiar use of Scripture expressions by the negroes, I have already indicated. This is not confined to them. A dram-seller advertises thus:—

'FAITH WITHOUT WORKS IS DEAD.'
In order to engage in a more 'honourable' business, I offer for sale, cheap for cash, my stock of
LIQUORS, BAR-FIXTURES, BILLIARD TABLE, &c., &c.
If not sold privately, by the 20th day of May, I will sell same at public auction. 'Shew me thy faith without thy works, and I will shew thee my faith by my works.'
E. KEYSER.

At a Sunday dinner-table, at a village inn in Virginia, two or three men had taken seats with me, who had, as they said, "been to the preachin'." A child had been baptized, and the discourse had been a defence of infant baptism.

"I'm damned," said one, "ef he teched on the primary significance of baptism, at all—buryin' with Jesus."

"They wus the weakest arguments for sprinklin' that ever I heerd," said another—a hot, red-faced, corpulent man—"and his sermon was two hours long, for when he stopped I looked at my watch. I thought it should be a lesson to me, for I couldn't help going to sleep. Says I to Uncle John, says I—he sot next to me, and I whispered to him—says I, 'When he gits to Bunker Hill, you wake me up,' for I see he was bound to go clean back to the beginnin' of things."

"Uncle John is an Episcopalian, aint he?"

"Yes."

"Well, there aint no religion in that, no how."

"No, there aint."

"Well, now, you wouldn't think it, but I've studied into religion a heap in my life."

"Don't seem to have done you much good."

"No it aint, not yet, but I've studied into it, and I know what it is."

"There aint but one way, Benny."

"I know it."

"Repent of your sins, and believe in Christ, and be immersed—that's all."

"I know it."

"Well, I hope the Lord'll bring you to it, 'fore you die."

"Reckon he will—hope so, sure."

"You wouldn't hardly think that fat man was a preacher himself, would you?" said the landlady to me, after they left.

"Certainly not."

"He is, though, but I don't think much of that sort;" and the landlady immediately began to describe to me the religious history of the neighbourhood. It was some different here, she said she reckoned, in reply to a remark of mine, from what it was at the North. Most respectable people became pious here before they got to be very old, especially ladies. Young ladies were always gay and went to balls till they were near twenty years old, but from eighteen to twenty-five they generally got religion, and then they stopped right short, and never danced or carried on any after that. Sometimes it wasn't until after they were married, but there weren't many ladies who had children that warn't pious. She herself was an exception, for she had three children and had not got religion yet; sometimes she was frightened to think how old she was —her children growing up about her; but she did so like dancing—she hoped her turn would come—she knew it would—she had a pious and praying mother, and she reckoned her prayers must be heard, and so on.

The religious service which I am about to describe, was held in a less than usually rude meeting-house, the boards by which it was enclosed being planed, the windows glazed, and the seats for the white people provided with backs. It stood in a small clearing of the woods, and there was no habitation within two miles of it. When I reached it with my friends, the services had already commenced. Fastened to trees, in a circle about the house, there were many saddled horses and mules, and a few attached to carts or waggons. There were two smouldering camp-fires, around which sat circles of negroes and white boys, roasting potatoes in the ashes.

In the house were some fifty white people, generally dressed in homespun, and of the class called "crackers," though I was told that some of them owned a good many negroes, and were by no means so poor as their appearance indicated. About one-third of the house, at the end opposite the desk, was covered by a gallery or cock-loft, under and in which, distinctly separated from the whites, was a dense body of negroes; the men on one side, the women on another. The whites were seated promiscuously in the body of the house. The negroes present outnumbered the whites, but the exercises at this time seemed to have no reference to them; there were many more waiting about the doors outside, and they were expecting to enjoy a meeting to themselves, after the whites had left the house. They were generally neatly dressed, more so than the majority of the whites present, but in a distinctly plantation or slave style. A few of them wore somewhat expensive articles, evidently of their own selection and purchase; but I observed with some surprise, that not one of the women had a bonnet upon her head, all wearing handkerchiefs, generally of gay patterns, and becomingly arranged. I inquired if this was entirely a matter of taste, and was told that it, no doubt, was generally so, though the masters would probably not allow them to wear bonnets, if they should be disposed to, and should purchase them themselves, as it would be thought presuming. In the towns, the coloured women often, but not generally, wear bonnets.

During all the exercises, people of both classes were frequently going out and coming in; the women had brought their babies with them, and these made much disturbance. A negro girl would sometimes come forward to take a child out; perhaps the child would prefer not to be taken out, and would make loud and angry objections; it would then be fed. Several were allowed to crawl about the floor, carrying handfuls of corn-bread and roasted potatoes about with them; one had a fancy to enter the pulpit; which it succeeded in climbing into three times, and was as often taken away, in spite of loud and tearful expostulations, by its father. Dogs were not excluded; and outside, the doors and windows all being open, there was much neighing and braying, unused as were the mules and horses to see so many of their kind assembled.

The preliminary devotional exercises—a Scripture reading, singing, and painfully irreverential and meaningless harangues nominally addressed to the Deity, but really to the audience—being concluded, the sermon was commenced by reading a text, with which, however, it had, so far as I could discover, no further association. Without often being violent in his manner, the speaker nearly all the time cried aloud at the utmost stretch of his voice, as if calling to some one a long distance off; as his discourse was extemporaneous, however, he sometimes returned with curious effect to his natural conversational tone; and as he was gifted with a strong imagination, and possessed of a good deal of dramatic power, he kept the attention of the people very well. There was no argument upon any point that the congregation were likely to have much difference of opinion upon, nor any special connection between one sentence and another; yet there was a constant, sly, sectarian skirmishing, and a frequently recurring cannonade upon French infidelity and socialism, and several crushing charges upon Fourier, the Pope of Rome, Tom Paine, Voltaire, "Roosu," and Joe Smith. The audience were frequently reminded that the preacher did not want their attention for any purpose of his own; but that he demanded a respectful hearing as "the ambassador of Christ." He had the habit of frequently repeating a phrase, or of bringing forward the same idea in a slightly different form, a great many times. The following passage, of which I took notes, presents an example of this, followed by one of the best instances of his dramatic talent that occurred. He was leaning far over the desk, with his arm stretched forward, gesticulating violently, yelling at the highest key, and catching breath with an effort:—

"A—ah! why don't you come to Christ? ah! what's the reason? ah!! Is it because he was of *lowly birth?* ah! Is that it? *Is it* because he was born in a manger? ah! Is it because he was of a humble origin? ah! Is it because he was lowly born? a-ha! Is it because, ah!—is it because, ah!—because he was called a Nazarene? Is it because he was born in a stable?—or is it because—because he was of humble origin? Or is it— is it because"——He drew back, and after a moment's silence put his hand to his chin, and began walking up and down the platform of the pulpit, soliloquizing. "It can't be—it can't be—?" Then lifting his eyes and gradually turning towards the audience, while he continued to speak in a low, thoughtful tone: "Perhaps you don't like the messenger—is that the reason? I'm the ambassador of the great and glorious King; it's his invitation, 'taint mine. You musn't mind me. I ain't no account. Suppose a ragged, insignificant little boy should come running in here and tell you, 'Mister, your house's a-fire!' would you mind the ragged, insignificant little boy, and refuse to listen to him, because he didn't look respectable?"

At the end of the sermon he stepped down from the pulpit, and, crossing the house towards the negroes, said, quietly, as he walked, "I take great interest in the poor blacks; and this evening I am going to hold a meeting specially for you." With this he turned back, and without re-entering the pulpit, but strolling up and down before it, read a hymn, at the conclusion of which, he laid his book down, and speaking for a moment with natural emphasis, said—

"I don't want to create a tumultuous scene, now;—that isn't my intention. I don't want to make an excitement,—that aint what I want,—but I feel that there's some here that I may never see again, ah! and, as I may never have another opportunity, I feel it my duty as an ambassador of Jesus Christ, ah! before I go—" By this time he had returned to the high key and whining yell. Exactly what he felt it his duty to do, I did not understand; but evidently to employ some more powerful agency of awakening than arguments and appeals to the understanding; and, before I could conjecture, in the least, of what sort this was to be, while he was yet speaking calmly, deprecating excitement, my attention was attracted to several men, who had previously appeared sleepy and indifferent, but who now suddenly began to sigh, raise their heads, and *shed tears*—some standing up, so that they might be observed in doing this by the whole congregation—the tears running down their noses without any interruption. The speaker, presently, was crying aloud, with a mournful, distressed, beseeching shriek, as if he were himself suffering torture: "Oh, any of you fond parents, who know that any of your dear, sweet, little ones may be, oh! at any moment snatched right away from your bosom, and cast into hell fire, oh! there to suffer torment for ever and ever, and ever and ever—Oh! come out here and help us pray for them! Oh, any of you wives that has got an unconverted husband, that won't go along with you to eternal glory, but is set upon being separated from you, oh! and taking up his bed in hell—Oh! I call upon you, if you love Him, now to come out here and jine us in praying for him. Oh, if there's a husband here, whose wife is still in the bond of iniquity," etc., through a long category.

It was immediately evident that a large part of the audience understood his wish to be the reverse of what he had declared, and considered themselves called upon to assist him; and it was astonishing to see with what readiness the faces of those who, up to the moment he gave the signal, had appeared drowsy and stupid, were made to express distressing excitement, sighing, groaning, and weeping. Rising in their seats, and walking up to the pulpit, they grasped each other's hands agonizingly, and remained, some kneeling, others standing, with their faces towards the remainder of the assembly. There was great confusion and tumult, and the poor children, evidently impressed by the terrified tone of the howling preacher, with the expectation of some immediately impending calamity, shrieked, and ran hither and thither, till negro girls came forward, laughing at the imposition, and carried them out.

At length, when some twenty had gathered around the preacher, and it became evident that no more could be drawn out, he stopped a moment for breath, and then repeated a verse of a hymn, which being sung, he again commenced to cry aloud, calling now upon all the unconverted, who were *willing* to be saved, to kneel. A few did so, and another verse was sung, followed by another more fervent exhortation. So it went on; at each verse his entreaties, warnings, and threats, and the responsive groans, sobs, and ejaculations of his coterie grew louder and stronger. Those who refused to kneel were addressed as standing on the brink of the infernal pit, into which a diabolical divinity was momentarily on the point of satisfying the necessities of his character by hurling them off.

All this time about a dozen of the audience remained standing, many were kneeling, and the larger part had taken their seats—all having risen at the commencement of the singing. Those who continued standing were mainly wild-looking young fellows, who glanced with smiles at one another, as if they needed encouragement to brazen it out. A few young women were evidently fearfully excited, and perceptibly trembled, but for some reason dared not kneel, or compromise, by sitting. One of these, a good-looking and gaily-dressed girl, stood near, and directly before the preacher, her lips compressed, and her eyes fixed fiercely and defiantly upon him. He for some time concentrated his force upon her; but she was too strong for him, he could not bring her down. At length, shaking his finger toward her, with a terrible expression, as if he had the power, and did not lack the inclination, to damn her for her resistance to his will, he said: "I tell you this is *the last call!*" She bit her lips, and turned paler, but still stood erect, and defiant of the immense magnetism concentrated upon her; and he gave it up himself, quite exhausted with the effort.

The last verse of the hymn was sung. A comparatively quiet and sober repetition of Scripture phrases, strung together heterogeneously and without meaning, in the form of prayer, followed, a benediction was pronounced, and in five minutes all the people were out of the door, with no trace of the previous excitement left, but most of the men talking eagerly of the price of cotton, and negroes, and other news.

The negroes kept their place during all of the tumult; there may have been a sympathetic groan or exclamation uttered by one or two of them, but generally they expressed only the interest of curiosity in the proceedings, such as Europeans might at a performance of the dancing dervishes, an Indian pow-wow, or an exhibition of "psychological" or "spiritual" phenomena, making it very evident that the emotion of the performers was optionally engaged in, as an appropriate part of divine service. There was generally a self-satisfied smile upon their faces; and I have no doubt that they felt that they could do it with a good deal more energy and abandon, if they were called upon. I did not wish to detain my companion to witness how they succeeded, when their turn came; and I can only judge from the fact, that those I saw the next morning were so hoarse that they could scarcely speak, that the religious exercises they most enjoy are rather hard upon the lungs, whatever their effect may be upon the soul.

(1856)

MARK TWAIN
(Samuel Langhorne Clemens)

Old Times
on the Mississippi

The Continued Perplexities of "Cub" Piloting

At the end of what seemed a tedious while, I had managed to pack my head full of islands, towns, bars, "points," and bends; and a curiously inanimate mass of lumber it was, too. However, inasmuch as I could shut my eyes and reel off a good long string of these names without leaving out more than ten miles of river in every fifty, I began to feel that I could take a boat down to New Orleans if I could make her skip those little gaps. But of course my complacency could hardly get start enough to lift my nose a trifle into the air, before Mr. B— would think of something to fetch it down again. One day he turned on me suddenly with this settler:—

"What is the shape of Walnut Bend?"

He might as well have asked me my grandmother's opinion of protoplasm. I reflected respectfully, and then said I did n't know it had any particular shape. My gunpowdery chief went off with a bang, of course, and then went on loading and firing until he was out of adjectives.

I had learned long ago that he only carried just so many rounds of ammunition, and was sure to subside into a very placable and even remorseful old smooth-bore as soon as they were all gone. That word "old" is merely affectionate; he was not more than thirty-four. I waited. By and by he said, —

"My boy, you've got to know the *shape* of the river perfectly. It is all there is left to steer by on a very dark night. Everything else is blotted out and gone. But mind you, it has n't the same shape in the night that it has in the day-time."

"How on earth am I ever going to learn it, then?"

"How do you follow a hall at home in the dark? Because you know the shape of it. You can't see it."

"Do you mean to say that I've got to know all the million trifling variations of shape in the banks of this interminable river as well as I know the shape of the front hall at home?"

"On my honor you've got to know them *better* than any man ever did know the shapes of the halls in his own house."

"I wish I was dead!"

"Now I don't want to discourage you, but" —

"Well, pile it on me; I might as well have it now as another time."

"You see, this has got to be learned; there is n't any getting around it. A clear starlight night throws such heavy shadows that if you did n't know the shape of a shore perfectly you would claw away from every bunch of timber, because you would take the black shadow of it for a solid cape; and you see you would be getting scared to death every fifteen minutes by the watch. You would be fifty yards from shore all the time when you ought to be within twenty feet of it. You can't see a snag in one of those shadows, but you know exactly where it is, and the shape of the river tells you when you are coming to it. Then there's your pitch-dark night; the river is a very different shape on a pitch-dark night from what it is on a starlight night. All shores seem to be straight lines, then, and mighty dim ones, too; and you'd *run* them for straight lines, only you know better. You boldly drive your boat right into what seems to be a solid, straight wall (you knowing very well that in reality there is a curve there), and that wall falls back and makes way for you. Then there's your gray mist. You take a night when there's one of these grisly, drizzly, gray mists, and then there is n't *any* particular shape to a shore. A gray mist would tangle the head of the oldest man that ever lived. Well, then, different kinds of *moonlight* change the shape of the river in different ways. You see—"

"Oh, don't say any more, please! Have I got to learn the shape of the river according to all these five hundred thousand different ways? If I tried to carry all that cargo in my head it would make me stoop-shouldered."

"*No!* you only learn *the* shape of the river; and you learn it with such absolute certainty that you can always steer by the shape that's *in your head*, and never mind the one that's before your eyes."

"Very well, I'll try it; but after I have learned it can I depend on it? Will it keep the same form and not go fooling around?"

Before Mr. B— could answer, Mr W— came in to take the watch, and he said,—

"B—, you'll have to look out for President's Island and all that country clear away up above the Old Hen and Chickens. The banks are caving and the shape of the shores changing like everything. Why, you would n't know the point above 40. You can go up inside the old sycamore snag, now."[1]

So that question was answered. Here were leagues of shore changing shape. My spirits were down in the mud again. Two things seemed pretty apparent to me. One was, that in order to be a pilot a man had got to learn more than any one man ought to be allowed to know; and the other was, that he must learn it all over again in a different way every twenty-four hours.

That night we had the watch until twelve. Now it was an ancient river custom for the two pilots to chat a bit when the watch changed. While the relieving pilot put on his gloves and lit his cigar, his partner, the retiring pilot, would say something like this:—

"I judge the upper bar is making down a little at Hale's Point; had quarter twain with the lower lead and mark twain[2] with the other."

1. It may not be necessary, but still it can do no harm to explain that "inside" means between the snag and the shore. —M.T.
2. Two fathoms. Quarter twain is 2 1/4 fathoms, 13 1/2 feet. Mark three is three fathoms.

"Yes, I thought it was making down a little, last trip. Meet any boats?"

"Met one abreast the head of 21, but she was a way over hugging the bar, and I could n't make her out entirely. I took her for the *Sunny South*—had n't any skylights forward of the chimneys."

And so on. And as the relieving pilot took the wheel his partner[1] would mention that we were in such-and-such a bend, and say we were abreast of such-and-such a man's wood-yard or plantation. This was courtesy; I supposed it was *necessity*. But Mr. W— came on watch full twelve minutes late, on this particular night—a tremendous breach of etiquette; in fact, it is the unpardonable sin among pilots. So Mr. B— gave him no greeting whatever, but simply surrendered the wheel and marched out of the pilot-house without a word. I was appalled; it was a villainous night for blackness, we were in a particularly wide and blind part of the river, where there was no shape or substance to anything, and it seemed incredible that Mr. B— should have left that poor fellow to kill the boat trying to find out where he was. But I resolved that I would stand by him anyway. He should find that he was not wholly friendless. So I stood around, and waited to be asked where we were. But Mr. W— plunged on serenely through the solid firmament of black cats that stood for an atmosphere, and never opened his mouth. Here is a proud devil, thought I; here is a limb of Satan that would rather send us all to destruction than put himself under obligations to me, because I am not yet one of the salt of the earth and privileged to snub captains and lord it over everything dead and alive in a steamboat. I presently climbed up on the bench; I did not think it was safe to go to sleep while this lunatic was on watch.

However, I must have gone to sleep in the course of time, because the next thing I was aware of was the fact that day was breaking, Mr. W— gone, and Mr. B— at the wheel again. So it was four o'clock and all well—but me; I felt like a skinful of dry bones and all of them trying to ache at once.

Mr. B— asked me what I had stayed up there for. I confessed that it was to do Mr. W— a benevolence: tell him where he was. It took five minutes for the entire preposterousness of the thing to filter into Mr. B—'s system, and then I judge it filled him nearly up to the chin; because he paid me a compliment—and not much of a one either. He said, —

"Well, taking you by-and-large, you do seem to be more different kinds of an ass than any creature I ever saw before. What did you suppose he wanted to know for?"

I said I thought it might be a convenience to him.

"Convenience! Dash! Did n't I tell you that a man's got to know the river in the night the same as he'd know his own front hall?"

"Well, I can follow the front hall in the dark if I know it *is* the front hall; but suppose you set me down in the middle of it in the dark and not tell me which hall it is; how am *I* to know?"

"Well, you've *got* to, on the river!"

"All right. Then I'm glad I never said anything to Mr. W—."

"I should say so. Why, he'd have slammed you through the window and utterly ruined a hundred dollars' worth of window-sash and stuff."

I was glad this damage had been saved, for it would have made me unpopular with

1. "Partner" is technical for "the other pilot."

the owners. They always hated anybody who had the name of being careless, and injuring things.

I went to work, now, to learn the shape of the river; and of all the eluding and ungraspable objects that ever I tried to get mind or hands on, that was the chief. I would fasten my eyes upon a sharp, wooden point that projected far into the river some miles ahead of me, and go to laboriously photographing its shape upon my brain; and just as I was beginning to succeed to my satisfaction, we would draw up toward it and the exasperating thing would begin to melt away and fold back into the bank! If there had been a conspicuous dead tree standing upon the very point of the cape, I would find that tree inconspicuously merged into the general forest, and occupying the middle of a straight shore, when I got abreast of it! No prominent hill would stick to its shape long enough for me to make up my mind what its form really was, but it was as dissolving and changeful as if it had been a mountain of butter in the hottest corner of the tropics. Nothing ever had the same shape when I was coming down-stream that it had borne when I went up. I mentioned these little difficulties to Mr. B—. He said,—

"That's the very main virtue of the thing. If the shapes did n't change every three seconds they would n't be of any use. Take this place where we are now, for instance. As long as that hill over yonder is only one hill, I can boom right along the way I'm going; but the moment it splits at the top and forms a V, I know I've got to scratch to starboard in a hurry, or I'll bang this boat's brains out against a rock; and then the moment one of the prongs of the V swings behind the other, I've got to waltz to larboard again, or I'll have a misunderstanding with a snag that would snatch the keelson out of this steamboat as neatly as if it were a sliver in your hand. If that hill didn't change its shape on bad nights there would be an awful steamboat grave-yard around here inside of a year."

It was plain that I had got to learn the shape of the river in all the different ways that could be thought of,—upside down, wrong end first, inside out, fore-and-aft, and "thortships," — and then know what to do on gray nights when it had n't any shape at all. So I set about it. In the course of time I began to get the best of this knotty lesson, and my self-complacency moved to the front once more. Mr. B— was all fixed, and ready to start it to the rear again. He opened on me after this fashion:—

"How much water did we have in the middle crossing at Hole-in-the-Wall, trip before last?"

I considered this an outrage. I said:

"Every trip, down and up, the leadsmen are singing through that tangled place for three quarters of an hour on a stretch. How do you reckon I can remember such a mess as that?"

"My boy, you've got to remember it. You've got to remember the exact spot and the exact marks the boat lay in when we had the shoalest water, in every one of the two thousand shoal places between St. Louis and New Orleans; and you must n't get the shoal soundings and marks of one trip mixed up with the shoal soundings and marks of another, either, for they're not often twice alike. You must keep them separate."

When I came to myself again, I said, —

"When I get so that I can do that, I'll be able to raise the dead, and then I won't have to pilot a steamboat in order to make a living. I want to retire from this business. I want a slushbucket and a brush; I'm only fit for a roustabout. I have n't got brains enough to be a pilot; and if I had I would n't have strength enough to carry them around, unless I went on crutches."

"Now drop that! When I say I'll learn[1] a man the river, I mean it. And you can depend on it I'll learn him or kill him."

There was no use in arguing with a person like this. I promptly put such a strain on my memory that by and by even the shoal water and the countless crossing-marks began to stay with me. But the result was just the same. I never could more than get one knotty thing learned before another presented itself. Now I had often seen pilots gazing at the water and pretending to read it as if it were a book; but it was a book that told me nothing. A time came at last, however, when Mr. B— seemed to think me far enough advanced to bear a lesson on water-reading. So he began: —

"Do you see that long slanting line on the face of the water? Now that's a reef. Moreover, it's a bluff reef. There is a solid sand-bar under it that is nearly as straight up and down as the side of a house. There is plenty of water close up to it, but mighty little on top of it. If you were to hit it you would knock the boat's brains out. Do you see where the line fringes out at the upper end and begins to fade away?"

"Yes, sir."

"Well, that is a low place; that is the head of the reef. You can climb over there, and not hurt anything. Cross over, now and follow along close under the reef — easy water there — not much current."

I followed the reef along till I approached the fringed end. Then Mr. B— said, —

"Now get ready. Wait till I give the word. She won't want to mount the reef; a boat hates shoal water. Stand by — wait — wait— keep her well in hand. *Now* cramp her down! Snatch her! snatch her!"

He seized the other side of the wheel and helped to spin it around until it was hard down, and then we held it so. The boat resisted and refused to answer for a while, and next she came surging to starboard, mounted the reef, and sent a long, angry ridge of water foaming away from her bows."

"Now watch her; watch her like a cat, or she'll get away from you. When she fights strong and the tiller slips a little, in a jerky, greasy sort of way, let up on her a trifle; it is the way she tells you at night that the water is too shoal; but keep edging her up, little by little, toward the point. You are well up on the bar, now; there is a bar under every point, because the water that comes down around it forms an eddy and allows the sediment to sink. Do you see those fine lines on the face of the water that branch out like the ribs of a fan? Well, those are little reefs; you want to just miss the ends of them, but run them pretty close. Now look out — look out! Don't you crowd that slick, greasy-looking place; there ain't nine feet there; she won't stand it. She begins to smell it; look sharp, I tell you! Oh blazes, there you go! Stop the starboard wheel! Quick! Ship up to back! Set her back!"

The engine bells jingled and the engines answered promptly, shooting white columns of steam far aloft out of the scape pipes, but it was too late. The boat had "smelt" the bar in good earnest; the foamy ridges that radiated from her bows

---

1. "Teach" is not in the river vocabulary.

suddenly disappeared, a great dead swell came rolling forward and swept ahead of her, she careened far over to larboard, and went tearing away toward the other shore as if she were about scared to death. We were a good mile from where we ought to have been, when we finally got the upper hand of her again.

During the afternoon watch the next day, Mr. B— asked me if I knew how to run the next few miles. I said:—

"Go inside the first snag above the point, outside the next one, start out from the lower end of Higgins's woodyard, make a square crossing and"—

"That's all right. I'll be back before you close up on the next point."

But he was n't. He was still below when I rounded it and entered upon a piece of river which I had some misgivings about. I did not know that he was hiding behind a chimney to see how I would perform. I went gayly along, getting prouder and prouder, for he had never left the boat in my sole charge such a length of time before. I even got to "setting" her and letting the wheel go, entirely, while I vaingloriously turned my back and inspected the stern marks and hummed a tune, a sort of easy indifference which I had prodigiously admired in B— and other great pilots. Once I inspected rather long, and when I faced to the front again my heart flew into my mouth so suddenly that if I had n't clapped my teeth together I would have lost it. One of those frightful bluff reefs was stretching its deadly length right across our bows! My head was gone in a moment; I did not know which end I stood on; I gasped and could not get my breath; I spun the wheel down with such rapidity that it wove itself together like a spider's web; the boat answered and turned square away from the reef, but the reef followed—still it kept right across my bows! I never looked to see where I was going, I only fled. The awful crash was imminent—why did n't that villain come! If I committed the crime of ringing a bell, I might get thrown overboard. But better that than kill the boat. So in blind desperation I started such a rattling "shivaree" down below as never had astounded an engineer in this world before, I fancy. Amidst the frenzy of the bells the engines began to back and fill in a furious way, and my reason forsook its throne—we were about to crash into the woods on the other side of the river. Just then Mr. B— stepped calmly into view on the hurricane deck. My soul went out to him in gratitude. My distress vanished; I would have felt safe on the brink of Niagara, with Mr. B— on the hurricane deck. He blandly and sweetly took his toothpick out of his mouth between his fingers, as if it were a cigar,—we were just in the act of climbing an overhanging big tree, and the passengers were scudding astern like rats,—and lifted up these commands to me over so gently:—

"Stop the starboard. Stop the larboard. Set her back on both."

The boat hesitated, halted, pressed her nose among the boughs a critical instant, then reluctantly began to back away.

"Stop the larboard. Come ahead on it. Stop the starboard, Come ahead on it. Point her for the bar."

I sailed away as serenely as a summer's morning. Mr. B— came in and said, with mock simplicity,—

"When you have a hail, my boy, you ought to tap the big bell three times before you land, so that the engineers can get ready."

I blushed under the sarcasm, and said I had n't had any hail.

"Ah! Then it was for wood, I suppose. The officer of the watch will tell you when he wants to wood up."

I went on consuming, said I was n't after wood.

"Indeed? Why, what could you want over here in the bend, then? Did you ever know of a boat following a bend up-stream at this stage of the river?"

"No, sir,—and *I* was n't trying to follow it. I was getting away from a bluff reef."

"No, it was n't a bluff reef; there is n't one within three miles of where you were."

"But I saw it. It was as bluff as that one yonder."

"Just about. Run over it!"

"Do you give it as an order?"

"Yes. Run over it."

"If I don't, I wish I may die."

"All right; I am taking the responsibility."

I was just as anxious to kill the boat, now, as I had been to save her before. I impressed my orders upon my memory, to be used at the inquest, and made a straight break for the reef. As it disappeared under our bows I held my breath; but we slid over it like oil.

"Now don't you see the difference? It was n't anything but a wind reef. The wind does that."

"So I see. But it is exactly like a bluff reef. How am I ever going to tell them apart?"

"I can't tell you. It is an instinct. By and by you will just naturally *know* one from the other, but you never will be able to explain why or how you know them apart."

It turned out to be true. The face of the water, in time, became a wonderful book— a book that was a dead language to the uneducated passenger, but which told its mind to me without reserve, delivering its most cherished secrets as clearly as if it uttered them with a voice. And it was not a book to be read once and thrown aside, for it had a new story to tell every day. Throughout the long twelve hundred miles there was never a page that was void of interest, never one that you could leave unread without loss, never one that you would want to skip, thinking you could find higher enjoyment in some other thing. There never was so wonderful a book written by man; never one whose interest was so absorbing, so unflagging, so sparklingly renewed with every re-perusal. The passenger who could not read it was charmed with a peculiar sort of faint dimple on its surface (on the rare occasions when he did not overlook it altogether); but to the pilot that was an *italicized* passage; indeed, it was more than that, it was a legend of the largest capitals with a string of shouting exclamation points at the end of it; for it meant that a wreck or a rock was buried there that could tear the life out of the strongest vessel that ever floated. It is the faintest and simplest expression the water ever makes, and the most hideous to a pilot's eye. In truth, the passenger who could not read this book saw nothing but all manner of pretty pictures in it, painted by the sun and shaded by the clouds, whereas to the trained eye these were not pictures at all, but the grimmest and most dead-earnest of reading-matter.

Now when I had mastered the language of this water and had come to know every trifling feature that bordered the great river as familiarly as I knew the letters of the alphabet, I had made a valuable acquisition. But I had lost something, too. I had lost something which could never be restored to me while I lived. All the grace, the beauty, the poetry had gone out of the majestic river! I still keep in mind a certain wonderful sunset which I witnessed when steamboating was new to me. A broad expanse of the river was turned to blood; in the middle distance the red hue brightened into gold, through which a solitary log came floating, black and conspicuous; in one place a long, slanting mark lay sparkling upon the water; in another the surface was broken by boiling, tumbling rings, that were as many-tinted as an opal; where the ruddy flush was faintest, was a smooth spot that was covered with graceful circles and radiating lines, ever so delicately traced; the shore on our left was densely wooded, and the sombre shadow that fell from this forest was broken in one place by a long ruffled trail that shone like silver; and high above the forest wall a clean-stemmed dead tree waved a single leafy bough that glowed like a flame in the unobstructed splendor that was flowing from the sun. There were graceful curves, reflected images, woody heights, soft distances; and over the whole scene, far and near, the dissolving lights drifted steadily, enriching it, every passing moment, with new marvels of coloring.

I stood like one bewitched. I drank it in, in a speechless rapture. The world was new to me, and I had never seen anything like this at home. But as I have said, a day came when I began to cease noting the glories and the charms which the moon and the sun and the twilight wrought upon the river's face; another day came when I ceased altogether to note them. Then, if that sunset scene had been repeated, I would have looked upon it without rapture, and would have commented upon it, inwardly, after this fashion: This sun means that we are going to have wind to-morrow; that floating log means that the river is rising, small thanks to it; that slanting mark on the water refers to a bluff reef which is going to kill somebody's steamboat one of these nights, if it keeps on stretching out like that; those tumbling "boils" show a dissolving bar and a changing channel there; the lines and circles in the slick water over yonder are a warning that that execrable place is shoaling up dangerously; that silver streak in the shadow of the forest is the "break" from a new snag, and he has located himself in the very best place he could have found to fish for steamboats; that tall, dead tree, with a single living branch, is not going to last long, and then how is a body ever going to get through this blind place at night without the friendly old landmark?

No, the romance and the beauty were all gone from the river. All the value any feature of it had for me now was the amount of usefulness it could furnish toward compassing the safe piloting of a steamboat. Since those days, I have pitied doctors from my heart. What does the lovely flush in a beauty's cheek mean to a doctor but a "break" that ripples above some deadly disease? Are not all her visible charms sown thick with what are to him the signs and symbols of hidden decay? Does he ever see her beauty at all, or does n't he simply view her professionally, and comment upon her unwholesome condition all to himself? And does n't he sometimes wonder whether he has gained most or lost most by learning his trade?

The "Cub" Pilot's Education Nearly Completed

Whosoever has done me the courtesy to read my chapters which have preceded this may possibly wonder that I deal so minutely with piloting as a science. It was the prime purpose of these articles; and I am not quite done yet. I wish to show, in the most patient and painstaking way, what a wonderful science it is. Ship channels are buoyed and lighted, and therefore it is a comparatively easy undertaking to learn to run them; clear-water rivers, with gravel bottoms, change their channels very gradually, and therefore one needs to learn them but once; but piloting becomes another matter when you apply it to vast streams like the Mississippi and the Missouri, whose alluvial banks cave and change constantly, whose snags are always hunting up new quarters, whose sand bars are never at rest, whose channels are forever dodging and shirking, and whose obstructions must be confronted in all nights and all weathers without the aid of a single light-house or a single buoy; for there is neither light nor buoy to be found anywhere in all this three or four thousand miles of villainous river. I feel justified in enlarging upon this great science for the reason that I feel sure no one has ever yet written a paragraph about it who had piloted a steamboat himself, and so had a practical knowledge of the subject. If the theme were hackneyed, I should be obliged to deal gently with the reader; but since it is wholly new, I have felt at liberty to take up a considerable degree of room with it.

When I had learned the name and position of every visible feature of the river; when I had so mastered its shape that I could shut my eyes and trace it from St. Louis to New Orleans; when I had learned to read the face of the water as one would cull the news from the morning paper; and finally, when I had trained my dull memory to treasure up an endless array of soundings and crossing-marks, and keep fast hold of them, I judged that my education was complete: so I got to tilting my cap to the side of my head, and wearing a toothpick in my mouth at the wheel. Mr. B— had his eye on these airs. One day he said,—

"What is the height of that bank yonder, at Burgess's?"

"How can I tell, sir? It is three quarters of a mile away."

"Very poor eye — very poor. Take the glass."

I took the glass, and presently said, —

"I can't tell. I suppose that that bank is about a foot and a half high."

"Foot and a half! That's a six-foot bank. How high was the bank along here last trip?"

"I don't know; I never noticed."

"You did n't? Well, you must always do it hereafter."

"Why?"

"Because you'll have to know a good many things that it tells you. For one thing, it tells you the stage of the river—tells you whether there's more water or less in the river along here than there was last trip."

"The leads tell me that." I rather thought I had the advantage of him there.

"Yes, but suppose the leads lie? The bank would tell you so, and then you'd stir those leadsmen up a bit. There was a ten-foot bank here last trip, and there is only a six-foot bank now. What does that signify?"

"That the river is four feet higher than it was last trip."

"Very good. Is the river rising or falling?"

"Rising."

"No it ain't."

"I guess I am right, sir. Yonder is some drift-wood floating down the stream."

"A rise *starts* the drift-wood, but then it keeps on floating a while after the river is done rising. Now the bank will tell you about this. Wait till you come to a place where it shelves a little. Now here; do you see this narrow belt of fine sediment? That was deposited while the water was higher. You see the drift-wood begins to strand, too. The bank helps in other ways. Do you see that stump on the false point?"

"Ay, ay, sir."

"Well, the water is just up to the roots of it. You must make a note of that."

"Why?"

"Because that means that there's seven feet in the chute of 103."

"But 103 is a long way up the river yet."

"That's where the benefit of the bank comes in. There is water enough in 103 *now,* yet there may not be by the time we get there; but the bank will keep us posted all along. You don't run close chutes on a falling river, up-stream, and there are precious few of them that you are allowed to run at all downstream. There's a law of the United States against it. The river may be rising by the time we get to 103, and in that case we'll run it. We are drawing—how much?"

"Six feet aft,—six and a half forward."

"Well, you do seem to know something."

"But what I particularly want to know is, if I have got to keep up an everlasting measuring of the banks of this river, twelve hundred miles, month in and month out?"

"Of course!"

My emotions were too deep for words for a while. Presently I said,—

"And how about these chutes? Are there many of them?"

"I should say so. I fancy we shan't run any of the river this trip as you've ever seen it run before—so to speak. If the river begins to rise again, we'll go up behind bars that you've always seen standing out of the river, high and dry like the roof of a house; we'll cut across low places that you've never noticed at all, right through the middle of bars that cover fifty acres of river; we'll creep through cracks where you've always thought was solid land; we'll dart through the woods and leave twenty-five miles of river off to one side; we'll see the hind-side of every island between New Orleans and Cairo."

"Then I've got to go to work and learn just as much more river as I already know."

"Just about twice as much more, as near as you can come at it."

"Well, one lives to find out. I think I was a fool when I went into this business."

"Yes, that is true. And you are yet. But you'll not be when you've learned it."

"Ah, I never can learn it."

"I will see that you *do.*"

By and by I ventured again: —

"Have I got to learn all this thing just as I know the rest of the river—shapes and all—and so I can run it at night?"

"Yes. And you've got to have good fair marks from one end of the river to the other, that will help the bank tell you when there is water enough in each of these countless places,—like that stump, you know. When the river first begins to rise, you can run half a dozen of the deepest of them; when it rises a foot more you can run another dozen; the next foot will add a couple of dozen, and so on: so you see you have to know your banks and marks to a dead moral certainty, and never get them mixed; for when you start through one of those cracks, there's no backing out again, as there is in the big river; you've got to go through, or stay there six months if you get caught on a falling river. There are about fifty of these cracks which you can't run at all except when the river is brim full and over the banks."

"This new lesson is a cheerful prospect."

"Cheerful enough. And mind what I've just told you; when you start into one of those places you've got to go through. They are too narrow to turn around in, too crooked to back out of, and the shoal water is always *up at the head*; never elsewhere. And the head of them is always likely to be filling up, little by little, so that the marks you reckon their depth by, this season, may not answer for next."

"Learn a new set, then, every year?"

"Exactly. Cramp her up to the bar! What are you standing up through the middle of the river for?"

The next few months showed me strange things. On the same day that we held the conversation above narrated, we met a great rise coming down the river. The whole vast face of the stream was black with drifting dead logs, broken boughs, and great trees that had caved in and been washed away. It required the nicest steering to pick one's way through this rushing raft, even in the day-time, when crossing from point to point; and at night the difficulty was mightily increased; every now and then a huge log, lying deep in the water, would suddenly appear right under our bows, coming head-on; no use to try to avoid it then; we could only stop the engines, and one wheel would walk over that log from one end to the other, keeping up a thundering racket and careening the boat in a way that was very uncomfortable to passengers. Now and then we would hit one of these sunken logs a rattling bang, dead in the centre, with a full head of steam, and it would stun the boat as if she had hit a continent. Sometimes this log would lodge and stay right across our nose, and back the Mississippi up before it; we would have to do a little craw-fishing, then, to get away from the obstruction. We often hit *white* logs, in the dark, for we could not see them till we were right on them; but a black log is a pretty distinct object at night. A white snag is an ugly customer when the daylight is gone.

Of course, on the great rise, down came a swarm of prodigious timber-rafts from the head waters of the Mississippi, coal barges from Pittsburgh, little trading scows from everywhere, and broad-horns from "Posey County," Indiana, freighted with "fruit and furniture" — the usual term for describing it, though in plain English the freight thus aggrandized was hoop-poles and pumpkins. Pilots bore a mortal hatred to these craft; and it was returned with usury. The law required all such helpless traders to keep a light burning, but it was a law that was often broken. All of a sudden, on a murky night, a light would hop up, right under our bows, almost, and an agonized voice, with the backwoods "whang" to it, would wail out:

"Whar'n the — you goin' to! Cain't you see nothin'; you dash-dashed aig-suckin', sheep-stealin', one-eyed son of a stuffed monkey!"

Then for an instant, as we whistled by, the red glare from our furnaces would reveal the scow and the form of the gesticulating orator as if under a lightning-flash, and in that instant our firemen and deck-hands would send and receive a tempest of missiles and profanity, one of our wheels would walk off with the crashing fragments of a steering-oar, and down the dead blackness would shut again. And that flatboatman would be sure to go into New Orleans and sue our boat, swearing stoutly that he had a light burning all the time, when in truth his gang had the lantern down below to sing and lie and drink and gamble by, and no watch on deck. Once, at night, in one of those forest-bordered crevices (behind an island) which steamboatmen intensely describe with the phrase "as dark as the inside of a cow," we should have eaten up a Posey County family, fruit, furniture, and all, but that they happened to be fiddling down below and we just caught the sound of the music in time to sheer off, doing no serious damage, unfortunately, but coming so near it that we had good hopes for a moment. These people brought up their lantern, then, of course; and as we backed and filled to get away, the precious family stood in the light of it—both sexes and various ages —and cursed us till everything turned blue. Once a coalboatman sent a bullet through our pilot-house when we borrowed a steering-oar of him, in a very narrow place.

During this big rise these small-fry craft were an intolerable nuisance. We were running chute after chute,—a new world to me,—and if there was a particularly cramped place in a chute, we would be pretty sure to meet a broadhorn there; and if he failed to be there, we would find him in a still worse locality, namely, the head of the chute, on the shoal water. And then there would be no end of profane cordialities exchanged.

Sometimes, in the big river, when we would be feeling our way cautiously along through a fog, the deep hush would suddenly be broken by yells and a clamor of tin pans, and all in an instant a log raft would appear vaguely through the webby veil, close upon us; and then we did not wait to swap knives, but snatched our engine bells out by the roots and piled on all the steam we had, to scramble out of the way! One does n't hit a rock or a solid log raft with a steamboat when he can get excused.

You will hardly believe it, but many steamboat clerks always carried a large assortment of religious tracts with them in those old departed steamboating days. Indeed they did. Twenty times a day we would be cramping up around a bar, while a string of these small-fry rascals were drifting down into the head of the bend away above and beyond us a couple of miles. Now a skiff would dart away from one of them and come fighting its laborious way across the desert of water. It would "ease all," in the shadow of our forecastle, and the panting oarsmen would shout, "Gimme a pa-a-per!" as the skiff drifted swiftly astern. The clerk would throw over a file of New Orleans journals. If these were picked up *without comment*, you might notice that now a dozen other skiffs had been drifting down upon us without saying anything. You understand, they had been waiting to see how No. 1 was going to fare. No. 1 making no comment, all the rest would bend to their oars and come on, now; and as fast as they came the clerk would heave over neat bundles of religious tracts tied to shingles. The amount of hard swearing which twelve packages of religious literature will command when impartially divided up among twelve raftsmen's crews, who have pulled a heavy skiff two miles on a hot day to get them, is simply incredible.

As I have said, the big rise brought a new world under my vision. By the time the river was over its banks we had forsaken our old paths and were hourly climbing over bars that had stood ten feet out of water before; we were shaving stumpy shores, like that at the foot of Madrid Bend, which I had always seen avoided before; we were clattering through chutes like that of 82, where the opening at the foot was an unbroken wall of timber till our nose was almost at the very spot. Some of these chutes were utter solitudes. The dense, untouched forest overhung both banks of the crooked little crack, and one could believe that human creatures had never intruded there before. The swinging grape-vines, the grassy nooks and vistas glimpsed as we swept by, the flowering creepers waving their red blossoms from the tops of dead trunks, and all the spendthrift richness of the forest foliage, were wasted and thrown away there. The chutes were lovely places to steer in; they were deep, except at the head; the current was gentle; under the "points" the water was absolutely dead, and the invisible banks so bluff that where the tender willow thickets projected you could bury your boat's broadside in them as you tore along, and then you seemed fairly to fly.

Behind other islands we found wretched little farms, and wretcheder little log-cabins; there were crazy rail fences sticking a foot or two above the water, with one or two jeans-clad, chills-racked, yellow-faced male miserables roosting on the top-rail, elbows on knees, jaws in hands, grinding tobacco and discharging the result at floating chips through crevices left by lost milk-teeth; while the rest of the family and the few farm-animals were huddled together in an empty wood-flat riding at her moorings close at hand. In this flatboat the family would have to cook and eat and sleep for a lesser or greater number of days (or possibly weeks), until the river should fall two or three feet and let them get back to their log-cabin and their chills again — chills being a merciful provision of an all-wise Providence to enable them to take exercise without exertion. And this sort of watery camping out was a thing which these people were rather liable to be treated to a couple of times a year: by the December rise out of the Ohio, and the June rise out of the Mississippi. And yet these were kindly dispensations, for they at least enabled the poor things to rise from the dead now and then, and look upon life when a steamboat went by. They appreciated the blessing, too, for they spread their mouths and eyes wide open and made the most of these occasions. Now what *could* these banished creatures find to do to keep from dying of the blues during the low-water season!

Once, in one of these lovely island chutes, we found our course completely bridged by a great fallen tree. This will serve to show how narrow some of the chutes were. The passengers had an hour's recreation in a virgin wilderness, while the boat-hands chopped the bridge away; for there was no such thing as turning back, you comprehend.

From Cairo to Baton Rouge, when the river is over its banks, you have no particular trouble in the night, for the thousand-mile wall of dense forest that guards the two banks all the way is only gapped with a farm or wood-yard opening at intervals, and so you can't "get out of the river" much easier than you could get out of a fenced lane; but from Baton Rouge to New Orleans it is a different matter. The river is more than a mile wide, and very deep—as much as two hundred feet, in places. Both banks, for a good deal over a hundred miles, are shorn of their timber and bordered by continuous sugar plantations, with only here and there a scattering sapling or row of ornamental China-trees. The timber is shorn off clear to the rear of the plantations, from two to four miles. When the first frost threatens to come, the planters snatch off their crops in a hurry. When they have finished grinding the cane, they form the refuse of the stalks (which they call *bagasse*) into great piles and set fire to them, though in other sugar countries the bagasse is used for fuel in the furnaces of the sugar mills. Now the piles of damp bagasse burn slowly, and smoke like Satan's own kitchen.

An embankment ten or fifteen feet high guards both banks of the Mississippi all the way down that lower end of the river, and this embankment is set back from the edge of the shore from ten to perhaps a hundred feet, according to circumstances; say thirty or forty feet, as a general thing. Fill that whole region with an impenetrable gloom of smoke from a hundred miles of burning bagasse piles, when the river is over the banks, and turn a steamboat loose along there at midnight and see how she will feel. And see how you will feel, too! You find yourself away out in the midst of a vague dim sea that is shoreless, that fades out and loses itself in the murky distances; for you cannot discern the thin rib of embankment, and you are always imagining you see a straggling tree when you don't. The plantations themselves are transformed by the smoke and look like a part of the sea. All through your watch you are tortured with the exquisite misery of uncertainty. You hope you are keeping in the river, but you do not know. All that you are sure about is that you are likely to be within six feet of the bank *and* destruction, when you think you are a good half-mile from shore. And you are sure, also, that if you chance suddenly to fetch up against the embankment and topple your chimneys overboard, you will have the small comfort of knowing that it is about what you were expecting to do. One of the great Vicksburg packets darted out into a sugar plantation one night, at such a time, and had to stay there a week. But there was no novelty about it; it had often been done before.

I thought I had finished this number, but I wish to add a curious thing, while it is in my mind. It is only relevant in that it is connected with piloting. There used to be an excellent pilot on the river, a Mr. X., who was a somnambulist. It was said that if his mind was troubled about a bad piece of river, he was pretty sure to get up and walk in his sleep and do strange things. He was once fellow-pilot for a trip or two with George E—, on a great New Orleans passenger packet. During a considerable part of the first trip George was uneasy, but got over it by and by, as X. seemed content to stay in his bed when asleep. Late one night the boat was approaching Helena, Arkansas; the water was low, and the crossing above the town in a very blind and tangled condition. X. had seen the crossing since E— had, and as the night was particularly drizzly, sullen, and dark, E— was considering whether he had not better have X. called to assist in running the place, when the door opened and X. walked in. Now on very dark nights, light is a deadly enemy to piloting; you are aware that if you stand in a lighted room, on such a night, you cannot see things in the street to any purpose; but if you put out the lights and stand in the gloom you can make out objects in the street pretty well. So, on very dark nights, pilots do not smoke; they allow no fire in the pilothouse stove if there is a crack which can allow the least ray to escape; they order the furnaces to be curtained with huge tarpaulins and the sky-lights to be closely blinded. Then no light whatever issues from the boat. The undefinable shape that now entered the pilothouse had Mr. X.'s voice. This said—

"Let me take her, Mr. E—; I've seen this place since you have, and it is so crooked that I reckon I can run it myself easier than I could tell you how to do it."

"It is kind of you, and I swear *I* am willing. I have n't got another drop of perspiration left in me. I have been spinning around and around the wheel like a squirrel. It is so dark I can't tell which way she is swinging till she is coming around like a whirligig."

So E— took a seat on the bench, panting and breathless. The black phantom assumed the wheel without saying anything, steadied the waltzing steamer with a turn or two, and then stood at ease, coaxing her a little to this side and then to that, as gently and as sweetly as if the time had been noonday. When E— observed this marvel of steering, he wished he had not confessed! He stared, and wondered, and finally said,—

"Well, I thought I knew how to steer a steamboat, but that was another mistake of mine."

X. said nothing, but went serenely on with his work. He rang for the leads; he rang to slow down the steam; he worked the boat carefully and neatly into invisible marks, then stood at the centre of the wheel and peered blandly out into the blackness, fore and aft, to verify his position; as the leads shoaled more and more, he stopped the engines entirely, and the dead silence and suspense of "drifting" followed; when the shoalest water was struck, he cracked on the steam, carried her handsomely over, and then began to work her warily into the next system of shoal marks; the same patient, heedful use of leads and engines followed, the boat slipped through without touching bottom, and entered upon the third and last intricacy of the crossing; imperceptibly she moved through the gloom, crept by inches into her marks, drifted tediously till the shoalest water was cried, and then, under a tremendous head of steam, went swinging over the reef and away into deep water and safety!

E— let his long-pent breath pour out in a great, relieving sigh, and said:

"That's the sweetest piece of piloting that was ever done on the Mississippi River! I would n't believed it could be done, if I had n't seen it."

There was no reply, and he added:—

"Just hold her five minutes longer, partner, and let me run down and get a cup of coffee."

A minute later E— was biting into a pie, down in the "texas," and comforting himself with coffee. Just then the night watchman happened in, and was about to happen out again, when he noticed E— and exclaimed,—

"Who is at the wheel, sir?"

"X."

"Dart for the pilot-house, quicker than lightning!"

The next moment both men were flying up the pilot-house companion-way, three steps at a jump! Nobody there! The great steamer was whistling down the middle of the river at her own sweet will! The watchman shot out of the place again; E— seized the wheel, set an engine back with power, and held his breath while the boat reluctantly swung away from a "towhead" which she was about to knock into the middle of the Gulf of Mexico!

By and by the watchman came back and said, —

"Did n't that lunatic tell you he was asleep, when he first came up here?"

"No."

"Well, he was. I found him walking along on top of the railings, just as unconcerned as another man would walk a pavement; and I put him to bed; now just this minute there he was again, away astern, going through that sort of tight-rope deviltry the same as before."

"Well, I think I'll stay by, next time he has one of those fits. But I hope he'll have them often. You just ought to have seen him take this boat through Helena crossing. *I* never saw anything so gaudy before. And if he can do such gold-leaf, kid-glove, diamond-breastpin piloting when he is sound asleep, what *could n't* he do if he was dead!"

"Sounding." Faculties Peculiarly Necessary to a Pilot

When the river is very low, and one's steamboat is "drawing all the water" there is in the channel,—or a few inches more, as was often the case in the old times,—one must be painfully circumspect in his piloting. We used to have to "sound" a number of particularly bad places almost every trip when the river was at a very low stage.

Sounding is done in this way. The boat ties up at the shore, just above the shoal crossing; the pilot not on watch takes his "cub" or steersman and a picked crew of men (sometimes an officer also), and goes out in the yawl—provided the boat has not that rare and sumptuous luxury, a regularly-devised "sounding-boat"—and proceeds to hunt for the best water, the pilot on duty watching his movements through a spy-glass, meantime, and in some instances assisting by signals of the boat's whistle, signifying "try higher up" or "try lower down;" for the surface of the water, like an oil-painting, is more expressive and intelligible when inspected from a little distance than very close at hand. The whistle signals are seldom necessary, however; never, perhaps, except when the wind confuses the significant ripples upon the water's surface. When the yawl has reached the shoal place, the speed is slackened, the pilot begins to sound the depth with a pole ten or twelve feet long, and the steersman at the tiller obeys the order to "hold her up to starboard;" or "let her fall off to larboard;"[1] or "steady—steady as you go."

When the measurements indicate that the yawl is approaching the shoalest part of the reef, the command is given to "ease all!" Then the men stop rowing and the yawl drifts with the current. The next order is, "Stand by with the buoy!" The moment the shallowest point is reached, the pilot delivers the order, "Let go the buoy!" and over she goes. If the pilot is not satisfied, he sounds the place again; if he finds better water higher up or lower down, he removes the buoy to that place. Being finally satisfied, he gives the order, and all the men stand their oars straight up in the air, in line; a blast from the boat's whistle indicates that the signal has been seen; then the men "give way" on their oars and lay the yawl alongside the buoy; the steamer comes creeping carefully down, is pointed straight at the buoy, husbands her power for the coming

1. The term "larboard" is never used at sea, now, to signify the left hand; but was always used on the river in my times.

struggle, and presently, at the critical moment, turns on all her steam and goes grinding and wallowing over the buoy, and the sand, and gains the deep water beyond. Or maybe she does n't; maybe she "strikes and swings." Then she has to while away several hours (or days) sparring herself off.

Sometimes a buoy is not laid at all, but the yawl goes ahead, hunting the best water, and the steamer follows along in its wake. Often there is a deal of fun and excitement about sounding, especially if it is a glorious summer day, or a blustering night. But in winter the cold and the peril take most of the fun out of it.

A buoy is nothing but a board four or five feet long, with one end turned up; it is a reversed boot-jack. It is anchored on the shoalest part of the reef by a rope with a heavy stone made fast to the end of it. But for the resistance of the turned-up end, the current would pull the buoy under water. At night a paper lantern with a candle in it is fastened on top of the buoy, and this can be seen a mile or more, a little glimmering spark in the waste of blackness.

Nothing delights a cub so much as an opportunity to go out sounding. There is such an air of adventure about it; often there is danger; it is so gaudy and man-of-war-like to sit up in the stern-sheets and steer a swift yawl; there is something fine about the exultant spring of the boat when an experienced old sailor crew throw their *souls* into the oars; it is lovely to see the white foam stream away from the bows; there is music in the rush of the water; it is deliciously exhilarating, in summer, to go speeding over the breezy expanses of the river when the world of wavelets is dancing in the sun. It is such grandeur, too, to the cub, to get a chance to give an order; for often the pilot will simply say, "Let her go about!" and leave the rest to the cub, who instantly cries, in his sternest tone of command, "Ease starboard! Strong on the larboard! Starboard give way! With a will, men!" The cub enjoys sounding for the further reason that the eyes of the passengers are watching all the yawl's movements with absorbing interest, if the time be daylight; and if it be night he knows that those same wondering eyes are fastened upon the yawl's lantern as it glides out into the gloom and fades away in the remote distance.

One trip a pretty girl of sixteen spent her time in our pilot-house with her uncle and aunt, every day and all day long. I fell in love with her. So did Mr. T—'s cub, Tom G—. Tom and I had been bosom friends until this time; but now a coolness began to arise. I told the girl a good many of my river adventures, and made myself out a good deal of a hero; Tom tried to make himself appear to be a hero, too, and succeeded to some extent, but then he always had a way of embroidering. However, virtue is its own reward, so I was a barely perceptible trifle ahead in the contest. About this time something happened which promised handsomely for me: the pilots decided to sound the crossing at the head of 21. This would occur about nine or ten o'clock at night, when the passengers would be still up; it would be Mr. T—'s watch, therefore my chief would have to do the sounding. We had a perfect love of a sounding-boat—long, trim, graceful, and as fleet as a greyhound; her thwarts were cushioned; she carried twelve oarsmen; one of the mates was always sent in her to transmit orders to her crew, for ours was a steamer where no end of "style" was put on.

We tied up at the shore above 21, and got ready. It was a foul night, and the river was so wide, there, that a landsman's uneducated eyes could discern no opposite shore through such a gloom. The passengers were alert and interested; everything was satisfactory. As I hurried through the engine-room, picturesquely gotten up in storm toggery, I met Tom, and could not forbear delivering myself of a mean speech:—

"Ain't you glad *you* don't have to go out sounding?"

Tom was passing on, but he quickly turned, and said,—

"Now just for that, you can go and get the sounding-pole yourself. I was going after it, but I'd see you in Halifax, now, before I'd do it."

"Who wants you to get it? *I* don't. It's in the sounding-boat."

"It ain't, either. It's been new-painted; and it's been up on the lady's cabin guards two days, drying."

I flew back, and shortly arrived among the crowd of watching and wondering ladies just in time to hear the command:

"Give way, men!"

I looked over, and there was the gallant sounding-boat booming away, the unprincipled Tom presiding at the tiller and my chief sitting by him with the sounding-pole which I had been sent on a fool's errand to fetch. Then that young girl said to me,—

"Oh, how awful to have to go out in that little boat on such a night! Do you think there is any danger?"

I would rather have been stabbed. I went off, full of venom, to help in the pilot-house. By and by the boat's lantern disappeared, and after an interval a wee spark glimmered upon the face of the water a mile away. Mr. T— blew the whistle, in acknowledgment, backed the steamer out, and made for it. We flew along for a while, then slackened steam and went cautiously gliding toward the spark. presently Mr. T— exclaimed,—

"Hello, the buoy-lantern's out!"

He stopped the engines. A moment or two later he said,—

"Why, there it is again!"

So he came ahead on the engines once more, and rang for the leads. Gradually the water shoaled up, and then began to deepen again! Mr. T— muttered:

"Well, I don't understand this. I believe that buoy has drifted off the reef. Seems to be a little too far to the left. No matter, it is safest to run over it, anyhow."

So, in that solid world of darkness, we went creeping down on the light. Just as our bows were in the act plowing over it, Mr. T— seized the bell-ropes, rang a startling peal, and exclaimed,—

"My soul, it's the sounding-boat!"

A sudden chorus of wild alarms burst out far below—a pause—and then a sound of grinding and crashing followed. Mr. T— exclaimed, —

"There! the paddle-wheel has ground the sounding-boat to lucifer matches! Run! See who is killed!"

I was on the main deck in the twinkling of an eye. My chief and the third mate and nearly all the men were safe. They had discovered their danger when it was too late to pull out of the way; then, when the great guards overshadowed them a moment later, they were prepared and knew what to do; at my chief's order they sprang at the right instant, seized the guard, and were hauled aboard. The next moment the sounding-yawl swept aft to the wheel and was struck and splintered to atoms. Two of the men, and the cub Tom, were missing—a fact which spread like wild-fire over the boat. The passengers came flocking to the forward gangway, ladies and all, anxious-eyed, white-faced, and talked in awed voices of the dreadful thing. And often and again I heard them say, "Poor fellows! poor boy, poor boy!"

By this time the boat's yawl was manned and away, to search for the missing. Now a faint call was heard, off to the left. The yawl had disappeared in the other direction. Half the people rushed to one side to encourage a swimmer with their shouts; the other half rushed the other way to shriek to the yawl to run about. By the callings, the swimmer was approaching, but some said the sound showed failing strength. The crowd massed themselves against the boiler-deck railings, leaning over and staring into the gloom; and every faint and fainter cry wrung from them such words as "Ah, poor fellow, poor fellow! Is there *no* way to save him?"

But still the cries held out, and drew nearer, and presently the voice said pluckily,— "I can make it! Stand by with a rope!"

What a rousing cheer they gave him! The chief mate took his stand in the glare of a torch-basket, a coil of rope in his hand, and his men grouped about him. The next moment the swimmer's face appeared in the circle of light, and in another one the owner of it was hauled aboard, limp and drenched, while cheer on cheer went up. It was that devil Tom.

The yawl crew searched everywhere, but found no sign of the two men. They probably failed to catch the guard, tumbled back, and were struck by the wheel and killed. Tom had never jumped for the guard at all, but had plunged headfirst into the river and dived under the wheel. It was nothing; I could have done it easy enough, and I said so; but everybody went on just the same, making a wonderful to-do over that ass, as if he had done something great. That girl couldn't seem to have enough of that pitiful "hero" the rest of the trip; but little I cared; I loathed her, anyway.

The way we came to mistake the sounding-boat's lantern for the buoy-light was this. My chief said that after laying the buoy he fell away and watched it till it seemed to be secure; then he took up a position a hundred yards below it and a little to one side of the steamer's course, headed the sounding-boat up-stream, and waited. Having to wait some time, he and the officer got to talking; he looked up when he judged that the steamer was about on the reef; saw that the buoy was gone, but supposed that the steamer had already run over it; he went on with his talk; he noticed that the steamer was getting very close down on him, but that was the correct thing; it was her business to shave him closely, for convenience in taking him aboard; he was expecting her to sheer off, until the last moment; then it flashed upon him that she was trying to run him down, mistaking his lantern for the buoy-light; so he sang out, "Stand by to spring for the guard, men!" and the next instant the jump was made.

But I am wandering from what I was intending to do, that is, make plainer than perhaps appears in my previous papers, some of the peculiar requirements of the science of piloting. First of all, there is one faculty which a pilot must incessantly cultivate until he has brought it to absolute perfection. Nothing short of perfection will do. That faculty is memory. He cannot stop with merely thinking a thing is so and so; he must *know* it; for this is eminently one of the "exact" sciences. With what scorn a pilot was looked upon, in the old times, if he ever ventured to deal in that feeble phrase "I think," instead of the vigorous one "I know!" One cannot easily realize what a tremendous thing it is to know every trivial detail of twelve hundred miles of river and know it with absolute exactness. If you will take the longest street in New York, and travel up and down it, conning its features patiently until you know every house and window and door and lamp-post and big and little sign by heart, and know them so accurately that you can instantly name the one you are abreast of when you are set down at random in that street in the middle of an inky black night, you will then have a tolerable notion of the amount and the exactness of a pilot's knowledge who carries the Mississippi River in his head. And then if you will go on until you know every street crossing, the character, size, and position of the crossing-stones, and the varying depth of mud in each of those numberless places, you will have some idea of what the pilot must know in order to keep a Mississippi steamer out of trouble. Next, if you will take half the signs in that long street, and *change their places* once a month, and still manage to know their new positions accurately on dark nights, and keep up with these repeated changes without making any mistakes, you will understand what is required of a pilot's peerless memory by the fickle Mississippi.

I think a pilot's memory is about the most wonderful thing in the world. To know the Old and New Testaments by heart, and be able to recite them glibly, forward or backward, or being at random anywhere in the book and recite both ways and never trip or make a mistake, is no extravagant mass of knowledge and no marvelous facility, compared to a pilot's massed knowledge of the Mississippi and his marvelous facility in the handling of it. I make this comparison deliberately, and believe I am not expanding the truth when I do it. Many will think my figure too strong, but pilots will not.

And how easily and comfortably the pilot's memory does its work; how placidly effortless is its way! how *unconsciously* it lays up its vast stores, hour by hour, day by day, and never loses or mislays a single valuable package of them all! Take an instance. Let a leadsman cry, "Half twain! half twain! half twain! half twain! half twain!" until it becomes as monotonous as the ticking of a clock; let conversation be going on all the time, and the pilot be doing his share of the talking, and no longer listening to the leadsman; and in the midst of this endless string of half twains let a single "quarter twain!" be interjected, without emphasis, and then the half twain cry go on again, just as before: two or three weeks later that pilot can describe with precision the boat's position in the river when that quarter twain was uttered, and give you such a lot of head-marks, stern-marks, and side-marks to guide you, that you ought to be able to take the boat there and put her in that same spot again yourself! The cry of quarter twain did not really take his mind from his talk, but his trained faculties instantly photographed the bearings, noted the change of depth, and laid up the important details for future reference without requiring any assistance from *him* in the matter. If you were walking and talking with a friend, and another friend at you side kept up a monotonous repetition of the vowel sound A, for a couple of blocks, and then in the midst interjected an R, thus, A, A, A, A, A, R, A, A, A, etc., and gave the R no emphasis, you would not be able to state, two or three weeks afterward, that the R had been put in, nor be able to tell what objects you were passing at the moment it was done. But you could if your memory had been patiently and laboriously trained to do that sort of thing mechanically.

Give a man a tolerably fair memory to start with, and piloting will develop it into a very colossus of capability. But *only in the matters it is daily drilled in.* A time would come when the man's faculties could not help noticing landmarks and soundings, and his memory could not help holding on to them with the grip of a vice; but if you asked that same man at noon what he had had for breakfast, it would be ten chances to one that he could not tell you. Astonishing things can be done with the human memory if you will devote it faithfully to one particular line of business.

At the time that wages soared so high on the Missouri River, my chief, Mr. B—, went up there and learned more than a thousand miles of that stream with an ease and rapidity that were astonishing. When he had seen each division *once* in the daytime and *once* at night, his education was so nearly complete that he took a "daylight" license; a few trips later he took out a full license, and went to piloting day and night—and he ranked A 1, too.

Mr. B— placed me as steersman for a while under a pilot whose feats of memory were a constant marvel to me. However, his memory was born in him, I think, not built. For instance, somebody would mention a name. Instantly Mr. J— would break in:—

"Oh, I knew *him.* Sallow-faced, red-headed fellow, with a little scar on the side of his throat like a splinter under the flesh. He was only in the Southern trade six months. That was thirteen years ago. I made a trip with him. There was five feet in the upper river then; the Henry Blake grounded at the foot of Tower Island, drawing four and a half; the George Elliott unshipped her rudder on the wreck of the Sunflower"—

"Why, the Sunflower did n't sink until"—

"*I* know when she sunk; it was three years before that, on the 2d of December; Asa Hardy was captain of her, and his brother John was first clerk; and it was his first trip in her, too; Tom Jones told me these things a week afterward in New Orleans; he was first mate of the Sunflower. Captain Hardy stuck a nail in his foot the 6th of July of the next year, and died of the lockjaw on the 15th. His brother John died two years after,—3d of March,—erysipelas. I never saw either of the Hardys,—they were Alleghany River men,—but people who knew them told me all these things. And they said Captain Hardy wore yarn socks winter and summer just the same, and his first wife's name was Jane Shook,—she was from New England,—and his second one died in a lunatic asylum. It was in the blood. She was from Lexington, Kentucky. Name was Horton before she was married."

And so on, by the hour, the man's tongue would go. He could *not* forget anything. It was simply impossible. The most trivial details remained as distinct and luminous in his head, after they had lain there for years, as the most memorable events. His was not simply a pilot's memory; its grasp was universal. If he were talking about a trifling letter he had received seven years before, he was pretty sure to deliver you the entire screed from memory. And then, without observing that he was departing from the true line of his talk, he was more than likely to hurl in a long-drawn parenthetical biography of the writer of that letter; and you were lucky indeed if he did not take up that writer's relatives, one by one, and give you their biographies, too.

Such a memory as that is a great misfortune. To it, all occurrences are of the same size. Its possessor cannot distinguish an interesting circumstance from an uninteresting one. As a talker, he is bound to clog his narrative with tiresome details and make himself an insufferable bore. Moreover, he cannot stick to his subject. He picks up every little grain of memory he discerns in his way, and so is led aside. Mr. J— would start out with the honest intention of telling you a vastly funny anecdote about a dog. He would be "so full of laugh" that he could hardly begin; then his memory would start with the dog's breed and personal appearance; drift into a history of his owner; of his owner's family, with descriptions of weddings and burials that had occurred in it, together with recitals of congratulatory verses and obituary poetry provoked by the same; then this memory would recollect that one of these events occurred during the celebrated "hard winter" of such and such a year, and a minute description of that winter would follow, along with the names of people who were frozen to death, and statistics showing the high figures which pork and hay went up to. Pork and hay would suggest corn and fodder; corn and fodder would suggest cows and horses; the latter would suggest the circus and certain celebrated bare-back riders; the transition from the circus to the menagerie was easy and natural; from the elephant to equatorial Africa was but a step; then of course the heathen savages would suggest religion; and at the end of three or four hours' tedious jaw, the watch would change and J— would go out of the pilot-house muttering extracts from sermons he had heard years before about the efficacy of prayer as a means of grace. And the original first mention would be all you had learned about that dog, after all this waiting and hungering.

A pilot must have a memory; but there are two higher qualities which he must also have. He must have good and quick judgment and decision, and a cool, calm courage that no peril can shake. Give a man the merest trifle of pluck to start with, and by the time he has become a pilot he cannot be unmanned by any danger a steamboat can get into; but one cannot quite say the same for judgment. Judgment is a matter of brains, and a man must *start* with a good stock of that article or he will never succeed as a pilot.

The growth of courage in the pilot-house is steady all the time, but it does not reach a high and satisfactory condition until some time after the young pilot has been "standing his own watch," alone and under the staggering weight of all the responsibilities connected with the position. When an apprentice has become pretty thoroughly acquainted with the river, he goes clattering along so fearlessly with his steamboat, night or day, that he presently begins to imagine that it is *his* courage that animates him; but the first time the pilot steps out and leaves him to his own devices he finds out it was the other man's. He discovers that the article has been left out of his own cargo altogether. The whole river is bristling with exigencies in a moment; he is not prepared for them; he does not know how to meet them; all his knowledge forsakes him; and within fifteen minutes he is as white as a sheet and scared almost to death. Therefore pilots wisely train these cubs by various strategic tricks to look danger in the face a little more calmly. A favorite way of theirs is to play a friendly swindle upon the candidate.

Mr. B— served me in this fashion once, and for years afterward I used to blush even in my sleep when I thought of it. I had become a good steersman; so good, indeed, that I had all the work to do on our watch, night and day; Mr. B— seldom made a suggestion to me; all he ever did was to take the wheel on particularly bad nights or in particularly bad crossings, land the boat when she needed to be landed, play gentleman of leisure nine tenths of the watch, and collect the wages. The lower river was about bank-full, and if anybody had questioned my ability to run any crossing between Cairo and New Orleans without help or instruction, I should have felt irreparably hurt. The idea of being afraid of any crossing in the lot, in the *day-time*, was a thing too preposterous for contemplation. Well, one matchless summer's day I was bowling down the bend above island 66, brim full of self-conceit and carrying my nose as high as a giraffe's, when Mr. B— said, —

"I am going below a while. I suppose you know the next crossing?"

This was almost an affront. It was about the plainest and simplest crossing in the whole river. One could n't come to any harm, whether he ran it right or not; and as for depth, there never had been any bottom there. I knew all this, perfectly well.

"Know how to *run* it? Why, I can run it with my eyes shut."

"How much water is there in it?"

"Well, that is an odd question. I could n't get bottom there with a church steeple."

"You think so, do you?"

The very tone of the question shook my confidence. That was what Mr. B— was expecting. He left, without saying anything more. I began to imagine all sorts of things. Mr. B—, unknown to me, of course, sent somebody down to the forecastle with some mysterious instructions to the leadsmen, another messenger was sent to whisper among the officers, and Mr. B— went into hiding behind a smoke-stack where he could observe results. Presently the captain stepped out on the hurricane deck; next the chief mate appeared; then a clerk. Every moment or two a straggler was added to my audience; and before I got to the head of the island I had fifteen or twenty people assembled down there under my nose. I began to wonder what the trouble was. As I started across, the captain glanced aloft at me and said, with a sham uneasiness in his voice, —

"Where is Mr.B—?"

"Gone below, sir."

But that did the business for me. My imagination began to construct dangers out of nothing, and they multiplied faster than I could keep the run of them. All at once I imagined I saw shoal water ahead! The wave of coward agony that surged through me then came near dislocating every joint in me. All my confidence in that crossing vanished. I seized the bell-rope; dropped it, ashamed; seized it again; dropped it once more; clutched it tremblingly once again, and pulled it so feebly that I could hardly hear the stroke myself. Captain and mate sang out instantly, and both together, —

"Starboard lead there ! and quick about it!"

This was another shock. I began to climb the wheel like a squirrel; but I would hardly get the boat started to port before I would see new dangers on that side, and away I would spin to the other; only to find perils accumulating to starboard, and be crazy to get to port again. Then came the leadsman's sepulchral cry: —

"D-e-e-p four!"

Deep four in a bottomless crossing! The terror of it took my breath away.

"M-a-r-k three! M-a-r-k three! Quarter less three! Half twain!"

This was frightful! I seized the bell-ropes and stopped the engines.

"Quarter twain! Quarter twain! *Mark* twain!"

I was helpless. I did not know what in the world to do. I was quaking from head to foot, and I could have hung my hat on my eyes, they stuck out so far.

"Quarter *less* twain! Nine and a *half!*"

We were *drawing* nine! My hands were in a nerveless flutter. I could not ring a bell intelligently with them. I flew to the speaking-tube and shouted to the engineer,—

"Oh, Ben, if you love me, *back* her! Quick, Ben! Oh, back the immortal *soul* out of her!"

I hear the door close gently. I looked around, and there stood Mr. B—, smiling a bland, sweet smile. Then the audience on the hurricane deck sent up a shout of humiliating laughter. I saw it all, now, and I felt meaner than the meanest man in human history. I laid in the lead, set the boat in her marks, came ahead on the engines, and said,—

"It was a fine trick to play on an orphan, *was n't* it? I suppose I'll never hear the last of how I was ass enough to heave the lead at the head of 66."

"Well, no, you won't, maybe. In fact I hope you won't; for I want you to learn something by that experience. Did n't you *know* there was no bottom in that crossing?"

"Yes, sir, I did."

"Very well, then. You should n't have allowed me or anybody else to shake your confidence in that knowledge. Try to remember that. And another thing: when you get into a dangerous place, don't turn coward. That is n't going to help matters any."

It was a good enough lesson, but pretty hardly learned. Yet about the hardest part of it was that for months I so often had to hear a phrase which I had conceived a particular distaste for. It was, "Oh, Ben, if you love me, back her!"

Official Rank and Dignity of a Pilot.
The Rise and Decadence of the Pilots' Association

In my preceding articles I have tried, by going into the minutiae of the science of piloting, to carry the reader step by step to a comprehension of what the science consists of; and at the same time I have tried to show him that it is a very curious and wonderful science, too, and very worthy of his attention. If I have seemed to love my subject, it is no surprising thing, for I loved the profession far better than any I have followed since, and I took a measureless pride in it. The reason is plain: a pilot, in those days, was the only unfettered and entirely independent human being that lived in the earth. Kings are but the hampered servants of parliament and people; parliaments sit in chains forged by their constituency; the editor of a newspaper cannot be independent, but must work with one hand tied behind him by party and patrons, and be content to utter only half or two thirds of his mind: no clergyman is a free man and may speak the whole truth, regardless of his parish's opinions; writers of all kinds are manacled servants of the public. We write frankly and fearlessly, but then we "modify" before we print. In truth, every man and woman and child has a master, and worries and frets in servitude; but in the day I write of, the Mississippi pilot had *none*. The captain could stand upon the hurricane deck, in the pomp of a very brief authority, and give him five or six orders, while the vessel backed into the stream, and then that skipper's reign was over. The moment that the boat was under way in the river, she was under the sole and unquestioned control of the pilot. He could do with her exactly as he pleased, run her when and whither he chose, and tie her up to the bank whenever his judgment said that that course was best. His movements were entirely free; he consulted no one, he received commands from nobody, he promptly resented even the merest suggestions. Indeed, the law of the United States forbade him to listen to commands or suggestions, rightly considering that the pilot necessarily knew better how to handle the boat than anybody could tell him. So here was the novelty of a king without a keeper, an absolute monarch who was absolute in sober truth and not by a fiction of words. I have seen a boy of eighteen taking a great steamer serenely into what seemed almost certain destruction, and the aged captain standing mutely by, filled with apprehension but powerless to interfere. His interference, in that particular instance, might have been an excellent thing, but to permit it would have been to establish a most pernicious precedent. It will easily be guessed, considering the pilot's boundless authority, that he was a great personage in the old steamboating days. He was treated with marked courtesy by the captain and with marked deference by all the officers and servants; and this deferential spirit was quickly communicated to the passengers, too. I think pilots were about the only people I ever knew who failed to show, in some degree, embarrassment in the presence of traveling foreign princes. But then, people in one's own grade of life are not usually embarrassing objects.

By long habit, pilots came to put all their wishes in the form of commands. It "gravels" me, to this day, to put my will in the weak shape of a request, instead of launching it in the crisp language of an order.

In those old days, to load a steamboat at St. Louis, take her to New Orleans and back, and discharge cargo, consumed about twenty-five days, on an average. Seven or eight of these days the boat spent at the wharves of St. Louis and New Orleans, and every soul on board was hard at work, except the two pilots; *they* did nothing but play gentleman, up town, and receive the same wages for it as if they had been on duty. The moment the boat touched the wharf at either city, they were ashore; and they were not likely to be seen again till the last bell was ringing and everything in readiness for another voyage.

When a captain got hold of a pilot of particularly high reputation, he took pains to keep him. When wages were four hundred dollars a month on the Upper Mississippi, I have known a captain to keep such a pilot in idleness, under full pay, three months at a time, while the river was frozen up. And one must remember that in those cheap times four hundred dollars was a salary of almost inconceivable splendor. Few men on shore got such pay as that, and when they did they were mightily looked up to. When pilots from either end of the river wandered into our small Missouri village, they were sought by the best and the fairest, and treated with exalted respect. Lying in port under wages was a thing which many pilots greatly enjoyed and appreciated;

especially if they belonged in the Missouri River in the heyday of that trade (Kansas times), and got nine hundred dollars a trip, which was equivalent to about eighteen hundred dollars a month. Here is a conversation of that day. A chap out of the Illinois River, with a little stern-wheel tub, accosts a couple of ornate and gilded Missouri River pilots:—

"Gentlemen, I've got a pretty good trip for the up-country, and shall want you about a month. How much will it be?"

"Eighteen hundred dollars apiece."　　　　　•

"Heavens and earth! You take my boat, let me have your wages, and I'll divide!"

I will remark, in passing, that Mississippi steamboat men were important in landsmen's eyes (and in their own, too, in a degree) according to the dignity of the boat they were on. For instance, it was a proud thing to be of the crew of such stately craft as the Aleck Scott or the Grand Turk. Negro firemen, deck hands, and barbers belonging to those boats were distinguished personages in their grade of life, and they were well aware of that fact, too. A stalwart darkey once gave offense at a negro ball in New Orleans by putting on a good many airs. Finally one of the managers bustled up to him and said,—

"Who *is* you, any way? Who *is* you? dat's what *I* want to know!"

The offender was not disconcerted in the least, but swelled himself up and threw that into his voice which showed that he knew he was not putting on all those airs on a stinted capital.

"Who *is* I? Who *is* I? I let you know mighty quick who I is! I want you niggers to understan' dat I fires de middle do'[1] on de Aleck Scott!"

That was sufficient.

The barber of the Grand Turk was a spruce young negro, who aired his importance with balmy complacency, and was greatly courted by the circle in which he moved. The young colored population of New Orleans were much given to flirting, at twilight, on the pavements of the back streets. Somebody saw and heard something like the following, one evening, in one of those localities. A middle-aged negro woman projected her head through a broken pane and shouted (very willing that the neighbors should hear and envy), "You Mary Ann, come in de house dis minute! Stannin' out dah foolin' 'long wid dat low trash, an' heah's de barber off 'n de Gran' Turk wants to conwerse wid you!"

My reference, a moment ago, to the fact that a pilot's peculiar official position placed him out of the reach of criticism or command, brings Stephen W—naturally to my mind. He was a gifted pilot, a good fellow, a tireless talker, and had both wit and humor in him. He had a most irreverent independence, too, and was deliciously easy-going and comfortable in the presence of age, official dignity, and even the most august wealth. He always had work, he never saved a penny, he was a most persuasive borrower, he was in debt to every pilot on the river, and to the majority of the captains. He could throw a sort of splendor around a bit of harum-scarum, devil-may-care piloting, that made it almost fascinating—but not to everybody. He made a trip with good old gentle-spirited Captain Y— once, and was "relieved" from duty when the boat got to New Orleans. Somebody expressed surprise at the discharge. Captain Y—

1. Door

shuddered at the mere mention of Stephen. Then his poor, thin old voice piped out something like this:—

"Why, bless me! I would n't have such a wild creature on my boat for the world—not for the whole world! He swears, he sings, he whistles, he yells — I never saw such an Injun to yell. All times of the night—it never made any difference to him. He would just yell that way, not for anything in particular, but merely on account of a kind of devilish comfort he got out of it. I never could get into a sound sleep but he would fetch me out of bed, all in a cold sweat, with one of those dreadful war-whoops. A queer being,—very queer being; no respect for anything or anybody. Sometimes he called me *'Johnny.'* And he kept a fiddle, and a cat. He played execrably. This seemed to distress the cat, and so the cat would howl. Nobody could sleep where that man—and his family—was. And reckless? There never was anything like it. Now you may believe it or not, but as sure as I am sitting here, he brought my boat a-tilting down through those awful snags at Chicot under a rattling head of stream, and the wind a-blowing like the very nation, at that! My officers will tell you so. They saw it. And, sir, while he was a-tearing right down through those snags, and I a-shaking in my shoes and praying, I wish I may never speak again if he did n't pucker up his mouth and go to *whistling!* Yes, sir; whistling 'Buffalo gals, can't you come out to-night, can't you come out to-night, can't you come out to-night;' and doing it as calmly as if we were attending a funeral and were n't related to the corpse. And when I remonstrated with him about it, he smiled down on me as if I was his child, and told me to run in the house and try to be good, and not be meddling with my superiors!"[1]

Once a pretty mean captain caught Stephen in New Orleans out of work and as usual out of money. He laid steady siege to Stephen, who was in a very "close place," and finally persuaded him to hire with him at one hundred and twenty-five dollars per month, just half wages, the captain agreeing not to divulge the secret and so bring down the contempt of all the guild upon the poor fellow. But the boat was not more than a day out of New Orleans before Stephen discovered that the captain was boasting of his exploit, and that all the officers had been told. Stephen winced, but said nothing. About the middle of the afternoon the captain stepped out on the hurricane deck, cast his eye around, and looked a good deal surprised. He glanced inquiringly aloft at Stephen, but Stephen was whistling placidly, and attending to business. The captain stood around a while in evident discomfort, and once or twice seemed about to make a suggestion; but the etiquette of the river taught him to avoid that sort of rashness, and so he managed to hold his peace. He chafed and puzzled a few minutes longer, then retired to his apartments. But soon he was out again, and apparently more perplexed than ever. Presently he ventured to remark, with deference,—

"Pretty good stage of the river now, ain't it, sir?"

"Well, I should say so! Bank-full *is* a pretty liberal stage."

"Seems to be a good deal of current here."

"Good deal don't describe it! It's worse than a mill-race."

"Is n't it easier in toward shore than it is out here in the middle?"

"Yes, I reckon it is; but a body can't be too careful with a steamboat. It's pretty safe

1. Considering a captain's ostentatious but hollow chieftainship, and a pilot's real authority, there was something impudently apt and happy about that way of phrasing it.

out here; can't strike any bottom out here, you can depend on that."

The captain departed, looking rueful enough. At this rate, he would probably die of old age before his boat got to St. Louis. Next day he appeared on deck and again found Stephen faithfully standing up the middle of the river, fighting the whole vast force of the Mississippi, and whistling the same placid tune. This thing was becoming serious. In by the shore was a slower boat clipping along in the easy water and gaining steadily; she began to make for an island chute; Stephen stuck to the middle of the river. Speech was *wrung* from the captain. He said,—

"Mr. W—, don't that chute cut off a good deal of distance?"

"I think it does, but I don't know."

"Don't know! Well, is n't there water enough in it now to go through?"

"I expect there is, but I am not certain."

"Upon my word this is odd! Why, those pilots on that boat yonder are going to try it. Do you mean to say that you don't know as much as they do?"

"*They!* Why, *they* are two-hundred-and-fifty-dollar pilots! But don't you be uneasy; I know as much as any man can afford to know for a hundred and twenty-five!"

Five minutes later Stephen was bowling through the chute and showing the rival boat a two-hundred-and-fifty-dollar pair of heels.

One day, on board the Aleck Scott, my chief, Mr. B—, was crawling carefully through a close place at Cat Island, both leads going, and everybody holding his breath. The captain, a nervous, apprehensive man, kept still as long as he could, but finally broke down and shouted from the hurricane deck, —

"For gracious' sake, give her steam, Mr. B—! give her steam! She'll never raise the reef on this headway!"

For all the effect that was produced upon Mr. B—, one would have supposed that no remark had been made. But five minutes later, when the danger was past and the leads laid in, he burst instantly into a consuming fury, and gave the captain the most admirable cursing I ever listened to. No bloodshed ensured; but that was because the captain's cause was weak; for ordinarily he was not a man to take correction quietly.

Having now set forth in detail the nature of the science of piloting, and likewise described the rank which the pilot held among the fraternity of steamboatmen, this seems a fitting place to say a few words about an organization which pilots once formed for the protection of their guild. It was curious and noteworthy in this, that it was perhaps the compactest, the completest, and the strongest commercial organization ever formed among men.

For a long time wages had been two hundred and fifty dollars a month; but curiously enough, as steamboats multiplied and business increased, the wages began to fall, little by little. It was easy to discover the reason of this. Too many pilots were being "made." It was nice to have a "cub," a steersman, to do all the hard work for a couple of years, gratis, while his master sat on a high bench and smoked; all pilots and captains had sons or brothers who wanted to be pilots. By and by it came to pass that nearly every pilot on the river had a steersman. When a steersman had made an amount of progress that was satisfactory to any two pilots in the trade, they could get a pilot's license for him by signing an application directed to the United States

Inspector. Nothing further was needed; usually no questions were asked, no proofs of capacity required.

Very well, this growing swarm of new pilots presently began to undermine the wages, in order to get berths. Too late—apparently—the knights of the tiller perceived their mistake. Plainly, something had to be done, and quickly; but what was to be the needful thing? A close organization. Nothing else would answer. To compass this seemed an impossibility; so it was talked, and talked, and then dropped. It was too likely to ruin whoever ventured to move in the matter. But at last about a dozen of the boldest—and some of them the best—pilots on the river launched themselves into the enterprise and took all the chances. They got a special charter from the legislature, with large powers, under the name of the Pilots' Benevolent Association; elected their officers, completed their organization, contributed capital, put "association" wages up to two hundred and fifty dollars at once—and then retired to their homes, for they were promptly discharged from employment. But there were two or three unnoticed trifles in their by-laws which had the seed of propagation in them. For instance, all idle members of the association, in good standing, were entitled to a pension of twenty-five dollars per month. This began to bring in one straggler after another from the ranks of the new-fledged pilots, in the dull (summer) season. Better have twenty-five dollars than starve; the initiation fee was only twelve dollars, and no dues required from the unemployed.

Also, the widows of deceased members in good standing could draw twenty-five dollars per month, and a certain sum for each of their children. Also, the said deceased would be buried at the associations' expense. These things resurrected all the superannuated and forgotten pilots in the Mississippi Valley. They came from farms, they came from interior villages, they came from everywhere. They came on crutches, on drays, in ambulances,—any way, so they got there. They paid in their twelve dollars, and straightway began to draw out twenty-five dollars a month and calculate their burial bills.

By and by, all the useless, helpless pilots, and a dozen first-class ones were in the association, and nine tenths of the best pilots out of it and laughing at it. It was the laughing-stock of the whole river. Everybody joked about the by-law requiring members to pay ten per cent of their wages, every month, into the treasury for the support of the association , whereas all the members were outcast and tabooed, and no one would employ them. Everybody was derisively grateful to the association for taking all the worthless pilots out of the way and leaving the whole field to the excellent and the deserving; and everybody was not only jocularly grateful for that, but for a result which naturally followed, namely, the gradual advance of wages as the busy season approached. Wages had gone up from the low figure of one hundred dollars a month to one hundred and twenty-five, and in some cases to one hundred and fifty; and it was great fun to enlarge upon the fact that this charming thing had been accomplished by a body of men not one of whom received a particle of benefit from it. Some of the jokers used to call at the association rooms and have a good time chaffing the members and offering them the charity of taking them as steersmen for a trip, so that they could see what the forgotten river looked like. However, the association was content; or at least it gave no signs to the contrary. Now and then it captured a pilot who was "out of luck," and added him to its list; and these later additions were very valuable, for they were good pilots; the incompetent ones had all been absorbed before. As business freshened, wages climbed gradually up to two hundred and fifty dollars—the association figure—and became firmly fixed there; and still without benefiting a member of that body, for no member was hired. The hilarity at the association's expense burst all bounds, now. There was no end to the fun which that poor martyr had to put up with.

However, it is a long lane that has no turning. Winter approached, business doubled and trebled, and an avalanche of Missouri, Illinois, and Upper Mississippi River boats came pouring down to take a chance in the New Orleans trade. All of a sudden, pilots were in great demand, and were correspondingly scarce. The time for revenge was come. It was a bitter pill to have to accept association pilots at last, yet captains and owners agreed that there was no other way. But none of these outcasts offered! So there was a still bitterer pill to be swallowed: they must be sought out and asked for their services. Captain—was the first man who found it necessary to take the dose, and he had been the loudest derider of the organization. He hunted up one of the best of the association pilots and said,—

"Well, you boys have rather got the best of us for a little while, so I'll give in with as good a grace as I can. I've come to hire you; get your trunk aboard right away. I want to leave at twelve o'clock."

"I don't know about that. Who is your other pilot?"

"I've got I. S—. Why?"

"I can't go with him. He don't belong to the association."

"What!"

"It's so."

"Do you mean to tell me that you won't turn a wheel with one of the very best and oldest pilots on the river because he don't belong to your association?"

"Yes, I do."

"Well, if this is n't putting on airs! I supposed I was doing you a benevolence; but I begin to think that I am the party that wants a favor done. Are you acting under a law of the concern?"

"Yes."

"Show it to me."

So they stepped into the association rooms, and the secretary soon satisfied the captain, who said,—

"Well, what am I to do? I have hired Mr. S— for the entire season."

"I will provide for you," said the secretary.I will detail a pilot to go with you, and he shall be on board at twelve o'clock."

"But if I discharge S—, he will come on me for the whole season's wages."

"Of course that is a matter between you and Mr. S—, captain. We cannot meddle in your private affairs."

The captain stormed, but to no purpose. In the end he had to discharge S—, pay him about a thousand dollars, and take an association pilot in his place. The laugh was beginning to turn the other way, now. Every day, thenceforward, a new victim fell; every day some outraged captain discharged a non-association pet, with tears and profanity, and installed a hated association man in his berth. In a very little while, non-associationists began to be pretty plenty, brisk as business was, and as much as their services were desired. The laugh was shifting to the other side of their mouths most palpably. These victims, together with the captains and owners, presently ceased to laugh altogether, and began to rage about the revenge they would take when the passing business "spurt" was over.

Soon all the laughers that were left were the owners and crews of the boats that had two non-association pilots. But their triumph was not very long-lived. For this reason: It was a rigid rule of the association that its members should never, under any circumstances whatever, give information about the channel to any "outsider." By this time about half the boats had none but association pilots, and the other half had none but outsiders. At the first glance one would suppose that when it came to forbidding information about the river these two parties could play equally at that game; but this was not so. At every good-sized town from one end of the river to the other, there was a "wharf-boat" to land at, instead of a wharf or a pier. Freight was stored in it for transportation, waiting passengers slept in its cabins. Upon each of these wharf-boats the association's officers placed a strong box, fastened with a peculiar lock which was used in no other service but one—the United States mail service. It was the letter-bag lock, a sacred governmental thing. By dint of much beseeching the government had been persuaded to allow the association to use this lock. Every association man carried a key which would open these boxes. That key, or rather a peculiar way of holding it in the hand when its owner was asked for river information by a stranger,—for the success of the St. Louis and New Orleans association had now bred tolerably thriving branches in a dozen neighboring steamboat trades,—was the association man's sign and diploma of membership; and if the stranger did not respond by producing a similar key and holding it in a certain manner duly prescribed, his question was politely ignored. From the association's secretary each member received a package of more or less gorgeous blanks, printed like a bill-head, on handsome paper, properly ruled in columns; a bill-head worded something like this—

Steamer Great Republic.

John Smith, Masters.

Pilots, John Jones, and Thos. Brown.

Crossing.   Soundings.   Marks.   Remarks.

These blanks were filled up, day by day, as the voyage progressed, and deposited in the several wharf-boat boxes. For instance, as soon as the first crossing, out from St. Louis, was completed, the items would be entered upon the blank, under the appropriate headings, thus:

"St. Louis. Nine and a half (feet). Stern on court-house, head on dead cottonwood above wood-yard, until you raise the first reef, then pull up square."

Then under head of Remarks: "Go just outside the wrecks; this is important. New snag just where you straighten down; go above it."

The pilot who deposited that blank in the Cairo box (after adding to it the details of every crossing all the way down from St. Louis) took out and read half a dozen fresh reports (from upward bound steamers) concerning the river between Cairo and

Memphis, posted himself thoroughly, returned them to the box, and went back aboard his boat again so armed against accident that he could not possibly get his boat into trouble without bringing the most ingenious carelessness to his aid.

Imagine the benefits of so admirable a system in a piece of river twelve or thirteen hundred miles long, whose channel was shifting every day! The pilot who had formerly been obliged to put up with seeing a shoal place once or possibly twice a month, had a hundred sharp eyes to watch it for him, now, and bushels of intelligent brains to tell him how to run it. His information about it was seldom twenty-four hours old. If the reports in the last box chanced to leave any misgivings on his mind concerning a treacherous crossing, he had his remedy; he blew his steam-whistle in a peculiar way as soon as he saw a boat approaching; the signal was answered in a peculiar way if that boat's pilots were association men; and then the two steamers ranged alongside and all uncertainties were swept away by fresh information furnished to the inquirer by word of mouth and in minute detail.

The first thing a pilot did when he reached New Orleans or St. Louis was to take his final and elaborate report to the association parlors and hang it up there, — *after* which he was free to visit his family. In these parlors a crowd was always gathered together, discussing changes in the channel, and the moment there was a fresh arrival, everybody stopped talking till this witness had told the newest news and settled the latest uncertainty. Other craftsmen can "sink the shop," sometimes, and interest themselves in other matters. Not so with a pilot; he must devote himself wholly to his profession and talk of nothing else; for it would be small gain to be perfect one day and imperfect the next. He has no time or words to waste if he would keep "posted."

But the outsiders had a hard time of it. No particular place to meet and exchange information, no wharf-boat reports, none but chance and unsatisfactory ways of getting news. The consequence was that a man sometimes had to run five hundred miles of river on information that was a week or ten days old. At a fair stage of the river that might have answered; but when the dead low water came it was destructive.

Now came another perfectly logical result. The outsiders began to ground steamboats, sink them, and get into all sorts of trouble, whereas accidents seemed to keep entirely away from the association men. Wherefore, even the owners and captains of boats furnished exclusively with outsiders, and previously considered to be wholly independent of the association and free to comfort themselves with brag and laughter, began to feel pretty uncomfortable. Still, they made a show of keeping up the brag, until one black day when every captain of the lot was formally ordered immediately to discharge his outsiders and take association pilots in their stead. And who was it that had the gaudy presumption to do that? Alas, it came from a power behind the throne that was greater than the throne itself. It was the underwriters!

It was no time to "swap knives." Every outsider had to take his trunk ashore at once. Of course it was supposed that there was collusion between the association and the underwriters, but this was not so. The latter had come to comprehend the excellence of the "report" system of the association and the safety it secured, and so they had made their decision among themselves and upon plain business principles.

There was weeping and wailing and gnashing of teeth in the camp of the outsiders now. But no matter, there was but one course for them to pursue, and they pursued it. They came forward in couples and groups, and proffered their twelve dollars and asked for membership. They were surprised to learn that several new by-laws had been long ago added. For instance, the initiation fee had been raised to fifty dollars; that sum must be tendered, and also ten per cent of the wages which the applicant had received each and every month since the founding of the association. In many cases this amounted to three or four hundred dollars. Still, the association would not entertain the application until the money was present. Even then a single adverse vote killed the application. Every member had to vote yes or no in person and before witnesses; so it took weeks to decide a candidacy, because many pilots were so long absent on voyages. However, the repentant sinners scraped their savings together, and one by one, by our tedious voting process, they were added to the fold. A time came, at last, when only about ten remained outside. They said they would starve before they would apply. They remained idle a long while, because of course nobody could venture to employ them.

By and by the association published the fact that upon a certain date the wages would be raised to five hundred dollars per month. All the branch associations had grown strong, now, and the Red River one had advanced wages to seven hundred dollars a month. Reluctantly the ten outsiders yielded, in view of these things, and made application. There was *another* new by-law, by this time, which required them to pay dues not only on all the wages they had received since the association was born, but also on what they would have received if they had continued at work up to the time of their application, instead of going off to pout in idleness. It turned out to be a difficult matter to elect them, but it was accomplished at last. The most virulent sinner of this batch had stayed out and allowed "dues" to accumulate against him so long that he had to send in six hundred and twenty-five dollars with his application.

The association had a good bank account now, and was very strong. There was no longer an outsider. A by-law was added forbidding the reception of any more cubs or apprentices for five years; after which time a limited number would be taken, not by individuals, but by the association, upon these terms: the applicant must not be less than eighteen years old, of respectable family and good character; he must pass an examination as to education, pay a thousand dollars in advance for the privilege of becoming an apprentice, and must remain under the commands of the association until a great part of the membership (more than half, I think) should be willing to sign his application for a pilot's license.

All previously-articled apprentices were now taken away from their masters and adopted by the association. The president and secretary detailed them for service on one boat or another, as they chose, and changed them from boat to boat according to certain rules. If a pilot could show that he was in infirm health and needed assistance, one of the cubs would be ordered to go with him.

The widow and orphan list grew, but so did the association's financial resources. The association attended its own funerals in state, and paid for them. When occasion demanded, it sent members down the river upon searches for the bodies of brethren lost by steamboat accidents; a search of this kind sometimes cost a thousand dollars.

The association procured a charter and went into the insurance business, also. It not only insured the lives of its members, but took risks on steamboats.

The organization seemed indestructible. It was the tightest monopoly in the world. By the United States law, no man could become a pilot unless two duly licensed pilots signed his application; and now there was nobody outside of the association competent to sign. Consequently the making of pilots was at an end. Every year some would die and others become incapacitated by age and infirmity; there would be no new ones to take their places. In time, the association could put wages up to any figure it chose; and as long as it should be wise enough not to carry the thing too far and provoke the national government into amending the licensing system, steamboat owners would have to submit, since there would be no help for it.

The owners and captains were the only obstruction that lay between the association and absolute power; and at last this one was removed. Incredible as it may seem, the owners and captains deliberately did it themselves. When the pilots' association announced, months beforehand, that on the first day of September, 1861, wages would be advanced to five hundred dollars per month, the owners and captains instantly put freights up a few cents, and explained to the farmers along the river the necessity of it, by calling their attention to the burdensome rate of wages about to be established. It was a rather slender argument, but the farmers did not seem to detect it. It looked reasonable to them that to add five cents freight on a bushel of corn was justifiable under the circumstances, overlooking the fact that this advance on a cargo of forty thousand sacks was a good deal more than necessary to cover the new wages.

So straightway the captains and owners got up an association of their own, and proposed to put captain's wages up to five hundred dollars, too, and move for another advance in freights. It was a novel idea, but of course an effect which had been produced once could be produced again. The new association decreed (for this was before all the outsiders had been taken into the pilots' association) that if any captain employed a non-association pilot, he should be forced to discharge him, and also pay a fine of five hundred dollars. Several of these heavy fines were paid before the captains' organization grew strong enough to exercise full authority over its membership; but that all ceased, presently. The captains tried to get the pilots to decree that no member of their corporation should serve under a non-association captain; but this proposition was declined. The pilots saw that they would be backed up by the captains and the underwriters anyhow, and so they wisely refrained from entering into entangling alliances.

As I have remarked, the pilots' association was now the compactest monopoly in the world, perhaps, and seemed simply indestructible. And yet the days of its glory were numbered. First, the new railroad stretching up through Mississippi, Tennessee, and Kentucky, to Northern railway centres, began to divert the passenger travel from the steamers; next the war came and almost entirely annihilated the steamboating industry during several years, leaving most of the pilots idle, and the cost of living advancing all the time; then the treasurer of the St. Louis association put his hand into the till and walked off with every dollar of the ample fund; and finally, the railroads intruding everywhere, there was little for steamers to do, when the war was over, but carry freights; so straightway some genius from the Atlantic coast introduced the plan of towing a dozen steamer cargoes down to New Orleans at the tail of a vulgar little tug-boat; and behold, in the twinkling of an eye, as it were, the association and the noble science of piloting were things of the dead and pathetic past!

(1875)

POETRY,
SONGS
and
SPIRITUALS

POETRY

MADISON CAWEIN

The Feud, Madison Cawein

Rocks, trees and rocks; and down a mossy stone
    The murmuring ooze and trickle of a stream
Through brambles, where the mountain spring lies lone,—
    A gleaming cairngorm where the shadows dream,—
And one wild road winds like a saffron seam.

Here sang the thrush, whose pure, mellifluous note
    Dropped golden sweetness on the fragrant June;
Here cat- and blue-bird and wood-sparrow wrote
    Their presence on the silence with a tune;
And here the fox drank 'neath the mountain moon.

Frail ferns and dewy mosses and dark brush,—
    Impenetrable briers, deep and dense,
And wiry bushes;—brush, that seemed to crush
    The struggling saplings with its tangle, whence
Sprawled out the ramble of an old rail-fence.

A wasp buzzed by; and then a butterfly
    In orange and amber, like a floating flame;
And then a man, hard-eyed and very sly,
    Gaunt-cheeked and haggard and a little lame,
With an old rifle, down the mountain came.

He listened, drinking from a flask he took
    Out of the ragged pocket of his coat;
Then all around him cast a stealthy look;
    Lay down; and watched an eagle soar and float,
His fingers twitching at his hairy throat.

The shades grew longer; and each Cumberland height
    Loomed, framed in splendors of the dolphin dusk.
Around the road a horseman rode in sight;
    Young, tall, blond-bearded. Silent, grim, and brusque,
He in the thicket aimed—Quick, harsh, then husk,

The echoes barked among the hills and made
   Repeated instants of the shot's distress.—
Then silence—and the trampled bushes swayed:—
   Then silence, packed with murder and the press
Of distant hoofs that galloped riderless.

        (1894)

War-Time Silhouettes

I The Battle

The night had passed. The day had come,
   Bright-born, into a cloudless sky:
We heard the rolling of the drum,
   And saw the war-flags fly.

And noon had crowded upon morn
   Ere Conflict shook her red locks far,
And blew her brazen battle-horn
   Upon the hills of War.

Noon darkened into dusk—one blot
   Of nightmare lit with hell-born suns;
We heard the scream of shell and shot
   And booming of the guns.

On batteries of belching grape
   We saw the thundering cavalry
Hurl headlong—iron shape on shape—
   With shout and bugle-cry.

When dusk had moaned and died, and night
   Came on, wind-swept and wild with rain,
We slept, 'mid many a bivouac light,
   And vast fields heaped with slain.

II In Hospital

Wounded to death he lay and dreamed
   The drums of battle beat afar,
And round the roaring trenches screamed
   The hell of war.

Then woke; and, weeping, spoke one word
    To the kind nurse who bent above;
Then in the whitewashed ward was heard
    A song of love.

The song *she* sang him when she gave
    The portrait that he kissed; then sighed,
"Lay it beside me in the grave!"
    And smiled and died.

III   The Soldier's Return

A brown wing beat the apple leaves and shook
    Some blossoms on her hair. Then, note on note,
The bird's wild music bubbled. In her book,
Her old romance, she seemed to read. No look
    Betrayed the tumult in her trembling throat.

The thrush sang on. A dreamy wind came down
    From one white cloud of afternoon and fanned
The dropping petals on her book and gown,
And touched her hair, whose braids of quiet brown
    Gently she smoothed with one white jeweled hand.

Then, with her soul, it seemed, from feet to brow
    She felt him coming: 't was his heart, his breath
That stirred the blossom on the apple bough;
His step the wood-thrush warbled to. And now
    Her cheek went crimson, now as white as death.

Then on the dappled page his shadow—yes,
    Not unexpected, yet her haste assumed
Fright's startle; and low laughter did confess
His presence there, soft with his soul's caress
    And happy manhood, where the rambo bloomed.

Quickly she rose and all her gladness sent
    Wild welcome to him. Her his unhurt arm
Drew unresisted; and the soldier lent
Fond lips to hers. She wept. And so they went
    Deep in the orchard towards the old brick farm.

IV   The Apparition

A day of drought, foreboding rain and wind,
As if stern heaven, feeling earth had sinned,

Frowned all its hatred. When the evening came,
Along the west, from bank on bank unthinned
    Of clouds, the storm unfurled its oriflamme.

Then lightning signaled, and the thunder woke
Its monster drums, and all God's torrents broke.—
    She saw the wild night when the dark pane flashed;
Heard, where she stood, the disemboweled oak
    Roar into fragments when the welkin crashed.

Long had she waited for a word. And, lo!
Anticipation still would not say "No":
    He has not written; he will come to her;
At dawn!—To-night!—Her heart hath told her so;
    And so expectancy and love aver.

She seems to hear his fingers on the pane—
The glass is blurred, she cannot see for rain:
    Is *that* his horse?—the wind is never still;
And *that* his cloak?—Ah, surely that is plain!—
    A torn vine tossing at the window-sill.

She hurries forth to meet him; pale and wet,
She sees his face; the war-soiled epaulet;
    A sabre-scar that bleeds from brow to cheek;
And now he smiles, and now their lips have met,
    And now…Dear Heart, he fell at Cedar Creek!

V Wounded

It was in August that they brought her news
Of his bad wounds; the leg that he must lose.
    And August passed, and when October raised
    Red rebel standards on the hills that blazed,
They brought a haggard wreck; she scarce knew whose,
    Until they told her, standing stunned and dazed.

A shattered shadow of the stalwart lad,
The five-months husband, whom his country had
    Enlisted, strong for war; returning this,
    Whose broken countenance she feared to kiss,
While health's remembrance stood beside him sad,
    And grieved for that which was no longer his.

They brought him on a litter; and the day
Was bright and beautiful. It seemed that May

In woodland rambles had forgot her path
Of season, and, disrobing for a bath,
By the autumnal waters of some bay,
    With her white nakedness had conquered Wrath.

Far otherwise she wished it: wind and rain;
The sky, one gray commiserative pain;
    Sleet, and the stormy drift of frantic leaves;
    To match the misery that each perceives
Aches in her hand-clutched bosom, and is plain
    In eyes and mouth and all her form that grieves.

Theirs, a mute meeting of the lips; she stooped
And kissed him once: one long, dark side-lock drooped
    And brushed against the bandage of his breast;
    With feeble hands he held it and caressed;
All his happiness in one look grouped,
    Saying, "Now I am home, I crave but rest."

Once it was love! but then the battle killed
All that sweet nonsense of his youth, and filled
    His heart with sterner passion.—Ah, well! peace
    Must balm its pain with patience; whose surcease
Means reconcilement; e'en as God hath willed,
    With war or peace who shapes His ends at ease.—

What else for these but, where their mortal lot
Of weak existence drags rent ends, to knot
    The frail unravel up!—while love (afraid
    Time will increase the burthen on it laid),
Seeks consolation, that consoleth not,
    In toil and prayer, waiting what none evade.

VI The Message

Long shadows toward the east: and in the west
    A blaze of garnet sunset, wherein rolled
    One cloud like some great gnarly log of gold;
Each gabled casement of the farm seemed dressed
In ghosts of roses blossoming manifest.

And she had brought his letter there to read,
    There on the porch that faced the locust glade;
    To watch the summer sunset burn and fade,
And breathe the twilight scent of wood and weed,
Forget all care and her soul's hunger feed.

And on his face her fancy mused awhile:
      "Dark hair, dark eyes.—And now he has a beard
      Dark as his hair."—She smiled; yet almost feared
It changed him so she could not reconcile
Her heart to that which hid his lips and smile.

Then tried to feature, but could only see
      The beardless man who bent to her and kissed
      Her and her child and left them to enlist:
She heard his horse grind in the gravel: he
Waved them adieu and rose to fight with Lee.

Now all around her drowsed the hushful hum
      Of evening insects. And his letter spoke
      Of love and longings to her: nor awoke
One echo of the bugle and the drum,
But all their future in one kiss did sum.

The stars were thick now; and the western blush
      Drained into darkness. With a dreamy sigh
      She rocked her chair.—It must have been the cry
Of infancy that made her rise and rush
To where their child slept, and to hug and hush.

Then she returned. But now her ease was gone.
      She knew not what, she felt an unknown fear
      Press, tightening, at her heart-strings; then a tear
Scalded her eyelids, and her cheeks grew wan
As helpless sorrow's, and her white lips drawn.

With stony eyes she grieved against the skies,
      A slow, dull, aching agony that knew
      Few tears, and saw no answer shining to
Her silent questions in the stars' still eyes,
"Where Peace delays and where her soldier lies."

They could have told her. Peace was far away,
      Beyond the field that belched black batteries
      All the red day. 'Mid picket silences,
On woodland mosses, in a suit of gray,
Shot through the heart, he by his rifle lay.

VII   The Woman on the Hill

The storm-red sun, though wrecks of wind and rain,
    And dead leaves driven from the frantic boughs,
    Where, on the hill-top, stood a gaunt gray house,
Flashed wildest ruby on each rainy pane.

Then woods grew darker than unburdened grief;
    And, crimson through the woodland's ruin, streamed
    The sunset's glare—a furious eye, which seemed
Watching the moon rise like a yellow leaf.

The rising moon, against which, like despair,
    High on the hill, a woman, darkly drawn,
    The wild leaves round her, stood; with features wan,
And tattered dress and wind-distracted hair,

As still as death, and looking, not through tears,
    For the young face of one she knows is lost,
    While in her heart a melancholy frost
Gathers of all the unforgotten years.

What if she heard to-night a hurrying hoof
    Wild as the whirling of the withered leaf,
    Bring her a more immedicable grief,
A shattered shape to live beneath her roof!

The shadow of him who claimed her once as wife;
    Her lover!—No!—the wreck of all their past
    Brought back from battle!—Better to the last
A broken heart than heartbreak all her life!

(1907)

PAUL LAURENCE DUNBAR

When Malindy Sings

G'way an' quit dat noise, Miss Lucy—
    Put dat music book away;
What's de use to keep on tryin'?
    Ef you practise twell you're gray,
You cain't sta't no notes a-flyin'
    Lak de ones dat rants and rings
F'om de kitchen to de big woods
    When Malindy sings.

You ain't got de nachel o'gans
    Fu' to make de soun' come right,
You ain't got de tu'ns an' twistin's
    Fu' to make it sweet an' light.
Tell you one thing now, Miss Lucy,
    An' I'm tellin' you fu' true,
When hit comes to raal right singin',
    'T ain't no easy thing to do.

Easy 'nough fu' folks to hollah,
    Lookin' at de lines an' dots,
When dey ain't no one kin sence it,
    An' de chune comes in, in spots;
But fu' real melojous music,
    Dat jes' strikes yo' hea't and clings,
Jes' you stan' an' listen wif me
    When Malindy sings.

Ain't you nevah hyeahd Malindy?
    Blessed soul, tek up de cross!
Look hyeah, ain't you jokin', honey?
    Well, you don't know whut you los'.
Y' ought to hyeah dat gal a-wa'blin',
    Robins, la'ks, an' all dem things,
Heish dey moufs an' hides dey faces
    When Malindy sings.

Fiddlin' man jes' stop his fiddlin',
    Lay his fiddle on de she'f;
Mockin'-bird quit tryin' to whistle,
    'Cause he jes' so shamed hisse'f.
Folks a-playin' on de banjo
    Draps dey fingahs on de strings—
Bless yo' soul—fu'gits to move 'em,
    When Malindy sings.

She jes' spreads huh mouf and hollahs,
    "Come to Jesus," twell you hyeah
Sinnahs' tremblin' steps and voices,
    Timid-lak a-drawin' neah;
Den she tu'ns to "Rock of Ages,"
    Simply to de cross she clings,
An' you fin' yo' teahs a-drappin'
    When Malindy sings.

Who dat says dat humble praises
    Wif de Master nevah counts?
Heish yo' mouf, I hyeah dat music,
    Ez hit rises up an' mounts—
Floatin' by de hills an' valleys,
    Way above dis buryin' sod,
Ez hit makes its way in glory
    To de very gates of God!

Oh, hit's sweetah dan de music
    Of an edicated band;
An' hit's dearah dan de battle's
    Song o' triumph in de lan'.
It seems holier dan evenin'
    When de solemn chu'ch bell rings,
Ez I sit an' ca'mly listen
    While Malindy sings.

Towsah, stop dat ba'kin', hyeah me!
    Mandy, mek dat chile keep still;
Don't you hyeah de echoes callin'
    F'om de valley to de hill?
Let me listen, I can hyeah it,
    Th'oo de bresh of angel's wings,
Sof' an' sweet, "Swing Low, Sweet Chariot,"
    Ez Malindy sings.

(1895)

An Ante-Bellum Sermon

We is gathahed hyeah, my brothahs,
    In dis howlin' wildaness,
Fu' to speak some words of comfo't
    To each othah in distress.
An' we chooses fu' ouah subjic'
    Dis—we'll 'splain it by an' by;
"An' de Lawd said, 'Moses, Moses,'
    An' de man said, 'Hyeah am I.'"

Now ole Pher'oh, down in Egypt,
    Was de wuss man evah bo'n,
An' he had de Hebrew chillun
    Down dah wukin' in his co'n;
'T well de Lawd got tiahed o' his foolin',
    An' sez he: "I'll let him know—
Look hyeah, Moses, go tell Pher'oh
    Fu' to let dem chillun go."

"An' ef he refuse to do it,
    I will make him rue de houah,
Fu' I'll empty down on Egypt
    All de vials of my powah."
Yes, he did—an' Pher'oh's ahmy
    Was n't wuth a ha'f a dime;
Fu' de Lawd will he'p his chillun,
    You kin trust him evah time.

An' yo' enemies may 'sail you
    In de back an' in de front;
But de Lawd is all aroun' you,
    Fu' to ba' de battle's brunt.
Dey kin fo'ge yo' chains an' shackles
    F'om de mountains to de sea;
But de Lawd will sen' some Moses
    Fu' to set his chillun free.

An' de lan' shall hyeah his thundah,
    Lak a blas' f'om Gab'el's ho'n,
Fu' de Lawd of hosts is mighty
    When he girds his ahmor on.
But fu' feah some one mistakes me,
    I will pause right hyeah to say,

Dat I'm still a-preachin' ancient,
    I ain't talkin' 'bout to-day.

But I tell you, fellah christuns,
    Things 'll happen mighty strange;
Now, de Lawd done dis fu' Isrul,
    An' his ways don't nevah change,
An' de love he showed to Isrul
    Was n't all on Isrul spent;
Now don't run an' tell yo' mastahs
    Dat I's preachin' discontent.

'Cause I is n't; I'se a-judgin'
    Bible people by deir ac's;
I'se a-givin' you de Scriptuah,
    I'se a-handin' you de fac's.
Cose ole Pher'oh b'lieved in slav'ry,
    But de Lawd he let him see,
Dat de people he put bref in,—
    Evah mothah's son was free.

An' dahs othahs thinks lak Pher'oh,
    But dey calls de Scriptuah liar,
Fu' de Bible says "a servant
    Is a-worthy of his hire."
An' you cain't git roun' nor thoo dat,
    An' you cain't git ovah it,
Fu' whatevah place you git in,
    Dis hyeah Bible too 'll fit.

So you see de Lawd's intention,
    Evah sence de worl' began,
Was dat His almighty freedom
    Should belong to evah man,
But I think it would be bettah,
    Ef I'd pause agin to say,
Dat I'm talkin' 'bout ouah freedom
    In a Bibleistic way.

But de Moses is a-comin',
    An' he's comin', suah and fas'.
We kin hyeah his feet a-trompin',
    We kin hyeah his trumpit blas'.
But I want to wa'n you people,
    Don't you git too brigity;

An' don't you git to braggin'
    'Bout dese things, you wait an' see.

But when Moses wif his powah
    Comes an' sets us chillun free,
We will praise de gracious Mastah
    Dat has gin us liberty;
An' we'll shout ouah halleluyahs,
    On dat mighty reck'nin' day,
When we'se reco'nised ez citiz'—
    Huh uh! Chillun, let us pray!

(1895)

When Dey 'Listed Colored Soldiers

Dey was talkin' in de cabin, dey was talkin' in de hall;
But I listened kin' o' keerless, not a-t'inkin' 'bout it all;
An' on Sunday, too, I noticed, dey was whisp'rin' mighty much,
Stan'in' all erroun' de roadside w'en dey let us out o' chu'ch.
But I did n't t'ink erbout it 'twell de middle of de week,
An' my 'Lias come to see me, an' somehow he could n't speak.
Den I seed all in a minute whut he'd come to see me for;—
Dey had 'listed colo'ed sojers an' my 'Lias gwine to wah.

Oh, I hugged him, an' I kissed him, an' I baiged him not to go;
But he tol' me dat his conscience, hit was callin' to him so,
An' he could n't baih to lingah w'en he had a chanst to fight
For de freedom dey had gin him an' de glory of de right.
So he kissed me, an' he lef' me, w'en I'd p'omised to be true;
An' dey put a knapsack on him, an' a coat all colo'ed blue.
So I gin him pap's ol' Bible f'om de bottom of de draw',—
W'en dey 'listed colo'ed sojers an' my 'Lias went to wah.

But I t'ought of all de weary miles dat he would have to tramp,
An' I could n't be contented w'en dey tuk him to de camp.
W'y my hea't nigh broke wid grievin' 'twell I seed him on de street;
Den I felt lak I could go an' th'ow my body at his feet.
For his buttons was a-shinin', an' his face was shinin', too,
An' he looked so strong an' mighty in his coat o' sojer blue,
Dat I hollahed, "Step up, manny," dough my th'oat was so' an' raw,—
W'en dey 'listed colo'ed sojers an' my 'Lias went to wah.

Ol' Mis' cried w'en mastah lef' huh, young Miss mou'ned huh brothah Ned,
An' I did n't know dey feelin's is de ve'y wo'ds dey said
We'n I tol' 'em I was so'y. Dey had done gin up dey all;
But dey only seemed mo' proudah dat dey men had hyeahed de call.
Bofe my mastahs went in gray suits, an' I loved de Yankee blue,
But I t'ought dat I could sorrer for de losin' of 'em too;
But I could n't, for I did n't know de ha'f o' whut I saw,
'Twell dey 'listed colo'ed sojers an' my 'Lias went to wah.

Mastah Jack come home all sickly; he was broke for life, dey said;
An' dey lef' my po' young mastah some'r's on de roadside,—dead.
W'en de women cried an' mou'ned 'em, I could feel it thoo an' thoo,
For I had a loved un fightin' in de way o' dangah, too.
Den dey tol' me dey had laid him some'r's way down souf to res',
Wid de flag dat he had fit for shinin' daih acrost his breas'.
Well, I cried, but den I reckon dat's whut Gawd had called him for,
W'en dey 'listed colo'ed sojers an' my 'Lias went to wah.

(1899)

JOEL CHANDLER HARRIS

Brer Rabbit and the Tar-Baby .

In Levemteen Hunder'd-an'-Full-er-Fleas,
When dey raise sech a crap er gooba peas,
De creeturs wuz all des ez chummy ez you please:
Dey raced an' dey rastled, dey jumped an' dey played,
An' dey wa'n't nothin' 'tall fer ter make 'um 'fraid.
Dey had der parties, bofe dar an' here,
Wid May-pop puddin' an' 'simmon beer;
An' de way dey keep der Fo'th-er-Julys
Wuz in eatin' goobas an' fresh tater pies—
An' dey wa'n't no doubt, an' no prehaps,
Dat dey holp one anudder out wid der craps.

An' dey had der frolics in de fall,
When dey 'scort'd Miss Meadows ter de ball,
Wid "Sasshay, ladies!" an' "Balance all!"
Dey had mighty little fer ter set um back,
Good health an' good craps—but what dey lack
Wuz good, clean water when de branch run dry,
Kaze de river wuz muddy when low er high.
Dey mought 'a' got a well by sellin' corn,
But de man what dugged um ain't been born;
So dey rocked along fum day ter day,
An' hoed der corn an' saved der hay.

When de Sun helt its own up in de sky,
An' de long drouth come, an' de branch run dry,
Mr. Fox an' Mr. Wolf look like dey'd die;
An' all de creeturs wuz in de same fix,
Ceppin' ol' Brer Rabbit, wid his errytatin' tricks;
He went his way, an' he had his fun
Ef de branch wuz dry er ef it run;
He loped along wid his lippity-clips,
A-wigglin' his nose an' a-workin' his lips,
An' his mornin' drink wuz allers new—
It wuz sweet-gum sap an' honey-dew!

De kin' what you fin' in de heart uv a flower,
Er de poplar-leaf, ef you'll wait fer de hour,
An' watch fer de moonshine's sweetenin' shower!
But de yuther creeturs ain't cotch de knack,
Dey wuz dull ez walkin' ter mill an' back;
Dey never tuck notice how de birds kin sing,
How de black bee zoons when he's on de wing,
How de stars swing 'roun', how de flowers smell,
An' dey'd dodge fum thunder wid "Well, well, well!"
Dey wisht mighty strong dat der cants wuz coulds,
Twel de day Mr. Fox got back fum de woods.

He come back, he did, an' sezee, "By jing!
You kin b'lieve me or not, but I done foun' a spring,
An' I feel like cuttin' de pidjin-wing!
An' it runs so clean, an' it runs so clear,
Dat it do like it's whisp'rin' in yo' y'ear,
Wid its 'Google-goody!' an' its 'Google-good!'
It's 'way over yander in de Chinkapin wood!"
An' de creeturs all, dey wuz happy, mon!
Dey trot, an' dey gallop, an' den dey run,
Wid a tippity-tip, an' a long-time swing,
Ter whar dey kin see de googlin'-spring!

Well, de spring wuz dar at de head er de dreen,
Whar de calamus shuck its flags er green,
An' de cat-tails tried fer to make a screen:
De creeturs all laugh, an' den dey squeal,
An' dey hopped all 'roun' on toe an' heel.
Brer Rabbit, he ax, "What's de hullabaloo?"
An' dey answer back, "It's a spring fer true!"
Den ol' Brer Rabbit tuck anudder chaw
Er his terbacker, an' he work his jaw,
An' sniff de a'r, an' shet his eyes,
An' fling back his head, an' look mighty wise.

Now, de spring had been dar sence de Flood,
But one fine mornin' 'twuz full er mud,
(An' ol' Brer Rabbit, he chawed his cud!)
An' atter dat 'twa'n't never clear,
An' der wa'n't no google fer de creeturs ter hear;
'Twuz mud in de mornin', an' mud at night—
'Tain't no use er talkin', dat mud wuz a sight!
Mr. Fox, ez de finder, watched over de spring,
An' he try ter diskiver what kinder thing

Wuz a-stirrin' up mud bofe night an' day—
An' he watch an' he wait twel he had his way.

An' one fine mornin' he foun' some tracks,
An' he shuck his head (I'm tellin' you de facts!)
An' he went off an' got 'im some shoemaker's wax,
An' pitch an' rozzum, an' den an' dar
He mould him a baby outer de tar,
Wid leg an' body, an' head an' han'—
An' it look like it settin' dar playin' in de san'—
An' he hide hisse'f whar he kin see
Whatsomever gwine ter happen ter de Tar-Baby-ee—
De Tar-Baby-ow, de Tar-Baby-oh—
An' den he hide an' lay mighty low!

Brer Rabbit, he skipped along at las'—
He skip sorter slow; den he skip kinder fas'—
Kaze he use de spring ez a lookin'-glass,
An' he seed de Tar-Baby settin' dar:
"Good-mornin', suh, an' how's yo' Ma?
An' how does yo' copperositee
Seem ter segashuate?" sezee;
"An' whar yo' manners? You mus' be deff!
You'll hear ef I hit you, an' you'll lose yo' breff!"
Brer Rabbit, he wait, wid "Tooby sho!"
Tar-Baby say nothin'—Mr. Fox lay low!

"You better tell me howdy! you better make yo' bow!
No trouble ter show you ef you dunner how—
Er maybe you er keen fer ter git in a row?
Good-mornin', dis mornin', I'll ax you once mo'!"
Tar-Baby say nothin'—Mr. Fox lay low!
Brer Rabbit, he stomp his foot on de groun',
"You er mighty stuck up, but I'll fetch you down!
You see dis han'? Well, I'll hit you a blip
Dat'll split you open fum hat ter hip!
What ail you, man? an' whar did you grow?"
Tar-Baby say nothin'—Mr. Fox lay low!

Brer Rabbit made a pass at 'im des fer luck,
An' he hauled off an' hit 'im in de eye—*kerchuck!*
An' tried ter jump away, but de han' done stuck!
"Turn me loose, you villyun, er I'll hit you ag'in!
I'll gi' you a jolt dat'll cave you in!"
Brer Rabbit draw'd back—"I'll try yo' pluck!"

An' biffed 'im ag'in, an' t'er han' stuck!
"You see dis foot? I'll gi' you a kick
Dat'll lan' you down yander close ter Ol' Nick!
Des turn me loose, an' I'll let you go!"
Tar-Baby say nothin'—Mr. Fox lay low.

Brer Rabbit hit de groun' wid his foot, an' say:
"You'll be sorry you pestered wid me dis day—
So des turn me a-loose an' go on away!"
Den he up wid his foot an' kicked 'im—*blam!*
"I lay I'll show you des who I am!"
But de foot done stuck! "Will you le' me go?"
Tar-Baby say nothin'—Mr. Fox lay low!
Den Brer Rabbit feel like he 'bout ter git vext,
Kaze he spected eve'y minnit would be de next,
An' he monstus sorry dat it wuz so!
Tar-Baby say nothin'—Mr. Fox lay low.

Well, de yuther foot stuck, an', atter dat,
Brer Rabbit, he grin like a Chessy-cat—
"Ef you don't turn me loose I'll butt you flat!
I'll scatter yo' brains! I'll ruin you, sho!"
Tar-Baby say nothin'—Mr. Fox lay low.
Brer Rabbit, he butted ez hard ez he could,
An' his head it stuck, let 'im do what he would—
An' de Tar-Baby helt 'im hard an' fast,
An' it look like his time done come at last:
Mr. Fox sa'nter'd out fum his hidin' place,
Wid a blood red smile runnin' 'cross his face!

He scraped his foot an' den he bow,
He licked his chops an' den he 'low:
"Howdy-do, Brer Rabbit? How you feel, nohow?"
Wid a th'obbin' heart an' a shakin' knee,
Brer Rabbit wuz skeer'd ez skeer'd could be.
"You er mighty stuck up," Mr. Fox, he say,
"An' I'm s'prized ter see it at dis time er day!"
He walked aroun'—"Here's a gooba shell,
I kin skacely believe it! Well, well, well!"
He pulled off his coat an' rolled up his sleeves—
"Now, I'm gwine ter show you des what I b'lieves!"

An' he grinned ag'in de grin dat wuz red,
An' he opened his mouf fer ter let it spread
Twel he show all de tushes in his head:

He grab Brer Rabbit by de leg,
An' you oughter hear dat creetur beg!
Mr. Fox, he say, "What I'm gwine ter do
Is to pay you bofe fer de ol' an' de new!
Oh, you nee'n ter talk: I know you er nice:
But you fooled me once an' you fooled me twice!
You steal my goobas, an' den you fling
A whole pile er mud right in dat spring!

"But I got you now, an' yo' hide I'll stretch—
I'll l'arn you sump'n, you triflin' wretch!
I'll gi' you de ol'-time Buckra tetch!
I'll skin you alive, I'll drown you dead!
I'll break yo' neck, I'll crack yo' head—
I'll wallop you twel I make you think
I'm de patter-roller, you wall-eyed slink!"
Brer Rabbit sniffle, an' den he say,
"I know mighty well you'll have yo' way:
You may drown me, suh, ef it's yo' desires,
But please don't fling me in de briers!"

De tar wuz so rank dat Brer Rabbit sneeze,
But he still wuz shakin' in de knees,
An' he keep on a-whimplin', "Please, suh, please!"
"Oh, yes! I'll please!" Mr. Fox, he say,
"An' I'll please myse'f dis very day!
You mayn't be mine, but I think you is,
An' I'm sho gwine ter bake you twel you sizz!
I'll kindle de bresh-heap, an' fling you in,
An' I lay dat'll cook an' crisp yo' skin!"
Brer Rabbit, he say: "Des fetch on yo' fires,
But please don't fling me in de briers!"

Brer Fox, he study an' rub his chin,
He rub it once, an' he rub it ag'in,
An' he wunk one eye, an' grinned a grin—
"I'll hang you high, an' maybe higher,
An' I'll fling you in de big quogmire!"
"Do des ez you please," Brer Rabbit cry,
"An' I'll ax no reason, fer which er why;
You kin drown me deep, you kin hang me high,
An' not one tear will drap fum my eye;
You kin hamstring me wid red-hot wires,
But please, oh, please, keep me outer de briers!"

Mr. Fox he tuck him at his word,
An' sont him sailin' like a bird,
Ez if he wuz feather'd instidder furr'd
Right spang in de briers growin' dar
Ez thick, ev'y bit, ez de thickest ha'r:
Brer Rabbit, he holla, "I ain't got a scratch!
I was bred an' born in de brier-patch!
You flung me in an' lif' de latch:
Oh, one fine mornin', when day was dawnin',
I was bred an' born in de brier-patch!"

(1904)

PAUL HAMILTON HAYNE

Vicksburg: A Ballad

For sixty days and upwards,
    A storm of shell and shot
Rained round us in a flaming shower,
    But still we faltered not.
"If the noble city perish,"
    Our grand young leader said,
"Let the only walls the foe shall scale
    Be ramparts of the dead!"

For sixty days and upwards,
    The eye of heaven waxed dim;
And e'en throughout God's holy morn,
    O'er Christian prayer and hymn,
Arose a hissing tumult,
    As if the fiends in air
Strove to engulf the voice of faith
    In the shrieks of their despair.

There was wailing in the houses,
    There was trembling on the marts,
While the tempest raged and thundered,
    'Mid the silent thrill of hearts;
But the Lord, our shield, was with us,
    And ere a month had sped,
Our very women walked the streets
    With scarce one throb of dread.

And the little children gambolled,
    Their faces purely raised,
Just for a wondering moment,
    As the huge bombs whirled and blazed,
Then turned with silvery laughter
    To the sports which children love,
Thrice-mailed in the sweet, instinctive thought
    That the good God watched above.

Yet the hailing bolts fell faster,
    From scores of flame-clad ships,
And about us, denser, darker,
    Grew the conflict's wild eclipse,
Till a solid cloud closed o'er us,
    Like a type of doom and ire,
Whence shot a thousand quivering tongues
    Of forked and vengeful fire.

But the unseen hands of angels
    Those death-shafts warned aside,
And the dove of heavenly mercy
    Ruled o'er the battle tide;
In the houses ceased the wailing,
    And through the war-scarred marts
The people strode, with step of hope,
    To the music in their hearts.

(1863)

GEORGE MOSES HORTON

On Death

Deceitful worm, that undermines the clay,
Which slyly steals the thoughtless soul away,
Pervading neighborhoods with sad surprise,
Like sudden storms of wind and thunder rise.

The sounding death-watch lurks within the wall,
Away some unsuspecting soul to call;
The pendant willow droops her waving head,
And sighing zephyrs whisper of the dead.

Methinks I hear the doleful midnight knell—
Some parting spirit bids the world farewell;
The taper burns as conscious of distress,
And seems to show the living number less.

Must a lov'd daughter from her father part,
And grieve for one who lies so near her heart?
And must she for the last loss bemoan,
Or faint to hear his last departing groan.

Methinks I see him speechless gaze awhile,
And on her drop his last paternal smile;
With gushing tears closing his humid eyes,
The last pulse beats, and in her arm he dies.

With pallid cheeks she lingers round his bier,
And heaves a farewell sigh with every tear;
With sorrow she consigns him to the dust,
And silent owns the fatal sentence just.

Still her sequestered mother seems to weep,
And spurns the balm which constitutes her sleep;
Her plaintive murmurs float upon the gale,
And almost make the stubborn rocks bewail.

O what is like the awful breach of death,
Whose fatal stroke invades the creature's breadth!
It bids the voice of desolation roll,
And strikes the deepest awe within the bravest soul.

(1829)

JAMES WELDON JOHNSON

The Creation

And God stepped out on space,
And he looked around and said:
I'm lonely—
I'll make me a world.

And far as the eye of God could see
Darkness covered everything,
Blacker than a hundred midnights
Down in a cypress swamp.

Then God smiled,
And the light broke,
And the darkness rolled up on one side,
And the light stood shining on the other,
And God said: That's good!

Then God reached out and took the light in his hands,
And God rolled the light around in his hands
Until he made the sun;
And he set that sun a-blazing in the heavens.
And the light that was left from making the sun
God gathered it up in a shining ball
And flung it against the darkness,
Spangling the night with the moon and stars.
Then down between
The darkness and the light
He hurled the world;
And God said: That's good!

Then God himself stepped down—
And the sun was on his right hand,
And the moon was on his left;
The stars were clustered about his head,
And the earth was under his feet.
And God walked, and where he trod

His footsteps hollowed the valleys out
And bulged the mountains up.

Then he stopped and looked and saw
That the earth was hot and barren.
So God stepped over to the edge of the world
And he spat out the seven seas—
He batted his eyes, and the lightnings flashed—
He clapped his hands, and the thunders rolled—
And the waters above the earth came down,
The cooling waters came down.

Then the green grass sprouted,
And the little red flowers blossomed,
The pine tree pointed his finger to the sky,
And the oak spread out his arms,
The lakes cuddled down in the hollows of the ground,
And the rivers ran down to the sea;
And God smiled again,
And the rainbow appeared,
And curled itself around his shoulder.

Then God raised his arm and he waved his hand
Over the sea and over the land,
And he said: Bring forth! Bring forth!
And quicker than God could drop his hand,
Fishes and fowls
And beasts and birds
Swam the rivers and the seas,
Roamed the forests and the woods,
And split the air with their wings.
And God said: That's good!

Then God walked around,
And God looked around
On all that he had made.
He looked at his sun,
And he looked at his moon,
And he looked at his little stars;
He looked on his world
With all its living things,
And God said: I'm lonely still.

Then God sat down—
On the side of a hill where he could think,

By a deep wide river he sat down;
With his head in his hands,
God thought and thought,
Till he thought: I'll make me a man!

Up from the bed of the river
God scooped the clay;
And by the bank of the river
He kneeled him down;
And there the great God Almighty
Who lit the sun and fixed it in the sky,
Who flung the stars to the most far corner of the night,
Who rounded the earth in the middle of his hand;
This Great God,
Like a mammy bending over her baby,
Kneeled down in the dust
Toiling over a lump of clay
Till he shaped it in his own image;

Then into it he blew the breath of life,
And man became a living soul.
Amen. Amen.

(1920)

The Crucifixion

Jesus, my gentle Jesus,
Walking in the dark of the Garden—
The Garden of Gethsemane,
Saying to the three disciples:
Sorrow is in my soul—
Even unto death;
Tarry ye here a little while,
And watch with me.

Jesus, my burdened Jesus,
Praying in the dark of the Garden—
The Garden of Gethsemane.
Saying: Father,
Oh, Father,

This bitter cup,
This bitter cup,
Let it pass from Me.

Jesus, my sorrowing Jesus,
The sweat like drops of blood upon his brow,
Talking with his Father,
While the three disciples slept,
Saying: Father,
Oh, Father,
Not as I will,
Not as I will,
But let Thy will be done.

Oh, look at black-hearted Judas—
Sneaking through the dark of the Garden—
Leading his crucifying mob.
Oh, God!
Strike him down!
Why *don't* you strike him down,
Before he plants his traitor's kiss
Upon my Jesus' cheek?

And they take my blameless Jesus,
And they drag him to the Governor,
To the mighty Roman Governor.
Great Pilate seated in his hall,—
Great Pilate on his judgment seat,
Said: In this man I find no fault.
I find no fault in him.
And Pilate washed his hands.

But they cried out, saying:
Crucify him!—
Crucify him!—
Crucify him!—
His blood be on our heads.
And they beat my loving Jesus,
They spit on my precious Jesus;
They dressed him up in a purple robe,
They put a crown of thorns upon his head,
And they pressed it down—
Oh, they pressed it down—
And they mocked my sweet King Jesus.

Up Golgotha's rugged road
I see my Jesus go.
I see him sink beneath the load,
I see my drooping Jesus sink.
And then they laid hold on Simon,
Black Simon, yes, black Simon;
They put the cross on Simon,
And Simon bore the cross.

On Calvary, on Calvary,
They crucified my Jesus.
They nailed him to the cruel tree,
And the hammer!
The hammer!
The hammer!
Rang through Jerusalem's streets.
The hammer!
The hammer!
The hammer!
Rang through Jerusalem's streets.

Jesus, my lamb-like Jesus,
Shivering as the nails go through his hands;
Jesus, my lamb-like Jesus,
Shivering as the nails go through his feet.
Jesus, my darling Jesus,
Groaning as the Roman spear plunged in his side;
Jesus, my darling Jesus,
Groaning as the blood came spurting from his wound.
Oh, look how they done my Jesus!

Mary,
Weeping Mary,
Sees her poor little Jesus on the cross.
Mary,
Weeping Mary,
Sees her sweet, baby Jesus on the cruel cross,
Hanging between two thieves.

And Jesus, my lonesome Jesus,
Called out once more to his Father,
Saying:
My God,
My God,

Why hast thou forsaken me?
And he drooped his head and died.

And the veil of the temple was split in two,
The midday sun refused to shine,
The thunder rumbled and the lightning wrote
An unknown language in the sky.
What a day! Lord, what a day!
When my blessed Jesus died.

Oh, I tremble, yes, I tremble,
It causes me to tremble, tremble,
When I think how Jesus died;
Died on the steeps of Calvary,
How Jesus died for sinners,
Sinners like you and me.

(1927)

SIDNEY LANIER

Thar's More in the Man
Than Thar is in the Land

I knowed a man, which he lived in Jones,
Which Jones is a county of red hills and stones,
And he lived pretty much by gittin' of loans,
And his mules was nuthin' but skin and bones,
And his hogs was flat as his corn-bread pones,
And he had 'bout a thousand acres o' land.

This man—which his name it was also Jones—
He swore that he'd leave them old red hills and stones,
Fur he couldn't make nuthin' but yallerish cotton,
And little o' *that*, and his fences was rotten,
And what little corn he had, *hit* was boughten
And dinged ef a livin' was in the land.

And the longer he swore the madder he got,
And he riz and he walked to the stable lot,
And he hollered to Tom to come thar and hitch
Fur to emigrate somewhar whar land was rich,
And to quit raisin' cock-burrs, thistles and sich,
And a wastin' ther time on the cussed land.

So him and Tom they hitched up the mules,
Pertestin' that folks was mighty big fools
That 'ud stay in Georgy ther lifetime out,
Jest scratchin' a livin' when all of 'em mought
Git places in Texas whar cotton would sprout
By the time you could plant it in the land.

And he driv by a house whar a man named Brown
Was a livin', not fur from the edge o' town,
And he bantered Brown fur to buy his place,
And said that bein' as money was skace,

And bein' as sheriffs was hard to face,
Two dollars an acre would git the land.

They closed at a dollar and fifty cents,
And Jones he bought him a waggin and tents,
And loaded his corn, and his wimmin, and truck,
And moved to Texas, which it tuck
His entire pile, with the best of luck,
To git thar and git him a little land.

But Brown moved out on the old Jones' farm,
And he rolled up his breeches and bared his arm,
And he picked all the rocks from off'n the groun',
And he rooted it up and he plowed it down,
Then he sowed his corn and his wheat in the land.

Five years glid by, and Brown, one day
(Which he'd got so fat that he wouldn't weigh),
Was a settin' down, sorter lazily,
To the bulliest dinner you ever see,
When one o' the children jumped on his knee
And says, "Yan's Jones, which you bought his land."

And thar was Jones, standin' out at the fence,
And he hadn't no waggin, nor mules, nor tents,
Fur he had left Texas afoot and cum
To Georgy to see if he couldn't git sum
Employment, and he was a lookin' as hum-
Ble as ef he had never owned any land.

But Brown he axed him in, and he sot
Him down to his vittles smokin' hot,
And when he had filled hisself and the floor
Brown looked at him sharp and riz and swore
That, "whether men's land was rich or poor
Thar was more in the *man* than thar was in the *land*."

(1869)

Song of the Chattahoochee

Out of the hills of Habersham,
    Down in the valleys of Hall,
I hurry amain to reach the plain,
Run the rapid and leap the fall,
Split at the rock and together again,
Accept my bed, or narrow or wide,
And flee from folly on every side
With a lover's pain to attain the plain
    Far from the hills of Habersham,
    Far from the valleys of Hall.

All down the hills of Habersham,
    All through the valleys of Hall,
The rushes cried *Abide, abide,*
The willful waterweeds held me thrall,
The laving laurel turned my tide,
The ferns and the fondling grass said *Stay,*
The dewberry dipped for to work delay,
And the little reeds sighed *Abide, abide,*
    Here in the hills of Habersham,
    Here in the valleys of Hall.

High o'er the hills of Habersham,
    Veiling the valleys of Hall,
The hickory told me manifold
Fair tales of shade, the poplar tall
Wrought me her shadowy self to hold,
The chestnut, the oak, the walnut, the pine,
Overleaning, with flickering meaning and sign,
Said, *Pass not, so cold, these manifold*
    Deep shades of the hills of Habersham,
    These glades in the valleys of Hall.

And oft in the hills of Habersham,
    And oft in the valleys of Hall,
The white quartz shone, and the smooth brook-stone
Did bar me of passage with friendly brawl,
And many a luminous jewel lone
—Crystals clear or a-cloud with mist,
Ruby, garnet and amethyst—
Made lures with the lights of streaming stone

In the clefts of the hills of Habersham,
In the beds of the valleys of Hall.

But oh, not the hills of Habersham,
And oh, not the valleys of Hall
Avail: I am fain for to water the plain.
Downward the voices of Duty call—
Downward, to toil and be mixed with the main,
The dry fields burn, and the mills are to turn,
And a myriad flowers mortally yearn,
And the lordly main from beyond the plain
Calls o'er the hills of Habersham,
Calls through the valleys of Hall.

(1877)

The Marshes of Glynn

Glooms of the live-oaks, beautiful-braided and woven
With intricate shades of the vines that myriad-cloven
Clamber the forks of the multiform boughs,—
Emerald twilights,—
Virginal shy lights,
Wrought of the leaves to allure to the whisper of vows,
When lovers pace timidly down through the green colonnades
Of the dim sweet woods, of the dear dark woods,
Of the heavenly woods and glades,
That run to the radiant marginal sand-beach within
The wide sea-marshes of Glynn;—

Beautiful glooms, soft dusks in the noon-day fire,—
Wildwood privacies, closets of lone desire,
Chamber from chamber parted with wavering arras of leaves,—
Cells for the passionate pleasure of prayer to the soul that grieves,
Pure with a sense of the passing of saints through the wood,
Cool for the dutiful weighing of ill with good;—

O braided dusks of the oak and woven shades of the vine,
While the riotous noon-day sun of the June-day long did shine
Ye held me fast in your heart and I held you fast in mine;
But now when the noon is no more, and riot is rest,

And the sun is a-wait at the ponderous gate of the West,
And the slant yellow beam down the wood-aisle doth seem
Like a lane into heaven that leads from a dream,—
Ay, now, when my soul all day hath drunken the soul of the oak,
And my heart is at ease from men, and the wearisome sound of the stroke
  Of the scythe of time and the trowel of trade is low,
  And belièf overmasters doubt, and I know that I know,
  And my spirit is grown to a lordly great compass within,
That the length and the breadth and the sweep of the marshes of Glynn
Will work me no fear like the fear they have wrought me of yore
When length was fatigue, and when breadth was but bitterness sore,
And when terror and shrinking and dreary unnamable pain
Drew over me out of the merciless miles of the plain,—

Oh, now, unafraid, I am fain to face
  The vast sweet visage of space.
To the edge of the wood I am drawn, I am drawn,
Where the gray beach glimmering runs, as a belt of the dawn,
  For a mete and a mark
    To the forest-dark:—
      So:
Affable live-oak, leaning low,—
Thus—with your favor—soft, with a reverent hand,
(Not lightly touching your person, Lord of the land!)
Bending your beauty aside, with a step I stand
On the firm-packed sand,
      Free
By a world of marsh that borders a world of sea.
  Sinuous southward and sinuous northward the shimmering band
  Of the sand-beach fastens the fringe of the marsh to the folds of the land.
Inward and outward to northward and southward the beach-lines linger and curl
As a silver-wrought garment that clings to and follows the firm sweet limbs
  of a girl.
Vanishing, swerving, evermore curving again into sight,
Softly the sand-beach wavers away to a dim gray looping of light.
And what if behind me to westward the wall of the woods stands high?
The world lies east: how ample, the marsh and the sea and the sky!
A league and a league of marsh-grass, waist-high, broad in the blade,
Green, and all of a height, and unflecked with a light or a shade,
Stretch leisurely off, in a pleasant plain,
To the terminal blue of the main.

Oh, what is abroad in the marsh and the terminal sea?
  Somehow my soul seems suddenly free
From the weighing of fate and the sad discussion of sin,
By the length and the breadth and the sweep of the marshes of Glynn.

Ye marshes, how candid and simple and nothing-withholding and free
Ye publish yourselves to the sky and offer yourselves to the sea!
Tolerant plains, that suffer the sea and the rains and the sun,
Ye spread and span like the catholic man who hath mightily won
God out of knowledge and good out of infinite pain
And sight out of blindness and purity out of a stain.

As the marsh-hen secretly builds on the watery sod,
Behold I will build me a nest on the greatness of God:
I will fly in the greatness of God as the marsh-hen flies
In the freedom that fills all the space 'twixt the marsh and the skies:
By so many roots as the marsh-grass sends in the sod
I will heartily lay me a-hold on the greatness of God:
Oh, like to the greatness of God is the greatness within
The range of the marshes, the liberal marshes of Glynn.

And the sea lends large, as the marsh: lo, out of his plenty the sea
Pours fast: full soon the time of the flood-tide must be:
Look how the grace of the sea doth go
About and about through the intricate channels that flow
                    Here and there,
                        Everywhere,
Till his waters have flooded the uttermost creeks and the low-lying lanes,
And the marsh is meshed with a million veins,
That like as with rosy and silvery essences flow
        In the rose-and-silver evening glow.
                        Farewell, my lord Sun!
The creeks overflow: a thousand rivulets run
'Twixt the roots of the sod; the blades of the marsh-grass stir;
Passeth a hurrying sound of wings that westward whirr:
Passeth, and all is still; and the currents cease to run;
And the sea and the marsh are one.

How still the plains of the waters be!
The tide is in his ecstasy.
The tide is at his highest height:
                    And it is night.

And now from the Vast of the Lord will the waters of sleep
Roll in on the souls of men,
But who will reveal to our waking ken
The forms that swim and the shapes that creep
                    Under the waters of sleep?
And I would I could know what swimmeth below when the tide comes in
On the length and the breadth of the marvellous marshes of Glynn.

(1878)

ALEXANDER BEAUFORT MEEK

The Mocking-Bird

From the vale, what music ringing,
    Fills the bosom of the night,
On the sense, entranc'd, flinging
    Spells of witchery and delight!
O'er magnolia, lime and cedar
    From yon locust-top it swells,
Like the chant of serenader,
    Or the rhymes of silver bells!
        Listen! dearest, listen to it!
            Sweeter sounds were never heard!
        'T is the song of that wild poet—
            Mime and minstrel—mocking-bird.

See him, swinging in his glory,
    On yon topmost bending limb!
Carolling his amorous story,
    Like some wild crusader's hymn!
Now it faints in tones delicious
    As the first low vow of love!
Now it bursts in swells capricious,
    All the moonlit vale above!
        Listen! dearest, listen to it!
            Sweeter sounds were never heard!
        'T is the song of that wild poet—
            Mime and minstrel—mocking-bird.

Why is't thus this sylvan Petrarch
    Pours all night his serenade?
'T is for some proud woodland Laura,
    His sad sonnets all are made!
But he changes now his measure—
    Gladness bubbling from his mouth—
Jest, and gibe, and mimic pleasure—
    Winged Anacreon of the South!

Listen! dearest, listen to it!
> Sweeter sounds were never heard!
'T is the song of that wild poet—
> Mime and minstrel—mocking-bird.

Bird of music, wit, and gladness,
> Troubadour of sunny climes,
Disenchanter of all sadness,—
> Would thine art were in my rhymes,
O'er the heart that's beating by me,
> I would weave a spell divine;
Is there aught she could deny me,
> Drinking in such strains as thine?
Listen! dearest, listen to it!
> Sweeter sounds were never heard!
'T is the song of that wild poet—
> Mime and minstrel—mocking-bird.

(1857)

EDWARD COOTE PINKNEY

Song

Day depart this upper air,
    My lively, lovely lady;
And the eve-star sparkles fair,
    And our good steeds are ready.
Leave, leave these loveless halls,
    So lordly though they be;—
Come, come—affection calls—
    Away at once with me!

Sweet thy words in sense as sound,
    And gladly do I hear them;
Though thy kinsmen are around,
    And tamer bosoms fear them.
Mount, mount,—I'll keep thee, dear,
    In safety as we ride;—
On, on—my heart is here,
    My sword is at my side!

(1825)

EDGAR ALLAN POE

The Raven

Once upon a midnight dreary, while I pondered, weak and weary,
Over many a quaint and curious volume of forgotten lore—
While I nodded, nearly napping, suddenly there came a tapping,
As of some one gently rapping, rapping at my chamber door—
"'Tis some visitor," I muttered, "tapping at my chamber door—
　　　Only this and nothing more."

Ah, distinctly I remember it was in the bleak December;
And each separate dying ember wrought its ghost upon the floor.
Eagerly I wished the morrow;—vainly I had sought to borrow
From my books surcease of sorrow—sorrow for the lost Lenore—
For the rare and radiant maiden whom the angels name Lenore—
　　　Nameless *here* for evermore.

And the silken, sad, uncertain rustling of each purple curtain
Thrilled me—filled me with fantastic terrors never felt before;
So that now, to still the beating of my heart, I stood repeating,
"'Tis some visitor entreating entrance at my chamber door—
Some late visitor entreating entrance at my chamber door;—
　　　This it is and nothing more."

Presently my soul grew stronger; hesitating then no longer,
"Sir," said I, "or Madam, truly your forgiveness I implore;
But the fact is I was napping, and so gently you came rapping,
And so faintly you came tapping, tapping at my chamber door,
That I scarce was sure I heard you"—here I opened wide the door;—
　　　Darkness there and nothing more.

Deep into that darkness peering, long I stood there wondering, fearing,
Doubting, dreaming dreams no mortal ever dared to dream before;
But the silence was unbroken, and the stillness gave no token,
And the only word there spoken was the whispered word, "Lenore!"
This I whispered, and an echo murmured back the word "Lenore!"
　　　Merely this and nothing more.

Back into the chamber turning, all my soul within me burning,
Soon again I heard a tapping somewhat louder than before.
"Surely," said I, "surely that is something at my window lattice;
Let me see, then, what thereat is, and this mystery explore—
Let my heart be still a moment and this mystery explore;—
    'Tis the wind and nothing more!"

Open here I flung the shutter, when, with many a flirt and flutter,
In there stepped a stately Raven of the saintly days of yore:
Not the least obeisance made he; not a minute stopped or stayed he;
But, with mien of lord or lady, perched above my chamber door—
Perched upon a bust of Pallas just above my chamber door—
    Perched, and sat, and nothing more.

Then this ebony bird beguiling my sad fancy into smiling,
By the grave and stern decorum of the countenance it wore:
"Though thy crest be shorn and shaven, thou," I said, "art sure no craven,
Ghastly grim and ancient Raven wandering from the Nightly shore—
Tell me what thy lordly name is on the Night's Plutonian shore!"
    Quoth the Raven "Nevermore."

Much I marvelled this ungainly fowl to hear discourse so plainly,
Though its answer little meaning—little relevancy bore:
For we cannot help agreeing that no living human being
Ever yet was blessed with seeing bird above his chamber door—
Bird or beast upon the sculptured bust above his chamber door,
    With such name as "Nevermore."

But the Raven, sitting lonely on the placid bust, spoke only
That one word, as if his soul in that one word he did outpour.
Nothing farther then he uttered—not a feather then he fluttered—
Till I scarcely more than muttered "Other friends have flown before—
On the morrow *he* will leave me, as my Hopes have flown before."
    Then the bird said "Nevermore."

Startled at the stillness broken by reply so aptly spoken,
"Doubtless," said I, "what it utters is its only stock and store
Caught from some unhappy master whom unmerciful Disaster
Followed fast and followed faster till his songs one burden bore—
Till the dirges of his Hope that melancholy burden bore
    Of 'Never—nevermore.'"

But the Raven still beguiling my sad fancy into smiling,
Straight I wheeled a cushioned seat in front of bird, and bust and door;
Then, upon the velvet sinking, I betook myself to linking
Fancy unto fancy, thinking what this ominous bird of yore—

What this grim, ungainly, ghastly, gaunt, and ominous bird of yore
    Meant in croaking "Nevermore."

This I sat engaged in guessing, but no syllable expressing
To the fowl whose fiery eyes now burned into my bosom's core;
This and more I sat divining, with my head at ease reclining
On the cushion's velvet lining that the lamp-light gloated o'er,
But whose velvet-violet lining with the lamp-light gloating o'er,
    She shall press, ah, nevermore!

Then, methought, the air grew denser, perfumed from an unseen censer
Swung by seraphim whose foot-falls tinkled on the tufted floor.
"Wretch," I cried, "thy God hath lent thee—by these angels he hath sent thee
Respite—respite and nepenthe from thy memories of Lenore;
Quaff, oh quaff this kind nepenthe and forget this lost Lenore!"
    Quoth the Raven "Nevermore."

"Prophet!" said I, "thing of evil!—prophet still, if bird or devil!—
Whether Tempter sent, or whether tempest tossed thee here ashore,
Desolate yet all undaunted, on this desert land enchanted—
On this home by Horror haunted—tell me truly, I implore—
Is there—*is* there balm in Gilead?—tell me—tell me, I implore!"
    Quoth the Raven "Nevermore."

"Prophet!" said I, "thing of evil!—prophet still, if bird or devil!—
By that Heaven that bends above us—by that God we both adore—
Tell this soul with sorrow laden if, within the distant Aidenn,
It shall clasp a sainted maiden whom the angels name Lenore—
Clasp a rare and radiant maiden whom the angels name Lenore."
    Quoth the Raven "Nevermore."

"Be that word our sign of parting, bird or fiend!" I shrieked, upstarting—
"Get thee back into the tempest and the Night's Plutonian shore!
Leave no black plume as a token of that lie thy soul hath spoken!
Leave my loneliness unbroken!—quit the bust above my door!
Take thy beak from out my heart, and take thy form from off my door!"
    Quoth the Raven "Nevermore."

And the Raven, never flitting, still is sitting, *still* is sitting
On the pallid bust of Pallas just above my chamber door;
And his eyes have all the seeming of a demon's that is dreaming,
And the lamp-light o'er him streaming throws his shadow on the floor;
And my soul from out that shadow that lies floating on the floor
    Shall be lifted—nevermore!

(1845)

Annabel Lee

It was many and many a year ago,
    In a kingdom by the sea,
That a maiden there lived whom you may know
    By the name of Annabel Lee;—
And this maiden she lived with no other thought
    Than to love and be loved by me.

She was a child and *I* was a child,
    In this kingdom by the sea,
But we loved with a love that was more than love—
    I and my Annabel Lee—
With a love that the wingéd seraphs of Heaven
    Coveted her and me.

And this was the reason that, long ago,
    In this kingdom by the sea,
A wind blew out of a cloud by night
    Chilling my Annabel Lee;
So that her highborn kinsmen came
    And bore her away from me,
To shut her up in a sepulchre
    In this kingdom by the sea.

The angels, not half so happy in Heaven,
    Went envying her and me:—
Yes! that was the reason (as all men know,
    In this kingdom by the sea)
That the wind came out of the cloud, chilling
    And killing my Annabel Lee.

But our love it was stronger by far than the love
    Of those who were older than we—
    Of many far wiser than we—
And neither the angels in Heaven above
    Nor the demons down under the sea
Can ever dissever my soul from the soul
    Of the beautiful Annabel Lee:—

For the moon never beams without bringing me dreams
    Of the beautiful Annabel Lee;
And the stars never rise but I see the bright eyes

Of the beautiful Annabel Lee;
And so, all the night-tide, I lie down by the side
Of my darling, my darling, my life and my bride
   In her sepulchre there by the sea—
   In her tomb by the side of the sea.

(1849)

LIZETTE WOODWORTH REESE

Tears

When I consider Life and its few years—
A wisp of fog betwixt us and the sun;
A call to battle, and the battle done
Ere the last echo dies within our ears;
A rose choked in the grass; an hour of fears;
The gusts that past a darkening shore do beat;
The burst of music down an unlistening street—
I wonder at the idleness of tears.
Ye old, old dead, and ye of yesternight,
Chieftains, and bards, and keepers of the sheep,
By every cup of sorrow that you had,
Loose me from tears, and make me see aright
How each hath back what once he stayed to weep;
Homer his sight, David his little lad!

(1899)

Thrift

A star proves never traitor, and a weed—
Even that vetch obscurely purple there—
Can hoard such loyalties against your need,
You may go rich, though all the world go bare.
A blackbird's whistle over the young grass,
Is but another wealth; so are these, too:—
The old rememberings that start and pass
At its short music, when the year is new.
If stars you love, and all their like, then know
Your love will be a thrift to set you clear

Of beggary, and whining at a door.
You change, life changes; it is ever so;
But these last on from whirling year to year:
Learn God of them, and add Him to your store.

(1927)

IRWIN RUSSELL

Christmas Night in the Quarters

When merry Christmas-day is done,
And Christmas-night is just begun;
While clouds in slow procession drift,
To wish the moon-man "Christmas gift,"
Yet linger overhead, to know
What causes all the stir below;
At Uncle Jonny Booker's ball
The darkies hold high carnival.
From all the country-side they throng,
With laughter, shouts, and scraps of song,—
Their whole deportment plainly showing
That to the Frolic they are going.
Some take the path with shoes in hand,
To traverse muddy bottom-land;
Aristocrats their steeds bestride—
Four on a mule, behold them ride!
And ten great oxen draw apace
The wagon from "de oder place,"
With forty guests, whose conversation
Betokens glad anticipation.
Not so with him who drives: old Jim
Is sagely solemn, hard, and grim,
And frolics have no joys for him.
He seldom speaks but to condemn—
Or utter some wise apothegm—
Or else, some crabbed thought pursuing,
Talk to his team, as now he's doing:

Come up, heah, Star! Yee-bawee!
        You alluz is a-laggin'—
Mus' be you think I's dead,
        An' dis de huss you's draggin'—
You' 'mos too lazy to draw yo' bref,
        Let 'lone drawin' de waggin.

Dis team—quit bel'rin, sah!
   De ladies don't submit 'at—
Dis team—you ol' fool ox,
   You heah me tell you quit 'at?
Dis team's des like de 'Nited States;
   Dat's what I's tryin' to git at!

 De people rides behin'
   De pollytishners haulin'—
Shu'd be a well-bruk ox,
   To foller dat ar callin'—
An' sometimes nuffin won't do dem steers,
   But what dey mus' be stallin'!

Woo bahgh! Buck-kannon! Yes, sah,
   Sometimes dey will be stickin';
An' den, fus thing dey knows,
   Dey takes a rale good lickin'.
De folks gits down: an' den watch out
   For hommerin' an' kickin'.

Dey blows upon dey hands,
   Den flings 'em wid de nails up,
Jumps up an' cracks dey heels,
   An' pruzently dey sails up,
An' makes dem oxen hump deysef,
   By twistin' all dey tails up!

In this our age of printer's ink
'Tis books that show us how to think—
The rule reversed, and set at naught,
That held that books were born of thought.
We form our minds by pedants' rules,
And all we know is from the schools;
And when we work, or when we play,
We do it in an ordered way—
And Nature's self pronounce a ban on,
Whene'er she dares transgress a canon.
Untrammelled thus the simple race is
That "wuks the craps" on cotton places.
Original in act and thought,
Because unlearned and untaught.
  Observe them at their Christmas party:
  How unrestrained their mirth—how hearty!
  How many things they say and do

That never would occur to you!
See Brudder Brown—whose saving grace
Would sanctify a quarter race—
Out on the crowded floor advance
To "beg a blessin' on dis dance."

O Mahsr! let dis gath'rin' fin' a blessin' in yo' sight!
Don't jedge us hard fur what we does—you knows it's Chrismus night;
An' all de balance ob de yeah we does as right's we kin.
Ef dancin's wrong, O Mahsr! let de time excuse de sin!

We labors in de vineya'd, wukin' hard an' wukin' true;
Now, shorely you won't notus, ef we eats a grape or two,
An' takes a leetle holiday,—a leetle restin'-spell,—
Bekase, nex' week, we'll start in fresh, an' labor twicet as well.

Remember, Mahsr,—min' dis, now,—de sinfulness ob sin
Is 'pendin' 'pon de sperrit what we goes an' does it in:
An' in a righchis frame ob min' we's gwine to dance an' sing,
A-feelin' like King David, when he cut de pigeon wing.

It seems to me—indeed it do—I mebbe mout be wrong—
That people raly ought to dance, when Chrismus comes along;
Des dance bekase dey's happy—like de birds hops in de trees,
De pine-top fiddle soundin' to de bowin' ob de breeze.

We has no ark to dance afore, like Isrul's prophet king;
We has no harp to soun' de chords, to holp us out to sing;
But 'cordin' to de gif's we has we does de bes' we knows;
An' folks don't 'spise de vi'let-flower bekase it ain't de rose.

You bless us, please, sah, eben ef we doin' wrong tonight;
Kase den we'll need de blessin' more'n ef we's doin' right;
An' let de blessin' stay wid us, untel we comes to die,
An' goes to keep our Chrismus wid dem sheriffs in de sky!

Yes, tell dem preshis anguls we're a-gwine to jine 'em soon:
Our voices we's a-trainin' fur to sing de glory tune;
We's ready when you wants us, an' it ain't no matter when—
O Mahsr! call yo' chillen soon, an' take 'em home! Amen.

The rev'rend man is scarcely through,
When all the noise begins anew,
And with such force assaults the ears,
That through the din one hardly hears

Old fiddling Josey "sound his A,"
Correct the pitch, begin to play,
Stop, satisfied, then, with the bow,
Rap out the signal dancers know:

> *Git yo' pardner, fust kwatillion!*
> Stomp yo' feet, an' raise 'em high;
> Tune is: "Oh! dat water-million!
> Gwine to git to home bime bye."
> *S'lute yo' pardners!*—scrape perlitely—
> Don't be bumpin' gin de res'—
> *Balance all!*—now, step out rightly;
> Alluz dance yo' lebbel bes'.
> *Fo'wa'd foah!*—whoop up, niggers!
> *Back ag'in!*—don't be so slow!—
> *Swing cornahs!*—min' de figgers!
> When I hollers, den yo' go.
> *Top ladies cross ober!*
> Hol' on, till I takes a dram—
> *Gemmen solo!*—yes, *I's* sober—
> Cain't say how de fiddle am.
> *Hands around!*—hol' up yo' faces,
> Don't be lookin' at yo' feet!
> *Swing yo' pardners to yo' places!*
> Dat's de way—dat's hard to beat.
> *Sides fo'w'd!*—when you's ready—
> Make a bow as low's you kin!
> *Swing acrost wid opp'site lady!*
> Now we'll let you swap ag'in:
> *Ladies change!*—shet up dat talkin';
> Do yo' talkin' arter while!
> *Right an' lef'!*—don' want no walkin'—
> Make yo' steps, an' show yo' style!

And so the "set" proceeds—its length
Determined by the dancers' strength;
And all agree to yield the palm
For grace and skill to "Georgy Sam,"
Who stamps so hard, and leaps so high,
"Des watch him!" is the wond'ring cry—
"De nigger mus' be, for a fac',
Own cousin to a jumpin'-jack!"
On, on the restless fiddle sounds,
Still chorused by the curs and hounds;
Dance after dance succeeding fast,

Till supper is announced at last.
That scene—but why attempt to show it?
The most inventive modern poet,
In fine new words whose hope and trust is,
Could form no phrase to do it justice!
When supper ends—that is not soon—
The fiddle strikes the same old tune;
The dancers pound the floor again,
With all they have of might and main;
Old gossips, almost turning pale,
Attend Aunt Cassy's gruesome tale
Of conjurors, and ghosts, and devils,
That in the smoke-house hold their revels;
Each drowsy baby droops his head,
Yet scorns the very thought of bed:—
So wears the night, and wears so fast,
All wonder when they find it past,
And hear the signal sound to go
From what few cocks are left to crow.
Then, one and all, you hear them shout!
"Hi! Booker! fotch de banjo out,
An' gib us one song 'fore we goes—
One ob de berry bes' you knows!"
Responding to the welcome call,
He takes the banjo from the wall,
And tunes the strings with skill and care,
Then strikes them with a master's air,
And tells, in melody and rhyme,
This legend of the olden time:

Go 'way, fiddle! folks is tired o' hearin' you a-squawkin'.
Keep silence fur yo' betters!—don't you heah de banjo talkin'?
About de possum's tail she's gwine to lecter—ladies, listen!—
About de ha'r whut isn't dar, an' why de ha'r is missin':

"Dar's gwine to be a oberflow," said Noah, lookin' solemn—
Fur Noah tuk the "Herald," an' he read de ribber column—
An' so he sot his hands to wuk a-cl'arin' timber-patches,
An' 'lowed he's gwine to build a boat to beat the steamah Natchez.

Ol' Noah kep' a-nailin' an' a-chippin' an' a-sawin',
An' all de wicked neighbors kep' a-laughin' an' a-pshawin';
But Noah didn't min' 'em, knowin' whut wuz gwine to happen:
An' forty days an' forty nights de rain it kep' a-drappin'.

Now, Noah had done cotched a lot ob evry sort o' beas'es—
Ob all de shows a-trabbelin', it beat 'em all to pieces!
He had a Morgan colt an' sebral head o' Jarsey cattle—
An' druv 'em 'board de Ark as soon's he heered de thunder rattle.

Den sech anoder fall ob rain!—it come so awful hebby,
De ribber riz immejitly, an' busted troo de lebbee;
De people all wuz drowned out—'cep' Noah an' de critters,
An' men he'd hired to work de boat—an' one to mix de bitters.

De Ark she kep' a-sailin' an' a-sailin' an' a-sailin';
De lion got his dander up, an' like to bruk de palin';
De sarpints hissed; de painters yelled; tell, whut wid all de fussin',
You c'u'dn't hardly heah de mate a'bossin' 'roun' an' cussin'.

Now, Ham, de only nigger whut wuz rinnin' on de packet,
Got lonesome in de barber-shop, an' c'u'dn't stan' de racket;
An' so, fur to amuse he'se'f, he steamed some wood an' bent it,
An' soon he had a banjo made—de fust dat wuz invented.

He wet de ledder, stretched it on; made bridge an' screws an' aprin;
An' fitted in a proper neck—'twuz berry long an' tap'rin';
He tuk some tin, an' twisted him a thimble fur to ring it;
An' den de mighty question riz: how wuz he gwine to string it?

De 'possum had as fine a tail as dis dat I's a-singin';
De ha'rs so long an' thick an' strong,—des fit fur banjo-stringin';
Dat nigger shaved 'em off as short as wash-day-dinner graces;
An' sorted ob 'em by de size, f'om little E's to basses.

He strung her, tuned her, struck a jig,—'twuz "Nebber min' de wedder,"—
She soun' like forty-lebben bands a-playin' all togedder;
Some went to pattin'; some to dancin': Noah called de figgers;
An' Ham he sot an' knocked de tune, de happiest ob niggers!

Now, sence dat time—it's mighty strange—dere's not de slightes' showin'
Ob any ha'r at all upon de 'possum's tail a-growin';
An' curi's, too, dat nigger's ways: his people nebber los' 'em—
Fur whar you finds de nigger—dar's de banjo an' de 'possum!

    The night is spent; and as the day
    Throws up the first faint flash of gray,
    The guests pursue their homeward way;
    And through the field beyond the gin,

Just as the stars are going in,
See Santa Claus departing—grieving—
His own dear Land of Cotton leaving.

His work is done; he fain would rest
Where people know and love him best.
He pauses, listens, looks about;
But go he must: his pass is out.
So, coughing down the rising tears,
He climbs the fence and disappears.
And thus observes a colored youth
(The common sentiment, in sooth):
"Oh, what a blessin' 'tw'u'd ha' been,
Ef Santy had been born a twin!
We'd hab two Chrismuses a yeah—
Or p'r'aps *one* brudder'd *settle* heah!"

(1878)

WILLIAM GILMORE SIMMS

The Lost Pleiad

I

Not in the sky,
Where it was seen
So long in eminence of light serene,—
Nor on the white tops of the glistering wave,
Nor down, in mansions of the hidden deep,
Though beautiful in green
And crystal, its great caves of mystery,—
Shall the bright watcher have
Her place, and, as of old, high station keep!

II

Gone! gone!
Oh! never more, to cheer
The mariner, who holds his course alone
On the Atlantic, through the weary night,
When the stars turn to watchers, and do sleep,
Shall it again appear,
With the sweet-loving certainty of light,
Down shining on the shut eyes of the deep!

III

The upward-looking shepherd on the hills
Of Chaldea, night-returning, with his flocks,
He wonders why his beauty doth not blaze,
Gladdening his gaze,—
And, from his dreary watch along the rocks,
Guiding him homeward o'er the perilous ways!
How stands he waiting still, in a sad maze,
Much wondering, while the drowsy silence fills
The sorrowful vault!—how lingers, in the hope that night
May yet renew the expected and sweet light,
So natural to his sight!

IV

And lone,
Where, at the first, in smiling love she shone,
Brood the once happy circle of bright stars:
How should they dream, until her fate was known,
That they were ever confiscate to death?
That dark oblivion the pure beauty mars,
And, like the earth, its common bloom and breath,
That they should fall from high;
Their lights grow blasted by a touch, and die,—
All their concerted springs of harmony
Snapt rudely, and the generous music gone!

V

Ah! still the strain
Of wailing sweetness fills the saddening sky;
The sister stars, lamenting in their pain
That one of the selectest ones must die,—
Must vanish, when most lovely, from the rest!
Alas! 'tis ever thus the destiny.
Even Rapture's song hath evermore a tone
Of wailing, as for bliss too quickly gone.
The hope most precious is the soonest lost,
The flower most sweet is first to feel the frost.
Are not all short-lived things the loveliest?
And, like the pale star, shooting down the sky,
Look they not ever brightest, as they fly
From the lone sphere they blest!

(1828;1853)

The Edge of the Swamp

'Tis a wild spot, and even in summer hours,
With wondrous wealth of beauty and a charm
For the sad fancy, hath the gloomiest look,
That awes with strange repulsion. There, the bird
Sings never merrily in the sombre trees,
That seem to have never known a term of youth,
Their young leaves all being blighted. A rank growth

Spreads vemomously round, with power to taint;
And blistering dews await the thoughtless hand
That rudely parts the thicket. Cypresses,
Each a great ghastly giant, eld and gray,
Stride o'er the dusk, dank tract,—with buttresses
Spread round, apart, not seeming to sustain,
Yet link'd by secret twines, that underneath,
Blend with each arching trunk. Fantastic vines,
That swing like monstrous serpents in the sun,
Bind top to top, until the encircling trees
Group all in close embrace. Vast skeletons
Of forests, that have perish'd ages gone,
Moulder, in mighty masses, on the plain;
Now buried in some dark and mystic tarn,
Or sprawl'd above it, resting on great arms,
And making, for the opossum and the fox,
Bridges, that help them as they roam by night.
Alternate stream and lake, between the banks,
Glimmer in doubtful light: smooth, silent, dark,
They tell not what they harbor; but, beware!
Lest, rising to the tree on which you stand,
You sudden see the moccasin snake heave up
His yellow shining belly and flat head
Of burnish'd copper. Stretch'd at length, behold
Where yonder Cayman, in his natural home,
The mammoth lizard, all his armor on,
Slumbers half-buried in the sedgy grass,
Beside the green ooze where he shelters him,
The place, so like the gloomiest realm of death,
Is yet the abode of thousand forms of life,—
The terrible, the beautiful, the strange,—
Wingéd and creeping creatures, such as make
The instinctive flesh with apprehension crawl,
When sudden we behold. Hark! at our voice
The whooping crane, gaunt fisher in these realms,
Erects his skeleton form and shrieks in flight,
On great white wings. A pair of summer ducks,
Most princely in their plumage, as they hear
His cry, with senses quickening all to fear,
Dash up from the lagoon with marvellous haste,
Following his guidance. See! aroused by these,
And startled by our progress o'er the stream,
The steel-jaw'd Cayman, from his grassy slope,
Slides silent to the slimy green abode,
Which is his province. You behold him now,

His bristling back uprising as he speeds
To safety, in the centre of the lake,
Whence his head peers alone,—a shapeless knot,
That shows no sign of life; the hooded eye,
Nathless, being ever vigilant and sharp,
Measuring the victim. See! a butterfly,
That, travelling all the day, has counted climes
Only by flowers, to rest himself a while,
And, as a wanderer in a foreign land,
To pause and look around him ere he goes,
Lights on the monster's brow. The surly mute
Straightway goes down; so suddenly, that he,
The dandy of the summer flowers and woods,
Dips his light wings, and soils his golden coat,
With the rank waters of the turbid lake.
Wondering and vex'd, the pluméd citizen
Flies with an eager terror to the banks,
Seeking more genial natures,—but in vain.
Here are no gardens such as he desires,
No innocent flowers of beauty, no delights
Of sweetness free from taint. The genial growth
He loves, finds here no harbor. Fetid shrubs,
That scent the gloomy atmosphere, offend
His pure patrician fancies. On the trees,
That look like felon spectres, he beholds
No blossoming beauties; and for smiling heavens,
That flutter his wings with breezes of pure balm,
He nothing sees but sadness—aspects dread,
That gather frowning, cloud and fiend in one,
As if in combat, fiercely to defend
Their empire from the intrusive wing and beam.
The example of the butterfly be ours.
He spreads his lacquer'd wings above the trees,
And speeds with free flight, warning us to seek
For a more genial home, and couch more sweet
Than these drear borders offer us tonight.

(1840;1853)

HENRY TIMROD

The Unknown Dead

The rain is plashing on my sill,
But all the winds of Heaven are still;
And so it falls with that dull sound
Which thrills us in the church-yard ground,
When the first spadeful drops like lead
Upon the coffin of the dead.
Beyond my streaming window-pane,
I cannot see the neighboring vane,
Yet from its old familiar tower
The bell comes, muffled, through the shower.
What strange and unsuspected link
Of feeling touched, has made me think—
While with a vacant soul and eye
I watch that gray and stony sky—
Of nameless graves on battle-plains
Washed by a single winter's rains,
Where, some beneath Virginian hills,
And some by green Atlantic rills,
Some by the waters of the West,
A myriad unknown heroes rest.
Ah! not the chiefs, who, dying, see
Their flags in front of victory,
Or, at their life-blood's noble cost
Pay for a battle nobly lost,
Claim from their monumental beds
The bitterest tears a nation sheds.
Beneath yon lonely mound—the spot
By all save some fond few forgot—
Lie the true martyrs of the fight
Which strikes for freedom and for right.
Of them, their patriot zeal and pride,
The lofty faith that with them died,
No grateful page shall farther tell
Than that so many bravely fell;
And we can only dimly guess

What worlds of all this world's distress,
What utter woe, despair, and dearth,
Their fate has brought to many a hearth.
Just such a sky as this should weep
Above them, always, where they sleep;
Yet, haply, at this very hour,
Their graves are like a lover's bower;
And Nature's self, with eyes unwet,
Oblivious of the crimson debt
To which she owes her April grace,
Laughs gayly o'er their burial-place.

(1863)

Ethnogenesis

I

Hath not the morning dawned with added light?
And shall not evening call another star
Out of the infinite regions of the night,
To mark this day in Heaven? At last, we are
A nation among nations; and the world
Shall soon behold in many a distant port
                    Another flag unfurled!
Now, come what may, whose favor need we court?
And, under God, whose thunder need we fear?
                    Thank Him who placed us here
Beneath so kind a sky—the very sun
Takes part with us; and on our errands run
All breezes of the ocean; dew and rain
Do noiseless battle for us; and the Year,
And all the gentle daughters in her train,
March in our ranks, and in our service wield
                    Long spears of golden grain!
A yellow blossom as her fairy shield,
June flings her azure banner to the wind,
        While in the order of their birth
Her sisters pass, and many an ample field
Grows white beneath their steps, till now, behold,
                    Its endless sheets unfold
THE SNOW OF SOUTHERN SUMMERS! Let the earth

Rejoice! beneath those fleeces soft and warm
<blockquote>Our happy land shall sleep
In a repose as deep</blockquote>
As if we lay intrenched behind
Whole leagues of Russian ice and Arctic storm!

II

And what if, mad with wrongs themselves have wrought,
<blockquote>In their own treachery caught,
By their own fears made bold,
And leagued with him of old,</blockquote>
Who long since in the limits of the North
Set up his evil throne, and warred with God—
What if, both mad and blinded in their rage,
Our foes should fling us down their mortal gage,
And with a hostile step profane our sod!
We shall not shrink, my brothers, but go forth
To meet them, marshalled by the Lord of Hosts,
And overshadowed by the mighty ghosts
Of Moultrie and of Eutaw—who shall foil
Auxiliars such as these? Nor these alone,
<blockquote>But every stock and stone
Shall help us; but the very soil,</blockquote>
And all the generous wealth it gives to toil,
And all for which we love our noble land,
Shall fight beside, and through us; sea and strand,
<blockquote>The heart of woman, and her hand,</blockquote>
Tree, fruit, and flower, and every influence,
<blockquote>Gentle, or grave, or grand;
The winds in our defence</blockquote>
Shall seem to blow; to us the hills shall lend
<blockquote>Their firmness and their calm;</blockquote>
And in our stiffened sinews we shall blend
<blockquote>The strength of pine and palm!</blockquote>

III

Nor would we shun the battle-ground,
<blockquote>Though weak as we are strong;</blockquote>
Call up the clashing elements around,
<blockquote>And test the right and wrong!</blockquote>
On one side, creeds that dare to teach
What Christ and Paul refrained to preach;
Codes built upon a broken pledge,

And Charity that whets a poniard's edge;
Fair schemes that leave the neighboring poor
To starve and shiver at the schemer's door,
While in the world's most liberal ranks enrolled,
He turns some vast philanthropy to gold;
Religion, taking every mortal form
But that a pure and Christian faith makes warm,
Where not to vile fanatic passion urged,
Or not in vague philosophies submerged,
Repulsive with all Pharisaic leaven,
And making laws to stay the laws of Heaven!
And on the other, scorn of sordid gain,
Unblemished honor, truth without a stain,
Faith, justice, reverence, charitable wealth,
And, for the poor and humble, laws which give,
Not the mean right to buy the right to live,
        But life, and home, and health!
To doubt the end were want of trust in God,
        Who, if he has decreed
     That we must pass a redder sea
Than that which rang to Miriam's holy glee,
        Will surely raise at need
        A Moses with his rod!

IV

But let our fears—if fears we have—be still,
And turn us to the future! Could we climb
Some mighty Alp, and view the coming time,
The rapturous sight would fill
        Our eyes with happy tears!
Not only for the glories which the years
Shall bring us; not for lands from sea to sea,
And wealth, and power, and peace, though these shall be;
But for the distant peoples we shall bless,
And the hushed murmurs of a world's distress:
For, to give labor to the poor,
        The whole sad planet o'er,
And save from want and crime the humblest door,
Is one among the many ends for which
        God makes us great and rich!
The hour perchance is not yet wholly ripe
When all shall own it, but the type
Whereby we shall be known in every land
Is that vast gulf which lips our Southern strand,
And through the cold, untempered ocean pours

Its genial streams, that far off Arctic shores
May sometimes catch upon the softened breeze
Strange tropic warmth and hints of summer seas.

(1861)

Ode

*Sung on the Occasion of Decorating the Graves of the Confederate Dead,
at Magnolia Cemetery, Charleston, S.C.*

I
Sleep sweetly in your humble graves,
 Sleep, martyrs of a fallen cause;
Though yet no marble column craves
 The pilgrim here to pause.

II
In seeds of laurel in the earth
 The blossom of your fame is blown,
And somewhere, waiting for its birth,
 The shaft is in the stone!

III
Meanwhile, behalf the tardy years
 Which keep in trust your storied tombs,
Behold! your sisters bring their tears,
 And these memorial blooms.

IV
Small tributes! but your shades will smile
 More proudly on these wreaths today,
Than when some cannon-moulded pile
 Shall overlook this bay.

V
Stoop, angels, hither from the skies!
 There is no holier spot of ground
Than where defeated valor lies,
 By mourning beauty crowned!

(1866)

ALBERY A. WHITMAN

The Runaway,

Awake, my muse, ye goodly sights among,
The land of Boone and Kenton claims my song.
Thro' other scenes our lovers take their flight,
See where their wand'ring footsteps pass in sight.
Lo! where yon pleasant valleys meet the eyes,
And goodly hills their forests lifting rise!
Here, as we pass, along our cheerful way,
Small farms adjoining, stretch in green array.
And small farm houses, looking great trees thro',
And neat dressed orchards, dot th' enlivened view;
And their quaint roofs by Autumn suns embrowned,
With wind-mills rude, and bird-box turrets crowned,
Look thro' the branchy elms and locusts high,
And send a rustic welcome to the eye.
See where yon flocks their even pastures browse,
And lowing homeward, hear the sober cows,
And hear yon plowman whistling as he plows.
Here circling plenty meets returning suns,
And lucid cheer in ev'ry valley runs,
Loud satisfaction fills the evening air,
And jovial comfort soothes the ear of care.

Thrice hail! proud land, whose genius boasts a Clay!
The Cicero of slavery's palmy day,
The gifted champion of Compromise,
Whose mien majestic filled a nation's eyes;
And on the eloquence of whose wise tongue
A learned Senate in rapt silence hung;
A Senate, too, whose fame no one impugns,
Of Websters, Randolphs, Marshals and Calhouns.
And could a land that boasts a mind like this—
That bord'ring on the clime of freedom is—
Suffer a harlot with her whorings vile
To peacefully pollute her gen'rous soil?
Yes, green Kentucky with her native pride,

Proclaiming trust in the great Crucified,
Flaunting her prestige in the world's wide face,
Boasting descent and precedence of race,
And by the greatest of all statesmen led,
Shared the pollutions of a slavish bed.
All o'er her fields, the blood-hound's savage bay
Pressed the poor sable trembling runaway,
And sometimes by the home of Henry Clay!
In all her woods, the wail of wild distress
Was heard, as tattered starving wretchedness
Fled in the shrieking wrath of wintry storm;
Wrapping her babe in rags to keep it warm!
Can I forget the tears a parent shed
When her dear hand she placed upon my head,
And me embracing, tremulously said:
"My heart is sick whene'er the sad winds blow,
And all the ground is buried deep in snow,
For I remember, when I was a child,
The night was dark, the raving winds were wild,
The earth was still, the snow lay deep and white,
When at our door there came a footstep light.
We opened, and a strange black woman's face
Looked in; she held a child in her embrace
And said: 'Ize nearly froz to deaf', oh wont
You let me in? Oh! don't say *no!* Oh don't!'
She came in, but before we said a word,
Her master's voice was in the quarters heard!
She knew the sound, her babe close to her drew,
And back into the wintry tempest flew.
The morning came, and chilly miles away,
In snow half hid the lifeless mother lay!
But in her arms the babe alive did sleep,
And when discovered, woke, but did not weep!
And lo! uncovered to the mournful light,
The mother's face was black—the babe's was white!"

I love Kentucky; tho' she merit scorn
I can't despise the land where I was born.
Her name I cherish, and expect to see
The day when all her sons will cherish me.
Her many sins have all in common been
With other sisters' who their sins have seen.
Yes, I will pray for that good time to come
When I can say: Kentucky is my *home*.
And this I now ask at my country's hand,

If I must die in some far distant land,
Then let my countrymen, when I am dead,
Where I was born, make my eternal bed.

But here our lovers are again;
Awake, my muse, thy wonted strain!
The hounds at day-break struck a trail
In deep Green River's lonely vale,
And thro' the dusk of dewy morn,
Echoed the hunter's rousing horn.
"What is it?" flew from tongue to tongue,
As to his horse each rider sprung.
A moment in their saddles still,
They heard the baying on the hill
Not far away, and full well knew
A runaway before them flew.
The chase began, the horses dashed
Away, and thro' the bushes crashed,
Like birds that flutter on the wing
All thro' the wild copse scattering.
Each horseman pressing for the lead
Bore on and on, with champing speed.
On, on and on, and on, o'er hills,
And winding valleys, leaping rills
And fallen trunks like startled hinds,
Wild as a flood, as swift as winds.
The hounds' loud clamor rolled and broke
Morn's drowsy stillness, and awoke
The sleepy hills, that answered back
The lusty tonguing of the pack.
Within his quiet farmhouse wood,
The early rustic list'ning stood,
The plowman whistling in his lane,
Paused, listened, paused and paused again,
Surmised, went on, went on, surmised,
And at their loud speed stood surprised;
As o'er his fences passing near,
He heard them in their mad career.

Their loud tongues on the morning breeze
Now Rodney heard, as if the trees
Were yearning in their sympathy,
And stretched, and sighed and whispered "fly."

And fly he did, and as away he sped,
Soon of the pack a length'ning space ahead;

His nimble limbs grown strong by punishment,
Bore manly up as on and on he went.
O'er fences high, and gullies wide he leapt,
Skimmed level fields and thro' the briars crept,
Now pricked by these, now by the wanton thorn,
And now by knotty bamboos hung and torn.
His footsteps now had gained a wooded hight,
Now fields and houses all were out of sight;
He paused to listen, heard his heart's quick beat,
And thought it was the sound of coming feet.
Another instant and the flying slave,
Was trying if his legs could well behave.
Thro' pond'rous woods and darkling shades he ran,
Three miles or more from where his flight began,
Sometimes along the wild boar's narrow way,
Sometimes where hunted wolves in cover lay.
He soon could hear the fierce hound on his rear,
Baying out inbred hate, and drawing near.
Loud in the distance angry signals wound,
And furious yells urged on the flying hound.
Dread oaths were muttering on the morn's still air,
Enough to hush the jungle's roaring lair.

Now Rodney, bursting from the wood,
An instant on the high bluffs stood
And gazed upon Green River's flood,
That tossed and growled and rolled beneath,
Like torments in the vaults of death.
The rocks look'd down with angry awe,
And feeble shrubs leant back and saw.
Few moments more the worst must bring,
For now the worst had poised its wing!
The hounds are on him! "Save! oh save!"
Right downward leaping cries the slave,
But not into a watery grave!
With arms of steel he mounts the wave,
He grapples with the dizzy tide,
Turns downward, where the cliffs doth hide,
And then with strokes manful to see,
He pulls for life and liberty.
Meanwhile the hounds have ceased to bay,
The hunters look and turn away,
And "Ah! *he's* drowned!" all seem to say.

Three nights or more curtain the skies,
And now we turn our weary eyes

To where the Creole mother flies.
Thro' dangers led by friends at night,
By day concealed from mortal sight,
Thus far, secure has been her flight.

A storm was low'ring, and the sun was low,
The Creole's weary steps were short and slow,
The air grew sightless, and the fields were still,
The woods were restless on the solemn hill,
The earth seems shrinking from the threat'ning skies,
As night on rayless wings athwart the sun's path flies.
All nature trembles! Lo! the cloud-folds break,
The mountains with their thunder-tongues awake,
While livid lightnings glare on every peak,
And with their arms of flame, their warring lances take.
The startled clouds flee out into the deep
Of troubled night; and headlong down each steep
Rush dizzy torrents from the flood-drenched hills,
And foam along the overflowing rills.
But hark! in all this storm a woman's wail!
A mother's anguish doth the ear assail!
Beneath yon beetling rocks, oh raise thine eyes,
To where Leeona lifts her tender cries!
See now she sinks into the cliff's embrace,
And turns to heaven her entreating face
In tearful beauty! Hark! for help she cries!
And thunders answer from the wrathful skies!
Between the surges of tumultous winds,
Her cry a passage thro' the tempest finds.
"Oh God! my child! my child!" she wails distrest,
And clasps the tender sorrow to her breast.
But like the vaulty whispers of the tomb,
Her words come back from hollow-throated night's deep gloom.
Oh! Heaven, can'st thou thus be pitiless,
And hear, unmoved, the cry of loveliness?
Cause thy rebellious winds to war no more,
The loud disturbers of a nightly shore!
Ah! how the torrents now are pouring down,
They seem as if the whole earth they would drown,
But this last flood descending, hope creates,
For when it slackens, then the storm abates.

The rain has ceased; but the belabored wood
Yet waves and trembles in a troubled mood.
The frantic Creole lifts a piercing cry,

Hoping to rouse some woodsman dwelling nigh;
But in the bluffs above her wolves reply.
"Oh! Heaven," shrinking in the rock she gasps,
And in her arms her infant tighter clasps,
"The wolves are howling, Ah! What shall I do?
Beset by beasts and human monsters too!"
Then like some doe when dogs and horns surround,
That starts, stops, listens, starts with sudden bound,
Flies from her covert, leaps rock, fence and hedge,
And leaves the baying dangers of the sedge.
Right so Leeona stops, and starts, and leaps,
And bounding onward leaves the howling steeps.
The flashing heavens make her footing good
In darksome paths, through the abodeless wood,
As on she flies, a spirit of the night,
But knows not where her heaven assisted flight.

Day came—an ugly, wet and sluggish day—
When in the woods, far on Leeona's way,
A band of sun-browned cleavers she beheld,
That near their lonely homes their forests felled.
Their great rough arms, as rough as oak limbs are,
Dropt on their knees, and to their elbows bare;
Held up their chins, as from their logs they gazed
Upon the fleeing woman, sore amazed.
And when she came to them with tales of woe,
They pressed around her eagerly to know
From whence she was, and whither she would go.
And then they grouped and muttered to themselves,
Smote on their breasts, and seized their pond'rous helves,
And breathing out a gale of oaths and threats,
They led her to their humble forest seats.

Of how the Creole, by these woodsmens' aid,
Her further flight toward Ohio made;
Of how she wandered two long months, beset
By shrewd suspicions, and by mistrust met,
By day concealed, by night hurried along,
Cannot be uttered on the tongue of song,
But raise your eyes to where the verging land
Of Bondage touches Freedom's holier strand.

Low in the cheerless West, deceitful rays
Kindle their fires to a feeble blaze.
The leafless woods send up a ceaseless howl,

As looking down upon them with a scowl,
From voiceless hills, the wintry blasts doth stand,
And shake their shrieking tops from hand to hand.
The hoarse Ohio chafes his bleak shores gray,
And sullen, rolls to warmer climes away.

But list! is that the moaning of a gale
Disconsolate, within yon leafless vale?
Draw nearer, listen, now it rises high,
Now lower sinks, recedes, and now comes nigh.
Is it the blast of all its mildness shorn?
Ah! no, 'tis poor Leeona that dost mourn!
See where on yonder rising rock she stands,
And holds her tattered garments in her hands;
Scarce able to rescue them from the wind,
That flings them, with her streaming locks behind;
Unwraps her perfect limbs, that white and bare,
Empurple in the bitter Northern air.
From her bare feet blood trickles down the stone!
Ah, God! Why is she here? Why thus alone?
Oh, what hath driven her from home away,
And Comfort's hearth, upon this ruthless day?

Ah! see her driven from warm Care's embrace
A lone sweet exile of the Creole race!
By heaven forsaken, and denied by earth,
As if too crime-stained to deserve a birth.
By native streams no more in peace to rove,
And hear the sylvan music of the grove.
No more to pluck the fruits of gen'rous growth,
And gather flowers of the fragrant South,
How can she meet the fierce wrath of the North,
Houseless and clotheless, thus to wander forth?
Ah! Ask you? Turn to where yon hounds pursue,
And circle swift the clam'ring forests thro'.
Hark! how loud horns resound upon her rear,
Oh! heaven save her! Is no helper near?
Must she beneath the angry tide be borne,
Or by the savage hounds be seized and torn?

Beyond the river is a fisher's hut,
Close in a cove beneath tall forests shut;
Beyond the hut a narrow path climbs o'er
The crescent bluffs, and winds along the shore.
Within this hut Ben Guildern sate all day,

Mending his nets and lines, and smoked away.
He dreamed of this wide world and all its cares,
Its hopes and doubts, its pleasures, pains and snares,
Of man's pilgrimage to a better bourne,
Where toil shall rest, and man shall cease to mourn;
And of the days and other faces gone,
Ere he was left to pass thro' life alone;
Of pleasant tasks his manly arms had wrought,
Of slumbers sweet that toil remitting brought;
And of the many times he climbed that hill,
And found a wife and children waiting still;
And supper smoking, and a ready plate,
When all day's luckless toil had made him late.
"All gone!" within his wave-tossed soul he sighs,
And o'er the waters lifts his tear-dimmed eyes,
"A cold and blustry night the boat went down,
And my poor wife and babes were left to drown!"

He sees a signal from the other shore—
A woman beckons him to set her o'er;
He hears the hounds, and not a word is said,
A fugitive he sees imploring aid;
His boat is launched, and from her moorings thrown,
The tide awaits her, rolling up and down,
A moment near the shore she slow doth move,
And waits another and another shove;
This way and that the eddy smooth she tries,
Ventures and darts, and with the current flies.
So when the speedy roe is brought to bay,
Where rising cliffs oppose her woody way,
Within some nook embraced by rocks and logs,
She turns her head upon the bristling dogs,
Bends here and there until her way is clear,
Flies through her foes and leaves them on the rear.

Seized by the heaving tide, the feath'ry boat,
Midway the river down begins to float,
But Guildern with his strong arms grasps the oars,
Plies all his strength, and up the current soars.
The angry billows clamor at his keel,
And on his prow in sudden fury wheel,
Till, at an angle of a good degree
Above the hound-pressed Creole pausing, he
Wheels short his flight, athwart the current shaves,
And shoreward glides before the rolling waves.

So when the untiring mistress of the winds
Discovers in the covert feeding hinds,
Midway she meets the current of the skies,
And by its adverse strength succeeds to rise,
Till high above the destined point she swings,
Drops from the clouds and shaves on level wings.

The shore is touched, the Creole boards the boat
With child in arms, and all are now afloat.
Old Guildern speaks not, but plies all his skill,
And looks the firm monition, "now be still,"
Leeona's heart with hope and awe is swelled,
She meets an eye that danger never quelled,
A face as rough as wintry hills, but bland,
An arm of massive strength, but gentle hand,
And mien of dreadful soberness, that braves
The sullen fury of the wind and waves.
The boat is now far out into the stream,
And as her quick oars in the low sun gleam,
Rides up and down the wave, and oe'r and oe'r,
And level swims towards the other shore.
Ah! nobly bearing up her precious freight,
How steadily she rocks beneath the weight!
Her keel has touched, it cleaves the yellow sand,
Thank God! thank God! they land, they land! they land!

Within a fisher's hut all night,
And leaving by the early light
Of bleak December's lurid morn,
Leeona passes into sight,
Cast down and faint, and travel-worn.

From naked hills loud shrieking flew the blast,
And out of hearing moaned along the waste,
Like some torn beggar all disconsolate,
That mutters from harsh Opulence's gate;
As 'Ona trudged along her lonely way,
Beneath a nightly vault of starless gray.

Her murmuring infant shivered in the blast,
As houses by her way she hurried past,
Where rustic comfort sat with smiling pride,
At honest labor's genial fireside.
Thus thro' the hoary landscape's wintry scorn,
She forced her mind's consent to journey on till morn.

The clouds dispersed as night wore slowly on,
And stars from their high glist'ring fields looked down,
Till late the moon-top'd hills in white arose,
And peerless night unveiled her shivering realms of snows.

Ah! bent and trembling, see that gentle form,
Where shelt'ring rocks oppose the wrathful storm,
Chased like some beast, that hovers with her young
In yawning caves, and desert rocks among.
Her tender infant in her arms is prest,
Hushed are its cries—it gently seems to rest.
Where vagrant swine their wintry beds have made
Of leaves and branches from the forest shade,
Now 'Ona stoops to rest her darling's head,
When lo! she starts, she shrieks—her child is dead!
Her wounded bosom feels a nameless dart,
A ghastly sorrow clutches at her heart—
Nor fear assails, tho' now to leave she tries,
But trying stays, her babe embraces, cries,
The cold cliffs groan, and hollow night replies.
The dismal gorges murmur at the sound,
And empty fields spread echoless around.

Beside her babe the weeping mother kneels,
With anguish dumb its pulseless hands she feels;
Its placid cheek against her face is prest,
Her ear is leant upon its silent breast;
Her hopes are gone! and Heaven's pure ear hears
Deep grief entreating thro' a flood of tears.
Above the cliffs where winds a country way,
A voice is heard in cautious tones to say:
"Leeona! Oh Leeona! Oh my dear!
Is it my 'Ona's mournful voice I hear?"
The Creole hushed, afraid to trust her soul,
That felt a mighty burden sudden roll;
Quick claspt her bosom in aching suspense,
But now distincter heard the voice commence:
"Leeona! Oh, my 'Ona! are you near?"
The Creole answers, "Rodney, I am here!"
Rodney had heard along Leeona's way,
Of her wild flight, and her pursued all day.
Now down the cliffs in breathless haste he flies,
And clasps his life, as thus to him she cries:
"Oh! see, my Rodney; see where baby lies!"

The bosom that had life-long sorrow borne,
The heart which had so long been taught to mourn,
With *real* manly sympathetic heaves,
Bent o'er the little corpse and raised it from the leaves.
"Poor harmless comer!" then he gently said,
"Better for thee that thy pure soul has fled
With angel watches to the waiting skies,
Where peace e'er flows, and happier climes arise.
Conceived in trouble and in sorrow born,
Thy life rose clouded in its very morn,
And wore along with unpropitious suns;
But to a happy close at last it runs!
Sweet be thy rest upon this lonely shore,
Rocked in the cradle of the winds no more,
And ne'er awakened by the tempest's roar."
This said, to roll the stone away he stoops,
And in its bed a hasty resting scoops,
Commits his tender burden to the ground,
In poor Leeona's last torn apron wound.
She from a mother's anguish pours out cries,
Bends o'er her infant where entombed it lies,
Its calm cheek moistens from her tender eyes,
Its pale lips kisses o'er and o'er and o'er,
And deeper sobs with each long last *once more*,
Till Rodney's kindly touch she feels implore;
Then murmurs "good-bye, good-bye, mamma's May!"
And with a loud wail tears her wounded heart away.

    Here sadness ends,
    A new sun lends
    His beams to light our way,
    And pleasant sights,
    And fair delights
    Unite to raise our lay.
    Where Freedom is what Freedom means,
    Our lovers pass to other scenes.

        (*from* "Not a Man and Yet a Man," 1877)

SONGS

The Ballad of Davy Crockett

Now, don't you want to know something concernin'
Where it was I come from and where I got my learnin'?
Oh, the world is made of mud out o' the Mississippi River!
The sun's a ball of foxfire, as well you may disciver.

Chorus:
> Take the ladies out at night. They shine so bright
> They make the world light when the moon is out of sight.

And so one day as I was goin' a-spoonin'
I met Colonel Davy, and he was goin' a-coonin'.
Says I, "Where's your gun?" "I ain' got none."
"How you goin' kill a coon when you haven't got a gun?"

Says he, "Pompcalf, just follow after Davy,
And he'll soon show you how to grin a coon crazy."
I followed on a piece and thar sot a squirrel,
A-settin' on a log and a-eatin' sheep sorrel.

When Davy did that see, he looked around at me,
Saying, "All I want now is a brace agin your knee."
And thar I braced a great big sinner.
He grinned six times hard enough to get his dinner!

The critter on the log didn't seem to mind him—
Jest kep' a-settin' thar and wouldn't look behind him
Then it was he said, "The critter must be dead.
See the bark a-flyin' all around the critter's head?"

I walked right up the truth to disciver.
Drot! It was a pine knot so hard it made me shiver.
Says he, "Pompcalf, don't you begin to laugh—
I'll pin back your ears, and bite you half in half!"

I flung down my gun and all my ammunition.
Says I, "Davy Crockett, I can cool your ambition!"
He throwed back his head and he blowed like a steamer.
Says he, "Pompcalf, I'm a Tennessee screamer!"

Then we locked horns and we wallered in the thorns.
I never had such a fight since the hour I was born.

We fought a day and a night and then agreed to drop it.
I was purty badly whipped—and so was Davy Crockett.

I looked all around and found my head a-missin'—
He'd bit off my head and I had swallered his'n!
Then we did agree to let each other be;
I was too much for him, and he was too much for me.

Bright Sunny South

In the bright sunny South in peace and content,
The days of my boyhood I scarcely have spent,
From the deep flowing springs to the broad flowing stream
Ever dear to my memory, and sweet is my dream.

I leave my confinement and comfort of life,
For the dangers of bloodshed, privation, and strife;
I come to conclude and reply with my word,
As I shoulder my musket and billet my sword.

My father looked sad as he begged me to part,
And my mother embraced me with anguish of heart;
And my beautiful sister looked pale in her woe
As she grabbed me and blessed me and told me to go.

Dear father, dear father, for me do not weep,
For on some high mountain I mean for to sleep,
And the danger of war I intend for to share
And for sickness and death I intend to prepare.

Dear mother, dear mother, for me do not weep,
For a mother's kind voice I ever will keep,
You have taught me to be brave from a boy to a man,
And I'm going in defense of our own native land.

Dear sister, dear sister, I cannot tell the woe,
Your tears and your sorrow they trouble me so;
I must be agoing for here I can not stand,
I'm going in defense of our own native land.

De Blue-Tail Fly

When Ah was young Ah use' to wait
On Massa an' hand him de plate,
An' pass de bottle when he git dry,
An' bresh away de blue-tail fly.

Chorus:

> Jimmy crack corn an' Ah don' care,
> Jimmy crack corn an' Ah don' care,
> Jimmy crack corn an' Ah don' care,
> Ol' Massa's gone away.

Den atter dinner Massa sleep.
He bid dis nigger vigil keep,
An' when he gwine to shut his eye
He tell me watch de blue-tail fly.

One day he ride aroun' de farm;
De flies so numerous dey did swarm.
One chance' to bite 'im on de thigh.
De Debble take dat blue-tail fly!

Dat pony run, he jump, he pitch,
He tumble Massa in de ditch.
He died, an' de jury wonder why;
De verdic' was de blue-tail fly.

Dey laid 'im under a 'simmon tree;
His epitaph am dar to see:
"Beneath dis stone Ah'm fo'ced to lie,
All by de means ob de blue-tail fly."

Ol' Massa gone, now let 'im rest;
Dey say all t'ings am for de best.
Ah nebber forget till de day I die,
Ol' Massa an' dat blue-tail fly.

Dixie

I wish I was in de land ob cotton,
Old times dar am not forgotten;
    Look away! Look away! Look away! Dixie Land!
In Dixie Land whar I was born in,
Early on one frosty mornin'
    Look away! Look away! Look away! Dixie Land!

Chorus:
    Den I wish I was in Dixie! Hooray! Hooray!
    In Dixie's Land we'll take our stand, to lib an' die in Dixie.
    Away! away! away down South in Dixie.
    Away! away! away down South in Dixie.

Ole missus marry "Will-de-weaber";
Willum was a gay deceaber;
    Look away, look away, look away, Dixie Land!
But when he put his arm around her,
He smiled as fierce as a forty-pounder;
    Look away, look away, look away, Dixie Land!

His face was sharp as a butcher's cleaber;
But dat did not seem to greab her;
    Look away, look away, look away, Dixie Land!
Ole missus acted de foolish part,
And died for a man dat broke her heart;
    Look away, look away, look away, Dixie Land!

Now here's a health to de next ole missus,
An' all the gals dat want to kiss us;
    Look away, look away, look away, Dixie Land!
But if you want to drive away sorrow,
Come hear dis song tomorrow;
    Look away, look away, look away, Dixie Land!

Dar's buckwheat cakes and Injin batter,
Makes you fat or a little fatter;
    Look away, look away, look away, Dixie Land!
Den hoe it down an' scratch your grabble,
To Dixie's land I'm bound to trabble;
    Look away, look away, look away, Dixie Land!

(Daniel Decatur Emmett)

I'm a Good Old Rebel

O I'm a good old rebel,
        Now that's just what I am,
For this "Fair Land of Freedom"
        I do not care a damn;
I'm glad I fit against it—
        I only wish we'd won;
And I don't want no pardon
        For any thing I done.

I hates the Constitution
        This Great Republic, too,
I hates the Freedmen's Buro,
        In uniforms of blue;
I hates the nasty eagle,
        With all his braggs and fuss,
The lyin', thievin' Yankees,
        I hates 'em wuss and wuss .

I hates the Yankee nation
        And everything they do,
I hates the Declaration
        Of Independence, too;
I hates the glorious Union—
        'Tis dripping with our blood—
I hates the striped banner,
        I fit it all I could.

I followed old Mas' Robert
        For four year, near about,
Got wounded in three places
        And starved at Pint Lookout;
I cotch the roomatism
        A campin' in the snow,
But I killed a chance o' Yankees,
        I'd like to kill some mo'.

Three hundred thousand Yankees
        Is stiff in Southern dust;
We got three hundred thousand
        Before they conquered us;
They died of Southern fever
        And Southern steel and shot,

I wish they was three million
  Instead of what we got.
I can't take up my musket
  And fight 'em now no more,
But I aint a going to love 'em,
  Now that is sarten sure;
And I don't want no pardon
  For what I was and am,
I won't be reconstructed
  And I don't care a damn.

      (James Innes Randolph)

John Henry

John Henry was a li'l baby, un-huh,
Sittin' on his mama's knee, oh, yeah.
Said: "De Big Bend Tunnel on de C. & O. road
Gonna cause de death of me,
Lawd, Lawd, gonna' cause de death of me."

John Henry, he had a woman,
Her name was Mary Magdalene,
She would go to de tunnel and sing for John,
Jes' to hear John Henry's hammer ring,
Lawd, Lawd, jes' to hear John Henry's hammer ring.

John Henry had a li'l woman,
Her name was Lucy Ann,
John Henry took sick an' had to go to bed,
Lucy Ann drove steel like a man,
Lawd, Lawd, Lucy Ann drove steel like a man.

Cap'n says to John Henry,
"Gonna bring me a steam drill 'round,
Gonna take dat steam drill out on de job,
Gonna whop dat steel on down,
Lawd, Lawd, gonna whop dat steel on down."

John Henry tol' his cap'n,
Lightnin' was in his eye:

"Cap'n, bet yo' las' red cent on me,
Fo' I'll beat it to de bottom or I'll die.
Lawd, Lawd, I'll beat it to de bottom or I'll die."

Sun shine hot an' burnin',
Wer'n't no breeze a-tall,
Sweat ran down like water down a hill,
Dat day John Henry let his hammer fall,
Lawd, Lawd, dat day John Henry let his hammer fall.

John Henry went to de tunnel,
An' dey put him de lead to drive;
De rock so tall an' John Henry so small,
Dat he lied down his hammer an' he cried,
Lawd, Lawd, dat he lied down his hammer an' he cried.

John Henry started on de right hand,
De steam drill started on de lef'—
"Before I'd let dis steam drill beat me down,
I'd hammer my fool self to death,
Lawd, Lawd, I'd hammer my fool self to death."

White man tol' John Henry,
"Nigger, damn yo' soul,
You might beat dis steam an' drill of mine,
When de rocks in dis mountain turn to gol',
Lawd, Lawd, when de rocks in dis mountain turn to gol'."

John Henry said to his shaker,
"Nigger, why don' you sing?
I'm throwin' twelve poun's from my hips on down,
Jes' listen to de col' steel ring,
Lawd, Lawd, jes' listen to de col' steel ring."

Oh, de captain said to John Henry,
"I b'lieve this mountain's shakin' in."
John Henry said to his captain, oh my,
"Ain' nothin' but my hammer suckin' win'.
Lawd, Lawd, ain' nothin' but my hammer suckin' win'."

John Henry tol' his shaker,
"Shaker, you better pray,
For, if I miss dis six-foot steel,
Tomorrow'll be yo' buryin' day,
Lawd, Lawd, tomorrow'll be yo' buryin' day."

John Henry tol' his captain,
"Looka yonder what I see—
Yo' drill's done broke an' yo' hole's done choke,
An' you cain' drive steel like me,
Lawd, Lawd, an' you cain' drive steel like me."

De man dat invented de steam drill,
Thought he was mighty fine.
John Henry drove his fifteen feet,
An' de steam drill only made nine,
Lawd, Lawd, an' de steam drill only made nine.

De hammer dat John Henry swung
It weighed over nine pound;
He broke a rib in his lef'-han' side,
An' his intrels fell on de groun',
Lawd, Lawd, an' his intrels fell on de groun'.

John Henry was hammerin' on de mountain,
An' his hammer was strikin' fire,
He drove so hard till he broke his pore heart,
An' he lied down his hammer an' he died
Lawd, Lawd, he lied down his hammer an' he died.

All de womens in de Wes',
When dey heared of John Henry's death,
Stood in de rain, flagged de eas'-boun' train,
Goin' where John Henry fell dead,
Lawd, Lawd, goin' where John Henry fell dead.

John Henry's li'l mother,
She was all dressed in red,
She jumped in bed, covered up her head,
Said she didn' know her son was dead,
Lawd, Lawd, said she didn' know her son was dead.

John Henry had a pretty li'l woman,
An' de dress she wo' was blue,
An' de las' words she said to him:
"John Henry, I've been true to you,
Lawd, Lawd, John Henry, I've been true to you."

My Old Kentucky Home, Good-Night!

The sun shines bright in the old Kentucky home,
'Tis summer, the darkeys are gay;
The corn top's ripe and the meadow's in the bloom,
While the birds make music all the day.
The young folks roll on the little cabin floor,
All merry, all happy and bright.
By'n by, hard times comes a knocking at the door,
Then my old Kentucky home, good-night!

Chorus:

> Weep no more, my lady,
> Oh! weep no more today!
> We will sing one song for the old Kentucky home,
> For the old Kentucky home far away.

They hunt no more for the possum and the coon,
On the meadow, the hill, and the shore,
They sing no more by the glimmer of the moon,
On the beach by the old cabin door.
The day goes by like a shadow o'er the heart,
With sorrow where all was delight;
The time has come when the darkeys have to part,
Then my old Kentucky home, good-night!

The head must bow and the back will have to bend,
Wherever the darkey may go;
A few more days, and the trouble all will end
In the field where the sugar canes grow;
A few more days for to tote the weary load,
No matter, 'twill never be light,
A few more days till we totter on the road,
Then, my old Kentucky home, good-night!

(Stephen Foster)

Old Folks at Home

Way down upon de Swanee ribber,
    Far, far away,
Dere's wha my heart is turning ebber,
    Dere's wha de old folks stay.
All up and down de whole creation,
    Sadly I roam,
Still longing for de old plantation,
    And for de old folks at home.

Chorus:
    All de world am sad and dreary
        Ebrywhere I roam,
    Oh! darkeys, how my heart grows weary,
        Far from de old folks at home.

All round de little farm I wandered
    When I was young,
Den many happy days I squandered,
    Many the songs I sung
When I was playing wid my brudder,
    Happy was I.
Oh, take me to my kind ole mudder,
    Dere let me live and die.

One little hut among de bushes,
    One dat I love,
Still sadly to my mem'ry rushes,
    No matter where I rove.
When will I see de bees a-humming
    All round de comb?
When will I hear de banjo tumming
    Down in my good ole home.

(Stephen Foster)

Omie Wise

Tell me no story, tell me no lies,
Tell me the story of little Oma Wise.
I'll tell you no story and I'll tell you no lie
How she was deluded by John Lewis's lies.

She promised to meet him at the head of Adams' branch
Some money he would bring her and other fine things.
She flew like an eagle to the head of Adams' branch
No money did he bring her nor other fine things.

No money, no money, my sweetheart said he,
Just hop up behind me and married we will be.
She hopped up behind him and away they did go
Down by the river where the deep water flowed.

John Lewis, John Lewis, I'm afraid of your way
I'm afraid that you will lead my poor body astray,
He beat her, he banged her, he drug her round and round,
He threw her in the river where he knew she would drown.

Two boys was a fishing all on one Sunday morn,
They found little Oma's body down by the old mill pond.
They threw the net around her, they carried her to the bank,
They drew her from the water and laid her on a plank.

They sent for John Lewis to come to the place,
They put her up before him that he knew her face.
My name is John Lewis, my name I do not deny,
I murdered my own true lover and her name was Omie Wise.

You can beat me, you can bang me for I'm the very one
That drowned my own true lover down by the old mill pond.

Sourwood Mountain

Chickens a-crowin' on Sourwood Mountain,
Chickens a-crowin' on Sourwood Mountain,
Call up yore dogs and let's go a-huntin',
Hey-ho, dee-iddle-um-day.

My true love lives over the river,
A few more jumps and I'll be with her.

My true love is a blue-eyed daisy,
Ef I don' git her, I'll go crazy.

My true love lives at the head of the holler,
She won't come and I won't foller.

My true love lives over the ocean,
I'll go to see her, if I take a notion.

Say, old man, I want yore daughter,
To wash my clothes and carry my water.

Fifteen cents, a dollar and a quarter,
Say, young man, take her if you want her.

Ducks in the pond, geese in the ocean,
Devil's in the women if they take a notion.

Strawberry Seller's Street Cry

I live fore miles out of town,
    I am gwine to glory.
My strawberries are sweet an' soun'
    I am gwine to glory.
My chile is sick, an' husban' dead,
    I am gwine to glory.
Now's de time to get 'em cheap,
    I am gwine to glory.
Eat 'em with yer bread an' meat,
    I am gwine to glory.
Come sinner get down on your knees,
    I am gwine to glory.
Eat dees strawberries when you please,
    I am gwine to glory.

SPIRITUALS

Go Down, Moses

Go down, Moses,
'Way down in Egypt land,
Tell ole Pharaoh,
To let my people go.

Go down, Moses,
'Way down in Egypt's land,
Tell ole Pharaoh,
To let my people go.

When Israel was in Egypt's land;
Let my people go,
Oppressed so hard they could not stand,
Let my people go.

Go down, Moses,
'Way down in Egypt land,
Tell ole Pharaoh,
To let my people go.
O let my people go.

"Thus spoke the Lord," bold Moses said;
Let my people go,
If not I'll smite your first born dead,
Let my people go.

Go down, Moses,
'Way down in Egypt land,
Tell ole Pharaoh,
To let my people go.
O let my people go.

In Dat Great Gettin' Up Mornin'

I'm-a goin' to tell you 'bout de comin' of de Saviour,
Fare you well, Fare you well.

Chorus:

> In dat great gittin' up mornin,
> Fare you well, Fare you well;
> In dat great gittin' up mornin,
> Fare you well, Fare you well.

Dere's a better day a-comin',
Fare you well, Fare you well;
Oh, preacher, fol' yo' Bible,
Fare you well, Fare you well.
Prayermaker, pray no mo',
Fare you well, Fare you well;
For de las' soul's converted,
Fare you well, Fare you well.

Dat de time shall be no longer,
Fare you well, Fare you well;
For judgment day is comin',
Fare you well, Fare you well.
Den you hear de sinner sayin',
Fare you well, Fare you well;
Down I'm rollin', down I'm rollin',
Fare you well, Fare you well.

De Lord spoke to Gabriel,
Fare you well, Fare you well;
Go look behin' de altar,
Fare you well, Fare you well.
Take down de silvah trumpet,
Fare you well, Fare you well;
Blow yo' trumpet Gabriel;
Fare you well, Fare you well.

Lord how loud shall I blow it?
Fare you well, Fare you well;
Blow it right calm an' easy,
Fare you well, Fare you well.

Do not alarm my people,
Fare you well, Fare you well.
Tell 'em to come to judgment,
Fare you well, Fare you well.

Gabriel blow yo' trumpet,
Fare you well, Fare you well;
Lord, how loud shall I blow it?
Fare you well, Fare you well.
Loud as seven peals of thunder,
Fare you well, Fare you well.
Wake de livin' nations,
Fare you well, Fare you well.

Place one foot upon de dry lan',
Fare you well, Fare you well;
Place de other on de sea,
Fare you well, Fare you well.
Den you'll see de coffins bustin',
Fare you well, Fare you well.
See de dry bones come a-creepin',
Fare you well, Fare you well.

Hell shall be uncapp'd an' burnin',
Fare you well, Fare you well;
Den de dragon shall be loosen'd,
Fare you well, Fare you well.
Where you runnin' po' sinner,
Fare you well, Fare you well.
Where you runnin' po' sinner,
Fare you well, Fare you well.

Den you'll see po' sinners risin'
Fare you well, Fare you well;
Den you'll see de worl' on fiah,
Fare you well, Fare you well:
See de moon a bleedin',
Fare you well, Fare you well;
See de stars a fallin',
Fare you well, Fare you well:

See de elements a meltin',
Fare you well, Fare you well;
See de forked lightnin',
Fare you well, Fare you well:

Den you'll cry out for cold water,
Fare you well, Fare you well;
While de Christians shout in glory,
Fare you well, Fare you well:

Sayin' Amen to yo' damnation,
Fare you well, Fare you well;
No mercy for po' sinner,
Fare you well, Fare you well:
Hear de rumblin' of de thunder,
Fare you well, Fare you well.
Earth shall reel an' totter,
Fare you well, Fare you well.

Den you'll see de Christian risin',
Fare you well, Fare you well.
Den you'll see de righteous marchin',
Fare you well, Fare you well.
See dem marchin' home to heab'n',
Fare you well, Fare you well.
Den you'll see my Jesus comin',
Fare you well, Fare you well.

Wid all His holy angels,
Fare you well, Fare you well.
Take de righteous home to glory,
Fare you well, Fare you well.
Dere dey live wid God forever,
Fare you well, Fare you well.
On de right hand side of my Savior,
Fare you well, Fare you well.

Never Said a Mumbalin' Word

Oh, dey whupped him up de hill, up de hill, up de hill,
Oh, dey whupped him up de hill, an' he never said a mumbalin' word,
Oh, dey whupped him up de hill, an' he never said a mumbalin' word,
He jes' hung down his head, an' he cried.

Oh, dey crowned him wid a thorny crown, thorny crown, thorny crown,
Oh, dey crowned him wid a thorny crown, an' he never said a mumbalin' word,
Oh, dey crowned him wid a thorny crown, an' he never said a mumbalin' word,
He jes' hung down his head, an' he cried.

Well, dey nailed him to de cross, to de cross, to de cross,
Well, dey nailed him to de cross, an' he never said a mumbalin' word,
Well, dey nailed him to de cross, an' he never said a mumbalin' word,
He jes' hung down his head, an' he cried.

Well, dey pierced him in de side, in de side, in de side,
Well, dey pierced him in de side, an' de blood come a-twinklin' down,
Well, dey pierced him in de side, an' de blood come a-twinklin' down,
Den he hung down his head, an' he died.

I Know Moonrise

I know moonrise, I know starrise,
Lay dis body down.

I walk in de moonlight, I walk in de starlight,
To lay dis body down.

I walk in de graveyard, I walk through de graveyard,
To lay dis body down.

I'll lie in de grave and stretch out my arms;
Lay dis body down.

I go to de judgment in de evenin' of de day,
When I lay dis body down;

And my soul and yore soul will meet in de day
When I lay dis body down.

Oh, Wasn't Dat a Wide Ribber

Oh, de Ribber of Jordan is deep and wide,
    One mo' ribber to cross.
I don't know how to get on de other side,
    One mo' ribber to cross.
Oh, you got Jesus, hold him fast,
    One mo' ribber to cross.
Oh, better love was nebber told,
    One mo' ribber to cross.
'Tis stronger dan an iron band,
    One mo' ribber to cross.
'Tis sweeter dan de honey comb,
    One mo' ribber to cross.
Oh, de good ole chariot passin' by,
    One mo' ribber to cross.
She jarred de earth an' shook de sky,
    One mo' ribber to cross.
I pray, good Lord, I shall be one,
    One mo' ribber to cross.
To get in de chariot an' trabble on,
    One mo' ribber to cross.
We're told dat de fore wheel run by love,
    One mo' ribber to cross.
We're told dat de hind wheel run by faith,
    One mo' ribber to cross.
I hope I'll get dere by an' bye,
    One mo' ribber to cross.
To jine de number in de sky,
    One mo' ribber to cross.
Oh, Jordan's Ribber am chilly an' cold,
    One mo' ribber to cross.
It chills de body, but not de soul,
    One mo' ribber to cross.

Poor Rosy, Poor Gal

Poor Rosy, poor gal!
Poor Rosy, poor gal!
Poor Rosy, poor gal!
    Heab'n shall-a be my home.
Before I spend one day in hell,
    Heab'n shall-a be my home.
I sing and pray my soul away,
    Heab'n shall-a be my home.
Poor Rosy, poor gal!
Poor Rosy, poor gal!
Poor Rosy, poor gal!
    Heab'n shall-a be my home.

Got hard trial in my way!
Hard trial in my way,
Hard trial in my way,
    Heab'n shall-a be my home.
O! when I talk I talk with God,
    Heab'n shall-a be my home.
O! when I talk I talk with God,
    Heab'n shall-a be my home.
Poor Rosy, poor gal!
Poor Rosy, poor gal!
Poor Rosy, poor gal!
    Heab'n shall-a be my home.

I dunno what de people want o' me,
Dunno what de people want o' me,
Dunno what de people want o' me,
    Heab'n shall-a be my home.
O! dis day no holiday,
    Heab'n shall-a be my home.
O! dis day no holiday,
    Heab'n shall-a be my home.
Poor Rosy, poor gal!
Poor Rosy, poor gal!
Poor Rosy, poor gal!
    Heab'n shall-a be my home.

A-singin' an' embracin', talkin' too,
Singin' an' embracin', talkin' too,
Singin' an' embracin', talkin' too,
  Heab'n shall-a be my home.
O! when I walk I walk with God,
  Heab'n shall-a be my home.
O! when I sleep I sleep with God,
  Heab'n shall-a be my home.
Poor Rosy, poor gal!
Poor Rosy, poor gal!
Poor Rosy, poor gal!
  Heab'n shall-a be my home.

Biographical Notes

JOSEPH GLOVER BALDWIN (1815-1864)
Joseph Glover Baldwin, a noted writer of sketches and tales about "the flush times" in Mississippi and Alabama, was born in Friendly Grove Factory, Virginia. He read law and published two Virginia newspapers in Lexington and Buchanan. From 1836 to 1854 he practiced law in DeKalb, Mississippi; Gainsville, Alabama; and Livingston, Alabama. During the period between 1851 and 1853, he wrote a series of twenty-six sketches which were gathered together under the title *The Flush Times of Alabama and Mississippi* (1853). His realistic, urbane, humorous depictions of inept and shifty lawyers, clients, and judges, as well as his ability to depict a practical joke or tell a tall story, captured the popular imagination, and he became identified with two other humorists of the Southwest: Augustus Baldwin Longstreet and Thomas Bangs Thorpe. In 1854, Baldwin moved to California, whose flush times he had reflected on in an article for *The Southern Literary Messenger* (1853). Baldwin is noted for two other works: *Party Leaders: Sketches of Thomas Jefferson, Alex'r Hamilton, Andrew Jackson, Henry Clay, John Randolph, of Roanoke, Including Notices of Many Other Distinguished American Statesmen* (1855) and the posthumously published *The Flush Times of California* (1966), a work that grew out of his 1853 text. He remained in California for ten years, working part of that time as an associate justice of the California Supreme Court. "How the Times Served the Virginians. Virginians in a New Country. The Rise, Decline and Fall of the Rag Empire" are taken from *The Flush Times of Alabama and Mississippi*.

GEORGE WASHINGTON CABLE (1844-1925)
George Washington Cable, one of the most influential writers of the Old South, was born in New Orleans, Louisiana. He entered the Confederate army at age nineteen; after the war, he returned to New Orleans, worked at the local customhouse and married Louise Bartlett on December 7, 1869. They subsequently had five children. In 1870, Cable began writing a column, as well as short stories, for the New Orleans *Picayune*. *Scribner's Monthly* and *The Century* began publishing Cable's short fiction about racial problems and social change among the Creoles, and soon Cable's fiction attracted national attention. In 1879, *Old Creole Days,* a collection of delightful short stories, was published; this was followed in 1880 by *The Grandissimes* (according to Louis D. Rubin, Jr., "the first modern Southern novel") and *Madame Delphine* (1881), a novella. Cable subsequently found himself in a position to write full-time and completed a novel about prison reform, *Dr. Sevier* (1884) and a history titled *The Creoles of Louisiana* (1884). After a reading tour with Mark Twain, Cable moved to Northampton, Massachusetts, in 1885. By this time, he had become a strong advocate for the New South, as demonstrated in "A Freedman's Case in Equity," *The Silent South* (1885), and *The Negro Question* (1890). Two popular novels, *John March, Southerner* (1894) and *The Cavalier* (1901), reflect the sentimental roman-

ticism prevalent in the fiction of the day. A number of his later works, *Bonaventure* (1888), *Bylow Hill* (1902), *Kincaid's Battery* (1908), and *Gideon's Band* (1914), show that even as he grew older, his imaginative energies did not flag. "Posson Jone'" was first published in *Appleton's Journal* (April 1, 1876); "Creole Slave Songs" was first published in *The Century Magazine* (April 1886).

MADISON JULIUS CAWEIN (1865-1914)
Madison Julius Cawein was born in Louisville, Kentucky. His father, William Cawein, a Huguenot, came to the United States after having fled Germany. In 1872, the Caweins moved to Oldham County, Kentucky, then a year later to New Albany, Indiana, and finally back to Louisville where young Madison attended Male High School. As a teenager, he discovered the Romantic poets, who were to have a profound effect on his own poetry. After graduating from high school, Cawein worked in a poolroom, while secretly writing poetry in his spare time. His first volume of poetry, *Blooms of the Berry,* was published in 1887, followed soon by others including *The Triumph of Music, and Other Lyrics* (1888), *Ascolon of Gaul, and Other Poems* (1890), *Lyrics and Idyls* (1890), *Days and Dreams* (1891), *Moods and Memories* (1892), *Red Leaves and Roses* (1893), *Intimations of the Beautiful* (1894), *Undertones* (1896), *Shapes and Shadows* (1898), *Weeds by the Wall* (1901), and *The Vale of Tempe* (1905). Cawein published his *Complete Poetical Works* in five volumes in 1907.

MARY BOYKIN MILLER CHESNUT (1823-1866)
Mary Boykin Miller was born in Statesburg, South Carolina. Her father, Stephen Decatur Miller, served as a state congressman, senator and governor. At age seventeen, she married James Chesnut, Jr., and moved to Camden, New Jersey; she and her husband eventually moved to Washington, D. C., so that her husband could serve in the U.S. Senate. When he resigned to lead the secessionist movement in South Carolina and serve under Jefferson Davis, Mrs. Chesnut moved south, eventually to Columbia, South Carolina. After the end of the Civil War, the Chesnuts returned to Camden. Mrs. Chesnut began her posthumously published *A Diary From Dixie* (1905, 1949) on February 15, 1861 and ended it on August 2, 1865; this work is an expansion of journals that she had kept during the Civil War and thus is not normally considered a traditional diary. In 1981, C. Vann Woodward edited this work and titled it *Mary Chesnut's Civil War.* In 1881, she returned to her journals and expanded them often by creating lively and imaginative vignettes that nonetheless remain faithful to her original work. As C. Vann Woodward and Elisabeth Muhlenfeld note, "Mary Chesnut had never been afraid of truth—had, in fact, told it fearlessly in the book written from 1881 to 1884 based on her diary." The section of Mrs. Chesnut's diary printed in this volume is from *Mary Chesnut's Civil War.*

CHARLES WADDELL CHESNUTT (1858-1932)
Charles Waddell Chesnut was born in Cleveland, Ohio, where his free-black parents had moved from Fayetteville, North Carolina, two years earlier. When he was eight years old, he returned with his parents to Fayetteville, where his father opened a grocery store. He attended a school established by the Freedman's Bureau, but at fourteen, pressed by financial difficulties, he was forced to take a full-time job as teacher first in Charlotte, North Carolina, and later, back in Fayetteville. In 1884, he returned to Cleveland with his wife and children, established a prosperous legal stenography firm, and became a well-known and respected businessman and local

personality. He first gained national recognition with his dialect story "The Goophered Grapevine" published in August 1887 in *The Atlantic Monthly.* Two collections of stories followed, *The Conjure Woman* (1899) and *The Wife of His Youth and Other Stories* (1899). Chesnutt subsequently published three novels largely concerned with racial prejudice and the rise of segregation in the postwar South: *The House Behind the Cedars* (1900), *The Marrow of Tradition* (1901), and *The Colonel's Dream* (1905). "Sis' Becky's Pickaninny" is taken from *The Conjure Woman.*

KATE CHOPIN (1851-1904)

Kate Chopin was born Katherine O'Flaherty in St. Louis, Missouri. Her father was an Irishman from Galway, and her mother, Eliza Farris, came from an old French Creole family long settled in the United States. As a young girl, Kate learned to read and to speak French from her maternal great-grandmother, Madame Charleville. When she was nineteen years old she married Oscar Chopin, a cotton trader from Louisiana. She moved with him to New Orleans where she began a family and played an active role in New Orleans society. In 1879, financial problems forced Oscar Chopin to move his large family—there were six children—to Cloutierville in Natchitoches Parish where the Chopin plantations were located. When her husband died in 1883 of swamp fever, Kate Chopin, after a year tending the family affairs in Cloutierville, returned to St. Louis and, strongly influenced by her reading of Maupassant, began her career as a writer. Among her works are two collections of Louisiana short stories, *Bayou Folk* (1894) and *A Night in Acadie* (1897), and her best known work, the short novel, *The Awakening,* published in 1899. "A Night in Acadie" is taken from the collection by the same name.

FREDERICK DOUGLASS (1818-1895)

Frederick Douglass, whose real name was Frederick Augustus Washington Bailey, was born a slave in Talbot County on the Eastern Shore of Maryland. In 1825, he was sent to Baltimore to work as a houseboy and unskilled laborer, and in 1834, he was hired out to a professional slave-breaker, Edward Covey. Douglass escaped from slavery in 1838 by impersonating a black sailor whose papers he had taken. Making his way to Massachusetts, he spoke out vociferously against slavery and published his *Narrative of the Life of Frederick Douglass, An American Slave, Written by Himself* in 1845. Two years later, he moved to Rochester, New York, and began to publish a weekly, *The North Star.* Like Harriet Jacobs, he was influenced by the suffragettes who lived in nearby Seneca Falls, New York. In 1855, Douglass published his second autobiography titled *My Bondage and My Freedom.* During the Civil War, he recruited black troops for the Union armies since he was too old to bear arms himself. After the war, he continued speaking out for the rights of the blacks and supporting ratification of the Fifteenth Amendment, which stipulates that the right to vote shall not be denied nor abridged by the United States nor any state on account of race, color, or previous condition of servitude. President Rutherford B. Hayes appointed Douglass U.S. Marshall for the District of Columbia in 1877; President James Garfield appointed him Recorder of Deeds for the District of Columbia in 1881, and President Benjamin Harrison appointed him Minister-Resident and Consul General to the Republic of Haiti and Chargé d'Affaires for Santo Domingo in 1891. Douglass published his third autobiography, *Life and Times of Frederick Douglass,* in 1881. The section of Frederick Douglass's narrative printed in this volume is from *Narrative of the Life of Frederick Douglass.*

PAUL LAURENCE DUNBAR (1872-1906)

Paul Laurence Dunbar, the son of former slaves, was born in Dayton, Ohio, where he attended local schools. According to his own admission, he wrote his first poem in 1878; he recited his poem, "Easter Hymn," in 1884 at the Eaker Street A.M.E. Sion Church in Dayton. In 1890, he began editing the *Dayton Tattler,* published by Orville and Wilbur Wright. A year later, he wrote a Western dialect story, "The Tenderfoot," for the A. N. Kellogg Syndicate, the first work for which he received payment. His first volume of poetry, *Oak and Ivy,* was published in 1892, soon followed by *Majors and Minors* (1895) and *Lyrics of a Lowly Life* (1896), with an introduction by William Dean Howells. In 1897, he toured England and read his poetry, and worked briefly as an assistant in the Library of Congress in Washington, D. C. His first novel, *The Uncalled,* was published in 1898, followed a year later by *Lyrics of the Heartside* and *Poems of Cabin and Field.* He published three other novels in succession: *The Love of Landry* in 1900, *The Fanatics* in 1901, and *Sport of the Gods* in 1902. Separated from his wife Alice, Dunbar returned to Dayton in 1903 lonely and in poor health; in spite of this, he published during this same year *Lyrics of Love and Laughter, When Malindy Sings,* and *In Old Plantation Days.*

DANIEL DECATUR EMMETT (1815-1904)

Daniel Decatur Emmett was born in Mount Vernon, Ohio, where his parents had moved from the South. His father was from Virginia, and his mother from Maryland. His early life is rather obscure, but after drifting from one job to another, including newspaper work and a period as a fifer in the army, he eventually became known on the minstrel show circuit as a songwriter. He wrote "Dixie's Land," both tune and text, for Bryant's Minstrel Troupe who first performed it in 1859 in New York under the title "Plantation Song and Dance/Dixie's Land/Introducing the Whole Troupe in the Festival Dance." The song soon became widely known and by the time it appeared in a pirated edition in New York in 1860, with music credited to J. C. Viereck, it had become a hit in New Orleans in a performance of John Brougham's burlesque *Pocahontas, or the Gentle Savage.* The origin of the word "Dixie" is not clear, but it was already in current usage among the minstrel show performers before Emmett wrote his song. It may have derived from the Mason-Dixon line, though other suggestions link it to the name of a wealthy New York slaveholder, or to a Louisiana ten dollar bank note with the word "dix" on it.

GEORGE FITZHUGH (1806-1881)

George Fitzhugh was born at Brent Town Tract, Prince William County, Virginia. Largely self-educated, Fitzhugh became a lawyer, and after marriage to Mary Metcalf Brockenbrough in 1829, he moved into the Brockenbrough mansion in Port Royal, Carolina County, Virginia. In the late 1840's, Fitzhugh gradually became noted for his proslavery views—which rejected the tenets of Locke and Jefferson—as reflected primarily in two pamphlets titled *Slavery Justified* (1849) and *What Shall Be Done with the Free Negroes?* (1851), both precursors to his better known *Sociology for the South: or, The Failure of Free Society* (1854) and *Cannibals All!, or, Slaves Without Masters* (1857). After the Civil War, Fitzhugh served for one year as an associate judge in the Freedman's Court in Richmond, Virginia. "Southern Thought Again" was first published in *DeBow's Review* (October 1857).

STEPHEN FOSTER (1826-1864)

Stephen Collins Foster was born in Laurenceville, Pennsylvania. He worked for a short time as a bookkeeper in Cincinnati, Ohio, before turning to a career as a professional songwriter. Master of many modes, Foster composed parlor songs, sentimental ballads, and minstrel showpieces, becoming in a few years one of the most popular songwriters of the nineteenth century. Though he had little direct contact with the physical South, he so effectively captured the American imagination with his nostalgic lyrical versions of the old plantation world that his songs were often mistaken for genuine folk songs, and were sung as such by both blacks and whites.

ELLEN GLASGOW (1874-1945)
Ellen Glasgow was born in Richmond, Virginia, where she resided for most of her life. One of many children in a household troubled by parental unhappiness, she acquired much of her intellectual education by herself, assisted by her father's large and liberal library. Her first two novels were portraits of New York bohemian life, but her third, *The Voice of the People* (1900), began a long series of Virginia novels that chronicled, with an insistent realism, the emergence of the Old South into the modern world, and that often featured strong-minded Southern women as the central figures. Among her many novels are *The Battle-Ground* (1902), *The Deliverance* (1904), *The Ancient Law* (1908), *The Romance of a Plain Man* (1909), *The Miller of Old Church* (1911), *Virginia* (1913), her widely acclaimed masterpiece, *Barren Ground* (1925), and a masterful Richmond trilogy, *The Romantic Comedians* (1926), *They Stooped to Folly* (1929), and *The Sheltered Life* (1932). Her autobiography *The Woman Within* (1954) was not published, in accordance with her instructions, until after her death. "Jordan's End" is taken from *The Shadowy Third and Other Stories* (1923).

HENRY GRADY (1850-1889)
Henry Grady was born in Athens, Georgia, where his father died in 1864 as a result of wounds he received while fighting for the Confederate forces. Grady graduated from the University of Georgia in 1868 and subsequently studied law at the University of Virginia in Charlottesville. He later served as associate editor of *The Rome Courier* and editor of *The Rome Commercial*. His career in journalism in Georgia continued when he became a part owner of *The Atlanta Daily Herald,* which was forced to close down in 1876. With the help of Cyrus Field, he became part owner of *The Atlanta Constitution*. Grady never ceased to speak out on behalf of a New South that would profit from advances in agriculture, industry, and education. "The New South" was delivered before the New England Society in New York City on December 21, 1886; the speech is taken from *The Complete Orations and Speeches of Henry W. Grady,* edited by Edwin DuBois Shurter (1910).

JAMES HENRY HAMMOND (1807-1864)
James Henry Hammond was born in Newberry, South Carolina. In 1815, the Hammond family moved to Columbia, South Carolina, and James began his studies at South Carolina College in 1823, having already been tutored at home by his father. In 1825, he graduated fourth in his class of thirty-one; in 1828, at age twenty-one, he was admitted to the bar and started practicing law in Columbia, and by 1830 he was editing the new pronullification *Southern Times*. In June 1831, Hammond married the wealthy Catherine Fitzsimons and, after closing his law office, he went to Beech Island to manage Catherine's dowry, particularly her plantation Silver Bluff. In 1835, he set off for Washington, D. C., with his wife and four children; he served in Congress as a representative of Barnwell District. On February 1, 1836, he succinctly revealed his proslavery stand: "If [slavery] is an evil, it is one to us alone, and we are contented with it—why should others interfere? But it is no evil." His tenure in Washington was short-lived, and he returned to Silver Bluff in 1837 after a tour of Europe with his

family. Hammond was Governor of South Carolina (1842-1844) and a U.S. senator (1857-1860), but he resigned from this latter post because he opposed the election of Abraham Lincoln as president. His "sacred and secret" diaries span the critical years from 1841 to 1864; they give tremendous insight into the life of a prominent figure before the Civil War. "Letter to an English Abolitionist" was first published in *The South Carolinian* (January 28, 1845).

GEORGE WASHINGTON HARRIS (1814-1869)
Born in Allegheny City, Pennsylvania, Harris, when five years old, was taken by his half-brother to live in Knoxville, Tennessee, where he remained for most of his life. Though he had little formal schooling, he showed early mechanical abilities, and began working for a living well before he was fully grown. Trained as a metalworker, he eventually worked his way into the ownership of a prosperous metalworking business in Knoxville. He tried his hand at a variety of other professions as well, including the running of a large farm in the Great Smoky Mountains, the operating of a sawmill, supervising a copper mine, and, intermittently, piloting a steamboat on the Tennessee River. He was known all during his adult life as Captain Harris. He began contributing to William T. Porter's New York sporting magazine, *Spirit of the Times,* in 1843, and in 1867 his major collection of Sut Lovingood stories, *Sut Lovingood. Yarns Spun by a "Nat'ral Born Durn'd Fool." Warped and Wove for Public Wear,* was finally published. An ardent secessionist, the Civil War and the defeat of the South deeply embittered Harris, and he died in 1869, after having prepared for publication a second collection of tales, which was lost and has never been found. "Mrs. Yardley's Quilting" is taken from *Sut Lovingood. Yarns Spun by a "Nat'ral Born Durn'd Fool." Warped and Wove for Public Wear.*

JOEL CHANDLER HARRIS (1848-1908)
Joel Chandler Harris was born in Eatonton, a small town in middle Georgia. His father was an itinerant Irish laborer who disappeared when Joel was born, and his deserted and unmarried mother barely managed to make a living as a seamstress. Unable to continue school because of his household's financial strain, Harris went to work when he was thirteen on a weekly paper published by Joseph Addison Turner, owner of Turnwold Plantation, where Harris spent four years that changed his life and that directed him toward a long and successful career in the newspaper trade. After having worked on newspapers in various Southern cities, including New Orleans and Savannah, in 1876 he took a position with *The Atlanta Constitution*, where he remained for twenty-four years, and where he first presented the Uncle Remus stories. The first volume of Uncle Remus stories, *Uncle Remus: His Songs and Sayings,* was published in 1880, and it was followed over the years by more than twenty other books on a variety of Southern subjects. Among his works are *Nights with Uncle Remus: Myths and Legends of the Old Plantation* (1883), *Free Joe and Other Georgian Sketches* (1887), and *Gabriel Tolliver: A Story of Reconstruction* (1902). "Mingo: A Sketch of Life in Middle Georgia" is taken from *Mingo and Other Sketches in Black and White* (1884); "The Wonderful Tar-Baby Story" and "How Mr. Rabbit Was Too Sharp for Mr. Fox" are taken from *Uncle Remus: His Songs and Sayings.*

PAUL HAMILTON HAYNE (1839-1776)
Paul Hamilton Hayne was born in Charleston, South Carolina. After the death of his father, he was raised by his uncle, Senator Robert Y. Hayne. After graduating from the College of Charleston in 1850, he studied law and was admitted to the bar in 1852. A published poet, he edited both *The Southern Literary Gazette* and *Russell's*

Magazine. As a Confederate soldier he served as aide-de-camp to Governor Francis Pickens for four months in 1861-1862. Hayne moved to Georgia after the Civil War and began editing and publishing again; his poetry appeared in such journals as *The Atlantic Monthly, Scribner's Monthly,* and *Harper's Monthly.* His poems, which often celebrate the virtues of the Old South and the beauty of the landscape, were published in three volumes: *Legends and Lyrics* (1872), *The Mountains of the Lovers: With Poems of Nature and Tradition* (1875), and a not-quite-complete volume titled *Poems* (1882). His letters to prominent Americans and Englishmen, including Longfellow, Whittier, Holmes, Bryant, and Swinburne, and especially Lanier, reveal a man deeply committed to poetry. The four letters of Hayne printed in this volume are from *A Man of Letters in the Nineteenth-Century South: Selected Letters of Paul Hamilton Hayne* edited by Rayburn S. Moore (1982).

JOHNSON JONES HOOPER (1815-1862)
Johnson Jones Hooper was born in Wilmington, North Carolina. Son of a prominent lawyer and plantation owner who had come on hard times, Hooper at the age of twenty left North Carolina to live with his brother in the small Alabama town of LaFayette. Hooper eventually became a lawyer himself, though he made his living primarily as a newspaper editor and publisher. In 1843, he began writing for William T. Porter's *Spirit of the Times,* and began developing his fictional character Simon Suggs, the rogue hero of Hooper's first book, *Some Adventures of Captain Simon Suggs, Late of the Tallapoosa Volunteers; Together with "Taking the Census" and Other Alabama Sketches* (1845). Hooper was active in Southern politics, and a determined secession-ist. The year before he died he held the position of Secretary to the Confederate Provisional Congress. Among his other works are *The Widow Rugby's Husband, A Night at the Ugly Man's, and Other Tales of Alabama* (1851) and *Dog and Gun: A Few Loose Chapters on Shooting* (1856). "The Widow Rugby's Husband" first appeared in *A Ride with Old Kit Kuncker and Other Sketches* (1849), and was later reprinted in *The Widow Rugby's Husband, A Night at the Ugly Man's, and Other Tales of Alabama.*

GEORGE MOSES HORTON (ca. 1797- 1883)
George Moses Horton was the slave of William Horton of Northampton County, North Carolina. In 1800, William Horton moved his family and slaves to Chatham County, North Carolina, not far from Chapel Hill. As a young boy, George learned to read and write poetry while working on the Horton farm. In 1814, James Horton, William's son, became the owner of George, and during trips to the University of North Carolina at Chapel Hill with his new owner, George recited and wrote poems for the university students. Some of those poems were commissioned by the students. In 1828 and 1829, white friends of George Horton twice attempted to buy his freedom, and a plan was devised to publish a volume of his poetry, and with the proceeds, help to emancipate him. In 1829, *The Hope of Liberty* was published, but the aspirations of the book's title were not fulfilled. Yet in a slave-holding state, a slave had published a book of poetry, the first of its kind in the South. In 1830, Joseph Caldwell, the president of the university and a friend of Horton, was replaced by former Governor David Swain, whom Horton expected to secure his freedom. This was not to be the case. In 1845, *The Poetical Works of George M. Horton* was published. In 1865, with the assistance of Captain Will Banks of the Ninth Michigan Cavalry stationed in Raleigh, North Carolina, Horton published *Naked Genius,* and after that he set out for Philadelphia, Pennsylvania. From there on, unfortunately, his life is lost in obscurity.

HARRIET ANN JACOBS (LINDA BRENT) (ca. 1813-1897)

Harriet Ann Jacobs was born a slave in Edenton, North Carolina. Her father most likely was Daniel, the slave of Dr. Andrew Knox; Daniel was probably the son of Knox's neighbor Henry Jacobs. Her mother, Delilah, was the slave of John Horniblow, an Edenton taverner. It is known that her maternal grandmother, Molly Horniblow, freed from slavery in her middle age, owned property in Edenton and worked as a baker. Orphaned as a child, Harriet learned to read and sew from her white mistresses. Subjected to sexual abuse as a teenager, she became involved with a white lawyer named Samuel Tredwell Sawyer and had two children by him. In 1842, after seven years in hiding, she fled to Brooklyn, New York, to be with her daughter, and then traveled to England and Rochester, New York, always fearing for her safety and that of her family. Eventually, she began publishing short pieces in various newspapers, such as Horace Greeley's *New York Tribune,* discussing among other topics sexual abuse among slave women. In 1861, Jacobs's narrative was pseudonymously published in Boston as *Incidents in the Life of a Slave Girl, Written by Herself.* After the Civil War, Jacobs lived and worked in Savannah, Georgia; Cambridge, Massachusetts; and Washington, D.C. The sections of Harriet Jacobs's narrative printed in this volume are from *Incidents in the Life of a Slave Girl.*

THOMAS JEFFERSON (1743-1826)

Thomas Jefferson was born at Shadwell, Virginia, a tobacco plantation near Charlottesville owned by his father. He was educated by private tutors and went to the College of William and Mary in Williamsburg, Virginia. He studied law with George Wythe and became a member of the Virginia House of Burgesses. As a delegate to the Second Continental Congress, Jefferson chaired the revolutionary committee that included Benjamin Franklin and John Adams and that chose Jefferson to write *The Declaration of Independence.* As a member of the Virginia House of Delegates, Jefferson took the initiative in passing the Act for Establishing Religious Freedom. In 1779, he was elected Governor of Virginia and subsequently wrote his *Notes on the State of Virginia.* In 1784, he was appointed Minister Plenipotentiary of the United States to the Court of France. When Jefferson returned to the United States in 1789, his subsequent career included serving as Secretary of State to George Washington, Vice President under John Adams and as President from 1801 to 1809. A man of immense knowledge and talent, not the least of which can be seen in the founding of the University of Virginia in Charlottesville, he had a personal library of some 6,500 volumes that became the seed collection for the Library of Congress.

JAMES WELDON JOHNSON (1871-1938)

James Weldon Johnson was born in Jacksonville, Florida, where his parents were hard-working members of Jacksonville's middle-class black community. His father was headwaiter in a large hotel, and his mother was a music teacher. Johnson attended local schools before enrolling in Atlanta University. After graduation, he founded a newspaper in Jacksonville, but in 1901 he moved to New York where he, his brother, and a friend, Robert Cole, became pioneering black songwriters for a series of successful musical comedies and minstrel shows, composing such popular standards as "Under the Bamboo Tree" and "Didn't He Ramble." After working abroad for several years, Johnson returned to the United States and left the entertainment world for a seven-year period of diplomatic service, as consul general in Venezuela and in Nicaragua. In 1912, he published his novel of "passing," *The Autobiography of an Ex-Colored Man,* and for the rest of his life devoted himself to writing, to working as an influential leader of the National Association for the Advancement of Colored People, and to teaching. Among his works are *God's Trombones: Seven Negro Sermons in Verse* (1927), *Black Manhattan* (1930), and *Along the Way* (1933).

EDWARD KING (1848-1896)

Edward King was born in Middlefield, Massachusetts. After the death of his father, his mother moved to Huntington, Massachusetts, and married Samuel Fisher. Educated by his step-father, King left home at sixteen, worked in a factory and became a reporter on *The Springfield Daily Union* and later on *The Republican.* He went to the Paris Exposition in 1867 and wrote his first book *My Paris* (1868) based on this trip. In 1870, he began working for *The Boston Morning Herald* and covered again in France the Franco-Prussian War. His first novel, *Kentucky's Love,* was published in 1873. J. G. Holland, the editor of *Scribner's Monthly,* invited King to tour the South and report on the effects of the Civil War; these articles eventually appeared in book form as *The Great South* (1875). His other works, based to a great extent on his foreign travels, include *French Political Leaders* (1876), *Echoes from the Orient* (1880), *Europe in a Storm and Calm* (1885); his novels include *The Gentle Savage* (1883), *The Golden Spike* (1886), and *Joseph Zalmonah* (1893). When he died, his friends found a volume of poetry, which they claimed was his best work. The sections of Edward King's travelogue are taken from *The Great South.*

GRACE KING (1852-1932)

Grace King was born in New Orleans, Louisiana, her home for her entire lifetime, and a city she always considered her special property. Her father was a successful lawyer whose fortunes collapsed when the Civil War forced him to move his family away from the city to a remote plantation. After the war, the family returned to New Orleans, but King's father never recovered his previous prosperity, and she would always remember the Reconstruction years as a bitter period of permanent loss. She had been educated in French convent schools, and though not a Creole herself, she strongly defended Creole society and culture. Her first published work was the story "Monsieur Motte" (1866), written in response to a challenge by a Northern editor that she write something herself after hearing her complain that Cable's Creole portraits were exaggerated. Among her works are two collections of stories, *Tales of a Time and Place* (1892) and *Balcony Stories* (1893), a novel, *The Pleasant Ways of St. Médard* (1916), several Southern and New Orleans histories, and an autobiography, *Memories of a Southern Woman of Letters* (1932). "Bayou l'Ombre" is taken from *Tales of a Time and Place.*

SIDNEY LANIER (1842-1881)

Sidney Lanier was born in Macon, Georgia, where his father had a law practice. He attended local schools before enrolling at Oglethorpe University, then located in Milledgeville. After graduation, Lanier enlisted in the Confederate army with the Macon Volunteers, one of the first units from Georgia to fight in Virginia. In 1864, he was taken prisoner by the Union army in Maryland where he contracted tuberculosis. After the war he drifted from job to job before settling down as a professional flute player for the Peabody Orchestra in Baltimore. By that time he had married, and had published a Civil War novel, *Tiger-Lilies* (1867). His first major poem, "Corn," was published in 1875, and in 1877 a collection of his poetry, *Poems,* appeared, but had little success. In 1879, he became a lecturer in English at Johns Hopkins University. Two of his books were based on courses given at Johns Hopkins: *The Science of English Verse* (1880) and *The English Novel* (1883).

AUGUSTUS BALDWIN LONGSTREET (1790-1870)

Augustus Baldwin Longstreet was born in Augusta, Georgia, where he attended local schools before entering Dr. Moses Waddel's well-known academy in Willington, South Carolina. He continued his education at Yale University, and after studying law in Connecticut, he returned to Georgia to practice law. In the 1830's, he began publishing humorous sketches in *The Milledgeville Southern Recorder.* He soon acquired his own newspaper in Augusta, *The State's Rights Sentinel,* whose title reflected his own long-standing political position. In 1835, *The Sentinel* published his *Georgia Scenes, Characters, Incidents, &c., in the First Half Century of the Republic,* which was reprinted in 1840 by Harper & Brothers. With *Georgia Scenes,* Longstreet launched the "Southwestern humorist" school of Southern writing. At the end of his life he presided over several Southern universities, including Emory College and the University of Mississippi. Among his other works are a pamphlet, *Letters on the Epistle of Paul to Philemon, or the Connection of Apostolic Christianity with Slavery* (1845), and a minor novel, *Master William Mitten; or, A Youth of Brilliant Talents Who Was Ruined by Bad Luck* (1864). "The Fight" is taken from *Georgia Scenes.*

ALEXANDER BEAUFORT MEEK (1814-1865)

Alexander Beaufort Meek was born in Columbia, South Carolina, but moved with his parents to Tuscaloosa, Alabama, when he was five years old. He studied law and was admitted to the bar in 1835. Active in Alabama politics and in journalism, Meek gradually gained a reputation as a talented, but occasional poet. Among his works are *The Red Eagles* (1855), *Songs and Poems of the South* (1857), and *Romantic Passages in Southwestern History; Including Orations, Sketches, and Essays* (1857).

JOHN SINGLETON MOSBY (1833-1916)

John Singleton Mosby was born in Edgemont, Virginia. He graduated from the University of Virginia in 1852, was admitted to the bar and practiced law in Bristol, Virginia. On July 21, 1861, he fought at the Battle of Bull Run and later scouted for General J. E. B. Stuart during the famous ride around General George McClellan's army in June 1862 during the Peninsular Campaign. He was given a lieutenant's commission in February 1863 and formed the Mosby Partisan Rangers, known for their guerrilla style of warfare. On March 9, 1863, they captured General Edwin Stoughton and about one hundred of his men at the Fairfax Court House. Mosby was promoted to lieutenant colonel in February 1864 and in December of that year to full colonel. The Union forces were never able to capture Mosby. After the Civil War, Mosby became a Republican and supported President Ulysses S. Grant for reelection in 1872. He wrote *Mosby's War Reminiscences* (1887) and *Stuart's Cavalry in the Gettysburg Campaign* (1908). The sections of John Mosby's narratives printed in this volume are taken from *Mosby's War Reminiscences.*

SOLOMON NORTHUP (ca. 1808-1863)

Solomon Northup was born in Essex, New York. His ancestors on his paternal side were slaves in Rhode Island and belonged to the Northup family. When one of the Northups and his family moved to Hoosic, New York, Solomon's father Mintus went with them. After Solomon Northup married Anne Hampton, a black, on December 25, 1829, in Fort Edward, New York, he worked repairing the Champlain Canal. Eventually, Solomon and Anne moved to Kingsbury, New York, to farm. In 1834, they moved to Saratoga, New York, where Isaac Taylor employed Northup as a hackdriver, and it was there that Northup met rich masters on vacation and their slaves. The Northups lived in Saratoga until 1841. Northup accepted an offer from two strangers passing through Saratoga to play in the band of a traveling circus. Shortly after, he was kidnapped, drugged, beaten, and sold into slavery by James H. Birch in Washington, D. C., and then shipped to New Orleans, Louisiana, where he was purchased by a trader in the Red River region of Louisiana. There he remained for twelve years as the chattel of William Ford and several other owners. Eventually, Samuel Bass of Marksville, Louisiana, originally from Canada, with the assistance of Governor Washington Hunt of New York State, secured Northup's release in 1853, the year his narrative was first published. What happened to Northup in his final years is not known, but he is believed to have died before 1863 when his wife sold family property. The section of Solomon Northup's narrative printed in this volume is taken from *Twelve Years a Slave* (1853).

FREDERICK LAW OLMSTED (1822-1903)

Frederick Law Olmsted was born in Hartford, Connecticut. At sixteen, Olmsted made four journeys, each over a thousand miles, through New England, New York, and Canada, thus gaining a knowledge of the American and Canadian landscape. Though he entered Yale in 1837, he never finished because of weak eyes; when he left college, he took up studying engineering with Frederick A. Barton. In 1850, he traveled to Europe with his brother and a mutual friend; their adventures were recorded in *Walks and Talks of an American Farmer in England* (1852). In 1852, he traveled through the American South at the invitation of Henry J. Raymond, editor of *The New York Times*, and subsequently wrote *A Journey in the Seaboard Slave States* (1856), *A Journey Through Texas* (1857), and *A Journey in the Back Country* (1860), which were condensed into two volumes as *The Cotton Kingdom: A Traveller's Observation on Cotton and Slavery in the American Slave States* (1861). In 1857, he was appointed Superintendent of Central Park in New York City; he worked with Calvert Vaux, a young English architect, to design and landscape this new park. Olmsted was appointed in 1861 by President Abraham Lincoln to the U.S. Sanitary Commission and in 1863 became the first Commissioner of the Yosemite National Park in California. He also designed the campus of the University of California at Berkeley and Stanford University in Palo Alto, California. In addition, he is noted for his work on George W. Vanderbilt's estate "Biltmore" in Ashville, North Carolina, and for designing the grounds for the Chicago World's Fair and the U.S. Capitol in Washington, D. C. Olmsted's skill and art are reflected in more than eighty parks in the United States and Canada. He published two important addresses: *Public Parks and the Enlargement of Towns* (1871) and *A Consideration of the Justifying Value of a Public Park* (1881). The sections of Frederick Law Olmsted's travelogue are taken from *The Cotton Kingdom*.

THOMAS NELSON PAGE (1853-1922)

Thomas Nelson Page was born at Oakland Plantation north of Richmond, Virginia. After attending Washington College and the University of Virginia, Page practiced law in Richmond. With the publication of "Marse Chan" (1884), Page became known as a defender of the Old South and as a writer of local color fiction, as seen in *In Ole Virginia, or Marse Chan and Other Stories* (1887) and *Unc' Edinburg: A Plantation Echo* (1889). After spending some years in Colorado and Europe involved in various business ventures, he began writing full time in the early 1890's. A prolific writer of essays, stories, sketches, and romantic novels, full of stalwart gentlemen and modest damsels facing life's tragedies with noble spirits, Page nevertheless wrote on a variety of topics. In 1913, President Woodrow Wilson appointed him Ambassador to Italy. His major works include *The Old South: Essays Social and Political* (1892), *Meh Lady: A Story of the War* (1893), *Red Rock: A Chronicle of Reconstruction* (1898), *Gordon Keith* (1903), *Robert E. Lee, the Southerner* (1909), *John Marvel, Assistant* (1909), and *Dante and His Influence* (1922). "Unc' Edinburg's Drowndin': A Plantation Echo" was first published in *Harper's New Monthly Magazine* (January 1886); "The Old South" is taken from *The Old South: Essays Social and Political* (1892).

WALTER HINES PAGE (1855-1918)

Walter Hines Page was born in Cary, North Carolina. Refusing to be strangled by antebellum traditions, Page became a leading spokesman for the New South and was particularly active in supporting public education. After studying at Johns Hopkins University in Baltimore, Maryland, he worked in journalism; he founded *The Raleigh State Chronicle* and edited *The Forum* and *The Atlantic Monthly*. Between 1913-1918, he served as the U.S. Ambassador to the Court of St. James, and proved a valuable advisor to President Woodrow Wilson. Page also started his own publishing firm, Doubleday, Page & Company, whose authors included Sidney Lanier, Ellen Glasgow, and Booker T. Washington. In addition to his educational and political essays, as well as his vast correspondence, Page is noted for his one novel, published pseudonymously, *The Southerner, Being the Autobiography of Nicholas Worth* (1909). "The Last Hold of the Southern Bully" was first published in *The Forum* (November 1893).

EDWARD COOTE PINKNEY (1802-1828)

Edward Coote Pinkney was born in London, England. His father served there as a U.S. commissioner and minister to the Court of St. James. Pinkney returned to the United States in 1811 and attended Baltimore College and St. Mary's College in Baltimore, Maryland, before joining the U. S. Navy and sailing the Mediterranean. He began writing poetry at an early age; one of his first successes, "Serenade," was set to music and published in January 1823. In the same year he published *Rodolph: A Fragment,* his most ambitious work. As Craig Werner has noted, the real strength of Pinkney's poems "reflects his ability to create verbal music resembling that of the Cavalier poets." In 1824, Pinkney resigned from the navy and started practicing law in Baltimore while continuing to write poetry, some of which was published in the local anti-Jacksonian *Marylander.* His volume, *Poems,* was published in 1825.

EDGAR ALLAN POE (1809-1849)

Edgar Allan Poe's parents were traveling actors who happened to be in Boston when he was born. Three years later, in Richmond, Virginia, after the death of his mother who had been deserted by his father, he was taken into the household of a Richmond merchant, John Allan, a stern businessman whose relationship with Poe was troubled from the beginning. Poe nevertheless received an excellent education, but after a year at the University of Virginia, his gambling debts forced him to leave. Subsequently, he enlisted in the U.S. Army and after two years enrolled as a cadet at West Point where he had himself dismissed after only eight months. By that time he had already published two volumes of poetry, but he had also broken with his foster father, and was now entirely on his own. From this point on, his life was a constant struggle to make a living, as poet, short story writer, editor, and critic. His marriage with his tuberculosis in 1847. Among Poe's works are *Tamerlane and Other Poems* (1827), *Al Araaf, Tamerlane, and Minor Poems* (1829), *Poems* (1831), *The Narrative of Arthur Gordon Pym* (1838), *Tales of the Grotesque and Arabesque* (1840), *The Raven and Other Poems* (1845), *Tales* (1845), and *Eureka: A Prose Poem* (1848).

JAMES INNES RANDOLPH (1837-1887)

James Innes Randolph was born on the Barleywood homestead, Frederick County, Virginia. He studied law in New York, but returned South to serve in the Confederate army as a topographical engineer for "Jeb" Stuart. After the war, he settled in Baltimore where he practiced law and journalism. He was a good friend of Sidney Lanier. Randolph's collected *Poems* was not published until after his death, in 1898. He first sang his song "I'm a Good Old Rebel" at the Mosaic Club in Richmond, Virginia.

LIZETTE WOODWORTH REESE (1856-1935)

Lizette Woodworth Reese, of Welsh and German ancestry, was born in Waverly, a suburb of Baltimore, Maryland. She taught English in Baltimore's Western High School and was instrumental in founding The Woman's Literary Club in 1891. Her first poem, "The Deserted Home," was published in *Southern Magazine* in 1874. A popular poet during her life, she published in *The Atlantic Monthly, Scribner's Monthly, Harper's Monthly,* and *The Smart Set.* Her lyrics, like those of Emily Dickinson or Sara Teasdale, are distinguished by intense emotion, simple personal interpretation, and concise expression. Her works include *A Bunch of May* (1887), *A Handful of Lavender* (1891), *A Wayside Lute* (1909), *Spicewood* (1920), *Wild Cherry* (1923), *Little Henrietta* (1927), *White April* (1930), *Pastures* (1993), and *The Old House in the Country* (1936), with an introduction by Hervey Allen. *The York Road* (1931) contains autobiographical narratives and *Worleys* (1936) is a fictional fragment.

IRWIN RUSSELL (1853-1879)

Irwin Russell was born in Port Gibson, Mississippi. Though the family lived for a while in St. Louis, Missouri, they resettled in Mississippi at the beginning of the Civil War. A precocious child, Russell read Milton at age six. In 1869, Russell graduated from what is now St. Louis University and returned again to Port Gibson to study law under Judge L. N. Baldwin. At age nineteen, he was admitted to the bar. After 1871, his dialectic poetry began appearing in national magazines, including *Scribner's Monthly.* Joel Chandler Harris praised Russell's "accurate conception" and "perfect representation of the negro character," though Harris admitted that Russell's use of dialect was often less than satisfactory. Often physically and emotionally exhausted because of a drinking problem and depression, Russell even worked briefly as a fireman on a steamboat to New Orleans as a form of escapism. Though primarily noted for his poem titled "Christmas Night in the Quarters" (1878), "an achievement that transcends any inadequacies in the transcription of dialect," according to Rayburn S. Moore, Russell's one volume of poetry published in 1888 shows a genuine appreciation for the role of blacks in Southern society.

WILLIAM GILMORE SIMMS (1806-1870)

William Gilmore Simms was born in Charleston, South Carolina. His mother died when he was two years old, and his father, an Irish-born tradesman, left Charleston for good, and served as a calvary officer under Andrew Jackson before settling on a plantation in Mississippi. Simms was raised in Charleston by his maternal grandmother. For a time he was apprenticed to a local druggist, but he eventually changed his mind about pursuing a career in medicine and turned to law. He was admitted to the bar in 1827, though he soon abandoned his practice for a full-time literary career. A prolific novelist and man of letters, he gradually became recognized as the leading Southern writer of his time. His first wife died in 1832, and in 1836 he married Chevilette Roach, whose family owned the large Woodlands Plantation where Simms set up house. Outspoken in favor of the Southern cause, he suffered enormous losses during the war. The end of his life was spent in a desperate and tireless effort to provide for his family by writing. Among his more than eighty volumes of work are *Martin Faber* (1833), *The Yemassee* (1835), *The Partisan* (1835), *Border Beagles* (1840), *The Wigwam and the Cabin* (1845), *The Golden Christmas* (1852), and *The Cassique of Kiawah* (1859). "Ephraim Bartlett, the Edisto Raftsman" was published as the fourth installment of "Home Sketches, or Life Along the Highways and Byways of the South" in *Literary World* (February 7, 1852).

ALEXANDER HAMILTON STEPHENS (1812-1883)
Alexander Hamilton Stephens was born in Wilkes (now Taliaferro) County, Georgia. After his parents died when he was fifteen, Stephens went to live with an uncle in Warren County. He graduated from the University of Georgia in 1832 and worked for two years as a schoolteacher. He then studied law and was admitted to the bar in 1834. Entering politics in 1836, he denounced nullification and protested tactics used against abolitionists. He was elected to the U.S. House of Representatives in 1843 and supported the annexation of Texas. He joined the Democratic Party in order to support Daniel Webster. Moderately proslavery, Stephens opposed secession and retired from Congress in 1859. He was elected in both 1861 and 1862 Vice President of the Confederate States, though he was often at odds with Jefferson Davis. He was arrested by Union soldiers after Appomattox and was confined to Fort Warren in Boston until October 12, 1865. When he returned to Georgia, Stephens advocated reconciliation and was elected to the U.S. Senate in 1866, but was denied his seat. He served in the U.S. House of Representatives from 1873 to 1882. Stephens wrote *Constitutional View of the Late War Between the States* in two volumes (1868-1870). The section of Alexander Stephens's diary printed in this volume is from *Recollections of Alexander H. Stephens: His Diary* (1910).

HENRY TIMROD (1828-1867)
Henry Timrod was born in Charleston, South Carolina, in a modest household. His father was a bookbinder and a minor poet who died when Henry was ten years old. He was educated at local schools and spent a short period at the University of Georgia, but never graduated. Before the Civil War he tutored, wrote for Charleston newspapers, and became a member of the Russell's Bookstore group. Aside from his poetry, he explored literary theory in such essays as "The Literature of the South" and "A Theory of Poetry." During the war he served for a short time as a war correspondent, but his fragile health kept him out of active service. He was working for the Columbia, South Carolina, newspaper, *The South Carolinian,* when Columbia was burned in February 1865. Thereafter his life became one loss and hardship after the other, a period he described to his friend Paul Hamilton Hayne as one of "beggary, starvation, death, bitter grief, [and] utter want of hope." Timrod's sole book during his lifetime was the collection, *Poems,* published in 1859. Hayne edited a fuller collection, *The Poems of Henry Timrod,* in 1873.

MARK TWAIN (SAMUEL LANGHORNE CLEMENS) (1835-1910)

Born Samuel Clemens in Florida, Missouri, and raised in nearby Hannibal, on the Mississippi, Twain lived his youth in a slave state settled by migrating Southerners, but deeply divided in its loyalty to Southern interests. His father was an impractical and improvident lawyer from Virginia who dreamed of owning a large plantation. Twain was much closer to his mother, a gentle, good-humored native of Kentucky. When his father died in 1847, he left school to work, and after holding a variety of jobs, signed on as an apprentice steamboat pilot in 1855. In 1857, he received his pilot's license and worked the Mississippi for four years. After a short spell in the Confederate army, he left the war behind and went to Nevada Territory, where his brother was secretary to the governor. There he wrote journalistic pieces and humorous sketches. His first full-length work, *The Innocents Abroad,* an ironic account of a cultural tour of Europe and the Holy Land, was published in 1869. After his marriage to Olivia Langdon in 1870, he settled in Hartford, Connecticut. Among his major works are *Roughing It* (1872), *The Adventures of Tom Sawyer* (1876), *Life on the Mississippi* (1883), *The Adventures of Huckleberry Finn* (1884), and *The Tragedy of Pudd'nhead Wilson and The Comedy of Those Extraordinary Twins* (1894). The four sections we include from *Life on the Mississippi* were first published as installments in his serial article "Old Times on the Mississippi" published in *The Atlantic Monthly* (1875).

BOOKER TALIAFERRO WASHINGTON (1856-1915)

Booker Taliaferro Washington, the son of a slave mother and a white father, was born near Roanoke, Virginia. In 1871, he began working for Mrs. Viola Ruffner and was inspired to enter Hampton Normal and Agricultural Institute in 1872; there he profited from the advice and wisdom of General Samuel Armstrong, the institute's founder and director, even returning in 1879 to teach at Hampton temporarily. In 1881, Washington went to Tuskegee, Alabama, and there founded and became President of Tuskegee Institute, which opened with thirty students on July 4, 1881. His speech at the Cotton States Exposition in Atlanta in 1895 propelled him into the position of being the leading spokesman of his race. His *Up From Slavery* (1901) has become an American classic and has remained widely read by all people of all races; it is often compared with Benjamin Franklin's *Autobiography* and Harriet Beecher Stowe's *Uncle Tom's Cabin.* Washington's other works include *The Future of the American Negro* (1899), *The Story of My Life and Work* (1900), *Tuskegee and Its People* (1905), *My Larger Education* (1911), in addition to *The Negro Problem* (1903), *The Negro in the South* (1907), *Frederick Douglass* (1907), *The Story of the Negro* (1909), *The Man Farthest Down* (1912). The section of Booker T. Washington's autobiography printed in this volume is from *Up From Slavery.*

ALBERY ALLSON WHITMAN (1851-1901)

Albery Allson Whitman was born near Munfordville, Kentucky. Though he suffered as a slave, after the Civil War he never sought recrimination against members of the white race. Once emancipated about 1863, he began to travel and worked for a while in Troy, Ohio. With some schooling and even a stint as a teacher, he entered Wilberforce University, Xenia, Ohio, about 1870 and met Daniel Alexander Payne, Wilberforce's founder and a bishop in the A.M.E. Church. Having joined this church, Whitman became a pastor in Springfield, Ohio. He subsequently published *Essay on the Ten Plagues and Other Miscellaneous Poems* (1871) and *Not a Man Yet a Man* (1877), a poem of more than five thousand lines. Whitman continued his ministry and preached in churches in Ohio, Kansas, and Texas, and eventually by the end of the 1890's in Savannah and Atlanta, Georgia. His other works included *The Rape of Florida* (1884), *The World's Fair Poem* (1893), and *An Idyl of the South, An Epic Poem in Two Parts* (1901).

Acknowledgments

The editors would like to thank the entire staff of Peachtree Publishers for all their extra help and expertise, with a special word of thanks to Laurie Edwards, whose skill and good cheer boosted our spirits during the final preparation.

Grateful acknowledgment is made for permission to reprint the following copyrighted works:

Ellen Glasgow: "Jordan's End" from *The Shadowy Third and Other Stories* by Ellen Glasgow. Doubleday, Page & Company. Copyright 1923. Reprinted with permission of the Richmond Society for the Prevention of Cruelty to Animals.

William Gilmore Simms: "Ephraim Bartlett: The Edisto Raftsman" as the fourth installment of "Home Sketches," or "Life Along the Highways and Byways of the South" in *Literary World 10* (February 7, 1852), in the version in Volume V: Stories and Tales, edited by John Caldwell Guilds, of the University of South Carolina's Centennial Edition of Simms. Copyright 1974. Reprinted with permission of University of South Carolina Press.

Mary Chesnut: "Mary Chesnut's Civil War" edited by C. Vann Woodward. Copyright 1981. Reprinted with permission of Yale University Press.

Harriet Jacobs: From "Incidents in the Life of a Slave Girl" by Harriet Jacobs, edited by Valerie Smith. The Schomburg Library of Nineteenth-Century Black Women Writers. Copyright 1988 by Oxford University Press, Inc. Reprinted by permission.

About the Editors

BEN FORKNER is professor of English and American literature at the University of Angers in France. A graduate of Stetson University in Florida, he received his M.A. and Ph.D. from the University of North Carolina at Chapel Hill. He has published essays on writers from Ireland and from the American South and has edited several anthologies of short stories: *Modern Irish Short Stories, A New Book of Dubliners,* and *Louisiana Stories.* With Patrick Samway, S.J., Professor Forkner has co-edited four anthologies of Southern literature, *Stories of the Modern South, Stories of the Old South, A Modern Southern Reader* (Peachtree), and *A New Reader of the Old South* (Peachtree). In addition, he edits the *Journal of the Short Story in English* and is currently compiling a collection for Peachtree Publishers, Ltd. titled *Georgia Stories.*

PATRICK SAMWAY, S.J., received his B.A. and M.A. from Fordham University, his M. Div. from Woodstock College and his Ph.D. from the University of North Carolina at Chapel Hill. Father Samway taught for eight years at Le Moyne College in Syracuse, New York, and also has received two Fulbright lectureships to France, in addition to having been a Bannan Fellow at the University of Santa Clara in California and Visiting Associate Professor at both Boston College and Loyola University in New Orleans. He is the Literary Editor of *America* and author of *Faulkner's "Intruder in the Dust": A Critical Study of the Typescripts,* co-editor with Michel Gresset of *Faulkner and Idealism: Perspectives from Paris,* and editor of *Walker Percy: Signposts in a Strange Land.*